Eugene Ely,
Daredevil Aviator

# Eugene Ely, Daredevil Aviator
## *First Shipboard Landing and Takeoff*

### William M. Miller

McFarland & Company, Inc., Publishers
*Jefferson, North Carolina*

LIBRARY OF CONGRESS CATALOGUING-IN-PUBLICATION DATA

Miller, William M., 1946–
Eugene Ely, daredevil aviator : first shipboard landing and takeoff / William M. Miller.
     p.     cm.
Includes bibliographical references and index.

ISBN 978-0-7864-9677-8 (softcover : acid free paper) ∞
ISBN 978-1-4766-1798-5 (ebook)

1. Ely, Eugene.  2. Air pilots—United States—Biography.  3. Test pilots—United States—Biography.  4. United States. Navy—Aviation—History—20th century.  5. Aeronautics—Competitions—History—20th century.  6. Distinguished Flying Cross (Medal)—Biography.  I. Title.
TL540.E6325M55 2014       629.13092—dc23       [B]   2014033836

BRITISH LIBRARY CATALOGUING DATA ARE AVAILABLE

© 2014 William M. Miller. All rights reserved

*No part of this book may be reproduced or transmitted in any form or by any means, electronic or mechanical, including photocopying or recording, or by any information storage and retrieval system, without permission in writing from the publisher.*

On the cover: Composite photographs of Eugene Ely (left) and a biplane he is piloting off the USS *Birmingham* in Hampton Roads, Virginia, on November 14, 1910 (Library of Congress and United States Navy)

Printed in the United States of America

*McFarland & Company, Inc., Publishers*
*Box 611, Jefferson, North Carolina 28640*
*www.mcfarlandpub.com*

# Table of Contents

*Preface*     1

1. Homecoming     3
2. Macon, 1911     8
3. The Old York Hills     12
4. A New Century     17
5. Scorching Through the Countryside     20
6. The City of a Hundred Hills     23
7. 5:12 a.m.—April 18, 1906     27
8. Native Son and Daughter     31
9. Driving the Right People     35
10. Racing Cross-Country     39
11. Challenging the Wrights     46
12. Dominguez     52
13. Wemme Wants a Prizewinner     56
14. Crowds Will Flock     60
15. "I was fascinated with the idea of flying"     65
16. On the Road to Curtiss     70
17. O, Canada     77
18. "Scrape that golden lining"     83
19. "A warm corner in the heart of Father Knickerbocker"     87
20. "Plucky pioneer conqueror of the air"     95
21. "There's your trouble, Gene"     103
22. "The ease of a swallow and the speed of an express train"     112
23. Bleak Days at Belmont     116

24. A Little Man with an Aero-Eye and the Plucky Little Woman Beside Him — 122
25. "He flew off with the greatest ease" — 130
26. Balmy Southern Skies — 140
27. Scientific Suicide — 149
28. A Platform for the *Pennsylvania* — 157
29. Two Days Out of Ten — 164
30. Waiting for a Rainbow — 169
31. "Easier than I thought" — 176
32. "Best girl" — 188
33. "The noble art" — 195
34. Good Luck Charm — 201
35. Land of Salt and Snow — 204
36. Flitting Along — 211
37. The Wayward Winds — 220
38. Sailing Air and Sea — 226
39. Redemption on an Oregon Trail — 232
40. Over the Rockies — 240
41. A Very Busy Month — 246
42. "We are merely circus performers" — 256
43. Not for $50,000 — 267
44. "Fate handed me this bump" — 272
45. "He was just Ely" — 280
46. Beginning the Afterlife — 292
47. "They're all gone now" — 298

*Chapter Notes* — 305
*Bibliography* — 327
*Index* — 333

# Preface

The threads of Eugene Burton Ely's life have been left dangling for too long. He had just captured the world's attention and gained the fame he sought when he smashed into the earth and was dead. He was buried the day after his 25th birthday, less than half a mile from where he was born.

Until 1911, the last year of his life, hardly anyone knew who this young man was and, a century later, nothing has changed. If he is known at all it's because he was the first to dare fly an airplane onto and away from a ship—and one has to wonder, how does an Iowa farm boy, afraid of heights, find the nerve to do that? To some, he's the father of naval aviation, the inspiration for today's nuclear powered aircraft carriers, but like most pioneers, the what, why, and how of his life have disappeared. Gene Ely is nothing more than a footnote, a few dates and facts with no more humanity than one can find in a bronze statue on a courthouse lawn. Recapturing the life of a man so young is not easy. His footprints are not deep and he has left few clues. We may never completely know the real Eugene Burton Ely, but maybe it's time we tried.

> For I dipped into the future, far as human eye could see,
> Saw the vision of the world, and all the wonders that would be;
>
> Saw the heavens fill with commerce, argosies of magic sails,
> Pilots of the purple twilight, dropping down with costly bales;
>
> Heard the heavens filled with shouting and there rained a ghastly dew,
> From the nations' airy navies, grappling in the central blue;
>
> Far along the world-wide whisper of the south-wind rushing warm,
> With the standards of the peoples plunging thro' the thunder storm.
>
> —from *Locksley Hall*, Alfred, Lord Tennyson (1842),
> republished in the *Macon Daily Telegraph*
> on the morning Eugene Burton Ely died.[1]

# { 1 }

## Homecoming

She grabbed his arm and pulled him to a sudden stop.

"Stick to straight flying, Gene," said Mabel Ely to her slumping husband. "I want none of those spirals and dips. Promise me you won't."

She had lost track of how many times she had made this plea, hoping he would finally listen, but Gene's sheepish grin gave her no encouragement and his half-hearted "Yes, dear" certainly wasn't convincing.[1]

He climbed into the seat behind the wheel of his biplane and pulled on his corklined leather helmet. Mabel's lecture already long forgotten, he tightened the strap under his chin. His mechanics had started the plane's engine and kept the machine from wandering by holding tightly to its wings. He worked the throttle up and down with his left foot and the 100 horsepower engine behind him raced, alternating between an irritating whine and a clattering rumble. The crowd in the grandstand put fingers in their ears, but their admiring eyes never left their hometown hero. Finally satisfied that everything was OK, Gene pulled his goggles down, gave thumbs-up, and the mechanics let go.[2]

In October 1911, Eugene Burton Ely had been flying for over a year and a half, but this Saturday exhibition at Davenport's Suburban Island was the first time he had flown in the Iowa town that since he was nine years old had been his boyhood home. A year before, he had flown just across the Mississippi River, in Rock Island, Illinois, but now, he was really home and showing off to family and friends. His mother had stayed at the family home near Williamsburg. Divorced from Gene's father, she was either unable or unwilling to attend, and never again would have a chance to see him fly. His father, a prominent local attorney, watched with Eugene's sister, Maidie.

Not far from the carousel and the roller coaster, the Suburban Island airstrip was just a level stretch of dirt next to an amusement park. Most people arrived early on one of the red trimmed, brassy-yellow electric trolleys run by the Tri-City Railways, a few came by boat, while others just walked across the narrow trolley rail bed from shore to the island. The baseball infield was scraped away for Gene's takeoff and portable grandstands were added for the aerial exhibition. As flight time approached, the penny arcade went silent and the sandy beach was abandoned.[3]

No one had ever taken off or landed an aeroplane here or anywhere else in Iowa.

Once mechanics put his plane back together, Gene would be the first. Faced with unreliable aircraft, aviators didn't fly between aviation shows in 1911. Instead, Gene's biplane had been taken apart on Long Island, New York, placed in packing crates, and shipped by railroad to Davenport. Actually, two biplanes had been shipped—the 100 horsepower Curtiss 8-cylinder that he would fly today and the Curtiss that had made him world famous the previous January, when he had landed on the Navy cruiser, U.S.S. *Pennsylvania* in San Francisco Bay. Charles Walsh, a last minute replacement for another Curtiss exhibition pilot, would fly with him in the less powerful plane.[4]

Gene's plane bounced and then eased into a glide over the field as he gained speed. At 100 yards, he pulled back on the wheel and the biplane sprang into the air. Reaching 1,000 feet, he turned sharply, circling back, and then dove at the grandstand. The anxious crowd ducked in fear, the screams turning into nervous laughter as he pulled his plane up and veered away to the west. He gained a few hundred feet of altitude then shot straight down again, refusing to pull up until he reached the danger point, less than 50 feet from the ground.

"That may be good flying," someone said, "but it is craziness!"

"If Mr. Walsh does that I'll get his machine and burn it," said Mrs. Walsh, "even if he has to work for a dollar a day." She too had warned her husband not to try anything fancy.[5]

Gene stayed in the air a few more minutes then landed to check on Walsh who was to join him in a race around the island. The oil tank on Walsh's plane had been damaged in shipment and mechanics were still working to replace it. As Gene saw a livid Mabel racing toward him again, he turned his plane around to the west and flew away. He pulled back on the wheel and under full throttle began to climb.

"He's trying for an altitude record," said an optimistic Mabel, but he wasn't. Reaching 2,200 feet, Gene sped toward the earth again, but this time leveling off well above the ground. For now, as he waited for Walsh, he seemed satisfied with a lot of speed, a few dips, and some sharp turns.[6]

For months, Gene and Mabel had been traveling together from one exhibition to the next, crossing the continent with little time for themselves. September had begun at the Boston aviation meet, followed by two different flying exhibitions near New York City, a long railroad ride to Canton, Ohio for a near disastrous exhibition, and then back to New York for another. Now, in Davenport, the strain was beginning to show. While taxiing across the field in New York, Gene fell off his plane and tangled himself in the biplane's control wires. Three days later, a fall from 100 feet and a minor collision with another aeroplane in Canton, brought headlines that said he was dead. He had indeed hit the ground, but fortunately had only suffered a few cuts and a black eye. Flying was becoming more dangerous and he and Mabel had already decided it was time to get out. When this Davenport aviation meet ended, they planned to spend a few days with Gene's family and then, for one of the few times in their four-year marriage, they would be separated by a thousand miles. Gene would head to Macon, Georgia for one more exhibition, while Mabel returned to New York City to book passage to Russia, where the Czar had asked Gene to perform.[7]

Gene said they would return to spend the winter with his family in Iowa before his overseas trip and when he returned, they would move permanently to the West

Coast. "I absolutely will quit flying," he told friends. "There is big money in the game, but it isn't worth the while. Something might happen when I am hundreds of feet in the air. There is always a possibility, and that would be the last of me." He said he would take his "considerable fortune," invest it in an exclusive territory, and sell Curtiss aeroplanes from an agency headquartered in San Diego. "I will also manage an aviation school in Southern California and will have an interest in the business," he said. More than anything, he wanted "to settle down to the quiet of a home life."[8]

The public didn't really know Eugene Ely. He played the part of the bold and daring birdman, but only his friends and relatives knew how painfully shy he was. Yes, proud of what he had done, and yes, he loved to fly, but until recently, he hadn't sought the limelight and the public praise that came his way. It had been enough to make good money and be respected for his skill. "Bright, determined and of high character," said Henry Wemme, the man who had bought the first aeroplane Gene would fly. "He needed only the opportunity to make a name for himself. When he was seized with the desire to pilot an aeroplane, he went about the work with the quiet determination that presaged success."[9]

Of course, many believed that Gene's quiet determination may well have been encouraged by not so subtle prodding from his wife, Mabel. "She was," wrote one reporter, "superintendent, captain, manager, overseer, boss, president, general, and everything else. She shows herself to be as proud of her high flying spouse as it is possible for a woman to be proud of anything. And, he seems to be well aware of it."[10]

The day before the Davenport exhibition was scheduled to begin, Gene arrived from New York at the Rock Island Railroad's passenger depot on the Illinois side of the Mississippi River. A mob of reporters, a small crowd, and several dozen of his old friends were waiting for him. With so many people insisting on shaking and re-shaking his hand, it was nearly impossible to break through. Nathan Ely, his father, finally managed to pull Gene to a waiting car and get him seated inside. He turned back to the reporters and said that if his son had known that there would be such a commotion, he probably would have gotten off the train at an earlier station. "Gene, as he is known here," said the senior Ely, "is not ceremonious and he lacks the penchant for the pageant."[11]

A marching band formed in front of the car that belonged to Pete Petersen, an old friend who owned a garage where a teenaged Gene had learned mechanics and how to race automobiles. With two touring cars overflowing with well-wishers following behind, Gene was wedged in the middle of a parade that after crossing over the bridge, wound its way through Davenport's downtown streets. The bashful aviator persuaded Petersen to let him drive, and slouching in the seat, Gene drove himself to the hotel.

"Mr. Ely is a modest young man," said a reporter, "without a show of one spoiled by the gaze of the public eye." The reporter speculated that Gene had taken the wheel to deflect attention "which might be centered on him."[12]

Before the two-day exhibition began, Gene was honored at a Friday night, seven-course banquet at the Main Street Commercial Club. After glowing speeches from his father and others, Gene received an engraved gold watch and was asked to speak. He told a few stories about his flying career, taking his mesmerized audience through the clouds and into the blue heavens. "It is certainly great," Gene said, "to pull open

Wearing a soft helmet and goggles, Eugene Ely is ready to fly in this undated photograph. By October 1911, after a year and a half of nearly nonstop traveling, Ely and his wife, Mabel, were ready to leave exhibition flying (Naval History and Heritage Command #NH 77494).

the lever and feel yourself suddenly rise in the air and soar gracefully away on the breeze. But one has to be constantly on the alert."

Then he answered a few questions. What did the Earth look like from 1,000 feet? "A level plain, hills flattening out," he said, "and it is seldom that a city is discernible." Was it easy to fly? "These cross country trips are generally made by novices seeking a reputation," he said, "although one has to give them credit for their nerve in doing it." How long did he expect to stay in the flying business? "Oh, I'll do like the rest of them—keep it up until I'm killed," he said. It was the answer he always gave these days, usually with a grin that said he didn't really mean it, but with eyes that weren't so sure.[13]

Walsh's machine finally rolled across the baseball field for 125 yards and climbed slowly toward the southwest. Soon he was so high no one could hear his engine. He crossed the Mississippi and circled over Rock Island, "just to show Illinois what they were missing." Ten minutes later, in a gentle glide, he landed in front of the grandstand, his test flight a success. After a brief visit with his 4-year-old son, Walsh was off again with Gene in hot pursuit. The race was finally on, first Gene, then Walsh, then Gene again, chasing each other around the field. After just two wide circles around the course, Walsh landed and Gene had the show to himself.

He climbed and then dipped toward the ground, missing the front of Walsh's parked machine by barely 25 feet before he rose again. From high in the sky, he twisted over and took aim at the grandstand, scattering spectators with his wheels just a few feet above their heads. Those who hadn't moved froze in terror, necks stretched back and mouths wide open. Moments later, Gene was spiraling again, this time striking within ten feet of the infield. On the ground, his father was mouthing angry threats at his grown-up boy, the daring and foolish young aviator. A disgusted Mabel began to fume. "There he goes," she said. "There goes a spiral."[14]

As Gene was landing, he saw Mabel holding onto the edge of her long skirt as she ran toward him. He knew he was in for it now and there was nothing to do but smile and take his punishment like a man. "I told you not to do that and you said you wouldn't," she scolded, her finger was tapping each word in perfect timing against his chest, as if her husband were a 3-year-old toddler. "If you won't promise not to do those crazy things you shan't go up again," she said. She turned and pretended not to hear Gene's pitiful attempt at reconciliation. "You know, dear heart, I don't take any chances," he said to her back. Mabel just kept walking.[15]

Saturday's domestic squabble assured Sunday's crowd of 10,000 people a much tamer exhibition. As promised, Gene took his old friend Pete Petersen along as a passenger. Petersen had gained the nickname, "Daredevil Pete," while racing cars at Davenport's one-mile dirt track. He said he might want to become an aviator someday, but soon changed his mind. "Gene went up in his Curtiss pusher and coaxed me to go along," Petersen later recalled. "There wasn't room for me in the plane, so I rode on a wing. I got the scare of my life when we cleared the trees by only a few feet."[16]

With Petersen safely returned to Earth, it was Mabel's turn for a ride. A seasoned pro by now, whenever she could, she flew alongside Gene. It was a good show for the crowd and it kept him flying safely. Away they went, rapidly reaching a "goodly height." Suddenly the plane began to shudder and wobble off course. Gene gripped tightly to the wheel and dove for the ground, bouncing hard in an unscheduled emergency landing. His mechanics quickly found the trouble. All but one of the six bolts holding the propeller onto the engine had sheared off. Disaster had once again been a mere few seconds away.[17]

The air show was over and Gene and Mabel had flown together for the last time. Mabel was off to New York City to arrange the voyage to Russia. Gene's visit with his mother was brief. He was due at the Georgia State Fair in just three days. He and his team of mechanics packed his plane into three crates and rode the train to Macon. In about two weeks, when the fair was over, Gene and Mabel would reunite in New York City. That was the plan, but Gene would never make it.

# { 2 }

## Macon, 1911

"Ah," said Gene Ely, "this was a grand and beautiful day. The weather is simply charming, and that air up there—it was delicious."[1]

The conditions at the Georgia State Fair in Macon had been nearly perfect since Gene's train arrived from Davenport on October 11. Skies were mostly clear and daytime temperatures lingered in the 60s and low 70s. The rainfall total was one-third lower than normal for that time of the year, so it was an unpleasant surprise to fair officials when opening day was washed out in a torrent of water. Visitors stayed away, not only missing their opportunity to see a tomato plant grafted onto a potato, but also all those other "spectacular" agricultural and livestock exhibits that make up a well organized state fair. The midway was empty and the ballpark in the middle of the racetrack, now the site of the aviation field, was a puddling mass of mud. Then, around 10 o'clock that evening, it got worse. The downpour turned vicious as it smashed into fragile roofs. A trickle of raindrops dripping from ceilings gathered into waterfalls, flowing through ever-larger holes until roofs collapsed and merchandise inside was soaked. A newspaper story lightheartedly warned the weatherman that "if he continues to show his teeth" the fair directors would likely ask Uncle Sam for a replacement prognosticator—someone who would not allow rain on such a special time as the state fair. It seemed to work. The weather changed and the festive atmosphere returned.[2]

This fair, the state's 56th, promised to be the most successful ever held. Not only would Macon see its first airplane flight, but Buffalo Bill Cody was also saying goodbye. Riding on what seemed to be an endless farewell tour, the old showman had brought his Wild West company for a one-day-only, last performance. Bill promised the exact same show recently performed for three weeks in New York City's Madison Square Garden. A record 30,000 Georgians turned out for Wild West Day. "It was people, people, people, everywhere," said the newspaper. At 2 o'clock, Colonel Cody rode out on his white Arabian to screams and cheers. The old scout, dressed in a buckskin coat and flannel shirt, with silver locks blowing in the breeze, stood up in silver stirrups and thanked the crowd by swinging his broad sombrero back and forth over his head. When he began to speak, the crowd hushed, straining to hear his brief farewell. Then, he shouted his familiar introduction. "Ladies and Gentlemen, allow me to introduce to you to the Congress of the World's Rough Riders." The show exploded into heart stopping battles between Indians and cowboys, stagecoach races, trick riding and sharpshooters who never missed their target—the same Wild West show that had traveled the world for nearly 30 years.[3]

Gene Ely wasn't scheduled to fly that day, but fair directors enticed him with an additional $500, and up he went. Not bad for just an extra half-hour of work and it certainly was an exciting surprise for the crowd.

Gene and Bill Cody had struck up a friendship. Cody admired young Gene's daring and his showmanship and Gene must have admired the old American hero. In the morning, before his first flight, Gene agreed to ride one of Buffalo Bill's best horses in the Main Street parade. Later, the two agreed to go foxhunting, as soon as Gene finished just one more day of flying.[4]

The difference between the daredevil in the sky and the shy and reserved man Gene was on the ground, continued to surprise people he met. Friendly and easy to talk to, it seemed the only time he stiffened with worry was just before he took off. He would circle the biplane in measured steps, his mouth firm and his eyes always searching. He might pull on a wire, hang from a wing, or point something out to his mechanics. Once satisfied, he climbed onto his seat and gave the order to start the engine. Still aware of the danger and focused on the task before him, his body was alert. He stared with the intense look of a professional. There was no relaxation until the flight was over and he could walk on the ground again. "The face that had at first seemed to show apprehension and then the placid purpose of the workman," wrote a reporter, "now took on a new expression, and the satisfaction and joy of the aviator was all-apparent."[5]

With his constant travel from one town to another, Gene had learned to make friends quickly. Whenever he wasn't flying or working on his biplane, he welcomed a chance to see whatever town he was in and meet new people. This time, with nearly two weeks to spend in Macon without Mabel's company, Gene relied on his new friends, the important men in town. They were in awe of the young aviator. "Personally Mr. Ely is an exceedingly modest chap, and he would never be singled out as a daring aviator. He would rather talk about almost anything else than his personal achievements and the great records that he has made recently with the biplane." He was guest of honor at luncheons they held at their elite social lodge, the Cherokee Club, and they took him to photoplay houses, where live performances alternated with short motion pictures. "Here in Macon," wrote a reporter, "he had formed a wide circle of friends."[6]

"How high did you go today?" asked one of the fair directors during a noontime gathering.

"I don't know," Gene said. "Up in the air, you are so much higher than anything around you. It is impossible for me to make any kind of accurate estimate. I suppose it was 600 or 700 feet."

Joe Flournoy, fair director, said he would like to have an airplane as soon as they were safe and he wondered when that would be.

Before answering, one can easily imagine Gene inhaling the smoke from one his ever-present "Egyptian cigarettes," a status symbol of the day.

"Give me your order, now," he said, "because they are absolutely safe. I consider them just as safe as the automobile. You wouldn't be afraid to ride in one of those, would you?"

Gene said that in his opinion the experienced aviator only had one thing to fear—overconfidence. "They get to that place where they feel absolutely safe and the next thing you hear of them, they have had a fall, which puts them out of business."

What would happen if his engine stopped or something broke while he was high in the air?

He offered to show them. "Well, if I can get a smooth place to alight tomorrow," he said, "I shall shut down my engine, away up in the air, and show you how I can get down to Earth in case something happens."[7]

The fair board had crossed their fingers when they had written the Glenn Curtiss Exhibition Company, asking for Eugene Ely. Of course they would accept any of the Curtiss birdmen, they said, but they really hoped Ely was available. Curtiss company officials wouldn't guarantee anything until just two weeks before the fair was to open, but the board got their man. Eugene Ely, the only person who had ever taken off and landed on ships, would come directly from Davenport to Macon with a brand new 100 horsepower biplane. He would fly three times a day, every day, October 12–19, 1911, with the exception of October 15, a Sunday; and October 18, which was "Wild West Day" and reserved for Buffalo Bill.[8]

With Mabel in New York, Gene felt free to do all those death defying tricks she hated—the tricks the public always expected to see. "At the recent aviation meet in Chicago, when two men were killed," wrote a reporter, "Ely performed feats, which were considered hazardous in the extreme.... It is certain that he will perform some unusual stunts while at the fair, and it is probable that his glides and dips and whirls will be the big sensation of the event." Gene was aiming to please with a full-page newspaper advertisement promising a "Blood Curdling 1,000 foot DEATH DIP!"[9]

In his first flight at the fair, Gene climbed to 400 feet and, at a mile a minute, flew from the fairgrounds over downtown Macon toward the women's Wesleyan College, five miles northwest of the city. The flight hadn't been part of his contract, but Gene had decided to give the town a dramatic first impression. Word spread quickly. Offices and stores emptied and thousands of people, some climbing to rooftops, looked skyward to see their first airplane. Many of them had seen balloons fly overhead, but this was their first heavier-than-air machine—their first "birdman."

Gene circled back toward the city, heading for the spires of Mercer University, then flying on to the Baptist school near Tattnall Square, and returning to downtown's civic center. The buzz of his engine echoed through a near motionless city. When he was over the fountain and pool in front of city hall, he dropped a letter addressed to the mayor. It fluttered down in the gentle breeze, drifting in hesitant starts, "and at last fell to the pavement with the ease of a snowflake." Someone picked it up and took it to the mayor who was watching from the city hall steps. What it said wasn't reported.

Only once did Gene show his "fancy work" during his two late afternoon flights. He climbed to somewhere between 500 and 1000 feet and circled the race track a number of times, before pitching down in a near straight drop toward the grandstand in the "Dip of Death." At the last second, he pulled up, away from the panicky crowd, landed hard on the grass field, and coasted to a safe stop. Those who only a moment before thought they might die, burst out in frenzied cheers and shouts of approval.[10]

Later, reporters reminded Gene that tomorrow was Friday the 13th. Did he have any fear that something would go wrong? He said the date didn't bother him at all and he would make his three flights as promised. "I will not defy the fates," he said. "I am willing to take things as they come."[11]

That Friday, spectators were disappointed. Gene couldn't fly. His hard landing the day before had broken a part of the plane and though he and his mechanics worked all day, repairs came too late in the evening. To make good on his contract, Gene would have to stay an extra day. Fair officials feared that the improvised field was too rough and might damage the biplane again. Taking advantage of the delay, they hired a crew of men to level the entire field.[12]

As if to prove his daring and silence the scoffers, Gene tore into the Saturday exhibition with reckless abandon. "At times the crowd expected to see both biplane and occupant dashed to the ground," a reporter said. It was non-stop. Spiral Twists, Death Dips, and turns so quick the crowd wondered how the aviator stayed in his seat. He would rise to 300 feet and then take aim at the grandstand in a 60-degree dive. He would clear their heads by ten feet, climbing again before taking aim for yet another pass, and then another. "It was simply a little joke of the aviator's and he seemed to delight in frightening them." Women screamed and "grabbed whoever happened to be standing close by." He came again and again. "He dashed down from a dizzy height, only to rise again before striking the earth. His control of the biplane was perfect." Gene left them breathless and wild. The few brave souls who earlier had said they would like a chance to fly in the clouds with Gene, after watching his contortions and swooping dives, had now completely changed their minds.[13]

His dives and dips continued. So often described as a cautious aviator, he was blind to his own overconfidence. He had only flown this new biplane for a few weeks, but already he decided to try an experiment. "Did you notice that I left off the front elevation?" he asked his friends on the fair board. "I thought I would try it without, because the Wright machines don't use it, and I wanted to see if the Curtiss would work without it." The front elevation was a square piece of canvas, out front of the machine, designed to add stability and give more control over the biplane for up and down steering. For two days, his experiment seemed a success, but then came Thursday, October 19.[14]

As he got ready for the first flight of the day, Gene went to the exhibition building. Earlier in the week he had discovered a boyhood friend had set up a booth there. Before he returned to his plane, Gene let the man hold his cork lined helmet. "What do you wear this heavy thing for, Gene?" the man asked.

Gene smiled. "Oh, that's just to protect my head in case I should fall."[15]

# { 3 }

# The Old York Hills

Month by month, Convey Creek slows to a trickle as it flows between rolling hills on its way to the Iowa River. In the early spring, its brittle waters rush south in a mad dash to catch an eastward ride in Old Man's Creek, but by fall, the water disappears and the creek bed is almost always dry.

Here, barely seven miles east of 1880s Williamsburg, Iowa, in Iowa County, farmers' wells are never deep and the gently rolling prairie freely bursts with flowing springs. This is farm country where the wagon roads are unpaved and free of gravel. In summer, they swirl with dust, and in winter, if not running with rain, they're blocked by snow.

In this place, known as York Center, Rutherford schoolhouse sits at the bottom of a gentle hill, on a small rise, not far from Convey Creek. Near the center of the one-room building, a pot bellied stove is fired each winter morning and those sitting nearby on pine seats are kept toasty and warm. The unlucky few, whose desks sit against an outside wall, shiver through frosty lessons, day after day. In spring, melting snow in the overflowing creek surrounds the school in muddy water. Children wearing rubber boots slop their way up the gentle hill, passing Orson Harrington's orchards, pastures, and bright white farm buildings. Harrington is Gene Ely's grandfather and here is where Gene's life begins. For the boy's first nine years, the homestead and the school were part of his wide-open playground.[1]

When Nathan Dana Ely married Gene's mother in the Harrington home, he was described as the "young man of fine ability and character" who had captured the heart of one of York's fair beauties. Later, when he divorced her, local gossip said he was an opportunistic scoundrel who had married for money and then began chasing after a younger woman. It didn't matter to family and neighbors that Nathan Ely came from a prosperous family, that the couple had been married nearly twenty years, or that they had conceived four children together. All that would really matter was Emma Lois Harrington had been abandoned and embarrassed. The long-held opinions of local busybodies were confirmed. She, who had "grown up in our midst"—Orson Harrington's youngest daughter—she had been abused and her feelings taken advantage of. She had innocently given meddlesome mouths something to talk about. She had married a much younger man—eight years younger as a matter of fact. How could anyone expect that kind of marriage to last?[2]

If there is some romantic tale of how Emma Harrington and Nathan Ely met, it's long been forgotten. Emma was just a toddler learning to talk in 1859, when the Harringtons moved from Indiana to the York homestead. Her grammar school years were spent at a one room schoolhouse built on her father's farm. When she was old enough, she was allowed to attend school in Iowa City, 25 miles east. Whether this was high school or the university is unclear, but her musical education, "noted for its proficiency," was always associated with her time spent there.

Nathan, also a child when his family moved to Iowa City in the early 1870s, was the oldest son of Captain Eugene Hanson Ely, a teacher and a Union veteran of the Civil War. Growing up in a well-educated family, it was natural after high school graduation in 1883, for Nathan Ely to begin two years of study at the State University of Iowa, in Iowa City. His first meeting with Emma might have been on one of those city streets, in a church, or a schoolroom, but it also might have been in the York Hills. Although exactly when, how long, and why the Ely boys lived so near to Orson Harrington's homestead isn't clear, but the evidence says that they did, and not just for a few days. A 1902 visit by Nathan's younger brother, Lt. Eugene J. Ely, prompted the Williamsburg newspaper to remember how "well-known" the young Army officer was in "York Township, where he spent many of his boyhood days." Nathan Ely likely accompanied his brother on some of those days, and if he did, meeting and falling in love with Emma Harrington would not have been difficult.[3]

By 1885, Emma and Nathan were engaged. When his father signed the document giving him permission to marry, Nathan was two weeks away from his 20th birthday. At about the same time, Emma was only a week away from her 28th birthday, and yet, it was her brother Frank, not her father, who signed the marriage license, attesting to the fact that Emma was over 18. The couple said their vows in Orson Harrington's living room on Christmas Eve before the Harrington family minister, the Rev. Thomas Hughes.[4]

After living with Orson Harrington for a few months, Nathan and Emma bought a farm not far away. There, Nathan would make a valiant effort to become a farmer, but it would never take. He did run the Farmer's Grange Store from the property, selling farm implements, feed, and supplies, but as he watched his younger brother receive an appointment to West Point, and his other brothers moving up in the world, he realized he needed more from his life. He wanted a profession and a chance to be somebody important, but for now, that had to wait, a baby was on the way.[5]

Eugene Burton Ely, the couple's first child, arrived October 21, 1886, almost ten months to the day after the wedding. Emma had named the boy after Nathan's father and her younger brother, Burton. Thirteen years older than Burton, Emma had become less of a sister and more of a surrogate mother to the boy, when their mother was stricken with tuberculosis. Mary Harrington had lingered in a long and painful decline until her death early in the winter of 1887. Barely a year after Rev. Hughes had married Nathan and Emma, he returned to the homestead to conduct Mary Harrington's funeral in the Harrington family cemetery.[6]

A year later, Mary's grandson, little Gene Ely, nearly joined her. In the first of many mishaps that would touch him over the coming years and would eventually bring his death, the baby boy waddled toward the family's uncovered well. Henry Brockshus, owner of a neighboring farm, was near enough to see the danger and raced to the boy, snatching him safely away at the last second. Years later, when Gene Ely had become a famous flier, Brockshus reminded him of the rescue. "You owe me a ride in your airplane for saving your life," he said. Gene agreed, but told him that his plane was only a one-seater and the ride would have to wait until he got a larger machine. Gene finally got his two-seater, but it came too late, and Brockshus never got his ride.[7]

Not long after the well incident, in August 1888, 21-month-old Gene found a stranger in his parents' bedroom. The crying creature clinging to his mother was baby sister Mary, named for Emma's mother, and nearly always called Maidie. While their father struggled to find his way off the farm, Nathan's two children grew close and increasingly looked to their mother for love and comfort.[8]

Nathan had heard the call of the Iowa Farmers' Alliance that was quickly gaining members. Promoting political action and government participation to ensure "just government" and respect for agriculture, they demanded legislative action to defend and improve the life of the average farmer. "Forces that prey upon them [the farmer] under pretense of serving them, must be kept under control," wrote a Des Moines newspaper editor, "else they will swallow up their substance.... Now is the time for the Alliances to be at work."[9]

Nathan had found his cause and his escape from the farm had begun. By spring 1891, Nathan was secretary of the Iowa County Alliance. He attended Alliance conventions and corresponded with newspapers, gradually awakening his own political passions. When county supervisors didn't award a bridge building contract to the lowest bidder, Nathan prepared and published a denunciation of the county board's tactics. "We favor, in the future, the publication of the letting of the contract for building our bridges yearly, in order that we may obtain the very best work for the least money," he said. For the moment, he followed the non-partisan path favored by the Iowa Alliance. But, as new opportunities arose, within a year he changed his mind and chose to become a dedicated and uncompromising Democrat.[10]

"I am a Democrat because I believe that through the Democratic Party the most good can be secured for the people of the city," he said in a speech to party faithful. "My views are to elect Democrats to office, men who will continue to be Democrats while in office, and to devise some means of disposing of such as do not remain true to the part.... I believe that we should harmonize and there are none that have a greater hope in the success of the party than myself."[11]

Perhaps it was serving as secretary to State Senator Michael Kelly during the 1891–92 session of the Iowa General Assembly that influenced Nathan's decision to become an attorney. His choice unintentionally set off decades of cynical whispers. When he entered the university's law department in 1893, the gossips' tongues began to wag, saying that he was nothing but a freeloader. It was, they said, Nathan's wife, who had actually paid his way through law school. They ignored all of the contacts he had made and the positions he had held during his political climb away from the farm. As he began his studies, the couple's third child, Julia, was born. She was destined for a painfully short life.[12]

In mid–June 1895, Nathan Ely graduated from the State University of Iowa's Law Department and briefly returned home to pack and move his family. An Iowa City newspaper announced that their former resident was headed for "Davenport, where he has built up a desirable law practice." Ely had joined forces with an Iowa native and his classmate at the university, Arthur Bush. By the end of September 1895, the Ely & Bush firm was advertising in the newspaper and taking on clients. It was the beginning of a lucrative, yet unusual partnership. Bush was a staunch Republican and Ely never stopped pushing Democratic candidates and the party's agenda. They would stay together until 1917.[13]

Early in July 1896, Nathan boarded a train as a member of the Iowa delegation to the Democratic National Convention in Chicago. Emma and her three children were off to the York Hills for a short family vacation with the Harringtons. It was a memorable convention that echoed many of the ideals Nathan had supported since his days with the Farmers' Alliance. William Jennings Bryan and his populist speech condemning the nation's Gold Standard as a "cross of gold" swayed the delegates. They nominated the 36-year-old Nebraskan for president of the United States. The Monday after the convention ended, Nathan returned to Davenport to find a telegram waiting for him. Since Saturday, Emma had been trying to contact Nathan with sad news. Baby Julia, not yet 3 ½-years-old, was dead.

One of the Harringtons' domestic workers had left a bucket of sudsy, boiling mop water on the floor. Curious Julia stumbled as she turned away from the bucket, toppling backwards into the scalding water. There she remained, trapped and undetected for a few minutes. Still alive, she was pulled out and placed on a bed. For 30 hours, Emma was at her side hoping that somehow the unconscious child with horribly burned skin would wake up, but she never did. Nathan rushed to the Harrington homestead. After funeral services in the same living room where he and Emma had been married, the miniature white coffin was carried from the house to the family cemetery.[14]

As much as possible, life for the Elys in Davenport gradually returned to normal. While Nathan was increasingly preoccupied with his politics and his career, the children, Gene and Maidie, got up each morning and went to school. Emma managed to carry on without her husband. When school was out for summer vacation, it was Emma and the children who spent most of their time visiting in York. Nathan sometimes came with them, but for the most part, he seemed to have more time for fishing trips with his Democrat friends than time to be with his family. The Ely & Bush law firm was doing well, actively litigating the usual murder trials, divorces, and political disputes.[15]

The year 1898 opened with the sinking of the battleship *Maine* in Havana Harbor. The incident festered until the war spirit was filling the Adjutant General's office in Des Moines with letters and applications from ex-soldiers, sailors, and those who had never served. Nathan tried to form a cavalry company, advertising for volunteers and asking them to "call at his office," but apparently, he was unsuccessful. Instead, he joined the local naval reserve unit as an "Ordinary Seaman," and on May 28, one month after Congress had declared war on Spain, he and 150 other volunteers left for Cuba. As noble and perhaps politically astute as Nathan's eager conversion to military service was, it didn't last long. He returned to Davenport in August with a medical discharge for a "disability [sustained] in the line of duty." He also had a long and angry tale to tell.[16]

Arriving in Key West, Florida, he had been assigned to the U.S.S. *Lancaster*, a wooden Civil War era sloop complete with sails and steam-driven propellers, but until the new recruits received their training, she didn't travel far. Nathan said he was an "assistant surgeon, in about the fourteenth degree," the only distinction between him and the common seaman was that he did not have to do "scrubbing of decks or brightening brass."

Nathan had been on board barely a month when he was overcome by the sweltering tropical heat and fell to the deck, remaining unconscious for six days. After two weeks in bed, he regained his strength and reported for duty, expecting a transfer to a warship. He was told to first go ashore and collect his pay from the paymaster. There he was surprised to find, not only his pay, but an honorable discharge. He was only allowed to return to the ship just long enough to fetch his hammock, blanket, and personal items. Fifteen hundred miles from Davenport, with a month's pay of $19 in his pocket and the $36 he had already saved, an angry Nathan Ely was a civilian again.

He knew he was luckier than most. He had money, or at least people at home who could send him enough money to get him home. "It isn't fair, nor just, nor right," he said, "that these lads who have made such a sacrifice for their country should be dumped ashore with only the pittance they receive for pay and then be expected to paddle their way home."[17]

Within a month, Nathan was again knee deep in Democratic politics and litigating increasingly higher profile court cases. His son, Gene, was still in school and not quite ready for publicity. Given Gene's heritage of educated family members, it seems inconceivable that he wouldn't finish high school or attend the university, but official records show he didn't. Whether his father was too busy to push or his mother too indulgent, Gene was beginning to go his own way and follow his own dreams. Perhaps the only thing he and his father now shared was an aversion to farming. Gene was developing his independence, immune from thoughts of military service and resistant to his father's political activism. Soon, relations between father and son would become so strained that they wouldn't speak with each other for years. Gene's fascination was turning to technology and he was about to fall in love with automobiles. People could try to tell him what they thought he should do and what he should be, but it didn't matter. He ignored them. His friends would remember him as a meek, courteous, and shy young man, but one who also had a wild streak. He would choose for himself, free of family pressures. With an inner strength, coupled with youthful impatience, a cool head, and fearless nerve, he was on a relentless path that would push him to worldwide fame—and ultimate disaster.[18]

# { 4 }

# A New Century

World opinion was still divided and the great debate continued. Did the new century begin in 1900 or 1901? Never mind that U.S. Supreme Court Justice David Brewer had "exhausted the legal aspects of the case," by declaring the century would begin in 1901; most people waking up on January 1, 1900, believed they were already living in the new century.[1]

In Davenport, the century opened ominously. A single case of smallpox, the first in over sixteen years, had struck quietly in the kitchen of a downtown hotel during the summer of 1899. The victim was quarantined and the threat apparently disappeared. Then, three months into the New Year, a second victim was quarantined, and then another. An epidemic seemed likely. One of the children exposed to smallpox attended Gene Ely's grammar school. The potentially infected boy had been vaccinated, but not until he already had attended one day of school. Chief City Physician Dr. Charles Preston moved quickly. He ordered vaccinations for every student in that school and eventually all students in the district. By the end of the year, his actions had limited the epidemic to 90 actual cases and only one fatality.[2]

Not all the news was bad that year. Gene's baby brother, Hubert, was born in April 1900, just nine months before Gene's graduation from grammar school. The baby boy was too young to care that his birth announcement in the newspaper had called him a girl; however, the same couldn't be said for his 13-year-old brother, Gene. How embarrassing it must have been when the newspaper's list of graduating ninth graders also labeled him a female.[3]

With Nathan's successful law practice and political affiliations, he was now one of the city's "society people," and he proved it with a good game of golf. Golf was the latest fad of the leisure class; those people successful enough in life to take time out from their daily obligations to play a game.

The game had come to the Davenport area in 1897, when a group of Army officers set up a course on the grounds of the Rock Island Arsenal, a government owned island situated in the middle of the Mississippi River between Davenport and Rock Island, Illinois. The island was a perfect place to hold annual men's and women's championship golf tournaments, prompting the Army officers to form the Rock Island Arsenal Golf Club and invite prominent area civilians to join. Nathan Ely became a member as early as 1899, unaware that the game of golf would lead to the end of his marriage.[4]

At the 1900 island tournament, Nathan's reputation as a "crack player" tempted a reporter to predict that, after failing the year before, this time Nathan would win the championship. The prediction looked promising when Nathan shot an 84 on the first day, breaking the record for the lowest score ever posted on the island links. By the third day, with a tenacious effort, he forced his opponent into an extra hole of sudden death, but there he faltered and lost.[5]

His biggest victory came the following spring when "Nate," the local boy, took on Willie Hoare from Dayton, Ohio, one of the best players in the country and a professional who had placed fifth in the 1897 U.S. Open. The two-hour contest ended on the 16th green with Nathan three strokes in the lead with only two holes to play. "Mr. Ely places himself among the foremost amateur golf players of the country," wrote a reporter. "The honor of defeating Mr. Hoare is one of considerable weight and stamps the successful winner as being a player possessing championship material." That fall, Nathan again reached the championship round and once again was eliminated. It marked his competitive peak. From then on, his passion for tournament play faded—replaced by a new obsession—one he had discovered on the Rock Island links. Her name was Mabel von Schaezler.[6]

Mabel von Schaezler had placed second in the 1902 women's golf championship. Three years younger than Nathan, she was described as "an unusually attractive brunette" with a "fascinating manner." Mabel had married Otto von Schaezler at Toluca, Illinois, in 1895. The oldest son of Barron von Schaezler, a German nobleman, Otto had fled his father's estate near Munich and come to the United States in 1881. He found employment as a clerk for a railroad before joining an Illinois coal company as a shipping clerk. In 1899 the von Schaezlers moved to Davenport where Mabel's brother was an accountant for the coal company's Iowa office. Shortly after learning that his father had died, Otto von Schaezler returned to Germany to claim his inheritance. He left the country with a strict warning from Mabel. Under no circumstance would she move to Germany. When negotiations were completed, Otto agreed to surrender his title in favor of his younger brother and returned to the United States a wealthy man. No one knew how large his fortune was, but rumor said "it would take several figures to express its size."[7]

The von Schaezler influence over the Ely family went farther than Nathan Ely's growing infatuation with Mabel. This was the time that Gene Ely was beginning what friends would remember as his fascination with things mechanical and it was the time Otto von Schaezler brought the first automobile to Davenport. When Gene first saw it racing through the city's neighborhoods, one can imagine how excited he would have been.

In May 1900, von Schaezler's unassembled, Stanley Stanhope Model No. 1, arrived by rail from its Connecticut factory. The open-air, steam powered horseless carriage was put together in one day and that evening it was seen speeding up the brick pavement of 3rd Street. Mabel von Schaezler's brother, Will Canniff, was the "expert driver" and Otto von Schaezler was along for the ride.[8]

So much money, acquired so quickly, and spent so lavishly, devastated the von Schaezler marriage. By the end of 1901, Mabel filed for divorce, convincing the court that she was a victim of "cruel and inhuman treatment" from a husband who was a "habitual user of intoxicants." Indeed, not long after the divorce, a drunken von Schaezler attempted suicide, but the gun missed its mark and he was disarmed, suffering little more than a minor flesh wound.[9]

By then, Nathan and Emma Ely were drifting apart. The signs were subtle, seldom talked about, and never reported in the press. In the winter of 1903, while leaving a streetcar, Nathan fell and struck his head. After a month in bed, diagnosed as suffering from "congestion of blood in the brain," his doctor prescribed a two-month vacation. Nathan traveled alone, the guest of Captain John McCaffrey, an old Davenport acquaintance and owner of the steamship *Ten Broeck.* They sailed down the Mississippi and up the Tennessee River to Florence, Alabama. There Nathan left the ship for a leisurely tour of historic sites from Lookout Mountain, Tennessee, through Florida, and on to New Orleans, before he returned home. Emma and the children's visits to her relatives in York were occasionally reported in newspapers, but Nathan was seldom with them. While he was arguing a case in an Iowa courtroom, off to another political convention, or just playing golf, Emma and her children were spending more and more time at Cedar Hill Farm, Nathan and Emma's home in York. By March 1906, Nathan had divorced Emma and married Mabel von Schaezler. Emma returned to Davenport for a few more months, and then moved to San Francisco where Gene had been living. Perhaps she thought her life would be better there, but after barely a year, she was back at Cedar Hill and there she would stay for the rest of her life.[10]

Angered by his father's abandonment, Gene refused to speak with or even visit Nathan. He stopped going to school, began working in a garage and, before he was 16 years old, had become a skilled mechanic. "Gene knows all about the gasoline wagons," said a reporter, "and can diagnose the ailments to which they are subject as correctly as any mechanic in Iowa." He learned to drive, and he drove like a madman. Gene was the boy in a hurry and he wasn't about to wait.[11]

# { 5 }

# Scorching Through the Countryside

No one was more important to Gene Ely's aviation career than the man who flew with Gene two weeks before he died; his mechanical mentor, Pete Petersen. Petersen was ten years older than Gene and had emigrated from Denmark to Chicago in the early 1890s. In 1902, he moved to Davenport with his brother and sister. Petersen was the youngest of the three siblings, but he was also the most successful, eventually owning an automobile dealership and part of a downtown hotel. He got his start by opening one of the first automobile repair shops in the city. From there, he began driving racecars, winning a number of races against professionals at the local mile track and participating in the first "cross-Iowa" automobile race. His antics and popularity earned him the newspaper nickname "Daredevil Pete." He had an outgoing personality with a knack for self-promotion. Although one can sometimes find a grain of truth in some of his stories, Petersen was a master of the tall tale. He claimed he was lifelong friends with racetrack notables, Eddie Rickenbacker and Barney Oldfield, and he convinced his friends that during the Spanish American War he had landed on the beaches of Cuba with Theodore Roosevelt and the Rough Riders. In fact, Petersen had been a private in an Illinois infantry regiment that never saw combat action, but after the fighting was over, did make it to Havana. Petersen also bragged of racing in the Indianapolis 500 and finishing sixth in 1924, but of course, his name does not appear as a starter for that race or any other 500 race. His most laughable exaggeration is the story of his short aeroplane flight made with Gene Ely—the one that he said had given him the scare of his life. While retelling that story in his senior years, he promoted himself to a "stuntman—strapped to the wing of a Curtiss biplane."[1]

To a young boy stricken with a mechanical fascination, Pete Petersen was obviously irresistible. Gene started skipping school and Petersen became his substitute teacher. Young Ely learned to take engines apart and put them back together again. He learned to drive and probably learned a few self-promotion ideas that would later come in handy. Petersen was Gene's guiding inspiration and for over a year, Gene Ely learned his lessons well.

By the summer of 1903, when Gene was only 16 years old, he was out on his own in Cosgrove, a small town about thirteen miles east of York Center. Driving the "best car in the state," his employer's $3,000 Franklin, Gene kept his foot on the accelerator and began setting speed records. His "scorching" commutes with the car's owner, Father Thomas Smyth, as a passenger, quickly gained this "youthful chauffeur" a reputation as "the best driver in Iowa."[2]

Father Smyth was born in County Clare, Ireland in 1838. His family claimed a long, uninterrupted line of Roman Catholic priests and after his uncle was appointed Bishop of Dubuque, Iowa in 1858, Smyth came to the United States and began studying for the priesthood. Ordained in 1869, he was appointed to St. Ann's in Long Grove, Iowa, twelve miles north of Davenport. After serving there for 24 years, he was transferred to St. Peter's in Cosgrove. Parishioners remembered Smyth as a silent, retiring, and prayerful priest, "with a keen sense of humor and a warm affection for friends." The 65-year-old priest liked to travel fast, with gray hair rippling in the wind as he sped through Iowa in his bright red car.[3]

With so few automobiles in Iowa at the time, the sight of a priest bouncing over dusty country roads was certain to draw a lot of attention, and with Father Smyth's gregarious nature, affectionate newspaper coverage naturally followed. Smyth eagerly shared his adventurous shopping trips and countryside wanderings by filling empty seats with friends or awestruck children. He enjoyed the look of terror on their faces as he urged Gene to race him from town to town. Because it was always Gene behind the wheel, these frequent journeys brought the boy his first taste of publicity. Newspapers reported that Gene had set the all-time speed record between Iowa City and Davenport with Father Smyth and four other passengers aboard, covering nearly 60 miles in two hours and 26 minutes. Two weeks later, "after a week's illness," he broke his own speed record and "clipped off the same distance in nearly a mile a minute over the uneven country roads."[4]

Gene had almost unlimited use of Father Smyth's Franklin auto, particularly on Sundays when the priest was busy with church. That's when Gene made frequent trips to York Center, Iowa City, and Davenport, visiting with parents, friends, and relatives. One morning, just before beginning one of these expeditions, Gene got a big surprise. Apparently, a leaky gas tank had spread fuel over the body of the machine and a spark set it off. While still in the Cosgrove barn that served as a garage, the automobile burst into flames. A quick-thinking Gene smothered the fire with a blanket and saved the day. The newspaper credited him with preventing an inevitable explosion that would have destroyed the automobile and flattened the barn, not to mention what it might have done to Gene.[5]

In late 1904, Father Smyth said he was planning a return trip to Ireland for a motoring tour of his ancestral home. He would ship the Franklin overseas and bring Gene along to do the driving. But that was before the big accident. One December evening, while racing over the road at his usual frantic pace, Gene lost control. Unable to brake in time, he crashed the car into a high dirt bank. The auto slammed to a sudden stop, throwing Father Smyth out onto the ground. Luckily, he, Gene, and the three young passengers only suffered a few scrapes and bruises, although, seven years later, Gene would report he had been struck in the head with no subsequent effect. The Franklin was done for. One of its wheels had snapped off, the chassis was twisted, and the front axle was bent almost in two. They hitched a ride home in a farmer's horse-drawn wagon. With Smyth's automobile out of service, Gene's brief year of publicity was over.[6]

It wasn't long before Gene decided to leave home. He said goodbye to his family and on October 17, 1905, Gene and his cousin, Orson Harrington, caught the train that would take them to San Francisco.[7]

For two Midwest boys striking out on their own, San Francisco was an exotic destination. "I've always heard that Frisco would never be outdid in any way," a wide-eyed Orson later wrote. They were sure that the wide streets of a big city offered more than enough opportunity to fulfill their dreams. They were talented mechanics and employment wouldn't be a problem. If nothing else, they could both drive cars for a living. But opportunities and boyhood dreams sometimes come with a high price and for the cousins—payment would be due on an April morning.[8]

# { 6 }

# The City of a Hundred Hills

Gene was their idol now and the boys of auto row wouldn't be stopped. The rumor was true. This Eugene Ely, the aviator who was returning to San Francisco for the 1911 International Aviation Meet, was the same Gene Ely that every automobile driver and every mounted policeman of the city knew so well. His flouting of speed limits and municipal traffic ordinances were legendary and his victories in auto races had made him a favorite driver, mechanic, and every driver's best friend. At least a hundred pairs of hands were reaching for their automobile horns as Gene drove onto the aviation field near Tanforan racetrack. These were the chauffeurs, the ones who knew him best, and they were determined to give Gene the "grand honking" they felt he deserved. He was returning in triumph with a newfound celebrity. He was their inspiration. If he could succeed, why couldn't they? He had left town a self-proclaimed failure, barely making $100 a month as a chauffeur. Now, newspapers said he was earning $50,000 or more each year and society elites were begging him to visit their homes and speak at their clubs. This onetime little guy, this motoring maniac, was now world famous. With blaring horns and a banquet at the Palace Hotel, his friend's were welcoming him home. How different it had been just five years earlier, in the winter of 1905, when he and Orson first saw San Francisco's Market Street.[1]

The railroad tracks from Iowa ended on the east side of San Francisco Bay. With a few hundred fellow travelers, Gene Ely and Orson Harrington left the train and boarded a ferry that in less than an hour's time would take them to the "City of a Hundred Hills." The brisk, salty sea air was a new experience for both of them. Leaning over the rail, the boys could see movement on the docks and on the ships moored at Goat Island, where the Navy was training their latest recruits. Farther west, they passed the Army fortress on the cliffs of Alcatraz Island. It was unbelievably crowded with a hodgepodge of wood and stone structures from bay waters to the crest of the hill. But nothing could compare with the compact city that kept growing larger in front of them. Houses, churches, and multistoried buildings lined a grid of streets that climbed up, over, and behind hills that looked more like mountains to a Midwesterner's eye. As the sounds of the city grew closer, orderly spaced piers, swarming with hundreds of workers, extended left and right until they curved around the shoreline and disappeared. The ferry slowed as it floated toward a sandstone, two-story rectangular building. Narrow arched windows spread out horizontally in two directions from a central tower. Halfway up the tower was a large clock, black hands pointing to Roman numerals. Above the clock, four Greek-like temples stacked one on top of the other and gradually growing smaller, climbed upward in a pyramid form until they were capped with a dome and flagpole. Hills and the skyline slid behind the building as the ferry docked. Gripping their few pieces of luggage, the boys walked down the gangway and toward the three giant arched windows under the tower. A wide and open space under the arches entered into the building and, almost like a tunnel, exited out the opposite side onto a cobblestoned plaza of noise.[2]

Davenport might as well have been a lemonade stand when compared with San Francisco. Nearly a half-million people lived here, the ninth most populous city in the United States, and it seemed most of them were here on this plaza.

Two men in uniform were pushing on a cable car that was resting on a circular platform. While they moved it a few feet to the right, they also were turning it around in a half circle until it lined up with two rails running away from the plaza. One of the men jumped on the car and pulled back on a long, floor-mounted lever and the car's metal wheels rumbled forward, then stopped. A rush of passengers climbed on. With the clanging of a bell, the trolley pulled away, heading up Market Street, a wide boulevard walled in on each side with tall buildings that framed two hilltop peaks in the distance. On the parallel set of tracks that had brought the first trolley to the plaza, another car was already arriving, many of its standing passengers jumping off before it stopped. To the far left were wooden trolley wagons pulled by teams of two horses, and to the right, rooftop arms on electrified streetcars were sparking as they rubbed on wires above. The rattle and clatter of carriages and freight-carrying wagon wheels blended with the occasional sputter and backfire of the latest in personal passenger service, open air automobile jitneys and taxis. With up to five men in suits stuffed into each vehicle, drivers for hire sped off in all directions. Newsboys shouted today's headlines and street vendors offered trinkets to buy or a bite to eat. People were everywhere, hurriedly weaving around each other's bodies, eyes set on their destination. This chaotic flow from plaza to street and street to plaza was intimidating, but these innocently optimistic boys were unafraid. They were at the beginning of their adventure and had no idea how severely their dreams of glamorous success would be tested.

"I became a chauffeur only after the money I started with was gone," Gene Ely said, "and everything I had tried, left me worse off than before."[3]

The meaning of the word chauffeur in 1906 San Francisco encompassed more than our narrow idea of someone just driving wealthy individuals from place to place. A chauffeur might also be someone hauling freight, operating a taxicab, or, could simply be a driver up for hire on a rental basis for anyone. Gene, would do almost all of them before he learned to fly. Though a chauffeur could make a decent living, there was still a lower class stigma attached to the profession.

Becoming a chauffeur was a disappointing last resort for Gene. He didn't see it as a steppingstone to better things. He knew it was virtually impossible for a chauffeur to become wealthy or be considered important, and perhaps that was his biggest problem. Much as his father had needed to escape the farm and be somebody, Gene felt he needed to escape the automobile. Like so many impatient 20-year-olds, a frustrated Gene didn't know what success would be, what he was looking for, and where he would find it. It was just too soon for him to realize that these automobiles were already taking him where he wanted to go. He just had to be patient and begin meeting the right kind of people.

The boys began to drive for Dr. Morris Herzstein, a man of enormous wealth who was also well connected with the highest echelons of society, the kind of people that would one day see something special in Gene and help move him toward his ambitious dreams.

On his way to becoming the most prominent physician and surgeon in San Francisco, Herzstein was a 24-hour bundle of energy. Patients received visits at all hours of day or night and wondered if he ever slept. Medical students affectionately remembered his humorous touch of vanity. "He went from toupee to toupee as one goes from haircut to haircut," wrote one scholar in his memoirs. "I heard debates among the students as to whether he wore his own hair or that of someone else." It was a quirk that only enhanced his reputation in medical circles and no one would ever question Herzstein's devotion to his patients.[4]

Born in Cologne, Germany, in 1854, Gene's new employer arrived in the United States in 1880, after graduating with a medical degree from Berlin's Frederick Wilson University. Three years later, he married Cora, daughter of William Wallace, one of the most prominent businessmen in San Francisco. Though it must have given a boost to his social standing, the marriage was childless and short-lived. After the divorce, Herzstein remained a bachelor for the rest of his life. He was a successful real estate speculator and, as a wealthy philanthropist, frequently made large donations to charities and medical programs, even endowing laboratories and scientific studies. By 1912, when the soon to be approved national income tax law was being discussed in Congress, there was agreement amongst a group of San Francisco physicians that Herzstein would pay more taxes than any of them, because he "makes the largest income in the city's medical profession."[5]

Herzstein owned one of the finest private hospitals in the city, the Waldeck. The Waldeck was a sanatorium, a private hospital for individuals wealthy enough to avoid public hospitals. "Public hospitals are, of course, a necessity for the poor," was the elitist attitude expressed in a medical journal of the day, "but private sanatoria under competent management must prove a boon to suffering humanity." The "suffering humanity" at the Waldeck were pampered in spa-like mud and mineral baths, steam chairs, hammocks, and a peaceful solarium, "where convalescents may have sun baths." In addition to providing surgical and outpatient services, the hospital could provide beds for over 300 long-term patients. Visiting surgeons were allowed to use the antiseptic and modern operating rooms and care for their patients with the cutting edge of technology, even taking some of the city's first X-ray photographs. For the comfort of patients, a ventilating system driven by a gigantic electric fan in the basement, supplied each room with individually temperature controlled fresh air. There were electric lights, an automatic fire alarm, telephones, and speaking tubes for the nurses. Food was prepared in a central kitchen and delivered to upper floors by an electric dumbwaiter. "No expense will be spared to make the institution first class in every particular," the management said. This indeed was a modern and forward thinking hospital.[6]

Although Gene and Orson may have occasionally driven for Herzstein as personal chauffeurs, it's more likely they just maintained and drove delivery vehicles and the hospital's ambulance van. The work wasn't glamorous, or what Gene might have dreamed of, but there was opportunity here, a chance to be noticed by an affluent patient or one of Herzstein's wealthy associates. Maybe success would come, but Gene couldn't count on it. He was only a chauffeur and there was no reason why anyone would remember him. Nothing made him special, nothing at all. Something needed to happen—something that could make a difference.

The wait would not be long.

# { 7 }

# 5:12 a.m.—April 18, 1906

Fifteen minutes before sunrise the earth began to pulse and sway toward the west. Sleeping eyes opened in an uneasy queasiness as body parts briefly wriggled and twisted in opposite directions. The gyrations peaked and then began to fade. Eyes closed and there was a peaceful moment of deep breaths and prayers of thanks. Then, the whole world seemed to heave and fall.

Rocking like a ship trapped in the waves of a boiling storm, the room launched bodies against walls. Beds hung in midair for a moment then spiraled down to the floor where they flipped and shattered. Furniture danced and tumbled. Plaster ceilings fell in chunks with heavy chandeliers still attached. Floors in multistoried buildings pancaked down on terrified victims. Windows shattered. Dishes flew from pantry shelves. Air and lungs were filled with dust and debris. Unheard over the unearthly roar from deep in the earth were the shrieks of women and the shouts of men pouring out through the sides of buildings where walls had fallen away. Although it was only a minute, it seemed it would never stop.

As the ground's convulsions began to subside, those lucky enough to be alive ran for the safety of the street. There, amongst debris and dead bodies, neighbors gathered in groups for mutual comfort, unashamed of the rainbow colored night clothing they wore.

Then the cinders began to fall. The city was on fire.

"I never was so near scared to death as I was that morning and own up to it," Orson Harrington wrote in a letter home. "It is no use to let on as though I wasn't."[1]

Orson Harrington and Gene Ely were rooming together when roused by the quake.

"Most of the roof was in our room when we got up," Orson said. "How we ever got out alive I never can tell you."

He compared his helplessness feelings in the shaking room to the weather that had frightened him as a child in Iowa.

"Don't talk to me about your cyclones and lightning storms. Wait until you get up against the real thing, an earthquake, and then you'll know where you are at."

It seemed that all of San Francisco had collapsed. "A city of over five hundred thousand and now [it] is about as large a place as Williamsburg."

"Some of the streets for several blocks are sunk down five or six feet below the sidewalks and lots of places you can't cross for big cracks," he said.

Fire and gas mains ruptured and there was little water left to fight the small fires that were merging into an inferno. The city was vanishing behind violent red flames shooting through a veil of dark and churning smoke clouds that rose a thousand feet into the sky. "The smoke of San Francisco's burning was a lurid tower visible a hundred miles away," wrote novelist, Jack London. "And for three days and nights this lurid tower swayed in the sky, reddening the sun, darkening the day, and filling the land with smoke."[2]

Fire crews pulled salt water from the bay and sucked sewers dry in vain attempts to stop the flames. At first, the fires had remained small, mostly in the tenements south of Market Street, but just before noon, flames leaped across that wide boulevard and began to eat into the Western Addition. The military, hoping to stop the fire's spread, began dynamiting buildings in its path to create a firebreak of rubble on the city streets. They ordered an evacuation of everyone east of Van Ness Avenue, one of the widest streets in the city, where the inferno was already climbing the hill toward Herzstein Waldeck Hospital.

Years later, when Gene Ely became famous, a newspaper reporter remembered Gene's heroics during that time, recounting how Gene had saved Herzstein's 300 hospitalized patients, with the fire just mere blocks away. Gene's ambulance shot to the hospital's front door. He "leaped out and said that he had come to carry the sick men and women to places of safety," said the reporter. Gene hurriedly crammed the first load of patients into the ambulance and sped off to a temporary field hospital in Golden Gate Park, nearly four miles to the west. Trip after overloaded trip, the ambulance flew between the hospital, the park, and back again. "Before the first tongue of flame touched the hospital building," the reporter said, "the last patient had been safely deposited upon the grass in the park."[3]

Dr. Herzstein's private secretary, King Hill, was impressed with Gene's effort.

"Ely was one of the cleverest men I ever saw at the wheel of a car," Hill recalled. "At the time of the fire, with but little assistance from the nurses, he conveyed more than 300 patients from the Waldeck. He displayed an immense amount of energy and surprised all of us. His eye was very sharp and his judgment of distance good. I have seen him swiftly pass through a very narrow place in his car, without so much as a scratch."[4]

With the evacuation completed, Gene and Orson moved north toward the bay, camping overnight in the open air. When the fire began to approach the next day, they moved again to a refugee camp that was near Ft. Mason, not far from the bay and Army headquarters in the Presidio. Within three days, Dr. Herzstein set up a hospital in an abandoned private home, four blocks west of the Van Ness Avenue firebreak and asked Gene and Orson to join him.

"We moved to where we are now and hope to stay a while," Orson wrote. "One thing nice, the government is feeding us. No stores are allowed to sell, and those that were, had everything taken from them, and all saloons were broken into and smashed. There has [sic] been lots of people shot here lately and any one poking around in the ashes after night, if caught by the soldiers, is shot."

Military authorities confiscated all available motor vehicles and ordered their drivers to take dynamite to points where it was needed most. Then, when the fire was stopped and the dynamite no longer needed, food and supplies were transported to the many refugee camps. Drivers drove day and night for days, many without sleep. Medical supplies, physicians, nurses, and injured patients, all under military control, had to be moved between temporary emergency tent hospitals to the Army hospital at the Presidio. Of course, someone also had to pick up the dead. Drivers piled bodies in sickening stacks of bloody and broken carcasses and then hauled them away to cemeteries like deliveries from a butcher shop. Gene and Orson drove for the Army during these weeks, but exactly what they had to do, didn't make it into print.[5]

"The chauffeur offered his services to the army surgeons who were working desperately with the sick and wounded," said a newspaper report. "The chauffeur was Eugene B. Ely, and in the dreadful days of unparalleled disaster, he proved the stuff of which he is made. He was just one of many unsung heroes."[6]

Driving on military controlled streets was a dangerous occupation for an unsung hero.

"Several chauffeurs have been killed," wrote Orson Harrington, "been ordered to stop and did not. They stuck their old musket up in my face several times and you don't need to ask me whether I stopped, for it's a certainty that I did—and was glad to—for that big gun didn't look good to me."

Although less than two weeks after the quake, streetcars on Market Street began to move again, conditions for most residents were still desperate. "Have just come from a big walk," Orson wrote. "No one is allowed out on the streets after 10 o'clock since the city is under martial law. No one is allowed any light except candles and these are to be put out at ten. Can't have any fire in stoves—have to do all the cooking out in the streets. The boys in blue are making everybody do as they say."

Newspaper columns filled with advertisements from frantic souls hunting lost family and friends. One, from Frank Towle, Pacific Coast representative of the Towle Maple Syrup Company, asked if anyone knew "where I can find Dr. M. Herzstein of the Waldeck Hospital, or any of his assistants. Please telephone 4153 or address 649 Oakland Ave. I am desirous of learning the whereabouts of my wife and two children."

Within a day, Towle could read his answer in a newspaper advertisement. "Your wife and children are safe and well, Hotel Rafael, San Rafael, care of Dr. Herzstein."[7]

A temporary hospital had been set up in the park behind that Marin County hotel. Some of Dr. Herzstein's patients had been ferried across the bay to recuperate in its more relaxed atmosphere. Perhaps Gene had accompanied them on the ferry and perhaps that's where he met his future wife, Mabel, who lived nearby. Sadly, there is no evidence either way.[8]

The boys only had a few coins in their pockets and though they were owed a month's wages, their bank had declared a 30-day holiday immediately after the quake. Orson joked that there really was no place to spend money anyway. But, looking through his bravado, it was obvious he was homesick. "I don't know whether my folks have left the farm or not, but I know I haven't heard from any one since March 30," he wrote. "I don't know where my letters could have gone, for they must have written since.... Never wanted to see my Mama so bad in quite a while."

He closed his letter by asking forgiveness for not writing in ink. "Excuse lead pencil, but they are all a premium these days."

A few weeks after the earthquake, Orson heard that the railroads had been offering free passes to anyone wanting to leave San Francisco, but thought he had missed his chance. Then he learned that the Santa Fe Railroad was still offering the passes to any point on the company's lines. It was too good to be true! Three Sundays after he had mailed his penciled letter, he was home again in Iowa.[9]

"Orson was in Frisco when the old earth was seized with the appendicitis," said the hometown newspaper, "and he can tell all about how the thing writhed and twisted and shook down the tall buildings in its agony. He admits being scared a bit and thought that he never again would behold the old York Hills or exchange greetings with the friends he loved. Not any more for him of the famous Pacific Coast, where even the earth is not secure for a night."[10]

Orson's exotic dreams were over. A year later, he would marry a local girl, raise a family, and except for a few months on the road as Gene's aviation mechanic, spend the rest of his life as an "easy going and friendly" auto mechanic in Iowa.

Gene, whose father had married another woman in Davenport just a month before the earthquake, wasn't going anywhere.

# { 8 }

# Native Son and Daughter

While Gene was falling in love with automobiles and long before he discovered airplanes or thought of soaring above the ground, Mabel Hall, his future wife, was growing up along the shores of San Francisco Bay. This had always been her home and, except for those few short years when she would travel with Gene, her entire life was spent within 25 miles of the Golden Gate.

Her family had been Californians since 1849 when Josiah Henry Hall left St. Joseph, Missouri bound for the California gold fields on the edge of the Sierra Mountains.[1]

The Hall family claimed a close connection to John C. Fremont, the "Great Pathfinder" and 1856 presidential candidate. Perhaps they inflated that relationship, but they did live near Fremont's home in Mariposa County's Bear Valley and Josiah worked in the Fremont mines. Fremont had returned to California in early 1849, eager to see if the 44,000 acres he owned might now be sparkling with gold. They were. Bear Valley became Fremont's headquarters for a network of mines that produced nearly $100,000 a month. Here, in May 1859 at the Pine Tree Mine camp, Josiah Hall's first son and Mabel Ely's father, Henry Clay Hall, was born.[2]

The family moved away from the mines and by 1866 was living in San Mateo County, south of San Francisco. Josiah tried to become a hop farmer, but his children remembered him as a man who could never really lose his gold fever. He was "still holding to the belief that eventually he would make a big strike," said a county history. "Again and again, almost to the day he died, he would disappear from for long periods of time and return to that line of work." With him absent so often, it must have been their mother, Ellen, who made sure the three children paid attention to their studies. All three became lifelong teachers.[3]

It was Henry, Mabel's father, who had the most success as an educator. He passed the State Teacher's Examination at age 18 and in 1876, began a 48-year teaching career. His reputation as an outstanding educator, respected writer, and eloquent orator grew quickly. "The sage of Menlo Park," wrote future San Mateo County school superintendent, Roy Cloud, "was, without doubt, the most gifted man that ever graced a school room in this county."[4]

Hall took a modern approach to teaching that produced results far "beyond the comprehension of his associates." He loved to teach history, especially territorial history, and was proud president of the local Native Son's of the Golden West, a group of native Californians dedicated to preserving California's history. He also had a passion for the outdoors and was an ardent conservationist, taking his students on hikes to mountains and beaches, hoping to fill them with a "healthy love of nature."[5]

"Generations of school children," said his youngest daughter, Mercedes, "remember Pop for the high value he placed upon an education."[6]

Politically, Henry Hall was a Democrat, not as intensely political as Nathan Ely, but a regular attendee of the county Democratic conventions and a member of the Democratic Central Committee. In 1890, he ran for State Superintendent of Public Instruction, but after losing the statewide election to the Republican by less than 10,000 votes, he turned his energy toward improving the local school curriculum and in 1893 was elected president of the San Mateo County Board of Education. "He gave the schools of the whole county a course of study that made every one of them better than it had ever been before," Cloud said. But soon Hall's progressive ways met with bitter opposition. Disputes reached a head in 1899 when Hall's choices for school trustee were defeated and his chief opponent, Professor Van Horn, replaced Hall as school principal. His 17 years of dedicated service had been ignored and the fight had been too personal. An angry Hall accepted a teaching position in Corte Madera and took his family to Marin County, north of San Francisco. There he split his time between teaching in San Francisco and in the Corte Madera schools.[7]

Daughter Mercedes remembered how "Pop" would leave his Corte Madera home in the evening with a "little black satchel always clutched to his side, and walk down to the Northwestern Pacific station for a long train and ferryboat ride to San Francisco." There he caught a horse drawn trolley that carried him three more miles to Mission High School where he taught algebra and English at a private evening high school.[8]

In 1907, Hall gave up his San Francisco credentials to teach fulltime in Marin County as the principal teacher at the Larkspur-Corte Madera School. He soon was promoted to principal of the school, and then to superintendant of the entire school district. There he devoted the rest of his teaching life.[9]

In August 1887, Henry Hall had married one of his recent students, Mary Loughren. Mary was also a California native, born to Irish immigrants. Mabel, their first child, was born in May 1889.[10]

Mabel could have followed in the family's teaching tradition, but, much like future husband Gene, she too traveled an independent and perhaps rebellious path. When they met, he was a car salesman, a common mechanic, a race car driver, a chauffeur, and she was upper middleclass. What must her parents have thought?

Mabel's childhood leaves few clues. The adult woman, who was described as ambitious and the force behind Gene Ely's success; as a young girl, was nearly invisible. Surrounded by a family of teachers, one suspects that she received a good education and could have pursued a profession, but she didn't. In addition to her father, her aunt was a teacher and her uncle was on his way to heading one of the largest county school districts in the state. For 22 years, her oldest brother headed the San Bruno city schools and for 24 years, her youngest brother was Tax Assessor for Marin County. Without a doubt, she had the social standing to draw upon. It seems impossible that this "little general," wife and manager of a world famous aviator, could have spent her youth as a shrinking violet. Whether she was simply rebellious, uninterested, or just waiting for the right time to escape from home, there are just too few clues to follow. Mabel lived in an era when young women of position were more often seen than heard. The goal was to grow up quietly and, while looking for a man to marry, do nothing that would embarrass the family. In that, she succeeded well. Not until Gene Ely began to fly did she find a way to stand on her own. That's when she showed her disciplined control and her unwavering determination to always push her husband to do more. Gene was a husband she could mould into the man she thought he should be. "My press agent," Gene would say.[11]

Mabel didn't need to marry this young chauffeur, a common mechanic, a struggling businessman. Perhaps her independent nature was taking her down that rebellious path traveled by many young women who consciously or unconsciously jump at the chance to choose the man least acceptable to their father or mother. But, even if that is true, it seems Gene and Mabel genuinely loved each other. It was only after Gene died that we see her impulsive and sometimes reckless side, a side that must have always been there. She married so quickly after he was gone, and some might say, for money or security more than love. Perhaps she missed the celebrity that Gene's growing fame and fortune had brought her, or, perhaps wealth and celebrity had been her goal all along. If so, she was following in the early footsteps of one of her best friends, the only friend we know anything about, and perhaps someone she envied—Mabel Cramer.

Young Mabel Cramer was about the same age as Mabel Ely and can only be described as a liberated woman, far more progressive than most women of her time. She exploded from obscurity to fame in mere weeks and, for the five or six years, before settling into a quiet life as a Navy wife, she lived a somewhat bohemian lifestyle.

Both Mabels were California born, and both grew up as teenagers in Marin County. Their families were Roman Catholic and their fathers were both active in the church and the Democratic Party. Although Mabel Hall came from a family of professionals, Mabel Cramer was the daughter of a teamster, but a teamster who still managed to instill confidence in his children and encourage them to accomplish something with their lives. His son Harry would become both an attorney and a dentist, while daughter Mabel would boldly captivate her world with her beauty.[12]

Although Mabel Ely was nearly always described as an attractive woman, if she ever happened to envy Mabel Cramer's beauty, it was understandable. Cramer was "the girl with the Cleopatra face," said a reporter, "and a countenance framed by great masses of raven black hair and lighted by large, luminous black eyes." She was unforgettable, a woman with the "symmetry and proportions of figure, which artists have pronounced the feminine ideal." It must have been a bit overwhelming for Mabel Hall to watch her friend soar from teenager to ravishing adult in mere months.[13]

In 1907, Cramer had won third place in a statewide beauty contest conducted by a San Francisco newspaper. A third place finish might have been the end for most women, but not for Cramer. With her free spirited and bold personality attracting men of every age, her phone began to ring with all sorts of offers and the newspapers couldn't resist her. Her most daring exploit was the time she suddenly appeared at a saltwater swimming pool wearing the latest French swimsuit. The bodice was tight and the skirt that ended just above her knees was slit fourteen inches up each side and worn over fleshy, pink colored stockings. Her exotic appearance dazzled the men and shocked all the women. "San Rafael Swimmers Nearly Drown When Surprised by Beauty," read the headline.[14]

In 1912, after a brief career as a musical comedy chorus girl and an actress, Cramer married a naval officer and finally ended her wild ways.[15]

Mabel Ely would never be as free spirited or provocative as Cramer, but watching her friend become the envy of the newspaper world may have been the inspiration that made her such a favorite with reporters who, expecting to report on Gene Ely, quickly found themselves much more charmed and captivated by his wife.

In December 1910, a month before Gene Ely would make his historic flight in San Francisco Bay, Mabel Ely dared her "close friend," Mabel Cramer, to fly as a passenger with Gene on his biplane. "Certainly I will fly," a laughing Cramer told a mesmerized reporter. "I am tired of being called a beauty," she said. "I want to be as free as any other young woman, and if I choose to fly, why not?"[16]

Reporters were intrigued to know what she would wear while flying.

"I understand that skirts or other flowing garments might interfere with the balance of the machine because of their being liable to be caught by the air currents," she said. "It is probable that I will be obliged to don knickers and leggings, but that is entirely in the hands of Mr. Ely."[17]

Though she might have been willing, Gene was not. Days before the exhibition was underway, two prominent birdmen had crashed and died and the weather in San Francisco was too unstable to take a chance. Sadly, the eager men of the world would never see Mabel Cramer fly.

# { 9 }

# Driving the Right People

After the earthquake, once the immediate crisis was over, Gene scrambled to find a new career. He hired on as a mechanic with Max Rosenfeld's Auto Livery Company. He couldn't have been luckier. There was no one in all of San Francisco who was more involved in the automobile business than Rosenfeld. Son of a self-made millionaire, Rosenfeld had formed his company in 1903. Fortunately his business was located on the west side of Van Ness Avenue, the safe side of the wide boulevard, where the army had stopped dynamiting buildings in their effort to stifle that fiendish 1906 fire. Rosenfeld claimed to be the first dealer in the city to offer a complete automobile salesroom; selling and renting cars, and also incorporating body, electrical, and repair shops all at the same location. He was the exclusive dealer for the Peerless Automobile Company and was president of the Automobile Dealers' Association of California.[1]

Working for Rosenfeld gave Gene the opportunity to meet the legendary racecar driver, Barney Oldfield. Oldfield, on his way to a Los Angeles race, stopped by Rosenfeld's Peerless automobile dealership in January 1907. The Peerless Company had hired Oldfield to race their cars. Although Gene Ely's relatives and friends would later tell newspaper reporters that Gene had "chummed around with the likes of Barney Oldfield and Eddie Rickenbacker," except for Oldfield's visit to San Francisco in 1907, and a joint appearance with Gene in St. Paul, Minnesota in June 1910, there is no evidence they ever knew each other. Likewise, a meeting with Rickenbacker cannot be found.[2]

The chummy Oldfield-Rickenbacker tale probably began in 1927, when Arthur "Bugs" Baer, nationally syndicated columnist, ghostwrote a series of stories for Oldfield's onetime manager and sports promoter, Bill Pickens. Pickens had taken over management of the Mercedes Benz team in 1909, the team Oldfield was then racing for. Pickens told Baer that in 1914 he began promoting a series of exhibition races between Oldfield and a group of aviators he called the "Pickens' Flying Circus." Baer's six-part *Saturday Evening Post* series said it was Pickens' brainstorm to have Gene Ely land and takeoff from Navy ships and that Gene had also flown with the Pickens' circus," even though Gene had been dead for nearly three years by then.

Pickens was well known for ballyhoo and a knack for making things up. One sports writer in a 1934 obituary, called Pickens the "modern" P. T. Barnum, a man who "trafficked in suckers."[3]

The 1927 fabrications might have been the end of it, but then, Baer wrote another column in 1954, repeating Pickens' claim that Gene Ely had flown with the Pickens' Circus and that Pickens had "dreamed up Ely's stunts." When Mabel Ely read that she was furious and picked up a pen.[4]

"Mrs. Ely," Baer wrote, "says Bill Pickens had absolutely nothing to do with either stunt. They were dreamed up by her husband who also executed them in person." Baer explained that he had been dubious of what Pickens told him in 1927, yet had had no evidence to doubt the claims.[5]

Working at Rosenfeld's auto dealership gave Gene a firsthand look at Rosenfeld's car rental business and, in a bold move early in 1907, Gene took delivery of two Matheson seven-passenger touring cars and began his own automobile renting company. Each of these machines would have cost him between $5,000 and $7,000 in 1907 money, so Gene, the mechanic and driver, was taking a major risk. But where did he find that kind of money? Perhaps he brought a well-hidden nest egg with him from Iowa, or his mother, recently divorced and arriving in San Francisco with Gene's brother and sister for an extended stay in the winter of 1906, may have invested in her eldest son's dreams. However it happened, he had his automobiles, but would have little luck. The rental business collapsed within months.[6]

Gene's association with San Francisco's automobile world also gave rise to another family legend that has been repeated so often it's accepted as historical fact. "At one time," it says, "Ely held the speed record at the San Jose racetrack." Never mind that a person can look forever for a San Jose automobile racetrack that was regularly clocking speed records between 1906 and 1908, and not find one. That's because the city's Driving Park, their first speedway, didn't hold its initial competition until November 1909. By then, Gene Ely had already moved to Oregon. The error comes from a newspaper story that initially identified one of the drivers in the speedway's premier 1909 event as E. B. Ely, confusing later researchers and perhaps Gene Ely's family. A subsequent story in the same paper correctly identifies the driver as E. M. Ely, "a noted Eastern racing driver."[7]

The initial confusion over Gene Ely's initials is easily understood. Gene was already a well-known race driver on the local auto racing circuit. While trying to set speed records, he had already driven through San Jose twice, but never on the speedway.

Gene's West Coast racing career had begun with the 1906–07 automobile races near Del Monte, California, a resort area east of Monterey, nearly 130 miles south by dusty road from San Francisco. In an endurance drive from the city by socially prominent automobile owners and their passengers, Rosenfeld brought two Peerless automobiles to Del Monte in September 1906. Both cars would race, with Rosenfeld driving one and perhaps Gene Ely, his mechanic, driving the other. But Gene was never mentioned in newspaper's race results. Then again, generally only the top two or three cars and drivers were mentioned and it wasn't uncommon for owners to hire a driver and take any earned race credit in their own name. If Gene raced, he didn't win in 1906—at least not officially. Rosenfeld did win a minor racing event that could have been driven by Gene, but he also won the Del Monte Cup, a five-mile race that specifically required Rosenfeld to be the driver of the car.[8]

The races in 1907 were reported differently. Most of the cars were driven by hired hands, but if the driver was also the owner of the car, that fact was noted in the newspaper. Rosenfeld again took home the Del Monte Cup and won two other races. Gene, driving a Rosenfeld Peerless, opened the day with a victory in the speed judging contest. With his speedometer covered, Gene completed a half-mile course in 3 minutes flat; his speed was the closest to the target of 10 miles an hour. That August, he would miss the next major racing event, the first automobile race ever held at the Tanforan horse racing track in San Mateo County, because, in August 1907, Gene was getting married.[9]

The announcement in July 1907 of Gene and Mabel's engagement could well have been the first time Gene or Mabel, or both, intentionally stretched the truth in a newspaper story. "Eugene Ely is the son of Congressman Ely of Iowa," the announcement read, "and he is a popular clubman of this city." Nathan, his father, certainly wanted to be a congressman, but he wasn't, and as far as social clubs were concerned, Gene's only known club association was the California Chauffeur's Association, where he was elected doorkeeper in February 1907. With the beginning of Gene's barnstorming career just a few years in the future, the well-placed white lie would become a valuable habit, but why stretch the truth now? Perhaps Mabel and Gene were trying to impress her father with the quality of her marriage choice, or perhaps it was Gene himself, insecure and impatient, wanting to be someone important. Perhaps he hoped that someone who really counted in the world would someday see who he was and take him where he wanted to be. For now, a few youthful embellishments might just pave his way.[10]

A giant step on that path was becoming chauffeur for Charles Conlisk. It put Gene up close to some of the most influential men in the Bay Area and may have helped him meet Mabel. Conlisk, a former executive of a gas and electric company in San Francisco, was the manager of the Hotaling Estate and the personal business manager for millionaire Richard Hotaling. The Hotaling family fortune, valued in 1900 at somewhere between 7 to 10 million dollars, was made in real estate and whiskey distribution. The Hotaling's whiskey business was so much a part of the San Francisco scene that many imbibing survivors of the 1906 earthquake laughed and thought it ironic that twenty barrels of Hotaling whiskey also survived the catastrophe without a scratch, while at the same time, forty-seven chapels and churches burned to the ground. Local poet and newspaper columnist, Charles Kellogg Field, couldn't resist the irony and wrote a poem for his column.[11]

> "If, as some say, God spanked the town
> For being over frisky,
> Why did He burn the Churches down
> And save Hotaling's Whisky?"[12]

By the mid–1900s, Richard Hotaling was manager of the family's estate. He was a respected businessman, but everyone knew that he would rather be an actor. "Hotaling was," said a friend, "a Shakespearean student, a born mimic, and a genial companion." He was always "playing a part and wearing its costume, even when his suit was business cut and his duties were over a ledger."[13]

The Hotalings owned a dairy ranch in Marin County, not far from Corte Madera, where Mabel Hall lived with her parents. Richard Hotaling had built a summer house on the ranch where he entertained friends, rehearsed plays, and enjoyed his artistic life. It's likely that Gene Ely crossed the Bay many times on a ferry from San Francisco to Marin County, while driving Conlisk to business meetings and society parties at the ranch. It's even possible that this is how Gene met Mabel Hall.[14]

In the middle of the week, August 7, 1907, after obtaining a marriage license that same day at the courthouse, Eugene Burton Ely and Mabel Hall were married at the altar of the old wooden Saint Rafael's Catholic Church in San Rafael, California. Witnesses to the marriage were a Marin County dairy farmer, Frank Seaton, and a Marion Hall, from San Mateo County. Her identity is unclear, but she may have been one of Mabel's aunts. The couple was married by Father Michael Walsh, the assistant pastor of the church. Their wedding certificate shows that Mabel had received her mothers' consent, but lists her as age 17, even though she was actually 18 at the time. Gene's age is given as 27, when in fact he was nearly three months shy of 21. After the ceremony, Gene and Mabel were off on a honeymoon in Colorado.[15]

Gene was making valuable friends from all social strata that would later help him in his aviation career. Henry Blakeslee, mechanic, driver, a member of the Chauffeur's Association with Gene, and co-founder of the Auto Livery Company with Max Rosenfeld, would later organize a few aviation exhibitions for Gene. Norman DeVaux, who owned an automobile dealership in San Francisco, would be one of Gene Ely's aviation managers before becoming president of three different automobile companies, including the Chevrolet Motor Company of California. And then there is Whipple Hall, the man who may have led Gene to Glenn Curtiss.

Gene's life had changed dramatically. In the nearly two years since he arrived in San Francisco, he had married his "press agent" and she, along with his San Francisco connections, were propelling him toward fame. But his Destiny was still a few years away. First, he would have to scramble farther to the north—across the high desert and the mountains between California and Oregon.

# { 10 }

# Racing Cross-Country

In early 1908, Gene and Mabel were settling into married life, but neither was making news or appearing in city directories or even telephone books. By February, after a year of living in San Francisco, Gene's mother had permanently returned to Davenport. Was this when Gene's rental car business began to fail?[1]

"I became a chauffeur only after the money I started with was gone," Gene would say in 1911, but did he mean before the earthquake, or after, or both? He obtained his chauffeur's license while living in San Francisco's Windsor Hotel at 5th and Market streets, but the Windsor was destroyed during the 1906 earthquake, a time when Gene was already driving for Dr. Herzstein. Sometime after the quake he was chauffeur for Charlie Conlisk and could have been a driver for unknown others. He still had at least one of his Matheson automobiles and, while earning regular money as a chauffeur, he still might have been trying to make his car rental business work. Not until the end of the year does his life become clearer. By then, there is no doubt that Gene is reorganizing his auto service, moving it north, and taking on a partner, Walker Lucas Clapp, Jr.[2]

Clapp came to San Francisco sometime after his father's death in 1901, but his early life in San Francisco is a mystery. Lucas Clapp's father and grandfather had both been attorneys in Tennessee and Clapp's father had even been speaker of Tennessee's House of Representatives and mayor of Memphis. Even with that background, politics and the legal profession apparently didn't interest the younger Clapp. He may have settled in San Francisco as early as 1902. That's when his mother and younger brother were visiting from Memphis and staying at a seaside resort near the town of Santa Cruz, some 70 miles south of San Francisco. Another brief newspaper report in 1905, listed Clapp as a visitor from San Francisco to the Byron Hot Springs Resort, across the Bay in Contra Costa County. Other than these brief mentions, he might as well have been a San Francisco ghost. When he did return to San Francisco in 1913, after a few years living in Oregon, he was listed in city directories as an autoworker and, later, as owner of an auto body parts company. It seems likely that he and Gene had some sort of automobile connection prior to their partnership, but what it was is unknown.[3]

In June 1908, the first national automobile race ever seen on the Pacific Coast was running near Portland, Oregon. With Gene's interest in racing and the fact that he would be living in Portland when the next major race was held there in 1909, there is always the possibility that he may have been at the 1908 race, but for now, his business and new partnership were probably more important. He and Clapp were on their way to the Modoc Plateau of northeastern California.[4]

A mile in the sky, with a landscape of hard lava flows, volcanic cinder cones, a few lakes, and dry plains dotted with pine trees, the plateau seemed to offer little commercial opportunity. But the railroad was coming, and railroads brought money and excitement. Moving northward from Reno through the high desert, the Nevada-California-Oregon Railroad had already reached Likely, California, a town humorously named by residents who thought it "most likely" that the U.S. Post Office would accept the name. By the end of 1908, the rails had stretched north into Alturas, where plans called for an extension through the Warner Mountains into Oregon. Railroad surveyors were already out in the field, plotting the rail line as far as Lakeview, Oregon. Work crews were preparing the rail bed, but it would be nearly four more years before trains actually made it that far. New settlers were arriving near Lakeview every day, buying at "government prices" what were sold as "the most fertile and productive lands in the entire State of Oregon." What a surprise it must have been when those new arrivals found themselves surrounded by a scorchingly dry prairie and a few pines, on the shores of a shallow and alkaline Goose Lake.[5]

With quicker and cheaper rail rides to San Francisco now a possibility, residents in this part of Oregon were anxious to find a more convenient connection to the new railhead in Alturas. For now, a horse drawn stagecoach was the only public transportation choice, offering a twelve-hour, tedious and uncomfortable ride of 72 rough and tumble miles. To Clapp and Ely the business opportunity seemed obvious. Clapp arrived in Lakeview in October with Gene Ely not far behind. They offered rides on an "auto stage line" that cost $10 for a one-way trip. That was $3 more than the stagecoach, but the automobile ride was 6 ½ hours faster, and much more comfortable.[6]

The local newspaper editor was amazed. "Deep mud and heavy roads seem not to bother this machine," he wrote. "A ride over the 80 miles of rough road to Lakeview in an auto makes the Golden Goose Lake Valley look bright to the home seeker, even on a cloudy day."[7]

The owner of the stagecoach line surrendered to the new competition and promised to put automobiles on his line by the next spring. Instead, he sold out to Clapp and Ely.

Clapp seems to be the partner who spent the most time in Lakeview. In between auto trips, he found plenty of time to hunt with the locals. Once, after a particularly successful expedition, Clapp hosted a dinner for a few friends at the Lakeview Hotel. He served up a main course of the fifteen ducks that he had shot the day before.[8]

The partners' automobile, a 65-horsepower, eight-passenger touring car, nearly matches the specifications for one of Gene's Matheson automobiles, and soon business was so good that one vehicle wasn't enough. Gene and Clapp managed to temporarily borrow a local car for a few trips until November, when Gene sent for his "other machine." That was good news for the Lakeview newspaper editor. "E. B. Ely's second car on the Likely-Lakeview auto stage line is expected from Frisco in the next few days," he wrote. No sooner had that car arrived than snow began to fall and temperatures plunged. The road to Alturas was blocked, the auto line shut down, and the boys packed it in for the winter. Clapp returned the following spring with his own automobile, but Gene and Mabel didn't.[9]

With Gene gone so quickly, the people of Lakeview might easily have forgotten him, had they not heard in 1910 that he was trying to fly an airplane. From then on, they would follow his exploits in the newspaper until the day he fell from the sky, remembering that "during his stay in Lakeview he had made many friends."[10]

Lucas Clapp continued the auto line, taking on another partner in 1909 and expanding his route an additional 95 miles westward, reaching from Lakeview into the Cascade Mountains and the town of Klamath Falls. Over the next few years, Clapp faced new and increasingly competitive auto companies that forced him to drop his fares. Then, a 1913 fire in his Lakeview garage left his two automobiles in ashes. He gave it all up and returned to San Francisco.[11]

When Gene returned to the city in 1909, he went back to the automobile business, selling and repairing cars, and driving races for Hazlitt Pelton and Harry Bogen. Pelton and Bogen were both San Francisco natives, barely older than Gene, and just as fascinated with automobiles. They were both dealers for the California built Tourist motorcar.[12]

At the end of January 1909, Pelton offered two championship trophies to encourage auto racers. "My aim is to lend every assistance to increasing the popularity of

In 1911, Walker L. Clapp reminded Eugene Ely of their partnership in 1908–1909, when they "mushed" their automobile "stage line" through the snow between Alturas, California, and Lakeview, Oregon. On this postcard, Clapp is driving and his wife, Ramona, is sitting in the very last seat. The identities of the woman holding the baby and the little girl are unknown (Diane Dunlop Collection).

the motor car," he said. The first trophy, the Pelton Cup, would go to the driver who, before March 15, 1909, made the fastest time in a cross-country race around San Francisco Bay. Drivers would start in Oakland, race south through San Jose, and then turn north to the San Francisco beaches. His second trophy, the Tourist Cup, would be a perpetual cup and would replace the Pelton Cup once it was won. No sooner had Pelton announced the competition than he began to hear complaints. The race route ran right through the city limits of many communities where strict automobile speed laws had just been passed and local police officers were having a field day chasing down and citing speeders. "To avoid any conflict with authorities," Pelton redrew the route around most cities, but did allow a final ten-mile dash through San Francisco to the Cliff House, up the rarely patrolled Great Highway that edged the Pacific Ocean on the western edge of the city. "This," he said, "will give any driver a good ten-mile stretch in which to make a final dash for speed and avoid breaking the law."[13]

The first run for the Pelton Cup was made just four days before the March 15 deadline. Charles Howard and his right hand man, Frank Murray, took off at 6 a.m. in Howard's Buick, the "White Streak." Howard was the San Francisco Buick dealer and the man who one day would own Seabiscuit, the racehorse. Their initial record time of 3 hours, 27 minutes and 6 seconds included a tire change and would only stand for two days.[14]

Early the next morning, the first attempt to break Howard's record came from Gene Ely and an unknown copilot. They made a speedy start, bouncing southward for nearly 30 miles in their 2-cylinder Tourist motor car. Suddenly the motor choked, sputtered, died, and the silent automobile rolled to a stop. A frantic inspection of the engine revealed that the air intake valve was missing. Gene and his partner wasted an hour, slowly retracing their route for a mile on foot, before finding the valve lying in the dust. Now, with no chance to break the record, they gave up. Gene tried to convince Pelton and Bogen to let him try again, this time for the perpetual Tourist Cup; however, they decided it was best to wait until the weather and road conditions improved.[15]

Automobile dealers sponsored these road races as a way to promote the quality and reliability of their brand. The Tourist was not one of the better company-financed automobiles and Pelton had been trying since early in the year to improve its image. In February, he sent Bruce Aurandt and Gene Ely on a long distance challenge to the roundtrip speed record between San Francisco and Del Monte. Norman DeVaux, one of Gene's future aviation managers, had set the record of 12 hours and 12 minutes at the beginning of the year, running through "a sea of mud." Although the roads were still bad at the end of February, the sun finally broke through, and Pelton decided the time had come. On this trip, Aurandt would drive and Gene would be his copilot. It had rained the night before, but they managed to reach Del Monte in less than six hours. Stopping for only a minute to rest, Aurandt turned the car toward home and sped away. Three miles north of Salinas, already beating DeVaux's record by a half hour, Aurandt ran past a well-hidden policeman. In what looked like a funeral procession, they were escorted back to the county seat "where a judge relieved the record breakers of five hard earned American dollars" and any chance of breaking the Del Monte record. Pelton said he wasn't likely to authorize another run. "Chances of arrest now seem to be too great."[16]

At the end of March, both Pelton and Gene entered a Tourist in the San Francisco Motor Club's Nineteenth Avenue Hill Climb competition. It was a disappointing day for both men. Pelton finished third out of four cars in the one-mile run up the avenue and Gene didn't finish at all. He managed to get his automobile started, but he couldn't get it to the finish line and was disqualified.[17]

Gene was back to competition in early May, this time putting his Tourist automobile on a ferry, crossing the bay to Marin County, and then driving north 50 miles to the town of Santa Rosa. Although it was time for the town's annual Rose Parade, Gene wasn't interested in flowered floats and marching bands. This year's celebration would, for the first time, include a 49-mile automobile road race with a top prize of $500. The course ran from Santa Rosa northward, through Healdsburg to the village of Geyserville. From there, it took a short tour west, finally looping back over the same route to Santa Rosa. Twelve cars would start the race, but before it was over, tire and mechanical problems would eliminate six.[18]

At 9 a.m. on Sunday, May 9, 1909, Fred Wiseman pressed his foot on the accelerator of his Stoddard-Dayton and the race was on. The plan had been to release each competitor at two-minute intervals, but at the last minute, officials decided there would be more excitement if they cut the interval to one minute. Gene, in his 4-cylinder, 35 horsepower Tourist, with a large white numeral *15* attached to the front of his radiator, was the last car to leave, waiting an agonizing 11 minutes on the starting line. The drivers had been told that the first seventeen miles of the race would be a virtual straightaway, but it was a "straightaway that was badly twisted." There were many, almost 45-degree turns, with embankments sloping dangerously downhill. "That none of the cars rolled over on these turns is hard to realize," wrote a reporter. Some of the bridges, originally built for horse teams, were not level to the ground and the racers found themselves launched into the air, praying that when they smashed back to earth, they wouldn't blow a tire or shatter an axle. Perhaps worst of all, the dirt road was rough, covered in potholes, littered with sharp tire-cutting stones and scarred with deep wagon tracks. A newspaper columnist compared the drivers to Roman chariot drivers. "It is safe to say that in no place in the world have a dozen men in an automobile contest displayed such skill, keen judgment, and lack of any visible sign of nerves."[19]

Only Ben Noonan, the race winner, completed the course without a stop. Cliff Ontank finished second even after ripping out two bridge posts in a collision that put a crack in his car's frame. Fred Wiseman had fallen from first to third because his battery had bounced out of the motor compartment. "Madman," Fay Sheets, lost his left front tire 17 miles from the finish, yet continued on, swaying side to side until he crossed the line. The road was so rough, Gordon Murray's Buick cracked its gasoline feed pipe, but even so, Murray managed to beat Gene Ely for fifth place by ten minutes. Overall, Gene had been lucky. One of his ignition wires had snapped apart midway in the race and it looked as if he wouldn't finish. He rolled to a stop near a spectator's large 6-cylinder touring car. The spectator, realizing Gene's trouble, rushed to the front of his own expensive automobile, lifted the hood, and jerked out all of his ignition wires. He ran to Gene, held out the wires, and told Gene to help himself. "But you won't be able to drive home," Gene said. "Then I guess we can walk," said the Good Samaritan. Only after he had crossed the finish line did Gene wonder who the man was. He asked around and tried to find him, but never did.[20]

With the Santa Rosa race over, drivers turned their attention back to the perpetual Tourist Cup, the run around the Bay from Oakland to San Francisco. Gene finally got the OK from Pelton to make a run for it. He found a motivated partner in Gordon Murray who wanted to reclaim the cup he had lost barely a week before. At 5 a.m., May 22, 1909, the Tourist sputtered to life and with Gene at the wheel, they were off. They sped down the East Bay roads, clouds of dust hanging behind them in the sunrise. When they reached San Jose, 40 miles down and on a record pace, they were halfway home. Gene slowed to 20 miles an hour so he could make a sharp turn to the north. Suddenly, around the corner, a farmer's horse-drawn cherry wagon was plodding along, directly in his path. Gene swerved, but instead of clinging to the safe side of the road, the startled farmer turned his team into the speeding car. There was no way to stop in time. The Tourist slammed into the wagon, shredding two wagon wheels, and catapulting the farmer from his seat onto Gene's steering wheel. Luckily, the farmer only had a few bruises and Gene and Murray were unhurt. The Tourist; however, had a punctured radiator and the record try was over. Gene paid the farmer for damage to the wagon, temporarily repaired the radiator, and slowly, very slowly, returned to San Francisco.[21]

Fred Wiseman must have heard that Gene and Murray were going to make another try for the Tourist Cup the next morning, because he got to the Oakland starting line long before they arrived. As the current record holder, Wiseman wanted to ensure defense of the cup with an even better time. At exactly 5 a.m., he was off and flying, his speedometer sometimes reaching 70 miles an hour. Thirty-four minutes after he began, and just one mile from the site of Gene's previous morning accident, the roadbed suddenly leaped upward. At 60 miles an hour the automobile swerved, hit a bump, and Wiseman lost control. The car wrapped around a locust tree, while he and his mechanic tumbled nearly 40 feet through the air with Wiseman still clutching the steering wheel that had sheared away in the crash. His vehicle was now twisted junk. Badly cut and dazed, Wiseman and his mechanic were rushed to the hospital where they remained for two days.[22]

Gene, who had left the starting line in Oakland eight minutes behind Wiseman, was also making good time on his way to San Jose. Reaching the city, not far from Wiseman's troubles, he rounded a corner and was startled to see two police officers pointing pistols directly at him. Apparently, in the excitement of Wiseman's crash, a few extra constables had made their way to the scene. Under these threatening circumstances, Gene thought it best to stop. After an eight-minute delay, he convinced the officers that he wasn't speeding, but once out of sight, he resumed his record setting pace. Fifteen miles from the finish line, with the record easily within claiming distance, Gene's motor fell out onto the ground. The mounting bolts had loosened in the previous morning's collision with the farmer's wagon and apparently no one had thought to check them. Others would continue to vie for the Tourist Cup, but Gene was through.[23]

By the summer of 1909, Gene and Mabel were living in Portland, Oregon. Once there, they took a trip to Iowa for a visit with relatives and then returned. Why they moved from San Francisco to Oregon isn't clear, but there are some circumstantial clues that may shed light on their decision.[24]

Two weeks after Gene and Gordon Murray last rode together for the Tourist

Cup, Murray announced he was going to Portland to drive an Auburn automobile in the Portland Automobile Club's second annual road race. It was an unsuccessful trip for Murray who was one of four men who never finished the race. Gene may or may not have been with him in Oregon, although the dates of the Oregon race match the time that a Portland newspaper later said Gene had arrived in the state.[25]

Then, there is Norman DeVaux, soon to be one of Gene's aviation managers. For the previous three years, DeVaux had been the Auburn automobile representative for the entire West Coast with his headquarters in San Francisco. In the fall of 1909, DeVaux ended his association with Auburn to become a partner in the Northwest Buick Company, serving the states of Washington and Oregon. Gene and DeVaux had crossed paths many times as racecar drivers and Gene's driving partner, Gordon Murray, had occasionally driven Auburn's for DeVaux. Now, with DeVaux's headquarters in Portland, he and Gene were about to see each other nearly every day. That's because Gene's first job in Portland was salesman and mechanic for Robert Simpson, the man who was taking over DeVaux's Portland Auburn automobile dealership. While Simpson looked for a permanent location, DeVaux let Simpson sell cars out of DeVaux's downtown Portland Buick store.[26]

The 1909 Oregon automobile races marked the beginning of Henry Wemme's quest to own Portland's first airplane. Wemme was a wealthy man who loved automobiles and was president of the Portland Automobile Club. He had decided to buy an airplane and had come to the races looking for a fearless driver who would make the perfect pilot. The local favorite to repeat as winner of the 44-mile road race was Howard Covey, a friend of Wemmes and exclusive agent in Oregon for Pierce-Arrow and Cadillac automobiles. Wemme was impressed at how tenaciously Covey raced to win. He drove alone, without a mechanic, carrying no tools or spare tires—all considered essential for a sensible driver. He pushed his 1400-pound Cadillac over the dirt road course, the roughness of the road ripping away at skin from his bleeding hands that were stuck firmly to the steering wheel. Covey's devil-may-care attitude seemed to be exactly what Wemme was looking for. A newspaper reporter agreed, comparing Covey to two of the world's most famous aviators, Glenn Curtiss, the American, and Frenchman, Louis Paulhan. "Covey is," said the reporter, "absolutely fearless."[27]

Wemme, the man who had brought the first automobile to Portland in 1899, was now prepared to spend $6,000 for the city's first airplane. He hinted that he might attempt to fly it himself, but at age 57, he didn't think it likely. He was more interested in finding a man to take care of his aeroplane and become his personal "sky pilot." Covey looked to be that man, but he wasn't. The airplane that everyone thought Covey was born to fly would soon belong to Gene Ely.[28]

# { 11 }

# Challenging the Wrights

Six years after the Wright brothers made the first successful powered flight, the airplane was poised to replace the automobile as the Nation's latest transportation fad. Glenn Curtiss, a bicycle-racing champion with a need for speed who liked to tinker with machinery, was challenging the Wrights. He had begun his engineering life while still a teenager, rearranging some camera assembly procedures at the Kodak Camera plant in Rochester, New York. He increased production from 250 to 2,500 cameras a day. He quickly moved from worker in a bicycle shop to shop owner and then manufacturer of his own line of bicycles. Always in search of speed, he experimented with various parts until he had assembled a gasoline motor and attached it to a bicycle. In 1905, in his hometown of Hammondsport, New York, he incorporated his business as the G. H. Curtiss Manufacturing Company—"Manufacturers of The Curtiss Motorcycles, Motors, and Accessories." He personally raced his motorcycles and in 1907, set the world motorcycle speed record of over 136 miles an hour, a record that would stand for another 23 years.[1]

Even before he thought of building airplanes, Curtiss offered to sell the Wright brothers a lighter engine for their machine, but they refused. That was a big mistake. Had the Wrights accepted his offer they might have avoided the upcoming years of litigation as they tried to protect their patents, primarily against Curtiss. It's possible that Curtiss might have been content with just supplying motors to the brothers and might never have thought of building his own airplane, but with his competitive nature and engineering mind, chances of that were slim.[2]

In the summer of 1907, Curtiss became Director of Experiments and Chief Executive Officer of the newly created Aerial Experiment Association, a group dedicated to building "a practical aeroplane, which will carry a man and be driven through the air by its own power." The association was headed and their experiments funded by Alexander Graham Bell of telephone fame. Together with two recent Canadian engineering graduates from Toronto University, J. A. D. "Jack" McCurdy and Frederick Baldwin, along with Lt. Thomas Selfridge of the U.S. Army, the men formed an operational aeronautical think tank. With gradual success, they finally constructed an airplane they named *June Bug*. It flew so well, they decided to enter it in competition for the Scientific American Cup, a trophy that would be awarded to the first aircraft to fly non-stop, five-eighths of a mile, or 1 kilometer. On July 4, 1908, with 30-year-old Curtiss as pilot, the *June Bug* flew past the 1-kilometer flag at 39 miles an hour. "The flag was quickly reached and passed and still I kept the aeroplane up, flying as far as the open fields would permit," Curtiss said. When he landed one mile from the start, he had far exceeded the trophy requirements. "I might have gone a great deal farther, as the motor was working beautifully and I had the machine under perfect control," he said, "but to have prolonged the flight would have meant a turn in the air, or passing over a number of large trees." As far as the Wright brothers were concerned, Curtiss had flown far enough.[3]

Following a *Scientific American* magazine article that described the *June Bug*'s flight and the structural features of the Curtiss biplane, Orville Wright accused Curtiss of violating the brothers' patents. In a letter to Curtiss, he wrote, "We did not intend, of course, to give permission to use the patented features of our machine for exhibitions, or in a commercial way.... If it is your desire to enter the exhibition business, we would be glad to take up the matter of a license, to offer it under our patents for that purpose."[4]

Writing on his copy of Wright's warning letter, Bell noted his alarm. "The full correspondence with Mr. Orville Wright upon the above subject should, I think, be made known to all the members of the A.E.A.," he said, "for it is obvious that we may expect to be brought into a lawsuit with the Wright Bros., if we make any public exhibitions of our apparatus for gain without an arrangement with them."[5]

Bell telegraphed Mauro, Cameron, and Lewis, patent attorneys in Washington, D.C., telling them to send a patent expert to Hammondsport "to examine *June Bug* and report to me what patentable features there may be about [the] machine."[6]

The Wright letter had fired a shot across Curtiss' bow and for a while that would be warning enough. Until the Aerial Experimental Association disbanded in early 1909, the members carefully made sure their activities were scientific and could not be considered exhibitions. Curtiss kept the waters calm by carrying on a friendly correspondence with the Wrights, sometimes sharing information about his progress, but also suggesting that their patent dispute should be "taken up privately between us, to save, if possible, annoyance and publicity of lawsuits and trials."

Meanwhile, there was a developing market for airplanes that just couldn't be ignored. Members of the Aeronautic Society of New York approached Curtiss, asking if he would build them an airplane. On January 21, 1909, Curtiss agreed and signed a contract, but asked that the agreement be kept secret until he had severed his connection with the Aerial Experiment Association. In March, he announced that he was entering the commercial side of aviation with a manufacturing plant in Hammondsport and that the company already had orders for two aircraft. On the surface, the Wright brothers appeared calm. They were busy negotiating with European syndicates that wanted to buy rights to the aviation patents and it seemed to Curtiss that they still might be willing to compromise.[7]

In July, the first commercial aircraft ever sold in the United States was complete and ready for delivery to the Aeronautic Society. Curtiss took it on a 29-mile flight that lasted nearly an hour, "just to wear smooth the bearings," he said. The flight would win Curtiss his second Scientific American Cup. The next day, July 18, the airplane was in the hands of the Aeronautic Society's chosen pilot, Charles F. Willard.

Willard was an occasional racecar driver, student at Harvard for a year, and a graduate of a correspondence course on gasoline engines. The airplane, named the *Golden Flyer* because of the yellow ochre tinting on the fabric wings and the yellow varnish on the struts and woodwork, was sold for $5,000, which included personal flight instruction from Curtiss.[8]

Willard instructions were brief. "Curtiss didn't say much," Willard said. "He just pointed to some people downfield, told me not to run into them, and then shouted over the barking engine, 'Get her up, straighten her out, then come down—and for God's sake don't break her up. She's not paid for yet.'" He needn't have worried. Willard flew for 28 seconds at 25 feet, and landed safely. Curtiss had his money by the end of the month.[9]

The Aeronautic Society announced it was negotiating demonstration flights across the country as owner of "the first aeroplane in the world available for public exhibitions." Small New York crowds gathered to watch while Willard continued to practice his technique. Soon the spectators were being charged admission. That was the final straw for the Wrights. On August 19, the brothers filed suit against the Aeronautic Society. "The public exhibition of the Curtiss machine now owned by the society constitutes an infringement of their patent rights and is otherwise detrimental to their interests," said a newspaper report. Two days later, a patent infringement action was filed against the Curtiss Company, and for the next eight years, with both sides draining their profits and unsuccessfully trying to settle, the "Patent Wars" dragged on. Curtiss and others continued to build their airplanes and conduct exhibitions with little interference. The Wrights would eventually be vindicated, but by then, Wilbur was dead and Orville had sold the company to Martin Aviation. The buildup for World War I brought together a consortium of aviation companies that agreed to pay the Curtiss Company and Wright-Martin a one-time $2-million each and finally end all patent disputes.[10]

The 1909 infringement suit had been filed while Glenn Curtiss was in Rheims, France, the only American flier to compete at the world's first international aviation meet. There, Curtiss would race for the Gordon Bennett Trophy and a $5,000 prize in the speed contest. He had taken the second airplane his company had ever built, a nearly identical copy of the Aeronautic Society's 4-cylinder *Golden Flyer*, except its silvery gray finish was purposely not tinted yellow. The wings were slightly shorter, and an 8-cylinder, 50 horsepower motor doubled the *Flyer's* power. It was an aircraft that had never been flown before and was propelled by a new engine that had barely been tested. "The motor was finished, but there was no time to put it in the new machine and try it out before sailing," Curtiss said. "It was, therefore, given a short run on the block, or testing frame, hurriedly packed, and the entire equipment rushed to New York, barely in time to catch the steamer for France." The 8-cylinder engine was supposed to be a secret, but to Curtiss' dismay, his chief rival, Frenchman, Louis Bleriot, had somehow found out and had quickly ordered an 8-cylinder, 80 horsepower engine of his own.

Bleriot was the first man to fly across the English Channel and had a tremendous reputation as a superior flier. Curtiss was a decided underdog even before Bleriot got his new engine, and now, even Curtiss doubted that he could win. "I believed my chances were very slim indeed, if in fact they had not entirely disappeared," he said.

But Curtiss, the speed demon, bicycle and motorcycle champion, would give it his best. He wasn't a quitter.[11]

Racing full throttle, twice around the rectangular ten-kilometer course with wings nearly scraping the tall red and white pylons that marked the corners of the course, Curtiss posted the first and ultimately best time in the speed contest, 15 minutes, 50 ⅗ seconds, or 46 ½ miles an hour. He beat Bleriot's best time in multiple tries, by a mere 6 seconds.[12]

Curtiss and company next traveled to Brescia, Italy where he carried his first passenger, Italian poet and author, Gabriele D'Annunzio, and won the grand prize of $7,600 in the aerial contests. He returned to New York City as the "Fastest Man in the World," and $15,000 richer. "We are only at the beginning of the marvels to be shown in the conquest of the air," Curtiss said. "From now on there is going to be a big interest throughout the United States in aviation."[13]

The next public exhibition was scheduled during the Hudson-Fulton anniversary celebration in New York City, held just days after Curtiss returned to the United States. The event commemorated the 300th anniversary of Henry Hudson's discovery of the Hudson River and the 102nd anniversary of Robert Fulton sailing a steam-powered ship up that river and bringing steam power to the waters of the world. A highlight of the festivities would be the scheduled aerial flights by Curtiss and Wilbur Wright. It was the first time the antagonists would fly at the same exhibition and, unfortunately, it turned out to be a disaster for Curtiss. Saddled with another new and never flown airplane, appropriately named the *Hudson-Fulton* machine, Curtiss failed to travel any significant distance. In contrast, Wright dazzled the public with several flights, including a 20-mile flight up the Hudson River and a circling of the Statue of Liberty. Curtiss had a contract to perform in St. Louis within days and didn't have time to get his airplane into flying shape for New York. He accepted $1,500 of the $5,000 agreed to in his contract and boarded a train for Missouri. "No one is more disappointed than I am that the weather conditions have prevented me from making a flight, which could be witnessed by a large number of people during the week," he said.[14]

Once reaching St. Louis, Curtiss gave the *Hudson-Fulton* machine a fine-tuning and a complete workout. The weather was bad and none of his flights went very far, but the nearly half million spectators on hand were satisfied with his performance. Exhibition promoters were excited and eager to make Curtiss happy. Within hours of his asking that trees be cut down for his safety, the trees came down. "St. Louisans," said a newspaper reporter, "have the aero fever so bad that had Curtiss so desired, skyscrapers would have been trimmed off."[15]

For a week after the St. Louis exhibition, Curtiss waited in Chicago for the wind to die down. "The usual Chicago half-gale prevailed," he said. The exhibition was a bust and little of aeronautical significance occurred—except for the discovery of Charles K. Hamilton. Hamilton was destined to become Curtiss' first official exhibition flier. Somewhere around five feet tall, barely 110 pounds, and 24 years old, chain-smoking Hamilton had already flown high in the sky in box kites towed by automobiles and sometimes by boats. He had been a fearless parachutist, balloonist, and dirigible driver, but now he wanted to fly airplanes. He begged Curtiss to teach him. With the winds keeping Curtiss on the ground, he put Hamilton on the airplane and explained how everything worked. Curtiss was surprised to see how quickly Hamilton caught on. He casually mentioned that if the eager boy were ever in Hammondsport, he just might allow him to fly. A few weeks later, when Curtiss returned home, he found Hamilton was already there and not so patiently waiting.[16]

Hamilton made his first attempt to get off the ground on October 29, less than three weeks after meeting Curtiss in Chicago. Three days later, he nearly equaled the longest flight Curtiss had ever made, flying the *Hudson-Fulton* machine for 25 minutes, eleven times around the Hammondsport facility. This was what Curtiss was looking for. "I was undertaking the exhibition business," Curtiss said, "and I needed assistants, needed another good flier at least." For Curtiss, exhibitions were the way to boost airplane sales and business inquiries were picking up, so much so that just a week after his maiden flight, Hamilton was already looking for a new plane. Curtiss sold the *Hudson-Fulton* machine for $7,500 to a Mrs. Arnold, "one of the richest women in Florida." The Curtiss factory was already working on ten additional planes based on the *Hudson-Fulton* design, so Hamilton had no reason to worry about a replacement. Besides, he could still practice with the *Rheims Racer* that had returned from Europe to Hammondsport, but was now equipped with a more manageable 4-cylinder engine.[17]

Before he hired Hamilton and put him on the road, Curtiss discussed the idea with his attorney. He was worried that by contracting with Hamilton, the flier would be considered an employee, making Curtiss legally liable for any accidents that might occur. He had reason to be concerned. Although barely a rookie, Hamilton was showing himself to be a daring flier, already known for throwing caution to the wind. Curtiss decided on a leasing contract that he would use as a model until incorporation of his exhibition company in 1910.[18]

Hamilton would be allowed to lease a Curtiss airplane as long as he agreed to all of Curtiss' terms. Hamilton was required "to make exhibition flights ... at such places and times as shall be designated by said Curtiss." Hamilton would pay Curtiss rent of 60 percent of the net proceeds from each exhibition. The net would be what was left over after deductions were made for transporting the airplane, salaries for the mechanical crew, as well as the cost of maintenance and repairs. Because of the way Hamilton flew, Curtiss believed there were going to be quite a few mishaps and a steady need for parts. If any parts were needed, then Hamilton would have to pay 40 percent of the cost of parts and their replacement from his share of the net profit. Signed November 17, 1909, the agreement would not go into effect until Hamilton provided a $5,000 surety bond, which apparently took about a month.[19]

Before Curtiss sent Hamilton out on his own, he wanted his newest pupil to know what an exhibition should look like. Curtiss and Hamilton met Charles Willard in Cincinnati, where the city was putting on its first aviation show. It was called the Cincinnati Air Exhibition, but it actually took place at the Latonia Racetrack, across the Ohio River, in Covington, Kentucky. Hamilton was there to observe and didn't fly, but he watched as Curtiss' first pupil, Willard, beat his instructor in height and distance. By then, Willard probably had more time in the air than Curtiss. Since taking control of the *Golden Flyer* in July, he had been flying whenever and wherever he had the chance. Now, with the addition of Hamilton and Willard, the nucleus of what would become the Curtiss Exhibition Company was poised to take on the mushrooming air show circuit.[20]

On December 12, in the seat of the airplane that in just a few months would belong to Gene Ely, Hamilton was up for his first exhibition. A thousand spectators watched from inside protective lakeside buildings on the frozen shores of Lake Contrary, near St. Joseph, Missouri, as Hamilton launched himself from the ice into a blowing snowstorm. He struggled against a 29 mile an hour headwind, a fouled sparkplug, a sputtering carburetor, and ice in his engine oil. A reporter and a local businessman, stopwatch in hand, had trudged through the mini-blizzard to measure out a 1-kilometer course, and when Hamilton landed, he claimed that Hamilton had set an unofficial world speed record of 62.72 miles an hour. The claim was dubious at best and the record remained unofficial. With the "northwestern gale" subsiding by midweek, Hamilton's performance continued, and though bones were "chilled to the mallow," the fearless rookie aviator returned to the thick lake ice, revving his engine and navigating several short flights at low altitudes until the day was cut short by a flight straight into a fence. After minor repairs, Hamilton was ready to go again the next morning, but the winds were back and now gusting at 35 miles an hour. Half of his first trip around the lake was little more than a series of hard hops over the ice, the airplane bouncing up and down after soaring only a few feet into the air. Intending to make some adjustments to the craft, Hamilton tried to land, but he set the brake too soon and too firmly. The plane slid over the ice toward barbed wire on the far shore. Hamilton jumped toward safety, but his coat sleeve snagged the plane's framework, dragging him 300 feet before he freed himself. When the boys on skates reached him, his nose was bleeding, he was bruised, and his clothes were covered in ice, but he was OK, and so was the plane.[21]

From St. Joseph, Hamilton continued west to Overland Park, a few miles south of Kansas City, Kansas. Here the winds were lighter and the weather warmer, but not by much. Beginning the day after Christmas, he completed a series of flights, flying 500 feet in the air for a mile, and then, after landing and taking off again, covering eighteen more miles in 23 minutes Spectacular flights continued until New Years Day, when a blown engine cylinder ended the weeklong exhibition.[22]

In less than a month, Hamilton had taken that biplane into the air over 80 times with a reckless attitude that was propelling him to national celebrity. Curtiss made the airplanes, but soon it would be Hamilton's antics that would sell them. Curtiss was OK with that. If the student was surpassing the instructor, so be it. Curtiss was already talking about ending his exhibition flying anyway, but until he could recruit more aviators, he had no choice but to keep on flying. Next stop—California.[23]

## { 12 }

## Dominguez

What aviator could resist a chance at $80,000 in prizes just for flying through the balmy blue skies of Los Angeles in January? Hamilton was certainly ready to get away from icicles, blizzards, and hard, lake ice and Curtiss was coming with the *Rheims Racer*. Willard would be there too, flying the *Golden Flyer*, still owned by the Aeronautic Society of New York.[1]

Of the 56 other entries, the three Frenchmen and a Frenchwoman barely validated the organizers' claim of an authentic international aviation event. Ten of the entries were hot air balloons and six were cigar shaped racing dirigibles. Although both were held in the sky by gases, the dirigibles were equipped with engines and their flight path was more easily controlled. Within a few months, many of these gasbag pilots, such as Lincoln Beachey in his dirigible and James "Bud" Mars in his balloon, would switch to the more lucrative world of aeroplanes.

Beachey was the man Mabel Ely would ultimately blame for her husband's death. In the coming months, he tried to build his own aeroplane and join the Wright brothers exhibition team, but he demanded more money than they were willing to pay. In the fall of 1910, while at Hammondsport, he begged Curtiss for a tryout and promptly crashed two biplanes. Only Jerome Fanciulli, Curtiss' business manager, saw some promise in Beachey and convinced Curtiss to give the boy another chance. It was a profitable move for Curtiss. Over the next few years, Beachey would become the maniacal aviation daredevil of his day with hair-raising stunts far eclipsing anything Hamilton would ever do.[2]

Bud Mars would also become a Curtiss aviator and one of Gene Ely's closest friends. During later exhibitions, his wife, Marie, probably spent more time with Mabel Ely than she did with her own husband. On the day Gene Ely died, the two women had been sharing an apartment in New York City for over a month. Mars had been drifting in hot air balloons since he was a teenager and had formed his own balloon company. It made him a small fortune, but he lost it all in the 1907 economic depression. By 1909, he was manager and designated pilot for the Oakland, California Aero Club and, at Dominguez, he would guide the club's balloon entry, the *City of Oakland*.[3]

There was a significant difference between Mars and Beachey. Mars was daring, but not reckless. When Curtiss agreed to train Mars he stuck with him, even after Mars had crashed his biplane at his very first air show. Perhaps it helped that just before the Mars' mishap, Curtiss and Willard had also crashed, both with severe damage. Years later, Curtiss told associates that Mars was always one of his favorite flying partners.[4]

Conspicuously absent from the Los Angeles exhibition were the Wright brothers who hadn't given their blessing to the Los Angeles air meet. Neither had officials of the Aero Club of America, headquartered in New York City. The national club had jurisdiction over all aeronautic events being promoted by affiliated clubs, including the newly formed Aero Club of California that had organized the Los Angeles event. Just before the planned start of the exhibition, the national club threatened to withhold its sanction, insisting that their rules must be followed to the letter. That meant no unlicensed pilots could participate. Los Angeles organizers resented the Eastern interference with their plans and told the national club that if amateur and unlicensed pilots weren't allowed to fly, their committee would hold the aviation meeting anyway, regardless of rules and without sanction. Cooler heads finally prevailed and a compromise was reached. Unlicensed pilots could fly as long as they didn't compete against licensed pilots, and licensed and unlicensed pilots could never fly at the same time. For the time being, "all doubt regarding the big aviation meet at Los Angeles was set at rest," said a reporter. But more doubt was on the way.[5]

On the first Monday of January 1910, while Curtiss was still on a train headed for Los Angeles, a United States Circuit Court ruling in Buffalo, N. Y. was causing shockwaves in Southern California. Judge John R. Hazel issued a preliminary injunction in favor of the Wright brothers, restraining the Curtiss Company from manufacturing or selling Curtiss aeroplanes. Although not clearly stated in the court document, most people assumed that Curtiss and his fliers would not be able to fly in any exhibition.[6]

Arriving in Los Angeles, Curtiss assured reporters that he would enter as many air meet events as possible. "I have just received a telegram from my attorneys in New York," he said, "and they assure me that no injunction has been granted. Some kind of an order was issued by a judge in Buffalo, but whatever it was, it will not interfere with my flights in Los Angeles." His business manager, Jerome Fanciulli, agreed. The temporary injunction "and the other suits instituted by the Wrights," he said, "will not interfere with the Los Angeles meet, and Curtiss will fly." However, the Southern California organizers weren't so sure.[7]

The injunction against Curtiss was only temporary, but legal opinion said that if and when it was made permanent, Curtiss and all other aviators would be barred from flying exhibitions. At the very least, an appeal to overturn the injunction would result in a long and expensive courtroom fight and until decided, would end any hope of exhibitions. But most of those worries disappeared when Curtiss agreed to put up a bond to cover any damages that the court might later award to the Wrights and attorneys worked out a compromise. Curtiss posted a $10,000 bond and agreed to deposit any exhibition money earned with the court. That gave him the right to fly until a final decision was made. The temporary injunction was suspended pending immediate appeal and the California exhibition was saved.[8]

The Los Angeles International Air Meet was actually held on what some out-of-town writers called a desert, thirteen miles south of the city among the gently rising Dominguez Hills. Cattle still grazed here as they had since 1784, when Juan Jose Dominguez, a retired Spanish soldier, received title to a Mexican land grant of 75,000 acres. Here, overlooking the frequently dry Los Angeles River, he built an adobe home on the side of a hill. His rancho was the scene of one of the few battles fought in California during the Mexican War. In October 1846, a company of U.S. soldiers, while camping on the Dominguez land, was attacked by a Mexican force and they were ultimately forced to retreat. The American capture of Los Angeles was delayed for another three months.[9]

The entrance to the 1910 aviation exhibition was just a few hundred feet below the old Dominguez adobe. "The ancient landmark, with its roof fallen in and its windows washed out, stands near the car tracks at the gate," a reporter wrote. "The new ranch house, a typical Spanish-American home, is nearby. Its many broad arches uphold a roof of red tiles, such as the early Californians used." Between the gate and the two adobes were the Southern Pacific railroad tracks. Steam trains delivered spectators every 45 minutes and the electric "Red Cars" of the Pacific Electric Railway, the local transit system, brought passengers to an enlarged platform at the edge of what was now called "Aviation Camp." A short walk through concession stands and tents brought spectators to the box seats and the massive grandstand, 40 feet high, 700 feet long. Built to seat 25,000 people, it still managed to offer a wide-open panoramic view of the sky and the snow dusted San Gabriel Mountains in the distant north. There were no obstructions to limit visibility for 26 miles in every direction. The 1.6-mile semi-elliptical aviation course circled three large tents; one for Curtiss, one for the French contestants, and one for all other competitors. Here, mechanics could assemble and make repairs to their machines. Dirigible maintenance tents stood in a gully behind the grandstand and balloons were based near the village of Huntington Park, eight miles to the north.[10]

The surviving Dominguez daughters and their families sat in the front row of the grandstand. That was the way the exhibition promoters chose to honor the family and it was the absolute least they could do. While these businessmen would pocket nearly $140,000 from the meet, the daughters, who had donated the family's rancho for this historic event, received nothing more than front row seats and some thanks.[11]

The gates opened on January 10, 1910, in less than perfect weather. The skies were gray and Jack Frost was more than nipping at every cheek. Men and women shivered under heavy coats and shawls, their noses pinched with prickly cold, their feet chilled and damp. But nothing could stop the 30 to 40,000 people who attended nearly every day of the eleven-day event. Even on Day 7, when gale force winds and morning rain were the perfect excuse to stay home, they came in droves, standing in the mud along the fence and holding down dripping seats in the grandstands. By the time the show began, the biggest crowd of the meet, over 50,000 people, had gathered in joyful anticipation. "A new word has been coined at the aviation field," said a reporter. "Aeronutty—a peculiar state of insanity."[12]

For most of the meet, skies were blue as aviators soared over dormant orange groves, farmer's fields, green meadow ranches, and the small growing villages surrounding the City of Angels. The aviation committee estimated that a total of nearly 200,000 people attended, but that was based on figures supplied by the railroad and transit company. No one had counted those who had just wandered in or the freeloaders on the nearby hilltops.[13]

Curtiss set two of the three world records recorded during the exhibition, rising into the air after just 98 feet of taxiing, and doing it in 6 ⅖ seconds. But it was Frenchman Louis Paulhan who set the most impressive mark. It had taken him 43 minutes to climb to a world record height of 4,164 feet. On January 19, the next to the last day of the meet, Paulhan set one of those asterisk filled "world records" by "carrying a passenger 76 miles in 1 hour 49 minutes." It was actually five flights with five different passengers, the longest of which was with his wife, 22 miles north to the town of Venice. The return flight zipped over the "hungry surf" of the Pacific Ocean, a half mile from shore. Meet officials were quick to point out that "no other aviator has taken up so many passengers during one day, and no other aviator has taken a woman."[14]

When the contests were over, Paulhan received most of the glory and won $19,000. Curtiss scored $6,200, Hamilton $3,500, and Willard, the most experienced American aviator of all, pocketed a mere $250.

The Los Angeles-Dominguez International Aviation Meet had done more for the science of aviation in an exciting eleven days of speed, endurance, and altitude, than anyone could have guessed. Now, the entire country was going "Aeronutty," and Gene Ely was about to join them. His biplane was already on its way to Portland.[15]

# { 13 }

# Wemme Wants a Prizewinner

A flurry of desperate telegrams flashed over the wires between Portland, Oregon and the Curtiss aeroplane factory in Hammondsport, New York. Henry Wemme needed an aeroplane and he needed it now. "If only I can land that ship here, that's all I want," Wemme said. He had closely followed Curtiss' victory at the Rheims aviation meet in August 1909 and a month later he was already pressing his fellow businessmen to sponsor an aeroplane exhibition in Portland. Even though it might cost as much as $200,000 to produce, Wemme thought it was justified, if for no other reason than for the international attention it would bring to the city. When Los Angeles beat him to the punch with the Dominguez air meet, Wemme dreamed up a new scheme, one that he vowed would be a "major surprise" to everyone. He would buy a Curtiss biplane and entice an aviator to fly it over the city.[1]

Wemme was a proud, self-made millionaire, a German immigrant who had never intended to stay in the United States. "I came here, went broke, and couldn't get away," he said. When he was 14 years old and living in Germany, Wemme was apprenticed to a flourmill. To become a master in his profession, tradition said he had to travel to other countries and study their processing methods. He began his tour in 1871 when he was 19. From Austria, through Italy, and France, Wemme eventually sailed to the United States, where, before his luck ran out, he easily found work in flourmill after flourmill. "When I got to Chicago, I went broke," he said. "After missing a few meals, I was willing to work at anything."

He kept moving west. "My bosses were always going broke or going crazy on me," he said. "So, I decided to go into business for myself." He worked his way to Portland, where, in 1886, desperation led him to his ultimate fortune. He started a one-man tent and awning "factory," doing all the work himself in his own rented room. "I have no patience with a man who throws up his hands and quits because he can't get work at his trade," Wemme said.[2]

In January 1898, the U.S.S. *Maine* blew up in Havana harbor and the United States declared war. Within months, Wemme was flush with government contracts. He suddenly had 400 people working for him and almost overnight had become one of the wealthiest and most influential men in the city.

The driving force behind Wemme's urgent need for a Curtiss aeroplane came from his own obsession with automobiles. He had tried to build his own steam horseless carriage in 1888 and managed to get the engine together, but at the time, he didn't have enough money to buy the rest of the parts he needed. "A few years later I decided to buy a real automobile," he said. In 1899, Wemme bought a Locomobile at the premium price of about $1,000, a car that usually listed for $600. It was the first automobile in the city. A few months later, he sold it at a profit and quickly replaced it with the city's second. He became a collector and trader of automobiles and by 1908, Wemme claimed he had personally owned twenty automobiles, in addition to those he had acquired for others.[3]

Wemme never intended to fly his aeroplane. "My chief object in bringing it to Portland is to attract people to the automobile show," he said.

Held at the end of January 1910 by the Portland Automobile Club, of which Wemme was the president, this was the city's second automobile exhibition. Wemme guaranteed that every penny of any profit would go to the club's "Good Roads Fund," including the extra 25 cent admission fee Wemme would charge if he could get a Curtiss aeroplane.[4]

Of course, a Curtiss biplane meant more to Wemme than just as an advertisement for the auto show. Wemme the collector, the self-proclaimed "father of the automobile" in Portland, wanted to be the city's "father of the aeroplane" too. He already had competition from John Burkhart, a young Cornell graduate who claimed to have already flown in the East and was building an airplane in Portland. Wemme was worried that Burkhart might finish his plane and fly it long before Wemme had a chance to buy his own. To top Burkhart, Wemme would spare no expense. "It is nothing. Nothing at all," he said.[5]

When an agreeable deal was finally put together with the Curtiss company, Wemme rushed to the Wells Fargo Express office to arrange expedited delivery direct from the factory to Portland. He was so happy and so enthused that he never asked the agent how much it would cost. When a friend speculated that the freight bill alone would likely come close to $500 or $600, a nearly speechless Wemme raced back to the express office. The agent told Wemme that the shipment would cost him as much as $1,500. Wemme had already agreed to pay $5,000 for the biplane and wasn't willing to spend that much more. He hastily prepared a telegram and sent it flying over the wires. "Stop shipment by express!" The factory replied that there was no way they could get the airship to Portland in time for the auto show, anyway, so Wemme called the deal off and fretted a short time before coming up with a new idea.[6]

Airplanes were already flying on the West Coast at Dominguez. If he could buy one of those and express ship it to Portland, the shipping cost would be less and the plane could arrive in time. He was ready to go to Los Angeles himself, but was summoned to Federal jury duty and, unable to convince the judge to release him, Wemme sent George Kleiser, a member of the Portland automobile club and co-owner of an outdoor advertising firm to Dominguez. "Bring home one of the prize winning aeroplanes," Wemme said. "Insist that it be a prizewinner and that it be expressed here before the opening of the show."[7]

When looking for Wemme's prizewinner, George Kleiser didn't have much of a choice. Other than the plane flown by Charles Hamilton, all first place prizes belonged to either Glenn Curtiss or his French rival, Louis Paulhan, and there was no way Kleiser could get one of those. Hamilton had collected his first prize by flying around the Dominguez aviation track in the slowest time—3 minutes 36 ⅕ seconds. It wasn't a world record and although aviators said it was the most difficult type of record to set; to the layman it wasn't very impressive. Later, the flyboys admitted that the event "was not really considered of any great importance." For Kleiser, that didn't matter. Wemme wanted a prizewinner and Hamilton's was available.[8]

On January 15, 1910, Kleiser wired Wemme, announcing he had purchased Hamilton's plane for $5,000 and would ship it to Portland as soon as the Los Angeles meeting was over. What Kleiser didn't know and so couldn't tell Wemme, was the kind of trouble Hamilton's machine had already endured.[9]

The biplane had been in the air nearly 100 times. In Missouri Hamilton had crashed it twice and bounced it off the ice. The engine blew a cylinder near Kansas City and over the past month there had been many hard landings, including two on the second and third days at Dominguez. His biplane would soon belong to Wemme, but Hamilton wasn't through with failure.[10]

While Curtiss and Paulhan went head to head in an aerial speed duel, Hamilton had disappeared for at least 30 minutes while attempting an altitude record. When he suddenly reappeared in the twilight, spectators heard his engine stop and saw his propeller freeze. The machine fell into a rapid, diving glide to earth. When it bounced to a stop on the soft sod, mechanics asked Hamilton what had happened. Hamilton seemed puzzled by the question. "My shaft broke and I had to get to the earth without killing myself. So, I just glided," he said.[11]

Two weeks of dashing through the clouds were over and Wemme had secured his prizewinner. With damaged parts replaced, it was packed into three large wooden crates for the two-day railroad trip to Portland. Curtiss gave Hamilton the 8-cylinder Rheims Racer as a replacement.[12]

The automobile show was just a few days away and Wemme was worried that the biplane wouldn't arrive in time. As soon as he received Kleiser's telegram, Wemme sent Howard Covey to Los Angeles to learn all that he could "and take a course of instruction in the art of manipulating the machine." Curtiss had promised an expert aviator would teach Covey how to fly and agreed that a mechanic would accompany the crated biplane to Portland and help set it up. It was assumed that once Covey could fly, he would also be able to teach others.[13]

Wemme again refused to say if he would fly the aircraft himself or even if he would ride with someone else. "Wait till I see what it looks like," he said, "I'll not say I will or will not ride in it. But, I have half a dozen Portland men who are just crazy for the chance to go up." Undoubtedly, one of those men was Gene Ely, but for now, he would have to wait his turn and watch.[14]

The prizewinner was two days late arriving in Portland. With the grand opening of the automobile show just a few hours away, mechanics rushed the crates to the second floor of the Portland Armory and frantically began reassembling the biplane. Wemme told friends that he had been "worried some for a while," but now that his aeroplane had finally arrived, he was very, very happy.[15]

Newspapers reported that Covey was returning from Los Angeles as "a full-fledged aeroplane navigator" who had received two days of flight instruction. Covey admitted to only one lesson, but bragged that one lesson was more than enough.[16]

"The operation of an aeroplane is simple enough when one understands it," Covey said. "I have not yet made enough trips in this machine to become expert in its operation, but think I have mastered the secret of guiding the machine."[17]

Covey kept promising to fly soon, but he never would. For over four months there would be a lot of bold talk without any action. Wemme would eventually tire of his biplane and Covey would return to his Cadillac dealership. Two other men would eventually try to fly the prizewinner, but their feeble attempts would only end in embarrassing failure. From the time the aeroplane arrived in Portland until Gene Ely got his hands on the wheel, there was no one talented enough to get Wemme's prizewinner into the sky.

# { 14 }

# Crowds Will Flock

At the end of January 1910, the Portland Armory was almost ready for the local dealers' second attempt to entice the horse riding public into a horseless carriage.[1]

The armory was a fortress castle; two and a half stories of red brick over black basalt stones. Tall, narrow windows were cut through sturdy walls, walls that might easily have withstood a medieval bombardment. Thick wooden doors led into a space free of support pillars, the building's roof held up by a set of arching trusses. Built in 1891 as an annex to a much smaller building, the armory was meant to be the all-weather headquarters for Oregon's First Regiment of National Guard and featured an indoor drill pad and an underground gun range. Temporary bleachers could seat 5,000 people and perhaps a thousand more could look down from the second floor gallery. It was one of the largest interior spaces available in the city.

The decorative scheme for the auto show was elaborate. The main hall, on the lower level, was transformed into a Roman garden. The center of the room was framed with sixteen simulated marble columns, each sixteen feet high, and topped with white, molded automobile tires that had sprouted bird's wings. On each tire was a statue of Mercury, messenger of the Roman gods, standing nearly four feet tall with his left arm in the air and legs poised for a leap into flight. At their base and surrounding the columns was a bas-relief fence with open gateways leading into the separate exhibit areas. Sixty small potted trees were scattered across the floor and nesting in their foliage were live canaries. The entire interior was lit with 167 recently installed incandescent bulbs and occasional sunlight shining through skylights in the roof.[2]

Twenty-eight auto dealers exhibited $300,000 worth of automobiles in elaborate displays, carefully crafted to capture interest and surprise the crowds. One of the most popular was the Winton Six, a torpedo-bodied roadster that because of its bright red paint was nicknamed the "Red Devil." Not far away, the polished body of a White model was elevated on a glass platform with its undercarriage reflected in a mirror underneath. Howard Covey, Wemme's sky pilot, had modified a Cadillac engine so that an electric motor kept its visible parts in constant motion. At the back of the hood a smaller motor pushed up individual numerals that spelled out the year—1–9–1–0. Visitors were more interested in when Covey would fly. "As soon as fair weather sets in," Covey would say. "I hope then to give a practical demonstration of operating this machine." Directly across the exhibit hall from Covey was the rather plain Auburn automobile display of Gene Ely's employer, Robert Simpson. Gene, as a salesman, likely spent quite a bit of time there.[3]

With the late arrival of Wemme's biplane from Los Angeles, there were only a few hours left to get the separate parts put together before the automobile show opened. While 100 workers added final touches to the decorative scheme of the hall, the three wooden crates that held the Wemme biplane arrived in the armory gymnasium. Piece by piece, in a separate room on the second floor, the aeroplane was put back together under the watchful eye of a reporter. "The Curtiss biplane is mounted on three wheels, placed as on a tricycle," he wrote. "The machine is noticeable for its apparent frailty, and yet, it is capable of withstanding a much greater shock than is believable by looking at it. Stout bamboo frames constitute the hectagon over which is stretched heavy canvas. Steel wires bind the different sections of the machine together. Immediately behind the operator's seat is placed the engine, which propels the machine and the weight of this is counterbalanced by the weight of the driver."[4]

On display next to Wemme's biplane, but separated by a partition, was John Burkhart's aeroplane. His craft had not flown and would not fly successfully for nearly two months.[5]

From the moment the doors opened, it was obvious the aeroplanes, whether they had flown or not, had captured everyone's imagination. Officials estimated that the aircraft displays had increased attendance over the previous year by 40 percent. Unfortunately for the automobile men, most people went directly from the main floor to the aeroplane room and, when they came back down, they left without ever seeing an automobile. The aeronautical curious were eager to pay the 50-cent armory admission and then hastily head upstairs to pay an additional 25 cents just to see the biplanes. The first paid admission came from a 16-year-old boy who told the ticket taker he was building his own machine and wanted to get a close-up look and get some pointers from the Curtiss aircraft. Officials guessed that scores of inventive boys of all ages were lured to the flying machines with the very same idea. During the six-day event, over 8,000 aeroplane admissions contributed more than $2,000 to Wemme's Mt. Hood Road Fund. Wemme had innocently thought one assistant would be more than enough to explain the science of the aeroplane and how it flew, but the intense public interest forced him to hire two more. "I am surprised," he said. "Scores of persons have gone night after night to view the machine."[6]

The show grossed $38,000, but after expenses, the profit was only $5,000, leaving Wemme $5,000 short of his $10,000 goal.[7]

Talk turned to aviation shows and how valuable an aerial exhibition would be for the city's economy and pride. Why not have Howard Covey fly Wemme's machine in competition with professional aviators like Hamilton, Paulhan, or even Glenn Curtiss? An air meet, they said, would even give Burkhart "a chance to show the merits of his Portland-built aeroplane." Wemme replied that his primary interest was the Mt. Hood Road Fund, but if the fund could share in the gate receipts, he would allow organizers to use his Curtiss machine.[8]

While theatrical agents began arranging details of the Northwest's first aviation meet, Wemme took Gene's future biplane on the road. Julius Meier, owner of the Meier & Frank department store, had donated $500 to Wemme's cause and offered to showcase his "skyscraper" during the store's "food fair and big aviation sale." It took two days to disassemble the biplane, repack it, haul it less than fifteen blocks, and reassemble it on the store's fourth floor. Admission cost only ten cents and children accompanied by their parents got in free. Wemme said the lower admission fee would allow "poorer persons who are interested in the mechanical bird to see it without great expense."[9]

At the end of February, Wemme sent the Curtiss machine to a Seattle exhibition sponsored by the Washington State Good Roads Association. Half of the gate receipts were promised to the Mount Hood Road Fund and the remaining half would support work on the highway between Portland and Seattle. A newspaper reported that "considerable money" was being raised, but because no figures were ever given, Wemme was likely disappointed with his share.[10]

From Seattle, the biplane was rushed back to Portland, where dreams of the Northwest's first aviation meet were about to become reality. With the Curtiss aeroplane ready to fly for the first time since Hamilton flew it in Los Angeles, promoters expected amazing gate receipts. Wemme wasn't so sure. Being Portland's father of aviation wasn't turning out to be as profitable as he had hoped.

By March, it was almost Gene's turn to fly the Wemme machine. Howard Covey wasn't the pilot of choice anymore. Now that fair weather had finally arrived in Portland, he apparently had lost his nerve and refused to try. A long line of potential aeronauts had also expressed their interest in flying, but when their chance finally came, like Covey; they too would keep their feet on the ground.

With Covey out of the picture, Portland-born Forest Smithson topped the list of willing aviators. Smithson was an Olympic gold medal champion who had set a new world record in the 110-meter hurdles at the 1908 games. A popular Oregon athlete and deeply religious, everyone assumed that he would make a good pilot, but at the last minute, he too said no.[11]

The mechanically inclined Walter Donnelly was next in line and seemed to fit the bill. Because he had been in charge of assembling and disassembling the biplane ever since it arrived from Los Angeles, and had given lectures on its operation, the Canadian immigrant, a former waiter with a high opinion of himself, believed he had the best flying qualifications. He bragged to reporters that he had become an "aviation expert" by studying aeronautics. His education had begun, he said, while watching dirigible flights at the 1904 St. Louis World's Fair. He even said he planned to buy his own airplane. When asked his profession by a 1910 census taker, Donnelly was confidently living in his unfulfilled dreams, or so it must have seemed to the census taker. On the census form, under the "occupation" heading, the enumerator had written "aviator," actually enclosing the word in quotation marks. It was a perceptive move on the enumerator's part. Donnelly would soon prove he was never meant to fly.[12]

Charles Hamilton's telegram arrived at the end of February. He said that once he finished his Southwest exhibition tour, he would perform for three days in Portland with a minimum of one guaranteed flight each day. He offered to race automobiles if the value of the prize was high enough and he tentatively agreed to attempt a new world record for distance and height. He promised to fly around "the mighty sentinel of the Columbia River," Mt. Hood, Oregon's highest mountain, but when he reached Portland he quickly abandoned that idea "I was not told the distance of the flight," he said. "That would mean flying 120 miles. I have never flown over 43 miles." Adding to the difficulty would have been an altitude gain of at least 2,000 to 4,000 feet, bringing the daring aviator dangerously close to the mountain and its shifting and sometimes vicious air currents.[13]

Promoters claimed the Portland aviation meet would be "second only to the international contests held in Los Angeles," but, if they wanted to finished preparations in time, they had to hurry. Secretaries, messengers, stenographers, clerks, carpenters, and laborers were hired. Posters were printed and advertising layouts for the newspapers prepared. Already wooden shelters for the aeroplanes were under construction on the infield at the Country Club fairgrounds. The racetrack was being raked and rolled to hard, smooth perfection. A 400-foot pine plank runway was laid out, for better traction in case it rained. Finally, the railroad agreed to add 100 coaches to their line and reduce passenger fares to accommodate the 50,000 or more people expected to attend."[14]

Because Hamilton would be reunited with his old biplane, everyone was sure he would be anxious to fly it again. If he declined, there was still Burkhart who said he was willing to give it a try. But when the meet began, he preferred to ride the sidelines as a "most interested spectator."[15]

As preparations continued, perhaps the biggest surprise for officials was the number of women who wanted to fly as passengers with Hamilton. A week before the Portland air show, Daniel Lively, the air meet manager, had already received a dozen written requests. "You would be surprised at the number of society women in Portland who want to take a ride in an airship," he said. "I do not care to name the women, but I can assure you that their names are known to practically everybody in Portland." A longtime promoter of fairs and expositions, Lively said he had never seen anything like it. "I cannot explain why women should take such an interest in aviation."[16]

Hamilton had been a very busy man since Los Angeles. The more daring and dangerous his flights became, the more cities wanted to see him fly. From San Diego he was off to Bakersfield and Fresno, then moving east through Arizona and on to Texas. The locations might change, but Hamilton still flew with reckless abandon.

In Fresno, he completely lost his bearings and had to land in a farmer's alfalfa field and ask directions back to the fairgrounds. When he returned, he crashed through a fence. With his machine repaired, Hamilton was on his way to Phoenix where an oil leak set his wings on fire. "I was flying about a hundred feet from the ground when my oil tank sprung a leak and burst into flames," he said. "Luckily I was flying into the wind at the time and the flames were driven back from my head." A tire exploded when he tried to land and Hamilton jumped to safety. In Tucson, he landed too fast, ran into a mechanic, and knocked him over, the biplane crashing into another fence post. An hour later, Hamilton was landing too quickly. He jumped to the ground and grabbed onto the plane, trying to stop it, but once again it crashed into a fence, leaving an elevator badly fractured, the front wheel carriage bent, and the front tire punctured and ripped away.[17]

Understandably, aviators wanted good money for the risk they were taking and, to get them to fly, local promoters had to guarantee an aviator's fee. To fly in Tucson, Hamilton demanded $2,000 and 50 percent of the gate, which meant the promoters, needed $4,000 in admissions just to break even. What they got was barely $1,600, half of which went to Hamilton. In Phoenix they were short $3,000 after their meet and in Douglas, Arizona, the newspaper would only say, "Here, as in those cities, the exhibition was not a financial success."[18]

What no one seemed to realize, when planning these events, was airplanes flew in the sky and unless a spectator really wanted to get a close-up look at the aeroplane, they could comfortably watch from the outside and never pay an admission at all. In Portland, they would call it "Tightwad Hill."

On March 3, after a three-day railroad trip from Arizona, Hamilton arrived in Portland aboard the Southern Pacific's *Shasta Limited*. As he came around the corner of the train lugging a large suitcase, the welcoming committee recognized him. Hamilton had heard band music when he arrived and suspecting an unwanted welcoming ceremony, had left the train on the opposite side of his car and had tried to bury himself in the midst of his assistants. It hadn't worked. "Hamilton is five feet and seven inches tall and weighs 110 pounds," wrote a reporter. "He doesn't look his height." That made sense because most sources say Hamilton was actually closer to 5 feet tall. "The most distinguished thing about his personal appearance is his ears," the reporter continued. "They are unusually large, even for a big man, and stand well out from the head." He had clear blue eyes, a pink complexion, a "high nose, and a well-formed, set mouth," giving "an attractiveness to his appearance."[19]

Howard Covey, who had met Hamilton in Los Angeles, took charge of the aviator and drove him to his hotel. Then he took him on a brief automobile tour of downtown Portland, showing him the aviation field at the Country Club. By then, it was already growing dark and time for a welcoming dinner in Hamilton's honor. Hamilton told the diners that flying was easy. "Learning to operate an aeroplane is just like learning to ride a bicycle," he said. "It is just as simple and little danger is attached to it." It sounded a lot like the words Covey had spoken less than two months earlier. Hamilton said he had begun to experiment with aeronautics five years before, while flying his dirigible in Japan. He said his interest in those experiments had led him to become a professional aviator. It was a story he told so many times that like a game of telephone, where a word whispered from one ear to another soon loses its meaning, reporters and promoters began saying Hamilton had flown aeroplanes instead of balloons in Japan. Once the story got started, it didn't end with Hamilton. Later, when Gene Ely began flying Hamilton's machine, he began telling reporters that he was the one who had flown in the Orient. "Last year, I made a tour of Japan with my machine and flew many times," he said. That of course was impossible.[20]

In Portland, the barometer was rising, fair weather was ahead, and officials were relieved. They assured the public that there would be no rain to prevent Hamilton from flying, but knowing the Northwest's unpredictable weather, even they couldn't be sure.[21]

# { 15 }

## "I was fascinated with the idea of flying"

From morning until sunset the sun never left the sky. Its warmth dried the ground and enticed a flood of 10,000 curious spectators to the show. A few innocent white clouds floated by and to the east, Mt. Hood's snow shimmered in the spring-like air. All agreed. There could not be a more perfect day for the Northwest's first ever aviation meet.

Wemme wasn't there. He had developed some undisclosed illness and his doctor had ordered a recovery in the therapeutic waters of Hot Springs, Arkansas. He telegraphed a message to air meet manager, Daniel Lively, asking that his Curtiss biplane be the first one to fly on opening day and that Charles Hamilton be the pilot.[1]

Hamilton managed to get the biplane barely ten feet off the ground, flying less than a hundred yards and landing hard with a sputtering engine. It was unfit for flight, he said. The engine was out of tune, the horizontal planes not adjusted properly, and the propeller was misaligned. Some speculated that Hamilton failed to fly because he didn't want to advertise a competitor's aeroplane, but a boy named Walter Donnelly was ready to fly holes in that theory and disastrously prove that Hamilton had meant what he said.[2]

Riding the 8-cylinder *Rheims Racer*, Hamilton flew six simple flights, never longer than five minutes or higher than 500 feet and when he had finished, the last and unscheduled feature of the day began—the wrecking of Henry Wemme's Curtiss biplane.

The ever-confident Walter Donnelly, ignoring what Hamilton had said about the machine's flight worthiness, got permission from Wemme to fly it. Late in the afternoon, Donnelly and friends moved the craft to the starting point. A crowd of perhaps 5,000 pressed in too closely, until the 400-foot runway was no wider than a narrow country lane. Donnelly climbed into the pilot's seat, gunned the engine, and was off. Running across the ground at an ever-faster rate, he lifted three feet into the air. The all too curious crowd surged in and Donnelly, too late, swerved right to avoid hitting them. His wing smashed 10-year-old Frankie Owen in the mouth, knocking out some of the boy's teeth and dragging him a short distance. Still in the air, Donnelly overcorrected, lost control, and swerved to the left, brushing against policeman Marcus

Rudolph's horse. The horse reared up, threw Rudolph off his saddle, and galloped away. Then, the biplane lifted up sharply, stalled, rolled over, and fell back into the terrified crowd. Donnelly was hurled from his seat, tumbled headlong into the scrambling mob. Spectators fell and were trampled as they tried to flee. Women in the grandstand fainted. A sharp wooden piece of the aeroplane speared one man in the face. Italian immigrant, Victor Cercis, fell down with a broken ankle. Of the six or seven injured people, only Frankie Owen and Victor Cercis required hospital attention. Donnelly was lucky. He escaped with just a few scrapes and bruises.[3]

Canvas and silk were sliced and torn away from the aeroplane. Bamboo cross bracing was snapped, all three tires were shredded, and the wheel carriage was squashed flat. Wemme's mechanics asked Hamilton to assess the damage. The engine was in fine shape, he said, and he saw no reason why the biplane couldn't fly again. Repairs would cost about $50 and the craft could probably be ready to fly in just a few days. Donnelly promised to fly longer and higher next time, if only he was allowed to practice with it. A reporter was dubious of Donnelly's chances. "It will require continuous practice all this week," he said, "for the young Portlander to master the craft."[4]

Perhaps because of how badly Donnelly had damaged the Wemme biplane, Hamilton angrily accused Wemme's crew of stealing biplane parts from his personal supply. Nose to nose with Hamilton, Wemme's manager, E. J. Arnold, said he resented the insinuation and, for at least half a minute, it looked like the shouting match would turn to fists, but thinking better of it, both men turned and walked away.[5]

Except for Donnelly's accident, it had been a good opening day, but the meet's promoters noticed a disturbing trend. Large crowds stood outside the grounds, peeked through the fence or snuck in, and paid nothing. The problem was obvious. The Country Club grounds sat in a natural amphitheater. "Unfortunately for the management," said a reporter, "from every hill within a radius of half a mile of the aviation field, from every telephone and electric lighting post, and peeking through the gates," the tightwads prevailed.[6]

Portland's aviation meet ended as most air exhibitions did, as a financial fizzle. "The meet was the greatest frost ever known in Portland," wrote a reporter. The gross receipts were less than $7,000, but backers of the exhibition refused to give an exact amount of their losses. This, they said, "depends entirely on what part of the guarantee Hamilton will demand." Hamilton demanded his full guarantee for the three-day event, leaving the backers to make up the difference; an embarrassing loss that never made the newspapers, except to say that Henry Wemme was its biggest victim. "I was told today that I would have to dig up my share of the loss on the aviation meet," he said. "It was the first information I had received that my name was connected with it in that respect."[7]

Repairs on Wemme's biplane took longer than Donnelly thought and, because of Wemme's losses, he refused to let Donnelly fly again. Trying to recoup some of his losses, Wemme sent Donnelly and the biplane to one last exhibition at an automobile show in Spokane, Washington. Wemme was promised 35 percent of the gate, a figure he expected to return somewhere around $2,000. Apparently, he didn't even come close. By the end of March, he decided his biplane had become a liability. Expenses were piling up and the aeroplane was the cause. Wemme was tired of his prizewinner and looking for a buyer.[8]

The offers came quickly. Jack Stark, said to be a wealthy mining man from New Mexico, was first. He arrived in Portland by train, telling reporters that one advantage to flying in the Southwest and not in Portland, was that an aviator wouldn't drown if he had to make an emergency landing. Stark's attempt at humor and the money he offered fell flat. Negotiations broke down and Stark left town. Although there were reports of other offers, Wemme was having a hard time finding satisfaction. "I do not intend to sell my Curtiss until I can get out of it all the money I have spent," he said. "It has cost me a lot of money, and while it has been worthwhile, I do not intend to lose anything."[9]

Gene Ely's employer, Robert Simpson, approached Wemme with an offer. He had an employee who was interested in flying. If Wemme would allow a few test flights to see if the employee could master it, Simpson would buy the Curtiss biplane.

Wemme agreed and Gene Ely was ready. "I was fascinated with the idea of flying through space," he said.[10]

Wemme's aeroplane was taken to the wide-open spaces east of town near the notorious Twelve Mile House. Beyond the reach of Portland's police department, the House was best known for its lack of respectability; where young men and women could always find a wicked good time. Flowers and cupid statues flanked the gaudy entry, and once inside, there were 28 luxurious rooms to choose from. Fine art and dozens of mirrors hung everywhere. Slot machines lined the silk covered walls of a well stocked bar, where underage drinkers had no problem sipping a glass of hard liquor or chugging a mug of beer. There was a toe-tapping orchestra near a maple wood dance floor, a smoke filled dining room that served "nothing but the best," and upstairs, those mysterious, private rooms. Gamblers could cut cards in high stakes poker games, pick their favorite in a cockfight, or bet the ponies at the nearby race-track. It was an unusual location to find the straight-laced Wemme and the shy Gene Ely, but it was just far enough from town to keep the curious crowds away.[11]

Walter Donnelly had reassembled the biplane on the infield of the racetrack. Perhaps he still believed Wemme would let him fly, but for now, the machine stood quietly in a canvas hangar.

Light rain stopped and skies began to clear, when Wemme, Simpson, Gene, and a party of motorists arrived at the racetrack. The biplane was rolled out and Gene climbed into the seat behind the steering wheel. He fiddled with the wheel and listened to the mechanics, who, even though they had never flown themselves, told him how to control the plane in flight. They fired up the engine and Gene revved the motor until the propeller was turning at nearly 1,200 revolutions per minute. While mechanics held tightly to the wings, the machine began to shudder and shake. As it struggled to break free, Gene pulled back on the wheel, elevating the altitude plane at the exact moment when the mechanics let go. No one would ever say whether it was an accident or a practical joke, but within seconds, the biplane was 30 feet in the air and running at full throttle. It took Gene a moment to remember how to kill the engine and then carefully glide to a miraculous landing, but when it was over, Gene Ely had flown his first 200 yards. He was a natural, or so he thought. It was April 12, 1910, and Gene Ely had become a dedicated birdman.[12]

The next day, he tried again. His first three flights were short and straight and he never got more than ten feet into the air, but by afternoon, his confidence was growing. During that fourth flight, he rose to 30 feet, flying directly into the face of a northerly wind. Suddenly a gust pushed him to the left toward a clump of trees. Gene tried to turn back and at the same time lower his altitude, thinking he might be able to land safely, but the wind was too strong. The aeroplane tipped and began to fall. Gene calmly shut off the motor and held on as the left wings tilted down and plowed a deep furrow into the ground. Then, the wings bounced back up and the plane flipped over to the opposite side, smashing to the ground, and jolting to a stop. Gene was unhurt, but repairing the fractured biplane would cost at least another $50 and take nearly a week to complete.[13]

Once all the pieces were back in place, nothing could keep Gene away. He made six successful flights that day, never very high, just straight and careful trials. "It is like learning to ride a bicycle," he said. "I am going to keep on trying until I am sure of myself. I believe I will be able to make an extended flight before the end of the week." When the census enumerator arrived at Gene and Mabel's Portland rooming house on April 28, Gene proudly proclaimed his new occupation—"Aeronaut."[14]

Simpson had seen enough to know that Gene would soon master the machine. He bought Wemme's aeroplane for an undisclosed amount of money, and with other investors, formed the Portland Aeroplane Company. Gene would be vice president and the company's exhibition pilot, but before he could turn professional, he needed to learn how to make successful turns and longer flights. With just two week's experience and less than a dozen flights under his belt, Gene was ready to try. On his first turn attempt, his rudder wouldn't respond, but after he landed and made some quick adjustments, he was back in the air again and turning it at will. He had taught himself to fly and he was modestly proud. "I am sometimes called a Curtiss pupil," he would later say, "though I never studied under Mr. Curtiss at all." Curtiss would agree. "Nobody taught Ely to fly," Curtiss said. "He was his own teacher, and he proved a good one."[15]

While Gene continued practicing, Simpson had been busy. In three weeks, the unknown Gene Ely would fly his first exhibition, and by the end of the year, after a number of embarrassing failures, he would be world famous

In mid–May 1910 practice time was over. They broke down the Curtiss biplane, packed it into its three traveling crates, and loaded it onto a southbound train. Seven hours after leaving Portland, Gene, Mabel, and the mechanical team arrived in what was about to become Oregon's newest city, Sutherlin, a small farming village between Eugene and Roseburg. After successfully flying over the relatively flat open spaces near the Twelve Mile House, Gene must have had a touch of claustrophobia as he looked up from the level floor of the Sutherlin Valley. The encircling sharp slopes quickly loomed upward into steep hills over 1,000 feet high. They formed an irregular seven-mile long corridor that ranged from three miles down to only a half-mile wide, but Gene was optimistic. He said the narrow walls wouldn't bother him, because the fir-clad hills would protect him from heavy winds.[16]

Oregon's second aviation exhibition was the highlight of the town's first annual strawberry festival and livestock fair. Sutherlin organizers wanted people to know that they were friendlier than their big city northern neighbors, and they were sure their air show would prove it. There would be no "high board fence" to keep the biplane out of sight and no one would need "several dollars" for admission. "Sutherlin people are not built on the order of grafters," wrote a reporter. Of course, on such short notice, a town that was still building its first racetrack and erecting livestock barns and carnival booths, had little time or money to put up a large fence. To accommodate the expected crowd of out-of-town visitors, a tent city would supplement the town's one hotel. There would even be a large temporary dining tent that could serve up to 300 people at a time.[17]

Early news reports of Gene's debut as a professional aviator were glowing. "The first flight of a biplane or aeroplane in Southern Oregon took place here this morning," one said, "and was a very successful demonstration of what a modern flying machine is capable of doing. The start was made without any delay or trouble and the biplane soared upward as a bird." The reporter marveled at the "inspiring spectacle" and the "remarkable feat of the birdman." However, that enthusiasm faded somewhat the next day, when the reporter seemed to express a general disappointment felt by the opening-day crowd. "It is expected," he said, "that the machine will make a better record [today] than it was able to do yesterday morning or afternoon." Later reports said that on day two, Gene had smashed into an "ordinary fence," the same fence he had "barely cleared" the previous day. In his defense, that negative report came nearly a week after the reported crash, when Gene had already announced a lawsuit.[18]

Day 3 had all the signs of success. The "thrilling flight" began late in the afternoon after the biplane was tested and adjusted. "The machinery was set in motion. Ely took his seat and a moment later the machine started on its perilous journey." He ran the length of the racetrack, "gracefully soared into the air," and then climbed "to a considerable height." As the valley began to narrow, he turned in a wide circle, intending to return to his starting point, but a gust of wind pushed his right wing down. For a moment, Gene lost control; the plane tilted and began to fall. Below were a group of fair buildings and the potential for serious injury. He frantically worked his controls, trying to find a safe way down and, although he continued to fall, he managed a successful hard landing in an open field. The propeller was battered and the aeroplane had several broken ribs, but Gene said it could all be repaired in just three days, more than enough time to prepare for his next flying exhibition, 110 miles to the south in Medford. There he expected to meet a Curtiss representative who was coming to witness what Gene hoped would be success.

As he was about to leave Sutherlin, Gene asked for his share of the gate receipts, but the promoters refused, saying his "flights were failures." The local newspaper mocked Gene's demand. "Considering the very mild degree of success attained by Mr. Ely," it said, "we presume the other side will have something to say if the case is ever brought to trial." On his way to Medford, Gene stopped off in Roseburg, the county seat, just long enough to file suit in district court. He demanded $480, the one-half share of $960 in paid admissions guaranteed him in his contract. It was the first, but not the last time he would have to fight for his money.[19]

# { 16 }

# On the Road to Curtiss

Look! Here he comes!

Hands grabbed shoulders, fingers pointed to the sky, and faces tilted upward. Traffic stopped, drivers stepped out, and joined in the heavenly search. There it was! In the north! An aeroplane! Wasn't that a man riding the lower wing? Wasn't that the sound of a sputtering engine? It's Ely! He's flying in from Sutherlin. It must be Ely! Such was the anticipation of seeing the first airship in Southern Oregon.

The news spread around town and up and down Medford's Main Street, but then—reality. The aeroplane was really a box kite, a huge box kite to be sure, but only a box kite. The little man on the wing was only a black camera. It was all controlled from the ground by a group of photographers who were just trying to snap a bird's eye view of the city. Two days later, Gene's train arrived carrying the actual biplane. "The machine came crated in three huge boxes," wrote a reporter. "Mr. Ely will soon unpack the animal and prepare for the flights at the end of the week."[1]

The local press touted Gene's "considerable success in flying" even though he was just a beginner. They theorized that his failures in Sutherlin were the fault of his motor and not because he lacked ability. He not only flew a Curtiss biplane, they said, but also the very same Curtiss machine he had used to set seven world records—records set by others, of course. The ultimate proof that they didn't really know who Gene Ely was is found in an advertisement that ran for nearly a month before he arrived, renaming "Portland manbird," Gene, "Paul Ely."[2]

Half of the proceeds from the Medford air exhibition would go to Gene. The remainder would be dedicated to the Crater Lake road-building fund. Crater Lake was only 80 miles from Medford, but the trip took nearly five days by wagon and was almost impossible by automobile. Wagons, with their higher clearance, easily passed over the boulders and stumps that were scattered in the roadway, but an automobile had to dodge every one. State funding for the highway had been approved, but was subsequently declared unconstitutional by the state's Supreme Court. Local businessmen were sure the road would increase tourism and bolster the local economy and had decided to raise $100,000 to build the road themselves.

This exhibition would be much like Gene's first. A sizeable crowd gathered in a farmer's field south of town to watch him climb to just 20 feet, fly 150 yards, and sud-

At Medford, Oregon, in June 1910, Eugene Ely poses beside his 4-cylinder Curtiss biplane. This was only his second exhibition since learning to fly. By the time he returned to Medford, one year later, the stress and strains of exhibition flying had caused this 160-pound aviator to lose as much as 40 pounds (Southern Oregon Historical Society #15623).

denly be hurled to the ground by a rift in the wind. The airship's "motive power ceased to flap," wrote a reporter, "and it lit in the form of a mass of tangled wreckage within a few yards of the starting point." Gene assured reporters that repairs could be made, but for the next two days he was grounded. "The fates and currents of air—some say hot air," wrote a reporter, "were against the enterprise." The promoters refunded all admission fees and arranged with Charles Bryce, the Curtiss advance man, to add aviator Whipple Hall to the exhibition. While nervous promoters waited a week for Hall to arrive from San Francisco, they hoped that two aeroplanes would give them a better chance of actually seeing something fly.[3]

There is no evidence that Hall and Gene Ely ever met in San Francisco, and judging by their relative social status, it doesn't seem likely. Hall had every reason not to risk his life in the air. Married and father of a 2-year-old daughter, 28-year-old Hall satisfied what one society editor called the ideals of society—"position and wealth." The son of a California Appeals Court judge, both he and his wife were "abundantly endowed with these factors," and yet, like so many men of the day who were living in the upper realms of society, Hall had caught aviation fever. It's possible he and

Gene may have crossed paths while Gene was a chauffeur, but Hall lived in Oakland, across the bay from San Francisco, and except for the car he drove, Hall had no interest in automobiles. They most likely met in Portland where Hall and his biplane were on tour with Hamilton. Wherever that first meeting took place, it led to a close friendship and one of the most important in Gene's life. Later, when Gene became successful, Hall would remind reporters that he had "picked up Ely in Oregon and taught him the first principles of flying." Most important for Gene's career, Whipple Hall knew Glenn Curtiss and soon Gene would know him too.[4]

Whipple Spear Hall was the most unlikely aviator anyone had ever seen. At a time when flimsy biplanes with underpowered engines were still struggling to get airborne, the ideal aviator was usually slender and lightweight. In the late spring of 1910, Hall was over 6 feet tall and weighed nearly 210 pounds, possibly more, so the idea that he would be able to fly his own low-powered Curtiss biplane seemed ludicrous to everyone but Hall. To his credit, some said he had managed to lose at least 30 pounds in the previous five months, but that was a dubious claim at best. Whenever questioned about his weight, he would say it made little difference, except in speed competitions, where he was only "slightly slower than a lighter man."[5]

Earlier in the year, Hall had arrived at the Los Angeles aviation meet desperate to fly. He somehow convinced Hamilton to teach him. From then on, Hall and Hamilton were inseparable, wherever Hamilton flew, Hall was there, watching and learning.

Whipple Hall's first flight was in San Diego as a passenger on Hamilton's biplane, but because of his weight, it was low to the ground and short. Still, Hall was ecstatic. "I have ridden in dirigibles, ordinary balloons, multi-planes, and mule carts," he said, "but for out-and-out dizzy riding I want to commend this biplane thing."[6]

A few days after his San Diego flight, Hall asked Glenn Curtiss if he could buy Charles Willard's biplane for cash. Curtiss agreed. Hall got his aeroplane and he and Hamilton were off for a tour of the southwest.[7]

On February 13, 1910, Hall sent his sister, Alice, a photographic postcard from Phoenix, Arizona of him sitting behind the steering wheel of Hamilton's 8-cylinder *Rheims Racer*. On the photograph, Hall's handwritten message to his sister was brief. "Just after my first flight." Hall would not fly solo for nearly two more months.[8]

After leaving Hamilton, not long after the Portland exhibition, Hall's first flight in Fresno almost killed him. With engine screaming, he smashed into a fence post, catapulted over the steering wheel, and somersaulted to the ground, his head just missing another post. Later reports would say he had suffered a fractured skull. It was an injury that within months would end his flying career.[9]

On June 4, 1910, a week after Gene's initial failure in Medford, the wind was worse than ever. Hall, after nine tries, never got off the ground. Gene managed only two short flights. "Mr. Ely proved that he had the nerve and did his best to soar, but the wind forced him to the ground." In his first flight, he traveled 200 feet at an average height of fifteen feet. After supper, when the winds had died down, Gene tried again, but once again was forced down. "His front control was set for an upward flight and his engine was running splendidly," said a reporter, "but down he came."[10]

The next day was just as bad as the first. Hall remained on the ground and Gene made only one, slightly longer flight. The spectators were disappointed and began laughing and taunting the so-called aviators.[11]

During his first Medford, Oregon, exhibition, June 4–5, 1910, Eugene Ely attempts a takeoff from a farmer's field, while Whipple Hall and an unidentified man in a white shirt watch to his right. Ely never got higher than 15 feet in the air and flew no further than 200 feet. He left town a laughingstock, but promised to return in a year and make good (Southern Oregon Historical Society# 1).

Red faced; dressed in derby hat, and a neatly pressed suit, the aviators' advance man, Charles Bryce, jumped to Gene's defense. "Yes, laugh at him," he said. "Next year he may be the most famous of them all—yea even more. I predict it!" Bryce had only recently signed a contract to manage fliers for Glenn Curtiss and even though he hardly knew Gene, his energetic personality couldn't be held in check. He had, what a newspaperman called, "a gift of gab, which is irrepressible and far superior to that of the ordinary man." Gene got his money, the spectators got a refund, and Gene promised he would return to show them he could really fly. Exactly a year later, he would do just that. By then he was world famous and his flights were spectacular. "I had to wipe out my record, made here," he said, "when I had a machine with no power and was new in the business." That's when everyone had to agree. Bryce had been a prophet.[12]

While Gene returned to Portland to prepare for the trip east and a meeting with Glenn Curtiss, Hall crashed his biplane in a Eugene, Oregon exhibition. Scheduled to fly in Minnesota with a plane that couldn't be repaired in time, Hall quickly had his agent buy another.[13]

Gene and Hall would reunite in St. Paul, Minnesota for the Twin City Aviation Meet, but first Gene had an exhibition scheduled in Billings, Montana. Organizers were promoting, "one of the great aviators of the world" who would fly the first aeroplane ever seen in the state. "Mr. Ely will soar over the city and valley for several hours," they said, but a day before Gene's scheduled appearance, the question was—where was he? Hartman Price, Gene's advance man, told officials not to worry. Ely was on the train, he said, and probably hadn't received their telegram asking for confirmation. Then, trying to lower feverish expectations, Price admitted that it would surprise him if Gene were able to leave the ground at all. "The altitude is too great," he said. Price explained that although aviators had already flown higher than the altitude of Billings, just over 3,100 feet, none of them had started their flight at such a high altitude. "Ely will do everything possible to fly and, if he can do so, we will be even more pleased than the spectators."[14]

Gene arrived just in time on the morning of the show and, after assembling his machine and waiting for the wind to die down, he began his first attempt at 5:30 that evening. Running down the dirt street that led to the fairground's entrance arch, one of his wheels broke off, slowing his speed just enough so that the machine barely left the ground. It bounced up two or three times, traveling about a hundred feet between each bounce before crashing back to earth. He couldn't clear the fairground fence and smashed into a concession booth. Montana's first airplane flight had covered only two blocks and it would be Gene's best flight of the day. "I rose easily several times during the first trial but the wind was so strong from the side that it swerved me off the road and I had not enough control of the machine," he said. "If the wind isn't so strong tomorrow, I feel confident of making a good flight."[15]

The next day, his first flight went less than a city block and never got higher than the heads of the several thousand spectators who lined the street. His second flight looked more promising as his machine raced down the street to the cheers and applause of the expectant crowd. It leapt into the air, sailed another two blocks, and then floated back to earth. "There is no use trying again," Gene said, "although I will do it if you want me to." He said the wind was ideal and his machine was working well, but that "the air is simply too light at this altitude and I cannot get to any appreciable height." He and Mabel boarded the train for the two-day trip to Minnesota.[16]

Planning for the June 1910 Twin City Aviation Meet had begun in February when the secretary of the Minnesota State Agricultural Society, Carson Cosgrove, was attempting to raise funds for the society by luring aviators to the Gopher State. By spring, he lost out to a group of Minneapolis and St. Paul businessmen who had incorporated as the Twin City Aviation Exhibition Company and announced that Glenn Curtiss and his aviators had agreed to appear in Minnesota. Cosgrove might have lost control of the aviation exhibition, but as State Fairgrounds manager, he still would win. With a little arm twisting, Cosgrove convinced exhibition company officials to rent the fairgrounds from him for $2,000 and, after paying Curtiss his $20,000 guarantee, give half the gate receipts to the agricultural society.[17]

June was becoming an important month in the history of aviation. Gene Ely was about to become a member of the Curtiss team, formation of the Curtiss Exhibition Company was being planned, and just before the Twin City Meet began, the Wright brothers lost in court.

Late in February, counsel for Glenn Curtiss had asked Judge Hazel for a rehearing on the Wright brothers' injunction. Hazel continued his order that Curtiss stop making aeroplanes until the U.S. Court of Appeals ruled on the injunction's validity, but he refused to restrain Curtiss from making exhibition flights as long as Curtiss maintained his $10,000 bond against any potential liability should he lose in court. Now, in June, the Court of Appeals unanimously dissolved the injunction, ruling that until a court could establish whether Curtiss had actually infringed on Wright patents, the injunction was not justified. The Wrights asked the court to reconsider, but once again, they lost. The court cancelled the $10,000 bond and the "Patent Wars" would drag on.[18]

Curtiss now had the ability to build more aeroplanes and enlist more aviators and he began to think about expanding his profitable exhibition business. Shortly after the court announced its decision, he wrote to his company's general manager, Jerome Fanciulli. "If you run across a man with money and a name worth something, or a few of them, who would take stock, we might organize a company." It would be two months before the official incorporation filing of the Curtiss Exhibition Company, but while the idea began to take shape, the percentage based leasing contracts between Curtiss and his aviators began to evolve. Instead of fixed percentages, aviators were paid based on their flying ability. The better an aviator flew, the more money he could make. Beginners, such as Gene Ely, might start at 25 percent of their take at an exhibition, and as their technique improved, their share might increase to 50 percent or more. Early on, daredevil pilots who risked their lives in perilous stunts could make as much as $1,500 a flight, and occasionally earn $5,000 a day, but that was before the public began to lose interest in aerial performances.[19]

Even though nearly 50,000 spectators attended the Twin City Air Meet, it never lived up to its publicity. "Minnesota has a fine climate to live in, but it is worthless for airship flying," Glenn Curtiss said. "Conditions were never worse for flying than they are right here." Minnesota was in the middle of a drought, what old-timers said was the worst weather they had ever seen. Temperatures near 100 degrees and little rain had left the ground parched and the air dry. With winds gusting to 15 miles an hour, there was little chance during the four-day event that the 4-cylinder Curtiss biplanes could make any substantial flights. Curtiss was up only twice on the first day, both times flying less than a half-mile at 50 feet before wind gusts pushed him to the ground. The best flight of the meeting came on the second day, when Curtiss flew an 8-cylinder machine up to 700 feet and for six miles, finally giving the spectators a chance to cheer and throw their hats into the air. During the entire meeting, Gene, Bud Mars, Charles Willard, and Lincoln Beachey, each made a few disappointingly short flights, but Whipple Hall never got off the ground, and a proposed challenge race between Curtiss and Barney Oldfield, the racecar driver, never took place.[20]

In his Iowa hometown newspaper, Gene had become a page 2 hero. "Among the daring aviators in the Minneapolis meet is the name of Gene Ely," the article read, "and one day, none flew farther or higher than Gene." It was an exaggeration, but understandably reflected the pride of Gene's friends and neighbors. "Mr. Ely is a York township boy and his mother and sister [and brother] live on the old homestead.... Six months ago he became interested in aerial navigation and, in this, his cool head and intrepid nerve gave him a prominent place." The reporter felt sure that Gene would visit Williamsburg before long so that everyone would have "an opportunity to see a son of York scudding on white wings through the upper air."[21]

From Minnesota, Curtiss headed east to fly at Atlantic City, while Mars, Beachey, and Willard boarded a train for Sioux City, Iowa. Gene was scheduled to fly at Superior, Wisconsin's auto racetrack, but Whipple Hall took his place. Apparently, Curtiss had decided that Hall had more experience and that Gene, his newest exhibition pilot, needed to learn more technique. Gene would join the boys in Sioux City and poor Hall, true to form, raced his aeroplane across the Superior, Wisconsin field, but never got off the ground. Local promoters confiscated Hall's machine and held it until the money they had advanced him was returned. Hall left for San Francisco and his biplane was sent to the upcoming Chicago aviation meet. Whether it was a result of all his troubles in Wisconsin or a reaction to his fractured skull, Whipple Hall was once again much too sick to fly in Chicago or anywhere else.[22]

Curtiss decided that after Gene flew in Sioux City and Chicago, he would be Hall's replacement at an already scheduled Canadian exhibition. Gene wasn't really ready, but the other Curtiss aviators already had assignments. Gene would go to Canada—fly there—and in a flurry of newspaper reports, apparently die there.

# { 17 }

# O, Canada

The Sioux City Commercial Club officials hoped that with the $10,000 they had raised for an aviation meet, Glenn Curtiss would send "his two chief assistants," Mars and Willard. But almost as soon as Willard reached town, he was gone. A local reporter suggested that Willard was a coward. "He took one peek at the wind velocity records," the reporter said, "and suddenly announced that he must join Glenn Curtiss in the East." Actually, Willard was scheduled to fly in Kansas City, Missouri on the Fourth of July. Had Mars and Gene been able to fly, Willard's absence from Sioux City probably wouldn't have been controversial, but the wind, described as being stronger than the smell of the nearby stockyards, never stopped blowing.[1]

"Both of them started out well," said a facetious reporter. "The pop, pop of their motors as they attempted straightaway flights was truly imposing. But after running half way across the fair grounds and finally getting to an altitude of ten feet, they invariably came down."

The meet began with five unsuccessful attempts to stay in the air and over the next two days, nothing much changed. Hour after hour, crowds of up to 10,000 people waited for flights that never came. While waiting, they watched never-ending motorcycle races. "Spectators of the meet," said a reporter, "are yet seeing and hearing motorcycles in their dreams." Finally, on the last scheduled night, long after most of the spectators and reporter had gone home, Mars managed to reach over 100 feet and "with the rapidity of an express train," circled the one-mile course two and a half times before landing. Gene managed one circuit of the course with a sputtering engine, before he was forced to give up. Then, Mars circled the field twice more, finally rising to 75 feet, dropping down in "an eagle-like sweep," and landing lightly on the ground.[2]

Newspapers christened the sorry exhibition as the "bogus aviation meet," a "fraudulent fiasco," "a frost," and "the foozle" in Sioux City. Commercial Club officials refused to pay the $6,000 still owed the aviators unless they flew successfully for two more days. Mars warned them that Curtiss would sue for the money and then he and Gene caught the train for Chicago.[3]

On the Fourth of July, with winds blowing in Chicago at a near constant 27 miles an hour, it was appropriate to call it the Windy City Exhibition. Chicago was living up to its nickname. The breezes were bad for aviators and even worse for the 25,000 neck-straining spectators who had come to the Hawthorne racetrack to see them fly. Bud Mars had invited his uncle and two cousins to see him fly. All three lived across the lake in Bud's hometown of Muskegon, Michigan. Because they had never seen a relative fly, they may have been the only spectators that day satisfied with the mediocre show. Mars got fifteen feet in the air and flew the length of the racetrack before giving up and Gene came down as fast as he got up.[4]

The local aero club had invited "other notable aviators," but only Gene and Mars showed up. Mars not only had the most experience of the two, he also had a childhood connection to the city. As a boy, he had sold newspapers on Chicago streets, but by age 13, he left on his own and began traveling the carnival and hot air balloon circuit. Chicago reporters lavished all of their attention on Mars, as if he'd been a hometown boy all of his life. The hometown connection was enough to impress Walter Darlington, a wealthy livestock broker at the Chicago Stockyards who offered Mars a $5,000 prize for an overwater flight from Chicago to the state of Michigan. Mars accepted immediately, but again, the wind didn't cooperate and kept him in Chicago, leaving Darlington's money safely in the bank.[5]

After two days of attempted flights, there was little to brag about. Perhaps Gene's biggest accomplishment that week was having his photograph taken and printed on promotional picture postcards that showed him flying his biplane. Gene had made one circuit of the racetrack at a low altitude and Mars had reached 100 feet, while traveling about two miles in the face of a 17 mile an hour wind. Surprisingly, no one in Chicago seemed disappointed and on the aviators' final evening in town, the meet promoters presented both Gene and Mars with a gold medal.[6]

During the mid–July lull between Chicago and the upcoming Omaha air meet, Gene and Mabel had planned to visit Gene's family in Iowa, but Glenn Curtiss needed Gene's help. Whipple Hall was sick again and scheduled for a Canadian exhibition. Curtiss asked Gene to go with Hall and back him up. Gene agreed to meet Hall at Winnipeg after he accompanied Mabel to York Center. While he was in Canada, Mabel would stay with Gene's mother and the couple would reunite in Omaha.[7]

While performing at the Chicago Aviation Meet at Hawthorne Park, July 4–6, 1910, Eugene Ely had his portrait taken and subsequently had this and other poses printed on promotional picture postcards (Diane Dunlop Collection).

Orson Harrington, Gene's cousin who had been with him in San Francisco during the earthquake, agreed to join Gene in Canada as chief mechanic. "Upon his careful and skilled work will depend the success of the flights," said an Iowa reporter. By the end of the year, Orson would return home to stay. With a 2-year-old baby girl and a wife in Iowa, it seems the exhibition circuit just wasn't as exciting as he thought it might be.[8]

Hall never made it to Canada, where Canadian newspapers were already introducing the aviators as "two of the most celebrated aeroplanists in the world." Millions of Chinese had seen them fly, they said, and "at Hong Kong, 72,000 paid for admission to the pavilion where the machine was on view." None of it was true, of course, but no one cared. The novelty was just too big to resist.

Gene was welcomed to Canada with a tempting chance at a $6,000 prize, most of it donated by John Eaton, owner of one of the country's largest department stores. To win, he would have to fly with a message to the town of Portage la Prairie, over 50 miles to the east, wait for a reply, and then return with an answer. Gene had never even flown 5 miles without landing, so for him to think that he actually had a chance to finish the flight shows his confident determination that in just a few months would make him an aviation celebrity. He said he thought the flight would take an hour or less each way, weather permitting. He would fly to Portage la Prairie, stay overnight, and return to Winnipeg the next day.[9]

Intermittent thunderstorms had blown through the area over the previous week, but on the day Gene and his mechanics assembled his biplane in the center of the oval racetrack, the skies were clear and the prairie dry. It was sweltering hot with afternoon temperatures soaring into the 90s, a great day for the pink lemonade stands that had no problem selling barrel after barrel of their cooling liquid comfort.

Through the morning and into the afternoon, spectators were allowed onto the infield grass for an up-close look at the aeroplane, described by a reporter as a "flimsy structure of oiled silk and slender framework." They marveled that anyone had enough courage to fly it.[10]

"This cannot fail to be one of the sensations of the fair," the newspaper predicted, but the weather had other ideas. All afternoon, wind gusts of over 25 miles an hour kept Gene's "sensation" on the ground. Orson Harrington and James Henning, his two mechanics, had to hold on to the machine, to prevent it from being blown away. The scheduled takeoff time came and went and with each passing hour the crowd grew more impatient. Finally, in frustration, Gene got permission to take down a portion of the wooden fence that surrounded the racetrack and had the plane pulled out onto the open prairie at the edge of town. Perhaps, at sunset the wind would die down and he could fly.[11]

The remaining curious crowd followed behind Gene, wandering slowly across the wild grass. "He'll make some excuse," someone muttered, "he will not go up." Gene heard the comment, but ignored it for a moment. He looked back to the flags snapping in the wind and then he looked to the sky. "Perhaps at sundown," he said to the skeptic, "at sundown, when the breeze falls." They found a level space where the grass was low, checked over the aeroplane, and waited. Sunset took its time and spectators began to melt away. Those who remained passed the time in idle conversation with Gene. "He is an unassuming mortal," said a reporter, "deliberate of voice and movement, deliberate even in his smiling." As Gene spoke, they watched him light one cigarette after another. "He knows the pick of the wind as a trainer [knows] his animal," they said, "and [he] can light his thick Egyptian cigarettes in the most boisterous breeze." They looked into his eyes and saw the faraway look of a daring heroic figure, what they said was a "brooding, sheathed glance, characteristic of eagles and aeronauts." Gene was nearly a god and his popularity had never been higher.[12]

"I have been up 2,200 feet, near half a mile in that thing," Gene told them, "but I like better to travel between 500 and 1,000 feet." They wondered if he ever got dizzy. "Don't notice it in the open like you would on a high building," he said, and then paused. "Although, sometimes, when you're among the clouds, it feels a bit high." They asked what effects the wind had on an aeroplane. Gene looked to the east and saw wispy clouds that told him the winds were still strong. "We like a calm, best," he told the crowd, explaining that when an aircraft flew with the wind, "it adds the speed of the wind to its own and thus it finds a calm. When facing the wind, it is exactly opposite," he said, "so the aviator is continually calculating and changing his speed." Twilight gave way to red streaked skies and still the wind blew. It was approaching 9:30 and the sun was disappearing below the razor edge of the prairie's horizon. As if thinking aloud, Gene spoke slowly and softly. "I'm afraid"—he paused and looked across the horizon. "I'm afraid that there will be nothing to see tonight. Maybe tomorrow." Then he turned away.[13]

The next day, only a handful of people would see Gene make that first aeroplane flight in Western Canada. His biplane was still quite a distance northwest of the racetrack and, after the previous day's failure, not many people were confident enough to take the long walk out onto the prairie. Even this far out, Gene could hear the derisive jeers of the large crowd in the grandstand. Wanting to silence the hecklers and impatient to fly, he waited all afternoon. That evening, as the wind was beginning to die down, he told reporters that if he was able to fly, he would climb to 700 feet, fly to the racetrack crowd, circle the track, and land in the infield. But, it was already too dark when Gene took to the sky. Henning fired up the engine, the arms of the propeller whipped through the air, and Gene began to roll into the 20-mile-per-hour wind. Bracing himself in his seat, he raised the front elevating plane, but the craft stayed on the ground, bouncing across the prairie for at least a quarter mile. Then the machine rose to twenty feet, flew 600 yards, dipped downward, bounced off its three tires a few times, and stopped. Refusing to give up, Gene again began to taxi over the unobstructed plain until he was airborne. Twenty-five feet in the air now, the whining engine straining to keep him up; the biplane dropped again. It smashed into the ground with such force that a wooden stay attached to the rudder instantly snapped. Gene, unhurt, jumped off to check the damage and decided he could still fly without making repairs. This time the flight looked good. He gradually climbed to 50 feet, angled his wings to the setting sun, and began to circle back to the place where he had started. His speed was increasing as he flew toward the handful of spectators watching below. That's when his engine began to sputter and backfire, and then suddenly—it went silent. "The spectators expected disaster and held their breaths." The plane struck hard on its left side, breaking two wooden ribs, a few braces, and splitting some support wires. Sure that Gene was injured, if not killed, spectators were surprised to see him calmly step from his seat and begin to inspect the damage. He limped a little from a bruise on his knee, but he was OK.[14]

Some overly excited individual had already run to the telegraph office and sent a brief story to the newspapers of the world, reporting Gene Ely's imminent death. While some editor's hedged their bet by headlining that Gene was "Probably Fatally Injured in Flight Near Winnipeg," or reporting that "he was picked up in a dying condition on the prairie," others didn't hesitate to bury him. "Aviator Killed," they wrote. "Fatal Fall in Manitoba." Most reports were sure he was in a hospital, in a coma, and that his condition was, at the very least, precarious. In nearby Minnesota, they were sure that "had he not extricated himself from his machine on his downward flight. He would have been pounded into a jelly."[15]

Gene had no reason to think his bruised knee in Canada would escalate into a near obituary back home. He didn't know that in York, Mabel learned he was dead. For two days, she heard nothing. Desperate and living in a panic, she was nearly prostrate and inconsolable. "She is but a young bride," wrote a reporter, "and the shock of the announcement was great." In Davenport, Nathan Ely, Gene's father, was trying desperately and unsuccessfully to reach his son. They hadn't spoken in years, but now their differences would finally be reconciled. Nathan contacted the Winnipeg chief of police and because the man had no information about Gene, Nathan said he was inclined to think that reports of the injury had been "greatly exaggerated." First word that Gene was safe came from Orson Harrington in a telegram to his father in York. Mabel was staying at the elder Harrington's home and the news that Gene had only been injured brought her instant relief. She packed her bags and as quickly as possible caught the train to Omaha for a thankful reunion with Gene.[16]

Two days of living through her husband's death had changed Mabel. She was still the enthusiastic supporter, perhaps still pushing him too hard to excel, but now, she lived with an unspoken fear. She stayed close to Gene, and except for his one trip to Texas to train Army fliers and the Georgia exhibition where he would die, she always traveled with him. "Yes, I go with him everywhere," she said. "I am his good luck. Things go wrong when I am not around." Because of her obsessive behavior and the way she clung to Gene, around the airfields, they soon began to call her "the little widow"—but never to her face.[17]

Gene's biplane went to the Curtiss factory for repairs and during the five days following his accident, Gene used Whipple Hall's machine. He managed a few bouncing flights over the prairie grass, never higher than 50 feet and only once as far as a quarter mile. The newspaper reports began to weary of his excuse that the wind was too strong to fly in. "An aviator traveling high over the Winnipeg exhibition grounds," they mocked, "would probably have likened what he saw to a densely populated nest of ants ... the grounds were literally choked with people." Gene was that aviator, but flying a measly 300 yards in ten seconds at a mere ten feet above the Winnipeg grounds, he wasn't making much of an impression or seeing many "ants."[18]

The promoters finally had enough. "Ely the Bird-Man Must Fly or Flit," read the headline. In a face-to-face meeting, Gene was given an ultimatum. Fly successfully in front of the grandstand for everyone to see, or not receive any more money. He had already pocketed $500 for showing up and $200 for each of the first two days of the exhibition. Gene reminded them that by contract he was due $200 for each day he was in Winnipeg, and that actual flights were only required when weather conditions would allow. He insisted on being paid what he was due, but the promoters said he first had to "deliver the goods." They told him they believed he had brought an underpowered glider that wasn't even capable of high flights. His 4-cylinder engine wasn't powerful enough, they said, and pointed out that Walter Brookins, who flew for the Wright brothers, had recently flown at over 4,000 feet and set a world record, while challenging a 22-mph wind. When they demanded Gene return the money he had already been paid, Gene threatened to sue, then stormed out of the meeting, and wired for manager Bryce who was in Chicago.[19]

The next day, while Gene waited for Bryce, he refused to bring his biplane out of its tent hangar in the middle of the racetrack infield. Instead, he charged a 25-cent admission to anyone who wanted to come in and have a look. He complained to reporters that his contract with exhibition management called for a suitable place in which to fly and it hadn't been provided. He said while corresponding with the promoters prior to his arrival, he had only promised to make spectacular flights when the air was calm, and only short flights when the wind was blowing less than 15 miles an hour.[20]

In the morning, Gene received a telegram from Glenn Curtiss telling him to report to Omaha for his scheduled performance. Gene said that until the dispute was settled, he would decline and stay in Winnipeg, but he was overruled. That same afternoon, he was on the train to Nebraska. "Pending the arrival of their manager with sufficient cash to get them all out of town," said the newspaper, authorities held hostage the biplane and mechanics Orson Harrington and James Henning. After negotiating with Bryce, the promoter's agreed to let Gene keep the $900 he had already been paid, released the biplane, and dared Bryce to follow through with his threat to sue. "It is thought that he is not likely to take this step," a reporter said, "as practically nothing was done by the aviator to carry out his part of the contract.[21]

A year later, when Wright flier, Frank Coffyn, flew impressive flights in Winnipeg, but was grounded for a couple of days because of bad weather, he too was threatened with a reduction in money owed him. When a reporter asked him if he knew that the exhibition board had also refused to pay Eugene Ely in 1910, Coffyn said, "Ely told me that. So I had it added to my contract with your fair board—that I was to be paid—flights or no flights." Coffyn got his money.[22]

While Coffyn was flying in Winnipeg in 1911, Gene was back in Canada flying in Lethbridge. He was an American hero by then and the same Winnipeg newspaper that had mocked him in 1910, now had a new opinion. "When Eugene Ely first came to Canada as the pilot of an aeroplane, his visit was looked forward to with the greatest interest, but he failed to show at that time what he would eventually become, one of the foremost aviators of the world."[23]

In July 1910, it was still a long way from bouncing over the grassy plain to becoming the world's foremost aviator, and Gene would certainly stumble a few more times. But people could see that there was something special about him—perhaps a logical stubbornness—a determination to succeed. Glenn Curtiss had seen it, and soon the world would see it too.

## { 18 }

## "Scrape that golden lining"

Omaha was another bust for Gene. His few flights were brief, low, and unspectacular. The biggest impression he made was when he arrived in company with Glenn Curtiss and Bud Mars. A reporter who knew of Gene's accident in Winnipeg was surprised that Gene seemed to be in great shape and that his only apparent injury was a scratch on his hand. "I fell eighty feet and smashed a couple of ribs," Ely said. "Your ribs?" asked the reporter. Gene laughed. "No, the machine's ribs." It was downhill from there, starting with the newspaper getting his initials wrong, calling him J. F. Ely, and ending in a minor fall in a biplane that was so badly damaged, he was unable to fly again. The prairie winds were relentless and though Curtiss and Mars were able to make a few successful flights, Gene was becoming little more than an expert at bouncing over the prairie. Luckily, the Nebraska spectators were fascinated with the first aeroplane flights they had ever seen and never complained. Curtiss received his $15,000 guarantee, and with a smile on his face, presented the local aviation club a model propeller made of mahogany and spruce. He said it was a compliment to their aviation knowledge. What he didn't say was how dangerous he thought the winds had been. A week later, when he and Mars were in a windy Pittsburgh and could barely fly, Curtiss used Nebraska in his angry defense. "Conditions here," he said, "were impossible for a good flight. It was Omaha weather."[1]

Reunited with Mabel, Gene left Omaha with Curtiss for Hammondsport, where his aeroplane was repaired and the motor replaced. With nine more horsepower to play with, a total of 39, Gene was looking forward to more speed and better control. After a few days of personal instruction from Curtiss and several beautiful trial flights, he had begun his transition from semi-pro amateur to "sky-rider of world fame." He christened his renovated machine the *Valkyrie*, a name he often heard while traveling with Bud Mars and Marie, Bud's wife. She had not yet flown in an aeroplane, but had made many balloon ascensions with her husband. When reporters asked how she felt about her husband flying in an aeroplane, she invariably would say, "I have perfect confidence, as a rule. You see, I too am something of a sky enthusiast, a sort of modern Valkyrie."[2]

The *Valkyrie* was packed into crates and shipped north to Rochester, New York. There, Gene was once again scheduled to fly with Whipple Hall. In spite of Gene's uninspiring demonstrations so far, the promotional campaign in Rochester was already in overdrive. "Ely is ranked a reckless and daring sky navigator," said promoters. "Omaha," they said, "acclaimed him a sky pilot possessing less sense of personal danger than any of the other fliers whose maneuvers have been witnessed there." Attributing parts of Hamilton's resume to Gene was also useful in promoting an aviator who had nothing of his own to brag about, and with each retelling, new variations improved the old stories. Gene had made a spectacular flight over the Imperial Palace, they said, and was personally rewarded with an ornate medal from the Japanese Emperor. They said he was the first ever to fly in Australia, where he was "looked upon as a sort of national figure." "Next in importance to Ely among the aviators," the promoters said, was Whipple Hall, a man "famous as a balloon racer years before he acquired notice as an aeroplanist." That too was Hamilton, of course. On and on it went, and perhaps the only factual statement made that week was the descriptions of Hall as "the heaviest aviator in the world."[3]

For any man or woman who could fly, the clouds were lined in gold, and in Rochester, Gene said he meant to "scrape that golden lining in more ways than one." First, as long as he flew at least one mile, his contract said he would pocket $2,000 each day, but Gene was also looking to pick up some extra publicity and perhaps a sizeable bit of extra cash. From Omaha, he sent the promoters a telegram. "Please challenge Ned Crane for race between myself in aeroplane and he in his racing car on any day of aeronautic meet for side bet of $1,000." Crane was already in Rochester and when shown the telegram, accepted immediately, suggesting that the race should be run at a distance of at least five miles. Crane was as wild on the racetrack as Gene was rumored to be in the air. He was almost as famous as Barney Oldfield. Crane was "one of the world's speed mongers ... daredevil driver of the Vanderbilt Cup and Indianapolis Speedway fame." He began professional racing in 1909 and in pursuit of a national reputation, he quickly began to win races; soon setting five international speed records. Unfortunately the aeroplane-automobile race would never be run. Crane's 120 horsepower race car was owned by a Buffalo businessman who, on the scheduled day of the race, accused Crane of being late with his rental payments. The businessman refused to let Crane use the car until he paid what he owed. Crane couldn't pay and the businessman reclaimed the car.[4]

By the first week of August 1910, both Gene and Whipple Hall were putting final touches on their biplanes in a large canvas tent in the middle of the Rochester racetrack. Gene's 39 horsepower engine had arrived late and Hall's machine, now called the *Falcon*, was being re-covered with new rubberized silk. Gene joked with reporters that when his engine was installed, he might try a flight over the city and maybe continue on to the baseball park, where he could check out the latest score.[5]

That evening, an electrical storm with torrents of rain muddied the baseball field and the next afternoon, relentless afternoon winds delayed any hope of aeroplane flights until the weekend. The exhibition managers assured the public that Gene and Hall would stay for as long as it might take to get into the air. They said each ticket sold was guaranteed and was issued with a wind-check. If flights were postponed, the wind check was valid for the next day's admission. In the meantime, the sides of the canvas tent hangar were thrown open and everyone got a chance to inspect the two biplanes. Gene and Hall stood by their machines all day, answering thousands of curious questions.[6]

Only 2,000 spectators dared the chilly temperatures on Saturday, August 6.

While they watched motorcycle and auto races, they kept a close eye on the frequent wind reports. No one expected a flight, but Gene had guaranteed that he would not disappoint them. "Gale or no gale I will fly at sundown," he said. Just after six that evening, the *Valkyrie* was pulled out onto the field and the motor started. "Look, the propellers going!" someone shouted. In just a few seconds, the grandstand emptied in a human stampede. The mechanics gave the biplane a push and Gene was off. In less than eighty feet, he bounced into the air and effortlessly climbed to 60 feet. The crowd watched in stunned silence until someone shouted, "She's flying!" Only then did they realize what they were seeing and they broke into amazed and hysterical screams, cheers, and applause. He flew three-quarters of a mile, the wind gusts almost pushing him into a tree. He tried to turn, but instead was forced to land in a bumpy field just outside the racetrack. It took an hour to make minor repairs before he took off again and flew back to the tent and a hero's welcome. The newspaper called it the first aeroplane flight ever made in Rochester, somehow forgetting Dr. William Green's experimental aeroplane that he had flown just a month earlier. Of course, Dr. Green, a onetime balloon pilot, had only traveled a quarter of a mile, but he did reach an altitude of 50 feet before crashing into a tree, falling to the ground, and vowing to rebuild and fly again someday.[7]

There was no flying on Sunday, but Gene and Hall agreed that they would race against each other on Monday. It would be Whipple Hall's first flight in Rochester, but when Monday came, Gene flew alone. Early Sunday morning Whipple Hall's mysterious illness struck again. The newspaper explained that it was caused by the "slightly fractured skull" he had suffered in May. Hall returned to San Francisco, never to fly again. He would spend a few years managing other aviators before he left the country, finding much better health in the Philippine Islands as owner of an import/export business.[8]

With Hall gone and the race with Ned Crane's automobile cancelled, it was up to Gene to give "ocular proof that the flying machine had progressed far beyond the toy stage." This time he did not disappoint. Fewer than 500 spectators were there to watch him start his engine, push off, and zoom over the trees at the edge of the track. With the rattling hum of the biplane's motor, he flew over the surrounding green pastures, panicking herds of cattle and horses that had been grazing peacefully in the grass. When he landed, Mabel, as always, was the first to reach him. "Wasn't it dandy?" she squealed. Gene told reporters that even though Mabel had never flown herself, she was more of an enthusiastic aviator than he was. "If I am advertised to fly and don't—well—there is something doing in the family," he said. Mabel offered a quick defense. "I take pride in my husband's accomplishments," she said. "I don't like to see people disappointed." She watched as Gene took off again, flying faster, and perhaps 10 feet higher. After a three-mile flight, he swooped back down over the grandstand and landed where he had started, but this time his rear wheels snagged a hole in the field. The snap of one of his support braces echoed across the racetrack. It was a minor repair and not enough to stop the adoring crowd's enthusiasm.[9]

Gene and Mabel caught the eastbound train heading for Long Island, New York, where Gene joined Glenn Curtiss and five other aviators at Belmont Park. The October International Aviation Meet would be held somewhere near New York City. Curtiss and his aviators had been asked their opinion of Belmont Park and nearby Garden

City as potential aviation fields for the event. After walking over both fields, Belmont seemed to be the favorite with at least four aviators, including Gene. Only Curtiss refused to announce his preference. "After what I have seen lately in the line of aviation fields," he said, "anything on Long Island looks good to me." Reporters pressed him further, but he only shrugged his shoulders and walked away.[10]

Curtiss, Gene, and their wives drove back to Hammondsport to prepare for the upcoming Sheepshead Bay aviation exhibition in New York. With his recent boost in confidence, Gene was lobbying Curtiss for a chance at a $25,000 prize that would go to the winner of a Chicago to New York cross-country race scheduled for October. While stopping overnight in Amsterdam, New York, Gene hinted to a reporter that Curtiss was probably going to enter two aeroplanes in that race and Gene would be flying one of them. He said they were traveling together with their wives by automobile so they could inspect the countryside over which the race would be flown. Curtiss didn't comment, and although he may have already agreed, the official announcement of Gene's entry into the Chicago–New York race didn't come for another month.[11]

The reporter asked Curtiss whether he preferred the relative safety of an automobile for traveling, or the speed of an aeroplane. Curtiss said he would choose to fly as long as he could find "proper places to make landings." Their automobile drive from New York City to Albany had already taken 24 hours, he said. "That makes the run somewhat slower than the one I took a short time ago in an aeroplane." Curtiss had earned a $10,000 prize the previous May, by becoming the first aviator to fly between Albany and New York City, completing the 150-mile flight in less than five hours. His biplane would forever be known as the *Hudson Flyer*, although a stubborn few, possibly from upstate New York, would always call it the *Albany Flyer*. In just three more months, with Gene in the driver's seat, the *Hudson Flyer* would again make history.[12]

It was almost as if Gene were being groomed to replace Charles Hamilton who was no longer a member of the Curtiss team, but still flying under his original contract with Curtiss. Between the end of April and the middle of June 1910, Hamilton didn't turn in an earnings report and was overdue in his lease payments. Even though Curtiss was becoming increasingly annoyed with his star flier's arrogance, when Hamilton was preparing a 170-mile roundtrip between New York and Philadelphia for June 13, Curtiss let Hamilton use the larger *Hudson Flyer* seven-foot propeller and sent him a twenty-gallon fuel tank to extend the range of *Rheims Racer*. After the race, Hamilton asked Curtiss for a release from his contract so he could fly in Europe. Curtiss refused and ordered Hamilton to perform in Nashville. Once he had performed there and paid what he owed, Curtiss agreed to release him to fly wherever he wanted. Hamilton did fly in Nashville, but he didn't pay up, ending his Tennessee exhibition by blowing a cylinder in his engine. Curtiss and Hamilton exchanged words and Hamilton quit, leaving the *Rheims Racer* with Curtiss. "Mr. Hamilton is a mere boy," Curtiss said, "and his sudden rise to fame appears to have been too much for him. I'm sorry he has acted the way he has, for his place will be hard to fill." Curtiss then filed suit, seeking $6,513.63, the amount in exhibition and lease fees he felt Hamilton owed him. Six months later, Curtiss prevailed and collected $6,211 plus court costs.[13]

Now it was Gene who was receiving unprecedented attention from Curtiss. Gene, in contrast to Hamilton, was willing to listen and learn. "I have every faith in Ely as an aviator," Curtiss said, and for most of the next year, that trust would be well rewarded.[14]

{ 19 }

# "A warm corner in the heart of Father Knickerbocker"

Sheepshead Bay is a saltwater inlet south of Brooklyn, New York. Locals say it was named for the zebra-like black and silver striped fish that once were prevalent in its waters. Directly to the south is Coney Island, where Atlantic Ocean waves, whipped thin by sea breezes, steal away the fine, soft sands of Manhattan and Brighton beaches. Here, centuries of overheated residents have found cooling relief from a muggy New York summer.[1]

In 1873, a doctor had sent a wealthy yet desperate banker to the seashore to save his dying newborn son. Safe from the dangerous criminals and prostitutes who wandered the nearby beaches and caroused through the night in a ramshackle collection of shacks, Austin Corbin and his wife found a decent hotel on the west end of Coney Island. Corbin was president and owner of his own Manhattan bank and a leading financier in New York City. He spent as much time as he could on the island, nursing his child back to health and he was surprised to see how quickly the boy began to recover. One day he set off to explore the barren east end of the island. Except for a U.S. lifeboat station on a bump of a hill on the far eastern shore, there was nothing here but miles of sand dunes and scenic beauty, but that's what gave Corbin his idea. If the sea air had healed his son so rapidly, perhaps this would be the perfect location for a resort hotel, a respectable seaside resort for respectable people, "accessible to the poor as well as the rich." He quietly had his agents buy property, acre by acre, until he owned nearly 600 acres and two and a half miles of beachfront. By July 1887, he bought a railroad, ran rails onto the island, and opened his luxurious Manhattan Beach Hotel.[2]

Corbin had turned this sandy wasteland into a goldmine. What had been little more than a shantytown at the edge of a fishing village was now prime real estate and a magnate for investors. Within months, on the beach to the west, he had friendly competition from the newly built Brighton Hotel. Millionaires began buying property along the northern shore of the bay and by the summer of 1880, the Coney Island Jockey Club opened one of New York's finest racetracks, the Sheepshead Bay track. Just two months after the racetrack opened, Corbin had a wooden footbridge built across the bay from the island, allowing his guests easy access to the races. Drawn by the luxurious surroundings, society's most influential people rarely let any of the 250 rooms stand empty. There were racing days when over 10,000 people dined at the hotel, every one of their wishes catered to by nearly 500 employees. Corbin spared no expense to entertain his guests. He was friends with John Philip Sousa, a frequent visitor who performed in the hotel's outdoor pavilion. During one of his stays in 1893, the "March King" performed his *Manhattan Beach March*, specifically dedicated "to Austin Corbin, Esq.," and released with a sheet music cover that included a drawing of the hotel. A few years later, Sousa premiered *Stars and Stripes Forever* at the hotel.[3]

By the time the Curtiss aviators made the Manhattan Beach Hotel their headquarters for the Sheepshead Bay aviation meet, both the hotel and the racetrack had fallen on hard times. The New York legislature had banned betting on horse races and the racetrack was closed to racing. Consequently, the Coney Island hotels were emptied of those regular customers who had for years reliably booked the entire racing season. The majestic Manhattan Beach Hotel would be torn down within a year and the Sheepshead Bay Racetrack would soon follow.[4]

For the true New York horse racing fan, the real end of the Sheepshead track was August 19, 1910—"when the sport of kings" gave way to the "sport of science." On that Friday, Glenn Curtiss, Charles Willard, Bud Mars, Jack McCurdy, and Gene Ely, would take to the skies and begin a three-day aviation meet, the first ever held near New York City and affectionately known as "The Curtiss Carnival." Two weeks earlier, Curtiss had announced that his minimum fee for a personal appearance as a flier was now $5,000 per day. He had been trying to find a way to spend more of his time in scientific investigations and experiments and said he intentionally had set a high fee, believing most promoters would refuse to pay it. But the Sheepshead Bay meet was one of the exceptions. Curtiss had arranged the exhibition and said it would be a good way to test the public's interest in flying. He wanted to establish a flying school with a permanent airfield somewhere nearby.[5]

The "Curtiss Carnival" began unofficially with the arrival of Bud Mars, almost a week before the meet was scheduled to begin. Mars had switched aeroplanes and was now flying the *Rheims Racer*, recently renovated and recovered from the alienated Charles Hamilton. While the meet was going on, Hamilton was on Long Island getting ready to return to the West Coast for his own exhibition tour. He was flying Whipple Hall's biplane on the Hempstead Plains. Perhaps when he had returned the *Rheims Racer* to Curtiss, he had also agreed to deliver Hall's plane back to his old California traveling companion.[6]

Before the meet began, Mars let Gene have a chance to fly the *Racer*. It was his first time in an 8-cylinder machine and he didn't get far, but because Curtiss was gradually switching to the larger engine, it was a valuable learning opportunity.[7]

On opening day, Gene's 4-cylinder biplane arrived while Mars was making his second practice run. Gene was watching as Mars began his descent and saw him nearly collide with a horse jumping hurdle that had been left on the infield of the racetrack. Once on the ground, the unfazed Mars hinted to reporters that once his engine was tuned perfectly, he was ready to set some aviation records. "I don't like to talk much about what I am going to do," he said, "but I will say that you may want to watch."[8]

The Curtiss Carnival turned out to be more of a three-ring circus. In the old betting circle, spectators were free to wander amongst the five biplanes that were being prepared for flight. They inspected the aviators like they were bugs under a magnifying glass. While the mechanics, "lithe young men with oil stained fingers bent over their canvas birds and spoke softly a language strange to the racetrack," the aviators answered the public's questions.[9]

By four in the afternoon, the birdmen were more than ready to start the show. An announcer hopped onto a small platform in front of the grandstand and holding a large megaphone to his lips began to bellow at the crowd. Bud Mars was ready to fly and for the first time, Marie, his wife, would be with him. He tucked Mrs. Mars into the passenger seat, told her not to squeal, and then climbing up beside her, motioned to his mechanics to start the motor. The couple bounced over the field for some 200 yards and then slowly rose to 40 feet. As they flashed by the grandstand, Marie Mars was laughing and waving her excitement to the crowd. "Evidently Mrs. Mars wasn't the squealing kind," wrote a reporter. It was a short flight and Mars landed at the end of the track. While Gene took off in his machine to test the wind, Mabel ran to Mars and insisted that he take her up. "Gene's machine is too small for passengers," she pleaded. Mars agreed and once again, it was a short flight, close to the ground, and hardly more than 30 feet in the air, but Mabel's "black eyes were snapping with excitement." Lena Curtiss, Glenn Curtiss' wife, declined to fly, but allowed photographers to take her picture sitting behind the wheel of her husband's *Hudson Flyer*.[10]

The next few hours were monotonous for spectators. First, there was delay of over an hour while the aviators waited for a frisky wind to settle down. Then, after Curtiss had made a short flight and pronounced the skies ready, Mars called out the name of his first passenger from a list prepared the previous day. Eduardo Breker, a reporter for *The World* newspaper was first up. When he got down, he was asked what it felt like to fly. Breker said flying "seemed a good deal like roller coasting at Coney Island. You seemed to be moving like an express train while the wheels hug the ground," he said, "but after that it was merely floating." Breker was the first of eight reporters and five others who flew the length of the racetrack that afternoon. In one near disaster, Frank Caruthers, a business manager with *The World* newspaper, and at 195 pounds perhaps the heaviest passenger ever to fly on a biplane, nearly tumbled to the ground when a wind gust threatened to push the Mars biplane onto its side. When safely on the ground, Caruthers confessed that he had no idea of the danger he had faced. Most of the other passengers had easy flights. "The thin ones tossed and bucked in a gusty wind, for perhaps half a mile," wrote a reporter. "The fat ones, held closer to the earth by their weights, merely cut the grass." In the meantime, the grandstand audience became restless and disinterested, waiting for some sort of excitement to break the boring succession of one short passenger flight after another.[11]

Just past seven, with the last passenger landing in the sultry air and the mosquitoes beginning their evening human picnic, Gene and Curtiss stepped aboard their biplanes. The announcer proclaimed the start of a three-lap race between four aviators. Gene, with the least powerful machine, got a head start. Just as he left the ground, Curtiss throttled up the *Hudson Flyer*, told his mechanics to let go, and 100 yards behind, he was off in pursuit. He had almost caught up to Gene by the first turn and before the first lap was complete, he was already well out in front. On the second turn, Gene cut the corner short; briefly regaining the lead, but Curtiss shot back to the front with a roaring motor and quickly outdistanced him. As they flew down the stretch, where thoroughbreds had dueled in the dirt for years, Mars fired up his engine, launched his machine into the air, and joined them for lap number three. On the fourth circuit, it was McCurdy's turn and for the first time ever, four aeroplanes were racing each other all at the same time. In the grandstand, the crowd came back to life, with a cane, a hat, or a handkerchief waving from nearly every hand. Suddenly the screaming sounds of biplane motors were lost in the unanimous cheers and shouts of 6,000 mouths. In the growing twilight, Mabel Ely, Marie Mars, and Lena Curtiss were just as excited as the spectators—jumping, waving, and cheering their husbands on, as their birdmen zoomed on by. One by one, the biplanes "came down as lightly as fluttering cards," first Gene, then Curtiss, followed by Mars. McCurdy, the only flier without a wife to report to, continued on, nearly a mile outside the racetrack, circled a grove of trees, and only then returned for a landing.[12]

Just before dusk on the second day of the exhibition, the Curtiss birdmen took to the sky to set a new world record, a five-minute single file parade around the Sheepshead Bay Racetrack. It was the first time five aeroplanes had ever been in the air at the same time. Earlier that afternoon, Curtiss had taken motion picture and still photographers aloft to document the scene from the air, and then, with Army sharpshooter, Lieutenant Jacob Fickel in full uniform as his passenger, Curtiss notched another historic moment in aviation. From 100 feet, Fickel aimed his 30-caliber Springfield rifle at a 3 by 5-foot target on the ground and pulled the trigger. These were the first bullets ever fired from an aeroplane. A couple of his shots came within a few inches of the target's ten-inch bull's-eye. He said that he had found it easier shooting from the air than shooting from the back of a horse.[13]

When the next day's events blew away in a blustery gale, the fliers agreed to stay another day, hoping for better weather, but Monday was only a marginal improvement. Gene tried a few straightaway flights across the field, but his biplane was too light for the wind. He left the sky to Mars and Curtiss in their 8-cylinder machines.[14]

The sun had set into a black night when Curtiss and Mars took off. They were almost invisible except for flames streaking from their engines that surrounded them in a ghostly glow. "The effect on those who witnessed this sight was extraordinary," said a reporter. "It makes a wonderful and impressive sight." For Mars, the event of the evening was the mosquito that smashed into one of his eyes, partially blinding him for a few seconds, and forcing an emergency landing. "It is all right in daytime," he said. "The mosquitoes here are so big that we can see them and dodge them, but when it is dark and there are millions of them around, what is to prevent them from blinding us?" Mars declared he would now wear goggles.[15]

Curtiss crated his machine and prepared to leave for Cleveland, where he would fly over Lake Erie. Before he left, he arranged for his aviators to continue the Sheepshead Bay exhibition for another three-day weekend and urged his "troupe of aerial dip divers" to push themselves and put on a good show. They would have to do it without Willard who also left for a series of exhibitions in Massachusetts. Augustus Post, a wealthy amateur who owned his own aeroplane, offered to replace Willard, and though his antics would be entertaining, Post would do more crashing than flying. During the extended meet, McCurdy made a few uncomplicated flights before finally stealing some national headlines with yet another aviation first. A mile out from the track, at 40 miles an hour, and 500 feet in the air, McCurdy tapped a specially installed telegraph key mounted on his steering wheel and without having to remove his hands, successfully transmitted a wireless Morse code message to a receiver situated on the grandstand roof. No one had ever done that before, yet even with all of this history being made at Sheepshead, it was Bud Mars and Gene who claimed the biggest headlines.[16]

Two hours after sunrise, on Saturday August 27, wind gusts were clocked at over 20 miles an hour. Unconcerned, Mars, as he had done nearly every morning since arriving at Sheepshead, rolled his biplane out in front of a sleepy gathering of dedicated aviation enthusiasts and lifted off. His goal was a cross-country flight to the west, over forts Hamilton and Wadsworth. He would return over the ocean and land near the Manhattan Beach Hotel, before returning to the racetrack. For a week, hotel management had been offering prizes of a free dinner and a silver cup to the first aviator who landed near the hotel. As Mars flew the most powerful plane, the hotel managers had originally intended the prizes for Mars alone. Gene was also invited to attempt the feat, but only as a guest, and no one believed his puny machine could make the flight. Mabel Ely, Gene's "little general," emphatically disagreed. She was furious when she heard doubts about Gene and said she would have none of it. Personally confronting hotel management, she reminded them that she and Gene were also guests in the hotel and that she did not approve of their arrangement with Mars. She insisted that her husband had every right to compete on equal terms and they had better let him compete. Not surprisingly, the management melted and promptly agreed.[17]

The windy weather had kept Gene and Mars from seriously contesting for the hotel prizes, but their temporary setbacks didn't stop newspapers from speculating that it wouldn't be long before hotel guests with unconcerned indifference would ignore the sight of biplanes flying overhead. "If pressed for the meaning of their indifference," said a reporter, "they may apologetically stifle a yawn behind a raised palm and reply, that it is only Bud Mars and Gene Ely, young and devoted husbands both, dropping in [to the hotel] to have afternoon tea with their wives."[18]

As Mars began his roundabout journey to the hotel, he flew out over Coney Island at 500 feet and climbed to 2,000 feet as he swung out over the ocean. "I was making good progress in the heavy wind," he said. "After I had gone as far seaward as I deemed necessary, I came about and headed for the forts." Then Mars heard one of the engine cylinders hissing, which meant lubrication wasn't working. When he pushed his right foot on the manual oil pump switch, he didn't know that the rod attached to the switch was bent and the kink in the rod pressed against the switch that cut off power to his engine. He was two miles offshore and falling in a long, curving dive. As the aeroplane went head first into the white-capped sea, he recalled his early days as a carnival high diver and remembered thinking, "Here goes Little Willie for the high dive." He fell from his seat and plunged several feet under water. The two inner tubes he was wearing as a life preservers, tried to force him back to the surface, but he was trapped against a wing under water. "My first thought was to get clear of the wreckage and I tore through the rubberized cloth and wire stays until I got to the surface," he said. A boy, passing by on a fishing boat, jumped into a small dingy, rowed to the wrecked biplane, and managed to grab on to the aviator's arm. Fifteen minutes later, Mars was safely aboard a tugboat and the boy was rowing away. Mars shouted his

**Eugene Ely confers with Glenn Curtiss before taking off at the Sheepshead Bay, Long Island, New York, aviation meet, August 19–30, 1910. Ely flew his Curtiss biplane from the Sheepshead Bay Racetrack and landed in front of the Manhattan Beach Hotel, just east of Coney Island. There he collected the management's silver trophy, offered to the first aviator to fly to the hotel (Naval History and Heritage Command #NH 77547).**

thanks and the boy modestly replied, "Oh, that's all right," and kept rowing. Mars, who later said he never learned the boy's name, turned to supervise the recovery of his wrecked biplane. The mangled craft was towed to the Atlantic Yacht Club on the west end of Coney Island.[19]

Gene knew that if he was going to win the Manhattan Beach trophy, his time was running out. Bud's 8-cylinder machine would be back in action in a few days and Mars was sure to try again. Gene knew it was now or never. Fifteen minutes before sunset, on the same day Mars had taken his unexpected swim, the wind died down and Gene was ready.[20]

He looked at Mabel. "It's dinner time, and I'm dining out," Gene said. "If I find the air lanes open, you'll see me to the left of the Dreamland towers." Dreamland was the amusement park on Coney Island, just to the west of the Manhattan Beach Hotel. "The slim birdman who used to drive racing automobiles until the game bored him," scrambled onto his biplane and was up and flying toward the northeastern horizon at 40 miles an hour. A mere shadow against the sunset, he made a wide turn toward the south while climbing to 700 feet. Mabel, Marie Mars, and three mechanics ran for the taxi stand where they ordered a driver to get them to the Manhattan Beach Hotel as quickly as possible. The hotel was barely two miles from the racetrack and with Gene's aeroplane already gliding down behind the houses and treetops in the south, the earthbound travelers would have to settle for a close, but second place finish. Perhaps 3,000 people were bathing, lounging, or walking the paths at Manhattan Beach when they heard the humming propeller and the phut-phut-phut of the motor. From the sand to the hotel balconies, eyes went skyward with open-mouthed amazement. Gene's graceful glide touched down with a gentle roll over the thick lawn between the Manhattan Beach and Oriental hotels and stopped next to a "Keep off the Grass" sign. Within moments, Mabel was at Gene's side and arm-in-arm they walked into the Manhattan Beach Hotel's bar. Inside, at least 50 people were cheering and offering to buy the couple champagne. Gene lightheartedly said he had indeed landed in front of the hotel to get a drink, but added, "I only drink water when I'm flying." The hotel management offered Gene the silver trophy for being the first aviator to land at the hotel, but once again, Mabel objected. She said she was tired of hauling suitcases full of cups and trophies and medals around the country and she preferred something more easily handled. The management offered $100 and she accepted. The next day Gene used the money to buy her the watch she had seen in a local jewelry store. Gene said he was hungry and he would gladly accept the hotel's offer of a free dinner, but, once again, Mabel said no. "Not now. I'm too excited," she said. "Let's have a drink of water and you fly back, and then, we'll come over a little later in a taxicab and have something really nice. We'll order it now so it will be ready."[21]

Minutes before sunset, Gene was in the air again and flying back to Sheepshead. He reappeared at the racetrack at 6:42 p.m. barely twenty minutes after he had left. He circled the field four times to the cheers of thousands in the grandstand and then landed. "When he flew back to the racetrack," said a reporter, "he dropped into a warm corner in the heart of Father Knickerbocker." Knickerbocker, a creation of author Washington Irving, was, by 1910, a cartoon character in newspapers that represented New York City.[22]

The final day of the meeting skies alternated between dirty gray and black as intermittent rain pelted down. During lulls in the downpour, the flights were short and unexciting, until Gene took off late in the afternoon. Later he would admit that he had a fear of heights, but now he climbed a thousand feet until he was just a dark speck against the clouds. Spots began to dance in his eyes and he lost all sense of direction. "For half a minute," he said, "I didn't know what I was doing. I had a fierce headache and my stomach was turning over and over." With the earth rocking and swirling below him, his muscles were weak. All he knew for sure was that he had to stay in control. He gripped the steering wheel and purely on instinct put his aircraft into a steep dive that only an emergency could justify. "I just had enough control of myself to get back to earth," he said. When his feet touched the ground, he couldn't stand or walk without help from his mechanics. They put him in a taxi and Gene and Mabel rushed to a doctor at the Manhattan Beach Hotel. "The doctor said it was a bilious attack," Gene said. "I used to have them once in a while when I was driving racing automobiles, but that was the first one I ever had in an aeroplane."[23]

For two consecutive days, he had finally made headlines. In the words of one reporter, Gene was entitled "to the fame that seems [to be] soaring toward him." He would push himself, go higher, and go farther than ever before. A few weeks ago, he had only been that unknown "addition to the Curtiss troupe," but within a few weeks, some would be calling him "the world's greatest aviator."[24]

# { 20 }

# "Plucky pioneer conqueror of the air"

At the end of the Sheepshead Bay aviation meet, Gene and Bud Mars were left with nearly a week before they would perform again, but still they had to hurry. The aviation partners had a date in Cleveland, Ohio, where Curtiss was getting ready to fly 70 miles across Lake Erie. If the boss were successful, it would be the longest flight ever made over water.

Curtiss would fly west from the Euclid Beach Amusement Park, nine miles east of Cleveland, to Cedar Point, a narrow peninsula across the bay from Sandusky. After landing, Curtiss would return over the same water route to Euclid Beach. He was guaranteed $5,000 for his appearance and was offered a chance at tripling his money. If he averaged a speed of at least 60 miles an hour for the roundtrip, the owners of the amusement park would give him another $5,000, and if he flew 3,000 feet above the Breakers Hotel at Cedar Point, its owner promised an additional $5,000. But Curtiss, always the cautious flier, said he was unlikely to try for either prize. "I have never tried for altitude records and shall not fly very high in the air en route to Cedar Point and return. If I get up over 500 feet it will be to avoid some air current." He said that with favorable winds, the speed record was possible, but even that was doubtful. "Winning the $5,000 for a speed record will be my good fortune rather than any effort or skill in navigating on my part."[1]

Gene and Mars arrived in time to help with final preparations at Euclid Beach for the August 31 takeoff. Large cigar-shaped rubber floats were attached to the lower wings so the machine would stay above water should an accident occur during flight. As an additional precaution, Curtiss wore an automobile tire inner tube over his shoulder and across his chest as a makeshift life preserver, just as he had on the Albany to New York flight. A crowd of 40,000 spectators jockeyed for position. The propeller began to spin, spraying a cloud of sand back into the faces of those lucky enough to be watching from the front rows. Hats flew off heads and women held their skirts down. "Let go!" shouted Curtiss, and with a quick wave to the crowd, he was off. Seventy-eight minutes later, he landed at Cedar Point in front of 10,000 people. Newspapers estimated that over 150,000 had seen him as he flew the first flight ever seen in Northern Ohio. When heavy clouds moved in and a few raindrops began to fall, Curtiss decided he would wait until the next day for the return flight.[2]

With the delay, Curtiss called his wife in Cleveland and suggested that she, Gene, Mars, and their wives should come to Cedar Point. Overnight, they decided that they would watch Curtiss fly back to Cleveland, while riding on the Lake Shore mail train. The rail trip was planned as a race between the biplane and the train, but the next morning, Gene, Mars, Mabel, Marie, and Mrs. Curtiss were late. Even with a speedy powerboat ride from Cedar Point across the bay to Sandusky and a headlong automobile dash through the city to the train depot, Curtiss was long gone by the time they arrived. Lena Curtiss had hoped to see her husband in flight, but "all she saw were farmers turning back from watching Curtiss high in the air." Flying into headwinds, the return flight took 24 minutes longer than the day before, yet Curtiss still arrived fifteen minutes ahead of the train. He also arrived an hour and fifteen minutes ahead of a flock of homing pigeons that had been released in Cedar Point, just before he took off.[3]

For $2.16 worth of gasoline, 13 ½ gallons at 16 cents per gallon, Curtiss was taking home $5,000. Friends said it was "one of the most moderately rewarded flights he had ever made," saying Curtiss had earned over $175,000 since flying at Rheims the previous year. After attending an evening dinner held in his honor by the Cleveland Aero Club, Curtiss left for Boston to prepare for the Harvard aviation meet. The next day, papers were filed in Albany, New York, officially incorporating the Curtiss Exhibition Company, organized to promote "exhibition flights with aeroplanes and the selling of aeroplanes for exhibition purposes." By then, Mars was on his way for an exhibition weekend at the Minnesota State Fair in St. Paul and Gene and Mabel were riding a train to Kalamazoo, Michigan. There, Gene was expected to be "one of the treats of the Southern Michigan–Northern Indiana Fair."[4]

Sheepshead Bay headlines had elevated Gene into the ranks of the best-known aviators in the United States. Every little thing he now did took on an exaggerated sense of importance. Newspapers framed his brief and simple flight to and from the Manhattan Beach Hotel as a daring and "perilous water flight." Readers were told that his aerial exploits had sparked "a sensation in New York" and "stirred the enthusiasm of practically all the larger cities in the United States." Even his bout with altitude sickness turned into an adventure story of how "his machine was nearly wrecked in a storm." He was becoming the invincible hero—every one of his moves proving his courageous skill. He was now nothing less than "one of the most daring of American birdmen."[5]

It took two days to move Gene's biplane from the railroad express office to the Kalamazoo fairgrounds. While three mechanics put the aeroplane together, Gene was asked about the carrying capacity of his 4-cylinder machine. "The future of the aeroplane is not to carry passengers," he said. "I would not go up with someone else flying the machine. I want to control the machine myself, and other people feel the same way about it." He said he thought aeroplanes might one day be useful to the military, perhaps in delivering mail. Then, the normally shy aviator began a long and technical explanation of the differences between the Wright and Curtiss aeroplanes. A reporter captured every word as Gene explained lateral steering, equilibrium control, and the intricacies of warped wings used by the Wrights versus ailerons used by Curtiss. If the reporter understood any of it he offered no further explanation.[6]

The 15,000 people who watched Gene "were greatly pleased with his work." Although a broken rudder cable marred his first day, it was quickly repaired and he was back in the air. The highlight of the exhibition was his victory in a five-mile race while flying 500 feet above a local automobile. "It was one of the most sensational flights ever made in Michigan, the first height flight ever attempted in Kalamazoo," said the newspaper. The two-day event was extended one day with a promise that Gene would perform "one of the feats that had set Sheepshead Bay on fire." Promoters said he would first climb to 1,000 feet. "The young aviator will seem but a speck while his massive machine will appear as a toy." From that high altitude, he promised a sensational dive, ending with a graceful birdlike landing on the turf. Unfortunately, on his third flight of that day, Gene's crankshaft broke and he lost his propeller just as he was taking off. Wemme's prizewinner was beginning to show its age. With no backup aeroplane or motor available, the Kalamazoo exhibition was over.[7]

Gene had less than a week before his scheduled appearance at Rock Island, on the Illinois side of the Mississippi River, and just across the water from his old Davenport home. While his aeroplane was being repaired, he had time to visit with his mother and the rest of the Harrington family at their annual reunion in York Center. Relatives and in-laws came from as far away as Colorado and Pennsylvania, and for the first time in 47 years, the Harringtons were reunited with their brothers and sisters. Orson Harrington, "chief mechanic to the chief birdman," was enjoying his own personal reunion with his wife, Maude, and their 2-year-old baby girl, Lucy.[8]

After a too short, three-day visit, Mabel, Gene, sister Maidie, and Orson, left for Davenport and the Rock Island exhibition. Gene had tried to convince his mother to come along, but failed. Maidie had never seen anyone fly and came to Davenport filled with excitement and pride. Other than her brother's daring and the cheers of the crowd, she would always remember the terrorized old man, pushing his way through the mesmerized spectators and warning all of them to, "Get under cover, that's not a man up there, that's the devil. Man can't fly!"[9]

On September 14, the first day of the exhibition, Gene almost made the man a prophet when he fell from 50 feet on his first flight. Once again, a rogue wind had tipped the plane on its side. Gene tumbled out, unhurt. Embarrassed in front of relatives and old friends, Gene said he would make repairs and promised to fly again that very day. Most of the spectators waited patiently for the next two hours. They didn't know what to expect, but whatever it was, they wanted to see it. Because aviation was still so new, and no aeroplane had ever flown in this part of the Mississippi Valley, many people didn't even know what an aeroplane was. Many thought it might look like something they had seen in balloon flights or the parachute jumps in previous air shows. A newspaper attempted to end their confusion. "The aeroplane should not be confounded with the balloon and the parachute," it read. "The aeroplane is a machine, or car, propelled by motors, and navigates the air as gracefully as a swan when directed by experienced hands."[10]

Just before 6 o'clock that evening, Gene and his crew pulled the biplane out of the tent. There was light applause from the expectant crowd who were wondering if this time the aeroplane would fly. As advertised, like a swan, the machine lifted off. The subdued spectators burst into cheers and Gene answered with a wave of his cap. "Five thousand persons craned their necks in awe-stricken wonder at the flimsy crate that was soaring and gliding, and turning above them." Up and up he went, perhaps as high as 1700 feet. "Women grew weak with fright," wrote a reporter, "and several covered their faces with kerchiefs rather than watch the heart-pounding thrill of an airship in flight." Fifteen minutes later, after circling over the Mississippi River on a ten-mile flight, Gene landed and stopped his machine at his exact starting point. Before he could step to the ground, the hysterical crowd surrounded him. Women hugged him and men tried to carry him on their shoulders. "People patted him on the back for twenty minutes," said a reporter. "He was glad to escape to his tent." The next day, a confident Gene telegraphed his formal entry into the $25,000 air race from Chicago to New York City, but he still had two more exhibitions to complete.[11]

Roanoke, in southwest Virginia, sits in a rolling valley barely eight miles wide and enclosed by picturesque mountain peaks. The fairgrounds were snuggly settled in a southward bend of the Roanoke River. To Gene, it must have brought back claustrophobic memories of the winds that had almost doomed his first exhibition in Sutherlin, Oregon. Across the river to the south were the steep slopes of Mill Mountain rising 800 feet above the city. As Gene walked across the fairgrounds that first afternoon, he looked up at the balloon sent aloft to test the wind. It floated perfectly still, but yet, Gene was uneasy. Strong, gusty low-level winds blew down from the mountainside. If they caught him sideways, they could flip his machine, or at the very least, keep him off balance. Though the fair promoters tried to persuade him to fly, Gene refused. "With a wind more than 15 miles an hour blowing I will not attempt a flight," he said. "Oft times when it appears to those on the ground that there is no wind at all blowing, the upper air currents are in full swing and too dangerous for flying."[12]

The thousands who had come to see him were not happy and not afraid to let Gene know it. "Of course I was pronounced a big fraud and a fake," he said later. "The grounds were in a hollow with hills of nine hundred feet all around the show grounds. I made my calculations and found that I could not attempt the flight with safety." He explained to a reporter that he believed an aviator should not fly when he was afraid. "A man in charge of a flying machine should have perfect confidence in himself and in the machine. If he does not know how to handle the craft, he should not attempt a flight.... Many a fatal accident has been avoided in the air merely because the operator of the machine did not lose his head."[13]

Well into the afternoon of the next day, the strong wind convinced most fair visitors to leave the grounds, sure, that once again, the biplane would not get off the ground. However, by 5 o'clock, the winds subsided and Gene announced he would fly within the hour. Those with enough patience to wait received their reward.[14]

Gene had taken a second look at Mill Mountain. A month earlier, a short, incline railway had begun taking passengers to the top for a panoramic view of the Roanoke Valley. "I noticed that there was a dance platform on a mountain in the vicinity and that an incline railway ran on the side of the mountain," Gene said. The dance platform was actually the large front porch of the Rockledge Inn, a small resort hotel that had struggled to survive since it was built in 1892. Gene wasn't able to get airborne from the fairgrounds, but that incline railway had given him an idea. He paid his 25-cent fair and rode to the top. There he talked with the management and, securing their approval, arranged to have his aeroplane put back in its crates, brought uphill on the railroad, and reassembled on the porch. "I glided off the platform after removing the enclosing rail," he said. "I flew off the top of a mountain because I could not get a good start at the exhibition grounds."[15]

He dropped down the slope and slowly rose into the air. It was a straight course in a northwesterly direction, crossing over the Roanoke River just to the west of the fairgrounds. There he turned to the east and began to descend into a safe and gentle landing in the center of the racetrack. "Thousands of people shrieked with delight," wrote a reporter. Both the young and the old were more than delighted to get a glimpse of the ship ... and every movement was watched with intense interest." The entire flight had traveled less than a mile, but Gene felt vindicated. "The people that a short time before had called me a fake," he said, "now lifted the machine off the ground and carried it around on their shoulders."[16]

Back in Oregon, the Portland newspaper was finally taking notice of Gene's achievements. "Reports emanating from the Eastern States tell of the grand success of Eugene Ely, the aviator," it said. "What makes his record of all the more interest to Portland people is the fact that in all his big record flights in the East, he used the Curtiss biplane, which E. Henry Wemme bought and had on exhibition in Portland." The article also reminded readers that Robert Simpson, Gene's former employer, now owned the biplane and while Simpson was back East on business, he had actually "seen his aircraft under the control of Mr. Ely."[17]

From Rock Island, to Roanoke, and then on to New York, Gene and Mabel were making a wide, counterclockwise, circular journey back to Chicago. Pausing in New York City's Times Square on September 25, Gene sent one of his promotional picture postcards to Whipple Hall who nearly a month after he left the Rochester exhibition, was still in a San Francisco hospital. "How is the hard luck family?" Gene wrote. "All well again I hope. Curtiss inquirers for you every time I see him. Good Luck, Eugene Ely." The next day, he and Mabel were in Poughkeepsie, New York. There, at the Dutchess County Fair, "the world's greatest aviator," took second billing to Theodore Roosevelt, former president of the United States. Both would receive a wild and enthusiastic reception.[18]

While Gene prepared to fly at Poughkeepsie, in Washington, D.C., the Secretary of the Navy notified the recently formed U.S. Aeronautical Reserve that Captain Washington Irving Chambers was now the Navy's contact person for aviation correspondence. The reserve was an association of private citizens formed to supplement national defense by advancing aeronautical science. It was the first time the Navy Department had made any provision for aviation. In just a month and a half, Gene would have his first meeting with Capt. Chambers, and together they would make aviation history.[19]

In the hangar tent at Poughkeepsie, James Henning and the mechanical team were making last minute adjustments to the biplane, while Gene talked to reporters. The newsmen were anxious to find out how Gene would approach his race with Ralph DePalma, the champion auto racer who was at the beginning of a legendary career and already the winner of three consecutive dirt track championships. "I intend to start the machine at the southern end of the track and make the circuit once," Gene said. "I believe the automobile, which I am to race, will start some distance behind the line and when we are on even terms start with full speed." The reporters reminded Gene that DePalma, a Fiat driver, was "fearless and drives with a recklessness that is terrifying to the onlooker." Did Gene think he could beat him? "I have heard that Barney Oldfield holds the track record here and I know that DePalma is the man to fight for that record," he said. "I think with favorable conditions existing, I can beat his Fiat."[20]

Just then, a young voice drew attention to a gap in the side of the tent, where three boys on their bellies were peeking in. "I sure would like to meet Ely," one youngster said. "Why he has got Curtiss whipped a mile and tied to a post." Gene laughed at the compliment and invited the boys in. "That reminds me of the time I flew at Davenport, where I was born," he told them. "After I had made a flight of over two thousand feet, the home papers had an account of how I was better than Curtiss ever was. It really made me laugh and I sent a copy of the paper to Mr. Curtiss."[21]

Mabel, "daintily dressed in a dark suit and an unassuming hat," was asked if she worried when Gene flew. "Why, no!" she said. "Mr. Ely has courage and a steady hand and I never have to worry a minute.... If I thought that he was not an excellent aviator, I do not think I would even allow him to go into the air for a moment." She even said she had made several flights with him in New York City. It was a fib, of course, but Mabel was learning quickly and successfully, how to promote herself and her "boy."[22]

"The most striking thing about the aviator and his wife," wrote a reporter, "is the pleasant manner characteristic of each. They are courteous and unassuming in their manner and favorably impress one who has the pleasure of meeting them."[23]

It was a miserable opening day at the fair, and yet, rain that had drizzled down all morning into puddles and slippery mud, didn't dampen attendance. "Ely, the aviator, is enticing many people to the grounds," said the newspaper, "for his reputation as a man bird is by no means confined to this state. He has made flights in almost every aviation meet held in this country and his skill as a driver of the aeroplane is common talk." Gene wasn't the only reason for the surge in ticket buying. Ralph DePalma was expected that afternoon for the first of many races between aeroplane and automobile. By noon, the driving track was still a deep, muddy pond filled with two inches of muck. While everyone waited for DePalma to arrive, race driver Eddie Parker drove DePalma's polished red Fiat onto the track. Parker was a member of the Fiat racing team and recently had become a test driver at Fiat's new Poughkeepsie auto manufacturing plant. He never had the success of DePalma, and was usually an also ran, but he was reliable and had a following of fans. Parker's fifteen-lap test run was nothing more than a series of long slides in the slime, but after he finished, he said as long as the mud dried out he would challenge Gene to an afternoon race.[24]

While Parker was still on the track, Gene began inspecting his biplane and making minor adjustments. At half-past two he wheeled the craft out of the tent, "and then with a gentle upward motion, rose gracefully into the air." It was a ten-minute flight, five times around the racetrack, with one brief pass over the trolley tracks just outside the fairgrounds. He thought about flying over the city, but decided potential wind currents coming from the Hudson River might make it too dangerous. From 500 feet, he turned off his engine and glided to a landing. Back at the tent hangar, Gene admitted that he didn't believe he could beat DePalma although he said he would try to get as much speed as possible and do his best to win, but he thought his engine was probably too small. "Consequently, I cannot attain the same speed that I can in the 60 horsepower motor in my other machine." His other machine still belonged to Curtiss and the fact that it was in Chicago for the Chicago to New York race was a convenient way of excusing his expected loss.[25]

With a smile, Mabel tried to encourage him. "There is a beautiful cup for the winner," she said, "and it certainly would be worth winning." The same woman who only a few weeks earlier had said she was tired of hauling suitcases full of cups and trophies, and medals, was once again playing newspaper reporters to great effect. "She is a brilliant conversationalist and is well informed on aerial subjects," wrote a reporter. "She is pleasant in manner and patiently answers hundreds of questions asked by curious sightseers."[26]

Gene and his team made a few minor adjustments before taking the aeroplane back into the air. Once he had altitude, he began to circle the track. Parker, in the Fiat below, slowed down until the aeroplane was directly overhead. That's when the signal for the start was given and both men began to sprint around the track. "From time to time the automobile driver cast his eyes upward and more than once Ely could be seen looking down upon his rival." By the third lap, Parker had a half-mile lead, and though Gene began to catch up, true to his prediction, Parker was an easy winner.[27]

Day Two was sunny and warm, but the winds had picked up. Mabel was afraid that air currents might push Gene's biplane into the trees near the track and she didn't want him to fly. But she relented when Gene said he didn't want to disappoint the 10,000 people who were waiting for him. No sooner had he lifted off and gained altitude than buffeting winds changed his mind. He began a turn, trying to return to his takeoff point, all the while frantically working his controls and trying to stabilize the craft. After four-minutes and a near crash, he dropped toward the ground and rolled to a stop. Hundreds of people rushed to the aeroplane. Soon, some were signing their names on the wings. It took a few minutes for police to regain control.[28]

An hour later, the wind had died down and Gene took off again for another race with Parker. This time he flew higher, believing it would give him greater speed, but even flying at 800 feet didn't make much difference. After the first lap, he was closer, but still nearly a half-mile behind. Mabel was explaining to reporters what Gene was doing in the air, when suddenly she gasped in fright and, as she began to run toward the falling plane, she shouted that Gene was in trouble. "Ely could be seen working with all his strength at the wheel and at the same time displaying a coolness that was remarkable," said a reporter. His engine went silent and he fell out of sight behind the trees near the stables. When Mabel and the reporters reached him, Gene was walking around, examining the plane. "My rudder wire snapped," he said. "I was forced to land in this plowed field. If the wind had been blowing at the time, I would have found myself in a bad predicament." Reporters stood silently, amazed at this "nervy aviator" as he continued to explain. "Any kind of fluffy wind might have overturned my machine," he said, "and even at that, I was not at all tickled with my situation." Without a rudder, he couldn't control the biplane's direction of flight. "The machine is at the mercy of the currents and the only thing that I can do is to let the machine glide to earth." He said the damage was minor and that he would fly again tomorrow. A few newspapers said that DePalma had actually been racing against Gene that afternoon; however, if that race ever actually took place, the local Poughkeepsie newspaper never mentioned it in its extensive coverage.[29]

Thursday was Roosevelt Day at the fair. In the morning, before the festivities, Gene and Mabel drove out to the Gill Farm, a couple of miles south of Poughkeepsie. Glenn Curtiss had made one of his two landings there in May on his trip from Albany to New York City. Gene said it was one of the best landing fields he had ever seen and, as his mind turned to the upcoming Chicago to New York air race, he decided he would land here on his way to New York.[30]

"With an azure sky above and the sun smiling at the happy throng," thirty thousand people entered the gates of the fairgrounds to hear the 26th president's noontime speech. Dressed in typical gray trousers, black coat, with a white shirt, and black necktie, Roosevelt waved his slouch hat to the enthusiastic crowd who answered with "three cheers for Teddy." The president called for responsibility and respect, with emphasis on the individual's duty to the country and to each other. "I have been in every state of the Union several times," he said, "and I am more and more struck, not with the superficial differences, but the essential unity of our citizenship. A good American is a good American in any state, north or south." He closed with his version of the Golden Rule. "Treat every man in accordance with his standard of conduct. Treat with contempt any man rich or poor whose attitude to his fellow man is wicked." With the crowd still cheering, Roosevelt smiled and waved his hat, climbed into an automobile, and was driven away. He didn't stay for Gene's aerial exhibition. Two weeks later, while in St. Louis, Roosevelt would accept a spur of the moment invitation from aviator, Arch Hoxsey, and became the first president to fly in an airplane.[31]

As Roosevelt was leaving, Gene had his biplane brought out. A mob of people rushed to the craft and surrounded it so closely that until police pushed them back, Gene couldn't get aboard. The unruly crowd in the infield made his takeoff and landing difficult and Gene worried that while in flight, something might force a deadly crash into the rowdy horde below. That evening, Gene took his machine over 1,000 feet into the sky. "People for the first time in the three days of the fair arose to the occasion and generously applauded the plucky pioneer conqueror of the air," said a reporter. There was a chill in the fall air, and when Gene stepped off his machine, his hands were blue. He had bundled himself in a heavy sweater coat for the high altitude flight, but forgot to wear gloves. As Gene "walked toward his quarters, he was rewarded with awe and due admiration," and although his own hands were numb, he shook the many hands offered him "with his characteristic sincerity."[32]

Nathan Ely, Gene's father, had arrived in time to hear Roosevelt's speech and then watch his son soar over the fairgrounds. He told reporters that he had "the utmost confidence" in his son's ability; however, the reporters noted how "the eyes of the father are constantly on the aviator," and every move was "keenly watched." Nathan Ely said he was thrilled and predicted that Gene would have no problems in the upcoming Chicago to New York Race. "He is now flying without even an effort," he said. "I can see nothing but a sure winner."[33]

It was windy on September 30, the final day of the fair, but although Gene was anxious to get to Chicago, he said he had to fly anyway. "I don't want the fair management to think I'm trying to duck on the last day," he said. The flight was short, but the spectators were satisfied and a newspaper declared his aerial exhibitions a success.[34]

Late that afternoon, Gene, Mabel, and Gene's father, drove to the new Fiat assembly plant that had just turned out its first automobile earlier that month. There was speculation that Gene wanted to buy a Fiat for himself, but more likely, his decade long fascination with fast automobiles had drawn him to the home of this speedy racing machine.[35]

Now it was on to the big Chicago race. "There'll be only one man to finish that race," Gene said with a smile, and without a doubt, everyone knew who he meant.[36]

# { 21 }

# "There's your trouble, Gene"

Gene arrived in Chicago with supreme confidence and the backing of not only Glenn Curtiss, but also his wife. "I am greatly interested in flying," Mabel said, "and I have made plans to follow my husband in his flight from Chicago to New York. Of course I will make the trip by automobile, and though I know the machine will not be able to keep up with an aeroplane, I will be able to catch up at the various stops."[1]

In October 1910, the two longest flights ever made in the United States each covered less than 190 miles. The first was a one-day roundtrip between New York and Philadelphia, made the previous June by Charles Hamilton. Walter Brookins, a Wright aviator, topped Hamilton's record at the end of September by flying from Springfield, Illinois to Chicago in less than six hours. The Chicago to New York race promised to be the most impressive attempt ever made in the history of aviation. Two months earlier, French aviators had completed a ten-day, 485-mile race to set the world distance mark, but if the Chicago race was successfully completed, the winner would more than double that mileage figure. "This was a very ambitious undertaking for this period," Glenn Curtiss said. "The distance between Chicago and New York was fully one thousand miles and landings were very difficult to accomplish in the broken country along the way."[2]

"It's a mighty long trip," Gene said, "but I am confident that I can make it and win." He assured reporters that he wasn't boasting. "I have high hopes and plenty of confidence.... It may take four days to do the distance and it may take less than that," he said. "When a man attempts to fly, it all depends on the same thing. He must have the sympathy of the weatherman." In any event, he was sure he wouldn't have to rush, even though the flight would be tiring. "There is a certain amount of human endurance in this flying business," he said. "If a man stays up three or four hours he's doing well. That is a day's work in my trade."[3]

On June 1, representatives of the *New York Times* and the *Chicago Evening Post* had announced that they were jointly offering a $25,000 prize to the first aviator who flew from Chicago to New York City in 72 hours or less. At the suggestion of Curtiss and other aviators, the promoters later agreed to extend the time to a full week. Charles Hamilton was one of the first to say he would fly and Glenn Curtiss promised his machines would also be there, but the champion aviator refused to say if he would personally operate any of his biplanes. The original idea for the race came from millionaire and amateur aviator, Clifford Harmon, the same Harmon who had been at the Dominguez air meet in January. After Curtiss' success on the Hudson flight, Harmon said he would give a $1,000 cash prize for an aeroplane flight between New York and Chicago. The *Times* and the *Post* took up the idea, but told Harmon to keep his thousand dollars, not realizing that Harmon was not one to sit on the sidelines. Two weeks before the race was to begin, Harmon was offering an additional $5,000 cash prize, but with his own conditions. The first birdman to fly 500 miles within 50 consecutive hours would receive $1,000. If the winner landed at Belmont Park, site of the upcoming international aviation meet in New York, Harmon would award the winner the remaining $4,000.[4]

"It will be the cool-headed, cautious, experienced aviator who will succeed in a competition of this character," Curtiss said. "If the race is finished, it will mark an epoch in the progress of aviation. It will be the forerunner of aeroplane tours and long-distance races." Even if the race were a failure, Curtiss said, it still would show "the possibilities of the aeroplane for practical purposes."[5]

The $25,000 prize initially stirred excitement in the aviation world and promoters anticipated heavy participation, especially from international aviators who would be flying in the international air meet at Belmont, later that month. But, by the first week of October, entries had dwindled down to only five aviators who were planning to fly; all were Americans, except for Canadian, Jack McCurdy. The Wright brothers at first had expressed some interest, but with the recent setback in their patent litigation with Curtiss, they decided a competitive race was just too dangerous. Curtiss had entered, but everyone expected him to choose someone else as a pilot. Curtiss aviators Willard and Post were there, along with onetime teammate, Charles Hamilton. Because he no longer was part of the Curtiss team, Hamilton had to bring his own aeroplane. He had crashed it and injured himself severely while making test flights on the West Coast. By the time he arrived in Chicago, he was leaning heavily on a cane and "hobbled onto the grounds like a pigeon with a broken leg." Too damaged to compete, Hamilton left Chicago before the race began. Although he hadn't appeared on anyone's "Who's Who" ranking of potential participants when officials announced race conditions early in July, Gene Ely was also there. At the time, no one could have predicted that Gene would become Curtiss' replacement in Chicago, or that by a stroke of luck he would be the only man to race.[6]

Curtiss had a lot of confidence in Gene's abilities. He let him practice with the more powerful 8-cylinder *Hudson Flyer*, and when the race was about to start, Curtiss offered Gene his newest biplane, the one Curtiss had personally flown in Boston a month earlier. To the untrained eye, the *Boston Flyer* looked like previous Curtiss biplanes, but modifications to the basic framework and wings, and adjustments in various flight controls, had lessened air resistance and allowed for greater speed. The craft was originally equipped with a 65 horsepower, 8-cylinder engine, but because the motor had given Curtiss so much trouble in Boston, some say that before it was given to Gene, the engine was replaced with one of lower horsepower. As with the numerical designations of early Curtiss biplanes, the reported horsepower ratings for a particular aircraft, at any particular time, varied and are not always reliable.[7]

Gene welcomed Curtiss' confidence and appreciated the lessons he received.

"Mr. Curtiss is a fine man and unexcelled as an aviator," Gene said. "He told me that if I won the race, the money at stake belonged to me.... It means a lot. You see, I have many ways in which I could use $25,000."[8]

For over a month, aviators and aviation fans discussed which route from Chicago they thought would be the best for an aviator to take once they reached Lake Erie—over the water or above the land. Glenn Curtiss agreed with the prevailing opinion; fly along the southern shore of the Great Lakes across Ohio to Buffalo, following the rails of the Lake Shore and Michigan Southern Railroad. The aviator should "keep close to the shore of Lake Erie," Curtiss said, "as this affords the best landing places." He didn't think flying over water, far from shore, was a good idea. "To equip the machine with floats and fly over the surface of the water would materially reduce the speed of the machine," he said.[9]

Curtiss sent his manager, Jerome Fanciulli, eastward to mark landing locations for the Curtiss aviators. Riding in an automobile that was called the "Pathfinder," Fanciulli was not only looking for unobstructed, level landing areas, but also areas easily accessible by automobile. The stops would be about 50 miles apart and once the race was underway, mechanics representing each aviator would take replacement parts to the next landing site and wait for the birdman to arrive and land safely. When the aviator took off again, the mechanics would speed ahead to the next stop.[10]

A preliminary exhibition in Chicago, beginning seven days before the big race got underway, offered the Curtiss team a chance to get ready. Winds and rain dampened at least two days of the exhibition, yet during the week, there was still time for dozens of flights. The highlight of the exhibition was the debut public flight of Blanche Stuart Scott, perhaps the only woman Glenn Curtiss ever personally taught to fly and now considered the country's first woman pilot.[11]

The rules of the Chicago-New York race required all aviators to either have a pilot's license, or to have completed a continuous one-hour flight. Gene qualified for his license on October 5, 1910, the 17th certificate issued in the United States.[12]

Race competitors would take off from inside the Hawthorne Racetrack, southwest of downtown Chicago. The one-mile oval offered a lush green infield that, had it not been marred by an almost circular lake near its western end, would have made a great place for takeoffs and landings. Instead, the aviators would have to use the dirt track. For their safety, the entire mile long inner rail was torn out, a few trees were removed, and the steeplechase jumping mounds were flattened. Because no one was allowed to fly over the city, the airmen would leave the racetrack track flying south for a short distance before turning southeast toward New York. The minor obstacles just outside the track were a few scattered houses and barns, some clumps of trees, and a twenty-foot high railroad embankment with rails and a network of wires running over its top. After inspecting the area, the aviators decided the obstructions were unlikely to cause any trouble. Once past the railroad tracks, the birdmen would fly into open country and with more than enough room to gain altitude, they could "circle the track, dodge the city proper, and start out on the 1,000-mile journey." The biggest danger for the contestants was the high wooden fence surrounding the track. Even though many other modifications were made, the fence that would keep nonpaying spectators out remained. At the LaSalle Hotel, headquarters for the Curtiss fliers, Curtiss got a laugh at a meeting of his exhibition team, when he made fun of the fence. "By George, boys," he said. "I'll tell you what. I'll jump the fence with you and keep you company, just for the sport."[13]

Realizing how hard the race would be on his biplanes, Curtiss had been trying to arrange spare parts and extra motors that he could place along the line of flight for use in emergencies, but there just weren't enough motors to go around. At one of their team meetings, someone suggested that only one aviator fly in the race and the remaining biplanes be disassembled and their parts added to the reserve. However, that presented a problem. Clause 10 in the race rules said, "At least three competitors must start, or no race." The Curtiss men decided that three men would fly out of Hawthorne Park, but only one aviator would continue on. The other two would quickly land and their aeroplanes would be taken apart for spare parts. The change was reluctantly accepted by representatives of the *New York Times* and the *Chicago Evening Post* newspapers. A *Times* news story rationalized its position. "This action insures a real effort to make the greatest aeroplane flight ever attempted."[14]

"We talked it over and decided that three [aviators] would have no chance," Gene said, "but one man, aided by the efforts of the other two, might get to the end of the course by the time allotted. Hence, three of us decided to draw lots to see which one would make the trip. Each promised to give his machine, if necessary, to the successful one, in the event of accident." By drawing the lucky long straw, Gene won the only chance at the prize money.[15]

"It's the only possible way that any of us could make New York," Willard said. "It is not a matter of our own physical endurance, but a question of how long our machines could stand the unusual strain." He said with good weather and no unexpected accident, Gene should have no trouble making New York. "He can replace his engine twice, completely, and have a machine as good as new," he said. Reporters asked Willard how he felt about losing the draw. "There's no use talking," he said, "I'd have liked to go, but he had the luck. Here's hoping he gets through."

"That's it," McCurdy said. "Ely has all the luck. Why, Willard and I would have given our right arms—almost—to go. Both of us realize what it means to the man who can say he has flown from Chicago to New York, and both of us want to be that man. We took the chance of a draw. Now all we can do is to wish Ely, Godspeed."[16]

Gene refused to consider failure. "I have trained for this event for months," he said. "I know that I am able physically to stand the strain and it will be a hard one. My machine is the fastest of those gathered here, and I intend to urge it to its limit." His Iowa hometown newspaper took proud notice of its native-born son. "The birdmen are planning a flight from Chicago to New York City and we notice that Gene Ely is listed," it read. "We expect to hear the boy from York is making a fine record on the trip."[17]

Early on Sunday morning, October 9, long before Curtiss and Gene arrived in the aviation tent, the mechanics began working on the *Boston Flyer*. Scrutiny was

*Opposite*: This postcard, possibly created during the October 1910 Chicago aviation meet, was designed to advertise the Glenn Curtiss Exhibition Company, formed to promote Curtiss airplane sales and featuring the company's premier aviators. With a portrait of Glenn Curtiss at its center and Eugene Ely at its top, the other members of the team are, clockwise, John "Jack" McCurdy, James Ward, Charles Willard, James "Bud" Mars, and Whipple Hall (Naval History and Heritage Command #NH 91002).

intense. Worn wires were replaced and nuts and screws tightened. Fasteners that were subject to any kind strain in flight were reinforced with yards of tape. Metal hold-down strips were attached to the motor to keep it firmly in place. Pulleys were adjusted and wings and elevators aligned. Anything that could possibly go wrong was checked and double checked, and checked again. Then, at full power, the 8-cylinder engine was tested. The seven and a half-foot propeller reached 320 pounds of thrust at its maximum velocity of 1,250 revolutions per minute. Only the strength of nine men holding tight kept the aeroplane from flying away. "It seems to be working perfectly," Curtiss said, but just to be sure, he took the *Flyer* up for one final test. He circled the infield pond, raced over the length of the track, then turned directly into the northwest wind that was blowing at about 20 miles an hour. Satisfied that the plane was ready, he circled back and landed lightly on the racetrack just before 4 o'clock.[18]

It was a nasty day, with black clouds rolling across a dim sky. The raw northwest wind had snapped at the tent all afternoon and for a while, Curtiss hadn't been sure it was the right day to fly. But Gene begged, saying the wind would add speed to his flight, "For the first 25 miles, the wind will be right behind me," he said. "What conditions I will face when I pass the end of Lake Michigan, I can't tell." He admitted that the wind might change direction after that and that there might be bad weather further ahead, but he was still anxious to go. "I thought of the special train with my wife aboard waiting for me out at Gary," he said. "And I thought of the anxious throngs in La Porte and South Bend. Also, I thought of that big prize and how little time I had to win it in." Curtiss had listened without saying a word and after a thoughtful pause, gave in. "I think the machine will do," he said. "You can start if you want to."[19]

Gene dressed head to toe in brown leather with a warm sweater underneath and gloves on his hands. A compass was strapped like a watch on his right wrist. He had already tried to memorize the map of his course. With the compass on his arm and the clock that was attached to his steering wheel, he would always have a rough idea of where he was. Mechanics topped off the fuel and rechecked the oil reservoir. Gene would be able to fly 150 miles on the twenty gallons of gas in his tank.

Curtiss, Gene, and Mabel walked to the *Flyer*. Gene gave Mabel a hug and a kiss. "Goodbye little woman," he said. Then he promised that he would join her again at the Hotel Astor in New York City on Friday, not later than noon. "Don't worry about me," he said. "I've been eating bird seed and I can fly to Europe." Mabel hugged him and told him to be careful. Curtiss laughed nervously. "Well, my boy," he said. "Are you going to make it?" Gene answered that one way or another he was going all the way to New York. "If I don't do it in seven days, I'll do it in seven weeks," he said. "I'll keep on going if it takes all winter."[20]

Curtiss shook Gene's hand. "Good luck to you," he said, and then turned to the mechanics and shouted, "Go!" Cranks were turned on the engines of three biplanes, motors sparked, and propellers began to spin. A few spectators who had gathered too closely behind the aeroplanes were nearly blown to the ground by the whoosh of air. Willard and McCurdy were already sitting on their machines. Gene turned to smile at his aviator friends and then with a question in his eyes, looked at Curtiss. Curtiss gave a silent nod and Gene climbed into his seat. He pulled the wheel toward him once, tested his aileron controls by rocking his body side to side a few times, then with a wave of his hand, he was ready. Mechanics let of the surging wings and the *Boston Flyer* was free. It rolled a short distance over the dirt for nine seconds and then jumped into the air. With one circuit of the racetrack, fighting the unpredictable wind at each turn, he gained enough altitude to clear the fence. As he turned southeast and climbed to 1,000 feet, the wind pushed him so rapidly that within four minutes he had completely disappeared from view. McCurdy and Willard followed him into the air, "hopping the fence" and officially demonstrating that three aviators had left Hawthorne Park. McCurdy barely left the grounds, but Willard sped away in a three or four mile circle. As soon as they returned to the track, mechanics immediately disassembled their biplanes, crated their parts, and shipped them 100 miles to South Bend, Indiana, where Gene hoped to stop for the night.[21]

Everything went wrong. "It was a great wind for speed," Gene said, "but the roughest I ever tackled. It was extremely choppy and kept me on the move every second to retain balance on the machine." After nine minutes in the air, eleven miles from Hawthorne, the engine began to cough and backfire. Gene knew immediately what was wrong, something was wrong in the carburetor, but at 1,500 feet, there was nothing he could do. He had control of the engine spark, but the mechanics had preset the carburetor and he couldn't reach it. An hour before sunset, Sunday duffers on the fairways and greens of the Beverly Golf Club looked up and recognized trouble in the air. They ran to their automobiles, forming a rescue convoy that followed after the biplane, knowing that it surely had to land, and land it did, but too far away from any road for the golfers to be of much help.[22]

Over the hills beyond the golf course, Gene scanned the ground for a safe place to land. "I found it in an open field, which I have learned is known as Frogtown," he said. Circling the relatively flat field, he gradually lost altitude. "I landed nicely and I set to work on my engine," he said. As he suspected, it was an easy repair, the needle pin in his carburetor had stuck and shut off the flow of gasoline. While he worked, a few children ran through the tall prairie grass to catch a look at the birdman and his machine. Moments later, some adults appeared and Gene asked them to help him get ready for another takeoff. The engine was firing smoothly again and the men who held the wings let go. As the biplane sped over the prairie, gaining speed, Gene saw a rock sticking up from the ground, but he didn't think it would be a problem. "It simply never occurred to me that it could do any harm," he said. "I hit it, that's all, and it hit me. It smashed my front wheel to smithereens." He was determined to get back into the air. He tried three or four more times, but without the front wheel, rather than running over the field, the biplane dug into the prairie like a farmer's plow and Gene finally had to give up. "I was hungry and tired, but not a soul offered me even a cup of tea," he said, "and it was not until I had walked, what felt as far back as Chicago, that I found a telephone." He called Curtiss who was still at the LaSalle Hotel. Off to the rescue, two mechanics, a spare wheel, and a *Times* reporter were sent to Frogtown. When their automobile arrived, they found a dejected and impatient Gene waiting for them. It only took a half hour to replace the wheel and fashion a connecting rod so Gene could control the carburetor in flight, but it was too late in the evening to try another takeoff. "A good night's sleep is the best preparation I can have for my flight tomorrow," he said, "and I can't get it here." He returned to Chicago, saying he would be back on the prairie early in morning and resume his flight. "It might have been worse," he told reporters. "I might have killed myself, you know, but that's about the only satisfaction I can get out of it. I'll make up for this piece of hard luck tomorrow." A reporter asked if he really thought he could make it all the way to New York City. "I do, more than ever," he said. "If this wind holds, I'll make up lost time tomorrow. ... My trunks and supplies have been sent to the Astor House in New York and I expect to be there with my trunks not later than Friday."[23]

The next morning, fog was so thick that mechanics standing on opposite sides of the aeroplane could barely see each other. Even the trains were off schedule. Nearly an hour and a half after he had planned to be in the air, Gene was still pacing nearby, surrounded by a crowd of several hundred, including some sleepy-eyed schoolchildren. Finally, the mist cleared and Gene took off. A half-mile later, only 75 feet above the ground, the engine began to misfire again. Power was wasting away and a landing was urgent. Gene saw a clear field ahead. When he turned toward it, his engine died and he began his silent glide. Gently, he touched down, rolled smoothly over the grass, but straight for a ditch. His foot pressed hard against the brake, but there was no escape. The front wheel fell into the ditch. Gene was thrown free and tumbled a dozen feet to the sound of his front wheel supports crumpling away and the shredding of rubberized silk. His front elevation planes were smashed and some of the frame and wing supports had snapped off. The crowd rushed to Gene's aid, but except for his disgust over a wrecked biplane, he was unhurt. A quick inspection found that the feeder pipe connecting the gas tank with the carburetor had come unfastened, causing the motor failure. "It must have been shaken loose by the rough ground over which I had to travel before I could mount into the air," Gene said.[24]

Mabel, who had been waiting on the special chartered train in Gary, rode back to the scene of Gene's trouble, accompanying Curtiss and his mechanics who were bringing spare parts. It took eight hours to repair the damage, but just after four in the afternoon, the *Boston Flyer* was in the air again. Gene circled the field twice to be sure that everything was working, slowly climbed to 1,500 feet, and accelerating to an estimated 50 miles an hour, shot away to the southeast. Nothing was heard until 5:45 when a news flash reached the railroad station at Gary. "He's dropped in East Chicago," it read. "Fell like a bullet out of the sky." A few minutes after six, the station telephone rang again. Gene was on the line. "I'm all right," he said. "Tell my wife. The machine is smashed and I can't get out of here until tomorrow. Don't know what's the matter, but my engine stopped again."[25]

Gene had fallen into a swampy area five miles west of Gary and once again, the front wheel and supports were torn away from the craft. Gene was tired and disgusted. "Do you know," he said, "I could see Gary from the seat of my biplane. I was getting along nicely, more than 1,000 feet in the air, and was just getting ready to look out for the white-painted roof of the special train, when my engine began to miss." There was little time to get back to earth. "Once again my landing was bad, this time because of the nature of the soil into which the wheels settled," he said. "Once more, I found myself pitched out on my face with the front of my craft a wreck." He said everything looked all right on his machine, nothing was broken, and he was beginning to wonder if there was something wrong with the gasoline he was using. Whatever the problem, as long as the biplane could be repaired in time, he would try again the next day. "It'll take me till tomorrow noon to get the plane in shape to go again, but once I do, look out," he said. "If the luck holds, I expect to keep up nearly 60 miles an hour right into New York."[26]

Barely twenty miles from Chicago, with less than five days left to cover nearly 1,000 miles, Curtiss returned to Chicago to see if the under rigging braces on August Post's 4-cylinder biplane could be transferred to Gene's larger machine. That afternoon, fighting back tears, Gene read Curtiss' abrupt telegram. "No parts here for repairs. Boxes shipped, Wells-Fargo, tonight." The boxes meant Gene should crate up his machine. The race was over. "I suppose now it's the best thing to do," Gene said. "Even if I got started again I couldn't keep going with no repair parts." He said he hated to give up. "I never started anything yet that I didn't finish until I struck this thing. I tell you it hurts." He vowed he would try again. "I've got the necessary endurance and I've got the nerve," he said. "I'm fighting mad now, and I shan't sit back and let anyone think that I gave up this trip for any reason other than plain hard necessity, the impossibility of continuing it further. If I could get new parts tomorrow I'd go on, though I know now that I couldn't reach New York inside of the required 168 hours."[27]

Earlier that morning, a close inspection of the engine revealed the real cause of Gene's engine failures. Particles of dirt had plugged an already oil-clogged pinhole in the biplane's gas tank. Much like trying to pour juice from a tin can requires two air holes poked into its top, without the vent hole in the gas tank, gasoline wouldn't flow to the carburetor. A simple pinprick through that hole would have kept Gene in the air. "There's your trouble, Gene," said the mechanic who discovered the clog. Gene stared blankly for a moment and then asked himself, "What do you think of that?" Thoroughly discouraged, he turned and walked away. "Two days of the kind of luck I've had will sap any one's strength," he said. "I feel as though I'd been pulled through a knothole. I got about four hours' sleep Sunday night and no more last night. Now I think I'll take a nap."[28]

The race was only an expensive dream now. Those particles of dirt plugging his air vent had not only cost Gene the $25,000 prize, but his Chicago expenses and the loss of available time for other exhibitions had cost him an additional $8,000 to $10,000. It wasn't his fault, but it was another embarrassing failure.[29]

Confidence shaken, Gene and Mabel returned to Chicago's train station. A night's sleep in a comfortable hotel bed would have been pleasant for the tired aviator, but Gene was already scheduled for another exhibition and was due in Youngstown, Ohio, the next day. He'd have to be satisfied with a rough and rocking berth on the Lake Shore & Michigan overnight train.

# { 22 }

# "The ease of a swallow and the speed of an express train"

The Youngstown aviation committee had expected to see Glenn Curtiss fly at their Columbus Day celebration. He had signed a contract with the Northeast Ohio steel town in September, but with the failure of the Chicago air race, Curtiss decided at the last minute to send Gene in his place so that he could fly in the more lucrative exhibition in Cleveland with McCurdy and Mars. Once Gene finished his Youngstown flights, he would join the team on the shores of Lake Erie.[1]

Gene and Mabel arrived early in the morning, and with a crated Curtiss biplane and mechanics in tow, headed for Willis Park, the old baseball grounds across the Mahoning River on Youngstown's South Side. Willis Park was barely three years old, but the baseball team that played there had failed after two seasons and a new baseball park was already being built closer to town. The aviation committee had leased the fields surrounding the old ballpark, believing those who didn't pay admission wouldn't be able to see the flights. But when the day came, the twelve Youngstown police officers who patrolled the grounds were no match for the 20,000 spectators who, for four hours, impatiently watched Gene's feeble attempts to fly. There was too much wind again and Gene never could travel further than 2,000 feet in a straight line or stay in the air longer than 30 seconds. Because the exhibition was a benefit for the proposed St. Elizabeth's Catholic hospital, committee members appealed to Gene to try again the next day. Now a Catholic himself and also never wanting to leave his audience disappointed, Gene agreed.[2]

There was no admission charge on the second day of the Youngstown exhibition, so a boisterous crowd of 10,000 crammed into the ballpark and filled the surrounding area. For his first flight, Gene had barely gotten off the ground when a gust of wind dashed a wing to earth, breaking one of its wooden ribs. The repair took less than an hour and Gene began again. It was a pretty flight, rising to at least 135 feet over the grandstand and then circling the ballpark for over a minute. As he gracefully began to descend, the crowd pushed through police rope barricades and swarmed over the field, leaving little open space for a landing. Just before he touched down, a woman with two children ran across the field in front of him. He frantically worked his controls and twisting and turning with every skill he had, he managed to avoid flying his aeroplane right into them. He jumped from his seat "trembling like an aspen leaf." They heard him shout. "I would not go up again under such conditions for $100,000! I thought I must surely strike that woman and two little children before they could get out of my way. I do not want any accidents of this kind and will not fly again at Willis Park." Surrounded by Youngstown police officers and still upset, he pushed his way through the crowd and the web of hands reaching out to touch him. "It was the first time they got on my nerve," he said later. As the crowd rushed to leave the grounds, a ticket taker was trapped against a pole. The cash box he was carrying pushed into his ribs, crushing his side and sending him to the hospital with serious internal injuries. It had been a dangerous situation, but on the positive side, over $3,000 was raised for the hospital. Gene and Mabel rested overnight in a local hotel and then left for Cleveland, about 75 miles to the northwest.[3]

Cleveland is the county seat for Cuyahoga County, Ohio and, in October 1910, a week-long celebration of the county's centennial was underway. The U.S.S. *Dorothea*, a former Navy gunboat, floated on Lake Erie and opened the festivities by firing a 100-gun salute to mark each one of those years. A new $4-million courthouse and a half-million dollar bridge across the Cuyahoga River would also be dedicated. Carnivals, a midway with sideshows, band concerts, and open-air theatrical performances drew merrymakers from miles around. In the public square, four grandsons of early pioneers were in charge of the ceremonial flag raising, while fifteen Chippewa Indians from a Michigan reservation watched from their three-tepee village. Two hundred automobiles, decorated in flowers and competing for dozens of prizes, stretched over the streets for five miles. Two hundred thousand people rushed to the Cleveland curbs to watch a mile-long parade of "native-born and naturalized Italians" who were celebrating Columbus Day with floats and marching children waving American and Italian flags. "Every sidewalk was black with humanity. Heads appeared at countless windows and from rooftops." Evenings exploded in fireworks with bursting bombs showering the lake in multicolored light. But even with all these festivities, most people were waiting for the Curtiss aviation show.[4]

A portion of Lakeview Park, on the shore of Lake Erie, was leveled and rolled flat into a runway. A canvas fence, running all the way down to the water, surrounded the park. Because weather was unpredictable, no official program of events was published. But at any given moment, spectators could check a large information board that stood in front of the 10,000-seat grandstand to learn who was flying and what aerial maneuvers were being performed. Once the motion picture men had erected their tall tower, not far from where the air show would begin, everything was ready.[5]

The ill wind that had shut down Gene's Columbus Day attempt to fly in Youngstown was blowing even stronger in Cleveland. A steady gale force wind from the northeast brought disappointment on Day 1 to the thousands who either paid admission or gathered on boats and nearby hilltops to see the birdmen fly. The next day was nearly perfect. A warm sun was shining and the wind was light. Curtiss made the one flight he had promised the centennial committee and then left for Hammondsport, where a new racing monoplane was being prepared for the upcoming international aviation meet at Belmont, New York. In all, there were ten conservative flights as Mars and McCurdy familiarized themselves with the area. That night, Gene's biplane arrived in Cleveland. The next day he was ready to fly, but it was Bud Mars who would steal the show.[6]

McCurdy began the afternoon by flying three times around the field in ever widening circles and landing within five feet of his starting position. Mars followed with an epic flight. He circled the grounds until he was flying at 500 feet and then shot off to the new county courthouse, five miles away. In the middle of a dedication ceremony, United States District Attorney William Day stopped midsentence, surprised by the rasping growl of the biplane's motor above as Mars swooped down and around the building. Returning to the aviation field, Mars began a slow climb through a broad, factory fueled smoke cloud that lingered just below 2,000 feet. For a moment, he disappeared over the lake. "Then on his return trip, a startled gasp went up from every throat as he was seen rising high out of the mists, his wings glinting in the sunlight." He descended to 1500 feet as he circled the field then cut his engine and floated down in front of the grandstand, and landed within a few feet of where he had started his ten-mile flight. Gene zoomed out to the west over the canvas wall, flying along the Lake Shore Railroad tracks. He passed through the smoke cloud that was now so dense and low that from just a few feet in the air, he could barely see the ground, but he managed to return and make a perfect landing. In his last flight of the day, Gene misjudged his landing and hit the ground so hard that he nearly turned over. "The bank of smoke along the lake front was so dense," said the newspaper, "that Ely became confused and thought that he was in Pittsburgh."[7]

During the Cleveland meet, Gene didn't have much to say, but Mabel, of course, always had at least a few words for reporters and, in the hotel that evening, she was once again harping on her on-again, off-again pet peeve, her opposition to the routine awarding of trophies to aviators. "Let them give medals instead," she said. "We'll save money on excess baggage." Apparently the aviation committee never heard her complaint. At the end of the meet they awarded each flier, including Gene, a $100 trophy.[8]

On the last day of centennial festivities nearly half a million people wandered the streets of Cleveland and most of them were there to see the Curtiss aviators. With the aeroplane flights free to all, down came the canvas wall. "There are many in Cleveland who were unable to see the birdmen in action during the week," explained one of the committee members. "The laboring man could not leave his work and his family, and, in many cases, he did not have the money to secure a seat."[9]

Because most factories agreed to close for half a day, smoke was thin and almost invisible. McCurdy, flying one of the 8-cylinder biplanes, was the first to try a high altitude flight and his half-hour of aerial antics at 2,200 feet were clearly visible to all. Gene took off in pursuit of McCurdy. They were nearly wing-to-wing as they raced in wide circles over the crowd. When, for a brief moment, Gene began to pull ahead, it seemed that his engine was more powerful than McCurdy's. Then, in the middle of a sharp turn, Gene's engine suddenly went silent and the biplane began to fall rapidly in an angled glide toward the hangar tent at the side of the grandstand. Mabel cried out in terror. Her experienced eye knew that Gene was in trouble, but somehow her boy managed to swing around the tent, float down the field, and land softly, with a shaken Mabel running to greet him.[10]

Gene took first place in the accurate landing contest, where the aviators first flew twice around the course and while landing, tried to stop as close as possible to a line of tape strung across the center of the field. Gene touched down "about fifty feet from the mark, put on his brake, and brought the aeroplane to a complete stop with the rear wheels resting on the line." McCurdy was close, but Mars came in with too much power and by the time his brakes took hold, he wound up ten feet past the line. For his win, Gene claimed another trophy for Mabel's growing collection. Fortunately for Mabel, in the bomb throwing contest, where aviators dropped three oranges from 200 feet toward a man-of-war ship target drawn in chalk in the center of the field, Gene was a "bad third" and won no trophy. Mars won the event and as he was flying away with his trophy, gave the crowd its most exciting moment of the day. The hyperactive aviator once again came in for a landing with too much speed and was on course for a crash into a wire fence and the automobiles parked behind. His wheels rolled across the field for twenty feet and just before he struck, he tilted upward and missed the fence by inches.[11]

The centennial committee desperately wanted to extend the aviation meet for one more day and they began soliciting donations from prominent citizens. "It was necessary to raise a large amount of money to keep the aviators and their aeroplanes in Cleveland over Sunday," said a reporter. "They are anxious to begin practice for the international meet, which soon opens at Belmont Park."[12]

Gene stayed and his historic flight over city streets and buildings was the sensation of the exhibition's last day. Ten seconds after he fired up his engine he was in the air, gaining altitude and circling the field. Off he shot toward the courthouse, circled it, and then at 2,000 feet passed over the *Cleveland Plain Dealer* newspaper building on the corner of 6th and Superior avenues. "Pedestrians on Euclid and Superior, and all of the downtown streets, stood with upturned faces," wrote a *Plain Dealer* reporter, "watching the twentieth century marvel as it sped on its way." Then Gene was on to the Cleveland headquarters of the Curtiss aviators, the spire of the Hollenden Hotel, over ten-stories in the air. "It was the first time in history that an aeroplane had ever passed over the city of Cleveland. Never before had man or woman been given the privilege of glancing into the air to see, speeding high above, the faint outline of a man-carrying machine." For a dozen blocks, the hills were black with people and not one of them lost sight of Gene as he flew "with the ease of a swallow and the speed of an express train." There was no smoke and not a cloud in sight. It was a ten-minute circular journey back to the aviation field, where, still high in the air, Gene cut his engine and glided to a point directly in front of the grandstand. The mass of people who had craned their necks to keep him in sight, exploded in the loudest ovation of the four-day meet.[13]

Cuyahoga County had finished its birthday party. "The songs and shouts of the young people have faded to an echo," said the newspaper. "The alluring call of the barker and the ballyhoo man has been silenced. The last horn has been tooted. The last bell sounded. Silence reigns in the littered streets," and the aviation world was on its way to Belmont Park.[14]

# { 23 }

# Bleak Days at Belmont

On the day after Gene Ely's 24th birthday, an afternoon Tule fog was swirling low over the Belmont Park racetrack. A bugle call blared out through the cold, drizzling, October rain, and the boom of a cannon and the bursting of an aerial bomb put all doubts to rest. Today they would fly. The Second International Aviation Tournament had begun.[1]

As the country's representative to the International Aeronautic Federation, the Aero Club of America had chosen the tournament's New York location, but it hadn't been easy. Ever since the previous year, when Glenn Curtiss had won the Gordon Bennett Cup at the first international tournament in Rheims, officials in dozens of cities across the United States had been clamoring for a chance to host the defense of the trophy. Early in June 1910, when William Vanderbilt offered to give his Long Island motor parkway to Aero Club officials and also loan them $20,000 to convert it into an aerial exhibition and training facility, all competition seemed to be over. In addition to the $20,000 loan, which would be repaid by admissions to aviation events, Vanderbilt said he would also pay for a fence around the motor parkway, put up a grandstand, roll the turf, build hangars, supply automobiles and gasoline for the use of aviators, and also pay salaries for mechanics, ticket takers, and any necessary course officials. The major objection to the plan was how remote the auto course was. The railroad and commuter trolley lines ended miles away and the only access was by walking, wagon, or automobile. Officials feared that it would be too difficult for great numbers of spectators to get to the course, and that was the only way to quickly repay the $20,000 loan.[2]

After meetings with Vanderbilt and discussions with its membership, the Aero Club declined Vanderbilt's offer and instead decided to lease property six miles to the west on the Hempstead Plain near Garden City, New York. To get the farmland into proper shape for an air meet, they would have to erect a fence, construct a grandstand, and turn fallow fields into a facility that could comfortably handle tens of thousands of spectators on each day of the tournament. It was a difficult task and expensive. Just the cost of staging an aviation tournament with adequate cash prizes for aviators would cost at least an additional $125,000. While club members began soliciting donations, August Belmont, Jr., offered the use of his Belmont racetrack that not only included the largest grandstand in the country, but also had parking space for hundreds of automobiles and easy access to public transportation. Garden City was out and Belmont was in. A few trees and track railings would have to be removed, and there would be some additions to the grandstand, but Aero Club finance chairman, Lawrence Gillespie, was sure the necessary changes would make Belmont Park "an almost perfect aviation ground." By saving money on the grounds, the club would be able to tempt foreign and American aviators with up to $72,300 in cash prizes.[3]

Right up to the start of the Belmont tournament, almost everyone assumed that Glenn Curtiss would personally defend his Rheims trophy as part of the three-man United States team. Aero Club members urged Curtiss to fly and said if he did, he wouldn't have to fly the mandatory qualifying flights. But, Curtiss once again said he was finally going to give up public flying to concentrate on his dream of an aeroplane that could land or take off on water. He sent a letter to the Belmont aviation committee saying he would attend the tournament, but that Gene Ely, Jack McCurdy, and Charles Willard would be the ones to fly. The promoters were disappointed, but not for long. In his message, Curtiss also announced "one of the greatest surprises of the international meet." He was sending a new racing machine of "the monoplane type" to compete for the Gordon Bennett Cup. It was unexpected news because Curtiss had always favored a biplane over a single wing design. To those who knew him well, the fact that he had actually built anything that even looked like a monoplane seemed incredible.[4]

"It is true," said Curtiss' manager, Jerome Fanciulli. "But, Mr. Curtiss does not designate his new aeroplane as a monoplane. He prefers to call it a single surface machine." Whatever he called it, the new machine was a radical departure from anything Curtiss had ever built before. The chassis was similar to his biplanes, but was "stripped to the bone and looked naked and bare when compared with the other machines." It was a smaller craft with a wing surface area reduced by nearly two-thirds. It retained the lower wing, about 30 feet long and five feet wide, but the upper wing looked more like a sun awning for the pilot rather than a wing. Positioned above and slightly behind the aviator's seat, the "awning" was just over five feet long and 2 feet wide. The pilot's seat had also been moved. Instead of sitting on the lower wing, the seat was now pushed forward of the front wing, lowered, and mounted onto struts that ran out to the hub of the front, middle wheel. A radiator at the pilot's back would separate him from a 65 horsepower, 8-cylinder motor. Fanciulli was careful to point out that the movable steering wheel and aileron controls on the new Curtiss plane worked exactly as they did on the biplanes. With the Wright patent lawsuit still in the courts, it was important to stress that the Curtiss aeroplane was steered differently than a Wright machine. Curtiss added another important surprise when he arrived to supervise assembly of the new racer. "The machine has not yet been flown," he said, "and therefore the question of whether it will fly well—or fly at all—remains to be found out at the present meet."[5]

The Curtiss team had almost skipped the Belmont tournament. If the aviation committee hadn't agreed at the last minute to pay each aviator appearance money, Curtiss would have sent his team somewhere else. "The trouble," wrote a reporter "has been caused by the Wrights' suits for alleged infringement of patents and their attempt to force the promoters of every aviation meet in the country to pay tribute to them for all biplanes entered, including foreign machines brought into the United

States…. There is bad blood between Curtiss and the Wrights." Curtiss was angry because the aviation committee had guaranteed the Wright brothers $25,000 if Wright aeroplanes appeared at the tournament. If the Wrights were getting paid, Curtiss was adamant that his fliers also get something for their appearance. The final agreement gave each aviator $1,000 just for showing up, even if they never flew at the meet. They would also receive $300 for delivering an aircraft to the grounds, an additional $300 if the aviator completed at least four laps of the racecourse, and $300 more when the aviation tournament closed. Each aviator also was covered by a $100 insurance guarantee against any damages. It wasn't equal to what the Wrights were getting, but Curtiss was confident that his team could win enough in cash prizes to make it all worthwhile.[6]

Perhaps Curtiss really thought his team or his experimental machine could easily recapture the Gordon Bennett Trophy, but he was in for a few surprises. Some of the Europeans were bringing engines rated at 100 horsepower and the Wright brothers arrived with a new racing machine that would prove to be very fast. It was a scaled down, "pocket version" of the Wrights' standard biplane that quickly earned the affectionate name, *Baby Wright.* The only full-size carryover from the standard model to the *Baby* were two propellers, each driven by a beefed up 60 horsepower engine. "This machine is what bicycle men might call a light roadster," Wilbur Wright said. He and Orville were confident that they had a winner, and after seeing the Wrights' *Baby* streak out at a speed somewhere near 70 miles an hour, most nonprofessionals in the stands agreed. Even a surprised Glenn Curtiss was impressed. While inspecting the *Baby Wright* he reportedly gasped as he said, "What a tremendous pitch to the propellers."[7]

Qualification flights to select an American team of racers for the Gordon Bennett Cup were postponed from day to day by heavy winds that blew continually during the entire Belmont meet. Time grew short and qualification flights were finally canceled. With hours to go before the speed race was scheduled to start, desperate Aero Club board members announced that they were going to arbitrarily choose the three American birdmen who would defend the cup. In a conference with Curtiss, the Wright brothers, and other aviators, they held a contentious meeting that lasted until midnight and disappointed almost everyone. The board's selections were Walter Brookins, flying the *Baby Wright,* Charles Hamilton and his *Hamiltonian* biplane, and John Armstrong Drexel, a Philadelphia millionaire in a French-made Bleriot monoplane. Drexel had been competing for altitude records in Europe and been given nonresident membership in the Aero Club of America. Brookins, "Brookie" as the Wrights called him, had known the Wrights almost since his 1889 birth in Dayton, Ohio. He had been flying for the brothers for just over a year.[8]

There was considerable surprise and some anger that no Curtiss aviator was named to the team, although Bud Mars had been selected as second alternate. "As the Curtiss camp had settled upon McCurdy as the best man to represent the Curtiss hangars in the race," said a reporter, "the Curtiss fliers were far from satisfied." Aero Club President Cortlandt Field Bishop had to refute charges that the club was discriminating against Curtiss and his team. "Curtiss refused to defend the cup," Bishop said. "He refused on the ground that he did not believe he could succeed." Bishop said he thought Curtiss was satisfied with the decision and had agreed with the committee's selections. Characteristically, Curtiss had little to say. "I'm not going to say a word about this action. I had hoped to see one of my machines enter the elimination trials at least. That's what I built a racer for."[9]

Whether Curtiss had withdrawn or was forced out, he told aviation columnist and managing editor of the *Philadelphia Inquirer*, John Trevor Custis, that "he had been entirely frank with the committee." Custis said Curtiss told the committee that he had never tested the new racer and when asked, refused to make any claim that it would win or how it would do if a Curtiss flier was chosen to defend the trophy. Custis believed that Curtiss' honesty was the real reason the committee eliminated him. Whatever the true story, after looking over the competition, it made little sense to challenge either the *Baby Wright* or the powerhouse European aircraft with an experimental airplane that had never been tested in flight. But then again, the Aero Club might have reconsidered had they known how disappointing the race would be for the Americans, especially the Wrights. Hamilton managed to take off, but he was too late to qualify. Drexel was only able to finish seven of the required twenty laps, and Brookins, the Wrights only hope, crashed and survived a 50-foot fall during a 70 mile an hour practice run before the race. The first American alternate, John Moisant, flying a Bleriot machine, took over for Brookins and salvaged a second place finish behind England's Claude Grahame-White.[10]

In his aviation book, written in 1912, Curtiss briefly mentions the single surface racer. "I had built a machine for the trials, which I thought would be very fast and had constructed it as a type of monoplane in order to cut down the head resistance." Although Curtiss wrote that he "did not try out my monoplane," he likely did—at least once. A writer for *Aircraft* magazine said that on the day after the Gordon Bennett Cup race was run, Curtiss personally took the racer into the air for the first time; it was a report later verified by Navy Captain Washington Chambers who had been ordered by the Navy to observe the Belmont tournament. "A new model Curtiss machine attracted much interest," Chambers said. "Unfortunately it left the ground for the first time after the cup race." A *Philadelphia Inquirer* story seems to indicate that the flight was far from successful. "Mr. Curtiss also brought out an un-flown machine, his famous single surface biplane with an awning over the aviator," wrote the reporter. "He spent the afternoon in manicuring it and getting it ready for use—apparently as a mantel ornament in his Hammondsport home." Except for a photograph of Gene sitting on the experimental racer and another with Mabel watching nearby, images of the single surface design are difficult to find.[11]

For Gene and the rest of the Curtiss team, their performance during the entire Belmont meet was second rate at best. True, they were facing bad weather, more powerful engines, more experienced pilots, and their biplane's basic design was getting old, but the real problem was the legal struggle with the Wright brothers. "There was a chasm between the Wrights and the Curtiss crowd, which the Brooklyn Bridge could not span," wrote a reporter. It's likely that Curtiss had finally realized that the real reason the brothers were getting $25,000 from the Aero Club was so they would not interfere with the Belmont tournament; in effect, it was a bribe, indirectly confirming the validity of the Wrights' patent infringement claim. Curtiss also likely heard the rumor that said the Wrights expected to receive the first $15,000 of any profit made by the Belmont tournament. If that were the case, a good performance from the Curtiss team would only attract more paying customers and that would mean the Curtiss men would be making even more money for the Wrights. Curtiss must have agreed with his old exhibition pilot, Charles Hamilton, who said the Belmont aviators had been duped. "It looks as if all of us," Hamilton said, "including the Curtiss group and the rest, have been unwittingly made parties to a tacit acknowledgement of the Wrights claims." Then, just as the meet began, Wilbur Wright announced disturbing news from Germany. "All of our suits for infringement of patent rights have been decided in our favor in the German courts," he said. It meant that no aeroplane could fly in Germany without Wright approval. The brothers were even more confident of ultimate victory in the United States and were pressing their perceived advantage. Hamilton said the Wrights had actually claimed "that they had licensed the Belmont tournament." Already they had begun pressuring promoters of the upcoming Baltimore and San Francisco air shows to either buy a license or face an expensive lawsuit. If the Wrights could decide who, when, and where someone could fly, they would defeat Curtiss without needing a final court decision. Once that was accomplished, they would own a piece of every airplane Curtiss manufactured. That would have been Curtiss' worst fear. So, it is possible that he told his aviators to slow down or perform poorly at Belmont, but perhaps his team was just overmatched. Whatever the reason, the few Belmont flights the Curtiss boys managed to complete, were unspectacular and mediocre at best.[12]

A steady downpour and heavy winds had threatened to postpone opening day of the tournament. Roads a half-mile in every direction were ankle deep in mud and few automobile drivers were willing to challenge the slop. When the first flight was about to begin, only 2,000 shivering spectators were huddling in scattered groups throughout the vast grandstand. Gene was the only Curtiss aviator to challenge the weather that day, but not for long. As he climbed, trying for the hourly altitude prize, his goggles loosened and fell away from his grasp. At 404 feet he had captured the $100 prize, but blinded by the rain, he was forced to land. That $100 was the only prize Gene would win during the entire tournament. When he landed, he stepped stiffly off his machine, shaking with cold. He said he had run into a sleet storm that had covered his aeroplane in ice. With another pair of goggles fastened securely to his head, he took off again. He was barely 200 feet in the air and piercing through the low hanging clouds, when spectators heard a dull thud and saw yellow smoke explode in long streams from Gene's motor. He aimed his lifeless machine toward earth and swooped to a hard and steep landing. He and his mechanics, soaked by the never-ending rain, frantically worked on his motor. It wouldn't start and they pulled the machine back to the hangar.[13]

The embarrassments continued. On the third day, Willard climbed to an unimpressive 629 feet to capture the $50 third place prize in the altitude contest, while Gene only managed 412 feet. Both were soundly beaten by Frenchman Jacques de Lesseps at 5,615 feet and Walter Brookins in his *Baby Wright* at 4,882 feet. Later, while Arch Hoxsey, a Wright flier, sailed on continuously for almost two hours to win the duration contest, Charles Willard, the only Curtiss aviator to compete, could only manage a mere 6 and a half minutes in the air.[14]

When it was over, there was little for Curtiss to cheer about. Of the $63,250 in cash prizes awarded to tournament participants, the Curtiss team captured only

$1,600, of which $1,350 came from Jack McCurdy alone. The Canadian was the only Curtiss aviator to win more than $100 during the entire meet, and $1,000 of that had come from a single event, a second place finish in a race with only one other competitor. The Wright team humiliated Curtiss, winning $17,666 and claiming the new world's altitude record—9,714 feet, set by Ralph Johnstone.[15]

Not everything had been bleak at Belmont. Mabel provided some comic relief with her first solo flight. Much like the time Gene had taken his first flight back in Oregon, Mabel was sitting alone in the pilot's seat while the mechanics were working. The phit-phit-phit of the propeller cut through the mist, gradually spinning faster and faster until the biplane suddenly pulled away and took to the air. Before mechanics could recapture it, pull it back to the ground, climb aboard, and shut down the engine, "Mrs. Ely was taken on a small circuit of the field at a distance of some ten feet above the ground." As it had been with Gene, no one would say whether it was an accident, an intentional joke, or something Mabel had secretly arranged with the mechanics. But when questioned, Mabel managed to sound innocent enough. "Gracious," she said, "what a temptation it was when I was in there all alone." She was enticed by the thought that a simple pull on the wheel would take her up. "It was the hardest job of my life to keep my hands off it," she said. "Just think of being that close to something you desire so much." She knew if she touched it, Gene would never again let her get into his machine alone. "So I kept my hands off," she said. With an innocent look, she explained that the aeroplane had just rolled into a channel of water on the field and, "well you know—just skipped across it. I know the wheels couldn't have been an inch off the ground, but Gene said I went up." Mabel, "the pretty little wife," had become a favorite with the support crew. They respected how she never hesitated to support and defend her husband, and how proud she was of him. She had a humorously firm control of everything Gene did or wanted to do, but she also knew how to play the helpless female when necessary. The crew never tired of teasing her. Time after time, they would wait for Gene to leave the ground and, once he was high in the sky, the crew would choose someone to look up, point, and say something like, "That's Bud Mars up there—isn't it?" Mabel never seemed to catch on to the joke. "It is not!" she would defiantly shout. "It is Mr. Ely."[16]

The Curtiss team certainly had no reason to hang around and celebrate. With the disappointing tournament finally over, the first machines to leave Belmont Park belonged to Gene Ely and Charles Willard. They left in a hurry and both men declined to make any comment to reporters. Curtiss explained later that he and his men couldn't linger long enough to attend a banquet that evening with the Wrights, or any of the other aviators, as they "had to pack up right away and leave for Baltimore." Actually, only Willard and Gene were scheduled in Baltimore. McCurdy and Mars were continuing south for a quick exhibition in Norfolk, Virginia. By leaving that night, before the other aviators, the Curtiss men hoped to avoid a strike of railroad express drivers that had begun just as the Belmont tournament was ending. As the strike slowly spread throughout Manhattan, a complete Teamsters Union shutdown of the entire metropolitan area seemed only a few hours away. The next morning, while other aviators were scrambling to find a way to get their aeroplanes hauled to a railroad depot and loaded onto a train, Gene, Willard, and their biplanes were already in Baltimore.[17]

# { 24 }

# A Little Man with an Aero-Eye and the Plucky Little Woman Beside Him

Arriving at the Baltimore railroad depot early the next morning, Gene and Mabel registered at the Belvedere Hotel and then hurried to the aviation field at Halethorpe, six miles southwest of the city. Five years earlier there had been talk of building a racetrack on the field, but nothing came of it. Located at the junction of the Pennsylvania and the Baltimore & Ohio railroads, the vast, flat field seemed ideal for some sort of public venue. Covered by a few trees, some scrub brush, and several tons of tomatoes and pumpkins planted in the spring by an ambitious farmer, the 40-acre field was leveled, plowed, and rolled smooth by two giant rollers early in October. When Gene arrived on the field, his mechanics, Jimmy Henning, "Doc" Wildman, and Frank Taylor, were already assembling his machine. Gene went on an inspection tour of the field with Colonel Joyce, chairman of the local aviation committee. They were followed closely by a swarm of newsmen with pads and pencils in hand. Whenever Gene or the Colonel spoke, their words echoed in the scratching sounds of a dozen pencils. While not usually very talkative, Gene quickly became a favorite with the scribes. It wasn't that Willard wouldn't talk to the press—he would, but he never said very much. "He talks in words, not sentences," said a reporter. "He is as sparing of his words as he is of his smiles." So, by default, Gene became the center of attention, and it probably didn't hurt that his "young and pretty wife," was nearly always beside him and always ready to chat.[1]

After a walk and short drive around the field, Gene said that except for the infield, where spectators would be parking their automobiles, he thought the course was acceptable and safe. "An excellent course," he said. "I have never seen it surpassed." However, he warned Chairman Joyce that Aero Club of America rules "positively stated that no automobiles could stand on the infield" and that if they remained, he wouldn't fly. Aviators needed the space, he said, especially in case of emergency. "If there should be any accident or a sudden descent, the manbirds would not want to fall onto an automobile or onto the heads of spectators." Colonel Joyce told Gene he didn't care what the rules of the Aero Club were—the cars would remain parked in the infield. For a few minutes, it looked as if the aerial exhibition might be in jeopardy, but after a brief private conversation, in which Gene told Joyce that all of the soon-to-arrive aviators would also refuse to fly if the cars remained, Joyce relented.[2]

Followed by the press corps, Gene returned to his hangar where mechanics were making final preparations on his biplane. Reporters began to ask more questions that would help them size up this sailor of the air. "Mr. Ely is a typical young American," said one. "He is full of enthusiasm and believes the science of flying will, within a few years, displace many other modes of travel." Physically, wrote another, Gene was "tall and slim, with a smooth shaven face—quite boyish in appearance." Another saw "a very little man with an aero-eye," which the reporter explained was "sort of squint." They asked Gene when he began to fly. "It was about a year ago in Portland, Oregon," he said. "At that time I was in the automobile business. I was fascinated with the idea of flying through space and it was only a short time after this that I was flying in a Curtiss machine. It is the greatest sport in the world. Were I French, I would describe it as they do—*se divine*." While Gene rambled into a technical explanation of how to factor the wind when computing an aeroplane's speed, one reporter took notice of Mabel, "the petite enthusiast." "She is," he said, "small, scarcely reaching to her husband's shoulder." Mabel turned on her charm and convinced the reporter that she had flown many times. Ever her husband's best press agent, Mabel was always willing to exaggerate. "I love to fly with Mr. Ely," she said, "for I have confidence in his driving. I don't know that I would fly with anyone else at the wheel, but I have often been up with him."[3]

Because only four aviators had managed to get to Baltimore for the meeting's opening day, officials cancelled the scheduled aviation competitions and said any flights made that day would not be eligible for prizes. But the 10,000 people who had come to see men fly that day were not disappointed. "The battle of the air kings," was nothing less than "an astounding exhibition of aviators at play," read the headlines. The starting bomb exploded and the clattering sound of "a thousand dishpans, tumbling about," erupted from the Curtiss hangar. Willard was first out. He shook hands with Glenn Curtiss, climbed aboard, throttled the engine, and watched as hats blew away from a few too close and too curious heads. He thrust his thumb into the air, the mechanics let go, and the unmuffled biplane rattled down the field. Willard's machine reared back at a steep angle and shot for the clouds. His legs were tense, his arms steered with a nervous energy, and his eyes stared straight ahead. At 500 feet, he circled back and when he was in front of the grandstand, he briefly dipped the craft down as if bowing before a queen, and then turned it back toward the sky. Just below the clouds, at 2,500 feet, he circled the field for ten minutes. Gene was already in the air. Fifty feet above the ground, at 60 miles an hour, he was on his second circuit of the tall, red and white canvas-covered pylons that marked the air racing course. On the ground, a mechanic saw a sliver of something fluttering down from Gene's aircraft and signaled him to land immediately. As Gene's plane touched down, the fascinated crowd cheered and 500 automobile drivers, all sitting in their cars, simultaneously pressed their horns, blaring out their appreciation.[4]

The English flier, Radley, in his Bleriot monoplane, bareheaded and with a cigarette dangling from his lips, was up and off to challenge Willard. He steadily climbed, but after nearly ten minutes in the misty air, he could only reach 1,600 feet. On the ground, Drexel, the American who had lived "so long in England that his manners are English and his speech is like that of his adopted country," walked toward his Bleriot machine, ready to join in the altitude duel. "Going to break the record?" someone shouted. "Good gracious, nooooo," said Drexel. "Just a bit of a spin." Fifteen minutes later, he had topped 3,100 feet.

Ten minutes after Gene landed, he was back in the air again. "This thin, slight man with the cheerful face and the low voice has something lurking inside that makes him almost superhuman in the air," said a reporter. Gene was out for speed and at 60 miles an hour and again at 60 feet, his left wing tip barely whispered past the pylons as he circled the course. He opened the throttle and his motor roared. Almost in unison, several hundred spectators shouted, "Look at that!" while others just gasped. He circled the mile course five times in 5 minutes, 32 seconds, and then began his glide to earth. The overmatched police had no way of stopping the mob that swarmed across the field. But shouts of "Good boy!" and "You're a wonder!" seemed to have no effect on Gene who only smiled as he walked to his hangar. There Glenn Curtiss was waiting to pat him on the back. Gene complained that trees at the far end of the field had impeded his flight and had cost him some speed. The trees were chopped down within hours.[5]

Later in the afternoon, Gene was flying at about 1,000 feet when his engine suddenly went silent. Some in the crowd panicked. "What's going on?" "What's the matter?" Curtiss looked up and tried to smile. He knew what Gene was doing—"The Glide." For a moment, the machine seemed to stick in the air, but then its nose tilted over into a dive. Gene was racing toward earth with ever increasing speed. Time stood still as the crowd waited for the inevitable end to this "terrible descent," but, just at that moment when they expected to see him smashed to his death, Gene pulled on his wheel and glided to a safe landing. There were twelve flights that afternoon, but none more spectacular or terrifying than Gene's glide. A newspaper editor asked him to write a story and tell how he accomplished the "Ely Glide."[6]

"The first man to glide did it because his motor stopped," wrote Gene. "That was an accidental glide and done only to save the man's life. An aviator would much rather be sailing through the air," he said, reminding his readers that intentional glides were dangerous. "When a man wants to glide in an airship," Gene said, "he should take out about a million dollars in life insurance, because his fall is worth that much as an advertisement for the insurance company." To begin the glide he circled the field just to see how the aeroplane was flying and to check out his motor. "You may need the engine badly before you make a landing," he said. He said he gained altitude in small stages of 100 feet at a time and warned amateurs not to climb in one continuous ascent. "Experience has shown me that it won't work—the oil will give out." The crucial moment came when he reached a high altitude and decided that it was time to glide. "I stop to look down. It is just a fifth of a mile on a straight drop to the field below. I am just 2,000 feet away from the place on the field where I want to land." He sees the crowd looking up. "I know every man who sees me start downward expects to help pick up my bones," he said. He turns off his motor, pushes on his steering wheel, and over he goes. "I am bending at an angle." Only the aeroplane's wings keep him from falling like a brick. "They hold their own, and me," he said. "It takes about 30 seconds to make the trip and every tick of the watch is like the beat of a dewdrop on a thirsty blade of grass. I feel my blood tingling and the air rushes by me." When he lands, he's amused to hear the crowds cheer. "I wonder," he wrote, "why people think flying is so much a matter of amazement." Finally, Gene revealed his personal secret for a successful glide. "Have a wife on the field when you start," he said. "Don't kiss her goodbye or you'll fail sure enough. That is the way Fate treats you. Just look at her gently, and if she is the right kind, she will smile. That's enough. Put your grip on the wheel and let her go."[7]

Mabel had spent that first day near the American hangar surrounded by reporters and sitting in a touring automobile with Lena Curtiss. Not content with one copy of the *Baltimore Sun* newspaper, she was slowly paging through two issues of the evening edition, looking for photographs and stories about Gene for her scrapbook and, according to one reporter, "almost literally devouring the accounts of the meet." Reporters asked if either of the ladies had ever flown. "Mr. Curtiss does not care for me to go up," Lena Curtiss said. Mabel said she had only been up a couple of times, never more than 150 feet, mind you, and she was never afraid. The reporters were impressed at how the women's "experienced eyes" followed every move of the machines in the air. They noted that Mabel was a Californian who spoke with "many Western colloquialisms." When "a program seller could not understand her when she said 'two bits,' instead of a quarter," a reporter wrote that she "was much amused" by the man. While Lena and Mabel answered questions, the reporters were taking notes on what the women were wearing. Mrs. Curtiss had chosen a long, brown velvet dress, trimmed in brown satin, and worn under a short fur coat, topped with a flowing, brown lace veil. Covering her head was a glossy gold turban, highlighted in brown brocade. Mabel was dressed more simply in a warm, but heavy, black and white serge dress, matched with a black and white satin scarf, and on her head a black satin turban.[8]

Even the aviators were not immune to the fashion report. Both Willard and Gene were dressed head to toe in heavy brown leather flying suits worn over their street clothes. For extra warmth, they added thigh-length brown leather coats, the kind worn by automobile chauffeurs. A racecar driver could just as easily have been found wearing their goggles and leather headgear. Radley, the Englishman, flew without headgear and let his blonde hair blow freely in the wind. His jumpsuit was dark blue, as was Drexel's, the American, who was always trying to follow the English style. With his tight fitting helmet that squeezed the sides of his chubby face, some reporters couldn't resist comparing Drexel to the Man in the Moon.[9]

Although Glenn Curtiss had already said he probably wouldn't fly, almost everyone hoped he'd change his mind. "The great reason that will keep me from flying is my wife," Curtiss said. "I have promised her that I will make no more exhibition flights and I like to keep my word." He said he would like to fly at Baltimore, but if he did, it would be nearly impossible for him to refuse to fly anywhere else. "Officials of other meets may say that they will not sign up my men unless I also promise to fly," he said. He was asked what he thought of Frenchman Hubert Latham's proposed 20-mile flight over the rooftops of Baltimore for a $5,000 prize offered by the *Sun* newspaper. "Did you see those foolish boys today," he asked, "flying all over the country, several miles away from the course? If anything bad happened, they could not have landed anywhere." Latham's flight, he said, would "be dangerous in the extreme, but not impossible," and although it would require a man "of cool daring," if anyone could succeed, it would be Latham. Gene wasn't as confident as his boss "In the first place," he said, "an aviator must have some proper place to land, and there is none near enough to Baltimore. I doubt whether Mr. Latham will be able to make his machine travel such a distance. However, you never can tell what these men will do."[10]

Near noon on November 7, Latham was off in his 50 horsepower Antoinette monoplane. He followed the Patapsco River to Chesapeake Bay, flew northeast to Fort McHenry, then west across the harbor to downtown Baltimore. He circled the Sun Building, continued on to Druid Hill Park in the west and, on his way back to the aviation field, took a detour over Ross Winans' house. Winans, a wealthy invalid, had offered Latham $500 to circle the Winan home, so the bedridden man could see an aeroplane fly from his bedroom window. Latham surprised everyone, completing the 25-mile roundtrip, nonstop, in 42 minutes and claiming the $5,000 prize.[11]

An overly optimistic weather forecast for the aviation meet's second day, predicted "clear and cool weather, with practically no wind." But, by the time the forecast reached the field, it was already raining steadily and hard. Arriving at their hangars early in the morning, the mechanics and aviators waded through knee-deep puddles of water and mud, and once inside their tents, huddled around a fire, waiting for competition to begin. "This certainly is awful," Latham said, while sitting near his two aeroplanes. "Here we come to Halethorpe and expect to find it nice and clear and the weather is as bad as it was at Belmont Park." By early afternoon, the day was a washout and the disgusted aviators returned to their Baltimore hotels.[12]

While Gene stood by Mabel in the hotel lobby, a reporter asked him why it was impossible to fly in the rain. He took a puff on his cigarette. "Well," Gene said, "rain causes mud. There is a great danger of skidding, both in landing and getting away in the mud." He said rain and dampness sometimes caused the wing coverings to shrink, and because of the shrinkage, they might possibly break away. "Last of all," he said, "it is awfully uncomfortable to be up in the air and have a hard rain beating in your face. I must say, the stronger the sun shines, the better I like it."[13]

The rusty autumn leaves were still on the trees that evening when the northwest wind began to spit a few icy flakes. The hypothetical clear skies had turned to blizzard. At 10 p.m. Lawrence Wheatley, an Army hospital corpsman assigned to observe the aviation meet, rushed out of his tent as it collapsed. "It was snowing like mad," he said, "and the wind—I think it must have been blowing fully 40 miles an hour." He and his fellow corpsman, James Wall, saw the foreign aviator's hangar tent fall under the weight of snow. "I saw the European tent go partly over," Wheatley said, "and then I knew that the situation was hopeless." They ran to the American hangar and saw that it was already covered in three feet of snow. "In the darkness we could see the big piece of canvas swaying in the wind and then there was a crack like a pistol shot." The men tried to tighten loose ropes and pound down holding stakes that had pulled out of the ground. "While we were doing this there was a sudden roar of the wind, the snow blinded me for a moment, and then there was a crash and the entire hanger settled to the ground." They tried to inspect the damage, but it was too dark. "We had only two lanterns with us," he said, "and could not determine whether the poles in coming down had hurt the machines or not." They had. The foreign machines were only slightly damaged, but the Curtiss biplanes were split and broken into pieces. First, Willard telegraphed to Norfolk asking for a replacement, but found none were available, not even the Curtiss *Hudson Flyer* that was to be flown by Bud Mars. He sent a wire to Curtiss who had returned to New York, and told him of the damage that had been done. "I told Mr. Curtiss that as the meet would continue, Ely and myself wanted two more machines shipped to us from the factory. One of the machines will probably arrive here on Sunday evening or early Monday morning," he told reporters, "and I wouldn't be surprised if the other one did not follow it immediately." Their damaged biplanes were sent back to the factory for repair, but Gene said he thought it was hopeless, that his machine was a total loss. The pole that had smashed through both of its wings, had also buried them in the ground. The uprights had snapped and the fractured motor had been thrown several feet away. "The damage done to our machines is about $10,000," Willard said, "and they will never be fit to use again until after they have been in the factory for some time."[14]

Gene said he was discouraged, but he was trying to be cheerful. "Gee," he said. "That was my pet, and I wouldn't have had this happen for any amount of money." He said he expected to have a brand new aeroplane to fly within three days. "Of course, no one could forestall the storm," he told reporters. "It came and that is all there is to it.... What is the use of kicking over our broken machines like a cat over spilt milk? The thing is done and it can't be helped."[15]

The aviation meet was postponed over the weekend while workers put the field back into flying shape. Aviators and mechanics were forced to linger around the hotel lobby like monkeys in a zoo, chattering with each other, answering reporter's questions, and smoking through it all. "To be a successful aviator" wrote a reporter, "it seems one must smoke at least one cigarette each minute." Radley always had a smoke dangling from his lip and Latham was forever sucking on a 5-inch long amber cigarette holder with a hand rolled cigarette always in its proper place. Neither man cared if it were Egyptian or Turkish tobacco, smoke was smoke. Bud Mars, who had come up from Norfolk after making some flights before the bad weather hit, said his doctor had told him that smoking was harmful to his health. "I have a tobacco heart and that I must not smoke," he told a reporter, between puffs. Gene, with his customary Egyptian cigarette between his fingers laughed, and said, "Well, that's a pretty fat cigarette you're puffing at now." Mars explained that he was smoking specially ordered tobacco. "When the doctor told me I must quit smoking I got some of this stuff, which I am told is only 7 percent tobacco, and started to roll my own cigarettes. At first I smoked them because I thought they would disgust me, but I have become rather fond of them."[16]

One of the reporters asked Gene whether he thought women could or even should fly. His thoughts turned immediately to Mabel. "Mrs. Ely, while not exactly an expert with a machine, knows how to control one and often takes flights alone," he said. "She enjoys the sport immensely, but of course, she does not fly in public. She has smashed a few planes," he said with a chuckle, "but she has the nerve of the family for all that."[17]

Mabel was chatting with Radley's manager, Reggie Hope, who said he thought most aviators had a pet name that they liked to call themselves. "Radley calls himself Sunny Jim," he said. Mabel told him that Willard liked to be known as the Daredevil. "What does your husband call himself for short?" Hope asked. "Why, King of the

Ozone," Mabel said. "That sounds like a Turkish bath," Hope said. "I can almost see him peddling about in soap."[18]

No one said much to the dejected Curtiss mechanics who sat quietly for hours beside the elevator in the Belvedere Hotel. "Poor fellows," Mabel said, as she and Gene walked past them on their way to a downtown shopping trip. "They haven't a thing to do and they sit around like stranded passengers from a shipwreck."[19]

Two days after asking for another biplane, Gene's replacement arrived from the Hammondsport factory and Willard's machine followed the next morning. "I'll be right there when the bomb goes off, and you can depend on that," Gene said. "So will my partner, Willard, and both of us will do some flying." Gene and Willard were expected to try out their new machines when the aviation meet restarted on Monday, but only Willard managed a few minutes in the air. Gene's aircraft wasn't ready until the next day, but even then, Mabel kept him from flying. Only three of the foreign aviators dared challenge the winds that blew steadily at near 30 miles an hour. Willard said he wasn't insane enough to commit suicide, but Gene, impatient to fly, paced around inside his hangar, closely followed by Mabel. He begged her, but she said no.[20]

The next day was nearly ideal for flying, but Gene was still concerned with the variable winds. He didn't want to take any chances with his new aeroplane until he had thoroughly tested it. Mabel agreed. He would be "flying in a new machine about which he knew nothing," she said. Gene tried to stay patient. He stood around for a while watching the other aviators fly, and twirling a cane. He restlessly wandered in and out and around the hangars. Finally, both agreed it would be safe and Gene put on his flying leathers. As he climbed onto the biplane, Mabel told him to, "Go on up, Gene, and stay up." Someone nearby hadn't quite been able to hear and asked, "Did you tell him goodbye?" "Of course I didn't," Mabel said with a smile. "I never say anything like that to him. I merely told him to go up, and stay up." Up in the air now, Gene had barely made one circuit of the course before he realized something was wrong. Mabel, with her "mechanical eye," had seen it too. When he tried to steer to the left, the tail refused to move. A reporter saw concern on Mabel's face. "Come down, Darl," she muttered, "the machine is not correctly balanced. There's something wrong with the tail." She was among the first to reach Gene after he landed safely. "There is something wrong with the tail of the machine," she told him. "Yes," Gene said, "I found that there is a little knot in the wire, which controls the steering gear." The reporter was amazed that Mabel knew how the machine should behave and also knew the instant when something went wrong. He asked her why she had called Gene, "Darl." She blushed for a moment. "It's the abbreviation for darling," she said. The next day, Gene entered the hangar and walked straight to a group of reporters. "Look here," he said, uncomfortably, "I'll stand for anything, but being called Darl." Mabel was standing near the reporter who had written about her secret nickname. "He doesn't like Darl," she whispered, "except when no one else is around."[21]

Gene and Willard flew occasionally, but were still having trouble controlling their machines. Willard's motor was erratic and Gene was having some sort of problem with his seat. "Both machines are said to be out of balance," a reporter said, adding that the two airmen who were stuck on the ground, would walk to the end of the hangars, look up, and admire the flying of the other aviators. With no good news coming from his mechanics and yearning to fly, Gene told friends that he had made a deal to fly in Radley's Bleriot. "No you won't," lectured Mabel. "When you fly in a Bleriot it will be one of your own, but you shall not fly in Mr. Radley's!" Gene said he'd rather break up someone else's machine than his own. "Yes," agreed Mabel, "that's just what you would do. You'd break the machine." The Boss had spoken and he did not fly the Bleriot.[22]

As the meet was about to end, Mabel was bursting to tell her latest secret. From the day they arrived she had been nagging Gene to take her up as a passenger. To her surprise, he had finally relented. Gene had whispered his promise in her ear, but had also made her vow not to tell anyone. "Oh, how can I promise that?" she said. "I feel just like shouting it from the top of the hangar, but I'll try to keep it." But she didn't. "I'm simply crazy to go up again," she told the president of the Aero Club and, from there, the story spread. By the next morning her secret was headline news. "MRS. ELY—AVIATOR. Daring Little Woman Expects To Fly Saturday." When Saturday came, it was windy, and the "plucky little woman," was disappointed again, but not as much as Gene. "I am getting tired of staying on the ground," he said "and I am going up, even if the wind is blowing 100 miles an hour." But Mabel, as usual, still had her own iron in this fire. "Gene, you cannot go up, and, that is all there is to it. I think a husband in the hangar is worth several in a hospital." Once again, she lay down the law and Gene did not fly.[23]

Back at the hotel, the aviators prepared to move on. Standing at the desk as Gene checked out, Latham, the Frenchman, with his perfect British accent was curious. "What is this I hear about your flying on a battleship?" he asked. "Why, yes, it is true," Gene said. "I am going to try next Monday, off the coast near Norfolk." Latham, the hero who had completed the nonstop flight over Baltimore, told Gene he thought flying from a ship would be a "wonderful" achievement. "I have only 50 feet to start in," Gene said. "But the question is," Latham said with a laugh, "is how much of a drop?" Gene said he would be about 48 feet above the water when he started. When he reached the end of the ship, he would swoop downward, and just before hitting the water, he would turn back up again. "Are you not afraid of getting a dunking? I suppose you can float?" said Latham. "Yes," Gene said, "and so does my machine."

"You Americans," said Latham. "You certainly have some very original ways of flying."

# { 25 }

# "He flew off with the greatest ease"

Timing is everything. The difference between first place and also-ran can be as little as a week, a day, or a second. For Gene Ely to reach his historic moment, the weather had to be bad, a mechanic unusually careless, and a deskbound Navy captain had to discover how well an aeroplane could fly.

In 1907, a global arms race was underway. Navies were building larger ships, armies fired bigger guns, and a few military minds were trying to figure out what an aeroplane could do. In the United States, the Army and Navy had little interest in fighting a war from the sky. An aeroplane seemed to be nothing more than a big boy's toy. That began to change when the Wright brothers took a biplane to Europe and began negotiating with French, German, and other European governments. "Consider," said an embarrassed American military man, "the first successful aeroplane was the product of American brains. It seems almost criminal that the Army and Navy should be unable to advance in the science, on account of a lack of funds." That December, the War Department finally solicited bids for a military version of a heavier-than-air flying machine. When the Wright brothers successfully bid $25,000 to build a two-man aircraft, there was little surprise. The real shock came on its demonstration flight in September 1908. Orville Wright was flying Army Lieutenant Thomas Selfridge as a passenger on the bid-winning aeroplane when a propeller broke free and the plane tumbled to the ground. Wright survived, but 26-year-old Selfridge became the first person to die in a powered airplane crash. The Army might have stopped right there and given up, but instead, they pressed on with their aviation experiments.[1]

The Navy; however, was still stuck in the water and would have to be dragged into the air. Although there were a few Navy men who thought the aeroplane might have some value, most agreed it could never be an offensive weapon. "It will be years before we will have to worry about them in warfare," said one naval officer. The consensus said that aeroplanes were too flimsy to fight. "The flying machine of fiction may be a very formidable monster, but the real thing is feeble enough," wrote one expert. "It is evident," said a reporter, "that the naval experts do not believe that the flying machine, in its present stage of development, has made obsolete and useless the World's navies." The reporter wondered if the Navy experts were really convinced that aeroplanes would "never dare to put to sea" or ever be able to "hover menacingly over" ships rapidly being built by Great Brittan, Spain, Argentina, Japan, and, most ominously, Germany. Apparently, until the end of 1910, that's precisely what the Navy experts thought.[2]

On October 21, 1910, Captain Washington Irving Chambers received orders to personally observe the aviation meet at Belmont Park and note "everything that will be of use in the study of aviation and its influence upon the problems of naval warfare." A month earlier, he took on a newly created position as the one naval officer who would monitor aviation progress in the country and review the Navy's growing aviation correspondence. As aviation exhibitions had become more successful, so many letters began flooding into the Navy Department that the Secretary of the Navy demanded that someone be assigned to take care of them. Chambers was an unlikely choice. He knew absolutely nothing about aviation, not even Navy dirigibles, but something had to be done with all those letters and Chambers was a reliable sailor. In his typical tenacious approach to his assignments, Chambers began an aviation crash course. He read everything he could find, studied the physics of flight, and quickly became not only the Navy's aviation expert, but also one of the world's biggest advocates for naval aviation. "I desire to place myself on record," he said, "as positively assured of the importance of the aeroplane in future naval warfare."[3]

Son of a Kingston, New York shoemaker with family ties to the earliest Dutch settlement of the state, Chambers was born an only child in 1856. His siblings, a brother and two sisters, had all died before he was born, none of them living to their eighth birthday. In June 1876, Chambers graduated from the Naval Academy at Annapolis, 28th in his class of 42. Over the years, he published a number of reports detailing his assignments, most notably his participation as an engineer in the Nicaraguan survey expedition of 1885 that drew the route of a proposed canal between the Caribbean Sea and Pacific Ocean. After years of slowly climbing the ranks, he finally was promoted to Captain in December 1908 and after a brief stint commanding the battleship *Louisiana*, was ordered to Washington, D.C. where he would push the Navy into the air.[4]

They "ordered me, against my protest, to special duty at the Navy Department," Chambers said, "which they considered of greater importance than sea service. During this slim duty, I seized the opportunity to investigate the practicability of aviation for Navy use, and against much skepticism and many more formidable obstacles, I succeeded in starting the work, which met with such success."[5]

While Chambers completed his observations at Belmont Park and then received orders to continue his work at Halethorpe, *The World* newspaper came up with a new scheme that had never been tried before, a scheme certain to tempt Glenn Curtiss. "It was suggested to me by the *New York World*," said Curtiss, "to launch an aeroplane from the deck of a ship at sea and have it fly back to shore carrying messages." *The World* management announced the plan on November 2, 1910. They secured an agreement with the Hamburg-American Line to build a launching platform on the bow of the company's *Kaiserin Auguste Victoria*, an ocean liner that was scheduled to return to Germany on the following Saturday. Curtiss picked Jack McCurdy to make the flight. "The plan was to take McCurdy and the aeroplane fifty miles out to sea on the outward voyage from New York," Curtiss said, "and then launch them from the platform." United States Postmaster General Frank Hitchcock gave McCurdy permission to carry an official waterproof mailbag filled with letters and postcards prepared by the ship's passengers. His only requirements were that the mails "have no intrinsic value" and that letter writers had to be told the mail would be carried by aeroplane.[6]

There was much more riding on this experiment than just one mail delivery. No one had ever flown an aeroplane from the deck of a ship and if the flight proved feasible, *The World* newspaper would get the publicity it was seeking, the Hamburg-American Line would begin equipping their new ships for regular aeroplane service, and the U.S. Navy would finally see that there was some value in an aeroplane. "It is a most interesting experiment," said Commander George Day, commanding officer of the Navy's Seventh Torpedo Division. "If successful it will cause a lot of thinking in naval circles the world over. I hope that it will be made and that it will be my good fortune to witness it."[7]

Day was in charge of the two destroyers that had been ordered to follow and observe McCurdy's flight, and if necessary, rescue the aviator should he fall. It would be the Navy's only participation in the event. However, one day before McCurdy's flight, President Taft overruled the destroyer escort order and refused to allow Navy participation. The official statement said, "Other requests for use of naval vessels in aeroplane trials have been refused and President Taft does not wish to be inconsistent." "The Navy Department is chiefly embarrassed in its aviation experiments by the lack of funds," explained a reporter. "The department has not one cent which it can spend in experimental or practical aeronautics."[8]

The cancellation of the destroyers was welcome news to some, but worrisome to those who had heard rumors that said German naval officers were secretly behind McCurdy's flight. One unnamed seaman spoke for many when he said, "The spectacle of naval vessels of the United States following the German flag and acting in the capacity of tenders would not be a patriotic sight."[9]

Taft had probably based his decision on advice from his Secretary of the Navy, George Meyer, who believed an aeroplane's use as a fighting machine, especially against the U.S. Navy, was "doubtful" at best. "In the first place," he said, "the aviator would have to go up several thousand feet to be out of rifle range and the size of the bomb he would be able to carry would not seriously hurt any battleship or fort…. No, I do not believe that these aeroplanes are going to put our battle fleet out of commission."[10]

Behind the scenes, John Barry Ryan, son of Thomas F. Ryan, of one of the wealthiest men in America, was working to change Meyer's mind. Ryan had recently created the Aeronautical Reserve, a civilian organization of enthusiasts who believed in promoting private aviation as a means of enhancing national defense. Ryan thought McCurdy's attempt was of "tremendous importance" and would "demonstrate the usefulness of the aeroplane as an auxiliary to the Navy." His opinions mattered because he had the money and the influential friends to back them up. "I was speaking to Secretary Meyer of the Navy not long ago about such a test," Ryan said. "He was deeply interested in having it attempted." Meyer was being careful. He was still resisting, but he wasn't about to upset Ryan, a man of significant political influence.[11]

The storm that had wiped out the start of the Halethorpe aviation exhibition and destroyed Gene's biplane, had swept up the Atlantic coast. It swirled 35 mile an hour winds and nonstop rain through the Hoboken, New Jersey docks, where the

*Kaiserin Auguste Victoria* steamship was preparing to cast off. The night before departure, German carpenters, drenched by rain and pelted by hail, had worked feverishly to finish the 80-foot-long wooden platform where McCurdy was to begin his flight. When it was obvious that the bad weather wouldn't let up, Curtiss and McCurdy decided to postpone the flight until the end of the month, when McCurdy would return from an exhibition in North Carolina. "Nothing but a gale will prevent the flight," Curtiss said. Disappointed passengers sailed away with the *Kaiserin Auguste Victoria*, the wooden platform still attached to her bow.[12]

Captain Chambers and John Barry Ryan were still trying to convince Navy officials to conduct their own experiment, but until Secretary Meyer returned from his inspection tour of the nation's naval stations and shipyards, no one in the department was willing to take a chance.

In Halethorpe, with the rain still coming down and Gene waiting for a machine to replace the one smashed by the storm, he and Mabel went out on a Baltimore shopping expedition. When they returned, they met Captain Chambers in the hotel lobby. Gene and Chambers had met at Belmont while the captain was talking with aviators and inspecting their aeroplanes. Chambers liked Gene's analytical approach to flying and his unassuming manner. They settled into the lobby sofas and began talking about McCurdy's upcoming flight. Chambers told Gene that he was trying to get the Navy to let him arrange a similar flight from a Navy ship, something he thought might get his superiors interested in aeroplanes. He had written to Wilbur Wright asking if he was willing to furnish a pilot, but Wright had refused to meet him and said the flight would be too risky. As he listened, Gene was getting excited. "I've wanted to do that for some time," he said. A hesitant yet hopeful Chambers told Gene that he didn't have an aeroplane or even a ship yet, and had no money to pay him. Gene said he didn't care. If Chambers could get a ship, Gene promised to supply an aeroplane and make the flight without charging a fee. He said he wanted the publicity and thought it was the patriotic thing to do. Besides, in discussions with other aviators, he had always argued that flying from a ship should be easy. Chambers worried what Curtiss would say. Would he let Gene fly? Did Gene need to get permission? "Not necessary," Gene said. "I make my own dates under our contract." Chambers couldn't believe his ears, but just to be sure, he still wanted to talk it over with Curtiss. Curtiss said that he thought the plan was too dangerous and if it failed, it would hurt the company's aeroplane sales, but he said he wouldn't stand in Gene's way. Later, Mabel would say she thought Curtiss was actually afraid that a successful flight might overshadow his current experiments, trying to build a hydroaeroplane that could land and take off from the water. As far as Gene was concerned, no matter what, he was going to fly that plane for Chambers. He accompanied Chambers to Washington D.C. for a meeting with the Secretary of the Navy.[13]

Secretary Meyer had just returned from his two-month-long, 10,000-mile inspection tour of naval facilities. After meeting with the president and a few of his department subordinates, Meyer planned to catch an afternoon train to his home state of Massachusetts, where he would vote in the midterm election and then return to Washington. Perhaps to his surprise, before he could leave, he found Captain Chambers and Gene Ely waiting for him. Chambers pressed Meyer to provide funding for the experimental flight and relied on Gene's technical expertise to show that a shipboard takeoff was feasible. Like most Navy men of the day, Meyer believed that battleships were the true backbone of the fleet and that aeroplanes were little more than carnival toys. There was no money and he was not about to sanction the flight, and that was final. Gene was respectful, but amazed at how little the secretary knew about aviation. Mabel said Gene remembered the secretary as a cold and arrogant man.[14]

Only one person could possibly change Meyer's mind, and Chambers knew who he was. A few days later, John Barry Ryan arrived in Washington ready to push the right buttons. Meyer had been a politician almost all of his life, starting in the Boston common council at age 30, moving on through the state legislature to appointments as ambassador to Italy and Russia, and prior to his Navy position, he had been the country's Postmaster General. He was already planning another political run after he left the cabinet, and of course, upsetting the influential Ryan was the last thing he wanted to do. He told Ryan there was no money available for experiments, but Ryan knew how to play that game. If Meyer would provide the ship, Ryan said he would use his own money to finance the operation. Meyer was trapped. He checked with the president who relented and gave his approval, and then Meyer ordered Assistant Secretary Winthrop to find an available ship and get it to Norfolk as quickly as possible.[15]

Things were also moving more quickly at the Hoboken docks. With word spreading that Gene would soon be attempting to fly off a Navy ship, there was now a race to see who would be first off of their platform. McCurdy's end of the month was scratched and the experiment was moved forward to Saturday, November 12. German carpenters hurriedly completed another platform on the liner *Pennsylvania*, the next available Hamburg-American Line steamship. Strong winds were hampering McCurdy's North Carolina flights and just for insurance, Curtiss ordered Bud Mars to leave the Norfolk exhibition and come to New Jersey where he might have to take McCurdy's place. When McCurdy couldn't make it, Mars was given his chance at history.[16]

Five minutes before the *Pennsylvania* was about to sail, the experiment was already over. With the biplane in position and lashed down to the deck, Curtiss and Mars decided to make one more check of the motor. As soon as the propeller began to spin, there was a loud snap and two pieces of wood flew out at great speed, one striking a sailor near his knee. Curtiss shouted to Mars to stop the engine immediately. "An oil can, carelessly left on one of the wings by a mechanic," Curtiss said, "was knocked off and fell into the whirling propeller." There was no spare propeller in the city and Curtiss said it was impossible to get a replacement before the ship had to sail. Mars was disgusted. "I would have been quite willing to go to Europe on the *Pennsylvania* and try the flight on my return," he told reporters. For Hamburg-American Line officials the experiment was over. They announced that no more attempts would be made. Winter weather was about to get worse, they said, and by the time summer came again, the experiment "will have been proved possible, or impossible, once and for all, from the deck of a warship." Gene Ely had inherited his moment of history.[17]

On November 9, Assistant Secretary Winthrop ordered the armored scout cruiser U.S.S. *Birmingham* sent to the Norfolk Shipyard and a temporary wooden platform installed on her bow. In charge of the work was Navy Constructor William McEntee who was working his men hard in what appears to be a race to get Gene into the air Saturday morning, hours before the attempt in Hoboken was scheduled. "IT WILL BE READY," McEntee said in a telegram to Captain Chambers, "and in case

Ely can get his machine here Friday, everything will be ready for a flight on Saturday, provided of course that the weather permits." Gene was still at Halethorpe where, because of all the weather delays, the air meet had been extended through that Saturday, so the earliest he could fly was Monday, November 14. That was fine with McEntee. It gave him a chance to go home and spend the weekend with his family.[18]

Except for a chance for Gene to talk to reporters, Halethorpe on Saturday was a waste of time. The winds were too strong and Mabel's eagerly anticipated flight as a passenger with Gene was canceled. Elegantly dressed in a seal coat, a fuzzy, white polar cap trimmed in blue, and wearing a corsage of violets, her favorite flower, Mabel jealously stood guard over her husband. It seemed that all the young ladies of Baltimore were crowding into the tent hangars trying to get aviator autographs.[19]

When reporters began asking about the Birmingham experiment, Mabel was first to answer. "I can't say just exactly when he will go up, for at this time of the year there are many different weather conditions that are unfavorable for flying. Mr. Ely will take his machine on the cruiser *Birmingham* and will put to sea on Monday afternoon. I will go along on another government vessel, and we will try to keep up with Gene as he flies over the water." Mabel said she had no fear for his safety. "I have personally seen to it that he will be properly equipped with life buoys, and he will wear them! The machine will have pontoons attached, so that in case anything should happen to it, it will float until it and Mr. Ely can be rescued. I have the greatest confidence in Mr. Ely and am sure that he will complete the flight all right."[20]

Reporters wondered if Mabel always spoke for Gene. In his modest way, Gene said yes, he always allowed her to do most of the family talking. "What she says is all right, so there you are," he said. "The flight in itself is nothing, and the mere object of it is to show to the government that a Curtiss machine can get away from the deck of a steamer without any difficulty. It will then be seen that the aeroplane is the best thing for scout work and dispatch carrying."[21]

The Halethorpe exhibition ended with a whimper and the airmen began to scamper away. Bolts were loosened, wires unfastened and rudders taken off. As each part was removed, it was carefully packed into its snug-fitting travel case. The aviators were packing too. Hoxsey was off to Denver where he would watch Ralph Johnstone fall to his death from a Spiral Death Glide. Willard and Radley were on their way to the Pacific Coast. De Lesseps, Drexel, and Latham planned to enjoy Baltimore for a couple of days and then leave for New York and then to Europe. Gene and Mabel boarded the evening steamer for an overnight cruise to Norfolk.[22]

Except for Gene's "favorite 4-cylinder motor," which was sent to Norfolk that night, his biplane and other equipment were put on a train for Raleigh, North Carolina, where, after completing the *Birmingham* experiment, he would fly an exhibition with McCurdy.[23]

Gene got permission from Curtiss to fly the prizewinning *Hudson Flyer* that was still at the Jamestown Racetrack in Virginia. Bud Mars had been flying it ever since Curtiss had finished his flight over Lake Erie in August. The plane had been damaged in the early November rainstorm and Mars had left it at the racetrack when he was called away to Hoboken. At the racetrack, located north of Norfolk, on the Sewell Point peninsula between Hampton Roads and Willoughby Bay, now part of the Norfolk Naval Station, mechanics Jimmy Henning and perhaps "Doc" Wildman and Frank

Taylor, were making repairs on the aircraft. Some sources say mechanic Frank Callan was also there, but Callan didn't join Gene's team until June of the following year. Once repairs were made, aluminum pontoons were attached under the wings and the *Flyer* was loaded onto a tugboat. Carried up the Elizabeth River to the Norfolk Navy Shipyard, it was hoisted aboard the *Birmingham* and placed at the farthest end of the wooden platform. The platform was 83 feet long, 24 feet wide, and built on the ship's bow with a downward slope of 5 degrees. Gene would have to be quick. From the front of the biplane's wheels to the end of the platform was a mere 57 feet.[24]

On Monday morning, November 14, Orson Harrington who was still Gene's head mechanic, arrived with Gene's 4-cylinder motor. There had been no time to test it, so once the team had it installed, and while the *Birmingham* steamed out onto the Hampton Roads, Gene eased the tension in his mind by inspecting the motor and poring over every inch of his machine. The original idea was to steam out as far as 50 miles onto Chesapeake Bay, turn the ship into the wind, and then attempt a takeoff and flight up the Elizabeth River back to the Norfolk Navy Yard. But the weather was bad. An observer on the edge of Chesapeake Bay reported fog so thick he couldn't see further than four miles, and though he should have been able to see the *Birmingham* by now, he couldn't. The clouds were dark and swirling and by 1:30 that afternoon, the light mist was turning to intermittent rain squalls speckled with hail. White caps licked at *Birmingham*'s hull as it sliced through the water. "The thickness of the weather rendered landmarks so obscure," Chambers said, "that the ship was anchored off Old Point Comfort to await a possible improvement." There at the entrance to Chesapeake Bay, within sight of the wharf at Fort Monroe, the Navy had dropped anchor and decided to wait out the rain. But Gene wasn't about to wait. It was now or never.[25]

Standing beside the biplane, he leaned in close to Orson Harrington's ear and told him his plan, then, he climbed into the seat on the *Flyer*'s wing. He started the engine and the ship's wireless operator tapped out a message for the escort ships. "2:43 p.m.— Engine of Ely's airship, *Hudson Flyer*, making so much noise that it is almost impossible to send wireless messages. The engine is going rapidly, apparently being tested out. Actual start not yet been made, but Ely is likely to fly away at any minute." The tail of the aeroplane was almost level with the ships bridge and the backwash from Gene's propeller blinded the helmsman standing at the wheel. If by chance the ship ever moved again, which to Gene seemed unlikely, there was no way the helmsman could steer an accurate course. Gene idled the engine for a moment, expecting the ship to begin its full-speed reverse that would give him an added boost of power as he ran down the runway, but the unmoving anchor was still 180 feet deep in the muddy water. The rain let up for just a moment, but black clouds were in the distance and another squall was coming on fast. Visibility was already down to less than a half-mile. Gene turned back to see what was happening on the bridge. Nothing! The Navy was too slow. If he didn't go now, he'd never go. "I was anxious to complete the test without waiting any longer for more auspicious conditions," he said later. He throttled his engine to full speed and gave Harrington the thumbs up. Harrington hesitated and Gene pushed his thumb even higher into the air and shook his fist. Harrington shouted to the sailors who were helping hold back the machine and all at once they let go.[26]

"He flew off with the greatest ease," Curtiss said. At 55 miles an hour, Gene roared straight down the centerline painted on the wooden platform, his tail clearing the

While flying off the U.S.S. *Birmingham* near Norfolk, Virginia, on November 14, 1910, and becoming the first man to ever leave a ship by airplane, Eugene Ely didn't pull up fast enough. His wheels hit the water and kicked up a spray that covered his goggles so that he was temporarily blinded. He somehow regained control and swooped up and away from the brown water until he was well over 150 feet in the air (Naval History and Heritage Command #NH 77601).

end of the runway by twenty feet. "Ely just gone," tapped the Navy wireless operator. "Ely off OK at 3:17:21 p.m." To gain more speed as he cleared the ship, Gene tilted down toward the sea, 40 feet below, he pulled back on the lever controlling his front elevator, but it was too late. Pontoons dug into the bay and sprayed his goggles with salt water. Temporarily blinded, he tried to clear his goggles with his glove hand. Fortunately, he still had enough speed to recover control, swooping up and away from the brown water, until he was well over 150 feet in the air. "I made a slight miscalculation in handling the control lever, which caused the machine to hit water," Gene said. "It has been more than a month since I used this machine and the control lever was slightly longer than I am accustomed to." Apparently, the lever had been lengthened for Bud Mars, but no one had thought to readjust it to fit Gene's longer arms.[27]

After four minutes in the air, uncomfortably cold and wet, Gene was lost. "By the time I had succeeded in drying my goggles, I lost track of the landmarks by which I intended to guide my flight over Norfolk to the navy yard," he said. "Anyway, it was a very dark day." He tried to get his bearings. Through the fog and rain, he could barely see a sandy strip of beach known as Willoughby Spit, directly across the water from Old Point Comfort. "I found myself making for a beach and choosing a convenient spot near the Hampton Roads Yacht Club." He made it sound so simple. "I felt that it would be better to land than to attempt to continue the flight," he said. It was a smart move. He didn't know at the time that when he had left the *Birmingham* and hit the water, the driving edges of his propeller tips had splintered, and one edge looked as if it had been cut off by a saw. He landed in the soft sand and until he saw the damage to his propellers, he thought he might try to takeoff and continue his flight. "I landed with no trouble," he said. "Had it been necessary I could have started the machine up again and tried to fly back to where I came from." He said he was not fond of the water, but he was proud that he overcame his fears "long enough to accomplish my purpose."[28]

The next day, Gene and Mabel, with reporters surrounding them, were bathing in their newfound worldwide fame. "I was absolutely satisfied with the test. We did what we went after," Gene said. They asked how far he had flown. He wasn't sure, but said it probably was between two and four miles. "We had no object in making distance, as everybody knows an aeroplane can fly," he said. "What we wanted to do was to show that the machine could be launched from the deck of a battleship. I feel confident that I demonstrated to the navy the practicability of aeroplanes as auxiliaries in war times. I feel proud also of having the distinction of being the first aviator to accomplish such a feat."[29]

Success for Gene was also success for the politically astute Secretary of the Navy George Meyer, and he was quick to bask in the reflected glory by sending a letter of congratulations that he conveniently supplied to the press. "I thank you for the services you have performed, gratuitously, in demonstrating the possibility of using an aeroplane from a ship," Meyer said. "So far as is known, you are the first aviator in the world to have accomplished this feat and I congratulate you.... Your achievement, which was actuated by purely zealous and patriotic motives, is much appreciated. A copy of this letter will be sent to the headquarters of the United States Aeronautical Reserve." Judging by that last line, more than just congratulating Gene, Meyer was trying to impress the head of the Aeronautical Reserve, John Barry Ryan.[30]

Several hours after his flight, Gene discovered there was even more glory to come from his experiment. Ryan arrived on the scene and personally gave Gene a $500 prize and commissioned him as a lieutenant in the Reserve. All he asked, Ryan said, was to keep the badly damaged propeller from the *Hudson Flyer*. It would join other unique aeronautical articles displayed in the Reserve's Fifth Avenue New York City headquarters. Ryan put the propeller in the back of his automobile, drove to Washington, and after meeting with government officials, carried his trophy all the way back to New York on the Pennsylvania Railroad's *Congressional Limited*.[31]

Now that Gene had flown from a ship, reporters and Navy officials wondered if it might also be possible to land that same aeroplane back on a ship. "I am confident that I could have flown back to the ship and landed on the runway with the same ease and safety as I experienced in leaving," Gene said. Then, thinking aloud, he began to work out some scenarios. "If, for instance," he said, "the vessel were backing up at full speed, the aviator could fly his machine onto the bow of the cruiser and the backward motion of the vessel would permit the aeroplane to make a safe landing." His other idea was a fast moving ship with the pilot gradually slowing his aeroplane until the airship could gently settle onto the launching platform. Either way, "It will be an interesting experiment," he said, "and I should like to try it." In two months, he'd have his chance.[32]

# { 26 }

# Balmy Southern Skies

Like a flock of white pelicans chilled by northern snow, the Curtiss boys were migrating south for the winter.

A day after the *Birmingham* flight, Gene and Mabel were on the train for North Carolina, where seven years earlier the Wright brothers had made the world's first powered airplane flight. After the brothers left, North Carolina had only seen three more attempts to fly; the first was by the Wrights who returned to the beach in 1908 to conduct experiments with their new biplane. The next came two days before Gene's world famous flight from the *Birmingham*, when Jack McCurdy, who had missed his chance at beating Gene off a ship, struggled for two minutes against a stiff wind in Charlotte before he crashed. The third attempt came at almost the same hour that Gene was landing on Willoughby Spit. Three Wilmington businessmen had built an aluminum-framed aeroplane, managed to get it into the air for a few short hops of five feet or less, before retiring the plane forever.[1]

Friendly rivals, Gene and McCurdy were scheduled to perform at the state fairgrounds in Raleigh. McCurdy got there first and was invited to speak to a group of college students at North Carolina A. & M. Few people could match McCurdy's aeronautical expertise. He had been there at the beginning, experimenting with Curtiss and Alexander Graham Bell, designing, building, and flying his own aeroplane. For 30 minutes, to a fascinated audience, he explained the science of aviation and traced the development of the "flying machine from infancy to the present day." The talk seemed to impress college administrators so much that they decided to give all students an afternoon away from classes so they could attend the flying exhibition.[2]

Gene and McCurdy's two days of effort would be overshadowed by an accident following an automobile race. Although Harvey Woolcott, manager of a local automobile dealership, only finished second in that race, Florence, his young wife, wanted to celebrate. She begged him to let her drive around the track. Harvey moved over to the passenger seat and held on tight as 24-year-old Florence circled the track at reckless speed. At the quarter-mile turn, after several laps around the track, she lost control, began to skid, broke through the protective fence, and plowed into spectators. "It was the most appalling thing I ever saw," said eyewitness J. R. Young. "Men, women and children tumbled over each other down the steep embankment in their efforts to get out of the way." As the car traveled another 40 feet, Florence Woolcott fainted. Her husband seized the wheel and shut off the power. "The wild machine seemed to literally dash over a bed of human bodies," Young said. The three women who were snagged underneath the car and dragged a short distance, were still alive, but no one thought for long. Ellie Mooneyhan was in critical condition with three broken ribs, a broken leg, and internal injuries. She would somehow survive, as would Alice Castleberry whose shoulders were smashed. Ada Bryant, with a fractured skull, never regained consciousness and died at the hospital the next day. The Woolcotts survived without injury.[3]

A newspaper editorial, titled "Making Us All Ashamed," seems to suggest that after the accident, spectators engaged in some sort of ghoulish souvenir collecting. It compared them to the mob in Denver, Colorado that stripped souvenirs from the dying body of aviator Ralph Johnstone, who, while flying an exhibition two days earlier, had plunged to his death. The Raleigh mob was, said the editorial writer, the same as the "mobs who pull a wooden stake from a still-breathing aviator," adding that the "hideous display" of the local mob was the behavior expected of animals "before civilization began."[4]

With the victims carried away and the crowd settling down, the air show began. Spectators were impressed with Gene's simple flights around the racetrack, but the heaviest applause went to McCurdy, who flew out over the city, circled it a few times, and then returned. The next day McCurdy "took a tumble" from 300 feet, putting his machine out of action. Gene continued with conservative flights, which apparently were long enough and high enough to astonish those who had never seen an aeroplane fly.[5]

With Gene's newfound fame, cities and towns weren't interested in just any old aviator anymore; they wanted Aviator Ely. He had no sooner finished flying off the cruiser *Birmingham* than a Curtiss representative found it easy to get him a last minute booking at Birmingham, Alabama.

Birmingham was proud of its phenomenal growth. The 1910 Federal Census showed a population increase in the previous ten years of nearly 250 percent. To celebrate, the city was combining the annual reunion of the Alabama Confederate Veterans of the Civil War with a celebration they called the "Census Jubilee." Hearing that Gene was nearby, the Jubilee committee decided to put together an air show that would bring thousands of people to town and highlight two days of speeches, parades, dances, and band music.[6]

The first day's excitement came in a race between an automobile and Gene in his biplane. The tires of a large touring car tossed clouds of dust into the air, as the driver pushed his engine to at least 50 miles an hour. High above, Gene's biplane was still far behind. The land machine was going so fast that it seemed impossible that Gene could ever catch up. Suddenly, the biplane swooped down toward the auto, gaining speed every second. The crowd gasped. The driver's head snapped back and forth on a rubber neck, his wide open eyes trying to follow the course of the racetrack, while; at the same time, wondering if the diving aeroplane was about to smash into him. "Taking a terrible chance with death," said a reporter, "Ely flew close in front of the auto, at times almost settling within touching distance of the earth." The cautious driver, expecting the biplane to land in front of him, killed his motor, and rolled to a stop. Gene was so low that spectators could see him laughing as he pulled back on his wheel and began to climb again. The auto driver started over and soon was back at 50 miles an hour. Suddenly, Gene's machine swooped down again, even faster than before, flying inches from the ground and just a few feet in front of the automobile. The terrified driver panicked, shut off his motor again, turned the steering wheel, and this time crouched down in his seat, sure that he was headed into a terrible collision. "Thus it went, Ely flirting with death, enjoying the prank hugely, and keeping the auto driver in a nerve-racking suspense the whole time." They were in the homestretch, Gene still high in the sky and the auto a few feet from victory. Down came the biplane in an Ely Glide, zooming at an unbelievable speed and crossing over the finish line first. Suppressed excitement exploded. Women screamed and waved their handkerchiefs. Men threw up their hats and yelled. "The flying machine skimmed the air like a swallow," said a reporter, "and no one who ever saw it, could ever forget it."[7]

It was a beautiful beginning, but once again it couldn't last. Gene hadn't realized that trouble was waiting for him in Birmingham. It wasn't a crashing biplane or a devastating storm. At Birmingham trouble was a woman, and Connie was her name.

Twenty-five-year-old Connie Sullivan was athletic and beautiful. Born Mary Corner Evans, Connie was the daughter of a Methodist Episcopal minister. She had only

Eugene Ely and his wife, Mabel, pose with Ely's 8-cylinder Curtiss biplane at Birmingham, Alabama, November 21–22, 1910. Later Ely would infuriate Mabel by taking a pretty Southern Belle with him on a flight around the field (*Naval History and Heritage Command #NH 77491*).

lived a few years in Alabama and after her marriage to a mining engineer earlier in the year, she was planning a return to high society in her childhood home of Richmond, Virginia. A tomboy by nature, as a teenager she had coached a championship boys' football team; the players all students in her Sunday school class. She played her first tennis tournament when she was 17 and when it was over, she cried at how poorly the other women had played. She continued her tennis competitions when she returned to Richmond, and for three years in a row, beginning in 1911, she won the women's singles championship at the Old Dominion Tennis Tournament. By then, she had already helped create the Women's Southern Golf Association. Athletics would always be a part of her life, but in 1910, she was the beautiful Southern Belle, oozing Southern charm, and the passenger selected to ride with Gene Ely.[8]

Details of the family confrontation are lost. In an era when newspaper reporters rarely mentioned domestic squabbles committed in public by important people, we are left to our imaginations. Did Connie hold too tightly to Gene as she sat beside him in the air? Did she hug him when they reached the ground? Did she dare kiss him on the cheek and, if so, did Gene smile just a little too much? All we know is what is contained in a single line of an aviation magazine. "Ely carried a woman passenger to the disgust of Mrs. Ely." It's hard to believe that the publically reserved Gene would have done anything to anger Mabel, but someone had done something and Gene was the one who suffered for it. It just wasn't good business to anger The Boss.[9]

Gene probably listened to a scolding all the way to Mobile, Alabama, where he stopped to watch McCurdy and millionaire pilot, Augustus Post, who were flying at the Mobile County Fair. McCurdy had to carry the show as Post was still having trouble getting his low powered, 4-cylinder biplane into the air. Although McCurdy reached as high as 2,000 feet once and occasionally battled the fierce winds to stay aloft for longer periods, there were still mumblings "of considerable discontent expressed over the exhibitions." Apparently, the only excitement to stir the crowd came when McCurdy's engine stopped, his aeroplane somersaulted into the ground, and the crowd thought McCurdy was dead.[10]

Gene's arrival in Mobile at the end of the week put a surge of optimism back into the spectators. Surely, the man who had just flown off a ship could handle these treacherous winds. Although he was just visiting and not scheduled to fly, Gene said he might challenge McCurdy in a ten-mile cross-country aeroplane race as long as the weather cooperated. The weather was ideal the next day, but there wasn't a race. Gene and McCurdy both made two flights that reached an altitude of 1,000 feet. "Their machines, visible from all parts of the city, were the object of curiosity to those who had never before witnessed a flight of a biplane." It was such a good day that even the hapless Post managed five laps of the field before landing. McCurdy and Post stayed over for one more day, while Gene left for Jackson, Mississippi, where he would headline the first aviation meeting held in that state.[11]

Less than two weeks after his *Birmingham* experiment, Gene was already legend, "the hero of the *Birmingham* episode," holding a "rank among the most noted daredevils of the air." Reporters put him "in a class with the ill-fated Ralph Johnstone who met a tragic death at Denver." Like Johnstone, said the reporter, Gene was "a youngster in the flying business, but none has shown more bravery and daring."[12]

Gene promised a high altitude flight in Jackson and without any problems, rose to 1,200 feet above a half-empty grandstand of 500 paying customers and 2,500 freeloaders on the hillside.

Temperatures were dropping, the wind swirling, and a little rain fell overnight, but the next day, summer had suddenly returned. It was warm, the winds had died, and Gene was back at a thousand feet, but no one seemed to care. The crowd was even smaller than the day before and thankfully for Gene, it was time to leave.[13]

On November 30, Gene and Mabel, along with McCurdy, Post, and their mechanics, arrived in New Orleans. Jimmy Ward, a rookie pilot who had made his first professional flight for Curtiss with Gene in Birmingham, had been sent ahead to supervise the preliminary setup at the City Park Racetrack. Because of anti-gambling laws, the track hadn't seen a horserace in nearly two years, but it had been the setting earlier in the year for the state's first air show. Louis Paulhan, the French aviator, had managed a few moderately successful flights at City Park in February, but all his attempts at world records were stymied by wind and rain. The Curtiss team expected to do better. "With four men entered in the races at New Orleans," McCurdy said, "we should have a magnificent meet. All indications point to good weather and that is all we shall need to make the New Orleans folk sit up and take notice." When he learned that Paulhan had attracted 27,000 people to his exhibition, McCurdy made a bold prediction. The Curtiss men would play to as many as 75,000 people. Gene agreed and added that the Curtiss team would outclass Paulhan in every way. "The Curtiss planes are the fastest biplanes built," he said. "Beyond a doubt, the Curtiss is the fastest biplane in the world."[14]

The *New Orleans Item* newspaper began promoting the event by offering a chance to fly as a passenger with one of the aviators. The Curtiss team wasn't consulted first, but the newspaper must have assumed that when the aviators were faced with dozens of applications to fly, perhaps they couldn't refuse. "DO YOU WANT TO FLY?" read the headline. "It's all up to you and the aviators. If the cloud men see no obstacles in the way of taking you on a trip to the clouds, you will be taken—not all of you, of course, but those whose applications are drawn out of the lot." The flight was, they said, a chance "for those discontented inhabitants of Earth who want a peep beyond the clouds."[15]

The response was overwhelming with over 200 people asking for a chance at the flying lottery. "I am 21 years of age," wrote one man, "and as my life is not insured, there is no objection to my flying on the part of any insurance company. Also, as I have my parents' permission to play football, naturally there are no objections on their part to my taking one of the trips." A few applicants, looking for an advantage, tried some humor. "Sir—As my only opportunity to rise in the world will probably be by aeroplane, I would greatly appreciate an opportunity to ride in one."[16]

This was all new for Ward, but he was ready with an answer. "We'll have to wait on the weather," he said. "We don't have much trouble getting up in the air with passengers, but it's the return that we're skeptical about, not so much on account of the danger to ourselves, but in the danger of wrecking our machines." Gene stretched the truth to make his point and said that even though he had taken many passengers on flights, which he hadn't, he had decided that passenger carrying was just too dangerous. "The last time I took up a young lady for a flight," he said, "it cost $250 in repairs to the machine. Another time, while away up in the air, my passenger, a woman, became hysterical and it's a miracle that we managed to get down safely." It almost sounds as if Gene was mostly worried about a potential woman passenger and the dangers of upsetting Mabel, the woman on the ground who didn't like him flying with other females.[17]

Other than a chance at seeing world records broken, the exhibition's biggest draw was expected to be a race between a biplane, piloted by either McCurdy or Gene, and Steve Speer, an automobile racer who had won the Louisiana cross-country road championship. Because he had heard about Gene's tricks during the Birmingham race, Speer refused to race against him. "I would never have a chance with Ely," he said. "I would have no chance with him. He would play with me." But Speer was confident he could beat McCurdy. Apparently, Speer didn't know, or didn't care, that by choosing McCurdy, he was challenging the aviator who had taken 2nd place at Belmont in the International Speed Contest. With McCurdy's ability to make sharp turns around pylons at 75 miles an hour he easily routed Speer's automobile by three-quarters of a mile.[18]

To the locals, nothing but the weather could ruin their aviation party and that didn't seem likely. "December weather in this climate is usually very good," wrote an unconcerned New Orleans reporter. That was good news for the birdmen who had come south looking for a better climate to fly in, but this December they wouldn't see very much of it. On opening day, cold gusty winds ripped across the racetrack, delayed flight attempts, and disappointed the 5,000 people who paid their admission and the 20,000 freeloaders watching from the outside. Ward made the first try with his aeroplane that was no more powerful than the old Wemme biplane that Gene had learned to fly. Into the wind he went, barely fifteen feet in the air, crossing the infield to cheers and applause before he had to give up and land. The spectators, standing and shivering in the cold, let out an audible sigh of disappointment. Gene, "the Big Bear" of the Curtiss aviators, tried next. Mabel, as usual, walked to the aeroplane with Gene, watched him take his seat, and then stepped back. Even with his 60 horsepower engine, Gene did no better than Ward. His mechanics pushed the biplane back to the hangar over the entire length of the infield and the aviators waited there for a calm that never came. "It is certainly unfortunate about the gusty weather," Gene said. "Straightaway flight against, or in the same direction as the wind, would not be dangerous. But our program calls for flights that the paid spectators inside the grounds may witness. So, it would be useless to fly up and away with little chance of turning and coming back again." He said the team was just as disappointed as the crowd was, "possibly more so, because our planes are in perfect condition. Better luck tomorrow."[19]

Even with a one-day extension of the exhibition, luck was fickle and hard to find. Ward climbed to over 4,000 feet, setting an unofficial low-powered aircraft altitude record, but the next day, he lost his motor. An optimistic Augustus Post said the New Orleans atmosphere was perfect for flying. "Why, holy smoke," he said. "It cannot be beaten in the whole world, this atmosphere that you have here, especially for racing and speed purposes.... Give us a fairly quiet day and we will equal some world's records." Post tried, but once again, crashed, smashed his aeroplane to bits, and scared the crowd half to death. Gene never got higher than 1,500 feet before having his own motor trouble, but he rallied in a race to defeat a motorcycle by a half-mile. The troubles continued. Brisk breezes and a rain shower cancelled Gene's head-to-head five-mile race with McCurdy, but Gene, the old automobile racer, thought he had another way to entertain the crowd. He borrowed an automobile and announced he would drive it to a new one-mile record. "He failed," wrote a reporter, without describing the race or giving a final time. That night, mechanics packed Gene's biplane and sent it on to Columbia, South Carolina. Before he left, Gene apologized for the poor showing of the Curtiss team. "We have the machines to make the flights," he said. "It is only because of the nasty puffs of wind, so variable and so extremely dangerous to flying, that we haven't already had half the country looking on."[20]

McCurdy and Ward agreed to stay over in New Orleans one more day, but it was a waste of time. On a day when the normal temperature should have been 56 degrees, the thermometer never rose above 42, and the fierce wind pushed temperatures to near freezing. "Six or seven aviation fans went to City Park race track yesterday," said the newspaper, "laboring under the delusion that the birdmen would get busy in spite of the biting cold." What they saw was McCurdy helping to crate up his aeroplane and send it to South Carolina where he would fly with Gene.[21]

Two days after his takeoff from the *Birmingham*, Gene had another signed contract, this one to appear in Columbia, South Carolina. Although McCurdy would fly with him, it was Gene's growing legend that was the big news. Laced with truth and fiction, the fanciful story in the local newspaper placed the "intrepid skyman" on a high and heroic pedestal. "Eugene B. Ely, although the youngest of the Curtiss aviators, is one of the most daring and successful," it said. He had set nonexistent speed and altitude records. He had "toured the Pacific coast and then sailed across the Pacific with his craft to the flowery land of Japan where he flew before the emperor and his court." When the Curtiss advance man saw the article, he must have been shocked at how McCurdy was totally ignored. He reminded the local editor that McCurdy was a "daring aviator" in his own right, having more flying experience than anyone except Glenn Curtiss or the Wright brothers. The subsequent article accurately and dryly told McCurdy's story, but by mistake, gave McCurdy credit for Gene's Norfolk flight from the *Birmingham*.[22]

Gene and Mabel arrived just before five in the morning and after checking into their hotel, went straight to the fairgrounds to watch the assembly of the aeroplane he would fly in a little over eight hours. Reporters, as usual, were surprised at how the various parts of a biplane didn't look "anything like a flier." It was, they said, "largely a pile of odd shaped sticks packed in several enormous trunks. The two wings, made of rubberized silk, have been stretched across some of the sticks and placed on upright supporters. The whole affair was braced by a maze of crisscrossing wires, each one a little cable twisted from the finest steel."[23]

That afternoon, Gene made headlines in three absolutely perfect flights—"LIKE GREAT WHITE HERON MAN-MADE BIRD CUT AIR." The crowd was small, but enthusiastic. "The secret was," said a reporter, "that Ely really flew." While an anxious Mabel watched with a reporter at her side, Gene climbed to a thousand feet and then floated to earth in the Ely Glide. "My nerves are getting used to it," Mabel said, "although, I still feel a little shaky when Gene is up in the air." Following the glide, there was a race with an automobile and once again, Gene toyed with the driver's courage, flying twenty feet over his head and ultimately winning the race.[24]

McCurdy arrived from New Orleans the next morning and while he and Gene were conferring in the Curtiss hangar, the county sheriff walked in and served Gene with a lawsuit, naming Gene, Glenn Curtiss, and the Curtiss Exhibition Company as defendants. The Georgia-Carolina Fair Association was claiming $15,000 in damages because Gene had not honored a contract to appear at the association's Georgia fair in early November. An armed guard of deputies surrounded the aeroplanes with orders that the machines not be allowed to move. Gene argued that the biplanes were his personal property and didn't belong to the Curtiss Company. He said he hadn't been able to appear at the Georgia fair because his aeroplane had been damaged by the storm in Baltimore. He argued that an inability to fly because of weather conditions was part of his contract with the association. As a favor to the Columbia promoters, the Fair Association's representative agreed to allow the exhibition to continue, but said until the aviators posted a $1,000 bond, the aeroplanes could not leave South Carolina. Gene posted the bond under protest, threatening to file a counter suit against the association when he reached Georgia in about a week. He didn't file, but the $15,000 claim continued until it was finally resolved in 1912 for $305.[25]

With four flights from Gene and a spiral glide by McCurdy, the crowd was suffering from "aviator neck, a new ailment for which the aeroplane is responsible." The flights were "nifty" and the crowd was pleased. Down to the last few moments of his last flight, it looked as if Gene would have a flawless exhibition. Then, at 100 feet, making his final turn in another race with an automobile, his machine suddenly nose-dived into a cornfield just outside the track. Cool and collected, he stepped off the shattered wing and began to pull cornstalks out of his support wires. He could hear Mabel shouting his name as she ran across the infield toward him. "A piston seized a cylinder and ripped its head off," Gene told her. Then gave her a hug and a laugh. "The wind was very choppy aloft, more so than yesterday," he said. "It seems that all Columbia breezes have the choppy habit." Surrounded by a crowd of people who had come to his aid, Gene calmly waited for his mechanics to arrive.[26]

While Gene waited for repairs to the biplane, McCurdy returned to New Orleans where Ward was waiting to continue their delayed exhibition. The three aviators would reunite in Atlanta in just a few days for the next stop on their southern expeditions. While still in Columbia, Gene received a booking from a Curtiss agent to perform immediately after the Atlanta meet at a one-day aviation show in Dillon, South Carolina, just over 100 miles northeast of Columbia. He also received an invitation to visit the town of Sumter, east of Columbia, where three aeroplane inventors wanted him to see their airplane and to look over their plans to build a manufacturing plant, an aviation school, and airfield on the site. Gene refused to tell reporters if he would join the new company, or if he was representing Curtiss, but he did say that he was enthusiastic over the possibilities of the inventors' company. "The inventors have a good thing," he said in his typical reserved manner. Mabel took the opportunity to elaborate. She said aviators needed flat fields not far from a town. "When you get the two in close proximity, the situation is ideal." In the coming months, Gene would be trying to get an aviation job away from day-to-day flying and somewhere on the ground. Perhaps his Sumter trip was the beginning of that search, or perhaps he was working as an agent for Curtiss, and it's even possible that he was simply enjoying his VIP status and living in his newfound fame.[27]

The aviators' dreams of easy money under balmy skies and southern sun were idealized delusions. Yes, the weather was warmer here in the south than in the snowy north, but intrepid sky pilots were still battling a heavy dose of Mother Nature's wind, rain, and cold. In Atlanta, just ten days before Christmas, the wind blew too hard, temperatures barely reached 44 degrees, and the crowds were small. Ward attempted two quick flights, but finally gave up. Dangerous wind currents continued for the next two days. McCurdy won his race with an automobile, while Gene lost one and won another. As Ward swerved dangerously in the breeze for 36 minutes, McCurdy could only run for twenty minutes, and Gene had an accident. At 100 feet, loose screws gave way and a small tube attached to his carburetor flew away and into his whirling, wooden propeller. The propeller splintered and Gene calmly made another emergency landing.[28]

A few days later, in Dillon, South Carolina, a crowd of over 3,000 people, three times the population of the town, came to the racetrack to see Gene Ely fly. Instead, in the severe winds and shivering they found that McCurdy had replaced him. Although his two flights were each less than three minutes in length, the crowd applauded and "many were heard to say that they were pleased that he flew with the ease and gracefulness of a bird." McCurdy pocketed his usual fee of $1,000 and left for Norfolk.

"Ely was to have come to Dillon," explained the newspaper, "but he was unexpectedly called away to California."[29]

{ 27 }

## Scientific Suicide

Just six weeks after Glenn Curtiss told Baltimore reporters that he would never fly exhibitions again, he was back in the air with Bud Mars and Charles Willard. He had come to Fresno, California to test the newest version of his aeroplane. Reporters speculated that Curtiss was bringing the "single surface" monoplane that he had planned to race at Belmont, but Curtiss said no, he was bringing a biplane. "Are you building a new type of machine?" he was asked. "Not exactly a new type," he said. "It preserves all the pronounced features of the old Curtiss type, but of course, there are several improvements." The biggest improvement was the addition of an 80 horsepower engine. Curtiss was sure it would be fast. "I believe it will have a speed of 100 miles an hour," he said. After two test flights, clocked 80 miles an hour, Curtiss announced he would attempt to break the world speed record for a five-mile flight. Never rising above twenty feet, he kept his promise and captured the record, circling the one-mile course five times in five minutes and five seconds. With the exhibition over, the Curtiss team packed their machines and headed for Los Angeles where Gene had been ordered to meet them.[1]

Undoubtedly, his flight from the *Birmingham* had earned Gene enough attention to secure an invitation to the second Los Angeles International Aviation Exhibition, but perhaps it was Captain Chambers who got Gene that unexpected call to California. Chambers had received a request from organizers of the upcoming San Francisco aviation exhibition, asking him "to designate a warship to serve as a landing place for an aeroplane." But the question was still, who would make that first landing? The organizers had requested Gene, but even in early December, Curtiss still wasn't sure if it would be one of his men or one of the Wright fliers, but he was confident that any of his aviators would be able to "do the trick." By mid–December, the Navy had let Chambers know that they wanted Gene for the landing, agreeing with the San Francisco organizers that because Gene had "successfully risen in an aeroplane from the deck of the *Birmingham*," he deserved an opportunity "for demonstrating the converse proposition." Curtiss decided that Gene would land with the new biplane, a machine that Gene had never flown. To get him the experience he needed, Curtiss entered Gene in the Dominguez air meet and ordered him to leave for Los Angeles immediately after completing his last flight in Atlanta.[2]

In Los Angeles, the aviation committee was trying to locate Thomas Baldwin, the one-time balloonist who now flew Curtiss aeroplanes. When contract negotiations with Baldwin broke down, rumor said he had gone up the coast to Santa Barbara to arrange his own exhibition. The committee sent a telegram offering more money if he would appear in Los Angeles, but the telegraph company couldn't find him. Four days before Christmas, Baldwin's secret was revealed. He and Bud Mars had boarded a ship in San Francisco, bound for Hawaii and a world aviation tour. Curtiss was furious because Mars had signed a $5,000 contract to appear in San Francisco's exhibition in just a few weeks. "Mars, whom I taught to fly," Curtiss said, "will no longer be connected with the Curtiss camp, but will act as an independent aviator, making his own contracts, and keeping them—let us hope." Embarrassed that Mars would "jump his contract," Curtiss said he would fulfill every contract promise he had made, to show that aviators were men of their word. "More daring and possibly more competent men," he said, "will do all the things Mars promised to do."[3]

Mars said he couldn't afford to miss the engagement in Honolulu. His agent, former Curtiss aviator and Gene's early aviation companion, Whipple Hall, had arranged a $50,000 contract for flights all around the world. Mars said he was sure that if he had cancelled the tour, some other aviators would have secured the exhibitions and taken away his money. In a few months, Bud Mars would become the first man to actually fly an aeroplane in Japan, finally ending the promotional lie that gave that honor to Gene and others.[4]

As the second Dominguez air meet began, Curtiss once again received good news. Before he had left for California, he had sent a letter to the Navy Department, offering free flight instruction for one or more naval officers as a way of adapting the aeroplane to military service. "I asked for and received no remuneration whatsoever for this service," he said. "I considered it an honor to be able to tender my services in this connection." The Navy responded quickly, ordering Lieutenant Theodore Ellyson to Los Angeles from his duty station at the Newport News Naval Station in Virginia. He was to report to Glenn Curtiss and learn to fly. Ellyson would later say he was honored to work with Curtiss. "It was not Curtiss, the genius and inventor, whom we knew," he said. "It was 'G. H.,' a comrade and chum, who made us feel that we were all working together, and that our ideas and advice were really of some value."[5]

Some of the world's most famous professional aviators and five local amateurs were getting their aeroplanes ready at Dominguez Field. Two European aviators gave the exhibition its credibility as an international contest and each flew monoplanes. Radley, the English flier who held the world's one-mile speed record, came with his Bleriot, while Latham, the Frenchman, would guide his slow but steady Antoinette.

Latham was one of the first to arrive and he came with his typical good humor. "I came to Los Angeles with no particular desire to fly," he said. "What I desire is to indulge in some of the good hunting and fishing, which I understand is to be found hereabouts." Members of the Bolsa Chica Gun Club were happy to oblige. The club was an upscale and exclusive group that owned over 3,400 acres of the finest birding preserve property in Southern California. They asked Latham if he would like to try an aerial duck hunt. Latham said yes. While sitting on his monoplane getting ready to take off, he "asked for his gun as nonchalantly as the backwoodsman would call for his rifle from the seat of a farm wagon." He slung the strap of the double barrel shotgun over his shoulder and took off toward the ocean. With his first shot, he downed a Bluebill that fell to the ground and was retrieved by club members. That night, Latham hosted a dinner at his hotel with his duck served as the main course. A few days later, the county game warden warned Latham not to go hunting in the air again unless he obtained an out-of-state hunting license.[6]

Latham wasn't the only airman to draw headlines from his preliminary aviation work. Through pelting rain, fog that obscured nearly all landmarks, and ice on his engine, Charles Willard in a Curtiss biplane made California's first intercity flight by soaring 55 miles from Los Angeles to Pasadena and back. "It was cold up there," Willard said, "but the trip was fine."[7]

Beginning an aviation meet on Christmas Eve and continuing through the New Year, probably wasn't a good idea. To be sure, the spectators who made their way to opening day at Dominguez were boisterous, but they didn't come close to filling even half of the available seats. Understandably, on Christmas Day, there were only 10,000 paid admissions, but on the day after Christmas, the crowd soared to a record 75,000, "the greatest ever assembled to see man attempt the conquest of the air." Twenty-thousand were in the grandstand and, crowding along the fence, eight to ten deep in both directions, spectators circled halfway around the course. It looked as though the record crowds would keep on coming, but they didn't.[8]

The weather was good, the winds relatively light, and the flying outstanding, but the meet would be a financial failure. Attendance was less than half of what it was at the previous exhibition in January. "The affair was arranged in the interests of charity," wrote a reporter, "but the people of Los Angeles did not rise to the occasion."[9]

Gene and Mabel arrived at Union Station in Los Angeles just one day before the Dominguez meet would begin. Curtiss had told him about the new biplane and Gene was anxious to try it. "The new machine is a dandy and I am going to do my best to become a habitual winner," Gene said. "California is my native state, you know, and I want to do my best while here." Although Gene would be flying the new aeroplane, he wasn't Curtiss' first choice to race her. The plan had been to let Bud Mars fly in the speed contests with the beefed up, 80 horsepower machine, and let Gene get ready for his shipboard landing by flying with a lower powered engine. But now that Mars was on his way to Honolulu, it was Gene in the racing seat with his hands on the wheel.[10]

The new Curtiss biplane incorporated many new features designed to streamline the craft for speed and stability. The front, double surface elevator, used to gain or lose altitude, was now a single surface, and the connections between the steering wheel and the elevator were simplified and shortened. Wing surfaces were double covered and enclosed the structural ribs and beams. To improve the lift capability of the machine, pivoting wingtip ailerons, that added precision to turns, were moved out from between the two wings and mounted behind the rear wing struts. The most recognizable feature of the new machine was the triangular-shaped front vertical stabilizing fin.[11]

At Dominguez, Curtiss was the first to put the new biplane into competition with an impromptu race against Phil Parmelee in a *Baby Wright*. He waited until Parmelee was in the air and circling the course before beginning his pursuit. "Look, look," the shouts came from the grandstand, "They're racing!" At least a half-mile behind, Curtiss pushed his motor to its limits and, as they approached in front of the long grandstand, Parmelee and Curtiss were now nose to nose. Parmelee raced his engine and, for a fraction of a second, he took the lead over a determined Curtiss who was "tearing through the air like a demon." He shot past the *Baby* and the crowd went crazy. Parmelee had been clocked at 54 miles an hour and Curtiss, unofficially at over 60, and this with the 50 horsepower engine. Without even using the 80 horsepower motor, he had dealt the enemy camp a defeat in their first head-to-head competition and the Curtiss team was jubilant. "He vanquished the Wright aviators," said a reporter, "and so far as one day's results are concerned, convinced the spectators that he has the speediest biplane yet constructed." Speediest biplane, perhaps, but it was Radley in his monoplane who took the five-mile speed race at the end of the day by three seconds, and except for one race, would win every speed event he flew in for the rest of the meet."[12]

Gene, "the fast jockey of the Curtiss stable," placed second to Radley twice and in every race against Parmelee, except for the one he didn't finish because of engine trouble, Gene defeated the *Baby Wright* to claim even more bragging rights for the Curtiss team. "This tall, angular challenger of the elements," said a reporter "threw fear to the winds that buffeted him and traveled a 50 mile an hour pace."[13]

Overshadowing everyone at the exhibition and out of sight most of the time was 26-year-old Arch Hoxsey. Hoxsey and Gene had begun learning to fly at about the same time, the difference being that Gene taught himself and Hoxsey learned from Orville Wright. Like Gene, Hoxsey had a fascination with automobiles and because of his mechanical skill had become chauffeur for Charles Gates, son of multimillionaire industrialist, John Warne Gates. Given a six-week vacation in early 1910, Hoxsey had returned to Pasadena, California where, since his father's death nearly twenty years before, he and his widowed mother had lived. Hoxsey had often told Gates that he wanted to be an aviator. "His pockets were always full of aeronautical journals," Gates said. That Hoxsey's vacation coincided with the first Dominguez air meet was probably no accident and likely was his plan all along. After watching Curtiss, Hamilton, and Paulhan fly, he was more enthusiastic than ever and came home to tell his mother that he definitely wanted to fly. "I spent many sleepless nights when he asked my consent to take up aviation," she said. As he drove back to New York City, he purposely stopped in Dayton, Ohio, met the Wright brothers, toured their factory, and told them his aviator dreams. Three days after returning to work in New York City, he received a telegram from the Wrights giving him his chance. Within 24 hours, he was on his way to Birmingham, Alabama, where the Wrights had set up a school for their first two pupils, Hoxsey and Walter Brookins. After completing his first flight at the end of April, Hoxsey rushed to the telegraph office to tell his mother that Orville Wright was his teacher and that he now planned to fly over the 1911 Pasadena Tournament of Roses Parade.[14]

Hoxsey and Brookins began their exhibitions in mid–June with what would become their trademark—attempts at record altitudes. While flying a St. Louis exhibition in October, Hoxsey was approached by former president Theodore Roosevelt who wanted an up-close look at the Wright biplane. "I'd sure like to have you as my passenger," he told Roosevelt. Without a word, the president took off his coat and climbed aboard, his uneasy staff holding their breath. Two laps around the mile and a half course and they landed. "By George, it was fine!" said the president who was rushing to his next appointment. "Hoxsey, you're all right."[15]

Hoxsey was a confident flier, daring and dashing in appearance. He worried more about the cleanliness of his stiff, white collar than the deadly risks he was facing daily. "His dandyism, his smile, and his achievements made him the idol of the crowds." Usually in white pants, he was known as the aviator with the "ice cream trousers." One reporter finally asked him how he kept himself so spotless. Hoxsey said it was habit. "For six years I have not worn overalls when working around an oily motor," he said, "and I can't recall having ever spotted my clothing."[16]

At Dominguez, Hoxsey had only two goals; capture the world altitude record, and end the exhibition by flying over the 1911 Rose Parade, which would march within two blocks of his mother's front door.

On Christmas Eve, the opening day of the Dominguez exhibition, Hoxsey's mother was in the crowd and for the first time about to watch her son fly. Two weeks earlier, Frenchman, Georges Legagneux, had set the altitude record at 10,499 feet and Hoxsey was determined to beat it. "I'll smash that record or something else will smash," he said with a grin. Hundreds of binoculars followed the aviator as he walked toward his machine, tightly wrapped in a fur coat, and pulling his hat down with his gloved hands. As he climbed aboard the double-propeller Wright, the crowd wondered why he was dressed for winter. Even though the temperature was still just shy of 70 degrees, spectators wiped perspiration from their brows and assumed that Hoxsey must also be sweltering. None of them had been two miles above the earth, where aviators shivered against icy wind, their arms and legs stiffening, and their eardrums pounding from the cold and thin air. "Two miles high, one feels the lightness of the atmosphere," Hoxsey said, "but with a good, strong heart and a good pair of lungs, that isn't to be minded." On this first day, Hoxsey made 9,288 feet before he could no longer stand the cold. It was a record for Dominguez and the Pacific Coast, but well short of Hoxsey's goal.[17]

The day after Christmas, dressed in a leather suit, arctic fur, black hood, and a pair of spectacles, Hoxsey brought the altitude record back to the United States. On a day when the wind was gusting to nearly 30 miles an hour, Hoxsey had made up his mind. "If the record of 10,499 feet was to be broken soon." he said, "it would have to be during this meet here in California." He flew out over the ocean for a mile hoping that the biting wind would be warmer and less fierce. It was a slow, hard climb. For two hours and 25 minutes he continued in circles, steadily gaining altitude until he was a mere speck in the sky. "My hands and feet and half my body were numb, but I had no difficulty in operating the machine." When he was confident that he had set a record, he climbed another 200 feet just to be sure. After a final lap for good measure, he came down. "My, but the warm air felt good," he said. "Did you get it?" Brookins asked. Hoxsey was too cold and exhausted to answer. He lay limp in his seat and nodded his head. Officials grabbed the barograph, the brown box that measured how high he had flown. The crowd was silent, all eyes on the man with the box. A snow-white signal flag slid up a pole and flapped in the breeze. "Like a roll of thunder, a mighty cheer went up from the multitude." The record had come home. He had climbed to 11,474 feet, nearly a thousand feet higher than the previous record. In comparison, Parmelee, in his Wright, had topped out at just over 6,500 feet and Gene only managed a meager 600.[18]

The next day, Gene did better; reaching an estimated 2,000 feet, but still came in third to Brookins at 3,200 feet and Hoxsey at 6,800 feet. Hoxsey kept flying high, every day disappearing into the sky with spectators wondering when he would return. While waiting, the announcers amused the crowds with a periodic shout through their gigantic megaphones of, "anyone here seen Hoxsey?"[19]

The Pasadena Rose Parade is never run on Sundays and for 1911 that meant New Year's festivities would begin on Monday, January 2. Hoxsey still had two days to top his altitude record before making his low-level flight over the flowered floats rolling up Colorado Boulevard. "Hoxsey seemed to go almost straight up," said Scott Davis, a visitor from Medford, Oregon. "When a machine gets away up like he was, you can hardly see it—it being like a speck of dirt to the eye." Davis said that it was tiring to keep looking up, so he and his relatives would take turns trying to locate Hoxsey. "He was the only aviator in the bunch who would go clear up out of sight and stay there for an hour or more," he said. A dust storm broke out on the ground and Davis thought that it might have also affected Hoxsey. "No one will ever know what caused him to start down," Davis said. "It had taken him an hour to rise and only about fifteen minutes to come down." The birdman made a graceful spiral glide to about 600 feet when suddenly something went wrong. The machine seemed to hesitate in the air, then turned vertical, nose toward the ground. "The cheer that was waiting to burst from 10,000 throats became a cry," said a reporter. To Davis, the sudden dive looked like a pigeon that had been shot and crippled while flying in the air. From no more than two blocks away, Davis watched the scene unfold. "His machine turned so that it headed vertically downward and the wind seemed to catch it," Davis said. "It shot for the ground." From its accelerating downward lunge, the machine pivoted under and almost tumbled over until Hoxsey's back was facing the earth. Then somersaults began, the biplane turning over and over into a final plunge. "When it crumpled on the hard field there were cries," said a reporter, "cries in which the very soul went up in a moan upon the wind. It is a terrible thing to hear such a cry; it is a breathless gasp, choking a shriek of terror." When they cleared the flattened wreckage from his body, Hoxsey was still in his seat, his hands still on the controls. The motor had crushed his right side and a sprocket from the propeller had smashed into his face. Those who put him into an ambulance said there was a look of horror, desperation, and despair on his face. There were those who wondered if Hoxsey were still alive—but not his fellow aviators. "They understood the miracle of flying, but they had never seen the miracle of a man falling 500 feet in an aeroplane—and living."[20]

"Oh, boys, it's awful," sobbed Brookins. "Don't ask me to talk. I can't talk and know what I am saying." His legs gave way and he fell to his knees and "cried like a child."[21]

Hoxsey was not the only aviator to die that day. Less than six hours earlier, in New Orleans, John Moisant, the man who had won the $10,000 race around the Statue of Liberty at the Belmont exhibition in October, fell 100 feet. He lost control of his machine and as it began to tumble, the strap that held him in his seat snapped. He slipped, lost his grip, and plummeted to his death. Both men had ignored warnings from fellow aviators that the winds were too treacherous. "It's what we aviators call a Swiss cheese atmosphere," Willard said. "The air is full of holes and it is not worth any man's life to attempt to fly." Even before Hoxsey began his deadly flight, he had read an account of Moisant's death in the afternoon edition of the newspaper. Reporters asked him what he thought had caused the accident. "Moisant must have been weary from too much flying," he said. "Poor chap. The strain was too much for him and his strength failed." They asked Hoxsey how much longer he would stay in the business. "I don't want to stay in it any longer than I can help," he said. "I want to get enough money to see my mother comfortably fixed. After that, a little while to get a nest egg for myself, then I shall quit and go into some other business." Hoxsey stood up and walked out of the hangar to his waiting aeroplane. "I won't go very high today," he said, "but the crowd must be entertained." An hour and a half later, he was dead.[22]

"Aviation is fascinating, thrilling, but always perilous," Willard said. "What goes up must come down, and every one of us aviators appreciates that. The moment that our machines leave the ground, we know that sooner or later we are going to fall." He said the best that an aviator could do was to carefully examine his aeroplane before flying, pay attention while in the air, and hope. Even then, "If I stick with aviation it will get me," he said. "It is just a question of time. You might call it scientific suicide."[23]

"If I thought that aviation was only a sensational way of committing suicide, I would not go up," Brookins said. "If the same thought struck me while I was in the air, I would come down in a hurry."[24]

"No," Gene said, "It cannot be called scientific suicide except for the reckless." He defended Hoxsey as a cautious aerial navigator, but said Moisant was a reckless daredevil. "Moisant was the fellow who flirted with death. He did not seem to care what he did in his machine or how he landed." Gene thought Hoxsey had been a victim of "mountain sickness" and was either unconscious or unable to move when he fell. "He made no movement to control his machine during the last 500 feet of his fall," he said, "and appeared to be in a helpless condition, like a man paralyzed." He thought a gust of wind, or a lack of it, had turned Hoxsey's machine toward the ground, but Gene was sure that a lack of oxygen had killed him. "Old balloon men tell me of having to beat their breasts to keep up heart action when they are at great heights in the air," Gene said. "The sudden change from the higher to the lower, or vice versa, acts on the heart and lungs and causes a sort of paralysis." Hoxsey's rapid climb into thin atmosphere had "caused partial paralysis and he was unable to move his limbs and control his machine."

Reporters wondered if Gene might think about giving up aviation. "Once a man becomes an aviator he cannot stop," Gene said. "It gets into the blood.... I guess we will all get it sooner or later. For myself, I have no fear of flying, and have had four close calls when I thought I was gone. If I have to get mine in the air," he said, "I should wish for no better time than after I had just completed some great feat. This was the case with Hoxsey. He had done something real and he will be remembered."[25]

Gloom descended on Dominguez. The aviators made a few feeble flights on the two days following Hoxsey's death, but their hearts weren't in it. With every sharp descent or hint of disaster, the uneasy spectators burst out in horrified shouts and screams. Latham was the only man to keep his craft in the air for more than half an hour and for a while Radley refused to fly. When he finally got into the air, a wind gust nearly turned him over and he landed immediately. "That is the last for me in winds like this," he said. "I am taking no more chances." Gene's short flight ended with a split guy-wire that wrapped around his propeller and broke off a piece of the blade.

He took a sharp angle to the ground and dropped to a hard but safe landing. "I was frightened," he said, "and decided to come down." Out of respect for Hoxsey and his funeral, the last day of the Dominguez meet was canceled.[26]

Hoxsey's day at the Pasadena Tournament of Roses Parade had been planned just the day before he died. He would fly to Pasadena, where the parade committee had prepared a floral aeroplane and mounted it on a special float for Hoxsey to ride on. When the parade was over, he would fly away from the tournament, over Pasadena, and back to Dominguez. Instead, his body lay in a mortuary a few blocks away and the flowery biplane, dedicated to the town's fallen hero, was pulled down the street with an empty seat. Someone suggested that the aeroplane be used as a hearse to carry Hoxsey's body, but his mother said no. "She wanted nothing that would be deemed theatrical in the last rites over her son."[27]

The next morning, fellow aviators, Glenn Curtiss, Phillip Parmelee, Walter Brookins, James Radley, Hubert Latham, Charles Willard, and Gene Ely, escorted Hoxsey's body to the mortuary chapel for a memorial service. The service was limited to friends and family, but outside, thousands of people waited their turn for a last look. It took the line of mourners over an hour to file past the casket.[28]

After the funeral services in Pasadena, Mabel and Gene immediately left for San Francisco. Mabel was coming down with a case of tonsillitis and by the time they checked into the Palace Hotel on Market Street, Mabel was so seriously ill, doctors confined her to her room.[29]

In many ways, Dominguez marked the progress being made in aviation. A year earlier, in Los Angeles, Louis Paulhan had flown less than a mile into the sky, setting the world's altitude record at 4,164 feet. Now, aviators were pushing through 10,000 feet and flying in thin atmosphere over two miles above the ground. Paulhan's record long distance flight of 48 miles in 1 hour 49 minutes, also set at Dominguez the previous January, was eclipsed at the end of the year by Maurice Tabuteau's 363-mile, 7-hour 45-minute, nonstop journey. Improved controls meant better and safer flights and bigger engines meant speed. At 48 miles an hour, Curtiss had been the fastest birdman in the world, but now, the aerial speed demons were pressing hard toward 80. Aeroplanes were better and so were the men who flew them, but still, there was danger.

Thirty-two aviators had fallen to their deaths in 1910. Four were Americans, and of those four, three had flown a Wright biplane. Ralph Johnstone, the first Wright birdman to die, said he believed that no matter how careful an aviator might be, there was always a mysterious fatal force riding with him. He called it, "IT." "IT gets us, sooner or later," he said, "all we men who fly." Hoxsey didn't agree. "Poor Ralph," he had said on the day Johnstone died, "he took chances." Hoxsey was a fatalist who believed that when it was his time to die, he would die, and it wouldn't matter where he was or what he was doing. "We don't stop," he said. "The game goes on just as if nothing had happened." Gene had little to add. "I look upon it as one of the chances that are taken by those in the profession," he said. "Still, I guess we will all get it sooner or later.[30]

In 1911, of 77 aviators who would die, only one was born in Iowa.

{ 28 }

# A Platform for the *Pennsylvania*

Ten Argentinean naval officers were getting their first look at San Francisco from the deck of a United States warship. The armored cruisers *California, Colorado,* and *Pennsylvania*, were dropping anchor a few hundred yards out from the San Francisco docks, at a place traditionally known as "man-of-war row." The ships had sailed from South America, where they had represented the United States at Chile's celebration of that country's 100th year of independence. There, the Argentinean officers had joined the mini fleet for a six-month educational voyage that would give them a chance to observe U.S. naval operations and participate in the Pacific Fleet's annual gun practice off the coast of California. In mid–October 1910, neither they, nor their American counterparts, knew how close they were to witnessing aviation history. But flying machines were far from the crews' thoughts. Now that they had reached San Francisco and would leave for San Diego within two weeks, these 1,400 sailors had but one urgent need, a chance at shore liberty. Within hours, San Francisco's Embarcadero was a mass of navy blue.[1]

This year, fleet artillery practice had been moved from its usual location, off the coast of Santa Barbara, north of Los Angeles, to the waters west of San Diego. Apparently, when Secretary of the Navy Meyer toured the nation's naval facilities that summer, he had visited the Navy's torpedo station in San Diego and had received a very warm welcome from city officials. Not long after he left the city, he ordered the entire exercise moved. In explaining the secretary's apparent snub to Santa Barbara, a disappointed and perhaps jealous local reporter would only say, "The secretary was recently entertained in San Diego."[2]

While the warships' sailed south from San Francisco, three additional cruisers, the *West Virginia, South Dakota,* and *Maryland,* joined them. Artillery target practice would begin when they reached San Diego; however, as a diplomatic courtesy toward two Japanese cruisers that were coming to the West Coast on a training mission, none of the big guns would be fired for three weeks. The U.S. crews would be kept busy with some small caliber firing, monotonous night and day drills, and mock battle maneuvers with the torpedo fleet.[3]

Early in December, after having their guns aligned for accuracy, the fleet sailed 30 miles out from San Diego between Coronado and San Clemente islands. There, they unleashed the big guns. During the exercise, a six-inch gun on the U.S.S. *Pennsylvania* exploded. It wasn't an unusual occurrence. The problem of exploding naval guns had become serious enough that the U.S. House of Representatives was holding hearings and asking, "Why is it that so many of our guns explode?" The previous March, during target practice near the Philippine Islands, a gun explosion on the cruiser *Charleston* had cut down eight helpless sailors when a piece of the gun flew across the deck, almost instantly piercing each man. Fortunately, no one was injured on the *Pennsylvania* and target practice was able to continue. While the guns were still firing, Navy brass decided on the ship they would provide for Gene's experimental landing and takeoff. Because replacing its six-inch gun would keep the U.S.S. *Pennsylvania* in port longer than the other cruisers, by default, the *Pennsylvania* was the obvious choice.[4]

The fourteen-ton cruiser, christened with a bottle of wine in August 1903, slid into the Delaware River from a Philadelphia shipyard, two years and nearly $4-million after her keel had been laid. She was armed with 58 guns and 2 submerged torpedo tubes. She was fast, easily able to reach her contract speed of 22 knots. By 1907, after service in the Atlantic and Caribbean, she was quietly ordered to the Pacific Ocean to become part of the Asiatic Fleet, soon to be designated the Pacific Fleet. Japan's victory in the Russo-Japanese War of 1904–1905 had revealed a powerful and militaristic competitor in the Pacific. Suddenly, United States military and government officials realized their lack of defense preparation. Their naval strength was in the Atlantic, leaving the United States unprepared for action in the Pacific. The Navy was actually less prepared for battle against Japan than Spain had been when it began fighting the U.S. in 1898, at the beginning of the Spanish American War. Residents of Hawaii and the West Coast, particularly California, feared a Japanese invasion and if Japan declared war, the country would almost immediately lose the Philippines, Guam, and possibly Alaska. To avoid any sudden movement that might antagonize the Japanese, the Pacific buildup of ships would be slow and quiet.[5]

Captain Charles Fremont Pond, "Frog" to his friends, took command of the *Pennsylvania* in the summer of 1909. Pond studied at the Naval Academy at the same time as Captain Washington Chambers, but unlike Chambers, he saw no need for aeroplanes in the U.S. Navy. Born in 1856, son of a cabinetmaker-undertaker, Pond was old school Navy, a no-nonsense, white-gloved man with a temper. He was furious when he heard that his ship was chosen for this aeroplane landing experiment. Why should he have to deface the beautiful white planks of his quarterdeck with a landing platform? He would dutifully follow his orders, but he would not be personally involved, someone else would have to do the work. Pond called his engineering officer, Lieutenant Rufus Zogbaum, to his cabin and ordered him to manage all arrangements for the experiment. Zogbaum and his assistant, Lieutenant John Rodgers, went to work as soon as the ship was back in port and the birdmen were on their way to San Francisco.[6]

Anchored again in San Francisco Bay, sailors aboard the six warships enjoyed a Christmas Day feast "of oysters, baked white fish, tenderloin of beef, roasted turkey, and black coffee with their choice of dessert." Those who couldn't get shore leave were entertained with heavy betting on a boxing match and a rowing completion between crews from each ship. The fleet officers retreated to sing songs and drink champagne aboard the admiral's flagship, the U.S.S. *West Virginia*, while enlisted men finished the day with sack races, wrestling, and pie eating contests.[7]

Just after New Year's Day, five of the cruisers pulled anchor and began to scatter. One left for Santa Barbara, another took on coal for a trip north to Washington State, and two others left through the Golden Gate to conduct tests on the quality and efficiency of Pacific Coast coal. The *Pennsylvania* crossed over the bay to Mare Island Naval Shipyard, near Vallejo, where she would be prepared for the San Francisco aviation exhibition.[8]

As he had in Baltimore, Gene, the former San Francisco chauffeur, was the first to arrive in the city. Once again, wherever he went he was the center of interest and peppered with curious questions. Yes, he said, there should be many world records set at the meet. "The air currents in the vicinity of San Francisco are ideal for aeroplane flights," he said. "As far as I can find there are no cross current's or wind pockets in the vicinity of the aviation field. I am confident that there will be a number of records made." Would he really be able to land a biplane on the deck of a ship? "I wouldn't contract to do it if I did not believe that I would succeed," he said. "It is only a matter of practice in accuracy landing.... I have proved that it is possible to fly from a man-of-war to the land and now I want to prove the reverse." He stressed to reporters how important this flight would be. "I want to make it plain," he said. "My job is to fly from the field to the warship, land on it, and then rise from the deck and fly back to the field. Merely to go from the field to the warship I would not consider a great feat. To land on the deck and then succeed in flying off will be something."[9]

With Mabel confined to her room because of her tonsillitis, Gene went by himself to inspect the aviation field, about twelve miles south of the city. On the field, mechanics were already putting together the Curtiss aeroplanes that had come from Los Angeles by train with Gene. The fifteen hangars that would house the professional and amateur aviators were almost complete. The large aviation field was ready, the land rolled flat between the Tanforan racetrack and San Francisco Bay. Instead of using the racetrack and its small grandstand that faced west, the meet's promoters built a 16,000-seat grandstand facing east, directly behind Tanforan. In between the two back-to-back grandstands, ran tracks of the Southern Pacific Railroad where commuters would have easy access to the show. Knowing that many motorists would be driving to the exhibition, aviation committee members had spent a day inspecting the various access roads, determining the best and quickest routes to the meet. An automobile grandstand of 600 special automobile parking spaces had been built, each space numbered and almost immediately reserved. Here, spectators would be able to watch the show while sitting in their car. Those without parking reservations could leave their auto in a large parking area near the grandstand. The airfield was surrounded by the usual air show facilities; concession stands, restrooms, judging platform, and bandstand, but this meet had something new.[10]

An army camp of tents was set up across from the grandstand. Here, 250 soldiers of the 30th U.S. Infantry Division would camp for the entire meet in four rows of conical-shaped tents, twelve tents to a row. Officers would sleep in more substantial quarters that were built at the head of each "company street." In addition, a small machine gun platoon had erected tents just to the north of the main camp. Field kitchens and bakeries were setup to feed the men. Nineteen soldiers from the Army's

San Francisco based "School of Cooks" would fire up the wood burning stoves. With the latest field and hospital equipment "known to modern science," including telephone and telegraph, everything was meant to simulate an army camp in time of war. Major Joseph P. O'Neill, in charge of the camp, named it Camp Selfridge, after Lieutenant Thomas Selfridge. Selfridge, a San Francisco native, was the man who died in 1908 while flying with Orville Wright. "The science of aeronautics caused his death in the prime of a brilliant career," O'Neill said. Within hours of O'Neill's order to his troops, the aviation committee voted to rename Tanforan Field as Selfridge Field.[11]

At its core, this was a military tournament, a training exercise to see how aeroplanes could be turned into war machines. It was also a chance to test a soldier's reaction to a sudden attack from the sky. The military would help the aviators whenever needed, but their most important assignment was conducting military experiments. While troops dug defensive trenches, invisible to approaching ground troops, officers would fly with the birdmen and attempt to sketch maps and take photographs of the ground defenses and surrounding countryside. Soldiers would march as a simulated invasion force from San Francisco to Selfridge Field, as aviators at the same time tried to find them from above. Two hundred human-shaped wooden silhouettes formed a make-believe army to be "discovered" from the air, and later, those silhouettes would become targets, used to evaluate the effectiveness of newly invented aerial bombs. There would be rifle firings from an aeroplane and new attempts at wireless air-to-ground communication. The military would be mimicking a war and at the same time entertaining civilian spectators. Never before had the military, Army, Navy, and Marines, cooperated to such an extent with aeroplane exhibition.[12]

Hearing that Gene had arrived and was at Selfridge Field, lieutenants Zogbaum and Rodgers left the *Pennsylvania* for San Francisco with an invitation for Gene. They wanted him to come to Mare Island to inspect the nearly completed landing platform on the cruiser's stern. While looking for Gene at Selfridge Field, they saw one of the amateur aeroplanes bounce over the field, skid into a ditch, and crumple. It wouldn't be the last aeroplane to land in "Calamity Gulch," but it was the first time the two naval officers had ever seen an aeroplane at all. They were relieved to find out that Gene had not been at the controls. Once they found Gene, they were impressed. "He seemed absolutely fearless with lionhearted nerves," Zogbaum said. Gene agreed to join the men for lunch on the *Pennsylvania* that afternoon. It was payday on board the ship and with cash in hand, the sailors paid little attention to the "youthful appearing" Gene. After inspecting the platform work, Gene, Zogbaum, and Rodgers began discussing improvements.[13]

While the aviators were still in Los Angeles, the aviation committee had sent retired Marine Corps lieutenant, John McClaskey, to Los Angeles to confer with Glenn Curtiss and obtain plans for the platform. When McClaskey returned, he turned the project over to Assistant Naval Constructor Richard Gatewood, son of one of the first Navy men to hold the Constructor title.[14]

Because the 119-foot oak platform was built on the stern of the *Pennsylvania*, it could be 36 feet longer than the one built on the *Birmingham*. "The proper place for the platform is aft," Captain Chambers said. "An after platform can be made longer, will not require a loosening of the stays of any mast, and its essential supports can be so rigged ... as to cause no inconvenience in arranging the other military essentials

Early in January 1911, in the Mare Island Navy Yard, north of San Francisco, the U.S.S. *Pennsylvania* was outfitted with a temporary landing deck 120 feet long and 30 feet wide in preparation for Eugene Ely's landing attempt (Diane Dunlop Collection).

of the ship's design." One of Chambers' chief concerns during the *Birmingham* experiment had been the original flight plan that would have had the ship moving while Gene took off. If Gene had fallen into the water at its bow, Chambers was sure that the ship could not change course in time to avoid running him over. A longer platform would also give Gene more room for error should he be flying too fast while landing.[15]

Thirty-one and a half feet wide, the platform sloped down from the bridge deck, over the quarterdeck and an 8-inch gun turret, to the stern. There it dropped down toward the water at a 30-degree angle in a fourteen-foot long fantail. It was thought that this fantail would protect Gene from a collision if he approached the ship at an altitude lower than the flight deck. Safety railings made from 4 × 12-foot boards were attached at the sides of the platform with the hope that should Gene's aeroplane veer left or right, the railings would keep him from sliding off the deck into the sea. If the railings didn't hold, Gene's last barrier against an unwanted water landing were canvas awnings, spread out like giant hammocks from the platform to lifeboat cranes. "In the event of a fall the birdman may take a bath," wrote a reporter, "but these awnings are so arranged that he will not strike rail or deck on his way to the water." If Gene weren't able to stop his aeroplane's speed after landing, engineers set up a series of crude canvas barriers at the end of the platform and hoped they would be effective. These two, 20-inch-high canvas screens, six feet apart, crossed the platform in front of a 2 by 12-foot plank. Ten feet further on, a wide canvas screen was stretched upward, perhaps twenty feet, to the temporary searchlight platform on the aft mainmast. The slight upward slope of the platform, the plank, and the canvas screens, were the only planned ways to stop the momentum of an out-of control machine. "These, and especially the plank," Captain Pond said, "were very crude devices, and had they come into use would probably have caused serious, if not fatal injury to the aviator and his machine." For added safety, life preservers and rescue swimmers were stationed on board. They were supplemented by two Navy launches that lay off either side of the ship. But it was obvious something more was needed to quickly reduce Gene's landing speed. When Gene and lieutenants Zogbaum and Rodgers first conferred aboard the *Pennsylvania*, they and their support crews considered several schemes that they ultimately rejected, but finally settled on the basic idea of what today is called the tailhook system.[16]

Three pairs of hooks were attached on the underside of Gene's biplane. On the *Pennsylvania*, sailor's duffle bags were each filled with 50 pounds of sand and attached to both ends of 22 ropes that were stretched across 75 feet of the landing platform at three-foot intervals. Rising a few inches above the platform, it was hoped that some of these ropes would catch the hooks on the biplane and drag against the heavy sandbags until Gene's headway was stopped. Each bag was precisely weighed to ensure that once captured, the aeroplane would not veer off to one side.[17]

Perhaps because the system proved to be so successful, more than one person lays claim to its creation. In his final report, Captain Pond said that in his consultations with Gene and Glenn Curtiss, it was "decided to adopt a system of sandbags" that "had been successfully used to check automobiles at racing meets." He didn't credit the idea to any one person, but his reference to racing automobiles seems to support Mabel Ely, who said Gene had been using this system to stop his racecars long before he ever took up flying. English flier, James Radley, also credited Gene. "His scheme ... proved successful," he told a San Francisco newspaper. However, Curtiss in his aviation book said that he and Gene had gone to Mare Island together "to tell the Navy officials at the station just what would be required for such a hazardous test." Although he didn't specifically claim the sandbag idea was his, there are those who think it might have been. Adding to the mystery is Lieutenant Zogbaum's autobiography, *From Sail to Saratoga*, published 50 years after the event in which Zogbaum remembers proposing the idea himself. Of all the claims, there's none more persistent than Hugh Robinson's. Robinson was a mechanic and engineer for Curtiss at the time of Gene's attempt, and later would become a Curtiss aviator in his own right. As early as September 1911, Robinson was claiming the sandbags, hooks, and ropes were completely his idea. He said he had once worked in a circus where a woman rode in a car on a track that did a loop-the-loop. She stopped the car by running into a pile of sawdust. Robinson said he put hooks on that car, which captured weighted lines and stopped the lady from having to fall into the wood chips. He said he had recommended the same idea to Gene. Perhaps it was a collaborative effort and no one person is entitled to credit. But, then again, had the sandbag idea failed, no one would have cared. Good ideas are like victory, they always have a thousand fathers.[18]

On January 7, 1911, Captain Pond, who was now enthusiastic about the aeroplane experiment, sent a telegram from Mare Island to Gene at the Palace Hotel in San Francisco. "*Pennsylvania* leaves seven o'clock tomorrow morning. Will be pleased to have you on board." Glenn Curtiss boarded the cruiser with Gene for a final inspection of the landing platform. Drawn by a rumor that Gene was about to either land or take off from the *Pennsylvania*, a few thousand people crowded the wharves opposite the anchored warships. They waited for a few hours and then drifted away in "keen disappointment." Anticipating Gene's upcoming experiment on the *Pennsylvania*, a San Francisco newspaper wasn't able to resist a tempting headline. "AVIATOR LANDS ON WARSHIP." The story quickly explained that Gene and Curtiss had been transported to the cruiser by a Navy launch and not by airplane. Before arriving, they had stopped briefly on the fleet flagship, U.S.S. *West Virginia*, where they picked up Ensign Roy Stover who, until the weather interfered, was to have been the passenger Gene would carry away from the *Pennsylvania* after he landed.[19]

A windstorm and pelting rain swept down the coast from Alaska, tangling tents, flooding the aviation field, and ending any hope of practice flights. The aviators stayed in their hotel rooms or toured the city. Only the drenched mechanics slogged their way through the mud to work on their aeroplanes. There, they could only tighten a few bolts and hope to keep their canvas-covered machines dry for the better days soon to come.

Gene told reporters that he was still optimistic and had no fear of the weather. "The wind is the only thing that I will have to contend with," he said. "If it is steady and does not blow in sharp, intermittent gusts, with a change of direction every other minute, I will be all right. It makes no difference whether it rains or not. Rain cuts no figure. We can fly in the rain as well as in the sun, only it is not very comfortable for the spectators." He had no doubt that he could land on the *Pennsylvania*. "When I flew from the *Birmingham* it was raining a little, and the naval officers told me that it would be impossible to make the attempt in such stormy weather and advised me to defer my flight. I told them that it was all right and that I was satisfied with weather conditions and would go ahead—and I did."[20]

Admitting that the *Birmingham* experiment had given him "much flattering prominence," Gene said he was more concerned with the practical value of the aeroplane. "I have always kept clear of spectacular work," he said. "I have tried to develop the general utility of the machine rather than its exhibition features."

But to reporters and spectators, everything an aviator did in the air was an exhibition and the exhibition was all they really cared about. Their follow-up question was inevitable. When would he fly?

"It has not been decided yet just when I shall attempt to fly to the *Pennsylvania*," Gene answered, "but it will probably be about the last of the present week." It wasn't.[21]

{ 29 }

# Two Days Out of Ten

The San Francisco flying exhibition would cover an area far away from Selfridge Field. Nearly surrounded completely by foothills, the San Francisco Bay stretches over forty miles, north to south, and is rarely more than five to ten miles wide. Selfridge Field was on the western edge of the bay, about ten miles south of downtown San Francisco. Between the city and the airfield, the San Bruno Hills rise over 1,100 feet. Marin County is directly north of San Francisco, across the Golden Gate, the famous one-mile wide inlet where San Francisco Bay meets the Pacific Ocean. Continuing north 10 miles to San Quentin prison, passes by Mabel Ely's Corte Madera home, and two miles further on is the county seat of Marin County and where Gene and Mabel were married, the city of San Rafael. Another 15 miles northeast, across the bay, is the Mare Island Naval Shipyard.

A month before the San Francisco International Aviation Meet was scheduled to begin, members of the Marin County Promotional League offered $5,000 to any aviator who would fly from Selfridge Field to San Rafael and return. San Rafael would be the only stopping point allowed. The return flight would pass over San Quentin Prison, cross the bay to San Francisco, and then continue to the aviation field. When San Quentin convicts heard of the plan, they asked the warden to forward a request to the aviation committee. "There are hundreds of men confined here who have never seen an aeroplane," they wrote, "and some of us probably never will, unless ... an aviator will come this way. We are writing to ask you if it can be arranged for the machine, which is scheduled to visit San Rafael, to circle over the prison." The committee said they would consider the request, but the flight was never made.[1]

The publicity potential of an aeroplane flight was something a wealthy business owner couldn't resist. Charles Runyon, secretary of the Goodyear Rubber Co. and president of the Mill Valley and Mt. Tamalpais Scenic Railway in Marin County, offered a $1,000 prize to the first "sky navigator" making a nonstop flight from Selfridge Field to the top of 2,600-foot Mount Tamalpais. Runyon assured the aviators that there was a bare spot in the midst of the pines, where they could safely land within 1,000 feet of his Summit Hotel and Tavern. Gene, who knew the Mount Tamalpais area well, said the greatest danger in making the flight would not be landing on the mountain, but rather the difficulty of a pilot trying "to find a landing place en route, if an accident should require a descent." It was another challenge that all the birdmen declined.²

The aviation meet was going to be an exciting time for Mabel's family, who would finally get to see Gene fly. Mercy Hall, Mabel's 10-year-old sister, in thanking the San Francisco *Call* newspaper for the wristwatch she had won in one of its weekly children's writing contests, was eager to associate herself with her sister's husband. "In her letter to the editor of the *Junior Call*," she wrote, "I wish to thank you for the pretty watch you sent me, which I received on Christmas day. I will use it to time my brother-in-law, Eugene Ely, in his flights at Tanforan next week. Wishing the *Junior Call* a prosperous New Year, I remain, your friend, Mercy Hall."³

Boys and girls were scrambling to win free tickets and a chance to work at the Selfridge aviation field. The aviation committee promised a free admission for every four tickets a youngster sold at 50 cents each. "Just get Dad and Uncle Bill to give you two dollars for four admission tickets," they said, "and you will receive a pass for yourself." The five children who sold the most tickets would be hired as "special messengers" at the aviation field and receive a salary of $2 a day. The youngster who sold the most tickets would be the head aviation messenger and, in addition to the $2 salary, would also get up to 25 free tickets for their friends.⁴

Ruth Beck, wife of Army Lieutenant Paul Beck, the secretary of the aviation committee and detailed as the Army's manager of the airfield, wrote a newspaper column explaining how women could sound like they knew something about aviation. She called it, "Timely Tips on Flying and First Lessons in the Strange Lingo of the Man-Birds." Lesson One: "Do not say *air-y-o-plane.* Pronounce it as if it "were spelled air-o-plane. Try it that way and even Glenn Curtiss or the Wrights will never be able to tell that you are a novice." With tongue in cheek, she suggested that the hangars shouldn't be pronounced in the American way, but instead, in the original French, "as in, *owng-ars.*" She continued with an extensive explanation of the different styles of aeroplanes and how aviators made them fly. "Most women are not popularly supposed to enjoy the blessing of a conscientious and understanding mind," she said, but she hoped her article would allow "feminine readers" to "thoroughly enjoy the aviation meet."⁵

Twenty amateur aviators had entered, but few would have any success. When Hugh Robinson, the man who claimed credit for the tailhook idea, and Lincoln Beachey, the ex-balloon pilot, signed up for the amateur ranks, the rest of the amateurs complained that they should have been competing against professionals. Though neither had previously won money as an aviator, Glenn Curtiss had already signed both to his exhibition team and he was also providing both with biplanes and training. But their status did not change. Robinson would capture $1,333 in total earnings as the top amateur at the meet and Beachey would place third with $858. The true amateur stars of the meet were Fred Wiseman and Clarence Walker.⁶

Wiseman was the Santa Rosa racecar driver who just a few years before had raced against Gene. Wiseman and some friends had been tinkering for quite a while and finally had managed to build their own aeroplane. "We thought all you had to do was build a kite and put a motor on it," Wiseman told a reporter, "But we found it was a bit more complicated than that." In this, his first competition as an amateur, Wiseman took second place, winning $1,283. After flying for about a year, he quit, saying there was no future in a business where so many of his fellow exhibition fliers were dying.⁷

Clarence Walker began building an aeroplane with friends in the summer of 1910 and planned to fly it at the San Francisco exhibition, but he could never get it into the air. When his father died in September, Walker expected an inheritance of a million dollars or more. He decided that rather than build an aeroplane, now he could buy one. Curtiss agreed to sell him the Lincoln Beachey biplane for $5,000, but Beachey crashed it twice and destroyed the machine while flying at the Los Angeles exhibition. Robert Simpson, Gene's old boss, offered to sell Walker his idle biplane, the Wemme machine that Gene was no longer flying. Simpson told Walker he would even pay to have it refurbished at the Curtiss factory. As part of the deal, Gene would give Walker flying lessons while he was at Selfridge Field. Walker made ten low-level flights and one unfortunate dive into a pool of water before he finally could control the machine. He picked up $250 as the "clever beginner," and fourth most effective amateur at the San Francisco meet. "Walker is a very nervy young fellow," Gene said, "and should make a great aviator some day." It was an accurate prediction, but only for a short time. Under the management of Gene's old mentor, Whipple Hall, Walker flew a few exhibitions in the U.S. and then ended his career six months later in Hawaii. He had gotten married only a few weeks earlier and when he crashed into a tree while his bride was watching; his flying career came to an abrupt end.[8]

Saturday, January 7, the "great meet" was on, and Gene had the honor of making the first flight. He flew ever-widening circles for eight minutes, dipping down to within 30 feet of the ground in front of the grandstand, where the photographers and spectators got a "splendid view." He closed by roaming off to the north and flying over the town of South San Francisco at the foot of the San Bruno Hills. Although Gene was first in the air, the real stars of the day were Radley and Latham.[9]

As Gene was landing, Radley in his Bleriot, took off. He went through a few simple maneuvers to please the crowd and then suddenly turned northeast and flew out over the bay. Every eye strained after him as he vanished from view. He flew until he reached the ferryboats traveling between San Francisco and Oakland. "Here I came lower and circled about the ferryboats as they came and went," he said, "circling down low so that all on board could see the machine plainly. This seemed to please the people, for they cheered and waved." Next he circled Goat Island, today's Yerba Buena, and then flew around the *Pennsylvania* and *West Virginia* to a "noisy reception" from the sailors on board. He was gone 28 minutes and said he had flown at about a mile a minute.[10]

Latham was the first to greet his British rival. "Why didn't you go out through the Golden Gate?" he asked, while pumping Radley's hand.

"I will, by golly," said Radley, "If you'll come with me."

"I'll go," said Latham, and, without another word, he ran to his Antoinette. With his incessant cigarette burning from the end of its long holder, he was off.[11]

He flew straight toward the San Bruno Hills, and then turned west toward the Pacific Ocean. With a right turn to the north he flew over the surf, past Seal Rocks and the Cliff House, until he finally reached the Golden Gate. "Many ships have passed through the Golden Gate," said a reporter who called the flight historic, "but never until Saturday did one come sailing in the air between those hospitable portals, which have seen a procession of Spanish galleons, clipper ships, great merchantmen, Pacific liners, and battleships."[12]

Latham continued toward the city, aiming for the tower of the Ferry Building, the most prominent building near the harbor. The waterfront streets were so jammed with spectators that traffic came to a standstill. As Latham came closer, the crowd rushed out onto the wharves for a better view. One young woman was so captivated by the scene that she walked right off the end of a pier and splashed into the bay. She was fished out alive and safe, and told reporters that she was now, quite sure, that the safest place to see airships was at the aviation field. After an hour of flying, Latham returned to Selfridge Field. Word of his flight had been telegraphed ahead, so as soon as he was seen in the sky, the band near the grandstand began playing the *La Marseillaise*, in honor of the Frenchman's achievement.[13]

This air meet was unlike any other. With its emphasis on military experiments and demonstrations that could establish the aeroplane as a military and naval factor in warfare, there would be few attempts at world records. "The airship is a war engine," said Lieutenant Beck. "We'll prove it." While the aviators flew, the Army troops went through mock maneuvers on the ground. "To give a martial setting to the campaign," said a reporter, "khaki soldiers, commanded by cocky officers, hustled army mules about and showed what a mountain battery in action is like." Latham, the aerial duck hunter, began the military experiments with pistol shots from his aeroplane. From 200 feet, flying like a hard riding cowboy in a Hollywood movie, Latham fired 25 shots and put ten holes through a wooden silhouette of a man on the ground. Willard and Gene dropped mock metal bombs from 500 feet, but both missed the twenty-foot circular target, Willard by seven feet and Gene by four.[14]

It was a good beginning. Weather conditions were surprisingly ideal. No fog, few clouds, and the sun shone with the warmth of a spring day. The breeze was light and barely moved the dozens of flags on the grandstand. Although there were no contests, there was at least one aeroplane in the air and sometimes three, nearly all afternoon. The aviators spent the day testing their machines and getting used to the local conditions surrounding the field. Gene beat the five-kilometer speed record in his new biplane, but because he had cut corners inside the pylons, the claim was not officially recorded.[15]

Almost until the very end, it had been a safe day. Although none of the amateurs had gotten more than a foot off the ground, the professionals had dipped and sailed without accident. Then, Walter Brookins' motor failed, forcing the Wright aviator into an emergency, diving glide toward the center of the airfield. Somehow, a young boy perhaps six years old, had slipped through police lines and was on the field, running directly to where Brookins would obviously touchdown. The crowd began to scream a warning to the tot, who, shaken by the sudden noise, began to run even faster. His cap flew off and that probably saved his life. He stopped to pick it up just as Brookins struck the ground, missing the boy by barely ten feet.[16]

The next day, the aviators and the crowd, optimistically estimated at 110,000, were welcomed by Willard's "Swiss cheese holes" in the atmosphere. Willard had risen into a whirlwind, limped around in the air a few feet off the ground, and unable to climb, banged down into a landing that broke his tailpiece in half. Latham skimmed the earth, bounced into a gully, bounced again over a hill, and plowed straight into a fence. Radley got into the air, but the wind batted him back down into a swamp. Gene, avoiding near disaster, landed lightly without a propeller. Luckily, he wasn't high in the sky when the standpipe on his motor broke away, tumbled into the propeller, and snapped off an entire blade. After Gene landed, Curtiss transferred his biplane's propeller to Gene's aeroplane and Gene was back in the air within minutes. Parmelee's wings wobbled some, but he was the only aviator to have an incident free flying day, completing the day's longest flight by circling the field at high altitude for nearly a half-hour. "The really ticklish part of yesterday's flying," he said, "was getting more than two or three hundred feet above the ground."[17]

It was Parmelee and Gene who provided the only real thrill of the day—a mock battle between the infantry on Selfridge Field and the two aviators in their biplanes. Gene and Parmelee circled high above the camp, "like war eagles," said a reporter, "about to pounce down and bear off the colors of the beautiful daughter of the commanding major general, or some other vital secret of the defense." A sentry on the ground sounded the alarm. Running soldiers grabbed rifles and cartridge containers filled with blank ammunition. Four companies of men raced to their four separate battle positions, but by then, Gene and Parmelee had already passed over them. The biplanes carried no bombs, but dove at the soldiers as if they did. When the biplanes came around again, the soldiers aimed their rifles and began to fire blanks. "With a bravery amounting to rashness," wrote a reporter, who saw this as a humorous battle, "the soldiers stood under the pitiless guns of the aeroplanes and fired volley after volley into the blue." The crowd was entertained with "five minutes of savage warfare," until the biplanes flew away and the soldiers claimed their dubious victory.[18]

Two days down and eight to go. The *Pennsylvania* was in position and Gene was ready to go. The plan had called for two flights to the cruiser, the first coming on January 9, Day 3 of the exhibition, but San Francisco weather has a way of changing its mind overnight. By the time the Monday morning newspapers hit the streets and readers read that "a storm of marked energy and very low pressure was moving rapidly southeastward," the arctic storm had already arrived and rain had been falling for hours. It was the first downpour of a very dry season and readers were warned to grab their umbrellas and galoshes. Nearly three-quarters of an inch fell in just over twelve hours, not exactly a flood, but enough to turn the aviation field into a muddy bog and cancel the day's program. Lieutenant Beck put an optimistic, public relations spin on the storm, saying the rain had actually helped, rather than hindered the meet. "It gave time to clean up the grounds and prepare for the important wireless experiments," he said.[19]

Aviation fans were urged to "take heart" and not worry about the weather. The contract with the aviators was "elastic," said officials. It called for ten days of flying that if necessary, could be extended over a "reasonable number of days." One way or another, the meet would continue until ten days had been flown, "unless," said the committee, "the weather man should conclude to open his water taps and let them run during the remainder of the winter." The ten days of flying trickled slowly through eighteen days of on and off rain.[20]

Prof. Alexander McArdle, the Weather Bureau's local forecaster, offered some hope. He thought the weather would subside enough to allow the aviators to fly. The predicted winds, he said, would probably not produce any more storms and there would be "frequent intervals of sunshine." It was a good guess, but those intervals of sunshine proved to be very short and very rare.[21]

# { 30 }

## Waiting for a Rainbow

While the birdmen waited for a day of warm sunbeams and light breezes, there was plenty of time for relaxation and idle chat. Most of the men stayed in their hotel out of the rain, others did some sightseeing, and a few took advantage of the many invitations to social events they had received. One of the more interesting invitations came from Admiral Edward Barry, Commander of the Pacific Fleet, who asked that the aviators visit his flagship, the U.S.S. *West Virginia*. He especially wanted to see Latham and Radley, the men who had flown over his ship a few days before. Latham sent his regrets, saying he had some personal business to attend to, but Radley came with his manager. The military's aviation trainees, Lieutenant Ellyson and Lieutenant Walker, joined them, along with Parmelee of the Wright team, and members of the aviation committee. Gene and Glenn Curtiss, still preparing for the shipboard landing, took a quick tour of the ship and then were off to the *Pennsylvania*,.[1]

Mabel had recovered from her tonsillitis attack and sat down for an interview in the hotel lobby. Reporters noticed that on the two days Gene had flown, she watched his every move, while sitting in an automobile parked near his hangar. Would she fly with him? "Oh, yes, I am going up with Mr. Ely," she said. "I often go with him and would have flown at Los Angeles if I had not been taken suddenly ill." However, she said that she would fly only after Gene had flown to and from the *Pennsylvania*. "I do not want him to take a chance of smashing his machine before he makes that flight," she said, "but I shall go up with him on one of the last days of the meet." It was almost the same story she always told, although, this time, reporters asked her something new. "What do you wear when you fly?" "Why, I go as I am," she said, "just the same as in automobiling." She assured them that there were no special preparations needed, "except to put on a cap, which keeps my hair from blowing about." She liked to fly and was never afraid. "I know that everything is secure before I go and that Mr. Ely is careful and will be able to land me all right if anything happens."[2]

One of those brief intervals in the bad weather came January 10. Mabel was once again sitting in a limousine while she watched Gene fly. With her were Lena Curtiss and Willard's younger sister, Emily. The recently engaged Emily had been traveling with Willard for about six months and had been a passenger on a few of his flights. Mary Miller, a reporter, approached the women and began asking questions. "Mrs.

Ely is a pretty woman with soft black eyes and vivid coloring," Miller wrote, "and she is a defender of the faith in aviating." Gene swooped past overhead as Miller shook hands with Mabel. "She was sitting with Mrs. Curtiss," Miller said, "and in reply to my question as to their emotional condition, they both laughed. 'Here we are perfectly calm,' said Mrs. Ely, 'and there goes my husband.'" Mabel waved "a careless hand toward this most modern conveyance as it dipped over the hill and disappeared." Mabel turned back to Miller. "My husband has been flying since last spring," she said, "but I am not at all nervous about it. I have a great deal of faith in his ability to take care of himself, and really, I never worry."

"My husband doesn't fly much anymore," Lena Curtiss said, almost ignoring the reporter. "I never worry over my brother," Emily Willard said, "and yet I cannot say I am not nervous. I simply will not let myself begin to worry."

Miller asked what it felt like to fly. Emily said that although there was no seat on the biplane for her, and she had to cling to the biplane's ribs for safety, she loved flying. Although, she admitted that when she came down, "it was like the drop of an elevator going a little too fast." Mrs. Curtiss said she couldn't describe the sensation and Mabel agreed. "I don't believe anyone can really describe it—what the sensation is like," Mabel said. "It is a little like the scenic railway without any railway, but I was so excited that it is hard for me to tell just how I felt."[3]

This third day of the meet was designated "Ladies' Day," where, between flights, San Francisco's society women served tea to the aviators in their hangars. Women of all ages and social standing were infatuated with the birdmen and, while one may think these ladies of the early 20th century were reserved and shy when showing their passion, they weren't. "Veritable armies of pretty women," wrote a reporter, "armed with every weapon known to the gentler sex, besiege the heroic birdmen." Phil Parmelee mostly attracted brunettes who, when invited, eagerly climbed up next to him on his biplane to have their photograph taken. When the feminine swarm grew too large, they all fanned out in front of the craft, pressing a smiling Phil into the center of their photo.[4]

So many women were out front of the aviators' hotel doors that Roy Knabenshue, manager of the Wright team, seriously worried that he and his men might have to change to a different hotel. The requests, he said, were "becoming an annoyance," and he was surprised by the boldness of some of the women who, "as an extra inducement," sent photographs of themselves. He said he had been chased by more than one persistent female whose "desire" was to meet a birdman or be given a ride on an aeroplane. Many, he said, were society girls and sometimes even their mothers. "It is surprising to see what ends women will go to for a chance to circle the field in an aeroplane," he said.[5]

At the security gate, between the grandstand and the hangars, hundreds of female imposters tried to bluff their way onto the field. On one day alone, guards stopped two of Mabel Ely's "mothers," thirteen of her "aunts," and one of her "maids." There were also a "brother," three "father's-in-law," and 50 very "intimate friends on important errands." Invariably a long procession of "best girls" who had been "invited" to the field by their soldier boyfriends, were turned back, as were the many elderly women who seemed to make up Charlie Willard's fan club. True to form, in March, Charlie would quietly marry Jeannette Sisson, five years his senior. The aviation committee finally had to issue clip-on badges to those who could legally be in the hangar and field areas, but even so, the bluff was still on and the women kept coming. The most amusing attempt came from three women, flawlessly dressed in the latest fashion, pointing to official badges on their sleeves. Sadly, for them, they just couldn't convince the gate guard that they were indeed, "laborers."[6]

The man with the most feminine admirers was definitely Walter Brookins, "a young, comely, and altogether well-fashioned young man," said the newspaper. While a mere 50 of Mabel's "intimate friends" were stopped at the security gate, Brookins was visited that same day by 87 relatives; mostly female, that included 19 "fiancées." Even when he took to the skies, Brookins was the subject of every woman's gaze. "Binocular eye," one reporter called it. He had been walking past the grandstand when he noticed a woman with her head thrown back and eyes straining, intently fixated on Brookins in his biplane, 350 feet above. "My! Isn't he handsome?" she said to her friend. The friend, who was also trying to pierce the blue sky for a glimpse of Brookins, was doubtful. "Can you see him so far away?" she asked. "Certainly I can see him, plainly," said the woman. "Don't you know I have binocular eyes?"[7]

One humorist suggested that with all the feminine interest in aviation, Gene should take a woman passenger on his flight to the *Pennsylvania*. No longer would a sailor have to wait for a girl in every port, he said, now they could "literally drop in from the air every time a ship got near shore."[8]

The aviators were ready to fly, but the automobile grandstand and the nearby parking lot were nearly empty. A road gang had worked through the night trying to repair the muddy highways leading from San Francisco, but the roads were still nearly impassable. The unsettled weather kept most enthusiasts at home and, had the trains not been running, the birdmen would have played to an empty field instead of the 10,000 hearty spectators bundled tightly against the chilling wind.[9]

"If the aeroplanes are any sort of bird today," someone joked, "they are ducks." The misty rain and the wind would have made a racing yachtsman happy, but the aviators were hesitant to set sail. Gene, "who sacrificed nothing of his reputation as a mighty willing aviator," begged Curtiss to let him fly. Conditions looked dicey, but Curtiss told Gene that if he wanted to take a chance, it was all up to him. Within seconds, the sound of Gene's crackling engine was echoing into the grandstand and he was airborne. As he began to climb, a sudden squall smashed against him, threatening to push him back down. He began to bob, weave, and shake. "There! He is striking that bad place now," Brookins said to the group of anxious aviators who were carefully watching the flight. Mabel, in a black velvet dress covered with a gray overcoat, and topped with a black turban on her head, abruptly gripped her binoculars more firmly as she followed Gene's struggle for control. Her mouth had been rapidly working on a stick of gum, but at that moment, it froze. For nearly five minutes she barely moved, then, with a snap of her gum, the binoculars came down, she climbed back into the limousine, and her mouth began to chew again.[10]

Gene made five laps of the course in his ten-minute flight, covering nearly eight miles before landing. Though his hands were stiff from battling the unsettled air, Gene said things weren't as bad as they looked from the ground. "Above 75 feet, for a considerable distance, a buffeting wind is met with," he said. "I got away from this by going higher. Flying at 500 feet, the air was very calm and, as the biplane glided along, it became almost supersensitive. Seldom have I enjoyed a flight more." He had found one of those predicted "intervals of sunshine" and the passing of the rain briefly made the day ideal for flying. "The sun shone brightly and the chill of the upper air was softened," he said. "As I passed over the grandstand, I could hear the band playing and the cheers of the people very distinctly."[11]

With Gene's apparent success, Radley and Parmelee fired up their motors. "After I had been in the air for about five minutes, I saw Parmelee and Radley rise," Gene said. "Thereafter, I watched them as we passed each other. This is one of the strange sensations of aviation. We pass and re-pass each other so quietly and easily that it can only be appreciated when it is experienced." Radley made only one pass in his Bleriot, a struggle of a flight for less than a mile before he landed. Parmelee's flight was just as short and just as uneventful, as were the two brief attempts by Willard and Latham.[12]

Latham left the ground about an hour after Gene had landed, aware of the dangerous winds aloft. He decided to change his original plan to take Lieutenant Beck along as a passenger. It may have saved the lieutenant's life. Latham's shotgun was by his side, but he wouldn't have time for target shooting today. After rising less than 30 feet, his Antoinette dove for the ground, struck a barbed wire fence, and split into three sections. When the rescue ambulances arrived on scene, they found Latham walking around the wreck, puffing hard on his cigarette. It was an $8,000 loss in less than eight seconds. "The machine parted behind my seat and I was safe enough," Latham said. "But if I had been carrying a passenger, both of his legs would have been broken off.... *Tres mauvais*," he said. "Very bad."[13]

Brookins had the major success of the day, rising to 1,413 feet, where he found the temperature too cold for safety. "I would have remained longer," he said, pulling off his gloves and revealing his blue hands. "The cold began to numb my hands and hurt my face. I wore a mask, but this did not protect my face from the cold."[14]

Rain showers returned and an ominous wind driven black cloud was moving in from the west. Radley brought out his Bleriot for another attempt, but once again he smashed to the ground. Like a wheelbarrow, his crew had to push "the bug-like monoplane back to the hangar," ending the day's flying.[15]

From Puget Sound in the north to San Diego in the south, a gigantic storm blew in. Two inches of rain battered the California coast and nearly four feet of snow fell in the Sierra Mountains. The aviation field was flooded and wind gusts up to 50 miles an hour put an end to all thoughts of flying. "The wind gauge was the only instrument that flew in the vicinity of Selfridge Aviation Field," wrote a reporter "and the birdmen stayed close to their nest." Spectators would have to wait another four days for sunshine before the flying began again. Meanwhile, each morning all telephone operators were told whether the meet was on or off, and aviation enthusiasts were encouraged to call "their telephone girl" for the very latest information.[16]

While the downpour continued, Gene spent a few hours working on the biplane, and then on January 12, he quietly slipped away with Radley for a duck hunting expedition in the wetlands surrounding the town of Los Banos, about 115 miles southeast of San Francisco. They returned two days later. It had been a wet trip, they said, but "the two birdmen showed no mercy on their feathered compatriots of the air and returned home with limit bags." Gene and Radley invited the professional aviators and their crews to a downtown café, where the duo's duck hunting marksmanship provided a complimentary feast. "There was plenty for all, and "the party was a merry one."[17]

For the grounded aviators it was a tedious wait. Over five inches of rain had fallen in four days and the aviation field resembled the mudflats surrounding much of the bay. The wind was no longer considered an enemy. For once, the aviators were actually hoping for a few stiff breezes that, if the rains ever stopped, might help to dry out Selfridge Field.

While everyone waited, the San Francisco Press Club invited all the aviators to a dinner and asked if they would give a speech. Only Gene and Glenn Curtiss agreed to speak, but not for long, and as one reporter said, "Their vocal engines misfired." Combined, they were on the podium for only one minute, 38 seconds. "Apparently," said the reporter, "Floating through the air a few thousand feet above earth in a frail craft requires one brand of bravery, and making an after dinner speech requires another." It seems unusual that Curtiss had nothing to tell the reporters. He was noted for his reserved manner in public, but he had just published a lengthy column in the local newspaper detailing what he saw as the future development of aeroplane speed.[18]

The storm that had gripped the city for most of the week and turned the aviation exhibition into a mud bath blew away as quickly as it came. The full moon poked through the clouds and though the field was still soggy, Sunday, January 15, promised a spectacular show. There were fifteen professional flights that day, but again few spectators. A brief and light early morning sprinkle was just enough to keep those who feared a pair of wet feet from leaving their home. Only the fearless 6,000 who made the journey were well rewarded.

Walter Brookins not only performed a spiral glide, he did it with a semi-terrified passenger, Lieutenant John C. Walker. Walker had received orders from the Army to take flying lessons from Curtiss beginning at the end of the month, but his flight with Brookins was the first he had ever made. He carried a camera as a military experiment that would determine if photographs taken from an aeroplane could help scout out enemy troop positions in time of war. Walker clicked off six snapshots in the first five minutes of the six minute flight. Flying at 1,000 feet, Brookins suddenly told him to, "Hold tight!" The aeroplane dipped directly downward, beginning a long and terrifying corkscrew to earth—the Spiral Dip. Later, Lieutenant Paul Beck confessed that he had suggested the surprise drop as a prank. "I guess I'll get mine," he said. Walker had no comment.[19]

Earlier, Parmelee had made the first passenger carrying flight ever attempted in San Francisco, carrying Army lieutenant, Myron Crissy to 550 feet for another military experiment. Oranges, baseballs, bags of flour, and other assorted missiles had been dropped from aeroplanes before, but Crissy carried the first real explosive. Filled with shrapnel and a quarter pound of black powder, the eight-pound bomb exploded on contact with the ground, releasing a puff of black smoke and blasting a hole three feet in diameter and nearly as deep. Because of the potential public danger, the target had been set up a half-mile away from the grandstand, and until they heard the explosion, few spectators were aware of the experiment. "This was my first experience in an aeroplane, but it isn't going to be my last," Crissy said. "Today has convinced me that the aeroplane may have an important part in war aside from its value for scouting."[20]

With no wind, a few cumulous clouds in the sky, and a rainbow in the afternoon, the birdmen were ready to unleash their skill and daring. Gene, Curtiss, and Parmelee raced around the course and out on some cross-country flights over South San Francisco. There were the dips, dives, ground skimming, and aerobatic maneuvers the crowds had been waiting for. For 12-year-old Katherine Roth, who had braved the damp morning with her parents, no one was a greater aviator than Gene Ely. She would win a watch for her prizewinning essay, "The World's Greatest Living Aviator." It appeared in the newspaper the following Saturday. "At last we reached our places in the grandstand," she wrote, "and looking up in the air, I saw a huge bird flying over the field. As it came nearer, I found it to be aeroplane No. 8. Glancing at my program, I found the aviator to be Eugene Ely." She marveled as Gene began to climb. "Higher and higher he rose, growing smaller as he went, till at last it looked like a miniature of an aeroplane ... till it looked as if he could grasp the sky, and yet he did not stop. Cheer after cheer rent the air as, with a sweep, he flew to the ground, running along the field till he was stopped by a number of men. I think that any man who is brave enough to do as Ely did is worthy to stand uppermost in the esteem of his fellow men."[21]

What Katherine hadn't seen that Sunday was probably the most spectacular flight of the day, and the one that nearly stole Gene Ely's date with history. Radley flew back out over the bay and took aim at the U.S.S. *Pennsylvania*. He circled the field twice and then shot off to the south. Realizing that some small wooden part had broken off his right wing, he decided to fly out over the water rather than risk a hard drop to the ground. He could have returned to the field, but instead turned north toward San Francisco. The bay was dotted with boats and the piers were lined with eager spectators. As soon as he came into view, the crowds cheered and whistles and sirens began to blare. Just south of the Ferry Building, the men of the *Pennsylvania* gathered on deck, believing Radley planned to land there. As he headed straight for the cruiser, it seemed certain that that was his intention. He began to descend and, as his approach got closer, the cheering and applause faded into the tension of the moment. The sputter of Radley's engine was the only sound heard. "Straight and steady he flew. The frightened, screaming gulls shot away from his path." He dipped down and just as he was about to touch the deck, he turned away, his motor roaring as he zoomed back up again. He crossed over the bay to the Oakland Hills, swooped down to the water near Alameda, and after 34 minutes in the air, returned to Selfridge Field. Gene was in luck. Radley had wisely abandoned his dangerous, unrehearsed landing. Gene still had his chance at history.[22]

Although the weather was slightly worse on Monday and the wind began to pick up, there were more flights than there had been Sunday. The military highlight came from Brookins and Gene, who both flew reconnaissance missions in a mock battle, the first time in United States Army history that ground troops had ever cooperated in a battle scenario with aeroplanes. The forces posted at Selfridge Field were designated as an invading force that had landed on the beaches of Half Moon Bay, marched east across the San Francisco Peninsula, and set up camp on the aviation field. A defending force, consisting of two batteries of artillery and two companies of cavalry, was marching south from the Presidio Army base, near the Golden Gate, to attack the "invaders." Brookins, representing the invading force, was ordered into the air in an attempt to locate the oncoming defenders. With him was Army Lieutenant George

Kelly who took photographs, sketched the terrain, and traced the aeroplane's course on a military map. It was a high-tech game of hide-and-seek, and although they flew almost 2,000 feet up, they couldn't locate the defenders who had hidden themselves well in a forested area on the west side of San Francisco. "Although they did not locate the troops sent out from the Presidio," said Army General Tasker Bliss, Commander of the Department of California, "the whole expedition showed that the aeroplane is especially fitted for reconnaissance work."[23]

Gene followed Brookins in an attempt to complete the same mission. According to the newspaper, "he nearly turned the trick." Being more familiar with the San Francisco terrain, he flew north to Lake Merced, five miles southwest of the Presidio. From there he turned inland and began circling. He got within a half-mile of the defenders, but never saw them. So, the soldiers, "defenders of San Francisco," were never discovered and never faced the threat of imaginary bombs falling on their heads.[24]

When Gene returned to the aviation field, Major O'Neill asked him to attack the major's "invading force," as if he were now flying for the "defenders." Gene approached from the north; O'Neill sounded the alarm, and by the time the soldiers were in position, Gene had dropped all of his imaginary bombs and was flying away. O'Neill's command was "dead" and Gene was the hero. "I did not know he was coming so fast," explained O'Neill.[25]

After the next day ended with more bombs, more dangerous glides, and a few cross-country flights, Gene's time had come. Landing on a ship had never been done before, but tomorrow, January 18, 1911, he would be the first.

Reporters asked Mabel to describe her emotions.

Pressing both hands over her heart, she said, "Oh, I shall be all stirred up in here when he flies to the warship."

"Then you are a little bit nervous sometimes, after all?" asked a reporter.

She shook her head. "Not afraid. Oh, no—Not at all. I am only so anxious for him to succeed. It will be such a wonderful thing if he can do it, you know. I am more excited over this flight than any he has ever made."[26]

## { 31 }

## "Easier than I thought"

He could fly a few thousand feet in the air, but Gene Ely was afraid of heights. The thought of riding in an elevator to the top of a 17-story skyscraper made his knees wobble, his face turn red, and drizzles of sweat break out from every pore. "For fear that I would fling myself down to death," he said, "never in my life have I been able to look down from the top of even a three-story building."

The day after he had successfully made his flight to the *Pennsylvania*, Herbert Mills, an actor and occasional writer for the San Francisco *Call* newspaper, invited Gene to take an elevator with him to the dome at the top of the Call Building. There he would be able to see the *Pennsylvania*, still anchored in San Francisco Bay, and picture for himself the flight he had just made.

Gene stood up, fumbled with his hat, and then sat down again. "It's no use," he said. "Without my biplane I'd probably fly seventeen stories to the street." He pulled out a handkerchief and dabbed it to his dripping forehead. "I have tried frequently to master this childish impulse and—and—well, I wouldn't go up into the dome of this building right now for a hundred dollars."

"But, the dome is only 235 feet high," Mills said, "and ten times that altitude is no unfamiliar altitude to you."

"True," Gene said, "but you are confusing biplanes and domes. The kind of support you have while up in the air has a great deal—I mean—has everything to do with your sensations while up." He said an aeroplane in the air was like a boat afloat in its natural element. On the ground, he grew "dizzy looking out of a second story window." But flying in the air, except for being more conscious of his breathing, he said he felt "no ill effects."

Mills asked if that was because the canvas wings of his biplane reassured him while in flight. Gene laughed. "I see no wings," he said, reminding Mills that in the Curtiss machine the aviator sits out front of the wings. "In front of me and on either side of me, I look down on air."

"Are you ever afraid in the air, Mr. Ely?" Mills asked.

"Yes," Gene said. "Afraid that I may not be giving as good a performance as I would like, but never afraid in the sense that you mean."

Then, they began to talk about the day before, the day that Gene finally "accomplished something real" and erased his "last sting of failure."

"What do you mean last sting of failure?" asked Mills.

Gene spoke slowly and with some discomfort. "I mean," he said, "that until I took up aviation as a profession, my whole business life had been a succession of failures. I became a chauffeur only after the money I started with was gone, and everything I tried left me worse off than before. I can freely confess the misery of my earlier career, for I have the solace of much good company."

He said all the famous aviators at Selfridge had told him that they too had been failures at everything they had tried before they took to the air. "James Radley failed in the automobile business in England and Hubert Latham in the same line in France." Brookins could never make a profit with his bicycle repair shop. Parmelee had failed at telegraph, and Willard was "mighty glad" that he was no longer a mechanical engineer. "A succession of failures put us all up in the air," Gene said, "and there we found success awaiting us."[1]

On Wednesday, January 18, 1911, an hour before Gene was scheduled to leave Selfridge Field, Captain Pond was welcoming guests on board the *Pennsylvania* and having them escorted to the navigating bridge, high above and behind the landing platform. Crewmembers, temporarily relieved of duty so they could watch the flight, scrambled for the best onboard viewpoint. "There were no reserved seats," said a sailor. "It was "every man for himself." Twenty sailors ringed the top of the rear smokestack, followed by several stragglers who were left clinging to its sides. Sailors in blue jackets under white hats dangled their feet from lifeboat cranes and every mast was climbed. The *Pennsylvania*'s silhouette was "blurred with humanity for an hour or so," said a reporter, "and looked as if a great swarm of bees had settled on the ship's spars and upper works." In the Bay, the water churned with ships and boats. If the *Pennsylvania* was swarming with bees, the surrounding water was swimming in schools of every kind of nautical craft, all of them bobbing and circling around the massive warship as they jockeyed for position. Hulls and decks of railroad tugs that yesterday pulled barges of railcars from one side of the bay to the other, today, were running low in the water, swamped with curious railroad executives and their families. River steamers and ferryboats, temporarily out of service, offered a new kind of paying passenger an up-close look at history. Old technology was meeting the new with a few hundred weather beaten merchant marines still floating on their old wooden sailing ships, and sitting as comfortably on their yardarm seats as sparrows on a power line. One joke of the day said that every gasoline launch in the entire bay area was floating somewhere nearby, and because it wasn't far from the truth, there was little room for error. "If Ely hit the water instead of the ship," said a reporter, "he would be involved in half a dozen collisions, so close did the smaller craft lie around the cruiser."[2]

Gene was ready and the weather was good, just a light breeze and a thin overcast with patches of fog. His crew was making a few, last minute checks. The aeroplane had been modified slightly for the *Pennsylvania* flight. A central skid was fitted underneath so that it hung about five inches above the bottom of the wheels. Three pairs of steel hooks were attached on each side of the skid, with the hope that they would catch the elevated ropes crossing over the landing deck on the *Pennsylvania*. So that the hooks wouldn't snag into cracks on the wooden platform, the points of each hook were filed down and dulled. Each U-shaped hook had a four-inch opening and a sixteen-inch shank. The shank was mounted parallel to and about four inches below the bottom of the central skid. There was a spring attached between the skid and the shank of each hook, so that if a hook unexpectedly hit an obstruction while rising from the ground, it would give way for a moment, but then automatically and immediately spring back to its proper position.[3]

The crew took a few extra precautions just in case the aeroplane missed the ship and landed in the water. Two seven-foot pontoons were attached under the lower wings and a hydroplane near the front wheel would keep the machine from somersaulting head first into the bay. "They nailed a couple of pontoons under my machine," Gene said, "and tied a bunch of bicycle tubes into a true lover's knot around my chest as a life preserver." He had chosen the inner tubes to replace the navy-issued pneumatic life preserver he had used during his flight from the *Birmingham*. It had "proved cumbersome," he said, "interfering with the free use of my arms and legs."[4]

Some have said that because Gene wore these inner tubes as a flotation device, he was afraid of the water and couldn't swim. Although it's one of the most persistent stories attached to the *Pennsylvania* flight, there seems to be no evidence that it's true. Most often quoted is Admiral van Deurs, who in his book, *Wings for the Fleet*, wrote, "Iowa-born Ely could not swim, feared the water, got seasick on ferryboats, and knew nothing about ships." Unfortunately, the Admiral doesn't cite a source for his information and neither do any of the others who make the claim. Gene did admit that he got seasick. "The only thing I should fear in going to sea with my machine," he said, "would be seasickness." Except for a brief mention after he flew from the *Birmingham* of his not being fond of the water, the contemporary evidence that he couldn't swim is missing. Perhaps he wore his improvised life vest for the same reason he wore a helmet—safety. If he fell into the ocean without protection and was knocked unconscious, it wouldn't matter at all whether he could swim or not. Although the swimming story may be true, the claim seems to be less fact and more of a dramatic enhancement—imagining the courage of a man who is unable to swim and yet flies across saltwater to land on and take off from a ship.[5]

As for Gene's helmet, it may be, as some claim, a football helmet; however, with its added height, it more resembles one of the French aviation helmets that were being introduced at about the same time. This may have been the first time Gene wore it. Earlier, and in some later photographs, he wears unpadded leather caps that appear to offer little more than warmth and protection from the wind. Gene's helmet for the *Pennsylvania* flight was made of heavy cork covered in thin brown leather. "What do you wear this heavy thing for, Eugene?" asked a friend who had picked it up. "Gene smiled and said, "Oh, that's just to protect my head in case I should fall."[6]

At 10:45 in the morning, Gene left Selfridge Field. "The atmospheric conditions appeared to be good," Gene said, "but, as I discovered after I got up in the air a few hundred feet, there was a good stiff breeze blowing." He flew out over the bay and turned north. Even with the southeast wind blowing at between 10 and 15 miles an hour, Gene liked the way the air held up his machine. "The quality of the air was good," he said. "It was heavy and moist and of even pressure. The temperature was cold enough to make me uncomfortable, but I cannot say that the coldness was severe enough to incapacitate me or to interfere with the free use of all the members of my body."[7]

As he passed the Hunters Point Peninsula on his left, he took aim at the red and black buoy that marked the final resting place of the iron-hulled cargo ship, *May*

*Flint.* In September 1900, she had drifted into the battleship *Iowa* near Man of War Row, her metal plating split and within five minutes, she sank in 15 fathoms of water. "As I came out over the bay above Hunters Point," Gene said, "I was about 1,200 feet up. It was cloudy, smoky and hazy. I could not see the ships at first and did not locate them until I was within about two miles of them."[8]

Visibility was only slightly better for the few hundred telescopes and binoculars scanning the southern sky on board the small boats and ships surrounding the *Pennsylvania*. Suddenly, the siren on the *West Virginia* screamed out a harsh, undulating wail. From the *Pennsylvania*'s crow's nest a sailor shouted, "There she blows! He's 10 miles southwest, sir." Captain Pond turned his binoculars to the speck in the sky. "That's a seagull," said one of the invited guests. "No," Pond said. "It's too steady for a seagull."[9]

The original plan had been to steam the *Pennsylvania* out to sea, turn into the wind at a speed between 10 to 20 knots, letting the biplane gradually approach in what was expected to be a less difficult landing than Gene was about to attempt. Pond said that it was Gene who had asked officers of the Pacific Fleet and members of the aviation committee to keep the ship anchored in San Francisco Bay. They agreed "with the wishes of the aviator."[10]

The wind was directly behind and pushing Gene along at about 60 miles an hour. The *Pennsylvania* was a mile away with her stern pointed south, into the wind. That would be a problem. Gene's landing would be with the wind, meaning he'd hit the landing deck faster than he wanted.

"I veered off to pass over what I supposed was the flagship *California*," he said. He later learned that this ship was actually the *Maryland* and not the *California*, which had sailed for Santa Barbara nearly two weeks earlier. In a salute to the admiral, who he believed was on board, Gene dove from 1,000 to 400 feet in mere seconds. The *Maryland* was anchored about a 1,000 yards behind and on the starboard side of the *Pennsylvania*. Gene passed directly over the *Maryland* and continued to descend, making a slow, wide turn a few hundred yards off the bow of the *Pennsylvania*. Suddenly he dove toward the water. "That dive never will be forgotten by those who saw it," said a reporter. "At a right angle to the water, Ely coasted down to within 50 feet of the waves. Women on the *Pennsylvania* screamed and men shouted out in fear." A calm Mabel, standing next to Captain Pond and his wife, assured the dignitaries that everything was all right. By the time Gene reached the cruiser *West Virginia*, about 500 yards off *Pennsylvania*'s port side; he had climbed back to 100 feet. He flew over the *West Virginia*'s bow and continued circling around the *Pennsylvania* until he was 500 yards behind her. "I pointed my machine for the *Pennsylvania*," he said. "I then made a sharp turn about 100 yards astern of that ship, gradually dropping down." Captain Pond estimated that it had barely been two minutes "from the time the aeroplane was first sighted, and no one expected him to land on the very first turn."[11]

Seventy-five yards from the *Pennsylvania*, Gene realized he'd have to compensate for the steady 15 mile an hour wind that was crossing from behind and diagonally across the cruiser's deck. "I had to calculate the force of this wind and the effect it would have on my approach to the landing," he said. If he flew straight onto the deck, the wind would push him left and he might miss his landing entirely. He decided to fly in a straight line toward the ship, but aimed slightly to the right. "I had to take the

**Eugene Ely's Curtiss pusher biplane approaches the Armored Cruiser U.S.S. *Pennsylvania* in San Francisco Bay, January 18, 1911. Despite a crosswind pushing his biplane to his left, Ely was able to compensate and make a successful landing, becoming the first person to land an airplane on a ship (Naval History and Heritage Command #NH 1385).**

chance that I had correctly estimated just how many feet the wind would blow me out of my course."[12]

There had been little time to recover from the shock of Gene's sudden dive before spectators realized that he was actually going to try a landing. Everyone fell silent and the biplane seemed to hang in the air as it slowly approached the deck. James Radley, the English aviator who was a guest on the *Pennsylvania*, said that with current wind conditions, he thought Gene wouldn't be able to land. Radley was still expressing his doubts when Gene crossed over the fantail overhang at the end of the landing deck and shut off his motor. The flow of the wind around the stern was broken, causing the gliding biplane to lift slightly and tilt to the left. "This puff of wind raised my machine a little," Gene said. "I thought for a moment that it was all up with me and that I could not hit the platform squarely. I cannot say that I was frightened, as it was so quick that I did not have time to think of the results of a failure. It was all over in a moment. Instead of catching the first ropes with my grappling hooks, I skipped three and she caught the fourth. I could feel her bringing up as she picked up the different drags, one after another, and as the strain became greater, she fetched up with a jerk that almost unseated me."[13]

About to land on U.S.S. *Pennsylvania's* wooden landing deck, Eugene Ely struggles against a crosswind. Note the duffle bags lining both edges of the deck. Each was weighed down with fifty pounds of sand and connected in pairs across the deck by a rope that stretched just a few inches above the deck. The ropes would catch a hook on the bottom of the biplane and bring it to a safe stop. A modern version of this "tailhook" scheme is still in use on Navy carriers today (Naval History and Heritage Command #NH 82737).

He had come to a stop in less than 30 feet from where he had landed, leaving another 50 feet of runway to spare. "If anything, I was brought to a stop a little too short," he said, "and it probably would have been better to have had a little less weight in the sandbags." Although he had landed with plenty of room to spare, Gene didn't think the landing platform should be any shorter. "I do not think a smaller one would be entirely safe for such an experiment," he said.[14]

It was a near perfect landing. "Three feet more of elevation would have forced him to plunge directly into the canvas screen," Captain Pond said, "and three to ten feet less elevation would have caused him to strike" the stern of the ship "with consequences which can only be surmised."[15]

The moment Gene touched down sirens shrieked and a hundred steam whistles all blew. Cheers, shouts, and applause echoed across the bay, not only from the *Pennsylvania*, where every sailor was waving his hat in the air, but also from every boat on the bay and the thousands of spectators who lined the San Francisco piers. Before

Gene had a chance to step off his machine, the deck swarmed with sailors who wanted a close-up look at the aviator and his aeroplane. Mabel, Captain Pond, and other dignitaries, rushed down from the navigating bridge to greet him. "From Captain Pond to his Chinese cabin boy," said a reporter, "the crew of the warship developed a sudden desire to dance and shout, and the guests that thronged the cruiser's decks joined with the navy in the most enthusiastic welcome that ever greeted visitor to a ship of the line." As Gene stepped onto the deck, Mabel was there with a kiss and arms around his neck. "You dear, brave boy!" she said. "I knew you could do it, Eugene." In what was the "hurrah" of its day, the crew began shouting "Hurroo! Hurroo!" Even Captain Pond was lost in the excitement. He too hurroo'ed and then, while hugging Mabel, he gave her a kiss on the cheek. Neither Mrs. Pond nor Gene made a complaint.[16]

Photographers took photographs from every angle and, "so that the men on the ships not present might at some future time have yesterday's performance reproduced for their entertainment and instruction," the Navy had a motion picture cameraman stationed high above. One wonders if that historic film may still survive on a long forgotten shelf in some Navy archive.[17]

Just minutes after the onboard celebration began, the *Pennsylvania*'s wireless operator tapped out a message to the Selfridge Field wireless station. "Ely at 10:59 landed on the *Pennsylvania* as pretty and light as a bird."[18]

Wearing two bicycle inner tubes as a life preserver and a heavy cork-lined helmet, Eugene Ely is congratulated on the deck of the cruiser U.S.S. *Pennsylvania* by his wife, Mabel, and Captain Charles Pond. Ely had just become the first man to land an airplane on a ship. The identity of the man behind Captain Pond is unknown (Diane Dunlop Collection).

After landing his Curtiss biplane on the U.S.S. *Pennsylvania* and dining with Captain Charles Pond and his officers for an hour, Eugene Ely prepares for takeoff. Only the second time anyone has ever flown an airplane off a ship (Naval History and Heritage Command #NH 77588).

"It was far easier than I thought it would be," Gene said, as he bowed to the spectators. "I want to thank Captain Pond for the opportunity he afforded me of making aeronautical history, and I also want to express my sincere appreciation of the applause given me by the thousands of people who were on the shore and in boats." Mabel took a small bouquet of California violets from her corsage and fastened it to one of the wing supports at the front of Gene's biplane, for which she "received a salvo of applause." She joined arms with Gene and Captain Pond, who led them below to the captain's cabin where they had lunch with admiring friends, military officers, foreign diplomats, and only the most important invited guests. It was a chance, said a reporter, to wash the "cloud dust out of his throat with a draught of Navy sherry."[19]

Gene's landing had converted a skeptical Captain Pond. The man who was furious when he learned his ship was chosen for the aeroplane landing, was now an enthusiastic supporter. "As a result of this experiment and of my observations on the aviation field," he wrote in his report, "I desire to place myself on record as positively assured of the importance of the aeroplane in future naval warfare."[20]

While Gene dined, a few of the *Pennsylvania*'s sailors cleared the sandbags and

**With tension in his face, Eugene Ely poses for one last photograph as he prepares to start his 8-cylinder Curtiss biplane for its takeoff from the U.S.S. *Pennsylvania* and the 10-mile flight back to Selfridge Field, south of San Francisco (Naval History and Heritage Command #NH 77579).**

ropes from the platform and turned the biplane around. They filled the gas tank and removed the arresting hooks from the landing skid. Just before noon, Gene suited up for his return to the aviation field. While he did a careful inspection of his machine, a sailor in search of souvenirs, pulled a few of Mabel's violets from the front of the plane, not realizing that Mabel was back on the navigating bridge and could plainly see him. "Don't you dare!" she screamed. "Put 'em right back!" He sheepishly did put them back and to make amends, offered Gene the cap band from his hat that said "U.S.S. *Pennsylvania*." Gene thanked him and asked him to tie the band around his left arm. The biplane's engine began its sputter. Gene climbed on, sat patiently as photogra-

**In a San Francisco Bay crowded with boats, Eugene Ely takes off from the U.S.S. *Pennsylvania* on the return flight to Selfridge Field. Barely an hour earlier, Ely had made the very first airplane landing on a ship (Diane Dunlop Collection).**

phers snapped a few last minute pictures, and then he leaned back for a moment, listening to make sure the motor was hitting correctly. When the deck was clear of sailors, he revved the engine, signaled his mechanics to let go, and began rolling down the platform. Unlike the *Birmingham* flight, this time there was barely a dip. "I dipped a trifle," he said, "but I did not wet my tires." Then he added, with a smile. "I am speaking of the tires on the wheels of the machine, not my chest protector." He began to climb. "I kept her elevated sharply for I wanted to get up one thousand feet or more.... She went as lightly as one of those gulls that were circling around the cruiser," he said. The delirious crowd cheered as he soared up into the sky and quickly flew away.[21]

"The cheers that sounded behind me as I sped away from the *Pennsylvania* were the sweetest music my ears have ever heard," Gene said. "I never regarded the undertaking as hazardous as the naval officers did, but those cheers persuaded me that I had accomplished something real at last." He unconsciously turned from the bay and flew toward the hills, his mind wandering. "In that moment of supreme joy and elation," he said, "I came more nearly losing control of myself and my machine than ever before in my flying career." A thousand feet in the air, he smiled at Mabel's violets as they quivered in the wind. He was daydreaming now, his ears straining to hear the cheers still coming from behind. Walter Brookins had warned Gene about the dangerous wind currents over the San Bruno Hills, but, "exulting and heedless," Gene said, "I rose to 1,400 or 1,500 feet and shot straight over the range of hills." Almost instantly, the whirling air snared him. "I was wobbling and battling for all I was worth.... For three minutes I experienced the roughest flying I have ever known. But I fought my way through to safety and shot down to the grass of Selfridge Field."[22]

Now the cheers were in front of him and the nearer he came, the louder they grew. "The world seemed to be celebrating the Fourth of July," he said. "The crowd had not waited to see the *Pennsylvania* cap band tied around my arm by a sailor—the wireless—the only thing that could beat me back—had already announced the success of the trip." At 12:12, Gene landed just 10 feet from where he had taken off. This time Mabel wasn't first to greet him, she was being rushed by automobile back to the aviation field. Army officers and soldiers charged out to his machine just as the sailors had done on the *Pennsylvania*. They grabbed him, raised him up, and put him on the shoulders of a husky Private Pounds who carried him to the headquarters tent. They put him down in front of Major O'Neill and every man who could reach Gene began patting him on his back and shaking his hand. They shouted questions and Gene in his quiet way, calmly answered. "There is very little to say about the flight and the result speaks for itself," he said. "I picked out the place where I intended landing and placed my machine right there. I judged the time it would take me to fly across the water and left the field with the intention of arriving at the battleship exactly on time. I am told that I have done so and am pleased that I was able to keep my word so exactly." They wanted to know if he thought he could do it again. "It was easy enough and I think the trick could be turned successfully nine times out of 10," he said. "I have no doubt it will be soon duplicated by others."[23]

Major O'Neill called the men to attention and ordered them to cheer for Gene. Then he took him inside the officer's mess, where Gene received more congratulations. "You are now a member of this mess," O'Neill said, "and you must avail yourself of our hospitality." He handed Gene a glass filled with some unknown beverage and proposed a toast. "Once before Mr. Ely sailed in an aeroplane from the deck of a war vessel, the first time that feat was ever accomplished," O'Neill said. "Today he landed on the deck of a war vessel, and not only did he land successfully, but he also repeated his former achievement by flying into the air again. This day will be an epoch mark in naval history."[24]

Because of the earlier weather delays, Curtiss had missed Gene's historic flight. "I was obliged to leave for San Diego," Curtiss said. "I regarded the thing as most difficult of accomplishment. Of course, I had every faith in Ely as an aviator, and knew that he would arrive at the ship without trouble, but I must confess that I had misgivings." He waited impatiently for the latest news and when the Associated Press bulletin announcing Gene's success arrived, Curtiss felt relieved and in his detached way, felt a sense of excitement. "I don't think there has ever been so remarkable a landing made with an aeroplane as Ely's," he said, "and probably never so much store put by the mere act of coming down in the right place." Any accident, he said, "might have spelled disaster for the whole undertaking, deprived the daring aviator of a well earned success, and the world of a remarkable and spectacular demonstration of practical aviation."[25]

Gene stayed on the ground for the rest of the day and the show went on, but the only topic of conversation anyone cared about was Gene's flight to and from the *Pennsylvania*. Frederick Scotford, chairman of the aviation committee, sent a telegram to San Francisco's popular Republican Congressman Julius Kahn, suggesting that Gene be rewarded for his achievement.

"Army and Navy officers detailed to San Francisco aviation meet, the businessmen's aviation board, as well as thousands of other San Franciscans, suggest Eugene Ely should receive national recognition for epoch making flight yesterday to deck of cruiser *Pennsylvania*, marking new era in military sciences. Respectfully suggest you father bill providing for special congressional medal."

The medal would never come.[26]

# { 32 }

## "Best girl"

After two more days of bad weather, the aviation meet began again on Saturday, January 21. The wind near the ground was deceptively gentle and although it was a bit cool in the shade, overall temperatures remained mild. The sun was bright, with only a few clouds drifting by, but the aviators still flew cautiously and low. At higher altitudes they had found it icy cold with blustery winds that just weren't safe. Yet as tame as this show might seem to some spectators, the birdmen marked the day with some humor and an aviation landmark.

The humor came from a frivolous adventure for Frederick Scotford, the heavyweight president of the aviation committee. Walter Brookins invited him to ride with him on his Wright biplane. It was a four-minute, machine-wobbling, low-level flight through choppy breezes, but Scotford said he thoroughly enjoyed it. "You've established another record," he said to Brookins, when they landed. "How so?" asked the puzzled Brookins. "You've just carried the heaviest man that ever flew in a heavier-than-air machine," Scotford said. "I weigh 249 pounds." Scotford had apparently topped the previous flying weight record of Gene's friend, Whipple Hall, by nearly 40 pounds.[1]

Not much later, Army Lieutenant Paul Beck, while riding with Phil Parmelee, performed an experiment of a more substantial nature that, for the military at least, came close to rivaling Gene's flight to and from the *Pennsylvania*. Beck was conducting a simple demonstration of air to ground, wireless communication. He and Earl Ennis had set up a wireless radio shack at the end of the Selfridge Field grandstand. Ennis was the owner and possibly the only employee of Western Wireless Equipment Company of San Francisco. He had assembled a 29-pound transmitter in a red mahogany box with a brass telegraph key attached to its top. As Beck flew with Parmelee, he carried the box on his lap. To ensure that the Beck and the ground radio operator had not conspired to send a prearranged message, a reporter handed Beck a folded piece of paper with a short message on it. Beck was told not to look at the message until he was in the air and ready to transmit.[2]

Flying near 55 miles an hour, about a mile from the radio shack, Beck tapped out his first message, but according to the San Francisco *Call* newspaper, it wasn't the one he'd been handed. "500 feet up and running level. It's getting chilly. *Blank, blank, blank*—awfully chilly." The three curse words were not reported in the newspapers, although one paper printed a selectively edited version of the message as, "It is getting (bumpy) up here." The word, "bumpy," said the paper, was put in parenthesis because the message was not completely received, "owing to a noise that occurred in the wireless station at the moment it came through the air." A moment later, Beck pulled the folded paper from his tunic and tapped out the reporter's message. Navy wireless operators at Mare Island and at the naval training station on Yerba Buena Island were surprised to hear Beck's messages breaking into their radio traffic. Forty miles to the south, a radio amateur also heard Beck. Military officials had not expected a signal to carry that far. With that kind of range, the scientific point was made. "From a military standpoint, the results obtained are invaluable," Ennis said. The aeroplane could fly high above the enemy's hostile fire and report important reconnaissance information back to headquarters. The wireless, Ennis said "is the most valuable contribution of the century to the science of modern warfare."³

It was Gene's turn, and as he walked to his machine, the crowd gave him a hero's

While Eugene Ely smiles, Mabel admires a gold medal presented to her husband on January 22, 1911. The medal commemorates Ely's landing on the U.S.S. *Pennsylvania* four days earlier and was paid for with donations from officers of the *Pennsylvania* and the U.S. Army's 30th Infantry Division, and from members of the San Francisco Aviation Committee (Naval History and Heritage Command #NH 77529).

welcome. Mabel was by his side cheering along with the spectators. He soared out to the edge of the San Bruno Hills and returned, dropping into a sudden dip before speeding twice around the 2 ½-kilometer course, and ending his day. It wasn't much of a performance, but it didn't seem to matter anymore. Just about anything he did these days was good enough for his adoring public.[4]

That evening, Gene and Mabel were guests of the Sigma Tau fraternity brothers in a theater box party at the Orpheum Theater on Market Street in downtown San Francisco. In addition to vaudeville antics and dramatic readings, motion pictures of Gene's *Pennsylvania* adventure were shown. Word quickly spread in the darkened theater that the famous aviator was in the audience. The frat boys stood, cheering and clapping until Gene finally stood up and bowed. "Speech!" they demanded and then drew quiet. "I can't talk as well as I can fly," Gene said, "but I thank you for—," and that was a far as he got, drowned out by more cheering and applause. The lights dimmed and the film flickered on the canvas screen. Gene saw himself land on the *Pennsylvania*, watched the officers and sailors greet him, and then saw his return flight to Selfridge Field. Flying into history—it must have been a dreamlike experience.[5]

Rather than wait for the congressional medal that members of the aviation committee had proposed, the membership, with additional donations from officers of both the U.S.S. *Pennsylvania* and the Army's 30th Infantry, had their own commemorative gold medal struck and presented to Gene at a special ceremony, on a Sunday afternoon, January 22.

A bashful Gene stood facing a grandstand packed tightly with boisterous spectators. Behind him was an honor guard company of soldiers and sailors standing at attention. Gene might have wanted to plug his ears against the military band blaring in full blast glory, but instead stood proudly with a smile on his lips. Mabel "beamed at him with love and pride in an affectionate glance that somewhat warmed the slightly chilled air of the aviation field." Captain Pond was first to speak. "Your feat—that of alighting on and then departing from a warship," Pond said, "marks an epoch in the history of aeronautics and of naval warfare. Untold possibilities arise in consequence of your courage, skill, and originality. From your deed may date an entirely new era in the history of warfare." The crowd cheered again as Major O'Neill took his turn. "I am glad, indeed," the major said, "that on Wednesday last, I saw Eugene Ely alight on the deck of the *Pennsylvania* and, after a brief visit, successfully fly away to a safe landing at Selfridge Field. That event will go down in the history of man's conquest of the air and it will date new plans and greater plans for offensive and defensive warfare."

Chairman Scotford said a few words and then introduced his wife as the person who would pin the medal on Gene. Mrs. Scotford stepped forward with Mabel following close behind. "I pin this medal on a brave bosom," she said with a laugh, as Gene's face turned red and he stammered out a couple of words of attempted thanks that showed how ill at ease he was. Mabel stepped forward and gave Gene a hug and a kiss on his cheek. No one could hear what they said to each other as Mabel admired the medal with her gloved hand. The crowd cheered again and Gene took off his hat and bowed. When the soldiers, sailors, and military band marched away, Gene hurriedly escaped to his biplane, "his medal stowed in his pocket along with a sack of tobacco, a monkey wrench, a pair of oil soaked gloves, and other things commonly acquired by aviators." He was anxious to fly away. He liked it better in the air anyway, but this trip was a reward, a special honor. Of all the aviators, he had been given the privilege of a date with San Francisco's favorite opera soprano, Luisa Tetrazzini, "Queen of the Songbirds."

A month before, Tetrazzini had mesmerized the city with a Christmas Eve concert like none ever seen before. Somewhere in America in December 1910, Christmas Eve might have been cold and smothered in snow, but not in San Francisco. For weeks that winter, as if to welcome Luisa Tetrazzini back to the town she loved, the weather in the city of a hundred hills had been as mild as a New York afternoon in May. "They are my family, all my children," she said, and because some of those children couldn't afford to hear her sing, she brought them a Christmas gift. She sang in the streets of San Francisco and risked her voice in the open air.[6]

Italian born, Tetrazzini, had made her American debut here in January 1905 with an eight-week season. An instant sensation, she sang 65 times in fifteen different operas. "They literally dragged her flower laden carriage through the streets," said William Leahy, owner of San Francisco's Tivoli Opera House. He had discovered Tetrazzini singing in Mexico and had brought her back to America. Tetrazzini returned twice that year then left for the glamour of New York City. Five years later, she returned an operatic prima donna, singing with the likes of Enrico Caruso and tangled up in a contract dispute.[7]

Believing her New York contract was no longer valid, Tetrazzini wanted to sign a new contract with Leahy who was ready to pay her at least $2,500 every time she sang. Impatient and furious, Tetrazzini told reporters that the courts couldn't stop her from singing. "I will sing in San Francisco," she said. "I will sing for nothing in that city where I was so warmly welcomed when I first came to America."[8]

She arrived in San Francisco in early December for a series of concerts and began planning the Christmas concert. More people would see Tetrazzini sing in that one short evening than probably attended a single day of the upcoming Selfridge Field aviation meet.[9]

A large platform was erected on Market Street in front of the *Chronicle* newspaper building, at the end of the Geary Street cable car line. The platform was backed with a 27-foot high sounding board to help project Tetrazzini's voice for blocks around. She offered to pay all costs, but city fathers asked for "the privilege of doing the work at the expense of the city ... in appreciation of the splendid Christmas gift she is making the citizens of San Francisco."[10]

The location of the platform, just east of Lotta's Fountain, was a sentimental choice. Shaped like a lighthouse, it stood at the center of one of San Francisco's busiest intersections, and miraculously had survived the 1906 earthquake. Lotta Crabtree had come to San Francisco as a child and after moving to the gold fields of Northern California, began entertaining at mining camps, where she was billed as "Little Lotta Crabtree." By 1875, when she was only 28 years old, Lotta was one of the best-known and wealthiest entertainers in the country; wealthy enough to give the city that she called home, a $10,000 bronze water fountain. On Christmas Eve, Market Street was silent, a reporter said, but "from the stand by Lotta's fountain came the sweetest sound from human lips."[11]

The crowd stood under twinkling stars, shoulder to shoulder, in temperatures floating in the low 50s. Some said over 250,000 people, over half the city's population, had squeezed into the outdoor concert hall. "There was not a window within range of her wonderful voice that was not filled with eager listeners, not a roof that did not add its quota to the audience." A *Call* newspaper conservatively estimated the crowd at nearly 100,000, although their reporter admitted that the estimate was probably much too low.[12]

Precisely on time, Tetrazzini appeared with a broad smile. She nodded, bowed, waved her handkerchief, and the crowd roared back with their approval. "A Caesar or an Alexander, an Antony or a Demosthenes, never raised such a roar out of human throats," said a reporter. The long white feathery plume on her hat wiggled as her head nodded from side to side and up and down to acknowledge the love of "my children." Her white dress sparkled in the bright beam of a spotlight mounted on a 10-story rooftop across Market Street.[13]

"Never, never in all my life, have I had an experience like that of Christmas Eve," Tetrazzini said. "I was almost afraid to do this …with so many thousand people it would be very difficult to maintain silence. Imagine my feelings when I stepped out on the platform and saw the great sea of faces." She had no reason to worry. From her first note, they were silent. "Never, even in the opera house or concert room, have I felt that so many people were listening so intently," she said. "You could have heard the song of a bird for several blocks."[14]

The aviation meet was almost over when San Francisco's "best girl" walked back into town after a month-long concert tour along the Pacific Coast. With two large bouquets of roses in one arm and "Aurora Borealis," her dog, in the other, Tetrazzini walked off a ferryboat at San Francisco's Ferry Building on January 18, just a few hours after Gene's *Pennsylvania* flight. "Ah, San Francisco, it is good to see," she told reporters. At an afternoon reception, where acting mayor, John Kelly, presented her a golden tablet in memory of her Christmas Eve concert, 550 schoolchildren sang a couple of Italian songs in her honor. With tears in her eyes and a struggling voice, Tetrazzini offered her gratitude. "It has been an afternoon that I will not forget as long as I live. This tablet already is engraved in my heart, and it shall be with me always."[15]

The next evening, the aviation committee formally invited her to attend the air exhibition at Selfridge Field "to watch the birdmen at play." She eagerly accepted. "I am just crazy about flying," she said. "I have never seen the wonderful flights that are startling the world, except in motion pictures, and even those thrilled me." Thrilled as she was, she gracefully declined the second part of the invitation. "They want me to fly with them," she said. "I know I have been called a bird—a songbird—but I almost tremble at the thought."[16]

Sunday, January 22, with perhaps the best weather of the entire meet, a crowd nearly rivaling that of Tetrazzini's Christmas concert, poured onto Selfridge Field for "Luisa Tetrazzini Day." That afternoon, after Gene had received his gold medal, he ran to his hangar where the crew was preparing his biplane. He would be surprising "the lovely Luisa" with and aerial escort to the exhibition.[17]

No one had told Tetrazzini that Gene was coming. The opera singer, her husband, and manager Leahy, had left their hotel by automobile for Selfridge Field shortly after 2 o'clock. It was a scenic drive just inland from the ocean, on the west side of San Francisco. They came to the Ingleside Golf Links, not far from the old horse track where Gene had raced a few automobiles after the earthquake. Gene had asked the aviation committee to have Tetrazzini's party stop here and wait for an escort, but no one told them what kind of escort it would be. In the half-hour it had taken Gene to receive his gold medal, the Tetrazzini party had arrived at the golf course. Leahy phoned from the clubhouse, wondering why the escort hadn't arrived yet. "Tell them it will be there in a few minutes," Gene said. In less than a minute he was on his way, a five-minute trip by air from Selfridge Field.[18]

Tetrazzini was chatting on the clubhouse lawn, when an employee of the club began shouting for everyone to look up at the approaching aeroplane. Tetrazzini, was as delighted as a child at a surprise birthday party. From 2,000 feet, Gene chose his landing spot and in preparation for the "Ely Glide," shut off his engine. "Like a hawk at play, he dropped, as it seemed, from the very clouds and came to rest on the putting green in front of the clubhouse."[19]

Gene put his helmet under his arm and walked toward Tetrazzini as she began to shuffle toward him. "It's Ely!" Leahy shouted. "The greatest birdman of them all." Gene smiled as he offered his hand. "I come to welcome the greatest songbird of them all," Gene said. Tetrazzini grabbed his hand and shook it hard. The excitement put tears into her eyes. Suddenly, she rushed to her automobile and pulled away two pennants that were mounted over the headlights, each bearing her photograph. Then, rushing back to the biplane, she pinned the pennants to the top wing, one at each end. "With my compliments and best wishes, Mr. Ely," she said. She and Leahy had forgotten all about their missing escort until Gene told them he would be their guide. Gene told their chauffeur to keep an eye on his biplane and to follow it as he flew above them. Back in the air, Gene flew as slowly as he could, but the dirt highway had seen too much weather over the past few weeks and the chauffeur couldn't keep up. Realizing that he had lost track of the automobile, Gene circled back trying to find it, but with hundreds of autos still headed south toward Selfridge, it was impossible to tell them apart. He returned to the field and when he landed, he said that Tetrazzini was just a few minutes behind him. A half-hour later, the diva arrived.[20]

Dressed in black with matching hat and feather plume, Tetrazzini stepped from her automobile to the deafening waves of applause that billowed across Selfridge Field and echoed into the hills. Accepting the crowd's reception with a smile, she clasped her hands and shook them overhead like a victorious prizefighter. Someone near her remarked how soft and balmy the weather was. "Ah, can you wonder that I love California?" Tetrazzini said, still bowing to the crowd. "It is just like my beloved Italy." She was led to a garishly decorated throne at the front of the grandstand where she received a line of city officials, aviation committee members, military officers, and aviators. When Gene reached her, she teasingly scolded him for deserting her as a guide. The crowd continued to roar, prompting Tetrazzini to stand on her throne and wave. Above, Parmelee had been flying for hours on a voyage that would break the American record for flight duration. "I couldn't hear any of the cheering," he said later, "but I noticed a good deal of commotion down there about the time I passed the record mark."[21]

Gene was the first to grab Parmelee's hand when he landed with only a few drops of gasoline left in his tank and the American endurance record—3 hours, 39 minutes, 49 ½ seconds. Gene boosted Parmelee's chilled body onto the shoulders of his fellow birdmen and, while the band played *Hail to the Chief* and *America*, they carried the protesting aviator to Tetrazzini's throne. The diva pinned a small bouquet of violets on Parmelee's coat and congratulated him on his success.[22]

Before she left for Los Angeles, Tetrazzini thanked everyone for her special day. "It is a day I can never forget," she said. "You San Franciscans are always doing something delicious for me, and I do not know how I can ever thank you. I wish to also thank the birdmen—as you call them—for flying so daringly for me, and especially Mr. Ely, who flew out and met me. It is all so wonderful that I cannot express how I feel.... I hope to come back to you soon."[23]

While Gene made one final flight at Selfridge Field before joining Glenn Curtiss at his new training school in San Diego, Mabel was chatting with friends and answering the usual "do you worry" questions from a reporter who thought she looked "pretty, fresh skinned, and vivacious." "Nervous? Why no." she said. "He can take care of himself." Gene landed gracefully, the crowd cheered, and Mabel smiled. "The little woman in the box was supremely happy," said a reporter, but Gene was having doubts.[24]

# { 33 }

## "The noble art"

"I wanted a place with the best climate to be found in this country," Glenn Curtiss said, "with a field large enough and level enough for practice flights by beginners, and with a convenient body of smooth water for experiments with a machine that would start from land or upon water."[1]

While he was in San Francisco, Curtiss had received the invitation he had been waiting for. Members of the newly formed Aero Club of San Diego thought they had found his perfect location. "San Diego was brought to my attention as affording every advantage for experimental work in aviation," Curtiss said. "A study of the weather bureau records showed a minimum of wind and a maximum of sunshine the year round." Excited by the potential, Curtiss decided it was time to personally check it out. Two days before Gene made his *Pennsylvania* flight, Curtiss and Lieutenant Ellyson left for San Diego.[2]

Curtiss signed a three-year lease for the use of North Island, a flat and sandy sliver of land a few feet above high tide in San Diego Bay. Just about a half-mile wide and a mile long, it was situated barely a mile away from the city. It was surrounded by water on only three sides, but much of the time it was still an island, connected to Coronado Island on its eastern edge by a thin sandbar that was always submerged during high tides. Northeast of the sandbar was a narrow and shallow slough called the Spanish Bight. The Bight, a few hundred yards wide and three quarters of a mile long, opened into the bay. Because the U.S. Navy began dredging San Diego Bay in 1944 to allow access to aircraft carriers, the Bight disappeared under sixteen million cubic yards of bay bottom mud, and the two islands became one—but it was here that Curtiss perfected his hydroaeroplane.[3]

The Spanish Bight and North Island offered more than just a perfect location for experiments and pilot training. Curtiss especially liked that both were remote and far away from prying eyes. "The island on which we were to do our experimenting and training was accessible only by boat," he said, "and it was a comparatively easy matter to exclude the curious visitor whenever we desired to do so." Excluding the public would allow him to work "unhampered by crowds," what he called, "a distracting influence."[4]

Army lieutenants Beck and Walker, were ordered to San Diego to learn flying from

Curtiss. They left San Francisco at the end of the month and joined Lieutenant Ellyson who was already helping Curtiss with his hydroaeroplane. Curtiss gave flying lessons early in the morning and late in the afternoon, the only times when wind conditions were acceptable. The rest of the day was left for experiments. It was a tedious process, but Curtiss was never discouraged. "Nearly every day for over two weeks we dragged the machine down to the edge of the water," he said, "launched it on the smooth surface of San Diego Bay, and drew it out again after testing some new arrangement of floats and surfaces." The men were waist deep in water for at least half of every day. Their clothes were always wet, their feet always cold. Eventually it was easier to wear swimsuits.[5]

January 26 was planned as just another day of tests. Ellyson spun the propeller and Curtiss began to accelerate over the Bight. He was bent over, looking down, intently watching how the hydroplane cut through the water. When he briefly looked up, he saw he was speeding directly toward shore. "I tilted the horizontal control and the machine seemed to leap into the air like a frightened gull," he said. "So suddenly did it rise that it quite took me by surprise."[6]

Rising to 50 feet, he flew for nearly a minute and a half before landing. He turned the floating craft around "as easily as a motor boat" and then pushed the machine to full power. He rose again, this time sailing over the bay toward San Diego at 100 feet. He circled around a couple of ships in the harbor, listening to their sirens wail, before returning to a gentle landing on the Spanish Bight. "I got more pleasure out of flying the new machine over water than I ever got flying over land," he said.[7]

It was an historic military moment. In the span of two weeks, Gene and Curtiss had changed the rules of naval warfare. Gene had landed on a ship and Curtiss had "succeeded in solving the one problem the Secretary of the Navy regarded as the most difficult, the one necessary to make the aeroplane of value to the navy." Now an aeroplane could be flown from land or water; landing on either at will.[8]

The San Francisco meet closed the day before Curtiss took off from the water. Gene headed to San Diego to fly a two-day exhibition with the Curtiss team. He and Mabel checked into the U.S. Grant Hotel, San Diego's newest and finest, and once again, reporters swarmed around him. Gene usually had a ready answer for everything, but occasionally, when he was stumped, he faked it. "Mr. Ely," someone said one morning, "I would like to hear your views on the possibilities of the ornithopter." In 1911, an ornithopter was a machine that tried to fly by flapping its wings like a bird. Gene, with a thinking frown on his lips, looked thoughtfully at the man, calmly took a drag on his cigarette, and then, with a flick of his finger, knocked off its ash. "Frankly," Gene said, "I would not risk my life in an ornithopter. The flying principles are not correct and the machine is not stable. That of course is my own personal opinion. I wouldn't have you condemn it on my say so." Happy to receive the opinion of an aviation expert, the man thanked Gene, smiled, and quickly walked away. Gene stared after him for a moment and then turned to a friend. "Now, what in the hell is an ornithopter?" he asked.[9]

With Mabel's ability to charm nearly every reporter she met, she never seemed to tire of answering the same questions over and over. "Mrs. Ely is young," said one scribe, "in fact, she is so very young that one involuntarily looks for her hair ribbon and sailor collar. She is pretty, petite, piquant, and lots of other adjectives that go to epitomize radiant youth." Mabel always made sure that everyone knew that Gene was her brave knight. "Bravery?" she said. "Why the knights of the olden days were children in comparison with the twentieth century heroes." But reporters still wanted to know how it was possible for her not to worry when her husband was "suspended so high in the sky." What was her secret? "Your desires are your prayers," she said. "I never allow the thought of an accident to enter my mind."[10]

The San Diego exhibition ran over the January 28–29 weekend. It was another aerial circus, this time sponsored by the San Diego Aero Club and held at the Coronado Polo Field, directly across the Spanish Bight from the Curtiss base on North Island. Waiting for the first sign of a birdman in flight, the small crowd stared intently toward the hangar across the Bight through misty air and occasional light showers. "There came a whirring, pounding noise not unlike the flushing of a covey of giant birds," said a reporter, "and almost instantly a great salvo of cheers rent the air as a big Curtiss racing biplane lifted itself above the sagebrush across Spanish Bight and ascended higher and higher." It was Curtiss. Following the line of the beach to the end of North Island, he crossed over the channel, soared to 200 feet, circled a few times around the grandstand, and then landed in front of the crowd. Gene was already in the air, gaining altitude, and zooming a mile west toward the Point Loma headlands. Circling back to Coronado, he prepared a terrifying surprise for everyone. Still 500 feet above the grandstand, his sputtering engine suddenly stopped, and his machine seemed to freeze for a moment in mid air. Then, one wing tipped toward earth and the biplane began to fall in tight, spiraling circles, plummeting ever nearer the ground. "It seemed the machine must have lost its intangible grip on the upper ether," said a reporter. Gene waited until the last moment, when everyone was sure that this last circle would drive him into the grandstand, but then, with a gentle flare, Gene leveled off and landed softly on the grass. For the first time, he had performed the "death defying Spiral Dip," thrilling everyone but Curtiss and Mabel, who both were at his side before he could even get off his machine. Curtiss was first with a loud and fierce scolding, warning him against any further attempts at "toying with death." Mabel was furious and demanded that he promise to "never, ever do" that again. Gene made the pledge, but he wouldn't keep it. The dip was a crowd pleaser and enhanced his reputation. In the coming months, Mabel would scream and scream again, but now that Gene had finally done it, he would continue to do it.[11]

On Sunday, the air was still and the weather ideal, bringing at least 10,000 people out to Coronado. Gene, Curtiss, and Hugh Robinson did some fine flying. The most entertaining flight that day was flown by Curtiss. A helium filled toy balloon was released and Curtiss took off in hot pursuit. As the balloon waggled and drifted through the atmosphere, Curtiss followed it with abrupt and steep-angled turns that always seemed to push the balloon a little farther away in a different direction. The spectators followed his stunt with applause and long and loud laughter. With Robinson flying below and Gene above, the two thrilled spectators with a five-mile neck and neck air race out over the bay that ended in a narrow victory for Robinson. Gene snuck in another spiral dip and, when he landed, stood silently as Mabel gave him another tongue lashing.[12]

As good as the flying was in San Diego, the only man to make an historic flight was Lieutenant Ellyson. Climbing onto his 4-cylinder training machine, affectionately called the "grass cutter" because it seldom flew very high, Ellyson pressed on the accelerator and began running straight down the dirt runway, never getting off the ground. When he reached the edge of the island, he stopped, turned the aeroplane around, and headed back. After a few hundred feet, he suddenly went airborne, climbing to 25 feet. For at least 200 yards, he swayed from side to side and surged in waves like a slow rollercoaster. That's when he crashed to the ground, breaking a few wooden ribs, but doing no other damage. The machine rolled to a stop and Ellyson jumped off. For the first time in Navy history, a commissioned officer had flown an aeroplane.[13]

Gene was in an exhibition rut. He had been traveling almost constantly for eight months, making money, but surely feeling the pressures and dangers he faced each day. Although he would never say so publicly, he was beginning to look for a way out. In his words, he had finely "accomplished something real at last," and maybe now was the time to cash in. Earlier in the month, when Congress approved an appropriation that might allow the Army to buy as many as 25 aeroplanes, Gene saw the possibility of a new career, and before leaving San Diego for an exhibition in Sacramento, California, he wrote to Captain Chambers.[14]

> Dear Sir:
>
> According to the newspapers, the Army has an appropriation for aeroplanes, and if the Navy has none, it will get one soon, I suppose. There will probably be an experimental station and someone who is competent will be needed to carry on the work.
>
> If you will let me know how to go about it, I shall try to be the one selected. Mr. Curtiss has proved that an aeroplane can rise from the water and we knew before that one could alight without trouble. I have proved that a machine can leave a ship and return to it, and others have proved that an aeroplane can remain in the air for a long time, so I guess the value of the aeroplane for the Navy is unquestioned.
>
> Let me hear from you soon and oblige.
>
> Yours, Sincerely,
> Eugene.[15]

He asked Chambers to send his response to Salt Lake City, Utah where Gene would be performing in two weeks.

On their way north to Sacramento, Gene and Mabel stopped for a visit with Mabel's parents in Corte Madera, where it was even more obvious that Gene was ready to settle down. In the heart of town, he and Mabel purchased two lots on a piece of ground known as Pixley Rock and announced they would soon build a house there. "However nervous Mrs. Ely may feel when her husband soars through the clouds," said a reporter, "she will be assured of his safety when he sleeps beneath the roof of a cottage built on a rock." It was a logical choice. Gene, as a former Marin County chauffeur, had many friends in town and, of course, Mabel had grown up there.[16]

Meanwhile, Gene had also enlisted his father's help in his career campaign, perhaps believing that Nathan Ely's political connections could do some good.

Writing from his Davenport, Iowa, law office, Nathan wasted no time in pressing his son's case with the Secretary of the Navy. "Will you kindly advise me," he wrote, "whether or not there is now in existence or contemplated such a position as superintendent of aeronautics or some position for such purpose in the Navy, and whether or not there has been any provision made for the payment of expenses involved." He never mentioned Gene by name in his letter, but identified him only as "my son" who "has been doing the flying on and off the battleships at Hampton Roads and at San Francisco." He closed, asking that Gene be given a job. "I am very anxious to connect him, if possible, in some way with the Navy or Army in his line of business. "Thanking you in advance, I am, yours truly, N. D. Ely."[17]

Before Gene left San Diego, eastern newspapers began circulating a rumor that the Curtiss aviators and their aeroplanes would be drafted into the Army and forced to fight the world's first aerial combat missions. The Mexican Revolution that had flared up in 1910 was now roaring like a prairie wildfire and the conflict was coming too close to the U.S. border. With a battle raging just fourteen miles south of El Paso, Texas, and rebels capturing Mexicali, Mexico, a few hundred yards across the border from Calexico, California, the Army high command ordered soldiers from the Southwest, including San Diego, to patrol the border. Rumor said Curtiss and Wright fliers would be drafted too, but with no imminent threat of invasion, the idea was dropped—at least for the time being. Gene could continue to fly as a civilian for money, but because of the revolution, he had to cancel a scheduled exhibition in Mexico City.[18]

Curtiss continued to experiment with his hydroplane at San Diego, making changes and flying almost daily flights with his Army and Navy students as passengers. By February 17, the U.S.S. *Pennsylvania* had finished its training exercises off Santa Barbara and was now in San Diego Harbor. "I sent word over to Captain Pond," Curtiss said, "that I would be pleased to fly over and be hoisted aboard whenever it was convenient to him." Pond wired back immediately, "Come on over." Curtiss flew to the cruiser, landed in the water alongside, and a crane pulled him and his machine aboard. After 10 minutes on the ship, the aeroplane was lowered back into the water, Curtiss fired the engine, and two minutes later was back on the North Island beach. Within a month, Congress authorized $25,000 for naval aeronautic experiments.[19]

Reunited at the Agricultural Park Racetrack in Sacramento, Gene and Charles Willard were about to fly in an exhibition that would end in angry frustration. Willard began the three-day meet with a dramatic one-hour roundtrip flight in a blustery wind to the state capitol's rotunda, his aeroplane dipping and sliding with Willard struggling for control. A crowd rimmed the lower dome, said a reporter, "and waited in the gale for two hours to greet the aviator." As he circled the gold-trimmed dome, Willard took careful aim at Governor Hiram Johnson's office balcony and dropped a message of greeting. With uncanny precision, it landed barely three feet from the governor's office. The next day, only 3,000 spectators braved a rainstorm to see three mediocre flights. That night, Willard and Gene discovered that the local aviation committee had no money and couldn't pay. "Willard and I were induced to come to Sacramento for $7,000, to be placed in a local bank," Gene said. When they checked at the bank, they found no funds deposited. They confronted the aviation committee whose members said they had no way to pay what was owed. Gene and Willard threatened to sue. The committee scrambled and within a day came up with a little over $900. With money in hand, Gene and Willard packed their aeroplanes and left town for Salt Lake City.[20]

Within a few days of his arrival in Utah, Gene received an answer to his letter from Captain Chambers and the news wasn't good. Chambers said the Navy was asking Congress for $25,000 with which to buy aeroplanes and to fund experimentation and development, but that the funding wouldn't go far. "I fancy we will have to get some practice machines from this appropriation," he said, "although it must cover all the other paraphernalia of development, such as hangars, repair facilities, and training." He didn't expect to do any independent experimental work "for a long time," and would instead rely on aircraft manufacturers for future developments. There would be some aviation training stations established, and it was possible that the Navy would want to employ a trained aviator, but probably not for at least another year. "You may rest assured," Chambers wrote, "that we will keep you in mind for any opportunity that may arise." Chambers asked Gene if he had any ideas as to how the Navy should proceed with its aviation plans and congratulated him on his *Pennsylvania* success, offering his regrets that he "was unable to be there to grasp your hand and that of Mrs. Ely on that occasion."[21]

The letter that had started off affectionately with, "My Dear Ely," ended with an ominous and concerned personal warning. "I understand you made some very risky flights out there at San Diego," Chambers said, "and I want to give you the advice of a friend, to cut out the sensational features. I don't want to hear of your meeting the fate of those other fine fellows, Johnstone, Hoxsey, and Moisant.

"Please remember me to Mrs. Ely and say that I shall expect her to continue keeping her eye on you, for our sake, and for the sake of the noble art of aviation."[22]

# { 34 }

# Good Luck Charm

Spiraling down from 1,000 feet, Gene Ely took aim at the paying customers. Applause grew louder as the speck in the sky that was his biplane grew larger. The clatter of his 8-cylinder engine went suddenly silent and the ominous whooshing sound of the propeller kept getting closer. In mere seconds, what seemed to be just another part of the show became a hysterical and scattered dash for safety. A few feet from the ground, Gene gunned the engine, pulled up, and shot back into the sky. The game had worked again. Nervous laughter in the relieved crowd said that they were finally in on the joke. They had watched him conquer the air and fool them all. It was worth every penny and they had no regrets. He circled the field, waving at his adoring fans below, and then, with the wind snapping at his wings, he bounced to a hard landing and rolled to a stop. As he climbed down off the wing, he felt Mabel's hand on his shoulder and braced himself for the inevitable. She pleaded, then warned, and then told him NOT to do that again. Gene shrugged and squeezed out a sheepish laugh, but he didn't do it again—at least, not that day.[1]

Because he had taught himself to fly and was still unsure of his ability, Gene flew for almost a year before he had dared attempt the Death Spiral. He had met aviators like Ralph Johnstone who had died while performing it in Colorado. He and Mabel had been there to watch Arch Hoxsey spiral to his death in December. Just a day later, Gene had nearly died himself when a broken wire tangled around his propeller, sheared off one of the spinning blades, and sent him plunging toward earth. Though the landing was rough, it was a miraculous recovery and even he was surprised that he was still alive. Many might have given up the flying game at that point, but not Gene Ely. "I have no fear of dying and have had four close calls when each time I thought I was gone," he told a reporter. Then, awkwardly trying to reassure Mabel who stood beside him, he continued. "I never fly, except where I know it to be safe. You know, dear heart, from inside me must come the necessary assurance that I am fit. I can't translate it into words, but when its voice says, 'Don't fly!' then Eugene Ely does not fly."[2]

But the audiences were changing and the thrill of merely seeing aviation science in action was fading. Spectators had developed a ravenous taste for aerial "dare deviltry." It wasn't enough just to see a man fly anymore. The crowds wanted excitement, what critics said was the act of waiting to see someone die. Aviators faced a hard choice.

Take chances or lose money, and by the end of January 1911, Gene had made that choice. Now, after being the only man to take off from two ships and land on one, he was confident enough of his ability to take chances. His risks would spiral up as fast as his biplane spiraled down. "I see the crowd below me looking upward," he said, "and I know every man who watches me ... half expects to see me killed. I suppose they all figure how they'll help pick up my bones some day."[3]

For the rest of her life, Mabel Ely would always blame aviator, Lincoln Beachey, for Gene's death. "God punish you," she told him. "I can't forget that Eugene would be with me now if he had never seen you fly." She wasn't the only one who thought Beachey was responsible. "Ely was one of the most careful of the Curtiss aviators," Hugh Robinson said, "but during the past summer he had been associating considerably with Lincoln Beachey and I believe the influence had some effect on him, for he has been practicing aerial gymnastics considerably. He was a fine young fellow and every one of us who knew him, were greatly grieved at the loss."[4]

Ely and Beachey had met at the country's second Los Angeles aviation meet in December 1910, not long after Curtiss had accepted Beachey into the flying exhibition team. It was the same event where Arch Hoxsey fell to his death. Beachey began his aerial career in balloons when he was 17 years old, but five years later, in January 1910, at the first Los Angeles aviation meet, he decided it was time to become an aviator. "Boy, our racket is dead," he told his balloon-flying brother. After failing to build his own biplane and at first flunking out of the Curtiss aviation school, Beachey got a second chance and this time he stuck. He quickly became the most daredevil of all daredevil aviators—the ultimate risk taker. He didn't invent the dangerous spiral, he just perfected it.

He said it began as an accident while flying over a layer of cottony clouds, thousands of feet above Los Angeles. Beachey said he felt like an angel—"so much so, that in the ecstasy of the moment I began to sing aloud. And, in a twinkling, death seemed to creep upon me and reach out and touch me with a bony finger tip. My motor had stopped." He began to drop, the air rushing past him faster and faster. He knew he was going to die and there was nothing to do but get over it quickly. "I tilted the nose of the plane down at an angle and began to glide." But the biplane's wings resisted the strain of the rushing air as he broke through the clouds. "The memory of it all is now but a mad, dizzy whirl through space," he said. "I know I came down out of the heavens with the swish of a great condor. I could hear the hysterical applause as I turned up the nose of my plane to ease the force of my drop from the blue." He had saved himself. With new confidence, he began to test the limits of aerial maneuvers, inventing aerial twists and turns never thought possible. Beachey had become the "World's Most Daring Aviator." The maneuvers he invented, so confused newsmen and the public that, unless they got it from the aviator himself, no one was really quite sure what they were watching—the Vertical Drop, the Dutch Roll, an Ocean Roll, the Turkey Trot, a Death Spiral, or the Dip of Death. They only knew it was daring and dangerous.

In a remorseful talk to members of San Francisco's Olympic Club in 1913, Beachey vowed he would never fly again. By then, nine of his aviator friends, including Gene Ely, had died while performing the Death Spiral. "One by one they have hurtled down, clutching at the robes of God, to smash on Earth," Beachey said. "I have quit as a pacemaker for Death." But soon, he was back in the skies, taking more dips, and earning more money, until two years later, he too was dead. The Dip of Death had shattered his plane over San Francisco Bay and this time there was no escape. He had joined his "brother aviators who went crashing into eternity trying to out–Beachey Beachey."[5]

After Gene's first Spiral Death Dip that January in San Diego, he repeated it so often that one has to wonder if Mabel's nagging was simply an act, a publicity ploy intended to generate newspaper and spectator interest in Ely the daredevil. Considering their relationship, it seems inconceivable that Gene would continually ignore her feelings. Even he had said that she was in charge of just about everything. "My press agent," he told a reporter. "I haven't had a personal press agent since I've been married. Haven't needed any. My wife is my principal booster and my general superintendent." "When he is on the ground I'm boss of this little family," Mabel said, "but when he's in the air he does those spiral glides and everything because he knows I haven't got my system of mental telepathy fully developed as yet." When reporters asked Gene why he ignored his wife's warnings, he would smile and say there was less to worry about in the air than on the ground. "Why, man," he said, "a building might fall on me down on the ground. I know nothing can fall on me up there."[6]

Mabel on the ground was just as much a part of the show as Gene was in the air. They both typically arrived at an airfield in Gene's automobile with Gene driving. At the beginning of his flights, she was always the last to bid him goodbye, wish him good luck, and always the first to greet him on his return. She accompanied him to his biplane and before he climbed aboard they would chat. Gene would sometimes whisper something in her ear and they would briefly embrace. While he was in the air, "his wife never once took her eyes off Ely." When it was over and her hero stepped from his aeroplane, "there to receive him was the devoted young wife." "I am not afraid," she said. But then again, "she supposed she would be, if her husband was ever picked up out of a mass of tangled wings, canvas, and sticks." She said whenever she did see trouble in the air; she closed her eyes and held her breath. "I just shut my eyes tight and wish him to safety," she said. "Your desires are your prayers, you know. I keep saying He must be safe. He shall be safe. He is safe. Sure enough, when I look up again, he is winging on." They were inseparable. At the end of the day, before he left an exhibition field, she made sure Gene removed his flying gear and was presentable, wearing just the right hat and coat. "She shows herself to be as proud of her high flying spouse as it is possible for a woman to be proud of anything," said a reporter. "I go with him everywhere," she said. "I am his good luck. Things go wrong when I am not around. He says so himself."[7]

The couple rarely voiced their inner fears. "I believe I am not afraid of death," Gene once said, "but I cannot think without a shudder of those endless seconds when a man might be dropping, dropping, dropping through the air from the clouds to the ground. Those are the seconds I fear. Those are the seconds I never want to live." If those seconds had to come, Mabel knew how she wanted to live through them. "If he ever did fall," she said, "I want to be with him in the machine. It would be better to go together."[8]

Gene was her "boy" and she was his good luck charm. Perhaps if she had been with him at the end, she might have saved his life.

# { 35 }

# Land of Salt and Snow

Whipple Hall had arranged the Salt Lake City aviation meet. Even though he had managed the Bud Mars flights in Hawaii against Curtiss' wishes, apparently he and Curtiss still had a cordial business relationship. Hall had also set up the canceled Mexico City flight for Gene. Braving the Mexican insurrection to pick up a $10,000 guarantee that was supposed to be waiting in a Mexico City bank, his train had been attacked several times by small bands of rebels. "When I arrived," Hall said, "the government did not believe it advisable to hold the meet and so renounced the contract."[1]

He had better luck with the Salt Lake promoters, Ben Tibby and James Wade, who were anxious to pay almost any price for the world's best aviators, especially for Eugene Ely, "the most expert driver of aeroplanes living today." Hall also signed Willard and local amateur Clarence Walker. "They have guaranteed to deliver the goods," Wade said, "and their money is ready for them in Salt Lake." There was the usual speculation that Curtiss himself would fly, but that was just good publicity and never had a chance. "Curtiss does not fly for exhibition purposes any more, but for experimental work only," Hall said. Tibby and Wade had also wanted Brookins and Parmelee to appear, but they couldn't work out a contract with the Wrights.[2]

The site chosen for the air meet was Barrington Park, out on the barren alkali flats west of Salt Lake City, about seven miles east of the Saltair Pavilion. The pavilion, a Moorish-style, two-story building with a five-story dome, was the city's favorite summer resort for dancing and swimming. It was built out over the water, on the shoreline of the Great Salt Lake. Because the Saltair Railway connected the pavilion to downtown, placing the aviation field not far from the tracks should ensure a heavy attendance, and that was important. The railroad was the only way to get to the exhibition, because all the roads were blocked by the remnants of winter, "duck ponds, sloughs, mud holes, and ... mud, mud, mud every mile."[3]

Accompanied by Whipple Hall and the mechanical team, Gene was taken out to the 800-acre aviation park. He stepped off the train and took a quick look around. "This is really one of the greatest fields I have ever seen," he said. "How far is it to the lake?" Seven miles to the lake, he was told, "with a mile and a quarter getaway course." Gene smiled and turned to his mechanics. "Boys, get ready to swim Saturday afternoon," he said. "I'm going out and take a turn around that pavilion and shoot out over the lake." He joked that he might fall in. "If I do, I'll want some of you fellows to haul me out. Besides, all of you boys need a bath." The mechanics joined in the joke, agreeing that a bath probably wouldn't hurt them, but they also said that they really didn't want to take a wintertime swim. One of the huskier and more serious wrench turners apparently didn't get the joke. "Mr. Ely," he said, "If you're going over that lake, I'll take a chance at getting you back here safe and sound myself."[4]

Workers were finishing the grandstand and box seats that would seat over 7,000. They had been waiting for Gene to tell them where to put the old Ringling Brothers circus tent that would serve as the hangar for the aviators. Gene walked out a few yards from the center of the grandstand, turned back, and pointed to the ground. As he stood there, looking at the mountains, someone asked how he felt about flying in this high altitude, over 4,200 feet above sea level. "Why, this altitude is all right," he said. "We ought to attain considerable heights here. Those mountains will look a lot smaller to me next Saturday afternoon than they do now." He also said he didn't expect wind to be a problem; however, he noted that wind and altitude weren't the only things that might worry him. "I dread the cold, most of anything here," he said. "I am not used to it and it gets awfully chilly when you are a few thousand feet in the air. But the cold will affect me more than it will my engine."[5]

When Gene got back to town, he went to a restaurant where he ordered 250 sandwiches. "Where's the circus?" asked the waiter. Before Gene explained that the sandwiches were for his hungry mechanics, he answered with a joke. "Out here, about six miles," he said. "We're going to feed the animals right after the big show." He sent the sandwiches out to the aviation field and then found a downtown candy shop where he bought the daintiest box of chocolates he could find. "You don't mean to say you are going to send your men candy?" someone asked. "Well, hardly," Gene said. "This candy is for my wife. I never get anything for the boys unless I take her something. It pays to stand in good with the head of the family."[6]

While reporters waited for Willard and Walker to appear, Gene and Mabel made the usual good copy. Gene and all aviators were superstitious, wrote one reporter. "There is tradition among them that if at any time three of them should light their cigarettes from the same match, it means certain disaster to one of the trio." He said Gene had told him of the time when he was preparing to fly and asked for a light from a mechanic's already lit match. As Gene blew out his first puff of smoke, the mechanic told him that two others had already fired their cigarettes from the same match. "No amount of persuasion," said the reporter, "could induce him to venture into the air until he was assured that the story was a hoax."[7]

After assuring reporters that she would be a passenger with Gene for at least one flight, Mabel was asked what she thought had been Gene's most dangerous flight. "I think the most hazardous flight my husband ever undertook," she said, "was his trip to the U.S.S. *Pennsylvania*. The excitement of the moment gripped me when he was flying that day, but I really didn't get nervous about him. I knew that he would take care of himself and come safely back to me." Although they asked a few personal questions, Mabel readily answered. "My flier and I have been married four years—short years," she said, "and every one of those years has been a honeymoon. We're just a couple of kids anyway and we have a heap of fun doing this aviation thing." Then, with a smile, she hinted at the scoldings reporters had seen her give Gene after his spiral dips. "He always likes to have me around," she said. "At least that's what he says."[8]

Gene and Willard's contract may have been more specific than any they had ever seen before. The promoters called it "ironclad." Each man was required to fly each afternoon of the three-day meet and, if weather forced a cancelled day, the aviators were required to make it up. Their combined flight time each day could not be less than an hour and they always had to be within sight of the spectators. The contract even specified exactly where in front of the grandstand they would take off and land. Some of Gene's flights must be made at 50 miles an hour or more and at least once a day he was required to fly past the grandstand no higher than 50 feet above the ground. In any wind of less than 30 miles an hour, Gene and Willard had to fly. None of these requirements seemed to discourage the Curtiss men. "If we can get good weather," Gene said, "you may rest assured that we will endeavor to break records." Willard agreed. "I feel much encouraged over the outlook for good flying," he said. If they satisfied the contract, Willard and Gene would share $2,500 each day.[9]

Poor Willard. At the time, he was probably the most talented aviator on the Curtiss staff, certainly a better flier than Gene, but he rarely got the credit. Where Gene was interested in making a name for himself, Willard wasn't. "I love this aviation business as a chorus girl loves the footlights," Willard told reporters. "All I want is a good opportunity to fly here and I will leave town the happiest boy outside of kindergarten."[10]

Hometown favorite, Clarence Walker rode into the Salt Lake train station a day before the exhibition was scheduled to start. Word had just reached Utah that Walker, for the first time, had flown Gene's old aeroplane in California to an altitude of over 200 feet. Walker had prepared himself for some sensational flights in Salt Lake City, but would soon find that his 4-cylinder engine was much too weak to battle Utah's high altitude.[11]

A midnight frost had left a low morning fog over the city, but at the aviation field, the sun was bright and warm. The Curtiss mechanics pulled off their heavy sweaters and began making final adjustments to the biplanes. Carpenters had almost put the finishing touches on the grandstand and a small midway of hot dog and lemonade stands had given the place the look of a circus. While final preparations were being made, Mabel, Gene, Willard, and Hall took a whirlwind trip through Salt Lake society. "They are not adverse to social activities in which they are asked to participate," wrote a society reporter, "providing that shop talk is tabooed." There was an automobile tour of the city, dancing at the University Club, and an invitation to the premier of a new play. Because the newspaper had said the aviators would attend, the playhouse was full of people trying to identify the famous aviator, Gene Ely. One young girl was so sure she had spotted Gene that she was willing to offer a box of cigars in a bet with her gentleman friend. "I can tell by the pictures I have seen," she said. "That big man is Ely." Her friend disagreed, pointing to a "tow-headed man" and betting a box of candy against her cigars. What they didn't know, and may never have found out, was Mabel, Gene, and Willard never made it to theater that night.[12]

On Friday, February 10, the day before the meet was to begin, 12 reporters and 200 specially invited guests came to the field to watch the aviators' trial flights. Gene showed them the aeroplane he had flown to the *Pennsylvania*, his "war boat" he called it. Although the visitors got close-up views of all the biplanes, they never saw any of them fly. Gusty winds blowing in from the lake convinced Gene and Willard that flying was too risky, especially when there was no money in it. "If I had smashed my machine," Gene said, "it would have put me out of business for the entire meet." He said he was sorry to disappoint the crowd, but he wouldn't take chances. "I am not in for this business of flying on Friday when conditions are not satisfactory. I may be a little bit superstitious, but perhaps that same feeling has saved my neck." Early the next morning, with Gene saying that no matter what, he would fly, winds approaching 40 miles an hour canceled the entire day. The weather bureau said the wind was the forerunner of a quick moving storm that overnight would bring much colder temperatures and either rain or snow. The only good news was that the winds were expected to be light. They were.[13]

The citizens of Salt Lake "were inoculated with the aviation germ," said a reporter, willing to ignore the nearly freezing temperatures at the aviation field. A few frugal spectators slogged eight muddy miles to the field, but most of the 10,000 spectators willingly paid the extra dollar that covered the cost of a roundtrip train ride to the field and admission to the exhibition. At precisely 2:30, Gene's biplane was pulled from the circus tent hangar, placed in front of the grandstand, and pointed to the northwest. The engine sparked to life, the propeller formed a circle of mist in the air, and "with little ado and a readiness that startled the vast crowds," Gene stepped onto his machine. "He settled his cap and gloves, and raised his hand in a signal," and began to move. "The whirring, leaping, little thing of bamboo and silk was bounding over the smooth starting stretch, disdainfully spurning the yellow mud." Seventy-five yards later the aeroplane gently lifted into the air and began to climb. The skeptics who had predicted failure were now convinced. Man could really fly. Gene flew out over the lake about three miles to Antelope Island and when he returned, passed over the grandstand at 400 feet. With a few dips, turns, and spirals, his eleven minute flight was over, but Willard's had just begun. He flew to the lakeshore and then returned, flying 10 feet above the ground at nearly 60 miles an hour in front of the grandstand. "His evolutions were probably the most thrilling of the afternoon," said a reporter. He would lunge toward the ground and spectators would scatter helter-skelter, sure that Willard was about to crash onto their heads. From 200 feet he dropped down into a vertical dive sweeping so low and so close to the "moving picture machine" that the camera man ran away in fear. Willard calmly reached out as he flew by and nearly put his hand in front of the lens. Before the day ended, both men had flown their required 30 minutes. "I'm very well pleased," Gene said. "Now that I know the air around here a little bit better, I feel that future attempts in my old airboat will be still more successful." Smiling, he had a lighthearted warning for the reporters surrounding him. "If you don't give us a good story and say a good word or two for the local boys who are promoting this meet," he said, "I'll sail over the city and drop dirt on your offices."[14]

The only disappointment of the day was Walker who, even after a half dozen up and down runs on the muddy straightaway, could never get his 30 horsepower machine to fly in the thin air. "It was a bitter disappointment to me," Walker said, "especially so because this is my home town." Gene defended Walker. "Young Walker from your city will make good," he said. "He is using the machine I used for many exhibition flights and I know that under the right conditions he will make successful flights." The next day, meet promoters had a plank runway put down over the mud, vainly believing this and the adjustments that Walker's mechanics were making to his engine would give him the necessary speed for success. Gene took pity on Walker and got approval from Curtiss to have an 8-cylinder, 75 horsepower motor sent from the New York factory. By the time it arrived, the meet was long over.[15]

The promoters, Wade and Tibby, were destined to lose money on the exhibition and their problems began even before the aviators arrived. The "shakedown" started at the courthouse when county officials decided the air exhibition required a circus permit costing $250, the most expensive permit they offered. They explained that the large fee was necessary because the county would be providing sheriff's deputies to handle the large crowds. Until opening day, that seemed to make a lot of sense. But as the gates opened, just two deputies arrived on their horses, meandered around for about an hour, and then disappeared.[16]

The deputies had left the birdmen and their aeroplanes unguarded. Spectators had pushed over the fence surrounding the aviation field in a mad rush to get close to the fliers. They stood only a few feet away from the wings of the aeroplanes as Gene and Willard were landing and taking off. In the grandstand, arguments between those who had paid extra for seats and the freeloaders who had already occupied them, turned into several violent fights. Wade and Tibby saw a chaotic and dangerous scene that promised to repeat itself over the remaining days of the meet. Their solution was to employ a company of soldiers from nearby Fort Douglas to patrol the grounds and maintain crowd control.[17]

Overnight temperatures dipped into the teens and a mini blizzard pelted the aviation field with four inches of snow. After a conference with Gene and Willard, promoters postponed the exhibition for another two days. During the lull, Gene received official word from the California National Guard that he had been chosen as chief flight instructor for their aeronautical squadron. The news was not a complete surprise. "I know the proposition of providing for an aviation squad for the National Guard of California has been under discussion for some time," Gene said. "Some of the officials ... talked the matter over with me and it was practically decided ... that favorable action would be taken." The 32-man squadron was officially organized on February 20 with headquarters in San Francisco. The men would begin training on the ground, studying aeronautical theory, and then be given flight training in an aeroplane. "Needless to say, I am heartily in favor of such squads," Gene said. "It is a step in the right direction for the advancement of the science of aviation." Gene was no doubt flattered to be selected by the Guard, but with too many scheduled exhibitions ahead, he didn't have time for the volunteers. He donated $1,000 to a $10,000 fund that would finance the experimental work, and left the aerial training to Curtiss and Robinson.[18]

Gene's official enlistment in the California Air Guard came a month later. In it, we learn that physically he stood five feet nine and half inches tall, weighed 130 pounds, had blue eyes with 20/20 vision, a fair complexion, and light brown hair. He said "glands" were removed when he was a child that likely left the "well defined scar" appearing on the right side of his neck. He reported receiving a head injury in 1904 when he had crashed Father Smyth's automobile, but he also noted there were "no resulting defects." He did drink "intoxicating liquors," "very moderately," he said, but apparently, in 1911, no one cared to ask about his heavy smoking habit.[19]

On Wednesday, February 15, Gene and Willard faced snow flurries. Luckily they were well prepared, both wearing fleece lined underwear, chamois skin protectors, bearskin gloves, head and face leather protectors, and the warmest wool socks they could find. At takeoff, only a few flakes fell on the field and none were sticking, but after reaching altitude, Gene faced the storm's full fury and a brief whiteout. He quickly descended in a long glide and landed after a fifteen-minute flight. As Willard forced his way into the teeth of the snowstorm, he too was lost for a minute or two, but returned to the field unharmed. Gene and Willard spent a few minutes thawing out in their hanger before going up again, this time, circling the field wingtip to wingtip. They finished with the usual twists, turns, and dives until each had flown a total of 30 minutes and satisfied their contract obligation.[20]

With more hope than optimism, promoters looked forward to February 16, the last day of the exhibition. Their profits were melting away as fast as the weather was closing in and spectators were staying away. With a little bit of luck, perhaps this day might be the beginning of a turnaround. Gene planned to fly across the city to Fort Douglas with a few extra stunts thrown in, and Willard would fly with passengers and perhaps make bombing runs. However, just minutes up into the icy air, one of Gene's guy wire supports broke and he was forced to turn back. During his emergency landing, he saw Walker's biplane being rolled out onto the field directly in his flight path. When Gene's machine touched down, he immediately swerved to avoid a collision, but his brakes slipped and he began sliding toward the spectators who were surrounding Walker's machine. In a last ditch effort to gain some kind of control, Gene took aim at a large fence post off to the side. The resulting collision shattered one of his bamboo wing supports. Although he was an instant hero who had "Risked Own Life to Save Others," the flight had only lasted four minutes, leaving him 26 minutes short of his contract obligation. If he and Willard were to be paid for the day, Willard would have to fly a total of 56 minutes to make up the difference. But, even though he flew three flights filled with reckless maneuvers, Willard came up 9 minutes short.[21]

While Gene and Willard had shivered through snowstorms at Salt Lake, Curtiss had flown through San Diego's warm and clear skies and had been hoisted aboard the U.S.S. *Pennsylvania*. Gene got word of the flight from reporters, while waiting for his own aeroplane to be repaired. "He was as enthusiastic as a boy with a new rifle," a reporter said. "That's the big event for which Curtiss has been waiting," Gene said. "His success in alighting on the water near the *Pennsylvania* and starting again from the water, settles the question about the practicability of the hydroaeroplane being used with scout cruisers."[22]

That evening, Wade and Tibby declared a breach of contract and refused to pay the Curtiss birdmen. Only 2,000 spectators had paid to see the last day of the meet and, together, Gene and Willard had flown less than the one hour specified in their contract. The aviators argued that the reason they hadn't been able to fly was the fault of the promoters who had allowed spectators onto the field, and that had forced Gene's collision with the post. "No money, no more flights," Gene and Willard said. The crowd had been satisfied, they said, and the promoters didn't return any of the gate receipts to the public. They felt entitled to their pay regardless of the technicalities of their contract. After hours of negotiation, neither side gave in. Lawsuits were threatened and a previously agreed to extensions of the aviation meet were canceled.

"So far as the aviators were concerned," Whipple Hall explained, "the meet was a success, but the spectators did not come out, so the promoters lost money." Perhaps the only people to make a profit from the exhibition were the owners of the Mission Theater in downtown Salt Lake City. They projected motion pictures of all the flights as a special added attraction, and within a week after the exhibition closed, they invited aviation lovers to take a warm seat in their theater and enjoy the show.[23]

Before Gene and Willard left for San Diego and a possible deployment to the Mexican border with the Army, Whipple Hall arranged a contract that would bring them back to Utah in April for a six-day aviation meet. The backers of this exhibition were said to be among Salt Lake City's elite and with their bankrolls and influence, no monetary problems were expected. The Wright fliers, Brookins and Parmelee, had already agreed to appear, ensuring an exciting and competitive contest between the country's greatest living aviators. "We are leaving you but for a comparatively short time," Gene said. "We'll be back in April and, with ourselves and the two representatives of the Wright people here, you can rest assured that there will be some real flying." He paused for a moment and then thanked the residents for their hospitality. "Mrs. Ely and myself have enjoyed our visit here very much, and barring the disagreement with the promoters of this week's meet, everyone would have been happy."[24]

{ 36 }

# Flitting Along

The situation on the Mexican border was getting worse and after a brief stop in San Francisco, Gene headed to San Diego. Rumor said that after securing an aeroplane, Gene would continue on to El Paso for observation duty with the Army. Actually, Curtiss had asked him to come to North Island to help train the latest batch of military aviators. With the cancellation of the 10-day Mexico City exhibition, Gene's expertise would be invaluable.[1]

Another false story said Gene had signed a $20,000 a year contract to operate an aviation school for the military. What the newspapers didn't know was that Gene's father, who had asked the Navy to find a position for his son, had finally received his answer from the Assistant Secretary of the Navy. "I have to inform you that the Department does not contemplate the establishment of such a position in the near future," he said. He complimented Gene's ability and said he appreciated how Gene had demonstrated the possible uses of aeroplanes in naval services, but "the Department regrets that it cannot contract for his employment at present."[2]

Gene had barely begun his work at North Island before Whipple Hall arranged another exhibition, this time in San Jose. Scheduled to begin the first week of March, it was delayed by a muddy field, allowing Gene just enough time in San Diego to watch Curtiss sink the hydroplane in the shallow Spanish Bight. The boss was finishing a test flight with Charles Witmer, one of his two civilian students. Witmer made the flight riding on another experimental pontoon under the wing, so that he could see how it behaved when it touched down in the water. In landing, Witmer got a closer look than expected. Curtiss had misjudged his altitude on the descent and smashed hard into the Bight, putting a hole in the pontoon. Water rushed in and the hydroplane quickly sank in six feet of water. Witmer was drenched, but both men were rescued and the flying boat was dragged to the hangar for repairs.[3]

With a few free days before the San Jose Exhibition would start, Gene went back to San Francisco to enjoy himself. One Friday evening, Harry Scott, son of the president of the Pacific Telephone Company was entertaining Gene, Mabel, and Willard at the Saint Francis Hotel. Because Bud Mars was still flying in Asia, Mabel had invited Bud's wife, Marie, to join them. Also with them at the party were some of society's elite, including William Larned, six-time U.S. Open tennis champion. The conversation turned to boxing and Harry offered to arrange a private match that very night. The merrymakers were excited, especially the women. After a few telephone calls, they drove to a rundown hall south of Market Street, one of the roughest parts of town. Scott had managed to put together two bouts, the first, a lackluster three-round affair with the "Panhandle Kid" dropping the "Mission Locomotive" with ease. The second was a bloody masterpiece of heavy slugging. The betting was heavy, with one of the women putting $300 on the "Cow Hollow Hammer." By the end of the sixth round, the "Hammer" was struggling to get to his feet and breathing hard through a face full of blood. The betting woman, who was never named, jumped into the ring, grabbed a towel, and while shouting encouragement, fanned the air in front of her worn out gladiator. A policeman, patrolling on foot nearby, heard loud shouts and high-pitched screams coming from inside the building. He burst into the hall and froze in amazement at what he saw. He blew his warning whistle and the fight fans panicked. "True to their instincts, the aviators went up in the air," said a reporter. Their wives and the social elite were close behind. By the time the officer had gone to the corner callbox to ask for backup support, the spectators were already in their automobiles and sputtering away. Towels, sponges, water buckets, and boxers had vanished too.[4]

In San Jose, Gene and Willard would normally expect to split their standard $5,000 a day fee and 60 percent of the gate, but for the first time, at least as far as the local organizers knew, the aviators were not asking for a guarantee. If true, this may have been a concession to the promoters, who a month earlier, had lost a lot of money preparing for an air show that was rained out.[5]

There were the usual promises of spectacular flying. Willard would soar in joy rides with the city's fairest society damsels as his passengers and Gene would fly fifteen miles to the dome of the James Lick Observatory, 4,200 feet up on Mt. Hamilton. They would both race against automobiles and motorcycles. As an extra incentive, the public was invited to watch the birdmen tune up their machines on the day before the exhibition began, and perhaps have a chance to see them fly for free.[6]

Less than 8,000 people came to the two-day exhibition, but those who did were more than satisfied. Willard did fly with one passenger, but it wasn't a woman. He also won the only race against an automobile. Although neither he nor Gene flew to Mt. Hamilton, Willard and his new bride, Jeannette, did take an automobile drive to the observatory. There they were treated to a dinner and a tour of the telescope. The couple had been married for less than a month, but at the urging of Jeannette, they had kept the marriage story out of the newspapers.[7]

Willard's flights were along the foothills and open areas, while Gene flew directly over the downtown business district. Overall, Gene flew higher, but Willard seemed more reckless. He was always aiming his machine at the spectators, taking both hands off the steering wheel, and waving to horrified faces. "I wish he would not do that," his new bride moaned. "It's the most dangerous thing he does." Gene had also added an old trick to his already treacherous spiral dips. Now, he ended his silent, twisting spirals, not with a last minute recovery and landing, but with a lunge directly at the grandstand, where the petrified spectators automatically began to scatter.[8]

Before he returned to San Francisco, Gene received an urgent telegram from Curtiss. Apparently, pressure from the government was increasing. Curtiss asked Gene if would consent to go to San Antonio, Texas and instruct Army officers in the use of the Army's recently purchased Curtiss biplane. Gene said he would, but first he had a number of exhibitions to complete. Although he didn't say so at the time, he must have been annoyed. On one hand, the government had told him that they had no job for him, but now, they needed him in Texas. Worst of all, no one was talking money. "I need the money," Gene would tell reporters a few weeks later, "and the Government has not yet said anything about compensation. In time of war, I would not hesitate a minute; of course, but this is a straight business proposition, and I shall not go unless they can offer me as much as I am getting at present."[9]

Gene was originally scheduled to fly at San Bernardino, in Southern California, on March 26, before he returned to Salt Lake City for the April aviation meet. At the last minute, Willard and Robinson were sent to San Bernardino and Gene went to Hanford, in California's Central Valley. There, his chief accomplishment was placing second to a motorcycle in an aeroplane, automobile, and motorcycle race. Next, Gene soared in Pasadena, giving the city its first aviation show. Gene had just missed former President Theodore Roosevelt who had, days earlier, stopped by the Pasadena home of Arch Hoxsey's mother and conveyed his condolences on her son's death. For nearly two hours, Gene flew through all of his daredevil tricks for some 5,000 spectators, but, as he lifted off on his final flight, the wind began to swirl. He struggled to keep control, but managed a few quick tricks before deciding that conditions were becoming too treacherous. "I could not see anything but those big oak trees," he said, "and if my engine had not responded quickly, I would probably have had to be fished out of them." A man interrupted Gene's interview, saying he would pay $1,000 for a "little ride" in Gene's machine. "I could not think of it in this wind," Gene said. "There are too many trees." The landing field is too small to take any chances with passengers."[10]

By mid–March, Phil Parmelee had arrived in San Antonio and had joined in military maneuvers with the country's first military flier, Army Lieutenant Benjamin Foulois. The two were testing the capabilities of the Wright aeroplane for military scouting missions, working through scenarios presented to them by the Signal Corps' aviation board. Although lieutenant's Beck, Walker, and Kelly had also been ordered to report for the Texas maneuvers, they were still in California receiving flight training at North Island. Because the Curtiss biplane purchased by the Army wouldn't be shipped from Hammondsport until the end of the month, Curtiss had asked for a delay until April. When the lieutenants finally arrived, they were told to help assemble the machine and wait for Gene to test it before flying themselves.[11]

To capture the largest possible attendance, promoters scheduled the Salt Lake City International Aviation Carnival to coincide with the semi-annual Latter-day Saints Church Conference Week in early April, when perhaps as many as 25,000 visitors would come to town. The aviation field was moved to a level bed of sagebrush-speckled shale, close to the Great Salt Lake and less than a half mile northeast of the Saltair Pavilion. An airfield close to the shoreline was essential, because Glenn Curtiss had agreed to bring his hydroaeroplane and personally fly it off the lake. Christened Bonneville Aviation Field, the exhibition site was named for Captain Benjamin Bonneville, a French-born American soldier who for four years in the 1830s had explored the Rocky Mountains and the West. Because the field was closer to the Saltair resort than the previous airfield, there was hope this exhibition would tempt the imagination of quite a few more aviation fans. The field had two major advantages. It sat on dry and hard land that was as flat as a billiard table, and even in wet weather it was relatively dry and rarely muddy. From the 1,000-foot long grandstand, there was a wide unobstructed view spanning up to three miles and every seat had an "entrancing view of the lake." Bubbling drinking fountains provided filtered water for aviation fans and there was a full midway of food and refreshment stands. With a spur line built from the railroad and a new automobile highway constructed, getting to the field would be easy.[12]

Even before the "Battle of the Birdmen" began, aviation headquarters was flooded with requests from young women to fly as passengers. The "aeroplane bee" was "buzzing in the bonnets of a number of young women in Salt Lake City," each of them just as eager to fly as any of the "sterner sex." However, a newspaper reporter didn't think it likely that the ladies would get their wish. "Aviators," he said, "were usually unwilling to have even a man go along with them and are even more unwilling to take any chances with a woman." No matter how brave and nervy she might be, he said, a woman would be more nervous than a man. "If a fair passenger did get frightened, the first thing she might do would be to clutch the aviator's arm," and, in the opinion of this reporter, the flight would end in catastrophe. True to his prediction, the few passenger-carrying flights were all made by men.[13]

Gene, Willard, and Curtiss were last minute arrivals, Willard on the night before the meet was scheduled to start, Gene the next morning, and Curtiss a day later. Brookins was already at the aviation field and Parmelee had arrived from San Antonio. Rain wiped out that first day, leaving plenty of time for reporters to ask questions. The major topic was the promised 50-mile match race between the Curtiss aviators and the Wrights, a race never run. Gene said he would press his competition hard in the race and expected to win. "The race is going to be a good test of aeroplane speed and, believe me, I've got a bunch," he said. "I can beat any Wright machine ever built." Gene made sure reporters knew that this wasn't friendly competition. "The race will be for blood," he said, "and for money, too—if there's any loose change around waiting to be taken up." The government was watching both sides, he said. "Why shouldn't we race to win? The government is going to buy 40 or 50 aeroplanes, as I understand it. That means an expenditure of maybe $200,000 or $300,000. Uncle Sam will buy either Curtiss or Wright machines." He said it was up to the Curtiss team "to try to prove the superiority of the Curtiss planes. We will do our best to run rings around the other fliers." He pointed out that the Navy had sent Lieutenant Ellyson from San Diego to Utah "to take notes on our work." The government was always interested in how they performed, he said, whenever and wherever they flew, and that was why the Curtiss men were flying to win every time they flew. "We want to show Uncle Sam what we can do."[14]

It was one of the few times that Gene was traveling alone. He had persuaded Mabel to stay home and rest while he flew for a few weeks in the Midwest and helped train Army officers in Texas. "I am booked to go down on the Mexican line after the Salt Lake meet," he said, "and there will, of course, be a lot of work mapped out for me there." He said he was anxious to get back into the air again after the doldrums of March, his quietest month of exhibition flying since he joined the Curtiss team. "I've just been flitting a little since I left here last February," he told reporters, "going up whenever opportunity was right." Just then, he saw Willard approaching with his bride on his arm. "We're going to have a good meet here," Gene said with a laugh, "because I'm in town." He jogged over to Willard, said hello to "Charlie" and his wife, and then both men instinctively lifted their walking sticks and began a mock sword fight. Except to joke that the falling rain was all Gene's fault, Willard didn't have much of anything to say. "We're going to fly and do things," he said. And that was it.[15]

The rain delay gave the traveling airmen a welcome day of rest and the downpour meant the mechanics had more time to fuss with their finicky machines. The crew at the aviation field finished off the grandstand and then put down a plank "getaway" so the fliers would have an easier start on that unexpectedly soggy, slate field.

On Thursday, April 6, the aviation carnival woke up to bright sunshine and a cloudless sky. Glenn Curtiss arrived at 9:00 in the morning and as soon as his hydroaeroplane was unloaded from the train, he went with it to the aviation field. This would be his first public demonstration of the machine and the stakes were high. Government contracts were likely to hinge on how well he performed here. The locals were speculating and probably laying a few side bets on what Curtiss would be up against when he flew from the Great Salt Lake. Depending on how high the water level is, where you take your measurement, and which expert you believe, the lake can be from one to twelve times saltier than the ocean. Some thought, because the salt would buoy him up, Curtiss would find it easier to slide across the water. Others were betting that the heavier density of the water would drag on his machine, much like a field of dirt on a plow. The answer would wait for two days, while Curtiss had the machine assembled and carefully inspected at Bonneville Field.[16]

Although train platforms were tightly packed with spectators and the dirt highway carried more than the usual amount of traffic, the crowd for opening day was a disappointing 4,000 people. This was the city's third aviation meet and many had already seen a man fly and had lost interest. "To see the great birdlike machines leave the ground and gracefully take to the air is no longer a sensation," said a reporter.[17]

Willard was first in the air, climbing to 500 feet, and chasing one of the thousands of seagulls that floated around the lake. Up and down like a rollercoaster they went, the frightened bird flying across and in front of the grandstand with Willard in hot pursuit. Suddenly, the gull veered away and doubled back behind the grandstand. Willard lost ground as he made a wide, steeply angled turn. "I can beat those birds on a straight run," he said, "but they can turn shorter than I can and that's where they get away." Brookins took Willard's bird flight as a challenge, saying that before the meet was over he would not only chase a seagull, but also would capture one in flight. "I can do it," he said. Someone reminded Brookins that seagulls were protected in Utah and that the authorities would surely slap him with a large fine. He said he didn't care. "I'll take a chance, anyway." Luckily, for the seagulls, and perhaps Brookins, no one could actually catch one.[18]

When Gene and his crew pulled his biplane out of the hangar tent, it was obvious that he was the crowd's favorite. They clapped, whistled, and shouted as they waited for him to finish final adjustments. "Ely is one of the easiest fliers in the business," said a reporter. "He goes along like a big hawk and sails away, and back again, enjoying the sensation more often than those who watch him." Willard joined Gene in the air, as did Brookins. "The trio cavorted around; doing stunts until their thirty minute contract required flights were accomplished."[19]

When Willard landed for his last flight of the day, he immediately stripped off his leather flying suit, revealing a slightly wrinkled business suit that he continued to wear as he and his wife left for town. The sight of Willard inspired a reporter to describe what the other aviators were wearing for warmth in the "ethereal blue." Gene wore goggles and a leather coat over his street attire, while Brookins wore a mask that covered his entire face and gave him the look "of a real dragonfly." Parmelee just flew, making no special preparations. "He doesn't seem to mind the wind whistling up his trouser's legs and screaming around his body and head."[20]

A slightly larger crowd of 5,000 on Friday saw more spiral dips, and bombing runs that featured flour bags and oranges dropped on a chalk-outlined battleship. A fouled spark plug on Gene's first flight of the day forced him down on the soft shoreline of the lake. Willard flew to his rescue, but saw from the air that Gene had already solved his problem and had begun to takeoff. Gene climbed high, circling farther out into the lake, and then flying northeast toward the mountains until he disappeared. After 40 minutes in the air, he returned to hear the cheers of a crowd that had been holding its breath and fearing the worst. He had flown 9,126 feet above sea level, 4,200 feet above Bonneville Field, setting an altitude record for the area, and promising to beat it the next day.[21]

On Saturday, April 8, the Curtiss hydroplane drew 12,000 people to the aviation field. As the band played the *Star Spangled Banner*, the new Utah flag, authorized by the state legislature just a month before, was unveiled. The four aviators were given the honor of hoisting it simultaneously with an American flag. After the birdmen finished their required flights it was announced that Curtiss was about to launch the hydroplane. Hundreds of spectators rushed across the field toward the banners on the beach that marked the Curtiss tent. They followed along as the crew pushed and pulled the craft a half-mile across the soggy sand to the water. Fashionably dressed women wearing the daintiest of shoes were ankle deep in muck, but still they slogged on. Old men, young men, fat and thin, rich and poor, could care less about a little bit of mud.[22]

Nearly exhausted, the mechanics had almost reached the shoreline. They revved the plane's motor, hoping the propeller would give them more push across the sand. With the added help of 20 to 30 volunteers, they finally got the machine to the water's edge. Curtiss got aboard and the craft was pushed away from shore, leaving the out-of-breath mechanics standing in shallow water, watching the boss sail away. Once in deeper water, Curtiss pushed the aeroplane faster than any boat ever seen on the lake. He crisscrossed back and forth over the surface, looking for the prevailing wind. Within five minutes he found it, turned into it, and skimming over the gentle waves, he was airborne. "Under the master hand of its inventor, it wheeled and dipped and danced above the gleaming lake in the most graceful flight of the day." At 200 feet, he turned back toward shore, circled around Saltair Pavilion, ending with a low flight over the thousands of cheering and applauding eyes watching from the beach. After nineteen minutes in the air and as casually as a seagull, he dropped into the water for a landing. When he had nearly slid to a stop, Curtiss juiced the engine again, rose from the water, and with a few turns and dips made another, but shorter flight. It had been a critical experiment. He had proved his hydroaeroplane could fly from any ocean or body of water in the world "There is no body of water in the world," Curtiss said, "heavier than this. And no important body any higher."[23]

Sunday's crowd was the largest so far, but when they arrived at Bonneville Field, they found ferocious gale force winds and steady whitecap waves sweeping over the lake. "It was a crime to ask the birdmen to go up," said one of the meet promoters, "but we took the chance anyway, just so that the large crowd present would not be altogether disappointed." The promoters couldn't rely on the Wright brothers who were sons of a Protestant minister and always refused to let their aviators fly on Sundays or religious holidays. To appease the impatient crowd, who couldn't understand why a little wind would keep the birdmen down, the entertainment was left to Gene, Willard, and Curtiss. Both Gene and Willard tried two short flights, but barely got into the air and each time were forced to land. Only the usually cautious Curtiss, perhaps wanting to experiment in bad weather, launched his hydroaeroplane onto the lake. When the choppy water nearly sank him, his mechanics quickly waded out to the machine to steady it. In spite of the danger, Curtiss did manage to make three short and relatively unexciting takeoffs and landings.[24]

Monday brought more wind, attendance of 3,000, and only a few low-level flights from the birdmen. Brookins took Lieutenant Ellyson along as a passenger, but never got higher than 50 feet off the ground. Willard lost a close wing-to-wing, 3 ½-mile race against Parmelee and Parmelee dropped a bomb that didn't explode on an old shack. Attendance continued to drop. On Tuesday, the grandstand was virtually empty, but the few hundred spectators who braved the chilly weather and persistent wind, saw all four aviators in the air at the same time. They circled the field in a slow promenade, interrupted only by engine trouble that forced Gene to land a mile away. Brookins completed a dramatic spiral dive and Parmelee surprised the small audience by dropping a live bomb that exploded fifteen feet from his target. Wednesday's weather forced another cancellation, when predicted April showers suddenly turned to snow. The meet was on hold for three more days, but by then, only the Wright team was still there. Curtiss was on his way home to Hammondsport, Willard was in Provo, flying a last minute exhibition, and Gene had returned to California.[25]

In Texas, the concerned military was wondering where Gene was. They had expected him to leave immediately after the delayed Salt Lake exhibition and arrive in San Antonio by April 10. Then they announced that they believed it would be the morning of the 12th, or maybe in the evening. All were bad guesses. Gene was in San Francisco, where he and Mabel, along with her parents, caught a train south to Bakersfield for a lucrative last minute air show.[26]

He should have been in Texas no later than the 17th, but because Gene was friends with Henry Blakeslee, promoter of the Bakersfield aviation meet, and the co-founder of the Auto Livery Company with Gene's old San Francisco employer, Max Rosenfeld, Gene wasn't about to pass up the $2,500 Blakeslee was offering for Gene's appearance.[27]

Making arrangements had been easy. Blakeslee was also close friends with Charles Young, the man who had taken over management of Gene and Willard, while Whipple Hall left again for Hawaii. There had been little time to promote the last minute show, but Young gave it his best effort. "I do not believe there is an aviator in the business today who can defeat Mr. Ely," Young said. "Once in the air, he has a series of spiral dips and turns that make every hair on your head stand out straight." Perhaps it was Young who was spreading the newest rumor that said the Army was going to pay Gene $3,750 per week to fill a position that would "last for some time." "That was," said the newspaper story, "more than has ever been paid to any one man by this government." Of course, it came after Gene had already been told twice that there was absolutely no position with the government available.[28]

When Gene arrived in Bakersfield on Saturday, April 15, Young had another offer for his consideration. A group of hotel owners would pay Gene $10,000, if he flew 344 miles from Santa Barbara on the coast to North Island in San Diego, and pass over the major hotels in the principle cities of Southern California. He would be able to stop along the way for oil, gasoline, food, and water. It would have been a spectacular flight, but Gene knew it was impossible.[29]

The gates opened on Easter Sunday at the tiny Bakersfield baseball park and almost immediately there was a problem. Only 1,200 spectators paid to get inside for a close-up look, while 5,000 others stayed outside for the free show. Blakeslee needed to clear at least $2,500 to meet Gene's guarantee, but 500 people in automobiles and 700 in the grandstand wouldn't come close. Outside the fence and for blocks around, automobiles edged both sides of the street. Families lounged on blankets thrown over the surrounding grass. Men climbed electric poles and "clung like woodpeckers," until ordered off by police officers who were sent by the power company. When Gene arrived with Mabel and her parents, Blakeslee asked him to postpone his flying while he sent men out to persuade some of the crowd to come in, but no one came. The impatience of those who had paid for the aviation show gradually turned to angry shouts and chants. Auto horns blared in "a most dismal and insistent croaking," and finally, Blakeslee gave up, started the show, and took his losses.[30]

One hour, eleven minutes late, Gene began his first flight. For eight minutes, he circled far out from the ballpark, flying over some of the more prominent buildings in town. As he returned, he startled a hawk flying ahead. The bird's wings flapped in panic as it rushed to escape, but the noisy flying monster behind him just flew on by. With its courage regained and curiosity apparently aroused, spectators said the bird set off to try and catch up, but finally gave up and drifted away. When Gene reached the field, he pitched down at too flat of an angle and struck the ground in the middle of the field, running too fast to stop. Mabel, sitting in an automobile, momentarily tensed her body and leaned forward as she watched Gene's aeroplane run up an incline at the edge of the field. His momentum was slowed just enough to bring him to a safe stop a few feet from the fence. Another potential tragedy had been avoided and Mabel relaxed—at least for the moment.[31]

Back in the air and flying northwest from the field toward a nearby town, Gene slammed into violent wind gusts that quickly alternated with pockets of dead calm. Abandoning the flight, he struggled to return to the field, where he began circling for a landing. Suddenly, his aeroplane dropped sharply and his motor went silent for a moment. Unseen on the ground, 600 feet below, a standpipe had blown away from his carburetor and gasoline was flowing out unchecked. He started his motor again and by carefully losing altitude, made what seemed to be a normal landing. He stepped off and casually walked down a long line of well-wishers until he reached Mabel, who probably had known something was wrong the moment it had happened, but had hid her emotions from those around her. Bill Hoff, Gene's current chief mechanic, found gasoline flowing in a stream and dropping off the lower wing like a small waterfall.

Miraculously, there had been no fire or explosion. Gene had cheated death again. When word of the near catastrophe reached reporters, as always, they wanted to know if Mabel had been worried. "Why should I feel anxious?" she said. "I have always had absolute, complete confidence in my husband's exceptional understanding of air conditions at all times and under all circumstances."[32]

That evening, Mabel and her parents caught the train to San Francisco, while Gene was driven to Los Angeles to catch the train to San Antonio. Uncle Sam was still impatiently waiting.

# { 37 }

# The Wayward Winds

Long before Gene arrived in San Antonio, President Taft was doing his best to save face and back away from what was perceived as an imminent invasion of Mexico. The president was the target of a growing anti–American sentiment in Europe and Latin America and growing political opposition in the U.S. Reacting to the uproar, he withdrew his order for Navy patrols of Mexican coastlines, but the cancellation had come so fast after the initial order that some said it was an unseemly affair, damaging to the dignity of the United States. With the realization that pulling Army troops away from the Mexican border too quickly would only fuel more political outrage, the administration ordered that a pullout be made without embarrassing haste. The Army would provide cover for the politicians with a few weeks of training maneuvers near the border in Texas and then quietly disperse.[1]

The Curtiss military biplane had arrived in San Antonio at the beginning of April and there it sat, waiting for Gene. Curtiss' manager, Jerome Fanciulli, said the aircraft was "the latest product of the Curtiss factory." Although based on the basic *Hudson Flyer* design, Fanciulli said it embodied "all of the new points developed by Mr. Curtiss except for the hydroaeroplane feature.... The machine is the model which we designate the Curtiss military passenger carrying type." Packed in two crates, only two men were needed to completely assemble it in two hours. All it needed was Gene's approval for the Army to accept it and designate it "Signal Corps Aeroplane No. 2." Aeroplane No. 1, a Wright biplane, was being retired after nearly two years of service.[2]

Gene arrived on April 19, nearly two weeks later than expected. After the tedious train ride from Los Angeles, a good night's sleep at the St. Anthony Hotel prepared him to meet with the Army's aviation board. Lieutenants Foulois and Walker had been put in charge of developing the tests that would determine whether the new Curtiss and Wright biplanes were acceptable and should be purchased by the government.[3]

Phil Parmelee was to have been the Wright flier, but he had come down with a virus in the closing days of the Salt Lake meet. Defying doctor's orders to remain in bed, he flew on the last day of the exhibition and, "as a result of his dances through the chilly air," was once again confined to his bed. Parmelee announced he would be taking a short vacation from flying to concentrate on his duties as business manager for the Wright Company. While he traveled to Boise, Idaho for an aviation meet with Brookins and Willard, Frank Coffyn replaced him in San Antonio.[4]

Coffyn was among the earliest Wright students, completing his training alongside Walter Brookins in June 1910. He was a reliable aviator and a regular on the Wright's exhibition circuit. Before coming to Texas, he had just completed 60 flights at Augusta, Georgia, including a 30-mile jaunt with his wife as passenger.[5]

On the morning of April 20, Foulois and Walker gave Gene and Coffyn a detailed briefing on the tests they would be required to fly, including the rules that would govern success or failure. The flying would all take place at Fort Sam Houston, an Army base a few miles northeast of downtown San Antonio. Because rain had followed Gene to Texas and turned the prairie into two inches of mud, it would have been a good day to stay indoors, but after their briefing, the aviators were anxious to get a feel for their new machines. With their hands on the controls of two aeroplanes that had never been flown before, Gene and Coffyn flew cautiously. In his four flights, Gene stuck to the basics, flying as high as 1,200 feet and covering fifteen miles each time, but avoiding all intricate or showy maneuvers. Coffyn was slightly more daring and did try a couple of spiral dips, but told reporters he hadn't pushed the machine to do its best work. Both men flew with passengers. Gene took Lieutenant Kelly on two flights and Coffyn flew once with Foulois.[6]

The next day, with mud clinging to every wheel, boot, shoe, and horse's hoof, flying was impossible. Rather than face the sticky muck, an entire infantry brigade stayed in camp, prompting a newspaper editor to wonder what was happening to the modern Army. "Since when was the war game called on account of wet grounds?" he asked. By the weekend, the ground had dried enough for a military review of 10,000 khaki-clad men on the fort's parade ground, a parade that included Gene and Coffyn, who had both received military orders to fly their machines over the marching soldiers. "The Curtiss plane seemed the fastest, but a bit unsteady," one spectator said. "The Wright brothers' device rode smoothly, but did not appear as easy to handle."[7]

The rain continued to fall, delaying Army tests. On Friday the 28th, conditions were favorable enough for Gene and Coffyn to successfully pass all the Army's requirements. Perhaps in celebration, each took a ride as a passenger in the other's aeroplane. With Coffyn at his side, Gene disappeared into the low hanging morning clouds. "He took Mr. Coffyn from one vapor bath to another," wrote a reporter. A few minutes later Coffyn did the same with Gene. "Just what the aviators thought of each other's machine could not be learned," said the reporter; however, "both of them seemed well satisfied."[8]

With the Wright and Curtiss aeroplanes passing the aviation board tests, an aero squadron was authorized. Army officers who volunteered had their choice of what model of aeroplane they would learn to fly. Although volunteers began with an earthbound orientation, learning to fly in the air was by trial and error. The Wright biplane had the advantage of dual controls. If something went wrong, the instructor could always take over. Curtiss students didn't have that luxury. Theirs was a teach yourself flying experience.[9]

Although Army officials hoped Gene would stay to train volunteers, he was already scheduled for more exhibitions. Training was left to lieutenants John Walker, Paul Beck, and George Kelly, the Army men who had learned to fly at North Island.

They had considerable air time, but not enough to be considered competent instructors. So, just before Gene left for Kansas, he gave the men a few final pointers and then watched as each lieutenant flew the new aeroplane for the first time. They seemed to have no problems and with a little more practice, Gene thought they would be qualified to teach. Perhaps he had given them too much confidence in their abilities. "There is but slight danger," Kelly told a friend.[10]

Army officials would later admit that the grounds at San Antonio were not suitable for aviation practice. With 20,000 soldiers camped on the ground, there was no place to start or land, except on the camp's streets.[11]

Walker was the first to risk his life. Flying at 60 miles an hour into a near gale wind, he turned to avoid what looked like an oncoming storm. The aeroplane suddenly went nose down and raced 150 feet until he "jammed down" on the elevator and somehow steadied the machine into a forced hard landing. The next day, Beck's engine stopped and at the end of a frenzied emergency landing, he smashed into a mesquite grove. The biplane had to be disassembled before it was carried to the hangar for repairs that took nearly a week to complete.[12]

On May 10, the biplane was ready for Lieutenant Kelly's turn to fly. After circling over the fort for less than five minutes, he came in for a landing at too steep of an angle, his wheels hitting so hard that he bounced back into the air. Kelly accelerated, circled the field again, and made another attempt. Once again, he bounced and was seen frantically working the controls. When the wheels finally began to roll over the ground, it looked as if he had made a rough, but safe landing. But in less than twenty yards, the fork that held the front wheel of the biplane struck some sort of obstacle. The propeller spun at a wild and wailing speed as the machine traveled a few more yards, sprang 30 feet into the air, and began to roll, tumbling midair toward the infantry tents. Kelly was thrown out and left lying face down with a fractured skull. He never regained consciousness and was dead an hour later.[13]

Beck, Foulois, and Walker were appointed to investigate the accident and after conferring for a few hours, decided that something in the control equipment had broken, leaving Kelly with no way to control the machine. Curtiss mechanic James Henning, often confused with John C. Henning, a Wright aviator, strongly disagreed. Henning had been in charge of assembling the biplane in San Antonio. In his report to Curtiss, he blamed Kelly for bringing the biplane in too fast and at such a low altitude that when he tried to turn away from a collision with the Army tents, the lower wing struck the ground and forced the biplane into an uncontrollable crash. The point was moot. Kelly was given a hero's burial in San Antonio's National Cemetery and the biplane was rebuilt within a month.[14]

Gene was on his way to the plains of Kansas when he heard of the crash. In a telegram home, he mourned Kelly's death. "Lieutenant Kelly of Army killed today in Curtiss biplane at San Antonio," he said. "My pet pupil. Am all knocked out."[15]

If Willard could blame Gene for having brought the rain with him to the Salt Lake exhibition, then perhaps Gene could also be blamed for the wind that followed him to Wichita. Early in the meet, without Mabel to nag him and before the winds turned treacherous, Gene felt free to fly several death defying spiral dips. But each day the wind got worse, until only Gene dared risk a flight on the last day of the exhibition. It was short one and he nearly crashed. Pocketed with Willard's Swiss cheese air holes, these winds were just too risky. The aviators refused to fly and 10,000 disappointed spectators grumbled their way home.[16]

Gene had nearly a week before he had to fly in Kansas City, Missouri. That was enough time for a mad, 400-mile dash by train toward home. Arriving in Ottumwa, Iowa just a day after his near disaster in Wichita, Gene met Orson Harrington at the depot. It took three hours for Gene to drive the 65 miles to Williamsburg, but by evening, he was home and just as excited to see his mother, sister, and brother, as they were to see him. For a few days they eagerly listened to his aviation stories and then he was gone. Mabel Ely and Marie Mars were still visiting old friends in Portland, Oregon as Gene was rushing on to Kansas City. Gene and Mabel wouldn't be back together again until the end of the month.[17]

While Gene prepared to fly in Missouri, word was spreading throughout the country that he now was a major in the U.S. Army. Officers in San Antonio were skeptical and told reporters that they doubted the report. Such an action could only happen if Congress passed a special bill, they said. "A civilian may obtain a commission in the army, but he starts in as second lieutenant." Some speculated that the announcement really had something to do with Gene's membership in the California National Guard; however, when Gene heard the story, he denied it all. He said he hadn't been informed of any commission and that to his knowledge, he hadn't been promoted in California either.[18]

Kansas City once again reunited Gene and Willard in what promoters were calling the National Aviation Meet. It was held south of town at the Elm Ridge Race Course, another of those tracks shuttered to horse racing when the legislature passed antigambling legislation. Struggling to survive, the track owners turned to automobile and motorcycle races. A few weeks before Gene arrived, Ned Crane, the racecar driver who the previous October was supposed to race against Gene in Rochester, New York, was thrown from his racecar and died instantly in the dirt with a broken neck. Luckily, the aviation meet would see no accidents, but neither would it stir much excitement.[19]

Opening day patrons saw Willard and Gene both win races against automobiles and do a few simple stunts, but there were no attempts to set records. Gene did fly to 1,000 feet, but Willard seemed content with twists and turns and a few dips toward the crowd.[20]

Over 100 Army officers had come down from Ft. Leavenworth, Kansas hoping to see the aviators fly warlike maneuvers. What they saw instead was Willard flying a half-hearted attempt at dropping a flour bag "bomb" on a simulated battleship below. He missed by twenty feet.[21]

In what was becoming a repetitive pattern, wind wiped out the second day of the exhibition. From the grandstand, a small angry mob, demanding that the birdmen fly, rushed toward the hangar tents where police were able to stop them. No one flew and the crowd was forced to take wind checks that would give them free admittance for the meet's final day. That only angered them more. The show came to an end on Sunday, May 15, with Gene and Willard each making one short flight before deciding that it was still too windy and too dangerous. The furious crowd demanded that the aviators fly or not get paid, but Gene and Willard had a guarantee of $1,500 each day they flew. The promoters paid the birdmen, refunded admission fees to the spectators, and when it was all over, lost over $10,000 for their trouble. "Never again," said Robert

Campbell, manager of the meet. "I hope someday to forget this nightmare." Willard left for Columbia, Missouri, 125 miles east, while Gene boarded the train for Dallas, 625 miles to the south.[22]

Charlie Witmer and Jimmy Ward would fly with Gene at Fair Park, the Dallas fairgrounds and home to the Texas State Fair. It was the second aviation meet in 1911 for the city, the first coming only five months earlier. Because that exhibition had been plagued by winter winds, promoters decided to hold this show in May "when the weather is supposed to be settled." As the gates opened, the sky was clear and temperatures were in the 80s, but winds were once again strong and blowing in erratic gusts. As senior man, Gene took off first. He passed in front of the grandstand, the nose of his plane pointed sharply skyward. The seven-minute flight to 1,500 feet was a fact-finding mission, proving that the wind was still gusty and rough, but that flying was entirely feasible. After landing, Gene gave the OK for the others to fly. In short flights, one after the other, they went aloft, performed a few tricks, and then returned to earth. Gene was more reckless now than ever before. His high flying was daring enough "to merit the term 'death defying,' in all that implies," said a reporter. "With his machine hurtling through the air at a marvelous rate of speed, he executed a series of spiral dips and glides that chilled the hearts of those who watched him from below." They cheered his recklessness and marveled at how he "left caution on the earth."[23]

The spectacular finale began with Ward, followed in mere seconds by Gene, and then Witmer two minutes later. Ward climbed higher, searching for altitude, while Gene began a mad dash at over 60 miles an hour, circling the track with his wings perpendicular to the ground as he banked around the corners. He soared skyward, then fell back to earth in a spiral dip. Turning, twisting, and gliding up and down, he gave an unbelievable performance, the kind no one in Dallas had ever seen before. "So perfect was his control that it seemed man and inanimate material were cast into one form." Witmer raced away at terrific pace and then returned with even a greater burst of speed, passing in front of the grandstand like a cannonball fired from a massive gun. It was difficult to decide where to look. "The view of three flying machines hovering over the aviation field at the same time is a sight that has been offered to comparatively few persons," said a reporter. The feat was even more impressive, he said, because "the flights were made in the face of a gusty, tricky wind that held the life of the daring men at the helm in constant danger." Everyone was optimistic. With good weather, the most spectacular flying was probably just ahead and the aviators were sure to set new records.[24]

The next day the wind was gaining strength. After waiting over an hour for the breeze to settle in, Gene launched himself into a four minute, eighteen second battle with Mother Nature. Running south into the wind's toughest bite, he was fairly level at 300 feet as he passed in front of the grandstand, but once past the fence that surrounded the track, "the biplane began to pitch and toss, like a Texas bronco." He was low enough for spectators to see his head, hands, and feet anxiously working the controls at a blurring pace, struggling to keep the machine from turning over. Then, finding the first of many holes in the air, he dropped like an iron bar, a hundred feet or more. At the bottom of the hole, he plowed into another current of air that lifted him up as rapidly as he had fallen down. He managed a turn in the buffeting wind, the machine rocking and jerking as he turned back to the north. Unwilling to give up, he began his second lap with a try for more altitude, but it was hopeless and he was forced to the ground. Gene told meet officials who met him at the tent hangar that he refused to let Ward and Witmer fly. "I won't attempt to say how strong the wind is up there," he said, "but it is something awful." Reporters asked if he would try again later. "There is not money enough to tempt me into the air again this afternoon with the wind like it is," he said. "I hate to disappoint those who came to see us fly, but I am not ready to commit suicide." He was visibly shaken and continued to speak without being questioned. "I think I can safely say that I have flown against worse winds than anybody else in the world and, I believe I am competent to say whether it is safe to fly." He remembered flying into a hard and steady wind once before, but said today's gusty and puffy wind was worse. "I am sorry," he said. "It's a question of life with us, and a man would be foolhardy to attempt to fly."[25]

Friday began with a light drizzle and temperatures that plunged by 40 degrees. The swirling northerly wind reached 35 miles an hour and without even pulling his biplane from the hangar, Gene said no one would fly. Saturday was even worse, the wind sweeping across the field at over 50 miles an hour. The crowd in the grandstand was small but hopeful. Curtiss manager, Charles Young, told reporters that the aviators were like caged birds, anxious to return to the air to "soar and soar to their heart's content." Texas was full of wonders, including the wind, he said. "But, I do not believe there is another city in the country that could garnish four such windy days in succession as we have encountered here, especially at a season of the year when the weather is supposed to be settled."[26]

The last day of the meet opened with a wind that promised to be just as dangerous as those that had blown for days, but still, the birdmen flew. Six times in a row, sweeping down from 100 feet, Ward aimed his machine at the grandstand where his bride sat, trying to smile through her fearful tears. The men flew spiral dips, long distance flights, and highflying aerobatics. The crowd was small, but enthusiastic. The photographers and movie men even got the aviators to pose for them. Gene cut a few last minute figure eights in the atmosphere and then returned to the hangar, where his mechanics immediately began to disassemble his biplane and pack it in crates for a return trip west. Although they admitted that this was the most dangerous air they had ever flown in, "dry, gusty, uncertain, and full of situations of the sort called tricky," the aviators said they were pleased with the treatment they had received. Even the promoters were happy. "Financially, we made nothing," said C. L. Norsworthy of the Young Business Men's League, "but professionally, we hold that it was a good show and that we have brought here the best fliers in the world. It pleases us that the crowds were pleased."[27]

Gene was on the evening train to Los Angeles. From there he would head north to San Francisco, meet up with Mabel after their month long separation, and the two would travel to Northern California on a steamship. Time was short. He had less than six days to get there.[28]

# { 38 }

# Sailing Air and Sea

While Gene was flying in Dallas, Norman DeVaux, manager for Gene's western exhibitions, was working out the logistics that would get the aviator from San Francisco, up the Northern California Coast, to the port city of Eureka. Early in May, DeVaux had received a letter from Captain Walter Coggeshall, promoter of the Eureka event, asking when Gene would arrive in San Francisco so that he could arrange transportation. Both men agreed that after Gene's long journey from Texas, he needed to arrive early enough for a few days' rest before he flew. "I immediately wired Ely asking when he could be here," DeVaux said, "but, by the tone of his telegram, it will be next to impossible to get away from here [San Francisco] until the 24th." Coggeshall wired back that if no ship were available, he would arrange an automobile trip that would get "the aviator to Eureka on schedule."[1]

Coggeshall, son of a Massachusetts shipbuilder, had come from Nantucket to California in the 1890s. He settled in Eureka and beginning with a rowboat, built up a small shipping empire by carrying lumber and supplies between Eureka and San Francisco. He also ran a ferry service to the Samoa Peninsula, a sandy sliver of land less than two miles across the bay from downtown. On the peninsula was a rundown recreational area that Captain Coggeshall had bought in 1908. He named it New Era Park and within three months of buying it, replaced a ramshackle wharf and an outdoor redwood dance floor with a casino and the largest dance pavilion in the county. The entire amusement park lit up with electric lights, electricity generated by a gasoline power plant. For decades, its beaches, sand dunes, and cypress groves made the perfect place for summertime fun. In 1911, this is where Coggeshall would host his aviation exhibition.[2]

Coggeshall hoped to see 5,000 people pay a dollar each to see the birdman fly, but he worried that Eureka's ever-changing weather and legendary harsh winds would keep Gene on the ground and disappoint the crowd. With the ocean on one side of the park and the bay on the other, it would be among the most difficult flights Gene had ever attempted. But DeVaux told Coggeshall not to worry. "It is going to be a very trying exhibition for Ely in Eureka," he said. "The conditions on the island, where you intend to hold the exhibition, make it a very dangerous and a trying ordeal for the most nervy aviator in the business. But, you can rest assured that Ely will fly and give the spectators something that they will remember for many a day."[3]

DeVaux wasn't happy with the idea of an overland trip from San Francisco to Eureka. "Is there no chance for a boat on the 24th or 25th?" he pleaded in a telegram to Coggeshall. Coggeshall admitted that the automobile trip was impractical. "Our mail steamer *Iaqua* leaves San Francisco Wednesday night, May 24th," he replied. "If Ely's train is late, we will hold the steamer for him if necessary. Wire me at once, definitely, what day and hour Ely leaves Texas for Eureka, and day and hour train is due in San Francisco. Ship aeroplanes and mechanics on *Topeka*, May 23rd." DeVaux worried that sending a crated biplane ahead to Eureka without supervision might invite trouble. "We want you to use every precaution to see that not a bolt or nut is touched until Ely's mechanics arrive," he told Coggeshall. "We have but two of the latest type Curtiss biplanes to work with for our engagements on the coast, and we would certainly be handicapped should anything happen to either one." The original plan had been to send a brand new Curtiss biplane to Eureka and when Gene's biplane arrived from Texas, it would be shipped to Medford, Oregon. In the end, the new aeroplane went to Medford and Gene accompanied his Texas machine on the steamer *Iaqua*.[4]

When DeVaux realized that Gene couldn't arrive until May 25, he telegraphed Coggeshall who immediately went to work. "Financial arrangements made this end," Coggeshall said, "for steamer *Iaqua* to wait in Frisco, Thursday, for Ely's train from Texas and sail immediately for Eureka on its arrival. Get in touch with Mr. M. A. Burns of the Eastern Steamship Co. Tell me hour train is due, also when *Iaqua* sails—Coggeshall."[5]

Gene's train arrived on Thursday, May 25, just after 9 in the morning. He barely had time to reunite with Mabel and her sister, Mercy, before DeVaux rushed them to the ferry dock in Oakland. They sailed across the bay to San Francisco where the steamer *Iaqua* was waiting. Launched in 1900 to run the coast of California, the *Iaqua* now sailed on a regular schedule between San Francisco and Eureka. There were dozens of these small steamers sailing the coast and connecting a few isolated California ports with the rest of the world. The *Iaqua* and her sister ships carried the cargo, mail, and passengers that were the lifeblood of towns like Eureka, where there were no railroads to the big city and a decent highway was still just a dream. Barely 200 feet long and 30 feet wide, the *Iaqua* was equipped to carry livestock and redwood lumber, with limited accommodations for passengers. Gene watched the steamer's crew stow away his crated biplane and then he, Mabel, Mercy, DeVaux, and DeVaux's wife, along with mechanics, Bill Hoff and P. J. Rooney, settled in at the rail to watch as they pushed off. Just after noon, they sailed out through the Golden Gate and turned north.[6]

A cruise up the Northern California coastline is never an easy thing. From San Francisco, it takes a coastal steamer nearly 24 hours to get to the sand dunes of Humboldt Bay and the port city of Eureka. Sometimes the sun shines, the sea is as smooth as a lake, and the wind hardly a breeze, but in the middle of the night, even if lighthouses on rocky cliffs aren't hidden behind impenetrable fog or a swirling rainstorm, the sea is likely to surge higher than a house. Day or night, gale force winds rip through the waves and unseen reefs tear hulls apart. For some captains, hard winds mean turning closer to the craggy beaches where the swells flatten, but where rocks are harder to avoid. Along these shores are strewn the mistakes of a hundred inattentive seamen and it only gets worse passing through one of the most treacherous water channels on the entire California coast, the narrow entrance to Humboldt Bay. By 1911, at least 30 and some say nearly a hundred ships, lost in a thick fog, a pelting rain, or the large, unpredictable Pacific waves, had slammed against the bay's rocks or beaches. Even Coggeshall had lost a ship while leaving the harbor and crossing across the bar into the rolling Pacific.[7]

It wasn't a pleasant trip for Gene, especially during a moonless night when the wind whipped the waves and the ship tossed, pitched, and rolled so violently that he was forced to stay on his cot, a seasick sailor vomiting through the entire night. It seemed strange, said a reporter, that an aviator "accustomed to all manner of plunges through space in his trusty machine, was in such a condition." Here was a man who was "more at home riding a 40 mile gale in his aeroplane, 1,000 feet above ground, than he is on an ocean going steamship."[8]

Near constant winds had slowed *Iaqua*'s progress and she arrived late. When word came shortly after 3 o'clock in the afternoon that the steamer was passing through the entrance channel, Captain Coggeshall, accompanied by a welcoming committee, boarded his finest launch and set off to meet her. Once alongside, without slackening speed, the launch and steamer were tied together and a gangplank placed between them. While the steamer and launch continued to rush up the bay, the welcoming committee crossed over to the *Iaqua*, their eyes searching the faces standing on the passenger deck, unable to pick out Gene. Not only was he train-weary, seasick, and hungry, Gene didn't look like the photographs published in newspapers and magazines. Coggeshall and friends were looking for a heavier man, but what stood before them was a lanky figure in a loose-fitting suit who probably didn't weigh more than 120 or 130 pounds, if even that. "The slightness of his figure was a matter of surprise," said a reporter. Gene admitted that he had lost weight, but believed he was actually heavier than he looked. "I now weigh about 140 pounds," he said. "A year or so ago, when I first began as an aviator, I weighed 160 pounds." All aviators seemed to lose weight, he said. "Although it does not make a man feel physically the worse."[9]

As they approached the Railroad Wharf and downtown Eureka, Gene, Mabel, Mercy, DeVaux, Hoff, and Rooney stood by the rail while a local newspaper photographer took photographs. Mercy stood close to her sister, wearing a sunbonnet tied with a broad ribbon and holding a baby doll. While Gene was answering questions, Mabel, as usual, interrupted. "Look at that beard he came back to me with," she said. Apparently, Gene hadn't shaved since leaving Texas. When he rushed from the train to the steamer in San Francisco, there had been no time and, while clinging seasick to his bunk on the *Iaqua*, shaving was impossible. "You've got to shave that off just as soon as we get to the hotel," Mabel ordered. Gene decided to tease her. "I'm going to let it grow," he said. Mabel was not amused. "Oh, no you're not!" she snapped, and a half-hour after reaching their hotel, Gene's cheeks were silky smooth again.[10]

After stepping ashore, they walked a block up the hill to the Vance Hotel where, after his shave and supper, Gene answered more questions. Yes, he would only have one night's rest before flying, but he said he was used to that and besides he seldom had more than a day between flights, anyway. Would he take a woman passenger on a flight? Only if the winds cooperated, he said. Would Eureka's winds keep him from flying at all? "Although I prefer no wind, I have flown in winds of over 60 miles an hour." Did he have a life insurance policy? No. Insurance companies refused to insure him at any cost, but he felt "perfectly safe when flying in the clouds" and never thought "of the grim reaper, hovering so near." He closed by saying that he was beginning to plan his retirement from exhibition flying and possibly would open an aeroplane plant in New York, where he could "manufacture machines for the coming generation of birdmen."[11]

As soon as the *Iaqua* docked, Gene's mechanics hauled the crated biplane to the grasslands on the Samoa Peninsula. On Saturday morning, May 27, after Gene's "good night's sleep," Coggeshall ferried him and DeVaux to the peninsula. There was a rumor that Gene would make a trial flight to be sure his machine was working properly. "People have some funny ideas," Gene said. "They seem to think that the machine can go of its own accord; that sometimes it can be made to fly and that at other times even the aviator cannot induce it to respond. I most certainly do not intend to make a flight this morning. That machine doesn't need any trying out. It will make the flight when the time comes and there'll be no trouble about it." Coggeshall had offered to place a redwood platform on the sand as a runway for Gene's takeoff, but DeVaux and Gene agreed it wouldn't be necessary. The grassland was firm enough for takeoff, although Gene did have some concerns. After rambling over the area for about an hour, he was asked what he thought of the field. "It's the worst I ever attempted to fly from," he calmly said. Sand dunes covered most of the peninsula. "If my motor stops when I am up over that sand," he said, "there will be a funeral." There was no fear in his voice. He was simply stating a fact. "Then you won't go up?" asked a reporter. "Oh, yes, I'm going up this afternoon at 2 o'clock," Gene said. "The getaway is OK, but as soon as I leave the ground I must fly up over the sand hills. Should the motor stop and the machine fall, there'll be an awful smash." He explained that normally when a biplane came in for a landing its wheels rolled over the ground until the machine came to a stop, but if he came down into the sand, the wheels would sink and the aeroplane would instantly stop. It would probably also turn over and possibly break apart. "Anyone who has ever attempted to ride a bicycle over dry sand can readily understand the logic of Mr. Ely's conclusions," said a reporter.[12]

Early in the morning, the wind was gusting at about 15 miles an hour, but by early afternoon, it was roaring steady at nearly 50 miles an hour. DeVaux pleaded with Gene not to fly, saying it was "foolhardy in the teeth of the strong wind." Although he was determined to fly, Gene agreed to wait an hour, hoping the wind would give in. After just 40 minutes, too impatient to wait longer, and with the confidence of a man who is only about to take a quick jaunt in an automobile, he mounted the machine. "There was no tinkering with the engine," said a reporter, "no irksome delays and false starts to mar the marvelous performance." The propeller churned through the air and the booming rumble of the engine overwhelmed all conversation as Gene rolled out across the field. In less than 100 feet, at full throttle, he was angling gently into the air. "It rose over the first sand hill as gracefully as a swan leaves the water." The rattle of his exhaust faded into a distant buzz as he nearly disappeared from view. "He rose 1000 feet, soared out over the timbered crags, and rose and dipped above the breakers of the Pacific Ocean." Fighting all the way against the wind, he pushed out a half mile over the ocean, and then, turning back to shore, he passed over the Samoa Peninsula and Humboldt Bay. Circling this imaginary racecourse four times, Gene was in the air over 15 minutes and covered an estimated sixteen miles before landing. He told reporters that it had been the most dangerous flight he had ever made, the sand dunes on the peninsula swirling in violent eddies and trying to pull him down as he flew over. Even without the fancy dips and spiral dives now expected at aviation meets, the crowd was thrilled. "After being buncoed by alleged aviators who didn't fly, time and again," said a reporter, "Eureka saw real aviation by a real birdman in the face of conditions most depressing."

That evening, Mabel revealed more of herself than she had before, when she agreed to talk with a woman reporter in her hotel room. "I was admitted to her private room at the Vance [hotel] with the utmost informality," said 18-year-old reporter, Jessie Campton. Campton said that she had previously seen Mabel's photo but that Mabel appeared "younger than one would imagine." Was this the famous "Mrs. Ely, or possibly her small sister, who is her companion on this trip?" She is "dark and slight," Campton said, "and by no means tall. She dresses with a simplicity that is especially becoming—her one extravagance being a profusion of handsome jewels, of which she is exceedingly fond." Campton was struck by Mabel's "quaint" speech, especially from someone who came from the San Francisco area. She said it was "delightful to hear odd little phrases and sentences and almost an absolute lack of the sound of 'r' in her vocabulary." It seemed "to mark her as a southerner." Mabel told Campton that she loved to fly with Gene and had been up eight times. "I think six with Mr. Ely and twice with other friends," but never higher than 250 feet, she said. No, she hadn't been afraid when Gene made his first flight. "Oh my, no! Not nearly so much so as I am now." She explained that in the beginning she hadn't realized the dangers of an aviator's life. Mabel told a few stories about how it felt to be the wife of a birdman and then finally admitted that, in fact, she had been a "little bothered" by Gene's afternoon flight. The wind had been strong and the area where he could land was "so small." From then on their conversation revolved around Gene. Except for how pleased she was with Eureka, the reception given her, and the enthusiastic crowds that cheered Gene on, "never another word could anyone persuade Mrs. Ely to say about herself."[13]

While flying Saturday afternoon, Gene decided to make some changes. He would add an additional morning flight to his scheduled exhibition on Sunday and leave the next day. It was earlier than originally planned, but he wasn't about to ride that steamer again and risk another bout of seasickness. At first he thought he might drive north through Crescent City, inland into Oregon, and then all the way to his next scheduled stop in Medford. This road was nothing like the relatively straight route he had driven between Alturas, California and Lakeview, Oregon in 1908. When someone told him that the northern road was in poor condition, running along narrow seaside cliffs, and twisting over rocks, and steep mountains, he decided it was better to drive south. He would follow dirt and gravel roads with some detours, but from Eureka to the San Francisco ferryboats, he felt the trip could easily be finished within a couple of days. "Ely has a couple of big 'bear cat' touring cars down in San Francisco," said a reporter, "and he figured out this little trip while up in the clouds yesterday afternoon." As soon as he got back to the hotel, Gene telephoned to San Francisco and ordered that his Reo touring car be immediately shipped north.[14]

It was foggy with winds near 40 miles an hour the next day, but Gene completed both his morning and afternoon flights. In the morning, he was up 15 minutes and made four circuits of the peninsula, flying out over the ocean a quarter of a mile from shore. In the afternoon, he took his biplane from New Era Park, across Humboldt Bay, to the city of Eureka, and there flew over the railroad tracks before returning to the peninsula. "The people were lining the waterfront," he said, "and many up and down the peninsula." This time he had also gone at least a half-mile out over the Pacific Ocean and, in spite of the weather, declared that conditions were fine.[15]

The steamer, *City of Topeka*, arrived with Gene's automobile just after 10, Monday morning. His biplane, crated and ready to go, was put aboard for its trip north up the Oregon coast to Newport. From there it would be shipped to Salem. "I suppose you are going away this afternoon on the steamer *Santa Clara*," said an admirer. "I should say not!" Gene said. "I am leaving overland by automobile." "But who is your driver?" the admirer asked. Gene pointed his finger to his own chest and with a smile said, "I am." As soon as the Reo was unloaded and filled with gas, Gene took the wheel with Mabel at his side and Mercy sitting in the back seat between DeVaux and his wife.[16]

Waiting in San Francisco was Jerome Fanciulli, general manager of the Curtiss Exhibition Company, who had come west to join Gene for a short tour. Gene and Mabel spent a couple of days with Mabel's family before boarding a northbound train with DeVaux and Fanciulli. They were returning to Medford, Oregon.[17]

# { 39 }

# Redemption on an Oregon Trail

A year ago, Gene couldn't get off the ground in Medford and he had left the town as a laughing stock. There had been some sympathy, a few weeks later, when reports said he was dead in that Canadian plane crash, but the bitterness returned as soon as residents found out that Gene was still alive and reached its peak when Gene failed again, in that aborted flight from Chicago to New York. "The star of ill fortune seems to guide the destinies of Aviator Ely," wrote a local reporter, "who ... appeared in this city in the early summer in a so-called 'aviation' meet ... but did not succeed in getting off the ground for any distance whatever." The reporter even accused Gene of lying about working for Curtiss. "Subsequent events disproved this statement," he said. In his opinion, the Chicago-New York failure was simply another repetition of Gene's inability to fly.[1]

Now, after Gene's flight from the *Birmingham* and his growing fame after the dramatic San Francisco exhibition, attitudes had changed. The world famous aviator was coming back to Medford. "He was here last year," they said in his defense, "but at that time his prowess had not developed." Now he was "a top-notcher" and the fame of his flights "encircles the globe." Gene endeared himself to local aviation fans by keeping his promise to return. "Mr. Ely has come back to Medford to show the people of this city that he has the nerve and the knowledge necessary to fly." Although he had become "the most noted aviator in the world," they said, "that makes no difference to him." His word was good and that was all that mattered. "While he is not from Missouri, he is an Oregon boy and he is going to show you." Word spread that Gene had personally requested this second Medford meet to make amends for his previous poor showing, his first repeat appearance in any town since Chicago. "I had to wipe out my record made here," Gene said, "when I had a machine with not much power and was new in the business."[2]

While Gene had been driving back from Eureka to San Francisco, the new Curtiss biplane and two mechanics arrived in Medford. To determine the best starting and landing points and the general direction that the flights should take, Gene's mechanics were escorted to the city's fenced in baseball park by Court Hall and Charlie Young, promoters of the event. The area's biggest sports promoter, Hall also owned the ballpark. Although the park could seat 1,000 and according to Hall there was room for perhaps an additional 4,000 standing spectators, the mechanics said nearby houses, utility lines, and the surrounding fence were all to close and made a takeoff impossible. Reluctantly, Hall and Young moved the exhibition to an open field south of town, not far from where Gene had tried to fly the previous year. It was a disappointment for the local men. The fence around the ballpark would have encouraged more paid admissions for an up-close look at the aeroplane. Instead, hundreds of people now flocked to the wide-open aviation field, freely watching mechanics make their final preparations.³

On Friday, June 2, the machine was ready and stood waiting for Gene to arrive. Court Hall, curious to see what it felt like to sit where the world's most famous birdman sat, climbed onto the aeroplane's wing. He barely got comfortable behind the wheel when a burst of wind grabbed the machine and began pushing it down the cinder path that covered the grass as a temporary runway. In a panic, he grabbed the wheel and pulled back. Up he went, a few feet off the ground and soaring 75 feet before the wind let go and dropped him in a hard bump to the ground. "Court Hall," joked a reporter, "baseball magnate, billiard shark, and automobilist, has added one more pursuit to his vocations in life. He is now a manbird, aviator, aeronaut, or aerial chauffeur. It may be that he and not Eugene Ely will cavort among the clouds for the delight of Medford people." Hall did not agree. "Ely may like to fly," he said, "but I don't."⁴

Gene and Mabel stepped off the train that evening like European royalty. A large

In June 1911, Eugene Ely kept his promise to return to Medford, Oregon, and make up for his poor flying performance the year before. He sits at the wheel of his REO Touring car beside his wife Mabel. In the rear seat, in the dark suit, is Ely's manager and future automobile executive Norman DeVaux. The man to the right of DeVaux and the man with the straw hat in the center are unknown. Reporters were surprised to see how much weight Ely had lost over the previous year. Ely said he was only 20 pounds lighter, but most observers thought it more like 30 or 40 pounds (Southern Oregon Historical Society #18651).

crowd cheered their arrival and then followed behind as they walked two blocks to their hotel. After dinner, while Gene rested for the following day's exhibition, Mabel sat with reporters and a few invited guests, happily answering questions and, as usual, impressing the all male members of the press. "Mrs. Ely is young, very charming, and very pretty," said a reporter. "She has a Parisian vivacity." Mabel's necklace was the gold medal presented to Gene in San Francisco, and as she talked, she held it in her hand and fondled it with her fingers. She said Luisa Tetrazzini on behalf of the city of San Francisco had given it to Gene, but of course, she hadn't. Mabel in her pride was becoming even more adept at those little white lies that helped make her and her husband seem more important. "I am proud of him," she said. "You see, I am the conceited one of the family. In spite of all the praise he gets, Mr. Ely refuses to get any different opinion of himself than he had before he took to flying. In spite of all that, he remains the same—quiet." Mabel said she wanted Gene to "hold his head up in the air," otherwise, "the people will simply think he is no better than all the other fliers." She paused with a broad smile. "And that you know isn't true."[5]

She was asked the inevitable question, had she ever flown with Gene? "Mrs. Ely smiled and her brown eyes sparkled. 'Oh, I have been up with my husband before, but not on the Pacific Coast.'" She planned to fly with Gene in Medford and said when she did; she would become the first woman ever to fly in the West. "I came near going up once before," she said, "but not with my husband. That was at the meet in San Francisco when Mr. Latham invited me to ride with him in his Antoinette. But, what a calamity. Instead of being taken up in an aeroplane I was taken down with tonsillitis." Wasn't she afraid to fly? "Not a bit," she said. "Love it." There was no reason to be afraid. "I know the machines Mr. Ely uses are the best and are in perfect condition or else he wouldn't use them. No, I never think of the danger. If I did—," she shrugged her shoulders and smiled again. "We wouldn't fly." Did she always travel with her husband? "Yes, I go with him everywhere," she said, "although I stayed at home in San Francisco in order to rest during his recent trip to Texas. I am his good luck. Things go wrong when I am not around. He says so himself."[6]

They asked what she thought of Medford and if Gene could actually fly here. "I like Medford," she said. "Mr. Ely made his second flight here, you know, and it was kind of a failure. The trouble was that the machine hadn't the power to get off the ground. He was very much disappointed and is determined that nothing will prevent his going up this time."[7]

On June 3, the following morning, Medford got its answer. "Where there was criticism a year ago," said a reporter, "today is only praise." The aviator had kept his promise and made good on the identical aviation field where he failed a year ago. When Gene and Mabel first walked across the field to the aeroplane, the small crowd was awestruck and silent. Some were overwhelmed with the excitement of seeing a man fly, others simply admired Gene's courage in defying death, and yet, there were also those morbid few who wanted to see him crash. For the moment, they all watched without a sound. Not one automobile horn blared, no one shouted, no celebrations of any kind. "There was simply interest, pure human interest in what was about to happen."[8]

This aeroplane was fresh from the New York factory and had never been flown. Gene carefully inspected each wire, ran his hand over the rubberized silk-covered wings, and listened carefully as the mechanics pulled down on the propeller and started the engine. He adjusted his helmet and looked at his watch. "I shall be in the air at 2 o'clock," he said to Mabel. With the temperature approaching 80° and no need for protection against the cold, he was dressed in a simple suit that might have been worn by a mid-level manager at a clothing store. The deafening bark of his engine pushed him 80 feet across the field and then up into the air. Except for a few whispers and mumbles of amazement, for nine long minutes, the spectators watched in mesmerized silence as Gene got the feel of this new machine. He flew west over the gold mining town of Jacksonville and returned in a graceful glide from 600 feet, touching down in front of a crowd that burst into bedlam. The second flight was full of dips and turns and a twelve-minute journey to the south over the city of Ashland. It ended in a spiral glide, reminding one reporter of the dive that "had sent Johnstone and Hoxie to their deaths." In Texas, Gene had adopted Willard's maneuver, taking aim at the startled crowd who scattered hysterically just before the aeroplane shot skyward at the last possible moment. Because the wind evaporated just as he was about to touch down, his landing was hard. Earlier a mechanic had attached a passenger seat to the aeroplane's wing and when Gene landed and stepped off the machine, Mabel was ready to climb aboard and fly with him. Gene refused all of her pleadings. "Why not, boy?" she asked. "It's too rough," he said. "It will scare you to death." Reporters asked her why she didn't persist. "I know when he is in earnest," she said. "He simply refuses to take me when there is any risk. Though, if he ever does fall, I want to be with him in the machine. It would be better to go together."[9]

Mabel wasn't the only disappointed passenger. Every newspaper editor in the county had asked for a ride, but Gene had turned all of them down, saying he didn't want to discriminate against any one of them. However, no potential passenger was more disappointed than 20-year-old Elsie Lamb. Elsie lived less than a hundred yards from the aviation field and had watched the mechanics assemble Gene's biplane. One day the mechanics let her sit in the seat as they pushed the machine around the field. "They promised me that they would ask Mr. Ely to take me up," she said. "I did so hope that I could go." She assured reporters that she was not afraid of flying. "I always have loved adventure, although I am not foolhardy," she said. "The element of danger in flying does not appeal to me in the least. If it did, I would not care to go. But the machine is handled so expertly, so carefully, and glides so gracefully about that I have the wildest desire to be up there soaring about in the heavens." Through each of Gene's flights, she pushed against the rope that held the crowd back, ready to run to the biplane and demand a flight. "I am not going to give up," she said. "An opportunity will come again and certain it is that I will make a flight. The folks say I am crazy for talking so, but I think it would be a source of the greatest pleasure to ride with the winds." Two weeks later, Elsie was a June bride and her aviation dreams were over.[10]

Gene and Mabel walked to his machine for the final flight of the day. The wind snapped across the field erratically as Gene whispered something in Mabel's ear. She insisted that he promise not to repeat the spiral dive. He laughed and said he wouldn't, but of course, he would. "Serenity had crept into Ely's countenance," said a reporter. "Drawn features relaxed. The daredevil prince of the air was ready for his battle with the elements." And a battle it was. To fight against the Swiss cheese holes that could drop him 500 feet or more, he climbed higher. At 2,000 feet he flew over Medford, circled the newspaper building, and returned in a terrifying spiral dip, what a reporter called "running a whizzer" over the crowd. "It was not a perfect day for an exhibition," Gene said, modestly. "It is a rough road up there."[11]

Gene drove Mabel back to the hotel where they picked up their luggage and then went to the depot to wait for the late afternoon train that would take them north to Salem. One year to the day after his failure, Gene had made good. He was relaxed now and with time on his hands, willing to talk to reporters. "I was really surprised when I got up among the clouds this afternoon," he told them, "to learn that this was such a beautiful valley. Generally, I consider the earth as a matter of fact and something to bump into if anything goes wrong, but today I could not help but remark to myself on the natural beauty of the scene." He said he regretted not having time for the five-day automobile roundtrip to nearby Crater Lake that a local politician had suggested. Mabel was excited about the idea. "Oh, I have heard of that place," she said, "and I do want to see it. We will be back, sure." Gene was more cautious with his promises. "I would give a great deal to drive a machine to Crater Lake and view the natural wonder from the sky," he said. "Someday in the dim far future, I may drive a machine up there. It would take about an hour to make the trip, if everything went well." It was all just small talk, but listeners were fascinated. These were the words of the heroic daredevil prince, the man who had finally earned the city's affection. "Soaring like a golden swallow," wrote a reporter, "Eugene Ely gave an exhibition of flying yesterday, which will long remain in the memories of Medford people as a phenomenon, the sensationalism of which has never before been equaled."[12]

Equally impressed with Gene was Jean Wilkinson, an 8-year-old girl visiting from West Virginia. "I think he was the greatest man I ever heard of or saw," she wrote in a letter to a newspaper. "He did not seem a bit afraid and went high, high in the air." She begged her father to take her closer to this newfound hero. "I shall always remember how he looked," she said. "Before I am much older I guess I will study something about him in history and then I will be so glad that I can say I saw him."[13]

When the Salem Board of Trade heard that Gene would be passing through Oregon's capital city on his way to the Portland Rose Festival, they had quickly negotiated a one-day exhibition. Ten prominent but anonymous businessmen each pledged $100 to assure Gene that he would get his required $1,000 guarantee. No one cared how long or how far, as long as he flew, he'd get the money.[14]

Because the Medford, Salem, and Portland exhibitions were to be held so close together, the biplane Gene used in Eureka had been shipped up the coast on the steamer *Santa Clara* to Newport, Oregon and then expressed east by railroad to the state fairgrounds in Salem. There it was already waiting for the aviator's hand, fully assembled, tested, and ready to go. While Gene flew in Salem, the Medford biplane leapfrogged ahead to Portland.[15]

A few puffs of wind blew through the afternoon, but overall the day in Salem was perfect for flying. Before Gene took off, a few dignitaries penciled their names on the biplane's wing, finding space amongst dozens of other penciled autographs acquired at earlier exhibitions. Gene flew by the grandstand, waved at the crowd, and then zoomed up for a few of his typical gyrations. He never climbed high, but the crowd was satisfied. The main features on the program were supposed to be Gene's separate races against an automobile and a motorcycle, but when the races were finished, he had a secret surprise for everyone.[16]

He flew a few more dips and swirls and then suddenly veered away from the fairgrounds toward the southwest. "The dingbusted machine has got away from him," someone shouted. But it hadn't. This was Gene's surprise, a surprise he hadn't even told to Mabel. By the time she finished running to the opposite side of the field to greet him, Gene was a mere speck above the distant horizon. As he flew over the rooftops, the sound of a rattling motor in a cloudless sky, like an alarm bell, had dotted the streets with people, all of them looking up and knowing exactly what they would see. Perhaps mimicking Willard's February flight to the capitol building in Sacramento, Gene was on a direct line to Oregon's capitol building. He circled behind the tall dome and then headed back to the fairgrounds. It had taken six minutes to make the four-mile roundtrip and when he swooped down to a landing, the thin crowd on hand gave him a rousing welcome. Mabel was at his side, making sure he made the right impression as he left the field. She had chosen his hat and made him put on his best dress coat, and not until she was satisfied that he was presentable, did the couple walk arm-in-arm to a waiting automobile. "She is a girlish little woman and calls her bird-husband, Gene," said a reporter, noting that she seemed to have total control over him. "She was superintendent, captain, manager, overseer, boss, president, general, and everything else," he said. But he wasn't making fun of what seemed to be a loving couple. "She shows herself to be as proud of her high flying spouse as it is possible for a woman to be proud of anything," he said. "And he seems to be well aware of it."[17]

Less than 50 miles to the north, along the Columbia River, Portland calls itself Oregon's Rose City, a name first suggested by Frederick Holman, a Portland attorney, president of the Oregon Historical Society, and an avid advocate of roses. In 1907, the Rose City decided to host an annual Rose Festival, at the time, little more than a large citywide rose exhibition, but by June 1911, a weeklong event with fireworks, a circus, a baseball game between the Portland and Los Angeles teams of the Pacific Coast League, and a parade. Rose covered floats and automobiles were pushed and pulled down Portland streets. On the Columbia River, a "royal barge" carried a mythical king, *Rex Oregonus*, a well-known local citizen whose identity was kept secret until he was unmasked at the end of the festival.[18]

Portlanders had seen aeroplanes fly before, but Gene would be the first to fly during the festival. He had left Portland an unknown just a year earlier, but now reporters hailed him as the hometown boy who, after "tinkering with the original Henry Wemme machine," had taught himself the art of flying, right here in Portland.[19]

Gene told reporters he would try to go higher than the 1,200-foot Portland altitude record set by Hamilton the previous year. He promised he would rise to a height of one mile, give an exhibition at that altitude, and then descend "to more moderate levels" where he would perform the spiral glide. The glide, reminded a reporter, is "the most hazardous venture that the birdmen of the world have ever attempted and every time it is tried the aviator faces death."[20]

No passenger flights were offered, except for a less than serious invitation to "Bat" Nelson, the former two-time world, lightweight boxing champion. Oscar "Battling" Nelson, the "Durable Dane," was celebrating his 29th birthday, but leaving the ground on an aeroplane wasn't the present he'd been asking for. "Give me two mitts and a canvas floor," he said, "and I'll meet any fighter in the world at my weight—on the ground. But that aerial stuff?—Nix on that! No! Tell him I'm a sick man."[21]

On the ground, it was a pleasant spring day with temperatures hovering near 70, but higher up, the wind blew in cross currents that beat hard against Gene and his machine. In his first of three flights, a screw in his seat came loose. While landing to make repairs, a sudden blast of air nearly turned him over as he rolled across the field. On his second trip, flying at 1,500 feet, the strap on his helmet broke and its flaps began beating so hard against his ears he had to land again. His last flight took him over the Columbia River to downtown Portland where he dropped a handful of flour that flew in all directions. Gene's machine looked like a mere speck in the sky and the flour was supposed to make it easier for spectators on the ground to see him, but because the flight was unannounced and the noise of the city drowned out the sound of his motor, few people actually looked up.[22]

Again, the bulk of the spectators paid nothing at all, watching the aerial festivities from outside the fences. On this first day in Portland, promoters took in only $500 in paid admissions, yet their expenses exceeded $5,000. They tried to discourage the freeloaders by pouring crude oil outside on the ground in front of the fences, but neighbors complained and the men who dumped the oil were arrested.[23]

On the second day, Portland teenager, Harry Rice, and his cousin, each paid a silver dollar for their grandstand seats. "At last the machine was wheeled out," Rice said. "It was a small biplane very similar to what the Wright brothers flew at Kitty Hawk. The wings were flimsy wooden frames covered with fabric and the tail was wood and cloth." It was the first time Rice had seen an aeroplane. "They got the engine started," he said. "The pilot climbed in and taxied down to the end of the field. A man ran along each side holding the wing tips to keep it level. They went down and turned around. Then he gave it the gun!" As the machine gained speed, the two men alongside continued to run as fast as they could until, "Glory be! Amid the cheers of the crowd, the wheels lifted off the ground and he was airborne." Gene had climbed to a few hundred feet and flown for less than eight minutes when his motor began to sputter and stopped. He quickly glided to a landing in a potato field outside the aviation grounds, where he tried unsuccessfully to restart the engine. When his mechanics got to the scene, they discovered a bent connecting rod had damaged the motor and it would have to be rebuilt. Because the Salem machine had already been shipped ahead to Montana for Gene's next exhibition, the Portland exhibition was over. "I am naturally somewhat disappointed at the outcome of the meet," Gene said, as he boarded an eastbound train, "although it means nothing to me financially as I am under a guarantee; however, I may be back some other time."[24]

Gene was putting on a remarkably brave front. Before he left town, he had a confidential talk with Henry Wemme, the automobile man who had originally bought Gene's first aeroplane and now was one of the aviation meet's promoters. Gene told Wemme that the sooner he quit aviation the happier he would be. "It's a risky game," Gene said. "I'm through with flying when the season is ended." He had a "constant dread of a fatal flight," Wemme told reporters, "and said that he never felt quite sure of himself when in the air."[25]

"I have amassed a considerable fortune," Gene told Wemme, "and I would retire now if I could satisfactorily arrange it. There is big money in the game, but it isn't worth the while. Something might happen when I am hundreds of feet in the air. There is always a possibility and that would be the last of me." Gene told Wemme of his plans to sell Curtiss aeroplanes and manage an aviation school in either New York or on the West Coast. Wemme asked him if he wouldn't miss the excitement and the crowd's respect and adulation when he retired. More than anything, Gene said he wanted to settle down to the comforts of a quiet home life. To do the things he couldn't enjoy while traveling across the continent.[26]

He was on his way east again. The boy in a hurry with dreams of glamorous success had finally found it, but at what cost? He was learning that dreams and reality are seldom the same thing. Dreams have consequences and it was already too late. Reality had taken firm control of his life. There was no escape.

# { 40 }

# Over the Rockies

America divides on the peaks of the Rocky Mountains, just five miles east of Butte, Montana. In springtime, the snowy slopes begin to thaw and water droplets dribble over the ground. Streaming together, they rush downward, trickling around boulders and forming tiny brooks that lose themselves in swelling creeks. On the eastern side of the mountains they meet the Missouri River and meander in the footsteps of Lewis and Clark until they reach the mighty Mississippi. The journey on the western slope is not so smooth. From Silver Bow Creek near the town of Butte, river after river merge in racing rapids and tumbling falls, snaking westward to Oregon, and the Columbia River.

Named for the conical shaped hill northwest of town, Butte sits on a gently pitched hillside at 5,549 feet, nearly 300 feet higher than the mile-high city of Denver. The Rocky Mountains sweep around east of town in a curve to the south and then head west, surrounding a small basin, edged by rolling foothills. Through this basin flows Silver Bow Creek. Here in 1864, a prospector pulled out a gold nugget, the beginning of a short-lived gold rush. A silver stampede in 1874 brought new miners and some families to Butte and the beginnings of a real town. But no mineral would be more important to the residents of Butte than the 1882 discovery of the fabulously rich copper deposit that would become the Anaconda Mine. Soon the hills were honeycombed with mineshafts, dug by hands, drills, and dynamite.[1]

Because workers never wore a mask against the dust hanging in the air of poorly ventilated mines, particles collected in their lungs, scrubbing them from the inside like sandpaper. The first signs of trouble were shortness of breath, wheezing, and coughing, ultimately leading to Miner's Consumption, a usually fatal disease that doctors said was affecting at least one-third of all Butte miners. In a quest for a hospital where ailing men could get help, Butte citizens created a hospital fund and solicited private donations for the cause. Before he left this exhibition, even Gene would make a contribution.[2]

Promoters of the air show made two major promises. Gene Ely would "flirt with death" in the spiral glide and would set a new world altitude record by becoming the first aviator to fly over the Continental Divide. Yes, there would be dangers, said a reporter. "The flight will be over the toughest country imaginable," he said, "rocky cliffs and precipitous slides everywhere greet the eye." A fall in such country, he said, would surely mean the end of a birdman. But Gene had some advantages in his favor. He would start on a field situated higher in altitude than any other field where previous attempts at an altitude record had been made. He would also be able to combat the thinner air and the chance that his carburetor would freeze at high altitude by using a more volatile gasoline. Even so, the reporter was still cautious. "It is a problem of more than mere altitude," he said. "It involves grappling with unknown air currents, due to the peaks and passes, and will call for the utmost degree of skill when piloting through a treacherous air."[3]

In the early evening of June 9, Gene, Mabel, three mechanics, and Gene's current manager, S. G. Rayl, arrived on the Northern Pacific from Portland. Local reporters met them at the depot where Gene declined an interview until he had settled into a hotel. "The foremost aviator in the world is a young man of slim build," said a reporter, "quiet and unassuming and appears to be a little bit reticent in discussing some of his famous aerial evolutions." Gene said he would try to deliver on anything the people wanted, but was surprised when he was told that someone had promised that he would try to set an altitude record. "I was not aware until you spoke of it that I was to attempt an altitude trial," he said, "but if the board of aviation managers want it, and the people want it, certainly I will do the best I can." He said he believed in short flights where he could best show his aeroplane's capabilities. "I will give three or four flights daily, according to the weather conditions," he said. "Likewise, I will remain aloft just as long as it takes me to accomplish what I set out to do." Reporters and promoters were glad to hear that he still planned to show the spiral glide. "I will show the people just what the hazardous dip is that resulted in the death of Johnstone and Hoxie," he said, "and I will give them every air maneuver that I know. If the people don't get their money's worth it will not be any fault of mine."[4]

Talking about the dangerous dip brought a smile to Gene's lips as he told reporters how amused he was at how spectators in different cities reacted to his flights. "Take for instance, Eureka," he said. "At Eureka, after I went up to a thousand feet and performed all sorts of difficult and dangerous feats and landed, I scarcely got a hand. When I went up again and went over the ocean, a feat not nearly so dangerous, and came back, the people nearly went wild." Then there was Portland. "I flew over the business district of the city, a distance of about four miles, and returned, and hardly a person in the audience applauded. Yet, when I went aloft, performed spiral glides and dips, and cut all kinds of capers, they seemed to appreciate the danger ... It's funny how different the people of different cities take to the various flights."[5]

Gene seemed to have a knack for attracting millionaires. While in Butte, Morris Largey, one of the prime promoters of the Butte exhibition, loaned Gene his personal chauffeur and an automobile. Born in Butte, Largey had inherited a sizeable fortune and a number of businesses from his father. He had earned degrees in engineering from Georgetown University and the University of Michigan, but when a man murdered his father in 1898, Largey gave up engineering and took over his father's bank, the State Savings Bank of Butte.[6]

Gene was impressed with Frank Callan, Largey's chauffeur. The man had a jovial personality and, in Gene's opinion, was an outstanding driver and a gasoline engine expert. Bill Hoff, who had been Gene's head mechanic for a while now, would soon be leaving for San Diego so he could learn to fly. Gene needed someone to replace Hoff and Callan was just the man. Largey was agreeable and Callan accepted the job, but because he didn't want to inconvenience his employer, Callan stayed over a few more days after Gene left town so that Largey could find his replacement.[7]

Donning his light aviator's cap and his leather coat, Gene began the two-day meet with seven trips around the racetrack as he gradually climbed to 1,000 feet. A few times, he tried a spiral glide, but the winds were too unpredictable. At the end of the fourteen-minute flight, he cut his engine at 500 feet and, in a long and steady glide, barely missed the heads of spectators who were hanging on the rail. "Those were the most peculiar wind currents I've ever seen," he told reporters as he stepped off the machine. Mabel stood unusually silent at his side, dressed in Sunday finery, a white hat, an ankle-length white serge suit, white high heel shoes, and a black parasol.[8]

Gene's second flight was a surprise for everyone but Mabel. When he took to the sky, it looked like a simple race against an automobile, but no sooner had he lost the race by just a few feet, than he was off to the Continental Divide. Mabel stood calmly beside the hangar tent as he climbed higher. Reaching 1,000 feet, he turned sharply east and continued to climb toward the high peaks. A few puffs of wind made the aeroplane swerve and dip. Mabel held her breath, clenched her hands tightly together, and leaned forward as she moved side to side, as if she were trying to push the machine back onto its course. Gene was a tiny speck, like a hungry hawk flying high above a farmer's field. He headed straight for the southernmost peak and there, at 7,800 feet, he reached the edge of the divide, but did not cross. The wind that swirled from the canyons and cliffs below, smashed into his fragile craft, the crosscurrents threatening destruction. Gene dropped 200 feet down below the peaks and flew along the continent's backbone until he found a canyon that released him to the west, toward Butte. As he came into view, 15,000 silent spectators who had nervously waited for his return began to chatter. With his gentle touchdown in the middle of the track, a thunderous roar echoed in the mountains. The crowd rushed to get a closer look at the first man to reach the Divide. Police, sheriff's deputies, and Gene's mechanics were just barely able to keep the aviation crazed fans from wrecking the aeroplane or carrying Gene away on their shoulders. It took a half hour for the crowd to cool down.[9]

The next day, after studying some local maps, Gene had come up with a daring plan. Instead of flying over the highest peaks to cross the Divide, he believed he had found a way to conquer it at a lower altitude. He would fly about six miles southeast and with some careful weaving through the tight curves of the Homestake Pass, he would cross the Divide at about 6,400 feet. Maintaining his altitude as he exited the pass, he would turn north and fly behind the high peaks, straight through the Jefferson Valley to the town of Woodville. There he would locate the tracks of the Great Northern Railroad and follow them southwest to Butte through the Elk Park Pass. It was only about seventeen miles, but it was through some of Montana's roughest territory and in a place where winds could still be a problem. A reporter compared Gene's attempt to the fatal 1910 flight of Jorge Chavez. Chavez had been the first man to cross through the Alps in an aeroplane, but had crashed just before he could land. "Although the altitude Ely will have to attain to cross the mountains will not be very high," said the reporter, "nevertheless it will be equally as dangerous as the flight of Chavez." It was a great plan, but Gene never got there.[10]

Rain, thunder, and lightning had swept over the fairgrounds in the afternoon, delaying Gene's start by over an hour. Members of the aviation committee, determined to keep a mob of spectators from swarming around Gene, warned the crowd that additional policemen would be stationed along the rail of the track and no one would be allowed into the center of the field. Unfortunately, as one reporter said, the "police were about as much use as one boy with a tin star." When the crowd saw the biplane pulled into position for takeoff, a thousand men and women rushed onto the field. The entire field, from grandstand to within twenty yards of Gene's machine, was crammed with people. There was no room to maneuver and Gene would have a dangerous take off, flying with the wind instead of against it. As Gene climbed aboard, Mabel told him she thought the wind currents were too dangerous. Gene told her not to worry. As she walked away, a reporter heard her say, "Gene will meet with an accident some day."[11]

As he started down the field, some of the crowd moved to get a better view. Before he was airborne they had lined up directly in front of him and were not about to move. He barely got off the ground and made a violent turn to the left. "I tried to turn out to avoid the crowd and save myself and them," he said. He rose to 30 feet, his wings at a steep angle as he tried to turn back into the wind and gain altitude. A blast of air almost rolled him over. Gene stood up, using his body to straighten his machine's flight. The biplane swooped down, nosed up for a second, and then dropped like a rock. The force of the impact hurled Gene away from the machine as if he were a cannonball. He landed on his back. Luckily, the rain had softened the ground; otherwise, he might have been killed. "If I had been able to get 50 feet higher," he said, "the puff of wind which careened the plane would not have bothered me much, for I could have straightened it out." Now, everyone rushed onto the field thinking that Gene might be dead or seriously injured, but they saw him stand up and began his inspection. Although the frame wasn't broken it was badly bent and it seemed that every guy wire had snapped. It would take five or six hours to repair, he said, and by then it would be dark. "I hate to disappoint the crowd," he said, "but the people themselves are to blame for crowding in and not giving me a fair show to get into the air." Those who hadn't seen Gene's spectacular Sunday flight would have to be satisfied with the motion pictures taken that day by a local photographer. Before Gene left town, he decided to donate $1,000 of his guarantee toward the Butte miners' hospital fund, but the aviation committee claimed that because Gene didn't fly on the last day, they were the ones who had forced his donation. Gene was already on his way to Great Falls, Montana, and probably didn't care who got the credit.[12]

Sitting on an eastward bend of the Missouri River, the town of Great Falls was named for five waterfalls that, before dams were built, tumbled freely in a 10-mile stretch of the ancient riverbed. In 1891, the first hydroelectric dam on the Missouri River was built just upstream from Black Eagle Falls and was followed 19 years later by another, further downstream. The electricity generated from these dams gave the town a nickname—"The Electric City."[13]

Across from the Black Eagle Dam, on the gently sloping south bank of the river, was Black Eagle Park. Pavilions and picnic grounds mixed together with the cottonwood and willow trees. In the open fields, baseball games and horseracing had their season and nearby, children climbed aboard swings and rode a merry-go-round. Here, just a month before Gene arrived, the Great Falls baseball team had finished a ballpark, and this is where Gene would begin his flights.[14]

Three thousand fans squeezed into the stands on June 17, 1911. Their automobiles surrounded the ballpark and pressed close against the outfield fence. The Great Falls Electrics were hosting the Salt Lake City Skyscrapers in a contest shortened to seven innings so spectators could watch the aviation show. The Electrics won 8–3 and when both teams cleared the field, Gene had his first chance to inspect the facility. It was too small and too dangerous. He said he was willing to fly, but not from within the ballpark. The promoters agreed to take down a part of the outfield fence and have the fans move their automobiles so that Gene could roll his aeroplane outside the park and take off from there. Gene made three short flights, "insignificant affairs and disappointing." No one was happy. "Ely's flights were made without accident," said a reporter, "but were in such directions that the spectators in the grandstand were able to see but little of them." He agreed to fly the next day and not charge the promoters, but the wind was up and the town was disappointed again. "The best that may be said of Aviator Ely's performances in Montana," wrote a newspaper editor, "is that instead of rising to the occasion, he stood his ground."[15]

It was summer and aviation exhibitions were mushrooming. From Great Falls, Gene recrossed the Rockies and rushed his aeroplane some 200 miles to the northwest corner of Montana for a one-day exhibition in Kalispell. On June 21, 5,000 satisfied spectators watched him perform a few low-level maneuvers in a single, four-mile flight from the fairgrounds and back. The upper winds were treacherous and a gathering thunderstorm had Gene's mechanics scrambling to get his machine under cover. Back on the train and headed east, over 300 miles and five days later, Gene had one of his most successful Montana exhibitions at Lewistown, the very center of the state. It may have helped that head mechanic, Bill Hoff, had gone ahead to Lewistown instead of Kalispell with Gene. It gave him almost a week to get things ready for Gene's arrival. The enthusiastic crowd numbered less than 3,000 on a weather perfect day and those who had seen other flights said, "Nothing better has ever been seen in the state." He took a 20-minute flight toward the South Moccasin Mountains, lost a race to an automobile, and then climbed high above downtown.[16]

For the fourth time in less than a month, Gene and Mabel crossed back over the Rocky Mountains. Heading west back to California, they had accepted a last minute booking on June 28 at Missoula, Montana. The reporters who had seen Gene misfire in his Montana flights were skeptical. "Aviator Ely is going at it again, this time in Missoula," said a reporter, "but it's not always UP with Aviator Ely." Because Missoula had no enclosed structure where Gene could take off and where admission could be charged, the exhibition was moved to Fort Missoula, about three miles southwest of downtown. For 70 cents, a spectator got a roundtrip train or streetcar ticket to the fort and admission to the show. A few of the 3,000 spectators showed up early in the afternoon just to watch the aviator and mechanics prepare the aeroplane for flight. Outside the fort, on the plains and small hills, the inevitable freeloaders patiently waited for the first flight. Nearby, a small group of Cree Indians had set up a few teepees the night before and sitting on horseback, waited for the birdman to fly.[17]

Just before 5 o'clock, a hard easterly wind was blowing across the Idaho-Montana border as Gene took off from the baseball field at the fort. "With a thrumming of giant propellers, the machine shot across the field and then rose swiftly and gracefully into the air." Gene made three flights, two of them ending with a skimming dive over the heads of the panicked crowd. In his third and last flight, Gene flew with Bill Hoff as a passenger. A reporter noted that the extra weight didn't seem to make much difference. "There was not a quiver or a flutter during the whole performance except perhaps on the turns when Hoff was in the machine."[18]

While the mechanics were disassembling the aeroplane, Gene was told that a local dentist, Dr. Joseph Oettinger, wanted to buy his machine. Oettinger had purchased Missoula's second automobile and was known to have collected a few speeding tickets. "I would sell him one like it," Gene said, "but not this one. I guess this machine has been in the air longer than any other in existence." He said that after the Missoula flights, the aeroplane had flown 109 hours and 20 minutes. "I have had it since December last and I have flown it so much that I have grown pretty fond of it." Just before midnight, leaving his mechanics to finish crating up the machine, Gene and Mabel boarded the train for Portland where, after a brief stopover, they would catch a Southern Pacific train to Chico, California.[19]

Because Gene was due in Reno, Nevada to fly at their Independence Day celebration, the July 3 exhibition in Chico was as uneventful as it was brief. Almost before it was over, Gene, Mabel, and Bill Hoff rushed to catch a train for the 97-mile trip to Sacramento. There they transferred to another train and slept through an overnight, 240-mile trip through the Sierra Mountains, arriving in Reno early the next morning.[20]

While Gene had been in Montana, Bud Mars, Gene's friend and flying partner, had returned from his six-month flying tour of the Orient. In a few weeks, the two men and their wives would get together for a short reunion and then head off in different directions. Mars would crash in *Pennsylvania* and survive, while newspapers wrote his obituary. "All aviators know what the public wants," Bud's wife said. "The people want the aviators to be doing dangerous things all the time." Gene would do them, Mars would not.[21]

# { 41 }

# A Very Busy Month

Gene was not the first to fly an aeroplane in Nevada. Ivy Baldwin, a 43-year-old balloonist and renowned high wire artist, had soared for a half mile near Carson City in June 1910. Many others had tried, but the only time those machines got off the ground was when mechanics decided to lift them into a railroad boxcar. Gene said these amateur attempts hurt the business and gave the public a false impression of the aviation art. To show what a true professional could do, he said he wouldn't accept his $2,500 fee unless he actually flew.[1]

Reno, the Washoe County seat and the largest city in Nevada, was celebrating the 135th anniversary of American independence and the 50th anniversary of Washoe County's founding. They were ignoring critics from other states that said the festivities were also celebrating the state's liberal divorce laws, what many called "a blacksmith shop for knocking off marital shackles."[2]

Toward the end of June, city fathers sent the county chain gang out to an overgrown piece of city property on the south side of the Truckee River, less than a mile west of downtown. Clearing and leveling the ground by hand, the men created a dirt runway 50 feet wide and over 600 feet long. Gene had only asked for 200 feet, but the aviation committee thought it safer to have more. Each day the field was sprinkled and rolled to keep it in tiptop condition.[3]

Gene, Mabel, and Hoff arrived the morning of July 4. Gene drove Hoff out to the aviation grounds so they could check field conditions. For a long time, questions lingered in Gene's eyes as he looked over the line of trees near the end of the runway, but he said nothing. His aeroplane was already assembled and waiting in a tent hangar at the edge of the field. This wasn't the machine that Gene had flown in Chico. Accompanied by two mechanics, the biplane that had flown in Missoula had been sent directly to Reno. "This will be the last flight that Mr. Ely will make in this biplane," Hoff said, "the one in which he made the record breaking flight to and from the deck of a battleship. It will be placed on exhibition at San Francisco."[4]

The excitement and thrills of July 4, 1911, were second only to those of a year earlier, when a Reno crowd of 20,000 saw Jack Johnson, the black heavyweight-boxing champion, humiliate Jim Jeffries, the "Great White Hope." By the time Gene climbed aboard his biplane, the temperature was fast approaching 90 degrees. There were reports that as many as 2,000 Indians from the Piute, Washoe, and Shoshone tribes were walking hundreds of miles across the desert to see the birdman. There wasn't an available hotel room anywhere in the city. Waiters and other restaurant employees were begging for the afternoon off, sure that no one would be eating while the aviators flew. Fifteen thousand spectators squeezed together for a good view and every high rooftop was thickly shingled in people. Both banks of the river and the island in its middle, swarmed with the aeronautically curious.[5]

In the next eight minutes, Gene would face more danger than he had ever experienced in such a short time. As his engine started, he leaned over to Hoff and nodded toward the clump of trees at the end of the runway. "This field is a death trap," he shouted over the engine's thunder, but he was still confident he could overcome the danger. His sea level propeller had been swapped out for a new version that should get more bite in Reno's thinner atmosphere and, once he got over the trees, Gene expected an easy flight. "There were people standing real close, with umbrellas to shade them from the sun," remembered Reno resident, Clarence Menke. "He warmed it up good and there was a cloud of those umbrellas that flew up in the air." Running in front of a swirling cloud of dust, the aeroplane labored halfway down the runway, looking as if it would never get into the air. At the last second, it angled up sharply, but like an overweight seagull it barely skimmed over the treetops before it dipped down and disappeared, falling below the trees and toward the ground. The trees, the nearby bluffs, and the river water, had created crosscurrents in the air that seemed to move in all directions at once. The wails, moans, and shouts of the uneasy crowd only lasted a few seconds, until the biplane suddenly bobbed back up and flew on. Riotous cheers echoed off the Sierra Nevada foothills. "The flight promised to be a very good one after all," Gene said, but, as he began to rise, things grew dicey. Over the Truckee River the air was cold, but after crossing over the opposite riverbank, it got hot again, pushing him upward and rocking his yellowed wings from side to side. He began a climbing circle to the southwest, all the while fighting against crosscurrents that streamed at him from the many mountain ravines. The machine turned in a wide sweep to the north, doubled back to the south, and completed another circle. It was a dangerous atmosphere with sudden and violent alterations, throwing and rocking the craft in unexpected directions. Briefly caught in a cold layer of air over the river and a hot layer above, the biplane suddenly dropped into a 100-foot freefall before Gene could regain control. Now, there was a grinding sound coming from the motor and the propeller didn't sound right either. Something inside had come loose. "Just as I reached the height at which I planned to encircle the city," Gene said, "there was a snap and something went wrong with my engine." He swung out wide, rising just enough to catch his bearings. "I circled around twice in order to find a good place to land," he said, "but determined to return if I could without power, for the engine was shut off." He aimed back toward the clump of trees at the end of the runway and began a long and noiseless glide. Rushing over the threatening trees, Gene pushed the biplane into an abrupt downward angle and skimming into the ground, slid over the smooth surface like a bowling ball. "Never again!" Gene said as he stepped from the seat. Mabel was by his side as the applauding crowd rushed in.[6]

When Hoff opened the biplane's motor, he found a wrist pin on a right side cylinder had snapped off, loosening a bearing that rattled inside the motor until the bearing was ground into tiny chunks. With cylinder walls deeply scratched, the motor was a total wreck. The crowd was thrilled by that first flight and wanted more. They lingered near the hangar tent hoping for some kind of miracle, but it never came. Gene's eight-minute flight had satisfied his contract requirements and he left town. The Reno promoters gladly paid his $2,500 fee from the $6,050 they had made from the event. For once, someone had made an aviation gamble that actually had paid off.[7]

Back in Sacramento on July 6, Gene rushed to the Adjutant General's Office in the state capitol building. There he successfully completed an examination that commissioned him a first lieutenant in the California National Guard and officially put him in charge of training pilots for the state's proposed aviation squadron. He left on the afternoon train to San Francisco, where he was expected to set up his headquarters, work with the Coast Artillery, and "devote a large part of his time teaching the members of the guard how to fly." If that indeed was the plan, it was quickly abandoned. Within three days, Gene was back on a train with Mabel and a newly purchased 6-cylinder Stevens-Duryea automobile that the newspaper said would follow him on his next exhibition tour. In Portland, Oregon, he and Mabel had a quick reunion with Bud Mars and Marie before both couples headed for Gene's one-day exhibition in Baker City, not far from the Idaho border, in Eastern Oregon. Mars had returned from his round the world tour just a few weeks earlier, after flying 250 times in a score of Asian and European cities. After Gene's competent, but unspectacular performance in Baker City, Mars continued east to fly in Pennsylvania, while Gene and Mabel made their way to Canada.[8]

Gene arrived in Canada's Alberta Province, in the city of Lethbridge, on July 14, just a day after Bill Hoff and his two mechanics unloaded the biplane that they had brought from Baker City. Gene crossed over the border with ease, but the aeroplane almost hadn't made it. Canadian officials had neglected to get the legal authority from the national government to let the aeroplane into the country. Custom officials wired to Ottawa, the Canadian capital, asking permission to release the machine. After a few hours, they were told that the biplane could enter the country, but it must return to the United States immediately after the exhibition was over.[9]

Gene skipped his hotel breakfast and rushed to the exhibition grounds. With memories of his disaster in Canada, exactly a year ago, he put a critical eye on his biplane and the aviation field. Gene was flying for $1,500, the most expensive attraction ever brought to Lethbridge, but the local agricultural board thought it a good investment. A new exhibition hall was opening at the fairgrounds and although promoters were already expecting the largest crowd ever assembled in southern Alberta Province, they still began with an overly optimistic full-page advertising campaign. "They promised that Gene would perform "every evolution known to the best in the game," including the daring and dangerous spiral glide, "ocean dips, speedy spurts, sudden tilts into the clouds, and wide circles into the surrounding country." A "well-known local lady" would be taken on a flight, seated next to "the world famous Anglo-American Aviator." The festivities would end with a grand public ball that officially opened the $30,000 exhibition hall. All of this for a mere 75 cent admission.[10]

At noon, the town's shops and businesses closed as thousands of well-dressed people, in a virtual holiday mood, hurried off to the fairgrounds. By 3 o'clock that afternoon, the crowd circled the entire half-mile racetrack, watching the infield preparations of Gene and his crew. They saw Mabel see Gene off and Gene climb onto the wing. The mechanics took their positions and the engine sputtered to life. The machine bumped over the ground, gaining speed, until finally, "the ingenious affair left the ground amid the shouts of the crowd." Over the years, there had been many manned balloon flights and terrifying parachute jumps at the fairgrounds, but few people here had ever seen a birdman challenge the territory of the birds. The impossible was now reality, just above their heads and right in front of their eyes.[11]

As Gene flew away to the north and climbed, the sound of his motor mellowed to a droning buzz. At 400 feet he turned back, began circling the track, and below, spectators wondered how he would ever get back to the ground. Gene swung out and around to the southwest, now flying straight toward the infield. With a slight downward dip, the engine went silent and the machine began to fall. Passing over the outside rail and skimming over the infield ground, its wheels touched down and rolled gradually to stop not far from where it had taken off seven minutes earlier.[12]

While the engine cooled and the mechanics made a careful inspection of the aeroplane, Gene told reporters that he wished he had eaten breakfast and lunch. "I'm not feeling up to the mark," he said, "but I will make another flight." He said the "air was full of holes" and he refused to take a passenger. Twenty minutes later, Gene was back in the air, this time flying far out over the city before returning to the racetrack, where he circled and dipped. He ended his thirteen-minute flight with another precise landing. The crowd was expecting a third, but the moment the machine hit the ground, the mechanics pulled it off the field. It was too dangerous to fly, Gene said, and that night he left for Seattle. The crowd was disappointed, but there were very few complaints. "Altogether the day was a very successful one," said a reporter, "one that will live for a long time in the memory of those who witnessed their first aviation exhibition."[13]

At almost the exact moment that Gene was ending his second flight in Canada, Bud Mars fell from the sky and was declared dead in Pittsburgh. On his second flight of the day, his biplane had jerked suddenly and began to whirl as it dropped from 500 feet. Spectators could see Mars frantically working his controls without success. He plunged into the ground, the shattered machine burying him in rubble. He was still conscious, but unable to speak as he was pulled from the wreckage and placed in an ambulance. His breastbone was broken, his skull fractured, and he had a brain concussion along with severe internal injuries. Even so, bruised from head to toe, he beat all newspaper predictions and lived. Doctors said it would be many months before he could fly again, but even with a leg that often gave him trouble, Mars was back on his biplane again before the end of the month.[14]

Gene and Mabel arrived in Seattle on July 16, one day before the beginning of the city's six-day celebration of what residents called "The Golden Potlatch of 97." The word potlatch came from northwest coastal Indians who said it meant a gathering or a festival. This event would commemorate the arrival of the steamship *Portland* in 1897, bringing the first ton of gold from the Alaskan gold rush.[15]

Gene would be flying with Hugh Robinson, but Robinson wouldn't arrive for another three days. That gave Gene his first chance to impress local reporters at the expense of his fellow Curtiss flier. Robinson was always late, Gene said. "He arrives at the last minute, takes his plane out of the trunk, and begins flying. He doesn't care whether the machine is ready or not." Gene said Robinson flew like Hoxsey, the dead aviator. "Hugh is a second Hoxsey," he said. "Someday he is going up like that and will fail to come down. He doesn't seem to believe that there is a danger of any kind in the air."[16]

Gene walked the waterfront with the meet's promoters who told him that the King of the festival would officially start the celebration with an arrival by ship. Gene said he would like to greet the King from the air. "It would make a pretty picture and as a feature would be unique," he said. "I should like to contribute my services and, if the king doesn't mind, I'll drop a message of greeting to him from his Queen, when I pass over the ship." The idea wasn't part of his contract, but the promoters quickly accepted. Gene made only one other request. After flying in the afternoon opening ceremonies, he wanted the rest of his flights to begin at seven in the evening. He explained that if he flew in the afternoon, as the promoters had arranged, the sun reflecting off the bay made it almost impossible to see anything in the air. It seemed a sensible idea and the promoters made the change.[17]

Temperatures had dropped to near 80 degrees after sizzling in an unseasonable 90-degree heat wave for three days. A predicted southwesterly wind promised to dip temperatures even further. The weather bureau's predictions held true and by the time the first biplane flew on July 19, the noontime temperature had barely crept past 60 degrees.[18]

With Robinson's arrival still a day away, Gene had the show to himself. Just after 1:25 p.m. spectators in the 10,000-seat grandstand and all along the waterfront saw a buzzing machine rise above the misty mudflats of Harbor Island, a few hundred yards across Elliott Bay. Gene climbed to a thousand feet on a northerly course that edged the headlands west of the city. "The wonderful bird-like picture of the fast moving aeroplane first hushed the crowds who watched him in silent admiration, then brought forth great cheers, which may or may not have reached the ears of the speeding birdman in his speeding aerial chariot." A year earlier, Charles Hamilton had plunged into a Seattle racetrack's pond and his failure to make good on his promised return, had festered in Seattle's memory. But now there was joy. "All former exhibitions were dismal failures," said a reporter, "but yesterday, aviation in the Queen City arrived for the first time." Applause was long, loud, and never ending, punctuated with bells, shrieking whistles, and automobile honks. As the "Gold Ship" steamed toward the docks, Gene dipped down, and flying slowly overhead, he dropped his message to the King. His mission accomplished, Gene turned back toward Harbor Island, but instead of landing, he started a gentle curve that took him back to the city and over the docks, the rapping of his motor drowning out all other sounds. It was a short, but impressive flight and set the stage for his evening performance. "To see Ely manage his flying machines, and especially to be near enough to hear the buzz of his motor," said a newspaper editorial, "is worth a journey of a thousand miles."[19]

"Gene Ely is flying for fun, for money, for the exploitation of the aeroplane as a commercial institution," said a reporter. "When Ely flies, he is out to demonstrate the aeroplane to the last of its possibilities, not how much a daredevil an aviator may make of himself."[20]

That evening Gene made two flights, both over the city and the bay. He dropped another message to the manager of his current hotel and then passed over three naval ships that had come as part of the Potlatch festival. It was the first time since San Francisco that Gene had flown over the fleet flagship, the U.S.S. *West Virginia*, and in his honor, the admiral ordered the firing of a seventeen-gun salute. Tomorrow Gene would share the sky with Robinson, but today he was the hero and reporters couldn't stop gushing in their admiration. "When Ely announces that he will fly, he flies," said one. "If he says it will be at 7 o'clock, it will be at 7 o'clock, and neither wind nor high water will stop him." Another admired Gene's professionalism. "He is not reckless. He is not convinced that aviation would profit at all by his death." Mabel, "his beautiful and charming wife," could also bask in Gene's glory. She had been afraid when he first flew, reporters said. "It had put a terror in her heart," but now, she saw his unshakeable nerves and how careful he was. Knowing for certain, as Glenn Curtiss had told her, "that disaster does not ride on a biplane correctly handled," she had found peace and confidence. Gene was, said a reporter, "one of the sort that cannot be replaced."[21]

Robinson arrived the next day with the hydroaeroplane. For the next few days, Gene from the island and Robinson from the waves, scattered the local waterfowl as they took to the sky. The streets and docks were crammed with humanity, faces turned up, and fingers pointing. Rooftops were swarming with spectators and on a few of the taller buildings, small grandstands had been set up. They called Gene "The Eagle," soaring high and then swooping down in wide circles around buildings. Robinson was "The Gull," or maybe a "Man-duck," skimming the bay with a tail of spray behind him, weaving through boats and ships until he found a clear place to take off from. Everything went well until the last day. There were perhaps 100,000 people lining the waterfront and it seemed that everyone in the area who owned a motorboat was on Elliott Bay. After Gene's late afternoon flight, he and Mabel, weaving through the mini blockade on the water, were rushed from island to shore in a special boat so as not to miss their eastbound train. But poor Robinson had trouble landing his "mechanical duck." It was getting dark and so many boats were blocking his way, it was impossible to land. In desperation, Robinson flew far out toward the entrance of the bay, dipping, diving, and swirling around, hoping to distract the mini flotilla below. Finally, with the sun going down and his fuel tank almost drained dry, he found empty water and set her down.[22]

Completely out of character, Mabel had left Seattle refusing all interviews, but she did write a short column that the local newspaper sent out over the United Press newswires. She began with an apology. "When you're in the public eye," she said, "even if you are pretty and 20 years old, that doesn't give you a license to snub the public all the time." After writing the usual story of how she loved to fly and how Gene had promised to build her an aeroplane, she dropped what should have been a bombshell. "Gene is never going to fly in an exhibition again," she said. "He terminated his contract with Glenn Curtiss with his last flight. Hereafter he will confine himself to the big contests and to experiments with a view to making the sport of aviation more of a sport for everybody. Just now, it is pretty dangerous for the novice, I must admit." Now Mabel was voicing Gene's apprehensions. "There is big money in the game, but it isn't worth the while," he had told Wemme in Portland. "Something might happen when I am hundreds of feet in the air." They arrived in Washington D.C. on July 29, where Gene told reporters that after a year in the business, he had flown a total of 123 hours.[23]

The Army's aviation school was located in College Park, Maryland, about eight miles northeast of the nation's capital. Bound on its western edge by the main line of Baltimore & Ohio Railroad, the government chose the site in 1909 as the most convenient location near Washington, D.C. for their aviation work. As an added bonus, officials were confident that it was far enough away from large cities that it would keep big crowds of spectators from interfering with training. It wouldn't. By the end of the year, three Army officers had already finished training on the field when the weather turned cold and training moved to Texas. For the next two years there was little activity on the field. In 1911, with a $125,000 appropriation in the military budget designated for the purchase and maintenance of aeroplanes, the Army began an expansion at College Park, where they were ready to evaluate the latest aircraft.[24]

It appears that Curtiss was content to let his Army-trained flyers demonstrate his aeroplanes without his or any other civilian's help, but complications developed almost immediately. While preparing to demonstrate one of the newest Curtiss 8-cylinder biplanes, Lieutenant Paul Beck received orders to stay on the ground. His superiors feared the new machine was too fast and they didn't want to risk an accident to one of their officers. Beck rushed to a telephone and made a long distance call to Glenn Curtiss in Hammondsport asking for help and urging him to come and fly at College Park. The stakes were high enough that Curtiss gave up his exhibition retirement and arrived in Maryland the next day. Gene had arrived hours earlier. Apparently, Curtiss had asked Gene to spend a few days flying in these important military demonstrations.[25]

Knowing that Army officials had said they were more interested in straight flights that showed an aeroplane's effectiveness in war, rather than "fancy dips and spiral effects," Curtiss made two very conservative flights. Gene's flight was decidedly different. He was out of the hanger and circling at 600 feet in just a few minutes. Once content that everything was working properly, he zoomed higher, flying at 70 miles an hour at over 1,000 feet. He dropped into a left hand spiral dive and then, still rushing downward, turned back into a right hand spiral. "The flying feats took the breath away from nearly all the spectators," as he twisted and twirled in circles. Then, in an instant, with one wing almost grazing the airfield grass, he leveled out and landed. That afternoon he received a telegram from Sacramento. He had been appointed chief signal officer for the California National Guard with a promotion to the rank of lieutenant colonel.[26]

No sooner had Curtiss made his two flights at College Park than he was called back to Hammondsport on urgent business. He left Gene to finish the rest of the demonstrations. What promised to be many days of Gene's experimental flights, ended with just one. After only three minutes in the air, Gene flew his endurance test of the new Curtiss 4-cylinder trainer right into the middle of an unexpected rainstorm. He hadn't seen the storm until he was in it and being pelted by showers and tossed by the wind, struggling to gain control. Still a mile from the aviation field and flying with the wind, he returned in a sharp dive, striking the field hard enough to crack his magneto and kill his engine. Pushed further by the wind, he rolled another quarter mile across the turf before he could stop. A soaked Gene stepped from his biplane as the oncoming rainstorm finally reach the spectators. The endurance test was canceled. When the weather cleared, Gene switched to the 8-cylinder machine that Lieutenant Beck had brought with him from San Antonio, and made two flights. His last made Gene "the sensation of the day," when he chased down another aeroplane and literally flew rings around it before speeding off into a high-speed circle of the aviation field. That night he received a telegram from Curtiss telling him to return immediately to Hammondsport. The local press reported that Gene would return to College Park within a week to demonstrate a new high-powered motor and perhaps fly the hydro-aeroplane, even though water was miles away. But Gene wasn't coming back.[27]

The Gimbel brothers were offering $5,000 to the winner of the first intercity aeroplane race. Three contestants would fly between New York City and Philadelphia. A major condition of the contest was that the winner must fly over the Gimbels department stores in each city. Gene was originally scheduled to race, but Curtiss had replaced him with Charles Hamilton. Curtiss apparently was trying to make peace with Hamilton by offering him a contract that would give him a chance to fly again for the company. But Curtiss was no fool. With memories of his previous difficulties with Hamilton, Curtiss must have worried about the flier's reliability and had decided not to take chances. That may be why he asked Gene to accompany him to New York. It turned out to be a good decision.[28]

The race started August 5 from Governor's Island, just off the tip of Manhattan. Because of overcast skies, winds steadily blowing over 12 miles an hour, and a threatening rainstorm, the start was delayed for a few hours. Hamilton looked at the weather and decided to withdraw from the competition. He had "developed a nervous feeling in regard to the weather conditions," said a reporter, "and also in regard to his machine." "I could not think of venturing up in this wind with the biplane provided for me," Hamilton said. "I have not been in a Curtiss flying machine for thirteen months, with the exception of a short spin six months ago. I am out of touch with the machine." Curtiss had given Hamilton Gene's powerful 8-cylinder motor and mounted it on a factory fresh, brand new machine, but Hamilton was still worried. "I have had no opportunity to test it out," he said. He even complained that he wasn't given enough gasoline. Flying over New York's tall buildings would be too dangerous, he said. The wind would swirl unpredictably. Later, perhaps trying to save face, he said that even with all of these problems, if the winds had died down, he probably would have flown. Although he would live for another two years, Hamilton's career was virtually over.[29]

Gene wasn't happy with the weather situation either. He was on a short vacation and it took considerable arm-twisting from the Curtiss crew to get him to take Hamilton's place. "Those dark clouds look like a coming thunderstorm," he said. "If they are, I don't think I want to lay up any trouble for myself." He told Ed Moore, the Curtiss representative, that he was taking a break from flying and wasn't in flying form. When Moore asked him to do it for the honor of the team, Gene agreed to at least test the air and then make a decision. He made a quick flight around the island and when he landed, he had changed his mind. "That thunder storm doesn't seem to be any nearer," he said. "I'm ready."[30]

This was an all Curtiss race. Lincoln Beachey, Hugh Robinson, and Gene were each flying a near duplicate 60 horsepower biplane, loaded down with twelve gallons of gasoline, three gallons of lubricating oil, and ten gallons of water. Only Beachey's craft had been modified into what was called the Curtiss headless design, the front elevator was gone now and incorporated in the tail. The competitors mounted their machines, started their engines, and moved into a line. Startled by the roar of the motors, a barking bull terrier charged toward Robinson's whirling and invisible propeller. Luckily, the canine slipped and fell ten feet from certain death, giving its owner just enough time to pull it to safety. Oblivious to the near disaster, the birdmen began to take off at one-minute intervals. They flew north up the Hudson River, turning northeast near 34th Street, crossing over the transatlantic docks, and then passing over tenements and factories until they reached the shopping district and were flying 2,000 feet above the Gimbels store at Broadway and 33rd Street. Here, as Jacob Gimbel watched from the rooftop, the official timing of the 83-mile race began. The birdmen turned south toward New Jersey. Crossing over the meadows of the Garden State, they planned to follow the tracks of Pennsylvania Railroad to Trenton and then trace the Delaware River until they reached Philadelphia. Twenty miles and twenty minutes from New York City, Gene and Beachey were neck and neck, flying within a few feet of each other over Rahway, New Jersey. Robinson was lagging seven minutes behind. They raced through another 10 miles. By now, Gene had taken a slight lead over Beachey, but then his motor began to sputter and suddenly stopped. As Gene touched down in a field just west of New Brunswick, he watched as Beachey sailed by. A frantic inspection showed that Gene's fuel tank had been leaking and was now empty. Racing to a nearby farmer's telephone, Gene called the Curtiss Company's representatives in Newark asking for help and a new tank. While he waited, Robinson landed nearby. He had seen Gene's machine on the ground and because he was low on gasoline himself, had assumed he had reached Trenton, his planned refueling stop. One of the local drivers who had watched Robinson land agreed to drive to New Brunswick and bring Robinson some fuel. Eighteen minutes later, a dejected Gene, still waiting, watched Robinson fly away. An hour and a half after Gene's emergency landing, with his leaking tank replaced and filled with gasoline, he hustled into the air. Thirteen miles later, at Princeton Junction, he was down again, this time with a clogged fuel line. Beachey had already reached Philadelphia and Robinson was a half hour behind. After a total of 56 minutes in the air, Gene's race was over.[31]

There were nearly 100,000 people watching in Philadelphia when Beachey's biplane, flying under a gloomy sky of black clouds, turned his aeroplane in from the river. "I knew nothing about the town," he said, "and looked around for the white flag that was to notify me it was the Gimbels store." As he flew over and around the building, he waved and dipped his wings to the large crowd gathered on the building's rooftop and on the surrounding streets. With victory assured, he aimed his biplane for the city hall tower and, in celebration, flew around the statue of William Penn that stood at its top. "He made his machine do the tricks of a bronco in the throes of being broke," said a reporter, and the crowd loved it.[32]

Beachey had finally learned to fly and now it was Beachey, not Gene, who was making the dramatic headlines. A month earlier, the "young daredevil," the upstart newcomer, had "flirted with death," flying over Niagara Falls, through the mist, through the gorge, and under the big steel bridge. He had taken motion pictures while high above Wilkes-Barre, Pennsylvania, flying with one hand on the wheel and the other turning the crank on a camera attached to his wing support. "Within the short space of six months," said a reporter, "Lincoln Beachey has become one of the most spectacular aviators in the world." His maneuvers, they said, "cause even the aviators themselves to catch their breath in astonishment." His dips and dives seemed to grow more complicated and dangerous with each flight. Nothing seemed too difficult. Gene couldn't compete with this kind of flying, but perhaps he tried. Mabel always blamed Beachey for Gene's death, as did a few other aviators' widows who had seen their own husbands fall. Mabel believed that Beachey had tempted her boy into trying foolhardy stunts. "Eugene would be with me now if he had never seen you fly," she told Beachey. Beachey later admitted that a few aviators had asked him to teach them his tricks, and judging by Mabel's anger, Gene was likely one of them.[33]

Losing the New York-Philadelphia race must have been embarrassing for Gene. Not only had Beachey become the latest darling of the press, Gene's losing because of a fuel problem brought back memories of last year's failed race from Chicago to New York City. Back at their New York hotel, Mabel told reporters that Gene might still finish his flight to Philadelphia someday, "just for the joy of finishing it," she said. "He hates to begin anything and then not go through with it." They were leaving that night for the Chicago International Aviation Meet, where Gene had had "such hard luck with his machine," she said. He had told her that he might even try that Chicago-New York race again. "If everything went off all right in Chicago," she said, "and if his engine worked as it really ought to, he might start from there on the last day of the meet and come to New York by air." Of course, there wasn't any prize for it, she said, "But he started to do it once, and he is determined to finish it before he gets through." In a couple of weeks that flight would be completed, but Gene wasn't the man who flew it.[34]

# { 42 }

# "We are merely circus performers"

Organizers of Chicago's aviation week promised the greatest aviation meeting in the history of aeronautics. Promoted by the Illinois Aero Club and led by aviation enthusiast and millionaire, Harold McCormick, Chicago's businessmen and social elite pledged $100,000 to guaranty funding. McCormick, alone, put up $25,000 of his own money. It was a massive affair, equipped as few other exhibitions had ever been. Overlooking Lake Michigan, in Grant Park, the grandstand would seat 70,000 spectators and was nearly a mile long. The standard tent hangars were replaced with a row of sturdy wooden sheds, capable of protecting up to 50 aeroplanes and their mechanics. The stands for the press and judges were wired for telegraph and telephone, and the Army Signal Corp had erected a high-powered wireless radio station. Two fully equipped hospital tents, one for men and one for women, each staffed by two interns, a nurse, and a surgeon, were ready for any medical emergency. Three ambulances, stationed at strategic points on the aviation field, could quickly transport injured aviators or spectators to the hospital tents or, in severe cases, rush them to the nearest hospital. Twenty-five nurses were scattered throughout the grandstand and medical staff patrolled the lakefront in speedy rescue motorboats.[1]

Forty-one aviators from all over the world said they would enter the aviation meet, but only 37 finally agreed to a contract. Knowing that almost all aviation meets in the past had struggled with money problems, particularly with guarantees to the aviators, McCormick and the Aero Club had come up with a new way to manage their costs. There would be no guarantees for an aviator's appearance. They would fly or they wouldn't be paid. Aviation companies wouldn't receive anything for their appearance and took the chance that they could win enough money to pay their expenses. To guarantee individual aviators would actually appear after signing a contract, each had to post a $1,000 bond. Once an individual's aeroplane was on the field, the aviator received $250 in cash. After flying for five minutes, he received an additional $250. If he flew longer than five minutes, each aviator was allowed $500 more for expenses.[2]

Aviators had two ways to make money from their flying—win some of the prize money, which amounted to over $80,000, or stay in the air as long as possible to collect "duration money." Computations for duration money began with a minimum $2 per minute awarded to an aviator for every minute they were in the air during designated flying hours. Three and a half hours were available each day, 3:30 to 7 p.m. In addition, the aviator with the longest duration time each day won a $500 prize. At the end of the meet, the aviator with the most total time in the air received half of the "grand duration prize," the remaining half was divided proportionately between the remaining aviators, based on their total flying time. Known by the aviators as "the financial plum of the meeting," the grand duration prize was originally $10,000, but when prize money was left over in other events, it was transferred to the duration prize so that on by the last day of the meet, the "plum" had grown to over $13,000.

On August 7, Gene and Mabel were among the first to arrive in Chicago. It was their fourth wedding anniversary. Unlike earlier meets when he flew alone or was the first aviator in town, this time Gene wasn't the center of attention. It seems that when surrounded by other aviators, his inherent shyness returned and he faded into the background. Because the other aviators were eager to talk, reporters found those "dapper young chaps—collegiate in attire," much more interesting. Young Jimmy Ward was perhaps loudest of all. "I am in Chicago to make altitude, distance, and duration records," he said. "You may count on me!" Bud Mars, less than a month after his near fatal crash in Pennsylvania, rather than brag, paid tribute to his old balloon mentor, Captain Tom Baldwin. "Uncle Tom, as we call him," Mars said, "is the dean of all airmen." Chicago reporters were hoping for an even more special interview, an interview they would never get. Harriet Quimby, the first and only American woman with a pilot's license, had told a reporter that she wanted to fly in Chicago, but McCormack's aviation committee had refused. The idea of a woman competing against the men just wouldn't fly.[3]

That evening, Gene and Mabel reunited once again with Bud Mars and Marie. The men had bought their wives gifts and were amused to see how eagerly the women ripped into the packages. "You know," Mabel said to the reporter who had come to interview Bud and Gene, "it's our wedding anniversary today." The women were wearing "marvelous creations of silk and satin" that Bud Mars had brought back from Japan. While the wrapping paper flew from the women's fingers, the reporter asked Gene about his new aeroplane. "Our new machines are quite different from the old Curtiss machines we had when you last saw us," he said. "The front elevator is now a monoplane and nearer in toward the wings. The wings, too, are double covered, which makes the machine faster. The tail has two flaps now, instead of one." Then he reminded the reporter that Mars was now flying a Baldwin designed biplane. "Captain Baldwin uses steel for his frame work," Mars said, "and hence, having so much less head resistance, his machine is faster than the Curtiss." They both had been using Hall-Scott motors, he said, but now Gene was flying a Curtiss designed engine. Gene broke in to say that he had already flown 1,000 miles with his Curtiss engine and it hadn't failed him yet. "The only stop I had was in the Philadelphia flight, when I had a brand new tank with dirt in it," he said. "But that wasn't the motor's fault." At the end of his interview, the reporter left without reporting what was in those wrapped packages that had so excited Mabel and Marie.[4]

On the Friday before the start of the meet, still away from the spotlight, Gene met with a group who had come from Iowa City just to see the local boy fly. His cousin, 14-year-old Hanson Ely, Jr., a future Navy lieutenant, came with them. Gene, or someone, had filled the boy's head with the idea that he would be flying as a passenger with Gene, but that could never happen. Hanson's Army father was still stationed in the Philippines. Without his permission, and considering the danger, a dejected Hanson certainly wouldn't "be taken into cloudland." Cousin Hugh Harrington had also come, returning home with grand stories of how he had met all of the famous aviators.[5]

With the aviation field right on the shore of Lake Michigan, everyone expected some sort of wind; after all, even back then Chicago was the Windy City. The only thing that took everyone by surprise was the end of a summer-long drought. On August 10, just before 9 in the evening, the most severe electrical storm in years began with a few flashes in the western sky. Ominous rumbles turned to bone rattling explosions as sheets of lighting began ripping through the atmosphere. The deluge of rain held off until midnight. Telephone and power lines went down, streets flooded, and water poured into cellars. In just a couple of hours, an inch of rain had beaten down upon a frightened city. By morning, with steady winds at 20 miles an hour and the aviation field ankle deep in mud, all test flights were cancelled. Mother Nature had washed it all away.[6]

On Saturday, August 12, in spite of the lingering mud, dismal skies, and hard winds, the nine-day Chicago International Aviation Meet was on. The aviators, representing five different nationalities, were up at sunrise and swarming into their hangars to prepare their machines. A visitor asked a reporter why it was that "nearly all of them were smoking." Weren't they in some sort of training? "Most of the aeronauts had been smoking since their arrival in the city," answered the reporter, "and they ate and drank just about as they pleased." The visitor and reporter overheard a puffing Earl Ovington telling one of the Army officers how he always remembered the man because of his brand of cigarettes. Then, Gene walked by with his Egyptian cigarette in his ever-present seven-inch long amber cigarette holder. It was in the Hubert Latham style and apparently "in evidence a great part of the day." One reporter marveled at how it seemed "to stand out from his face like a sixteen-inch gun." Only Jimmy Ward had given up cigarettes, but that didn't mean he had stopped smoking. "I've been off them for three days, now," he said, as he took another puff on a black cigar. All of this smoking, concluded a reporter, "was a liberty that would cause a riot in a real training camp."[7]

Reporters approached Gene as he was working on his biplane with his mechanics. "I want to get a little of your history, if you please, Mr. Ely," said one. Mabel had just approached with a large bundle under her arm and spoke first. "Mr. Ely is one of the best in the business," she said. "He has—," and a proud Mabel began rattling off fact after fact in a detailed account of Gene's career. The men waited patiently for her finish. "That's my press agent," Gene said with a big grin. "I haven't needed a personal press agent since I've been married. My wife is my principal booster and my general superintendent." Mabel was visibly annoyed. "I have to consult her about all of my exploits," Gene said. "Whatever you read about Ely in the papers, just depend that Mrs. Eugene E. is back of it." That's when he went too far. "Besides running me," he said, "she has all of my mechanics on HER personal staff." That was too much for Mabel who loudly slammed her bundle down on a nearby table and unwrapped it. "Something new for the boys, Gene," she said, holding up a neon red pullover sweater. "I bought them yesterday." Across the front of three sweaters, in large white letters was the word, ELY. When she tried to hand them to the mechanics, the "cautious boys" suddenly had a nervous look in their eyes, a look that darted back and forth between Mabel's demanding face and the greasy smears on their wool jackets. "Well, just watch us on dress parade," one of them said with a laugh. The tension broken, the boys thanked Mabel for her gift.[8]

At least a quarter of a million people were watching on the shores of Lake Michigan, but only 80,000 tickets had been sold. The welcoming gun fired at 2:30 p.m. and the exhibition began an hour later. Two accidents marred the first hour of the show. Frank Coffyn, flying low on his Wright biplane with two passengers aboard, stalled and fell on Rene Simon's aeroplane as the Frenchman was getting ready to take off. No one was hurt, but Simon was furious, claiming that Coffyn had intentionally smashed into his monoplane. A few minutes later, another aviator, speeding around one of the 70-foot pylons with his mechanic as a passenger, struck the ground with his left wing and his machine began a somersault that threw both men to the ground. These were omens of things to come. There were three more minor accidents that first day, none requiring an ambulance or preventing any repairs to the aeroplanes, but peaking one perceptive newspaper's interest. In its daily summary of events, the *Rockford Republic* began to include aeroplane accidents, and there would be more than enough of those in Chicago to choose from.[9]

Gene began his day as the second aviator into the air, his machine staggering against the face of a stiff north wind. Mabel, standing in a row of field glasses held by aviator wives, watched him closely, but from time to time, she took a glance at Marie Mars who was standing next to her. "I am not a bit nervous," Mabel whispered to a reporter. "I am accustomed to this. But I have to keep close watch on Mrs. Mars or she would fly to pieces. After having seen her husband picked out of a mass of broken sticks and canvas, I really don't see how she manages to watch the flights at all." Mabel didn't have to worry about Gene today. His best finish was fourth place against eleven competitors in the 15-mile cross-country race over land and water.[10]

The star of the day was Earle Ovington, who defeated Gene in the cross-country race by nearly three minutes and followed it up with a victory in a 20-mile cross-country race. Ovington flew a Bleriot monoplane and was regarded as the best American aviator flying that French machine. Ovington was now also learning to fly his own Curtiss biplane. Glenn Curtiss had been so impressed with Ovington's ability that just before the Chicago meet he had signed Ovington to run an aviation school at the Nassau Boulevard Aviation Field on Long Island, New York.[11]

If Ovington was the star, Beachey was the thrill. He made a dozen circuits of the course, rarely rising above 10 feet. He flew so close to the earth that workers on the field had to fall flat on the ground to avoid being hit. Around and around the pylons he zoomed, his angle so sharp it looked as if he was rolling out of control. He skimmed across Lake Michigan, the waves nearly touching his wheels. Twice he climbed to 4,000 feet, turned off his motor, fell into a perpendicular dive for 1,000 feet, and then, recovering in a spiral glide, aimed directly at the center of the grandstand. A few of the aviators were unhappy that Beachey wasn't disciplined for violating the aviation committee's rules against aviators taking unnecessary risks, but these kind of thrills sold tickets and the committee needed all the money they could get.[12]

Sunday there were no accidents and no significant flying by Gene, but on Monday, any of five accidents could have proved fatal. Ovington's wing grazed a pole, sheared off, and the machine fell. Somehow, Ovington was able to get enough power out of his engine and he safely wrestled his broken machine to the ground. For Howard Gill, a Wright flier, his propeller chain snapped at 600 feet, forcing the aviator into a powerless glide and a hard but successful landing. Not long afterwards, while over the lake, Jack McCurdy's engine began to miss. Instantly recognizing a damaged cylinder, he shut off his motor and began a glide toward land, but he was going so fast he couldn't see the threads of electric wires leading away from the Chicago Yacht Club. A fountain of sparks sprayed out as his machine ripped through the wires, tearing them away from their fastenings and splitting a power pole in two. The aeroplane turned over in an awkward, upside-down glide and landed almost gently on the ground. McCurdy scrambled out, surprised to find little damage. But, as he began to walk away, a sparking electric wire dropped on a wing and started a small fire. The flames crawled toward a stream of leaking gasoline, igniting the wing fabric and wood supports. Someone ran out of the yacht club with a fire extinguisher, but it was too late. McCurdy's biplane was charcoal.[13]

Two other machines dropped into Lake Michigan that day. Lee Hammond's motor suddenly stopped and just before it hit the water, he made a last minute high dive away from his plane. Rene Simon had flown out over the lake, circling the masts of ships in the harbor and beginning a series of erratic climbs that ended in dives toward the lake. On his last dive, his engine failed. In a quick glide, he settled onto the surface of the lake and climbed out onto a wing. He sat down, flicked some water from his tan shoes, lit a cigarette, and waited for the rescue boat.[14]

A half hour before sunset, Harry Atwood arrived in his Burgess-Wright biplane from St. Louis, Missouri. Atwood, who had only been flying for four months, was out to set a world record for distance, by flying from St. Louis to New York. Without goggles, overalls, or helmet, and dressed in a business suit and tie, Atwood was a mere twinkling speck in the southwestern sky as he approached the aviation field. Spectators began to chant, "Atwood! Atwood!" as he twice circled the field before landing. The aviators, who were already in the air when Atwood arrived, formed an aerial parade behind him. Atwood had planned to stay overnight and then leave early the next morning, but meet officials asked him to delay until the afternoon so that more people could see his departure. He wasn't happy about it, but agreed as long as he was paid. Atwood's departure at 3:30 the next day was to be the first event of the flying day. He was told he must leave by 3:30 or wait another day. "I'll leave when I choose," Atwood said, "or someone will get hurt." With Atwood's engine running, Frank Mudd, the contest committee chairman, handed over a check for $500 and Atwood exploded. "I landed here yesterday to please the crowd," he said, "and I was promised $1,000 for doing it." Mudd and Atwood "indulged in hot words and loud language," with "much gesticulation," until Atwood threw the check back at Mudd, telling them he wouldn't accept it until it was certified. While Atwood sat on his machine, shaking hands with the other aviators, the meet officials hastily huddled. Mudd certified the check and pushed it into Atwood's hand. With a final handshake from William Badger, the amateur birdman, Atwood was off and headed east over Lake Michigan. Billy Badger would be dead within the hour.[15]

Born in Pennsylvania, 26-six-year old Badger had inherited $250,000 from his father's estate and a few months earlier had bought one of Captain Baldwin's biplanes and learned to fly. After Atwood left the field, Badger followed the other aviators into the air. He began circling the field, each time diving toward a deep depression in front of the grandstand. With each dive, he became more reckless, skimming close to the ground. On his third attempt, he dropped his nose into a careless dive, angling at more than 45 degrees from 300 feet, gaining speed as he fell. At 50 feet above the ground, he began his upward tilt, but the forces on his aeroplane were too great and his wings crumpled together and he fell like "a pigeon shot while on the wing." The machine smashed into the dirt depression, its motor buried in the mud. The biplane shattered into a stack of sticks, twisted red metal tubing, and canvas rags. Badger was crushed between the radiator and the motor. His leg and back were broken, a steel engine rod had pierced his crushed skull, blood poured from his nose and eyes, and yet, he was still breathing. A few hundred spectators jumped the fence trying to get near the wreck, but police forced most of them back with nightsticks and a few well placed cracks to the head. An ambulance rushed Badger to the hospital, but it was too late. He died moments after his arrival. Gene and the other aviators, continued to fly circles over the lake and around the field. They could see the large truck and a work crew gathering up the wrecked biplane below, but none of them knew that Badger was dead. On the ground, worried about Gene, Mabel was upset. "Oh, this is horrible," she said. "Why don't the officials stop the meet?"[16]

Among the aviators looking down on the tragedy was St. Croix Johnstone, only son of a Chicago physician and no relation to aviator Ralph Johnstone who had died in Denver. St. Croix Johnstone was still flying as an amateur, but just a few weeks earlier had flown 195 miles in four hours, setting a new American endurance record. "I turned to aviation simply to find a new game," said the 24-year-old former racecar driver. "I wanted to find a new kind of excitement, and I found it." He learned to fly in France and when he returned to the United States in March 1911, he asked his father to buy him an aeroplane, but his father refused. "My conscience will not permit me to contribute to your certain death by providing you with a flying machine," his father said. "I can't buy you one, St. Croix." Johnstone found a way to buy his own aeroplane and began his flying career with the Moisant International Aviators. When he wrecked that machine, Alfred Moisant, head of the Moisant Company, built him another.[17]

When Badger had plunged into the ground, Johnstone had already been in the air for over an hour. He expected to fly until 7 o'clock, gathering more minutes toward the grand duration prize. His mother and father watched with Mary, Johnstone's wife, as the aviator sailed along at 1,500 feet. Just before 6 o'clock, Dr. Johnstone turned to his wife and daughter-in-law and told them that he had some prior business he had to take care of. "Don't go yet," pleaded Mrs. Johnstone. "St. Croix will be down in a few minutes." The doctor shook his head. "No, I must go," he said. "It doesn't look as though St. Croix will lose his life today. He seems to be flying too smoothly for any mishap." Reluctantly, Mrs. Johnstone left with the doctor, leaving Mary Johnstone alone to watch her husband fly. Twenty minutes later, with the sun near the horizon, the sky turning red, and Johnstone flying over the lake about a mile offshore, there was a flash and a dull thud, like a faraway cannon blast. Mary Johnstone, standing in the doorway of the Moisant hangar, hadn't taken her eyes off her husband. She screamed with one hand grasping at her throat. Her body twisted in agony and she pointed at the falling machine that dropped like a lead weight, but in her eyes it seemed to be taking minutes to hit the water. "Oh, Pity! My boy will be killed!" she cried. The wives of the other aviators were at her side trying to console her, but it did no good. "You could see," she wailed, "the way the machine plunged—St. Croix had completely lost control. Oh, why don't they hurry up and get out to him. Some of you men must take me to a boat so I can go out and help him." For nearly 10 minutes, she continued to plead. That's when Hugh Robinson, in the hydroaeroplane, floated to the dock where Mary Johnstone was standing.[18]

Robinson had been flying near Johnstone and had seen his gasoline tank explode. "I saw the engine drop through the frame and the wings fold up," he said later. He saw Johnstone falling head first into the water. "Johnstone and his machine were both under water, Johnstone unable to free himself.... Although I hovered over the spot where he disappeared, his body did not reappear. Robinson believed Johnstone was dead before he hit the water. "I struck out for the field, believing that he was gone." While his hydroaeroplane was drifting near the dock, Robinson yelled at the stunned members of the yacht club. "What's the matter with you fellows there? Why don't you get busy and tie me up." Mary shouted her plea to Robinson. "My husband—he's all right,—right?—isn't he?" Robinson took off his helmet and lied. "Certainly, ma'am," he said. "He's in a boat out there. There's a whole swarm of launches around him and they're trying to tow in his machine." Mary laughed in relief. "I bet he got a good wetting," she said. "I'd better get over to the hotel and get him some dry clothes." It was eight minutes before the wreckage was dragged to the surface and there, entangled in heavy wires, was Johnstone's body. Within a half hour, it was brought to the yacht club where Dr. Johnstone and his wife had rushed when they heard the news. After viewing his son's body, the doctor went to his daughter-in-law's hotel room to tell her the truth—her husband was dead.[19]

Aviators thought the meet should have stopped after Badger died, but it wasn't and they were furious. "Had the day's events been called off following Badger's death," one of them said, "Johnstone would not have perished." A few men continued to fly after Johnstone's death, but out of respect, the majority refused. "The meet will not be called off," said James Plew, president of the Illinois Aero Club. "These accidents are most terrible, but the meet must go on. This is the sacrifice necessary to the advancement of aviation." Plew and the aviation committee now had become the perfect target for angry aviators and their wives.[20]

"Only barbarians would have permitted the day's events to be finished yesterday after Billy Badger was killed," Mabel Ely told a reporter. "The management of this meet seems to take the attitude that simply because they have promoted a purely sporting event they need take no responsibility for the safety of the participants. Common humanity would have demanded that at least the balance of the day's events be called off and flags lowered to half-mast out of sympathy to a bereaved family, which sacrificed one of its loved ones to amuse the multitude. If this had been done, another death would have been averted."[21]

Marie Mars had even more reason to complain. On the same day that Badger and Johnstone died, Bud Mars had hit the field hard and narrowly escaped death. His injuries weren't critical, but coming only a few weeks after his near disaster in Pittsburgh, he wouldn't be flying again for several weeks. "Must the people see blood to get their money's worth?" Marie asked. "One tragedy in a day should have been enough, and a second would have been averted if out of respect for the dead the crowd had been deprived of the last hour of its Roman Holiday. What can an hour's amusement compare with the terrible feeling that our husbands endure when they are compelled to circle the field after witnessing the death of one of their comrades? The meet should have been stopped. Aviators are only human and they cannot be unaffected when, after one tragedy, they look toward the crowd and see their thumbs down."[22]

Walter Brookins, flying with a passenger, also had a narrow escape that day, crashing into a dirt pile near where Badger had died. "We were all unnerved by the accidents," Brookins said, "but we were not signaled to come down, and so continued our flights. There was not an aviator on the grounds who felt fit to handle a machine after Badger's death. We knew him and liked him. Still the program never halted."[23]

Dr. Johnstone, St. Croix Johnstone's father, wrote a protest letter "To the Press of Chicago and America. My boy, who never gave his parents a moment's concern and who was as brave as a lion, is dead. As a flier, he was conservative, studying the art from the viewpoint of the elimination of its dangers. He was a type of a dozen of others who are gone and dozens more now on the brink of the same sacrificial slaughter at this aviation meet, which must suggest to the thousands of spectators as a Roman gladiatorial arena. Society should endeavor to prevent this loss. 'We cannot,' you say. 'Man must conquer the air.' It is perfectly obvious that these frail machines will break with a terrible strain put upon them. In the hands of the best mechanics motors will act erratically, break, and stop." Until aviators could safely fly, the doctor demanded that all exhibition flying be stopped "in the name of humanity."[24]

Harry Atwood, still angry over his treatment in Chicago, was told of the deaths when he landed in Indiana. He sent the Chicago newspapers a telegram. "My warmest sympathy to the many friends of my brother aviators who lost their lives yesterday," he said. "I can only term the attitude of the Chicago meet management as ferocious and uncivilized."[25]

In defense of the aviation committee, Frank Mudd told reporters that the meet had been carefully planned; beginning with committee members being sent to other aviation meets to get copies of their rules. "We selected the best of the rules in the other contests and took every precaution to make the flying safe for the aviators," he said. Then he enraged the aviators by blaming Badger and Johnstone for their own deaths. The committee had determined that there were structural problems with the two aeroplanes, of course, but "the underlying cause," he said, "was too much sport and daredevil recklessness. There seems to be too much commercialism and too little science in aviation." He said the committee had suggested that aviators wear life preservers when flying over the water, and had even provided them. "Not one of them wore a life preserver, although we requested them to do so." In short, the rules and the committee were "in no way responsible for the fatalities."[26]

Aviators signed a petition asking that Mudd be removed from his position as chairman of the contest committee. "The promoters seem to think that we are merely circus performers," said Ovington. Others said they would "no longer submit to Mudd's heartless and brutal tactics." There was a precedent, they said, established almost at the very first aviation meet. If an aviator died, all other fliers were always brought to the ground immediately.[27]

Gene said he had gone to Mudd right after Badger crashed, demanding that flying stop for the day. Mudd told him that there was $30,000 sitting in the grandstand and the flying would not stop. "What can we think of a man like that?" Gene asked. "What can the public think of a man who refuses to show even common respect to the dead and declines to make an effort to save more lives for a reason like that?" Johnstone, Gene said, would still be alive if Mudd had listened. "It is true that Johnstone did not have to make the flight, but there is a code of ethics among the flyers that is as complete, in its way, as that which guides the actions of physicians, army men, or any other profession. It was this code of ethics, which caused me to go up after Badger fell, although I am frank to admit that the death of jolly little Bill Badger had its effect upon me, just as it did upon every aviator on the field." Gene said he was bitter toward all the members of the aviation committee and was thinking about leaving the exhibition.[28]

At his funeral, Johnstone's casket was carried to and from a brief ceremony by six aviators, including Gene and Bud Mars. The casket, mauve colored and covered with flowers, was topped with a miniature aeroplane, the number *18* on its steering rudder. It was the number of the machine that plunged Johnstone to his death. Badger's body, accompanied by Captain Baldwin, was sent to his home in Pittsburgh for burial.[29]

The meet continued in an uneasy truce between the aviators and meet promoters. The fifth day brought swirling winds, an approaching rainstorm, and four more accidents.[30]

Angry aviators and aeroplane accidents weren't the only things to worry the aviation committee. On day six, the Wright brothers filed suit against the Illinois Aero Club in an attempt to restrain them from holding any aviation meet where disputed patent rights were involved. The suit wouldn't stop the current exhibition because the circuit court wasn't in session and no official injunction could be issued. Even before the Chicago meet began, Orville Wright had demanded 20 percent of the prize money as a royalty for the use of his claimed patents. A few other cities had paid, but the Chicago association refused. Wright, arguing in person before the committee, threatened to pull his aviators and four boxcars full of aeroplanes out of the exhibition. "But you have signed contracts to appear," said a committee member. "If you have any valid reason for withdrawing you may do so." Wright stormed out of the meeting. "I am here to defend my rights," he told reporters. "This meet marks a fresh infringement of our rights." Even so, the exhibition continued and the suit never made it to trial.[31]

The exhibition was already half over and Gene had very little to show for it. In five days he had flown less than five hours and in the next four days, he only added two and half hours more to his total flight time. But finally, he began to win some prize money. Using the new Curtiss 75 horsepower motor for the first time he had set the meet's one lap speed record and posted the best time in climbing from the ground to an altitude of 50 meters. He placed second to Beachey in a twelve-mile race, losing by only six seconds, and then beat Beachey by almost a minute in the 18-mile over water race. He finished third in the twelve-mile race for biplanes and monoplanes and, in the final speed race of the meet, he again topped Beachey in the twelve-mile race for biplanes, claiming first place by barely 15 seconds. It took that kind of hustle over the last four days of the meet, for Gene to finally tally $4,172 in prize money—$7,000 less than Beachey and over $9,000 less than Rodgers, the overall money winner.[32]

For three days, the birdmen flew cautiously, but by the time the meet was ending, thoughts of Johnstone's and Badger's deaths had worn off. The daredevils flew with abandon, giving the spectators "thrills galore," especially when four more aeroplanes were wrecked. Ovington crushed his landing gear, split a wing, and broke his propeller. Rene Simon demolished his landing skid and wrecked his rudder, while Charles Witmer collided with the excursion steamship *Mary M*, and Jimmie Ward flew Gene's biplane into a steamroller.[33]

The Chicago International Aviation Meet was the largest aviation exhibition ever held in the United States. The nine days of contests set three world records and ten American records, the most notable being Lincoln Beachey's nearly two-hour climb to 11,578 feet, breaking the world altitude record that had been set only fifteen days earlier. However, even with an estimated four and a half million spectators, Chicago's exhibition still was a financial disaster. The final cost was $195,000, and with daily receipts averaging about $15,500, promoters of the event were stuck with a $51,000 deficit.[34]

On August 21, the aviators held a benefit exhibition for Johnstone's widow who sat in the stands, dressed in black, behind a black veil, and surrounded by family and friends. Flags on the grandstand snapped in a 30 mile an hour wind and it looked as if all flying, including the advertised passenger flights of citizen volunteers, was off for the day. Lincoln Beachey, "the star of Chicago's meet all during its nine days," said he would wait to see if the wind died down, but no matter what, he was going to fly. Gill, Ward, and Rodgers made short, low-level flights, but Beachey was the hero again, rising to over 2,000 feet and staggering through the wind to perform. Mrs. Johnstone received nearly $12,000.[35]

The terror of Chicago, prompted Marie Mars to write about the fears of an aviator's wife. "I always held firm in the thought that no harm can come to my husband," she said. "I pray earnestly and constantly for his safety each time he goes into the air and my prayers have been rewarded, for while Bud has had many slight accidents since becoming a sailor in the sky, he fortunately has experienced only one horrible one." Faith and superstition went hand-in-hand, she said. "Even while praying, I see signs and know what they foretell." When Badger and Johnstone died, the wives had "waited in grim silence for the third [to die]. Things always go in threes," she said. "We felt that after those two died, one more flyer was fated to be killed. We wondered who he would be." No one else had been killed that day, but Marie's concern came from a dinner party in an Italian restaurant a few days earlier. Marie and the celebrating aviators had seen an ominous sign. "We were such a merry crowd and having such a happy time when Mrs. Eugene Ely suddenly counted and found that there were thirteen at the table," Marie said. "We wives were terrified. We knew that one of them had to be killed before the year was over. All merriment ceased." Bud Mars and Mabel left "to break the spell" and only returned when more guests arrived. Billy Badger had remained at that table. Marie said she had even more reason to worry. "There is no worse sign at an aviation meet than a one-eyed man," Marie said. "I am always so sorry for a man or woman so deformed, but my sympathy does not lessen my knowledge that his presence is harmful." Of course, she saw her one-eyed man not long before Johnstone and Badger made their fatal flights. "Every time I saw him, I knew that something dreadful would happen, and it did."[36]

Gene and Mabel left for the Boston aviation meet, while Bud and Marie Mars were off to Kentucky. Gene Ely had been one of those thirteen aviators who sat in the Italian restaurant that night, and Mabel could only hope that by having left the table to "break the spell"; she had managed to save his life.

## { 43 }

## Not for $50,000

While on their way to Massachusetts, Gene, McCurdy, and Beachey stopped off in New York City where a ceremony was being held to welcome Harry Atwood, after his 1,265-mile cross-country flight from St. Louis. Unfortunately, Atwood's motor failed just 25 miles from his goal, delaying his arrival by at least another day. Needing to make final preparations for the upcoming exhibition in Boston, the Curtiss aviators had to leave.[1]

The Harvard-Boston Aero Meet was Boston's second aviation exhibition. It was held on the Squantum Peninsula, five miles south of Boston. In 1910, the Harvard Aeronautical Society had leased about 700 undeveloped acres on the peninsula for their aviation experiments and that fall had held the first Boston meet. With the Chicago tragedies in mind and because Squantum was wedged between the Neponset, Massachusetts, and Quincy bays, aviators were required to wear life preservers whenever they flew over water. Accidents, such as those in Chicago "must, if possible, be averted at the meet here," officials said. "It will be impressed upon the minds of the aviators that the public does not ask them to endanger life or limb."[2]

To *Boston Journal* columnist, Persis Dwight Hannah, the 1911 meet didn't look much different from the 1910 exhibition. "Same old fleecy clouds," she said, "looking as if they might have something to say almost any moment about this extraordinary invasion of their precinct." Englishman Claude Grahame-White was back with his matinee idol good looks and his "natty clothes." The field was muddy again and photographers haunted every nook and corner. The parking area was chock full of every kind of horse drawn carriage ever built, along with automobiles of the latest make. On the midway, obnoxious barkers were offering the "same old popcorn and lemonade." At least the popcorn looked like the same old popcorn, Hannah said, and without a doubt, it was definitely old. She noticed at least a dozen different "official souvenirs of the meet." They came in the shapes of canes, flags, and badges, much as they always had, but this year there was something new—the shaker, multicolored pom-pom-like "mops of paper" that justified their name whenever they were "shaken in your face." The crowd's attitude had changed too. Last year, applause broke out whenever an aeroplane moved or a motor roared, Hannah said, but this year, "the aviation palate demands spicier food." Spectators needed a race or an accident before their adrenalin began to flow.[3]

In the midst of a steady trickle of rain, the aviators' wives were asked the usual questions and gave their usual answers. Scores of people milled about the hangars, watching mechanics and aviators preparing their machines. Some were allowed to add their signatures to the wings of the aeroplanes, already scribbled over with the names of those "autograph fiends" who always "harassed the aviators wherever they performed." Aviator Beatty had his own name painted in three-foot-high letters under his wings. Englishman Grahame-White had tacked up a good luck horseshoe over the entrance to his hangar and Earle Ovington had done the same, using a rusting shoe his wife had found along the road near the exhibition entrance. For added good fortune, Ovington had attached a policeman doll to his aeroplane's tail. This mascot, dressed in a long blue coat with bright metal buttons, swung back and forth in the winds as Ovington flew.[4]

While flying in Rochester in 1910, Gene had missed the first Boston Aviation Meet and if he hadn't shown up in 1911, probably no one would have noticed. He began with a promising $150 second place finish to Claude Grahame-White in the 12-mile speed race, but it was downhill from there. Had Gene known that the $150 was the last money he would win in Boston, he might not have walked so confidently back to his hanger after the race, wearing a big smile and puffing on that ever-present cigarette in its long, amber holder.[5]

Mabel was drawing more attention than Gene. Reporters thought it a touching sight every time they saw the "girlish wife of the aviator" carefully adjusting Gene's life preserver just before he would start on an over water flight. It seemed to give a hint of the tension that aviators' wives had to face every time their husbands flew. One afternoon, during a lull in activities, spectator eyes were drawn to a vivid patch of purple color that was constantly moving around the Curtiss hangar. "Who is that woman in the purple dress?" they asked. "The woman was Mrs. Ely," wrote columnist Hannah, "and with a nearer view, I am glad to inform her interested audience, she was even more striking than at a distant glimpse. She was purple from the word go—purple gown, purple hat, purple parasol, amethyst earrings and rings, and eyes as close to violet as long lashes can make very deep blue eyes look—and that is very near." Mabel was the only aviator wife to fly twice as a passenger at the exhibition, not with Gene, but first on a Wright machine with George Beatty and then with Tom Sopwith on his Bleriot. Perhaps in curiosity, or just suffering from embarrassment, Gene finally took his own ride with Beatty.[6]

Again, it was Beachey and his headless biplane that were thrilling the crowds. Against gale-force winds he climbed above the fog to 2,000 feet and performed "seemingly impossible feats," twists, turns, and spiral dives. "He had earned his reputation of being the world's most daredevil aviator," said a reporter, and even Gene was impressed. "There is the best flier of all," Gene said. "He is a wonder." Reporters asked Gene if he thought it worth the risk to fly like Beachey. "No, personally I do not believe in it," he said. "The man who does it, gets it, sooner or later." That afternoon, when aviators voted to cancel the race around the Boston Lighthouse because most of them thought the winds too dangerous, Gene and Beachey filed a protest. They threatened to cancel their contracts and leave the exhibition on grounds that the meet was unfair to aviators operating biplanes. The aviation committee compromised and scheduled an additional race for biplanes only.[7]

When the 33-mile race around the Boston Light was run, a monoplane was the winner, while both Beachey and Gene flew into trouble. Beachey, misunderstanding his instructions and believing that the Boston Light was the farthest light from the aviation field, instead of the nearest, had actually flown too far. Realizing while flying that his mistake had cost him too much time to ever win the race, he returned to the field where he dove into a landing "with the recklessness of a daredevil." Jumping from his machine, he began a brief and animated conversation with meet officials who almost instantly raced to telephones and nearby motorboats. On his return flight, Beachey had seen Gene dropping down toward the bay in obvious trouble. He wasn't sure if Gene had been able to find land or had crashed into the water. One motorboat after another headed east. Reporters scrambled into two automobiles, followed by Mabel in another, each vehicle bouncing over the rough ground in a breakneck race toward Squantum Head. There, a sliver of beach ran out to Moon Island. It was on that narrow neck of sand that they found a smiling Gene standing beside his biplane. A simple metal pipe leading to his radiator had burst shortly after takeoff, and fearing damage to his engine, Gene had cut power and dropped to a soft landing just above the high water mark on the seaweed-strewn beach. A frantic Mabel jumped from the car before it completely stopped and ran toward Gene. They kissed and hugged, and kissed again, Mabel not wanting to let go. "The meeting between the two was most affecting," said a reporter.[8]

On the next to the last day of the meet, Gene flew a thrilling race against Claude Grahame-White in the figure eight contest. His wings tilted at nearly 90 degrees as he banked around the pylons, shooting for maximum speed. He upset White for the $300 prize, winning by just over a minute and a half, but the Englishman protested, saying that Gene broke the rules by not making an additional run around the course after completing his figure eight. The contest committee upheld the challenge and Gene was disqualified. Gene said that this was just another example of favoritism toward the monoplanes and that he had flown for the last time in Boston. He would take his $150, pack up, and leave. Perhaps he found some satisfaction in news that the Boston Meet had once again lost money, ending with an $11,000 deficit.[9]

The only headlines Gene made in Boston came from the announcement that he and Mabel would be heading to Europe later in the year and from there they would begin an aviation exhibition tour of the world. He had also penned a column for a Boston newspaper. He predicted that aeroplanes would soon have an enclosed cabin capable of carrying a pilot, ten passengers, their seats, and luggage, at 70 miles an hour. "The excessive speed of the new aeroplane," he said, "will not only make it useful in the carrying of the mails, but also of small cargoes of perishable goods from points far apart." It was a perceptive prediction, but Gene would never see it.[10]

Gene's outrage at the Boston aviation committee and his hasty exit from the exhibition was a dramatic way of expressing his anger and frustration, but he would have left Boston that evening anyway. The next day, he had a contract to fly in Rhode Island.

Less than 100 miles southwest of Boston, Hillsgrove was the home of Rhode Island's annual state fair. In addition to midway shows and sweating harness horses, the 1911 edition also included the state's first aeroplane flight. Gene, with a new engine in his Curtiss and no competition from other aviators, rose quickly into the scattered clouds at 2,000 feet, circling over the racetrack several times. He had invited two councilmen from nearby Pawtucket. Both told him that they were curious to see how an aeroplane was controlled after the engine stopped in mid air. Apparently, they weren't disappointed. Gene's motor ran so poorly that its occasional skipping, sputtering, and machinegun-like backfires kept him from a promised flight over the city. After 28 minutes, he shut off his engine and descended in a slow and graceful spiral glide, whooshing past the grandstand, and landing near his hangar. The crowd of a few thousand swarmed over his machine, shaking Gene's hand and patting him on the back. While trying to gain control of the crowd, police managed to rough up a few reporters who immediately filed protests, but got no satisfaction. Waiting through one day of bad weather, Gene was back in the air. He flew away from the track, over the town, and then high above the local prison and reform school, where many of the inmates were allowed to watch from the prison yard.[11]

Because rain had extended the exhibition in Rhode Island, the Brighton Beach aviation meet on Long Island in New York was already underway before Gene arrived. He hadn't missed much. Aviators were counting on gate receipts to make their money, but this time, the crowds were sparse. New Yorkers weren't rushing out to see the birdmen fly anymore. On his first day, Gene had no trouble flying at the racetrack near Coney Island, but his major competitors did. Beatty ran straight through the fence in front of the grandstand and was out of action for two days. Grahame-White buried the nose of his Nieuport monoplane into the deep muck of a marsh inside the infield, and to the amazement of bathers on the beach, Tom Sopwith, flying with a passenger, somersaulted his Wright biplane into the ocean. Fortunately, none of these accidents caused serious injury, but by the end of the day, only Gene had survived without a scratch. When he made his last landing after four flights, "sighs of mixed relief and disappointment fluttered from a thousand breasts." Unlike the previous year when Gene had won glory by flying to the nearby Manhattan Beach Hotel, Brighton Beach was a virtual waste of his time. A few of the spectators waited around, hoping for someone to fly again, but after fighting all day against an army of "man-eating" mosquitoes, most of the crowd was in full retreat from the insect assault. The voices of young men holding megaphones echoed into the deserted stands. They announced that although flying was cancelled for the day, meet officials had extended the meet for an additional week of daily flying. It was a hollow promise. The most talented aviators couldn't commit. Grahame-White had another engagement in Boston, Sopwith didn't think he could be ready in time, and Beatty just wasn't sure. Gene's machine was the only aeroplane left on the field in flying condition and Gene was crating it up for an exhibition in Vermont.[12]

The 65th annual Caledonia County Fair in St. Johnsbury, Vermont opened September 12. In a light rain, residents toured the aviation shed where mechanics answered questions about the art of aviation and explained how the Curtiss biplane was able to fly. This was the second time Vermont had seen an aeroplane. The previous year, at the same fair, Charles Willard had made two flights totaling less than 10 minutes. The breezes circulating over the surrounding hills had barely bothered Willard, but Gene was faced with a harsh and variable wind. In his first two-minute flight, Gene reached perhaps 1,000 feet, but immediately returned for a landing. He was asked how high he had gone. "I was too busy to notice anything but my machine," he said, "but I wouldn't repeat that flight for $50,000." After skipping over a day with winds too treacherous to fly in, Gene made three flights and closed with something new. Dropping from 2,000 feet in a 400-foot spiral glide, he leveled off for just a moment, and then started another spiral, but then changed his mind and simply dropped several hundred feet more. From there, he dropped into a long glide, passing so low over the fence surrounding the field that he scattered the spectators who perched there. He rolled to the hangar and prepared to return to New York.[13]

Gene boarded a train and was headed for a one-day exhibition in Utica, but before he reached Albany, two freight trains collided, killing a railroad fireman and blocking the tracks for at least two days. Curtiss arranged a substitute for Utica and Gene returned to Brighton Beach.[14]

There were only 3,000 paid admissions to the Brighton Beach track on September 16, while nearly 100,000 freeloaders were watching from nearby streets and beaches. With nothing to do while waiting for his biplane to arrive, Gene watched Mabel take another ride with George Beatty and New York socialite, Grace Marx. The Wright birdman took the women on a short flight some 500 feet in the air. Reporters said it was the first time that two women passengers had flown together at the same time. Then, Beatty took Mabel on an even longer ride, this time bringing Marie Mars along as a passenger.[15]

Impatiently waiting until the next day when his machine was finally put together, Gene was the first aviator to fly away. He climbed a thousand feet above the boardwalk and for a half-hour, every eye in Coney Island watched his twists, turns, and rollercoaster-like undulations. "In spite of explicit orders from his boss, Glenn H. Curtiss," said a reporter, "Ely went up and did every stunt on the calendar except turning a loop-the-loop in the air." "Many hearts throbbed with his fearless handling of the biplane." Before Gene had gone up, he said his stomach had been upset and he was feeling faint, but "the flight entirely cured me." After this final day of good flying, the "long drawn out nine-day series of aviation exhibitions" at Brighton Beach racetrack ended. One by one, aviators who still had an aeroplane that could fly, lifted off and sailed a few miles east to the recently established Nassau Boulevard Field. There, the next international aviation contest was about to begin.[16]

# { 44 }

# "Fate handed me this bump"

The 350-acre Nassau airfield was situated on Long Island, just over five miles west of Mineola Field, the official field of the New York Aeronautical Society. The Nassau event was the brainchild of Timothy Woodruff, an ex-lieutenant governor of New York and president of the New York Aero Club. "The field looks like a circus lot," wrote a reporter, "with its tents and waving banners, and the green slat seats of the bleachers only adding to the illusion." Spectators had access to a walkway, fenced off from the main field and lined with wooden hangars for each aviator. The flier's last names were painted over each hangar door. There were cook tents and dining pavilions filled with luncheon parties munching on sandwiches and washing them down with sarsaparilla and ginger ale. Diners kept "one eye on the clouds and the other on the catsup bottles." It had taken less than a week to build a 2 ½-mile long wooden fence around the large field. The Aero Club had hired 100 local farmwomen to whitewash it. No one in the neighborhood had ever seen this many women do this kind of work, so the ladies quickly developed a large contingent of curious bystanders.[1]

If running a paintbrush over a fence seemed unique, then the sight of three women flying at Nassau must have seemed a miracle. Certainly, the "spice of femininity added zest to the entertainment," but, the fact that women could fly as well as any man, and better than some, was a shocking revelation to the males in the audience. Americans, Matilda Moisant and Harriet Quimby, each claimed a victory at the exhibition. Moisant won a trophy, but no money, by climbing to 1,200 feet to win the trophy for the highest altitude reached by a woman. Quimby pocketed $600 as the winner and only woman to finish the 30-mile cross-country race, while Helene Dutrieu, of France, took home $500 and the women's American record for endurance flying, by staying aloft 1 hour, 4 minutes and 57 seconds.[2]

The most popular feature of the entire exhibition was the country's first regularly scheduled airmail delivery. Many aviators had already carried letters, notes, and packages before, and even Fred Wiseman, Gene's old California racecar competitor, had made an 18-mile airmail flight earlier in the year, but the Nassau meet marked the first regularly scheduled mail flight over a specified route by a carrier who was sworn into service by the U.S. Postmaster General, Frank Hitchcock. Earle Ovington had volunteered to make the daily 6-mile flight from the aviation field to the post office at Mineola during the exhibition. Two postal substations and twenty regulation mailboxes were set up on the Nassau field in areas convenient to spectators. Letter paper, cards, envelopes, and stamps were sold and regularly collected. They were brought to a white post office tent with "U.S. Mail, Aeroplane Station No. 1," lettered on its outside canvas ceiling. The items were cancelled, bagged, and flown to Mineola, where they were dropped at the local postmaster's feet from 500 feet in the air. Workers sorted them by destination before sending them across the country and around the world. For the first run, on September 23, 6,165 post cards, 781 letters and 55 pieces of miscellaneous printed material had been packed into two mailbags. This was too much weight for one aeroplane to handle so Englishman Tommy Sopwith volunteered to carry the extra bag. During the week, Ovington and other aviators carried 32,415 postcards, 3,993 letters, and 1,062 miscellaneous items.[3]

The flying at the Nassau meet was riddled with problems from its start. The Wright brothers had demanded and received $5,000 to give their blessing to the exhibition. The promoters were relieved and glad to spend the money. "A few days ago," wrote a reporter, "it was not known whether the Wrights would send aviators or whether they would sue."[4]

The meet opened on Saturday, September 23 with 10,000 paid admissions, but paying customers quickly dwindled and on the last day of the exhibition barely 1,000 people wandered in through the gate. The loss that day alone was estimated at $20,000. The total financial loss would remain a well-kept secret. Worsening weather was part of the problem, but so was the management's inept handling of the press. Had they not irritated most of the reporters, perhaps they may have gotten better publicity. "To get any information as to what was going on was a catch-as-catch-can proposition," wrote a reporter. "Photographers were not allowed on the field, although lady friends of the [meet] officers had no difficulty on that score." The most disgraceful sight, he said, "was the repeated chasing given to the photographers by alleged cops on horseback, with the Ex-Lieutenant Governor Woodruff cheering the gallant horsemen on."[5]

An overconfident and arrogant Woodruff soon had more than photographers to worry about. Two hours before the show began on Sunday, the second day of the meet; Nassau County Sheriff Charles De Mott warned Woodruff that a formal protest against the exhibition had been filed by Frederick Burgess, Bishop of the Episcopal Diocese of Long Island. Burgess said the meet was a flagrant violation of the state's Sunday Law that forbid charging admission for sporting events or allowing contests for prize money on the Sabbath. There was a heated discussion between the sheriff and Woodruff with the sheriff saying that he thought the bishop and his followers would be satisfied to let the meet continue, if no prize money was awarded. "Oh, all right," Woodruff said. "Officially there will be no prizes offered today." Then he laughed. "I suppose, I'll have to go to jail for six months after this meet is over." After visiting with the aviators in their hangars, Woodruff had his men announce that the meet would continue, but that the flights would only be exhibitions and winners wouldn't be paid prize money. However, it was privately understood that the aviators would indeed be "compensated in some way, later in the week."[6]

Bishop Burgess and his allies were furious. Petitions circulated in nearly every nearby church and Burgess, vowing to appeal to the Supreme Court and the governor if necessary, filed charges against Woodruff with the local justice of the peace.

Woodruff wasn't worried, but the pressures of the church protest and its threat of lawsuits were more than some of the meet officials could stand. From a distance, reporters saw the publicity manager for the aviation committee in a loud "heart to heart" argument with Woodruff. They couldn't hear what was being shouted, but saw the manager pull off his badge and push it hard into Woodruff's chest. Woodruff grinned, turned, and walked away.[7]

Amidst this anger and confusion there was actually some Sunday flying. Gene won the quick-starting contest and then followed up with a thrilling win in the 10-mile race for biplanes. "Ely, helmeted like a gridiron warrior," said a reporter "was the choice of the sharps in the final, and he proved to be the proper sort of a favorite, never leaving the result in question at any stage of the contest." On his last lap, Gene cut too close to a pylon and passed it on the inside. He had to swing back and around in a wide detour to pass it properly, but still he won the race with over a minute to spare. Then, Gene and his partner, Henry "Hap" Arnold, competed in the team relay race along with eight other aviators, but they lost to Sopwith and Grahame-White. It was the first time a relay race was run at any aviation event and it proved to be a helter-skelter crowd favorite. The race began with judges handing messages to the aviators. Each aviator ran to his aeroplane, flew five miles around the course, landed, and ran to his partner's machine, where he passed the message on. The partner took off, flew his five miles around the course, landed, and ran the message back to a judge. All of the teams flew at the same time and it was "daredeviltry in the extreme," said a reporter. When landing, power was turned off and as the aeroplanes continued to bounce over the field, the birdmen would leap to the ground, not waiting for a stop. Where Gene finished in the race wasn't reported, but the fact that he was "tangled up in the wires near his levers, was flung to the ground," and nearly run over by his still rolling machine, was.[8]

Monday was Ladies Day, but there were few women or girls upon the grounds, and less than 2,000 men. Woodruff's day began in a mess and as the hours passed, it only got worse. First, a reporter met Woodruff at the entrance gate and asked if he had heard about aviator dissatisfaction around the hangars. "I believe those stories are mere rumors," Woodruff said, "with no foundation in fact." The rumors had been festering amongst the aviators ever since the meet began. They said that meet officials had paid Helene Dutrieu $2,000 just to appear and the American aviators, who had received nothing, also suspected that Englishmen Grahame-White and Tom Sopwith had received even more. Within a few moments of his arrival, Woodruff was surrounded by seven or eight angry aviators who stopped him in front of the box seats. Dutrieu had confirmed that she had received the $2,000, but said she was told it was only to pay her for passage to America, not appearance money. The men of aviation row had had enough and Woodruff was the target of their fury. The military aviators were sure everyone, except them, was getting something, and the American civilians, who were getting nothing at all, were sure the British, Harry Atwood, and probably everyone else, were. They threatened to stop flying unless Woodruff could convince them that there was no truth to the rumors that Sopwith and Grahame-White were receiving large guarantees, perhaps as high as or higher than $3,000 each. When Sopwith and Grahame-White happened to walk by, they joined the group and began a conversation that no one could hear. The shouting eased and soon some sort of agreement was reached.[9]

Woodruff, with the aviators behind him, walked back to the rail where reporters wanted to know what was going on. "I ought to have a platform to make this speech from," said a condescending Woodruff. "I'm not used to addressing the crowd down on the same level as—." Reporter's groans stopped him. "Someone," Woodruff continued, "had told the men around me that we were discriminating unjustly by paying the expenses of some fliers here and not paying many others. Mr. Grahame-White and Mr. Sopwith have just assured these men that these stories are false. Am I right, gentlemen?" They were all smiles and everyone agreed. "How were things patched up?" shouted a reporter as Woodruff turned to leave. One of the birdmen turned around with a wink and a smile, before heading out to his aeroplane. At least for the moment, everything seemed settled.[10]

There was more trouble in the bomb-throwing contest. Participating aviators had been told they were required to fly with a woman passenger and the woman would throw the bombs. Gene and Mabel had made some very successful practice flights together and expected to win, but at the last minute, the judges dropped the passenger requirement. Gene refused to fly.[11]

That evening, just as the day's exhibition was about to close, a Bleriot-style machine with a large number *13* painted on its tail and apparently attempting a spiral glide, turned into a sharp bank and began to climb. The machine shuddered, dropped, and then began to tumble. Nose first it smashed into the ground, parts of the machine piercing the pilot's body and forcing rescuers to chop away the wreckage to get the dead man out. Opposite the number *13* on the official program was Eugene B. Ely's name, but Gene wasn't flying this aeroplane. When numbers were assigned at the beginning of the meet, a superstitious Gene had refused to carry number *13*. At the time, Earle Ovington had laughed at him saying that for Ovington, *13* was "the luckiest number in the series." Gene accepted number *14* and Ovington painted *13* on both of his aeroplanes. But Ovington wasn't flying the doomed aircraft either. The victim was Dr. Charles Clarke, an amateur flier with no pilot's license, who repeatedly begged for a chance to fly an Ovington aeroplane. Ovington had taken off in his spare machine, leaving the airmail plane on the ground. Clarke managed to sneak it into the air and flew it for four minutes before dropping to his death.[12]

There was mayhem as mounted police and guards on the ground tried to hold back the crowd that was scrambling across the field toward the wreck. "Drive them back, drive them back!" Woodruff shouted to the club swinging police. Heads were bloodied. All cameras except one were smashed—that one held by a short and wiry photographer who managed to slip between the mounted police officers and capture a single photograph. Grabbed by two officers as he ran back through the line, he managed to toss his camera to a friend, just before he was wrestled to the ground. Woodruff hadn't seen the camera toss and shouted a "well done" to the police. "Tomorrow I shall have you armed with guns," he said, "and if the photographers don't keep away, I want you to shoot them all. They shall not be allowed to take any pictures of accidents." The next day, Woodruff saw that he had failed. The single photograph of Clarke's wreck, copyrighted and perhaps taken by noted New York based photojournalist, Paul Thompson, was printed in New York City newspapers.[13]

The accident appeared to threaten the aviation meet and with it, Woodruff's tenuous truce with the aviators. The next morning's headlines said that five of the most prominent aviators were quitting the meet in protest and moving on. George Beatty said he couldn't make enough money at Nassau to pay his expenses. Bud Mars withdrew without ever flying. Atwood was going west and McCurdy had refused to fly in any of the contests all afternoon. Gene was quoted as believing "the meet incompetently managed" and he too was leaving in protest. By the time afternoon newspapers hit the street, the story proved false. Only three of the five were actually leaving and that was because weeks before they had signed contracts to appear somewhere else. Gene and Atwood were due in Canton, Ohio and McCurdy had a date in Rhode Island, but all three were coming back at the end of the week so they could fly the Sunday program, a program with special biplane only races and races handicapped for speed that offered them the best chance at prize money. Of all the aviators, Mars had the best reasons for leaving. He still was recovering from his accident, hadn't returned to competitive form, and wouldn't fly in another exhibition for almost another month, but instead of leaving, he stayed to watch. By midweek, with the aviators flying elsewhere and Beatty having engine trouble at Nassau, the exhibition was at a standstill. It didn't really matter because the weather had turned stormy and any hope of flying was postponed until the weekend.[14]

Canton was a welcome relief from the chaos of Nassau Boulevard. Smaller meets meant guaranteed appearance money and far less risk. "This meet is going to be good fun," Gene told reporters as he stepped down from the Baltimore and Ohio railcar. "It will develop a great deal more interest than a prize contest," he said, "where often the meet develops into a one-sided affair." He would fly his 100 horsepower machine, "the fastest in the world," his manager said, "the only one of its kind ever turned out by our company." After checking in to his hotel and having lunch, officials drove Gene to the fairgrounds. The 40-acre aviation field was to the west of the racetrack and surrounded by a canvas fence. "I expect to see some good flying here this week," Gene said, "especially since, from what I have seen of the field, I believe it to be excellently adapted to my machine." With his high speed machine, he was sure he would be able to "make a short turn much quicker than any aviator on the field." When his words were written down, Gene always seemed full of confidence, but in person, reporters noticed unease in the way he answered. As one reporter noted, "In the air, he is known as one of the most daring performers in America—on the ground, he is nervous in manner." But reporters liked Gene, especially his humility. "Ely does not like to speak of his own achievements," one reporter wrote, "and would rather praise his fellow aviators. He has praise for all the men with whom he is associated." In Gene's eyes, even his landing on the *Pennsylvania* wasn't that important. "It probably brought me more publicity than anything else," he told reporters. "It was risky in a way, because no one had ever done anything like it before, but it worked out all right."[15]

When he entered his tent hangar, he found mechanics and helpers standing around and waiting. Where was his machine? The aeroplane was supposed to be on the same train that brought Gene to Canton. The plan had been to quickly move it to the field where it would be put together and made ready to fly no later than a half hour before the official flying time began at 3:00 in the afternoon. He had traveled from New York with Jesse Siegelmann, a novice aviator who flew a Moisant monoplane. Siegelmann's machine had arrived, Gene's hadn't. No one had ever seen him more furious. "When I sent my machine from Nassau Field, I shipped by way of Pittsburgh," Gene said. "When I arrived in Pittsburg, Tuesday morning, I saw my machine on the same car with the Moisant monoplane. The machine did not arrive here with the monoplane, so the express company men must have transferred it in Pittsburgh.... The express company that slipped up on my shipment ought to be sued," he said. He walked in circles and worried all through the early afternoon. Finally, just after 3 o'clock and too late, the crates arrived. There wasn't enough time to assemble the machine and test it out before the day's flying period was over. Brookins and Atwood would amaze the crowd with slow glides, perilous dives, and perfect landings, while Gene lost a day of guaranteed money.[16]

The next morning, Wednesday, September 27, only a few hundred spectators had braved the nonstop rain. Four of the aviators were still in their hotels, waiting to hear that the day's flying was still on. Only Gene was on the field and he was in a panic. His machine had been assembled, but the motor still hadn't been tested. The special oil and gasoline he used hadn't arrived either and Gene, followed everywhere by a small group of curious umbrella carrying spectators, went from one official to another trying to get an answer. When someone told him there his delivery was at the main gate, Gene ran through the downpour to get it.[17]

The opening of the meet had brought nearly 35,000 people to the fairgrounds, but today there were barely 4,000, and the question was being asked, "Are they going to fly?" In the early afternoon, the rain stopped and the thick gray overcast began to thin. Patches of blue appeared in the north and although there were occasional misty drizzles and light winds, the aviators were called to the aviation field. "It's good for flying," Brookins declared. Gene agreed. His biplane was ready and his mechanics were rolling it onto the field. He climbed aboard.[18]

There was excited applause as Gene's propeller began to cut through the mist. Rushing 450 feet over the grass, Gene pulled the machine into a steep climb, zooming up to nearly 100 feet before reaching the end of the field. Banking into a sharp turn, he found a choppy wind pulling the lift away from his wings. He was falling straight down. Just beyond a small mound of earth that hid him from the crowd's sight, he struck the ground and bounced briefly back into view like a rubber ball. Thrown from his seat, he landed on his head, bleeding over his right eye, with several bumps and scratches on his face and hands. As he fell, Atwood and Brookins had begun a simultaneous rolling takeoff. Atwood was barely two feet in the air when Gene's falling machine struck one of his wings. The damage was minor and Atwood would fly again, but Gene's machine had severe frontend damage, two broken stays, and the leading tricycle wheel was twisted and smashed beyond repair. By the time mechanics reached Gene, he was already on his feet and ready to help haul the machine back to the hangar. He had no excuse for reporters and took full blame for the accident. "I simply turned a screw too far," he said.[19]

Gene telegraphed Hammondsport, asking for a special express shipment of replacement parts so he would be ready to fly again the next day. "Did you ever hear of anything like it?" Gene asked reporters. "Until two weeks ago I always carried a big stock of supplies in order to make quick repairs if an accident should happen. But I had not had any trouble since October 9 of last year," he said, a flashback to the failed Chicago-New York race. "I just quit carrying the supplies." Gene was disgusted. "Fate handed me this bump and the broken wheel," he said. "I haven't got another wheel and I can't make another flight this afternoon. I could not fly Tuesday afternoon because I didn't have the oil and gasoline I wanted and now this happens." Reporters asked if he would stay in Canton and finish the meet. "I don't know positively," Gene said. "There are three things I have to consider." He worried that he hadn't fulfilled his contract yet and whether he could get replacement parts in time. "The other thing is that I can be getting $1,800 a day at Nassau Boulevard," he said. Within the hour, he learned that replacement parts would not arrive in time. The machine was sent back to New York, where either parts, or another aeroplane, would be waiting for him at Nassau Boulevard. Gene followed the next morning.[20]

Arriving on Friday with a plaster bandage still clinging above his right eye, Gene was anxious to get back into the air, but Mother Nature still wasn't cooperating. With pelting rain and winds that blew away nearly every tent on the aviation field, there was no hope. One refreshment stand sailed over a high picket fence and was found a block and a half away, its contents of bottles, cigars, candies, and picture postcards strewn across the grass. When horses stabled in a tent stampeded across the field, luckily, no one was hurt, although it was exhausting work to get them rounded up.[21]

While the meet was on hold, Woodruff appeared before a justice of the peace, answering a warrant issued for his arrest. The justice released him on his own recognizance and scheduled a hearing in a week on a charge that he had violated the Sunday Law. Meanwhile, Woodruff's attorneys had taken his case to New York Supreme Court Justice Lester Clark. They argued that the Sunday Law was a criminal law that must name specific violations, and aviation meets were not listed as a crime. Aviation meets were not contests, they said, but rather "highly moral educational exhibitions," much like art exhibits or Sunday performances of motion pictures. Justice Clark listened to arguments for over three hours, finally agreeing to issue an injunction that bared the sheriff from interfering. "It will surely be a hard blow to some people to learn that I was not put into jail this morning," Woodruff said.[22]

The weather cleared Saturday and though the wind twisted in 20 mile an hour gusts throughout the afternoon, birdmen and birdwomen flew. Helene Dutrieu set her endurance record and Harriet Quimby won the cross-country race. Airmail deliveries flew on schedule and military men dropped wet, salt bombs at a flat ground target, never getting closer than sixteen feet in the tricky wind. While carrying a passenger in the endurance contest, Gene finished fourth and out of the money. He only managed to stay airborne for just over ten minutes, while the winner, Lieutenant Hap Arnold, flew for over an hour.

Winds were stronger and the clouds more threatening on Sunday. The rain started as a drizzle and then fell like a soft hail, beating into the faces of the few hundred spectators who slogged through ankle deep mud. If they had come to see aviators fly or perhaps the arrest of some exhibition promoters, they were disappointed.[23]

With such a small crowd, Woodruff really didn't want the aviators to fly. Rain checks and sunshine would make him more money. Woodruff gathered the Americans together in the field headquarters tent on aviation row and suggested that today might not be a good day to fly. The discussion seemed friendly enough and the aviators were still weighing their options, when Grahame-White drove up in his personal automobile. As he stepped off the running board, officials rushed to him, leaving the American aviators in midsentence. Grahame-White was steered to the back of the hangar where

Sopwith joined him. "I'll fly!" Gene said. "I'll go through the whole darn program." Beatty said he was with Gene. "I'm ready, too," said another airman. "So am—," The sentence was interrupted. The conference with the Englishmen was over and Woodruff was back. "Today's flying is cancelled," said Woodruff. Grahame-White and Sopwith had said it was a "blubby day" and they would stay on the ground. It was a slap in the Americans' faces. They outnumbered the Englishmen at least two to one, but it seemed the management only cared about the foreigners' opinion. "If they treated American aviators in England as handsomely as they treat English aviators in America," Gene said, "it would be hard to restrain me from sailing on the next steamer." Five angry Americans decided that the meet wasn't going to end this way. "You don't tell me!" they said.[24]

The men holding the megaphones announced the day closed and reminded spectators that rain checks were available at the gates. As the dejected crowd began to leave, a few heard a loud engine roaring at the end of the field. One after another, "like a covey of very angry game birds," the Americans rushed aircraft into the wind and rain. Deprived of prize money, the birdmen went into the passenger carrying business, and even at $100 a ride, business was very, very good. Beatty was up first and collected the most money. Gene followed, rocketing into a steep climb through the misty drizzle as Lieutenant Ellyson, like a cattle herding cowboy, whooped his way into the sky. Hammond was already diving at the heads of the megaphone men who were still announcing that the meet was over, while Lieutenant Arnold and his passenger had already joined the flock.[25]

Drizzle turned to downpour and passengers were soaked before the last aeroplane landed. Spectators were allowed to walk along hangar row and watch as the aviators and their mechanics packed up their machines in crates and prepared to leave. For the entire meet, Gene had won $1,400, fourth highest among the Americans, but a figure nowhere near the English totals. Grahame-White pocketed nearly $4,000 and Sopwith $5,200.[26]

Five days after the Nassau Boulevard Meet closed and before Woodruff could run another Sunday exhibition, he was stopped. New York Supreme Court Justice Garret Garretson ruled that Sunday aviation contests where admission was charged and prizes won violated state law. By then, Gene was already in Iowa, getting ready to fly for his friends and visiting with his family for the last time.[27]

# { 45 }

## "He was just Ely"

On October 6, 1911, at 1:45 in the afternoon, Gene was home. He stepped off the *Rocky Mountain Limited* at the Davenport depot and into a crowd of friends, fans, and reporters. As he squeezed through the arms of his admirers, a shout came from the crowd. "Were you much hurt in your accident in Canton?" "No—," Gene began to say, his answer drowned out in cheers and interrupted by one excited handshake after another. Given the wheel of old friend Pete Petersen's automobile, Gene followed a brass band that paraded him and Mabel through downtown streets to the Kimball Hotel for an evening gala reception and banquet. "The air king was wined and dined," and presented with a gold watch. When a few of his old friends asked for a chance to fly with him, Gene said he couldn't promise because he hadn't decided on what he would do. He was sure Mabel would ride along as a passenger and had already convinced his mechanical mentor Pete Petersen to give it a try, but anything beyond that would depend on time and weather.[1]

Flying the 100 horsepower Curtiss with the number *14* still painted on its tail, Gene's weekend flights were stunning successes. It was his first chance to show old schoolmates and his father's friends how well he had conquered the air. His father and Mabel weren't happy with his spiral dives and "crazy flying," of course, but the tens of thousands of spectators who were seeing their first aeroplane flight were thrilled. Sadly, homecoming was over too soon and Gene had little time to spend with his mother who had remained at home in York. Mabel left for New York where she would arrange passage to Europe for the couple's last planned exhibition tour, while Gene and his mechanics packed up his biplane and boarded a train for the Georgia State Fair in Macon.[2]

Early in September, the Georgia fair directors had asked Curtiss to send them Gene Ely, but if he wasn't available, they wondered if Lincoln Beachey could come. The Curtiss people said that they would do their best, but wouldn't make any guarantees. Finally, at the end of the month, it was official. Gene would come to Georgia immediately after his exhibition in Davenport. He would fly at least once in the morning and twice in the afternoon, each day for six days, between October 12 and 19. The only exceptions were Sunday the 15th and Wild West Day, October 18, when Buffalo Bill's Wild West Show would take over the aviation field in the middle of the racetrack.

## NIGHT LETTER
### THE WESTERN UNION TELEGRAPH COMPANY

Form 2289 B

25,000 OFFICES IN AMERICA    CABLE SERVICE TO ALL THE WORLD

THEO. N. VAIL, PRESIDENT                         BELVIDERE BROOKS, GENERAL MANAGER

RECEIVED AT the WESTERN UNION BUILDING, 195 Broadway, N. Y. ALWAYS OPEN

a 6 An ym 33 NL

Macon Ga Oct 14 1911

Mrs Eugene Ely
   164 West 74 St
         New York

Having lots of bad luck but think the run is
over. Did not fly yesterday so wont leave here till
the nineteenth your letter very welcome write some more regards
to Mars love

            Eugene Ely
               253a

In one of the last telegrams Eugene Ely sent to his wife before he died, the lonely aviator tells Mabel that because of bad luck with a broken part on his biplane, he would have to fly for one extra day to fulfill his contract in Macon, Georgia. That day, October 19, 1911, was the day Ely would crash and die (Diane Dunlop Collection).

The directors promised Gene a cool $500 extra if he would also agree to fly on the 18th and, without hesitation, "the master of the air" said yes he would.[3]

With nearly two weeks in Macon without Mabel, and a growing overconfidence in his abilities, Gene was free to do any and all of his dangerous dips and dives, free of relentless nagging. He would make the most of it. The newspaper had renamed his spiral dip the "Blood Curdling Death Dip," and at every opportunity, Gene was diving at the grandstand or just about anything else that moved below. "At times," said one reporter, "the crowd expected to see both biplane and occupant dashed to the ground," the aviator "catapulting his cloud-cleaver into convulsions above the heads of state fair visitors."[4]

Gene was enjoying his popularity. He had made friends with Buffalo Bill and had ridden one of Bill's horses in the grand opening day parade down the midway. The old American hero and the young aviator got along so well, they had agreed to go foxhunting together as soon as the Georgia exhibition was over.[5]

Gene began by flying over the city and dropping an aerial message to the mayor and this birdman, who had refused to paint the number *13* on his aeroplane in New York City, assured reporters that he would also be flying on the next day, Friday the

13th. He said he wasn't superstitious and had no fear of that ominous date. Still, when Friday came, Gene didn't fly. He said he had broken an unspecified part on his biplane and needed time to "readjust it again." His mechanics worked through the day and into the evening, but it was too dark and too late before everything was put back into flying shape.[6]

Reporters asked Gene about the dangers of flight. "I am in no danger," he said. "If I thought I was in danger I would not be going into the air, for I want to live. It's not a case of thinking. I know I am not in danger." A reporter reminded him of all the many things that might go wrong. "There is nothing that may happen if one is careful," Gene said. "There is but one danger and that is overconfidence. Of course there is some danger from adverse air currents and weather conditions, and some from breaking of the machine, but I have no fear in that direction." Those problems were easily overcome, he said. "When weather conditions are not perfect, I simply refuse to fly and I never ascend unless I know that everything is all right with the machine." He was not afraid. "I shall never be killed by the aeroplane."[7]

After flying two flights on Monday, October 16, Gene decided to try an experiment. He had the front elevator removed from his machine. The Wrights didn't use one and he had seen Beachey soar to fast-paced fame by removing his. Perhaps a headless machine would improve his performance. "He told me he thought it would work out all right," said Edgar Turner, one of Gene's mechanics. But a cascading two inches of rain the next morning left the field soggy and saturated and Gene canceled his test flight. "I do not fear the rain," he said, "but that I might encounter unfavorable winds in the upper currents." On Wednesday, the sun was back for Buffalo Bill's farewell show and Gene made a conservative half-hour test flight with his modified machine. By avoiding any severe maneuvers, everything seemed to work just fine.[8]

That afternoon he sent a telegram to Mabel. He told her that when he left Macon in a couple of days, he had been booked to fly a three-day exhibition in Norfolk, Virginia, and then he would join her in New York. From there they would make one last trip home to Iowa before leaving for Europe.[9]

On Thursday morning, October 19, the local newspaper was inspired to print an excerpt from Alfred Lord Tennyson's poem, *Locksley Hall*. "With his poetic insight," said the reporter, Tennyson had seen the future and had written a poem that "naturally comes to mind as one watches Ely make his wonderful flights."

> *For I dipped into the future, far as human eye could see,*
> *Saw the vision of the world, and all the wonders that would be;*
> *Saw the heavens fill with commerce, argosies of magic sails,*
> *Pilots of the purple twilight, dropping down with costly bales ...*[10]

It was a beautiful way to start a beautiful, clear morning.

Gene returned to the fairgrounds just after noon and headed straight for a booth in the exhibition building, where he had found a boyhood friend. The man was a traveling salesman for International Harvester out of Chicago. The day before, the friend had received a $200 company check for his expenses, but being a stranger in town and without identification, he worried that he wouldn't be able to cash his check. Gene said that nearly everyone in town knew who he was and taking the check, told his friend that he would gladly get the money for him. "Here, old boy," Gene said, as he began counting bills into the man's hand. "I want to get square with you before I go into the air." They talked for a few more minutes and the old friend asked if he could hold Gene's cork lined helmet. "What do you wear this heavy thing for Gene?" he asked. Gene answered with a smile. "Oh, that's just to protect my head in case I should fall."[11]

When Gene got to his hangar, he found Will Dunwoody, president of the Georgia State Fair Association, waiting for him. "I told him," Dunwoody said, "that although there was one more day before he would leave us, I wanted to take the opportunity to thank him for the fair treatment that we had received at his hands here, and to tell him in what esteem we held him, both as a man and an aviator." Then Dunwoody asked Gene what was the greatest danger an aviator faced. "A swelled head," Gene said. "Every one of the men who have lost their lives in the air has been killed through overconfidence." Then Gene took a moment to tease Dunwoody for not accepting his invitation to fly with him as a passenger. He also repeated his offer to cover his machine with phosphorescent paint and when darkness had settled in, he would fly over the city. "I'll make them think that there is a comet shooting through the air," Gene said. Dunwoody said that the fair board still had not made a decision and was unsure if it could come up with the $1,000 Gene had asked for. He wished Gene luck on today's flights and left.[12]

Earlier that morning, Gene had done something he had never done before. Perhaps sensing trouble, he approached Turner, his mechanic, with a request. He asked if Turner had a notebook handy. "I told him I did and pulled out this one," Turner said, with a red pocket notebook in his hand. Gene took the book and wrote down Mabel's New York address, "164 West 74th St., Hotel Marbury Hall, New York City." Since returning to New York a month earlier, the Ely's had shared a suite of rooms at the hotel with Bud Mars and his wife. "If anything happens today," Gene told Turner, "be sure to send a telegram to my wife and have her come here at once." "While Ely did not say that he feared to go up," Turner said, "I really believe that he feared something would happen."[13]

After a few final adjustments, mechanics pulled Gene's machine out of the hangar and onto the field. At almost exactly 3 o'clock, he was off. "He started at the near end of the track," said head mechanic, Frank Callan. He climbed to several hundred feet, making a complete circuit of the one-mile racetrack. "He executed what is known to the aviators as an ocean wave," Callan said, "which is merely a quick, sharp, dip and rise." Gene had circled the track once and while completing his second turn he fell. A police lieutenant was sure he had seen something wrong with the plane, "but I had no idea he was going to fall," he said. "Suddenly, it dropped like a ball of lead." An actor friend of Gene's, Mae Carter, was standing on the fairground stage watching the flight. "I saw him when he dropped," Carter said. "I feel sure that a wire on his machine snapped. I could distinctly see him trying to fix something and I believe he took his arms out of the shoulder straps that he usually wore." Dunwoody, who only a few minutes before had finished his conversation with Gene, saw Gene starting to drop. "He came down in a wonderful sweeping circle," Dunwoody said. "He had gotten about twenty feet off the ground and everything seemed to be going well. He started on the return swoop up and the machine was running just about horizontal with the ground, when suddenly, and without any cause, it turned its nose toward the ground."[14]

For the second time in two weeks, Harry Layton, a visitor from a nearby town, was watching a man fall from the sky. He had witnessed a balloonist drop 700 feet to his death earlier in the month and now he was only 40 feet from where Gene Ely was about to crash. He said Gene appeared to be about 150 feet in the air when he made a turn at the west end of the track. As Gene began to drop, his motor stopped. When the machine was about twenty feet from the ground, Layton said, "the engine started again at full speed, but the machine crashed into the ground." "He was starting his volplane." said mechanic Callan, "The last one of his life. The volplane correctly done," he explained, "is a long swoop downward to about twenty feet off the ground and then a rise. But what's the use?" Tears were forming in his eyes. "You know what happened. He never rose."[15]

In those very few last seconds before he hit ground, Gene must have experienced the same terrified fascination felt by Bud Mars in Pittsburgh, when Mars realized he was going to smash his machine and had "practically no chance of coming out alive." Mars too was falling straight to the ground. "I remember how my body pulled against my shoulder straps as I started down," Mars said. "Ordinarily, the resistance of the atmosphere makes the control of a machine an easy matter as you ride down through it. But here I was simply carried with the current—with no resistance at all." To Mars, and probably Gene, the logical thing to do was pick up momentum and regain control, but the controls wouldn't respond. "At that instant, I knew I was in for a smash," Mars said. "I didn't feel any fear and the events of my life didn't go rushing across my vision like a panorama. All I thought was dodge the crowd if you can and tip her sideways somehow so the engine won't smash you!" He was helpless, but never gave up, still straining to gain control as he crashed. Mars woke up in the hospital, amazed that he "never felt the slightest bit of pain," but Gene wasn't so lucky. "I believe I am not afraid of death," he once said, "but I cannot think without a shudder of those endless seconds when a man might be dropping, dropping, dropping through the air from the clouds to the ground. Those are the seconds I fear; those are the seconds I never want to live." Now, he was barely conscious with his machine shattered around him. "I lost control," someone heard him say. "I know I am going to die."[16]

The falling biplane had barely missed killing Frank Callan and fellow mechanic Edgar Turner. While standing in the racetrack infield, both men suddenly fell flat on the ground, listening to Gene's engine roar just a few feet above their heads as the biplane flashed by. "I don't know whether he was trying to make a dip or whether the machine wouldn't work without the front elevator as he expected," Turner said. "When he started sailing down our way, I thought he was trying to kid us as he has always done in his flights. He always told us to look out for him, always in a jesting way, and we didn't think there was anything wrong until we saw him working with the gearing."[17]

Turner remembered his promise to Gene and broke through the crowd, running to the Western Union Telegraph Company's tent, a branch office not more than 150 feet from the wreck. He sent a brief telegram to Mabel. "Ely has fallen. Come at once."[18]

In a mad rush, a few thousand people climbed over fences and raced across the infield to get close to the broken machine. It had landed on its right side with only the left wing still intact. The number *14* was still visible on its tail, but the rest was shredded canvas, twisted wire, and bits and pieces of shattered wood. "I ran up and

A crowd surrounds the tangled wreckage of Eugene Ely's biplane on the Georgia State Fairgrounds in Macon. The biplane smashed into the ground on October 19, 1911, killing the young aviator just two days before his 25th birthday (Diane Dunlop Collection).

started trying to pull the mass of debris away," Dunwoody said, "for I thought he was underneath the wreck. Then I saw him where he lay on the ground. I then turned my efforts to keeping the crowd back."[19]

How Gene's body wound up so far from the crumpled wreck of his aeroplane was unclear. Although the consensus seemed to be that he had stayed with the biplane and was thrown free when it hit, a few eyewitnesses were just as sure that Gene had jumped before crashing. "I saw him throw the straps from his shoulders," said one, "and when the aeroplane was about forty or fifty feet from the ground, he leaped. The aviator and the plane landed at about the same time, but the aviator was some fifteen feet in front of it. After he jumped, he turned several times in the air like a sack of flour and then struck on the back of his neck. He straightened out with a flop and relaxed." Those who were closest to the accident disagreed. Lieutenant Thompson of the Macon police was one of the first to reach the wreck. He said Gene was definitely thrown from the airship, somersaulting from his seat, and rolling 15 or 20 feet away from where the machine hit the ground. That matched Harry Layton's account. "Ely made no attempt to jump from his seat," Layton said, "and the force of the impact with the ground threw him out and from under the biplane, the body rolling half doubled up for a distance of fifteen or twenty feet."[20]

Police had their hands full holding back a curious crowd filled with souvenir hunters who would have carried the entire wreck away if given a chance. An erroneous story of ghoulish behavior by spectators was almost immediately flashed across the national newswires of the Associated Press. "In a few minutes, the field was cleared of every bit of the wreckage," said a San Francisco newspaper. "Ely's collar, tie, gloves, and cap, similarly disappeared; the collar even being taken from his body. The crowd forsook humane instincts in its morbid desire for souvenirs of the horror." That exact account also appeared in the *New York Sun*, and many other newspapers, coast to coast. A *Macon Telegraph* reporter was furious. "This is an outrageous exaggeration," he wrote. "No such things as these happened." He admitted that a boy did pick up a splinter of wood that had never been part of Gene's machine, put red ink on it, and offered it for sale as a true relic. A crowd quickly gathered around the boy and opened up a hot bidding contest for the splinter and the boy pocketed $7 for his fabricated artifact. The reporter said there had also been another boy who "picked up a collar, which had been taken from Ely's neck," by someone who hoped to relieve Gene's labored breathing. The boy had discovered the collar on the ground and hadn't stolen it from Gene's neck.[21]

It had taken a few minutes for the police to establish a rope barrier ringing the demolished machine, "but knowing the morbid fancy of crowds for souvenirs," they had to move as quickly as possible to save the aeroplane from hands that were "itching to tear it into shreds." A night guard was established and police said that no one was able to disturb the machine from the moment it had fallen. They must have forgotten or overlooked the city firemen who managed to get two pieces of bamboo from the crumpled biplane and later fashion them into two walking sticks. "Not as relics of the tragedy," you understand, "but of a flying machine that had flown through the air to great heights."[22]

Gene lay on his back, eyes tightly closed with one arm covering his face as if he had tried to protect himself from impact. The other arm was tight against his chest. There were no visible cuts and only a few bruises on his body, but blood was trickling from his nose and mouth. His lips quivered and his breathing was hard and erratic. Those who knew first aid, tried to open his mouth and force his tongue out of his air passageway, but the jaw was locked tight. Frank Callan, Gene's mechanic, crying uncontrollably now, cradled Gene in his arms like a baby. Knowing that Gene was a Roman Catholic, he asked that someone find a priest. A man had no sooner left the scene than two priests who had been watching from the grandstand pushed their way through the crowd and kneeled beside Gene. One of the priests said something to the aviator and Gene's eyes opened for a moment. As the Last Rites of the church were administered, Gene Ely died.[23]

Turner sent his second telegram to Mabel just ten minutes after the first. "Ely is dead. Meet the body in Davenport." Callan sent telegrams to Gene's father in Davenport and to Gene's uncle, Walter Harrington, in Williamsburg. In his telegrams, Callan reassured the family that Gene's body had not been disturbed. The Williamsburg newspaper summarized Callan's report. "All the sensational matter paraded in the daily press was entirely lacking in truth. The crowd did not swarm around the stricken aviator, nor was there one particle of his clothing removed. All such reports are positively denied."[24]

As they met the press, Turner and Callan were both still in tears. "He was a prince of good fellows and the most daring man I have ever known," Turner said. "I have been with flying men for quite a while and know most of them, but Ely was the best of them all in my opinion. He simply made the mistake that the others have made— he flew once too often." Frank Callan's voice shook. "Here are these great men," he said, "and their death is just a pure loss to the world. If in their death the world was taught something about aeronautics it would not seem so cruel, but nine times out of ten they are killed and we can't even draw a lesson from it. When reporters asked Callan for details of Gene's life, he refused. "A history of his life?" he said. "No, I should say I could not. He was just Ely, and he is dead. That is all."[25]

Although alone when Turner's telegram reached her, Mabel was quickly surrounded by friends who found her so heartbroken she couldn't stand or talk. Her best friend, Marie Mars, was in Michigan, where husband Bud had finally resumed his flying exhibitions. Marie telegraphed her sympathy to Mabel and said she was leaving Bud in Michigan and would meet Mabel in Davenport. Mabel had finally recovered enough to send a telegram to Gene's father, Nathan, saying that she was leaving immediately for Iowa. Until she arrived, friends and family in Williamsburg worried that she might want to bury Gene in California. Family tradition also says that Nathan and the United States Government wanted to bury Gene at Arlington National Cemetery. In the end, Mabel would agree with Gene's mother that Gene should rest near his boyhood home, in the family cemetery near the Harrington farm.[26]

Mabel telegraphed Turner asking that Gene's personal effects be forwarded to Davenport. Then she telegraphed her parents in Corte Madera. "Gene is dead," she said. "Am going to Davenport, Iowa, at once. Remains there." At her home in Corte Madera, Mabel's mother found reporters had come to the house. "This never would have happened if Mabel had been with him," she told them. "She always inspected his machine before every flight. He called her his guardian angel and she wouldn't permit him to ascend when there appeared to be danger." Henry Hall, Mabel's father, sent his own telegram to his daughter. "The whole Pacific Coast mourns with you tonight," he said. "The press glows with touching tributes to your hero."[27]

The glowing tributes spread from coast to coast. "Ely gained fame here," said headlines in the *San Francisco Call*. "San Francisco, to which he belonged, is especially grieved. Ely was well liked and well known in this, his hometown. He was modest, as most truly daring souls are, and gentle of speech and manner. The lionizing that came to him as a consequence of his exploits did not alter his bearing toward the world." In another of his "hometowns," Portland, Oregon, Gene's death was said to be "the first sacrifice Portland makes to the science of aviation." He was "bright, determined, and of high character, needing only the opportunity to make a name for himself." Alongside the Columbia River, Henry Wemme remembered the boy who had flown the aeroplane that had once been his, and how Gene "was always in dread of a fatal flight." As newspapers recounted Gene's short aeronautical career, they remembered his "great services to aviation," and how he "stood head and shoulders above most of his fellows as an aviator." It didn't matter where Gene had flown, or hadn't flown, they mourned the passing of a brave and perhaps foolish young man, a man who had "toyed with the elements," in "exhibition stunts." Had he only done something practical, some said, "He wouldn't have fallen." But *Williamsburg Journal-Tribune* publisher John Gallagher, who knew Gene well, ended his story of the tragedy with a personal touch. "As a rule, the wife accompanied her husband on all his tours and doubled the thrill and joy of his successes by sharing them. To her he was the hero of a new world; the daring mariner of an untried sea, and, for him, her love and devotion were inspirations that he prized above the world's acclaim." Then Gallagher offered what he said was the community's prayer. "May the young wife's grief, the mother's burden of sorrow, the sister's affliction, and the brother's woe, find easement in the soothing touch, which God imparts to the healing years."[28]

Gene's body was brought to Jesse Hart's funeral home in Macon. There he was placed in an expensive open casket and put on display in the home's chapel. The chapel soon filled with floral memorials and hundreds of curious people. Mechanic Turner stood by the casket, this big and rugged man unable to hold back his tears as he recalled the many times he had watched Gene fly. Someone had placed a white rose on Gene's chest. The press of people overcrowded the home's entrance and Hart had to force people into a line and demand that they enter the chapel one at a time. The visitors showed no morbid curiosity, but seemed genuinely grieved by Gene's death. "Many of the visitors who called to look on the pale face of the dead man had known him in life," said a reporter, "and out of all the hundreds who stood in the long line, not one had anything but praise for him." Gene had made many friends during his short stay in Macon and each felt a sense of personal loss. "More than one eye was moistened with tears last night as the visitors paid their last tribute of respect to the man who gave his life in the cause of aviation." The line of mourners continued until early the next morning, when the casket was closed and taken to the train station. At 4:12 a.m., accompanied by Frank Callan and a wreath from the State Fair Association, Gene began his long, day and a half journey home. From Macon, through Evansville, Indiana, never leaving his side, Callan accompanied Gene to Chicago. Mabel, along with Gene's father and stepmother, were waiting. From there it was on to Davenport.[29]

What had gone wrong? In Hammondsport, a Curtiss spokesman could only speculate. "Mr. Ely enjoyed the confidences of Glenn H. Curtiss as a conservative aviator," he said. "Mr. Curtiss himself being the most conservative of men, always urged caution to all of the aviators who were associated with him. The only reasonable surmise is that Mr. Ely in some unaccountable way lost control at a critical moment." Other, unidentified people "who knew Eugene Ely well," said that recently he had become "very confident" of his ability to control his new machine, "the fastest biplane in the world." He talked, they said, "of the possibility of performances never before accomplished, even venturing once the opinion that a complete somersault might be turned in the air without injury to the operator." Hugh Robinson, who was flying the hydroaeroplane over the Mississippi River from Minnesota to New Orleans when Gene died, placed the blame on Gene's fascination with Lincoln Beachey. "Ely was one of the most careful of the Curtiss aviators," he said, "but during the past summer he had been associating considerably with Beachey and I believe the influence had some effect on him, for he has been practicing aerial gymnastics considerably. He was a fine young fellow and every one of us who knew him were greatly grieved at the loss."[30]

"The cause of the accident has not been ascertained, and it is hardly probable that it ever will be," wrote a *New York Times* reporter, but a reporter for *Aeronautics* magazine was fairly sure he had the answer. It was probably Gene's removal of the

*Opposite*: **The day after Eugene Ely died in Macon, Georgia, the Georgia State Fair Association sent Mabel Ely their condolences and an itemized list of what they had found on her husband's body. From the $156.25 Ely was carrying when he died, the Association gave $100 to Ely's head mechanic to cover the expense of accompanying the body to the aviator's home in Iowa (Diane Dunlop Collection).**

front elevator. "Though there is plenty of control without the front elevator for ordinary purposes," the article said, "the elevator of a headless does not respond so quickly. It is possible that either Ely waited too long before straightening out, or that the wind velocity changed close to the ground and he dropped further than he expected." Mabel would always blame Beachey. "Eugene would be with me now if he had never seen you fly," she told Beachey.[31]

```
                        "MEET ME AT THE FAIR"
W. E. DUNWODY, PRESIDENT      HARRY C. ROBERT, SEC'Y & GEN'L MGR.      CHAS. B. LEWIS, TREASURER

      DIRECTORS                GEORGIA STATE FAIR                        OFFICERS
Georgia State Fair Association                                   Georgia State Fair Association
                                    MACON
                              OCTOBER 10-20, 1911
                                  UNDER AUSPICES
                         GEORGIA STATE AGRICULTURAL SOCIETY
                              "Every Day a Big Day,
                              Every Night a Huge Night"

                           FREE FIRE WORKS EVERY NIGHT

CURTISS AEROPLANES                                         BUFFALO BILL'S WILD WEST
   October 12-18                                                  October 18
```

Macon, Ga., October 20, 1911

Mrs. Eugene B. Ely,
     Davenport, Iowa,

Dear Madam:—

    It is with great sympathy and grief, for you and your family, that we beg to confirm our wire of October 19, in which we announced the accident to and death of your esteemed husband, Mr. Eugene Ely, which occurred on our grounds at 3:30 yesterday afternoon, and we deplore the seeming harshness in the wording of the wire, but under the great mental strain and excitement, we felt that you should be advised of the truth and atonce, hence the brief telegram.
    Mr. Ely gave us the finest exhibition of his mastership over his machine that has ever been seen in the South, and we regret that the warm friendship and attachment that we had formed of him during his brief stay with us, was so abruptly terminated by this unfortunate accident.
    We sympathise with you Mrs. Ely in your great loss and to show but feebly our esteem of the Mr. Ely we are preparing a set of resolutions which will be sent to you in due season.
    It is impossible to assign a cause for the accident, but we are sending our daily newspaper which gives various accounts of the mishap and am enclosing a postal card photo of the wrecked machine.
    On Mr. Elys remains were found the following personal effects of which we have used $100.00 by handing same to Mr. Frank Callan to pay the expenses of the body and attendant, Mr. Callan to Davenport, the balance being sent to you at Davenport by express to-day:

        One Check payable to Eugene Ely    1,000.00
        Cash in currency and silver        156.25
        Cash delivered to Frank Callan for expenses   100.00
        1 Gold watch, chain and medal
        1 Silver wrist watch and leather strap
        1 Diamond ring, with two stones
        1 Pair silver cuff buttons
        1 Gold knife with stone in handle
        1 watch chain, ladies, with gold cross and gold pencil holder

While Gene's body was carried north, mechanic C. C. Orr was told to pack up the wrecked biplane and send it back to the Hammondsport factory. He and his helpers gathered up the larger pieces, leaving only splinters of wood and small tatters of canvas. The scraps were thrown outside the police rope line, where a small crowd, "like a flock of buzzards over a carcass," rushed to pick them up. When reporters asked why Orr was so carefully packing all of these broken parts, he said, "The broken parts tell, to a certain extent, the story of the accident and they will be carefully studied at the factory with the idea of the invention of some device which will make the repetition of such an accident impossible." The large crates were quickly loaded onto a wagon and driven to the railroad freight depot where they were met by Sheriff Hicks. The Georgia-Carolina Fair Association had filed suit, demanding that the shattered machine not be released until the association received payment on what they claimed was a breached contract by the Curtiss Exhibition Company and Gene Ely. The Curtiss aviator was supposed to have flown at their fair the previous November, they said. At the time, Gene had told them his machine had been damaged by a storm at the Halethorpe exhibition, near Baltimore, but the association didn't believe him. Orr had heard that legal papers were going to be served and had worked as quickly as possible, trying to get the machine out of town before the legal papers arrived. He failed. The wrecked biplane remained in Macon until July 1912, when the fair association finally accepted $305 in lieu of their claimed $15,000 in damages.[32]

A number of photographers managed to get photographs of Gene's wrecked machine, including Macon City electrician, Charles Humphreys, an amateur, who was able to sell some of his images to newspapers and leading aviation periodicals. In less than three weeks, motion pictures of Gene falling to his death were in movie houses across the United States. Even in Iowa City, hometown of Gene's father and where Gene had visited his Ely grandparents, the public could watch "Eugene Ely in his famous and ill-fated dip of death," in Pathé's weekly silent newsreels of current events. With so many copies of that newsreel circulated in the United States in early November 1911, one wonders if any still exist.[33]

On the *Rocky Mountain Limited*, the very train that brought Gene to Iowa just two weeks before, Gene's body, accompanied by Mabel, Nathan Ely, Gene's stepmother, and Frank Callan, arrived in Davenport just before 2 o'clock in the afternoon on Saturday, October 21, Gene's 25th birthday. That evening, Gene was resting in the parlor of his mother's York Center home, just downhill from the Harrington house. "Sad, beyond telling was the scene," wrote publisher Gallagher, "the mother broken with grief; sister and brother in an agony of anguish; and the young wife dripping the distilled pearls of sorrow."[34]

Early Sunday morning, Henry Brockshus, Fred Newkirk and Gus Kleinmeyer began digging Gene's grave in the Harrington Cemetery. Presbyterian minister, James Wylie, conducted the funeral service from Emma Ely's home with music provided by the Congregational Church Choir of Williamsburg. The pallbearers were cousin Harry Groves; a Mr. Nolan, representing the Curtiss Company; Gene's mechanical mentor, Daredevil Pete Petersen; and cousins, Fred, Hugh and Frank Harrington.[35]

It was a large funeral with most of the mourners waiting outside the house for the service to end and the procession to the cemetery to begin. "I well remember the funeral," Carl Brockshus said. "I was a boy 12 years old. There were cars in the funeral cortege, but the hearse was a wagon pulled by a team of black horses." Most in the slow moving procession drove wagons or carriages, but there were at least 50 sputtering automobiles. The gathering was so immense that as the hearse was entering the cemetery, a mile and a quarter from the Ely home, the tail end of the long, long line was just leaving.[36]

In the cemetery, next to the grave of Gene's 3-year-old sister, Julia, the coffin was flanked with floral offerings from family, friends, and associates. Glenn Curtiss and Buffalo Bill Cody sent beautiful arrangements. Buffalo Bill had also sent Gene's mother a book with photographs of his Wild West show. In one of those photographs, he had marked the horse Gene had ridden in the Macon parade just days before. From the cemetery, one could see the home where Gene had been born 25 years earlier. Looking between the house and the coffin being lowered into the grave, Publisher Gallagher seemed to hear "wailing winds." Winds that shared "the sorrow over the passing of one whose skill and intrepid daring carved his name highest on the list of the hardy few who gave the world a new science." The grave was covered and Gene Ely was gone.[37]

"As a practical aviator Eugene Ely had no peer in all the world," Gallagher said. "His two years in the field make his name famous in all lands. Twice he demonstrated to the U.S. Navy and many officials the potential worth of the airplane in naval and military work by making flights to and from a battle ship. These successful feats gave him a prestige as an aviator that must last as long as human ambitions tempt humans to fathom the unexplored."[38]

Mabel returned to Corte Madera to live near her aging parents for a while. She had many years ahead of her, but through them all, she would never forget her hero—her "Darl," her "boy." She would guard his memory and cherish his name.[39]

{ 46 }

# Beginning the Afterlife

Two months after Gene's funeral, Mabel was again looking to the skies. The sun was about to set when she heard the familiar buzz of an aeroplane flying nearby. Standing at the gate of her mother's back yard in Corte Madera, California, she was watching an aviator do what Gene had been unable to do 12 months earlier—circle Mt. Tamalpais in a biplane. It was Weldon Cooke, a 27-year-old aviator from Oakland, who had only been flying for two months. Assuming that Cooke would land at the mountaintop resort, Mabel ran to the telephone and called the Summit Tavern. She wanted to be the first to congratulate Cooke when he landed. When Cooke finally reached the summit, the winds were too strong and a landing there was impossible. He saw an open field at the base of the mountain, dropped 2,000 feet, and just as he was about to land, a gust of wind pushed him off course and dropped him into a muddy swamp. Although Mabel never reached him, for a few brief moments her memory had returned to her lost world of aviation—a chance to forget "her own sadness in her admiration of the thrilling sight." A few days later, to show his appreciation, Cooke sent Mabel a postcard showing his flight over Tamalpais[1]

Mabel's spirits were on the rise. Old friends Bud and Marie Mars had just arrived from Chicago. Bud told Mabel he was arranging a local aviation exhibition in her name as a benefit performance that he hoped would make her "comfortable for the remainder of her life." Although most people seemed to think that Gene had made tons of money while flying that doesn't seem to be true. There had been transportation costs, repairs to his aeroplanes, salaries to his mechanics, hotel bills, and Mabel's new clothes and jewelry. Nathan Ely, Gene's father, was visiting eastern cities where Gene had performed, searching for a rumored estate of $75,000 that had somehow disappeared. Nathan was sure the money was "doubtless on deposit somewhere," but no trace was ever found. There was one newspaper report that said Gene lost all of his money through speculative investments, but whether that was true or not, three events suggest that Gene's death had left Mabel practically penniless. First, her sudden and unexpected marriage just 10 months after Gene died; a marriage that would end in a contentious divorce and reveal that she had come to the marriage with little money of her own. Then there was the court-ordered inventory of Gene's estate during a San Francisco probate filing. The 1915 inventory found a mere $450 in Gene's estate.

Finally, the two residential lots Mabel and Gene had purchased in Corte Madera in 1911 weren't legally turned over to Mabel until 1916.[2]

After watching so many of their fellow aviators die, Mars and Gene had made a pledge to each other. The two friends had agreed that if one of them fell, the other would take care of the dead man's widow. It was something professional aviators and their wives were always willing to do when tragedy struck. Mabel had helped organize a benefit for St. Croix Johnstone's widow after he crashed and she even stood for hours on a Chicago street corner, soliciting donations. Many people probably assumed that after Gene's death she would never want to watch another man fly, but that wasn't Mabel. She wanted Gene remembered, and the best way to do that, at least for now, was to let Bud Mars organize his aviation benefit.[3]

Mars planned to hold the benefit in Oakland, believing the city across the bay from San Francisco would subscribe the $50,000 needed for prize money. The aviators would all be paid to perform and Mabel would receive 20 percent of the gross receipts for the entire exhibition and all the receipts on a designated "Gene Ely Day." There was no trouble finding interested aviators. Gene's old mechanic, Bill Hoff, and others, even offered to pay their own expenses so Mabel would receive more money, but Bud and Mabel refused. They appreciated the gesture, but said it would be too much of a hardship for the fliers.[4]

While the aviators gathered in Los Angeles for the third Dominguez Aviation Meet, Mars stayed in the Bay Area, night and day planning his exhibition. At first, it seemed that he would have the most impressive list of participating aviators ever seen. Mars estimated that at least 60 had agreed to fly for Ely, including Grahame-White, Brookins, Willard, Hamilton, and Robinson. The country's most famous women aviators, Blanche Scott, Matilda Moisant, and Harriet Quimby had said they were also eager to come. But then, negotiations with the Aero Club of America broke down. Aero Club officials insisted that if it sanctioned the meet, scientific competitions and tests to further the cause of aviation would have to be scheduled. Aviators were not happy, saying that there had been constant friction between them and club officials who were always trying to dictate when and how they could fly. The birdmen were tired of interference and when they said they would fly without a sanction, the national club fired off a telegram, threatening legal action, license suspensions, and declaring that any aviator who participated in the Oakland exhibition was an "insurgent," an "outlaw," and warning that any record set at the meet would not be recognized. After a short meeting, the aviators answered with their own telegram, defying the Aero Club and welcoming the insurgent label. They received support from Ex California State Senator Frank Leavitt, who had taken over the Oakland exhibition from Mars. Leavitt flatly rejected the Aero Club's demands. "This is an aerial three ring circus, one mile high and three miles wide that we are going to hold," he said. "There will be none of the so called scientific demonstrations. The spectators demand sensational flying and real nerve racking thrills."[5]

The show would go on, but rather than 60, only ten aviators dared challenge the Aero Club's wrath. The gates opened on February 17, 1912, under a high, foggy overcast with no shadows below. Mabel took her honorary grandstand seat at the remodeled Emeryville Racetrack that stood on the eastern mudflats of San Francisco Bay, just north of Oakland. Most fences and track railings had been removed and the field was rolled flat, but much to the dismay of the aviators, the old flagpole remained standing.[6]

A visibly nervous Hoff was third into the air after Beachey and Parmelee. Trying to lift off too soon, he struggled to get into the air and once up, found himself too close to Parmelee's Wright machine and ran into a swirling wash of air. The inexperienced Hoff was surprised and when he reacted by suddenly trying to climb too quickly, his already sputtering engine stopped. The machine pitched to the right, rolled into a somersault, and fell 50 feet, straight down. As the right wing crashed into the grass, Hoff was ripped from his seat, but before he hit the ground, his unleashed motor tumbled through the air after him. While both were in midair, the engine smashed into Hoff, fracturing his pelvis. The unconscious birdman was buried under pieces of the crumpled machine. Besides massive internal injuries, his jaw was broken, an arm fractured, and his head battered and bloody. Horrified shrieks and shouts had echoed across the field. With Gene's death fresh in her memory, Mabel fell back into her seat, unable to move and sure that Hoff was also dead. Mechanics, other aviators, meet officials, and a mob of about 100 people raced to rescue Hoff. Finally, this "crumpled mass of bleeding flesh and broken bones" was loaded into a car and driven to the emergency hospital tent. After a quick examination, an ambulance rushed him in critical condition to the East Bay Sanatorium in Oakland.[7]

Mabel Ely's souvenir ticket for Eugene Ely Day, a benefit aviation meet for the widowed wife of Eugene Ely, held on February 23, 1912, near Oakland, California. Mabel received just over $7,000 (Diane Dunlop Collection).

Mabel Ely (left) sits with aviator Blanche Scott at the controls of Scott's Martin-Curtiss biplane on Eugene Ely Day. Note that Mabel is wearing the gold medal, encrusted with diamonds, which the Chauffeurs Association of San Francisco had intended for her husband before he died, but instead had presented to her that afternoon (Diane Dunlop Collection).

When Hoff regained consciousness, he was delirious and refused to let doctors touch him. He screamed for "Mrs. Ely!" He had to see "Mrs. Ely!" Mabel was already on her way. Hoff raved, rambled, and cried as if he were personally seeing Gene fall from the sky, even though he hadn't been in Georgia when Gene died. Finally, with Mabel sitting beside him and holding his hand, he calmed down and doctors began their work. Lucky to be alive and "tossing on a bed of pain," Hoff would be lying down in the hospital for most of the next three months. A donation list was started and the birdmen agreed to give Hoff his full share of the exhibition proceeds. Hoff had devised the "no fly, no pay" contract for the meet, but his flying friends knew he was going to need money. It took five years for Hoff's multiple fractures to finally heal and World War I to make him fly again. After the war, Bill Hoff quit aviation for good.[8]

On Friday, February 23, "Ely Day" arrived. Special souvenir admission tickets were printed, each carrying a picture of Gene, and because the gross receipts of the day would be given to Mabel, the admission price was raised from 50 cents to a $1. Even aviation committee members would buy tickets as they entered the field. The aviators had already decided to give Mabel their share of the day's gate receipts.[9]

Blustery north winds kept flying to a minimum. "It's the worst wind I have ever flown in," Phil Parmelee said. Had the day not been a benefit for Mabel Ely, the birdmen might well have stayed on the ground. Even Mabel's promised ride with Blanche Scott and Scott's promise to shower the crowd with thousands of Mabel's favorite flowers, violets, were canceled. Both women were ready to fly and had taken their seats on the biplane, but they finally listened to the more experienced aviators who told them it would mean their death. As usual, only daredevil Beachey seemed unafraid of the brisk wind, flying as if he were living a charmed life. Parmelee and Fish nearly collided and Cooke's motor failed.[10]

During the exhibition's intermission, meet officials and the aviators escorted Mabel to the center of the field in front of the grandstand. On behalf of the San Francisco branch of the Professional Chauffeurs' Association of America, she was presented with a diamond encrusted gold medal that the group had designed as a gift for Gene after his flight to and from the U.S.S. *Pennsylvania*. After they pinned the medal to her black dress, Mabel thanked the association, meet officials, and all the spectators attending the benefit, bowing to their applause.

The Oakland Exhibition had grossed $22,000, what Mabel received wasn't revealed. Her 20 percent share of the gross receipts would have been $4,400 and after the aviators 65 percent share of $14,300 was deducted, Mabel may have received most of the remaining $3,300 as her "Ely Day" share. Mabel was still in trouble and certainly wasn't left, as Mars had hoped, "comfortable for the remainder of her life." She was about to leave national prominence, but her future was still not assured.[11]

In August 1912, Mabel's name leaped back into the national press with the announcement of her marriage to 23-year-old Philip Cross. Mabel's secret elopement, less than a year after Gene's death, had surprised everyone, including her parents. She and Cross had driven over 120 miles north of San Francisco to the town of Ukiah for the private ceremony. Although they had often been seen together over the previous few months, their marriage was a shock to all of Mabel's friends. Many of them knew that Cross had only been single since the spring of 1911, when his wife of four years successfully filed for divorce.[12]

By the time of Mabel's marriage to Cross, he was already heavily involved in real estate with his stepfather, William Obear. Obear was successful and wealthy, but more than once had been accused of questionable if not illegal business practices. In late 1918 Obear and Cross' names came up in an investigation of secret bidding for oil leases in California, accusing them of receiving illegal loans that they had used to purchase promising oil property in the state. The investigation revealed that Cross was worth nearly a million dollars, but Cross had always told Mabel he had very little money. She was furious and filed for divorce, charging fraud and infidelity.[13]

Long before the oil lease investigation began, the couple's marriage was already in trouble. Earlier that year they had talked separation and possible divorce. Mabel said she had brought $7,000 to the marriage, most likely that was her share of the 1912 Oakland aviation benefit. Cross had asked her for the money, promising to invest it and giving her an IOU with a promise to repay. Mabel testified that in May 1912, before she knew of Cross' land holdings and his million dollars, she had agreed to settle for $25,000. She said Cross had convinced her that he was on the brink of poverty and that $25,000 was more than half of all they possessed. Now that she knew the truth, Mabel was demanding $500 a month temporary alimony and three-fourths of their community property.[14]

At the court hearing, she repeated her allegations that Cross had used abusive language, told mutual friends that he had no use for her, and had hired detectives to follow her wherever she went. An additional one of Mabel's accusations seems to be valid. Cross had "lavished money and rich gifts upon other women," she said. The most notable was a vaudeville actress who used many names, but was best known as Grace McGary. Mabel said that Cross had set the woman up in a love nest apartment. The address Mabel gave for that apartment matches Grace's address as it appears in the 1920 federal census. Mabel got her divorce, but no community property. According to Cross' attorneys, her share of the settlement came to about $45,000.[15]

Just before Thanksgiving, 1920, Mabel returned from a New York City vacation to her new home in San Francisco's Palace Hotel on Market St. She had already enjoyed two years of marital freedom, but now was anxious for a relationship. A newspaper story says that, while partying in a friend's hotel apartment, she met a man and impulsively decided to marry him.[16]

She may have believed that Wilford Andre de Meloche was the Belgian nobleman he claimed to be, but he wasn't. Meloche, without the "de," was born in Montreal, Canada in 1889. By his mid-twenties, he was in Jualin, Alaska, not far from Juneau, on the north shore of Berners Bay and working as a mining engineer for a company based in Belgium. There were many trips to the company's West Coast headquarters in San Francisco's Monadnock Building. It stood on Market Street, right next door to the Palace Hotel, a coincidence that perhaps led to his introduction to Mabel. After a mine fire in April 1920, the company's mines in Jualin were shut down, giving Meloche more time in San Francisco.[17]

Their midnight marriage was a "whirlwind affair." They induced a friend, Superior Court Judge John Van Nostrand, to grant them a marriage license, leave his bed, come to the hotel, and, "at the stroke of midnight," perform the ceremony. It was a short marriage. Mabel last saw Meloche four months later on April 8, 1921. He had left, telling her he had business in Mexico, but, when she hadn't heard from him for a few weeks and worrying that he had been kidnapped or injured, she began a search. "She found that he would probably not return." That's all the newspaper said, offering no further explanation. Mabel's divorce on the grounds of desertion was finalized in November 1922. "No children, no community property, no husband, were the simple elements of the complaint," wrote a reporter. Mabel was free again and for a few more years she disappeared into temporary obscurity.[18]

# { 47 }

## "They're all gone now"[1]

Three months after returning from the Mayo Clinic in Rochester, Minnesota in 1916, Emma Ely, Gene's mother, died. Two operations had failed to cure her of an undisclosed condition. She was buried in the Harrington Cemetery, next to Gene and her daughter Julia who had died in 1896. Since Gene's death, Emma had concentrated her life on her York Center farm and her surviving children. Now, Maidie and Hubert were left on their own.[2]

After his father divorced his mother, it's likely that Hubert's relationship with his father was no better than his brother Gene's had been. Having spent most of his young life with Emma on the Ely farm, Hubert was naturally closer to her. Unlike his older siblings, all of his early school years were spent in York and Williamsburg, not Davenport. By the time he was 13, he began a succession of military schools and just a month after his mother died he tried to run away. Somehow he managed to get to Chicago and cross into Canada, where he enlisted in a Canadian regiment that was about to be sent to the trenches of World War I. Before he could sail, military officials discovered his age and sent him home.[3]

In April 1917 he told the family he was joining the army and leaving for Fort Leavenworth, Kansas. No one was surprised. "Hubert has always felt a fondness for military service," said a reporter. But instead of enlisting he continued on to California where he registered for the draft in September 1918. He was working as a ranch hand on a sheep ranch just a few miles west of the California-Nevada border. Here he married a woman we only know as Amy and by 1930 he and Amy were living in Detroit, where Hubert was a city policeman. A year later, now living in a rooming house and apparently divorced, he was working for the Chrysler Corporation.[4]

Between 1939, when he was living in Bessemer, Alabama, and November 1967, when he died in San Francisco, his trail goes cold. His all too brief obituary offers no clues. He was described simply as "aged 67 years ... a retired member of the Hotel Clerks' Union." Hubert would be the only one of Emma and Nathan Ely's children not buried in the Harrington Cemetery.[5]

Gene's sister, Maidie, had a less adventurous life than her brothers. Born Mary Ely, Maidie was eleven years older than Hubert. Although she lived briefly with her father in Davenport after her mother's death, she was closest to her Harrington aunts, uncles, and cousins, living on the Ely farm almost continuously until she died. In 1918, she married James Austin, a farmer who had come to Iowa County four years earlier. They had two children, James Jr. and Lois Gene. Lois was Maidie's mother's middle name, and because the baby was born near Gene Ely's birthday, Maidie named her "Gene" in remembrance of her brother. Maidie's life was as peaceful and uneventful as one would expect for a loving mother and contented Iowa farm wife. In November 1939, at age 51, Maidie died.[6]

Although Gene's father, Nathan Ely, was still officially a law partner with Arthur Bush until the end of 1920, his 25-year participation in the Davenport firm had actually ended two years earlier, when, in July 1918, Nathan received a commission as major in the U.S. Army. To some, the commission was too conveniently helpful to his political ambitions. Earlier in the year, the Democratic Party had nominated Nathan as their candidate for the House of Representative to run against Iowa's 2nd District, two-term incumbent. Nathan had refused to run two years earlier, but now, with the country finally entering World War I under a Democratic president, he must have sensed the possibility of victory.[7]

While Nathan was posted in Alabama, his surrogates ran a nasty campaign, prompting the opposition to resurrect those old rumors and accusations that Nathan had been unfaithful to Gene's mother before their divorce. "If what his neighbors say of Mr. Ely is true," said one editor, "he is in no position to make any charges reflecting on the character and standing of another man…. To be 100 percent American a man must not only be loyal to his country, but above reproach in the *numerous other relations in life.*" Nathan lost the election by over 5,000 votes. He retired from the Army in March 1929 as a full Colonel after serving in the Judge Advocate General's Office in Washington, D.C.[8]

Gene's father may have been the one who started the campaign to posthumously award the Distinguished Flying Cross to Gene, a drawn out affair that took two separate sessions of Congress to complete. While considering the original version of a Senate bill, House members insisted it was more appropriate that the award be presented to "Mabel Ely, wife of the said Eugene B. Ely," rather than Nathan Ely, his father, as originally proposed. But the Congressional session ended before the two bodies could reach reconciliation. A year later, the bill was reintroduced and finally made it to President Hoover's desk in February 1933, just two weeks before the end of his presidency. In a brief ceremony on the White House lawn on February 16, Hoover turned to Nathan Ely and handed him the award. "It is a very great pleasure to present this to you," the president said. "Colonel Ely quietly spoke his thanks," said a reporter, "and the ceremony, what there was of it, was over."[9]

While the Distinguished Flying Cross bill was wending its way through Congress, a giant Navy dirigible was floating across the continent toward California. Named for the city where she was built, the *Akron* was christened on August 8, 1931.[10]

In May 1932, the airship had left its base in Lakehurst, New Jersey, for maneuvers with the Navy's Pacific Fleet. She arrived over San Francisco Bay on May 13 and was tied off at the new dirigible base near Sunnyvale, some 35 miles south of San Francisco. A week later, her crew was asked to fly over San Rafael, in Marin County, as a tribute to Captain Robert Dollar, a poor Scottish immigrant who had made millions in maritime shipping before his death. Mabel Ely was among the spectators watching as the *Akron* dropped rose petals and a wreath on Dollar's funeral service.[11]

Mabel had returned to Marin County to live near her mother after Mabel's father had died in the fall of 1926. Perhaps because Gene's Distinguished Flying Cross was still pending in Congress, someone in the Navy realized that Gene's wife was nearby and chose to honor her. "Among the small number of persons possessing one of the coveted official passes to inspect the *Akron* at Sunnyvale," said a reporter, "is a San Rafael widow whose name, Mrs. Eugene B. Ely, is 'open sesame' to the Navy." More than just inspecting the *Akron*, Mabel was allowed on board the securely moored airship, standing in the control car, and waving at photographers below.[12]

Mabel seemed content to slip into middle age and relative obscurity, seeking no fame or glory. She had married a man named Richard Pierce in the late 1930s and, while he was stationed on Palmyra Island, where a naval air station was being constructed in the early days of World War II, she volunteered as a teletype operator at an Army post on the edge of San Francisco Bay. After the war, the marriage ended in separation.[13]

Each year, usually in January, Mabel was reminded of the time she had spent with Gene, at the center of everyone's attention as they traveled across the country. Newspapers would delve into archives and remind readers that "years ago, January 18, 1911, Eugene Ely made a successful landing on a warship and subsequently took off again."

Perhaps the gradual passing of friends and early associates also stimulated Mabel's nostalgic memories of those happier days. When Charles Hamilton, the man who had flown the very biplane in which Gene began his career, died in 1914, it probably hadn't meant much to her; however, a year later, she may well have found some quiet satisfaction when the man she blamed for Gene's death, Lincoln Beachey, plunged to his own death, while performing over San Francisco Bay.[14]

Beginning in 1930, when Glenn Curtiss passed away following an emergency appendectomy, the deaths must have become more personal. Gene's father died in his Washington, D.C. home, March 5, 1941, and was buried in Arlington National Cemetery. Whipple Hall, Gene's mentor and once the "heaviest aviator on record," died in the summer of 1942. In 1944, Bud Mars, who had given Mabel her first aeroplane ride, died in Southern California. He had remarried at least once since those early days and the fate of his first wife and Mabel's close friend is unknown. A year later, Gene's cousin, Orson Harrington, who was with Gene in San Francisco when the earthquake hit and later became his mechanic, passed away at age 69. Orson had owned a Williamsburg auto repair shop for his entire life.[15]

In the last decade of her life, Mabel began a campaign to have Gene placed on a United States postage stamp. She also carefully watched over his name when it was mentioned in newspapers. "Just heard from the widow of Eugene Ely, the first man to fly on and off a U.S. battlescow," wrote national columnist Bugs Baer in 1954. Mabel had written to correct Baer for saying that Barney Oldfield's manager, Bill Pickens, had helped Gene prepare for the U.S.S. *Pennsylvania* landing in 1911. "It was a long time ago," said Baer, "and I don't keep memorandums. So, we straighten this out for

Eugene Ely's widow, Mabel, near her home in San Rafael, California, in the mid–1950s. "She was a sweet little lady," said Diane Dunlop who had married one of Mabel's nephews, "not very tall at all. Quite pretty though" (Diane Dunlop Collection).

Mrs. Ely who is writing the biography of her intrepid husband." Mabel was pleased with Baer's response. "I cannot tell you how I appreciate the story you put in your column," she wrote later. "Many Navy personnel think you are dandy to do so. The Navy is quite interested in Eugene's biography and look upon him as the father of the carrier. You have also the gratitude of many San Franciscans who are proud their city is the first to have a carrier. Thanks again—Mabel Hall Ely."[16]

Although Mabel never finished the biography, her efforts must have had some influence. In 1953, former Iowa U.S. Senator Guy Gillette unsuccessfully asked the Navy to name a ship in Gene's honor. Periodically the request is still made, but without success. In 1954, the Navy did dedicate a newly constructed bachelor officer's quarters at the Norfolk Naval Station as "Ely Hall," but did little else to commemorate Gene's accomplishments. By 1960, had there not been a few magazine articles, occasional brief mentions in books, and those annual newspaper reminders of his *Pennsylvania* landing, hardly anyone would have known who Eugene Ely was.[17]

Mabel's efforts ultimately ended in frustration. "It was a bittersweet irony that haunted his wife until her death," said George Hall, one of Mabel's nephews. "Mabel threw in the towel on her campaign to have a stamp issued in Ely's memory. She tried very hard and was very discouraged that he was never acknowledged."[18]

When Diane Dunlop married George Hall in the 1950s, she met Mabel.

"She was living in San Rafael in her own little apartment—a small little place on 5th Street," Dunlop said. "Actually it looked like an attic room. She would walk to church every morning to go to mass and she really couldn't walk very well, she was awfully stiff. She was a sweet little lady, not very tall at all. Quite pretty though."[19]

Mabel lived the last years of her life in a San Rafael assisted care facility, dying there March 27, 1960, two months before her 71st birthday. A Requiem High Mass was read at St. Raphael's Church. She had married Gene in the original church in 1907, but it had burned down in a 1919 fire. Mabel's body was taken to the Holy Cross Cemetery in Colma, south of San Francisco. There she was buried in the family plot beside her father and mother.[20]

For years, Mabel had been corresponding with Mrs. Allegra Harrington who lived in Williamsburg and was wife of one of Gene's first cousins. When Mabel died, Mrs. Harrington continued to press the Post Office to issue a stamp and asked Iowa congressman Fred Schwengel to help. When Schwengel learned that a four-cent stamp commemorating 50 years of naval aviation would be issued in San Diego on August 20, 1961, he wrote the Postmaster General, suggesting that Williamsburg was a more appropriate "point of issuance." His request was denied. "We regret we cannot comply," said the letter, explaining that the stamp would be issued to coincide with a joint meeting of the Institute of Aerospace Sciences and Navy officials. "This is in accordance with the recommendation of the office the chief of naval operations, with whom we have worked on this stamp."[21]

When the stamp was revealed in San Diego, Mabel's wish had almost come true. On a field of blue, below the words "1911 * Naval Aviation * 1961," the stamp featured a large image of a pair of naval aviator wings. Above the words was a much smaller image of a Curtiss pusher biplane. Gene's image wasn't on the stamp, unless one had a vivid imagination and could believe that Gene was that stick-figure-like smudge piloting the biplane. The only way to actually see an image of Gene was to get the stamp attached to a cancelled envelope imprinted with a commemorative cachet that featuring Gene standing in front of his biplane on the deck of the *Pennsylvania*.[22]

Perhaps with some embarrassment over disappointing Williamsburg residents and additional pressure from Congressman Schwengel, the Navy announced that they were casting a commemorative bronze plaque to honor Gene Ely's achievements. Officers from the Norfolk Naval Air Station, site of Gene's flight from the U.S.S. *Birmingham*, would present the plaque in his memory at a dedication ceremony in the town's central park on October 19, 1961, the 50th anniversary of Gene's death. It was a chilly day with temperatures stuck in the 40s and wind gusts appropriately whipping through the town square at 35 miles an hour. While telling the story of Gene's career, praising his courage, and reminding everyone that Gene's daring exploits were accomplished less than eight years after the Wright Brothers' made their first flight, Captain Norman Gillette, commander of the Norfolk Naval Air Station, presented the 50-pound plaque to the city of Williamsburg. Congressman Schwengel brought special edition stamp albums commemorating the 50 years of naval aviation and gave them to the seven Eugene Ely relatives who were attending. The plaque remained at city hall until the spring of 1964, when a stone covered structure was built in the park to surround the town's water well. The plaque was mounted on the building's south facing wall. There are two errors on the Williamsburg plaque. One perpetuates the story that Gene became a pilot in 1909, and the other moves his actual birth date from October 21 to the 22nd. If anyone noticed or cared, they didn't speak up. Williamsburg residents had finally received some recognition for their local hero and weren't about to complain.[23]

In 1977, when Allen Haworth took over as postmaster at the Williamsburg Post Office, he had two murals painted on the lobby walls above the mailboxes. One depicted Gene landing on the *Pennsylvania* and the other was Gene's portrait. "I paid for the materials and donated the murals to the city of Williamsburg," Haworth said. "The artist donated her time and is now deceased."[24]

Haworth and a few other residents tried hard to get their hometown hero the national recognition they felt he deserved. A campaign began in 2001 asking the Navy to name the next super carrier after Gene Ely. "I had over 2,000 signatures from local residents," Haworth said, "to no avail." When carrier CVN-77 was launched in 2006, it took the name of the nation's 41st president, the U.S.S. *George H. W. Bush*. In 2007, the Iowa Senate and House again passed joint resolutions asking the government to name the next aircraft carrier the U.S.S. *Eugene Ely*, but CVN-78 is the U.S.S. *Gerald R. Ford*. Haworth, now in his 70s, said he lost all hope in the spring of 2011 when the Navy announced that the carrier to follow the *Ford* would be named the U.S.S. *John F. Kennedy*, replacing the earlier carrier named after Kennedy.[25]

The Iowa legislature had also asked the Postal Service to issue a commemorative stamp for Gene that would mark the centennial of Gene's accomplishments in either 2010 or 2011. Again, the effort, including a Haworth petition drive, failed.[26]

When Williamsburg area residents gathered at Gene's grave in October 2011 to mark the 100th anniversary of his death, nine months after Williamsburg's mayor declared January 18, 2011, "Eugene Ely Day," they wonder why these events received no national media attention and why it seems their hero is being ignored. They should take heart. The country has not totally forgotten Gene Ely.

In October 2010, Bob Coolbaugh, a retired Navy commander, made his initial flight with a replica of Gene's biplane. A month later, November 15, he had the plane lifted onto the flight deck of a U.S. aircraft carrier to commemorate the 100th anniversary of Gene's *Birmingham* flight. Ironically, the carrier was the U.S.S. *George H. W. Bush*—the ship Iowans had hoped would be named for Eugene Ely.

Museums such as the Hiller Aviation Museum in San Carlos, California; the Glenn H. Curtiss Aviation Museum in Hammondsport, New York; and the Smithsonian in Washington D.C. have all presented exhibits that include Gene Ely. Also, here and there across the country, one can still find an occasional commemorative marker or statue. Perhaps these remembrances are all that Eugene Ely deserves. Soon enough, some other aviator would have worked up enough courage to try a shipboard landing or takeoff—but then again—Eugene Ely was first. With a fear of heights, he had flown to the pinnacle of his profession in an age of wire, cloth, and bamboo aeroplanes, knowing all along that it might not last. Like an immortal god, he could dare the heavens, glide and dip, plunging toward earth with a steely hand, but in the end, he was a human who was trapped and he couldn't escape. "'IT' gets us all sooner or later," aviator Ralph Johnstone had said, and Gene had agreed. "Oh, I'll do like the rest of them," he said, "keep it up until I'm killed." The day after his 25th birthday, Eugene Burton Ely was finally home again. Home and asleep in Iowa.

# Chapter Notes

## Preface

1. *Macon Daily Telegraph*, 19 October 1911, 5.

## Chapter 1

1. *Iowa City Daily Press*, 10 October 1911, 4.
2. Ibid. Glenn H. Curtiss et al., *The Curtiss Aviation Book* (New York: Frederick A. Stokes, 1912), 290. In addition to the foot throttle, the Curtiss had a hand throttle lever mounted on the right side of the steering wheel.
3. David Heitz, "Ask the Times," *Quad-City Times* (Davenport, IA), http://www.qctimes.com/articles/2008/01/30/news/ask_the_times/doc47a1583692b2f940128540.txt, 30 January 2008 (14 July 2008).
4. *New York Times*, 28 September 1911, 1. "Ely Demonstrates Conquest of the Air to Home Folks," *Davenport* (IA) *Democrat and Leader*, 8 October 1911, 9.
5. Davenport (IA) Democrat and Leader, 8 October 1911, 9.
6. Ibid.
7. *New York Times*, 25 September 1911, 11. "Aviator Eugene Ely Was Killed at Canton, Ohio," *Evening Post* (Frederick, MD), 28 September 1911, 4. "A Tribute to a Young Man from Iowa County Who Made Aviation History," Iowa County Historical Society, Vignette No. 122, September 1986.
8. *Oregonian* (Portland), 20 October 1911, 4.
9. Ibid. San Francisco Chronicle, 20 October 1911, 1.
10. *Daily Oregon Statesman* (Salem), 6 June 1911, 1.
11. Davenport (IA) Democrat and Leader, 6 October 1911, 5.
12. "Eugene Ely 'Brass Banded' to Hotel," *Davenport* (IA) *Democrat and Leader*, 6 October 1911, 5.
13. *Iowa City Daily Press*, 10 October 1911. *New York Times*, 20 October 1911, 1.
14. *Iowa City Daily Press*, 10 October 1911, 2.
15. Ibid. Davenport (IA) Democrat and Leader, 8 October 1911, 9.
16. *Humeston* (IA) *New Era*, 18 October 1911. *Morning Democrat* (Davenport, IA), 11 October 1955.
17. Waterloo Evening Reporter, 20 October 1911, 2.

## Chapter 2

1. *Macon Daily Telegraph*, 20 October 1911, 2.
2. *Macon Daily Telegraph*, 11 October 1911, 1.
3. *Macon Daily Telegraph*, 18 October 1911, 12; 19 October 1911, 1.
4. Brockshus, "The Bird Man."
5. *Medford* (OR) *Mail Tribune*, 4 June 1911, Daily Edition, 1.
6. *Macon Daily Telegraph*, 12 October 1911, 1; 20 October 1911, 2, 9.
7. *Macon Daily Telegraph*, 20 October 1911, 2.
8. *Macon Daily Telegraph*, 30 September 1911, 8.
9. Ibid. Macon Daily Telegraph, 14 October 1911, 10.
10. *Macon Daily Telegraph*, 13 October 1911, 1.
11. Ibid.
12. *Macon Daily Telegraph*, 14 October 1914, 1.
13. *Macon Daily Telegraph*, 15 October 1911, 1.
14. Glenn H. Curtiss et al., *The Curtiss Aviation Book* (New York: Frederick A. Stokes, 1912), 289. F. Robert Van der Linden, in his book *Best of the National Air and Space Museum* [(New York: HarperCollins, 2006), 43] says that after a crash that destroyed his front elevator, Lincoln Beachey found the biplane actually flew better, prompting Curtiss in 1912 to eliminate the elevator in production aircraft.
15. *Macon Daily Telegraph*, 20 October 1911, 2.

## Chapter 3

1. Carl Brockshus, "Early History of a Part of York Twp. Known as York Center," n.d., believed to be from the *Iowa County Farmer*, February 1972, copy from the Williamsburg, Iowa, Public Library. Carl Brockshus, "Mentions Incidents Rutherford School," *Williamsburg* (IA) *Journal-Tribune*, 11 November 1971, 6. *The History of Iowa County, Iowa: Containing a History of the County, Its Cities, Towns, &c., Biographical Sketches of Its Citizens, War Record of Its Volunteers in the Late Rebellion, General and Local Statistics* (Des Moines: Union Historical Company, Birdsall, Williams, 1881), York Township, 691–709.

The 1860 census in Iowa County, Iowa, calls Orson "Anson" and the 1880 Census in Iowa County calls him "Orsen." Most contemporaneous accounts call him Orson.

2. *Williamsburg* (IA) *Journal-Tribune*, 1 January 1886, 2. Carl

Brockshus, "The Bird Man, Eugene Ely," Iowa County Historical Society, Vignette No. 166, August 1994.
　3. *Williamsburg* (IA) *Journal-Tribune*, 23 March 1916, 3; 10 October 1907, 3. *Vidette-Reporter* (Iowa City), 24 November 1883, 6. Student newspaper, Iowa State University. The State University of Iowa, in Iowa City, is often confused with Iowa State University in Ames.
　4. George A. Katezenberger, ed., *Catalogue of the Legal Fraternity of Phi Delta Phi* (Ann Arbor: Inland Press, 1898), 430. Copies of E. H. Ely document giving permission for Nathan to marry and the Iowa County Record of Marriage were obtained in personal correspondence with Netha M. Meyer of the Iowa County Genealogical Society. *Williamsburg* (IA) *Journal-Tribune*, 1 January 1886, 2.
　5. *Williamsburg* (IA) *Journal-Tribune*, 26 February 1886, 2.
　6. *Williamsburg* (IA) *Journal-Tribune*, 4 February 1887, 3.
　7. Brockshus, "The Bird Man."
　8. *Williamsburg* (IA) *Shopper*, 7 September 1939.
　9. *Homestead* (Des Moines), 21 June 1889, 10.
　10. *Homestead* (Des Moines), 17 April 1891, 9; 26 June 1891, 9. *Iowa Citizen* (Iowa City), 25 December 1891, 9.
　11. *Davenport* (IA) *Weekly Leader*, 15 December 1899, 3.
　12. *Daily Citizen* (Iowa City), 23 June 1892, 3. Brockshus, "Early History of a Part of York Twp."
　13. *Davenport* (IA) *Daily Tribune*, 4 June 1895, 3; 15 August 1895, 4. *Davenport* (IA) *Daily Republican*, 28 September 1895, 6. Harry E. Downer, *History of Davenport and Scott County, volume 2* (Chicago: S. J. Clarke, 1910), 187. www.celticcousins.net/scott (13 March 2004). *Iowa City Press-Citizen*, 17 January 1921, 5.
　14. *Davenport* (IA) *Daily Leader*, 14 July 1896, 5. *Williamsburg* (IA) *Journal-Tribune*, 17 July 1896, 4.
　15. *Davenport* (IA) *Daily Republican*, 6 October 1896, 7.
　16. *Davenport* (IA) *Daily Leader*, 7 April 1898, 4. "Tears Mingle with Cheers. Last Farewell Is Said to the Moline Naval Reserves," *Davenport* (IA) *Daily Leader*, 29 May 1898, 3.
　17. *Davenport* (IA) *Daily Leader*, 14 August 1898, 13.
　18. Personal correspondence with the Davenport History Museum, 23 March 2009, "We do have a book of [high school] graduation lists, but Eugene B Ely is not listed in any of the years from 1901–1906," and with Jeremy Brett, Project Archivist Special Collections and University Archives University of Iowa Libraries, 7 August 2008, "I could find no mention of Eugene Ely as a graduate of the State University of Iowa." Confirmed, same date, by Sarah N. M. Harris, Senior Associate Director, Enrollment Services Coordinator, Transcripts & Verifications, University of Iowa.

## Chapter 4

　1. *Times-Democrat* (Lima, OH), 12 February 1900, 4.
　2. *Davenport* (IA) *Times*, 26 April 1900; 20 February 1901. *Davenport* (IA) *Daily Leader*, 30 July 1901, 4. *Davenport Times* news reports come from www.celticcousins.net/scott/smallpox1900.htm, website of the Scott County, IA, USGenWeb Project.
　3. *Williamsburg* (IA) *Journal-Tribune*, 6 April 1900, 5. *Davenport* (IA) *Daily Leader*, 21 January 1901, 4.
　4. Erwin Weber, *Rock Island Arsenal Golf Club: A National Historic Place* (Rock Island, IL: Rock Island Arsenal Golf Club, 1997), 13, 15. *Davenport* (IA) *Sunday Leader*, 1 October 1899, 7.
　5. *Davenport* (IA) *Daily Leader*, 4 October 1900, 7.
　6. "Through the Green," *USGA Journal and Turf Management* 3.1 (April 1950): 4. *Davenport* (IA) *Daily Leader*, 25 April 1901, 6.
　7. *Davenport* (IA) *Daily Republican*, 13 September 1902, 7; 28 November 1902, 7. *Daily Iowa Capital* (Des Moines), 6 November 1899, 8. *New Bethlehem* (PA) *Vindicator*, 23 March 1900, 6.
　8. *Davenport* (IA) *Republican*, 2 May 1900, 8.
　9. *Davenport* (IA) *Daily Leader*, 30 August 1901, 8.
　10. *Davenport* (IA) *Republican*, 21 January 1903, 8. *Iowa City Daily Press*, 17 March 1906, 3. *Williamsburg* (IA) *Journal-Tribune*, 11 July 1907, 4.
　11. *The Call* (San Francisco), 20 October 1910, 2. *Williamsburg* (IA) *Journal-Tribune*, 4 November 1976, 3; quoting a 1904 newspaper.

## Chapter 5

　1. George. M. Houston, *History of the Second Regiment Illinois Volunteer Infantry from Organization to Muster-out*, ed. H. W. Bolton, Chaplain (Chicago: R. R. Donnelley & Sons, 1899), 365–66, 369. *Morning Democrat* (Davenport, IA), 11 October 1955, 30. *Times-Democrat* (Davenport, IA), 15 June 1968, 12.
　2. *Williamsburg* (IA) *Journal-Tribune*, 26 October 1911, 1.
　3. St. Ann's Catholic Church, www.stannslonggrove.org/aboutus.html (4 March 2005).
　4. *Iowa City Daily Press*, 26 August 1904, 4. *Waterloo Evening Courier*, 24 October 1911, 2.
　5. *Iowa State Press* (Iowa City), 18 November 1903, 8.
　6. *Iowa City Daily Press*, 5 December 1904, 1; 15 December 1904, 7. Diane Dunlop, Ely Collection, "Oath and Enlistment Papers—Eugene Burton Ely."
　7. *Williamsburg* (IA) *Journal-Tribune*, 12 October 1905, 2; 19 October 1905, 2; 10 May 1906, 1.
　8. *Williamsburg* (IA) *Journal-Tribune*, 10 May 1906, 1.

## Chapter 6

　1. *The Call* (San Francisco), 9 January 1911, 5.
　2. *The Call* (San Francisco), 20 November 1905, 5.
　3. *The Call* (San Francisco), 9 April 1911, 8.
　4. Ray Lyman Wilbur, Edgar Eugene Robinson, Paul Carroll Edwards, *The Memoirs of Ray Lyman Wilbur:1875–1949* (Palo Alto: Stanford University Press, 1960), 88.
　5. *San Francisco Examiner*, 26 October 1927, 4. *Oakland Tribune*, 2 November 1927, 8. *Oakland Tribune*, 4 August 1912, 23.
　6. M. Lewis Emerson, M.D., "Sawing Off a Plaster Cast," *Journal of the American Medical Association* 41.12 (1903): 734. "Sanatoria," *Pacific Medical Journal* 39 (1896): 327–329. "The Waldeck Sanatorium," *Pacific Medical Journal* 37 (1894): 574.

## Chapter 7

　1. *Williamsburg* (IA) *Journal-Tribune*, 10 May 1906, 1.
　2. Jack London, "The Story of an Eyewitness: The San Francisco Earthquake," *Collier's*, 5 May 1906, www.jacklondons.net (12 June 2009).
　3. *The Call* (San Francisco), 9 April 1911, 8.
　4. *The Call* (San Francisco), 9 January 1911, 5.
　5. *The Call* (San Francisco), 22 April 1906, 2.

6. *The Call* (San Francisco), 9 April 1911, 8.
7. Henry Anson Castle, *History of St. Paul and Vicinity, v. 3* (Chicago: Lewis, 1912), 1058. *The Call* (San Francisco), 22 April 1906, 7; 23 April 1906, 5.
8. Transcript, Martha Foster Abbot Oral History Interview, 7 January 1977, by Carla Ehat & Anne Kent, Anne T. Kent California Room of the Marin County Free Library, www.co.marin.ca.us/depts/lb/main/crm/oralhistories/mfabbotft.html (11 June 2009).
9. "Transportation Issued Free," *Oakland Tribune*, 21 April 1906, 2.
10. *Williamsburg* (IA) *Journal-Tribune*, 24 May 1906, 4.

## Chapter 8

1. Margaret Blake-Alverson, *Sixty Years of California Song* (Oakland: self-published, 1913), 7–11.
2. Newell D. Chamberlain, *The Call of Gold: True Tales on the Gold Road to Yosemite* (Mariposa, CA: Gazette Press, 1936), 11. Jessie Benton Fremont, *A Year of American Travel* (New York: Harper & Brothers, 1878), 11, 69–81, 102, 123. Horace Greeley, *Life of John Charles Fremont* (New York: Greeley and McElrath, 1856), 24–25. *Marin Journal* (San Rafael), 25 November 1926, 1.
3. Roy W. Cloud, *History of San Mateo County, California, v. 2* (Chicago: S.J. Clarke, 1928), 436.
4. Roy W. Cloud, *History of San Mateo County, California, v. 1* (Chicago: S.J. Clarke, 1928), 303.
5. Ibid. *The Call* (San Francisco), 19 July 1908, editorial, 1.
6. Catherine Pixley Robson, as told by Mercedes Hall Brevig, *Marin People, Volume 2*, "Henry Clay Hall" (San Rafael: Marin County Historical Society, 1972), 149.
7. Woodland (CA) *Daily Democrat*, 6 November 1890, 3. Cloud, 303. *The Call* (San Francisco), 10 July 1899, 3; 10 December 1901, 9; 5 March 1902, 9.
8. Robson, *Marin People*, 149.
9. Ibid.
10. *Mariposa* (CA) *Gazette*, 20 August 1887.
11. *Marin Journal* (San Rafael), 2 September 1937, 2. San Bruno (CA) Park School District, http://sbpsd.k12.ca.us/schoolhouse/index.html (8 July 2009).

California Assessors' Association, www.calassessor.org (8 July 2009).
12. Federal census records, *The Call* (San Francisco), 6 August 1894, 8; 22 July 1899, 11; 26 May 1900, 11; 29 June 1901, 9. *Langley's San Francisco City Directory, May 1890* (San Francisco,)12 (m, ollection, S December v.lu here, but still, stay on your toes and be meticulous in fixing errors. As always, riminal Je 1890), 351. San Francisco Genealogy databases, www.sfgeneaology.com (22 July 2009).
13. *The Call* (San Francisco), 6 May 1907, 7; 21 July 1907, 35.
14 *The Call* (San Francisco), 5 May 1907, magazine section, 6; 16 August 1908, 36.
15. *The Call* (San Francisco), 27 December 1908, 41; 15 March 1909, 14; 5 September 1910, 1. *Oakland Tribune*, 22 November 1912, 5.
16. *The Call* (San Francisco), 19. December 1910, 2. *Bakersfield Californian*, 20 December 1910, sec. 2:1.
17. Ibid.

## Chapter 9

1. *Oakland Tribune*, 31 December 1908, 13. *Washington* (D.C.) *Post*, 19 January 1911, 9.
2. "A Tribute to a Young Man from Iowa County Who made Aviation History," *Iowa County Historical* Society, Vignette No. 122, September 1986. *Times-Democrat* (Davenport, IA), 15 June 1968, 12. *Post Standard* (Syracuse), 23 June 1910, 13. The Peerless Motor Car Club, "The Complete Peerless History," www.peerlessmotorcar.com (13 August 2009). Oldfield's previous visit to San Francisco was in December 1904 when Gene Ely was still in Iowa.
3. "Joe Williams Says," *El Paso Herald-Post*, 23 July 1934, 6.
4. The Pioneer Aviation Group, "Lincoln Beachey," www.lincolnbeachey.com/lbbo.html (23 October 2009). *Salt Lake Tribune*, 21 July 1934, 19. "Accelerating Sentiment," (serialized) *The Saturday Evening Post* [1927] October 29 (200: 18), 6–7, November 12 (200: 20), 26–27, November 26 (200: 22), 20–21, December 10 (200: 24), 28–29, December 24 (200: 26); [1928] January 7 (200: 28), 28.
5. *Lowell Sun*, 30 November 1954, 4; 1 February 1955, 15.
6. *The Call* (San Francisco), 9 April 1907, 8; 14 April 1907, 43. *Antique Automobiles*, September 1950, http://digital.hagley.org (14 August 2009). *Williamsburg* (IA) *Journal-Tribune*, 11 October 1906, 1.
7. Just a few examples of this San Jose legend: *Williamsburg* (IA) *Journal-Tribune*, 25 November 1976, 1C. Iowa County Historical Society, Vignette No. 122, September 1986. "San Jose Drivers Park Opened for Racing at the end of November 1909," *San Jose Mercury News*, 17 November 1909, 8. "The E. M. Ely—E. B. Ely Confusion Is Illustrated," *San Jose Mercury News*, 26 November 1909,4; 28 November 1909, sec. 2:12. E. M. Ely would finish 4th in his race, issue a protest and be placed 3rd.
8. *The Call* (San Francisco), 13 September 1906, 13; 14 September 1906, 7; 15 September 1906, 11; 16 September 1906, 41. *Oakland Tribune*, 31 December 1908, 13.
9. *Los Angeles Herald*, 5 July 1907, 6. *The Call* (San Francisco), 5 July 1907, 12.
10. *The Call* (San Francisco), 28 July 1907, 36. Arthur Inkersley, "Automobiling," *Western Field: The Sportsman's Magazine of the West* 10.1 (February 1907): 66.
11. *Oakland Tribune*, 22 January 1911, 23. Telephone Directory, San Francisco, California Pacific States Telephone and Telegraph Company, February 1903, 882. Eugene Ely was licensed as a chauffeur with badge number 2474; however, exactly when the license was issued was not reported by the California Secretary of State, *Register of motor vehicles and names of licensed chauffeurs registered in the office of the Secretary of State to December 31, 1909* (Sacramento: W.W. Shannon, 1910), 363. *The Call* (San Francisco), 17 February 1900, 17. *Oakland Tribune*, 23 March 1924, 49.
12. A bronze tablet with this verse, written by Charles Kellogg Field, is attached to the former A. P. Hotaling warehouse on Jackson Street in San Francisco, www.sfmuseum.org/sunset/magazine.html (5 September 2009). A contemporary story in the *Oakland Tribune* agrees with the quote and the attribution; however, at nearly the same time, the San Francisco *Call* published a different version. "If it be true God spanked this town, For being over-frisky, Why did he shake the churches down, And save my good friend's whisky?" *Oakland Tribune*, 6 May 1906, 16. *The Call* (San Francisco), 11 July 1906, 8.
13. *Oakland Tribune*, 22

November 1925, 66; "Howard Auto Co. Has New Head," 23 May 1915, 42. NEWSPAPER?
   14. Advertisement, *Overland Monthly, and Out West Magazine* 43.4 (April 1904): xiv. Maureen Dixon, "Sleepy Hollow," *Pacific-Sun.com*, 23 January 2009 (5 September 2009).
   15. Dunlop Collection, Correspondence with Cathy Gowdy, Marin County Genealogical Society, "Marin County, CA Marriage Book O," p. 219. *Williamsburg* (IA) *Journal-Tribune*, 29 August 1907, 10.

## Chapter 10

   1. *Williamsburg* (IA) *Journal-Tribune*, 13 February 1908, 1; 23 July 1908, 3.
   2. The Call (San Francisco), 9 April 1911, 8. Register of motor vehicles and names of licensed chauffeurs registered in the office of the Secretary of State ..., 363.
   3. R. L. Polk and Company, *Memphis City Directory for 1901*, 262, 412. *The Call* (San Francisco), 17 August 1902, 29; 13 August 1905, 21. Lucas Clapp's mother and her son Robert were still living together in Memphis in 1910. Robert was office manager at the cotton factory.
   4. *The Call* (San Francisco), 17 May 1908, 52; 5 June 1908, 8.
   5. David L. Durham, *California's Geographic Names* (Clovis, CA: Quill Driver Books, 1998), 393; *Oakland Tribune*, 1 April 1908, 13.
   6. *Lake County Examiner* (Lakeview, OR), 15 October 1908, 7.
   7. *Lake County Examiner* (Lakeview, OR), 29 October 1908, 8.
   8. Robert C. Laurens, "A History of the Matheson Automobile," *The Antique Automobile* 14 (September 1950), 102. *Lake County Examiner* (Lakeview, OR), 29 October 1908, 8; 29 October 1908, 5.
   9. *Lake County Examiner* (Lakeview, OR), 26 November 1908, 4; 20 May 1909, 8.
   10. *Lake County Examiner* (Lakeview, OR), 2 June 1910, 4; 26 October 1911, 8.
   11. *Klamath Echoes* 12 (1974), 9. *Evening Herald* (Klamath Falls, OR), 10 July 1909, 1; 3 October 1913, 1.
   12. *The Call* (San Francisco), 8 January 1909, 10; 12 March 1909, 7. Details of Pelton and Bogen derived from census and directory sources.
   13. *The Call* (San Francisco), 26 February 1909, 7.
   14. *The Call* (San Francisco), 12 March 1909, 7.
   15. *The Call* (San Francisco), 13 March 1909, 11; 16 March 1909, 4. Howard lowered the record by 1 hour and 3 minutes.
   16. *The Call* (San Francisco), 8 January 1909, 10; 19 February 1909, 7; 20 February 1909, 11.
   17. *The Call* (San Francisco), 28 March 1909, 8; 29 March 1909, 10.
   18. "Luther Burbank Home and Gardens," http://ci.santa-rosa.ca.us/departments/recreationandparks/parks/lbhg/Pages/History.aspx (26 January 2010). The Santa Rosa Rose Parade had begun in 1894 to honor horticulturalist Luther Burbank, a resident of the town from 1884 until his death in 1926.
   19. *The Call* (San Francisco), 9 May 1909, 39; 10 May 1909, 8, 9.
   20. Ibid.
   21. *The Call* (San Francisco), 23 May 1909, 39. *San Jose Mercury News*, 24 May 1909, 8.
   22. *The Call* (San Francisco), 24 May 1909, 1.
   23. *The Call* (San Francisco), 24 May 1909, 5.
   24. *Oregonian* (Portland), 20 October 1911, 4 (notes that Gene arrived in Portland in July 1909). *Iowa City Citizen*, 19 July 1910, 1 (notes that Gene had visited Iowa in 1909).
   25. *The Call* (San Francisco), 8 June 1909, 5; 13 June 1909, 39. Championship points were not awarded during the 1909 season, but assigned retroactively in 1927 and revised in 1951. Motor enthusiasts continue to argue over who was really the first national race champion and when the first race was actually held. In this race, Gordon Murray is often confused with Frank Murray, a driver of Buicks (not Auburns) for Charles Howard.
   26. *The Call* (San Francisco), 5 September 1909, 37. *Oregonian* (Portland), 21 November 1909, sec. 4:5; 31 December 1909, 6.
   27. *The Call* (San Francisco), 5 June 1908, 8; 13 June 1909, 39. *Portland Oregon Journal*, 23 January 1910, sec. 7:15. The 1909 race results are from Team Dan Race Team, www.teamdan.com/archive/gen/indycar/1909.html (1 December 2006).
   28. *Oregonian* (Portland), 22 January 1910, 18.

## Chapter 11

   1. Glenn H. Curtiss et al., *The Curtiss Aviation Book* (New York: Frederick A. Stokes, 1912), 11–28.
   2. Glenn H. Curtiss to Wright Brothers, 16 May 1906, The Wilbur and Orville Wright Papers at the Library of Congress, General Correspondence: Curtiss, Glenn H., image 1, http://memory.loc.gov/ammem/wrighthtml/wrighthome.html (25 July 2009).
   3. Curtiss, 38–39; 51–53. J. A. D. McCurdy (John Alexander Douglas) preferred to be called "Jack."
   4. Orville Wright to Glenn H. Curtiss, 20 July 1908, The Alexander Graham Bell Family Papers, Aerial Experiment Association, Bulletins, Bulletin No. V, 10 August 1908, images 217–218, http://memory.loc.gov/ammem/bellhtml/bellhome.html (26 October 2009).
   5. Ibid.
   6. The Alexander Graham Bell Family Papers, Aerial Experiment Association, Notes, 1908, image 22 (27 October 2009). Bell's actual telegram may be seen in "Telegram from Alexander Graham Bell to Mauro, Cameron & Lewis," *Aerial Experiment Association vs. Meyers, 1908–1912*, image 1 (27 October 2009)
   7. Glenn H. Curtiss to Wright Brothers, 10 July 1909, The Wilbur and Orville Wright Papers at the Library of Congress, General Correspondence: Curtiss, Glenn H., image 12–13. http://memory.loc.gov/ammem/wrighthtml/wrighthome.html (25 July 2009). *New York Times*, 4 March 1909, 9.
   8. *New York Times*, 18 July 1909, 1; 19 July 1909, 1. *Trenton* (NJ) *Times*, 1 February 1977, B4.
   9. *Trenton* (NJ) *Times*, 1 February 1977, B4. *Cleveland Plain Dealer*, 19 July 1909, 2. *New York Times*, 8 August 1909, 1.
   10. *New York Times*, 8 August 1909, S3; 20 August 1909, 2; 22 August 1909, 2; 7 August 1917. *Kansas City Star*, 18 August 1917, 12.
   11. Curtiss, 66–67. C. R. Roseberry, *Glenn Curtiss: Pioneer of Flight* (Garden City, NY: Doubleday, 1972), 185–186.
   12. *New York Times*, 29 August 1909, 1–2.
   13. *Syracuse Herald*, 30 August 1909, 1.
   14. *New York Times*, 2 October 1909, 2; 3 October 2009, 20.

15. "Curtiss Flies," *Aeronautics* 5.5 (November 1909): 193. Roseberry, 223. *Lima* (OH) *Daily News*, 11 October 1909, 4. *University Missourian* (Columbia), 10 October 1909, 2.

16. "Curtiss Flies In Chicago," *Aeronautics* 5.6 (December 1909): 216. Roseberry, 224–225.

17. *New York Times*, 2 November 1909, 5. *Gainesville Sun*, 8 November 1909, 1. "Curtiss Company Adds Agency," *Aeronautics* 5.6 (December 1909): 215.

18. Roseberry, 227–228.

19. Affidavit of Glen H. Curtiss, The Wilbur and Orville Wright Papers at the Library of Congress, Legal Cases-*Wright Co. v. Curtiss Aeroplane Co.*, images 44–45, http://memory.loc.gov/ammem/wrighthtml/wrighthome.html (5 October 2009).

20. *Boston Evening Transcript*, 13 November 1909. *Aeronautics* 6.2 (February 1910): 50.

21. *New York Times*, 17 December 1909, 1; 20 December 1909, 1. *Herald-Republican* (Salt Lake City), 13 December 1909, 6. *Nebraska State Journal* (Lincoln), 18 December 1909, 3. *Aeronautics* 6.2 (February 1910): 50. The editor of Aeronautics added a footnote to the reporter's story. "This speed has been questioned. We have no further authority than the above at present."

22. *Aeronautics* 6.2 (February 1910): 50–51.

23. *Aeronautics* 5.6 (December 1909): 217.

## Chapter 12

1. The Wilbur and Orville Wright Papers at the Library of Congress, General Legal Cases: *Wright Co. v. Herring-Curtiss Co.*, Miscellaneous Documents, 1910–1911, image 38, http://memory.loc.gov/ammem/wrighthtml/wrighthome.html (9 December 2009).

2. *Oregonian* (Portland), 24 December 1909, 6. Roseberry, 297.

3. *The World* (New York), 20 October 1911, 1. Roseberry, 35, 264. *New York Times*, 15 July 1911, 1. *Evening Independent* (St. Petersburg, FL), 26 July 1944, 1.

4. *Paducah Evening Sun*, 11 April 1910, 2. Roseberry, 286.

5. *Aeronautics* 6.2 (February 1910): 52. *Deseret Evening News* (Salt Lake City), 23 December 1909, 15. *Herald-Republican* (Salt Lake City), 23 December 1909, 7. *Oregonian* (Portland), 24 December 1909. *Reno Evening Gazette*, 25 December 1909, 2. *New York Times*, 31 December 1909, 7.

6. *Aeronautics* 6.2 (February 1910): 63–68. *New York Tribune*, 4 January 1910, 14. *New York Times*, 5 January 1910, 4. *The Call* (San Francisco), 6 January 1910, 5. Roseberry, 230–231. The Wilbur and Orville Wright Papers at the Library of Congress, General Legal Cases: *Wright Co. v. Herring-Curtiss Co.*, Miscellaneous Documents, 1910–1911, images 1–8, http://memory.loc.gov/ammem/wrighthtml/wrighthome.html (9 June 2009). Judge Hazel was the judge who administered the oath of office to President Theodore Roosevelt in Buffalo, New York, after the assassination of William McKinley in 1901. Library of Congress, http://memory.loc.gov/ammem/pihtml/pioaths.html (8 December 2009).

7. *Evening Observer* (Dunkirk, NY), 4 January 1901, 6. *Oxnard Courier*, 7 January 1910, 9.

8. *New York Times*, 6 January 1910, 4. *New York Daily Tribune*, 9 January 1910, 2. *Oregonian* (Portland), 9 January 1910, 5.

9. "Desert Presents Field for Airships Glenn Curtiss Talks of Great Usefulness of Aeroplane on Waste Places," *Oregonian* (Portland), 7 January 1910. Robert Glass Cleland, *A History of California: The American Period* (New York: Macmillan, 1922), 211–216. "Historic Adobes of Los Angeles County," http://www.laokay.com/halac/default.htm (10 June 2009).

10. Charlton Lawrence Edholm, "Latest Successes in Flight," *Technical World Magazine* 13.2 (April 1910): 190. *Oregonian* (Portland), 9 January 1910, 5.

11. *Los Angeles Herald*, 11 January 1910, 2; 21 January 1910, 6. The Dominguez sisters, Maria Guadalupe, Maria Dolores, Maria Victoria, Susana del Amo and Maria de los Reyes, ranged in age from 63 to 79. The *Los Angeles Herald* photograph of three of the sisters misidentifies them as granddaughters of Manuel Dominguez.

12. *Los Angeles Herald*, 11 January 1910, 1. *Oregonian* (Portland), 17 January 1910, 1.

13. Ibid.

14. *The Call* (San Francisco), 13 January 1910, 1, 5; 20 January 1910, 1–2.

15. *Aeronautics* 6.3 (March 1910): 104–106.

## Chapter 13

1. *Oregonian* (Portland), September 5, 1909, sec. 4:5. *Portland* (OR) *Spectator*, 8 January 1910, 12.

2. Fred Lockley, ed., *History of the Columbia River Valley, v. 1*, "Portland's First Automobile" (Chicago: S. J. Clarke, 1928), 675–678.

3. Ibid. *Oregonian* (Portland), 8 November 1899, 5; 16 February 1908, 6.

4. *Oregonian* (Portland), 22 January 1910, 18.

5. *Oregonian* (Portland), 25 January 1910, 14; 30 January 1910, sec. 3:9.

6. *Oregonian* (Portland), 25 January 1910, 14.

7. *Oregonian* (Portland), 16 January 1910, 3. *Portland Oregon Journal*, 16 January 1910, sec. 6:6.

8. *Oregonian* (Portland), 23 February 1910, 14. *Aeronautics* 6.3 (March 1910): 104–106.

9. Ibid.

10. *Los Angeles* (*Herald*, 12 January 1910, 1; 15 January 1910, 6.

11. *Oregonian* (Portland), 4 March 1910, 12. *Los Angeles Herald*, 21 January 1910, 1, 6. *Aeronautics* 6.3 (March 1910): 106.

12. *The Call* (San Francisco), 21 January 1910, 1–2.

13. *Oregonian* (Portland), 17 January 1910, 14.

14. Ibid. *Oregonian* (Portland), 16 January 1910, 3.

15. *Portland Oregon Journal*, 23 January 1910, sec. 7:15. *Oregonian* (Portland), 24 January 1910, 9; 25 January 1910, 14.

16. *Portland Oregon Journal*, 23 January 1910, sec. 7:15.

17. *Oregonian* (Portland), 25 January 1910, 14.

## Chapter 14

1. Bob Kingston, from the Gerding Theater Opening Celebration Program, Portland Center Stage, www.pcs.org/history/ (9 January 2010).

2. *Oregonian* (Portland), 23 January 1910, 3; 24 January 1910, 9; 25 January 1910, 14.

3. *Oregonian* (Portland), 23 January 1910, automobile section, 3; 25 January 1910, 1, 14.

4. *Oregonian* (Portland), 24 January 1910, 9.

5. *Oregonian* (Portland), 10 March 1910, 1; 23 March 1910, 11; 18 May 1926, 20.

6. *Portland Oregon Journal*, 30 January 1910, sec. 2:7.

7. *Oregonian* (Portland), 30 January 1910, 4.
8. *Oregonian* (Portland), 28 January 1910, 12; 29 January 1910, 13; 30 January 1910, sec. 3:10.
9. *Portland Oregon Journal*, 30 January 1910, sec. 2:7. *Oregonian* (Portland), 2 February 1910, 9.
10. *Oregonian* (Portland), 20 February 1910, sec. 4:6.
11. *Fairbanks Daily News*, 26 July 1908, 1. *Oregonian* (Portland), 3 March 1910, 7; 16 January 1910, 3.
12. *Los Angeles Times*, 5 March 1910, sec. 4:12. *Oregonian* (Portland), 5 March 1910, 12.
13. *Oregonian* (Portland), 23 February 1910, 14; 25 February 1910, 13; 5 March 1910, 12.
14. *Oregonian* (Portland), 23 February 1910, 14. *Portland Oregon Journal*, 28 February 1910, 2.
15. *Oregonian* (Portland), 10 March 1910, 1; 23 March 1910, 11.
16. *Oregonian* (Portland), 1 March 1910, 7.
17. *Arizona Journal-Miner* (Prescott), 5 February 1910, 1. *The Call* (San Francisco), 6 February 1910, 22. *Bisbee* (AZ) *Daily Review*, 12 February 1910, 1. *Waterloo Evening Courier*, 12 April 1912, 14. *Tucson Daily Citizen*, 21 February 1910, 1.
18. *Tucson Daily Citizen*, 12 February 1910, 1; 21 February 1910, 1. *Bisbee* (AZ) *Daily Review*, 4 March 1910, 3.
19. *Oregonian* (Portland), 3 March 1910, 7; 4 March 1910, 12.
20. *Oregonian* (Portland), 4 March 1910, 12. *Tucson Daily Citizen*, 17 February 1910, 1. *The Call* (San Francisco), 9 April 1911, Sunday Magazine, 8.
21. *Oregonian* (Portland), 5 March 1910, 12.

## Chapter 15

1. *Oregonian* (Portland), 6 March 1910, 8.
2. *Portland Oregon Journal*, 6 March 1910, 1; 8 March 1910, p. 2. *Oregonian* (Portland), 8 March 1910, 12.
3. *Los Angeles Times*, 5 March 1910, sec. 4:12. *Oregonian* (Portland), 6 March 1910, 1, 8. *Portland Oregon Journal*, 6 March 1910, 1. Frank A. Owen was identified in the newspapers as W. M and sometimes W. A. Owen. In fact, based on the address given in the newspaper articles compared to the 1910 census, Will M. Owen was Frank Owen's father. Victor Cercis, also identified as Carois and Carios, has not been identified.

4. *Oregonian* (Portland), 6 March 1910, 1, 8; 8 March 1910, 12.
5. *Oregonian* (Portland), 8 March 1910, 12.
6. *Oregonian* (Portland), 6 March 1910, 1. *Portland Oregon Journal*, 6 March 1910, 4. *Oregonian* (Portland), 7 March 1910, 1.
7. *Oregonian* (Portland), 8 March 1910, 12; 20 March 1910, sec. 3:11.
8. *Oregonian* (Portland), 20 March 1910, sec. 3:11; 27 March 1910, sec. 3:9.
9. *Oregonian* (Portland), 29 March 1910, 12; 2 April 1910, 11.
10. *The Sun* (Baltimore), 2 November 1910, 1.
11. *Oregonian* (Portland), 22 March 1936, magazine section, 6; 18 November 1938, 4.
12. *Oregonian* (Portland), 13 April 1910, 1.
13. *Oregonian* (Portland), 14 April 1910, 15.
14. *Oregonian* (Portland), 18 April 1910, 5. 1910 Federal Census.
15. *Oregonian* (Portland), 28 April 1910, 13; 8 May 1910, 14. *Lake County Examiner* (Lakeview, OR), 2 June 1910, 4. *The Sun* (Baltimore), 2 November 1910, 10. *The Call* (San Francisco), 9 April 1911, 8. Biennial Report of the Secretary of State of the State of Oregon (Salem: State Printer, 1911), 143. Incorporation filed 5 May 1910, fee $11.56. The Portland Aeroplane Company incorporated with capital of $5,000 which may represent the cost to buy the Wemme biplane.
16. *Roseburg* (OR) *Evening News*, 9 May 1910, 1. *Oregonian* (Portland), 10 May 1910, 6.
17. Ibid. *Roseburg* (OR) *Evening News*, 16 May 1910, 1.
18. *Roseburg* (OR) *Evening News*, 17 May 1910, 1; 18 May 1910, 1.
19. *Roseburg* (OR) *Evening News*, 25 May 1910, 4. *Oregonian* (Portland), 26 May 1910, 6. *Oakland* (OR) *Advance*, 27 May 1910, supplement, 2. Gene hired Roseburg partners, Judge James C. Fullerton and Albert Newton Orcutt.

## Chapter 16

1. *Medford* (OR) *Mail Tribune*, 24 May 1910, 1; 25 May 1910, 1.
2. *Eugene* (OR) *Register Guard*, 7 June 1910, 1. *Medford* (OR) *Mail Tribune*, 5 May 1910, 1; 26 May 1910, 1; 30 May 1910, 1.
3. *Medford* (OR) *Mail Tribune*, 27 May 1910, 1. *Ashland* (OR) *Tidings*, 30 May 1910, 1.
4. *The Call* (San Francisco), 4 February 1906, 24. *Evening Bulletin* (Honolulu), 20 April 1911, 10.
5. *San Diego Union*, 31 January 1910, 7. E. J. Edwards, "Millionaires Who Own and Operate Flying Machines Springing Up All Over," *Oregonian* (Portland), 26 June 1910, sec. 6:4. *San Jose Mercury News*, 11 May 1910, 8.
6. *San Diego Union*, 26 January 1910, 8; 29 January 1911, sec. 2:13. *The Call* (San Francisco), 28 April 1910, 18. The story mistakenly says Hall "has been a student of Charles K. Hamilton for the last *four years*."
7. *The Call* (San Francisco), 21 April 1910, 4. ["Hall has just signed a contract to fly in this city on that date. He will use a four cylinder Curtiss machine, which was navigated by Charles Willard when he flew in Fresno in the early part of February. Willard sold the machine to Hall, who has been traveling for some time with Charles K. Hamilton."] *Hawaiian Gazette* (Honolulu), 23 December 1910, 5. *Philadelphia Inquirer*, 13 March 1910, 4. ["I took my machine, *a new one*, and tested it out one morning in several flights" – Willard.] http://earlybirds.org/johnsonf.html (1 December 2006). ["Whipple Hall, who also owned and flew Herring Curtiss No. 5."]
8. Image of postcard from Whipple Manning (2004). *Seattle Daily Times*, 21 March 1910, 3.
9. *The Call* (San Francisco), 2 May 1910, 4. *San Jose Mercury News*, 2 May 1910, 8. *Hawaiian Gazette* (Honolulu), 23 December 1910, 5.
10. *Medford* (OR) *Mail Tribune*, 5 June 1910, 1.
11. *Medford* (OR) *Mail Tribune*, 6 June 1910, 1.
12. *Medford* (OR) *Mail Tribune*, 4 June 1911, 1. Southern Oregon Historical Society, Oral History of Seely Hall, no. 36, p. 26. Following the flying fiasco in Medford, a real estate promoter was advertising the farmer's field on the Old Cox Ranch, as the place "where the bird men fly," and offered for sale parcels in the new city addition. *Medford* (OR) *Mail Tribune*, 5 June 1910, 13.
13. *Eugene* (OR) *Register Guard*, 7 June 1910, 1; 20 June 1910, 1; 30 June 1910, 2. *Aeronautics* 7.2 (August 1910): 46.
14. *Billings Daily Gazette*, 10 June 1910, 2; 17 June 1910, 1. *Ana-*

conda (MT) *Standard*, 20 June 1910, 1.
15. Billings Daily Gazette, 19 June 1910, 1.
16. *Anaconda* (MT) *Standard*, 20 June 1910, 1.
17. *Duluth News-Tribune*, 3 June 1910, 2. C. N. Cosgrove, comp., *Annual Report of the Minnesota State Agricultural Society for the Year* 1910 (Minneapolis: Syndicate Printing, 1910), 12. Gerald N. Sandvick, "The Birth of Powered Flight in Minnesota," *Minnesota History* 48.2 (Summer 1982): 51.
18. *New York Times*, 27 February 1910, 8; 1 July 1910, 4. "Wright Patents Litigation," *Flight Magazine* 80 (9 July 1910): 527.
19. *Auburn* (NY) *Citizen*, 3 September 1910, 4. Roseberry, 286.
20. Minnesota Department of Transportation, www.dot.state.mn.us/aero/aved/museum/aviation_firsts/minnesota.html (13 January 2009). *Aberdeen* (SD) *Daily News*, 21 June 1910, 1. *Manitoba Free Press* (Winnipeg, Canada), 23 June 1910, 1. *Minneapolis Journal*, 14 June 1910, 4; 19 June 1910, sec. 8:10; 22 June 1910, 1; 26 June 1910, 1. *Minneapolis Tribune*, 23 June 1910, 2. *Aeronautics* 7.2 (August 1910): 46–47.
21. *Williamsburg* (IA) *Journal-Tribune*, 30 June 1910, 2.
22. *Duluth News-Tribune*, 27 June 1910, 5; 28 June 1910, 5; 30 June 1910, 5; 1 July 1910, 5.

## Chapter 17

1. *Correctionville* (IA) *News*, 23 June 1910, 1. *Waterloo Evening Courier*, 27 June 1910, 1. *Sioux County* (Orange City, IA) *Herald*, 6 July 1910, 1. *Moberly* (MO) *Weekly Monitor*, 10 June 1910, 3.
2. *Sioux County* (Orange City, IA) *Herald*, 6 July 1910, 1. *Aeronautics* 7.2 (August 1910): 48.
3. *Cedar Rapids Evening Gazette*, 2 July 1910, 1. *Sioux County* (Orange City, IA) *Herald*, 6 July 1910, 1. *Correctionville* (IA) *News*, 7 July 1910, 4. *Le Mars* (IA) *Semi-Weekly Sentinel*, 12 July 1910, 2.
4. *Chicago Daily Tribune*, 5 July 1910, 3. *Muskegon* (MI) *News Chronicle*, 6 July 1910, 5.
5. *Chicago Daily Tribune*, 3 July 1910, B3. *Iowa City Citizen*, 27 June 1910, 2. *Daily Free Press* (Carbondale, IL), 1 July 1910, 8.
6. *Chicago Daily Tribune*, 6 July 1910, 3; 7 July 1910, 5.
7. *Williamsburg* (IA) *Journal-Tribune*, 28 July 1910, 5.
8. *Williamsburg* (IA) *Journal-Tribune*, 14 July 1910, 2.
9. *Manitoba Free Press* (Winnipeg, Canada), 14 July 1910, 1; 15 July 1910, 8.
10. *Manitoba Free Press* (Winnipeg, Canada), 14 July 1910, 1.
11. *Manitoba Free Press* (Winnipeg, Canada), 14 July 1910, 1; 15 July 1910, 8.
12. *Manitoba Free Press* (Winnipeg, Canada), 15 July 1910, 20.
13. Ibid.
14. *Manitoba Free Press* (Winnipeg, Canada), 16 July 1910, 1. J. A. D. (John Alexander Douglas) "Jack" McCurdy made the first flight in Canada, at Bras d'Or Lake, Nova Scotia, 23 February 1909. He flew the Silver Dart while still associated with Alexander Graham Bell in the Aerial Experiment Association.
15. *Washington* (D.C.) *Times*, 16 July 1910, 1. *New York Times*, 17 July 1910, 2. *Idaho Statesman* (Boise), 16 July 1910, 3. *Springfield* (MA) *Republican*, 17 July 1910, 1. *Duluth News-Tribune*, 17 July 1910, 1.
16. *Cedar Rapids Evening Gazette*, 23 July 1910, 1. *Iowa City Citizen*, 19 July 1910, 1. *Williamsburg* (IA) *Journal-Tribune*, 28 July 1910, 5. Even after his recovery got nationwide news coverage, Gene's "death" was still being reported in newspapers. A few listed him in their year-end tally of aviation fatalities, and until late that summer, one widely printed newspaper article, "The Price We Pay to Conquer the Air," in indicating "that the mastery of the air must be bought with human life," used Gene as an example of one its "martyrs of aviation" (See *Stevens Point* [WI] *Daily Journal*, 30 August 1910, 3. *Elgin* [IN] *Echo*, 8 September 1910, 6. *Oelwein* [IA] *Daily Register*, 9 September 1910, 7.)
17. *Medford* (OR) *Mail Tribune*, 4 June 1911, Daily Edition, 1. *Evening Statesman* (Marshall, MI), 20 October 1911, 1.
18. *Manitoba Free Press* (Winnipeg, Canada), 18 July 1910, 1; 19 July 1910, 1; 20 July 1910, 1.
19. *Manitoba Free Press* (Winnipeg, Canada), 21 July 1910, 1.
20. *Manitoba Free Press* (Winnipeg, Canada), 22 July 1910, 1.
21. *Evening Times* (Grand Forks), 25 July 1910, 8. *Manitoba Free Press* (Winnipeg, Canada), 23 July 1910, 21; 26 July 1910, 11.
22. *Manitoba Free Press* (Winnipeg, Canada), 12 July 1961, 45. An article looking back to the 12 July 1911 edition of the newspaper.
23. *Manitoba Free Press* (Winnipeg, Canada), 29 July 1911, automobile section, 1.

## Chapter 18

1. *Nebraska State Journal* (Lincoln), 24 July 1910, 5; 28 July 1910, 2. *New York Times*, 8 August 1910, 2.
2. *Democrat and Chronicle* (Rochester), 4 August 1910, 14; 31 July 1910, 16. *Chicago Daily Tribune*, 3 July 1910, B3.
3. *Democrat and Chronicle* (Rochester), 30 July 1910, 14; 31 July 1910, 1.
4. *Democrat and Chronicle* (Rochester), 27 July 1910, 15. *Philadelphia Inquirer*, 15 April 1911, 1. *Buffalo Express*, 9 August 1910, 7.
5. *Democrat and Chronicle* (Rochester), 5 August 1910, 18.
6. *Democrat and Chronicle* (Rochester), 6 August 1910, 13.
7. *Democrat and Chronicle* (Rochester), 7 August 1910, 22. *Aeronautics* 7.2 (August 1910): 49.
8. *Democrat and Chronicle* (Rochester), 9 August 1910, 15. *Oakland Tribune*, 13 December 1917, 4.
9. Rochester Daily Union and Advertiser, 9 August 1910, 10. Democrat and Chronicle (Rochester), 9 August 1910, 15.
10. *New York Times*, 10 August 1910, 20.
11. *Amsterdam* (NY) *Evening Recorder*, 13 August 1910, 5. *New York Times*, 16 September 1910, 5.
12. *Amsterdam* (NY) *Evening Recorder*, 13 August 1910, 5. *New York Times*, 30 May 1910, 11.
13. Roseberry, 282–84. *Atlanta Constitution*, 24 June 1910, 3. *New York Times*, 12 July 1910, 2; 10 January 1911, 6.
14. Curtiss, 120.

## Chapter 19

1. New York Historical Society, https: www.nyhistory.org (14 April 2010).
2. *New York Times*, 5 January 1896, 1. *Brooklyn Daily Eagle*, 12 July 1877, 4; 19 July 1877, 2.
3. "The Coney Island Jockey Club," *New York Tribune*, 19 June 1880, 2; "Opening a Race-Course," 20 June 1880, 12. *Evening Telegram* (New York), 9 August 1880, 4. "Manhattan Beach Hotel Soon to Go," *New York Times*, 17 September 1911, 7. "Illustrated Covers from

the Brooklyn Sheet Music Collection," http://sheetmusic.brooklynpubliclibrary.org (15 April 2010).
   4. *New York Times*, 17 September 1911, 7; 26 August 1923, Real Estate and Apartments, 2. The Sheepshead Bay Racetrack, where some of the great equine battles had been fought, where the owners had only allowed thoroughbreds to run, officially shut down in 1911. There would be a few unsuccessful attempts at automobile races, but finally, in 1923, a new owner divided its 438 acres into small lots and sold them at public auction.
   5. *New York Daily Tribune*, 3 August 1910, 3. *Trenton* (NJ) *Evening Times*, 12 August 1910, 6. *New York Times*, 12 August 1910, 3.
   6. *New York Times*, 24 August 1910, 6.
   7. *Aeronautics* 7.3 (September 1910): 90.
   8. New York Times, 16 August 1910, 4 Evening Telegram (New York), 17 August 1910, 4.
   9. *The Sun* (New York), 20 August 1910, 2.
   10. Ibid. *New York Times*, 20 August 1910, 16.
   11. *The Sun* (New York), 20 August 1910, 2. *Cleveland Plain Dealer*, 20 August 1910, 4. *Aeronautics* 7.4 (October 1910): 128.
   12. *New York Times*, 20 August 1910, 16. *The Sun* (New York), 20 August 1910, 2.
   13. *Oakland Tribune*, 21 August 1910, 18. *Aeronautics* 7.4 (October 1910): 128–29.
   14. *New York Times*, 24 August 1910, 6.
   15. *Brooklyn Daily Eagle*, 23 August 1910, 16. *New York Tribune*, 23 August 1910, 4.
   16. *Aeronautics* 7.4 (October 1910): 129. *New York Tribune*, 23 August 1910, 4; 28 August 1910, 1. *New York Times*, 28 August 1910, 20. *Brooklyn Daily Eagle*, 26 August 1910, 3. *The Sun* (New York), 28 August 1910, 1.
   17. *Evening Telegram* (New York), 23 August 1910, 3. *New York Times*, 24 August 1910, 6.
   18. *Brooklyn Daily Eagle*, 23 August 1910, 16.
   19. *Trenton* (NJ) *Evening Times*, 27 August 1910, 2. *Oakland Tribune*, 28 August 1910, 17. *New York Times*, 28 August 1910, 20. *New York Tribune*, 28 August 1910, 1. *Washington* (D.C.) *Post*, 28 August 1910, 1.
   20. *Nebraska State Journal* (Lincoln), 28 August 1910, 1. *Brooklyn Daily Eagle*, 28 August 1910, 6.

*New York Times*, 28 August 1910, 20.
   21. *New York Times*, 28 August 1910, 20. *New York Tribune*, 28 August 1910, 1; 29 August 1910, 3. *The Sun* (New York), 28 August 1910, 4.
   22. *New York Tribune*, 28 August 1910, 1. "Father Knickerbocker," http://pbskids.org/bigapplehistory (27 April 2010).
   23. *Washington* (D.C.) *Post*, 29 August 1910, 3. *The Sun* (New York), 29 August 1910, 5. *New York Tribune*, 29 August 1910, 3. *Brooklyn Daily Eagle*, 29 August 1910, 16.
   24. *New York Tribune*, 28 August 1910, 1. *Aeronautics* 7.3 (September 1910): 90. *Kingston* (NY) *Daily Freeman*, 23 September 1910, 12.

## Chapter 20

   1. *Cleveland Plain Dealer*, 29 August 1910, 1, 3. *Coshocton* (OH) *Daily Age*, 22 August 1910, 3.
   2. *Cleveland Plain Dealer,* 29 August 1910, 1, 3; 31 August 1910, 1; 1 September 1910, 1. *Washington* (D.C.) *Post*, 1 September 1910, 1.
   3. *Iowa City Citizen*, 2 September 1910, 1. *Cleveland Plain Dealer*, 2 September 1910, 1–2. *Aeronautics* 7.4 (October 1910): 119.
   4. *Cleveland Plain Dealer,* 1 September 1910, 1; 2 September 1910, 2; 3 September 1910, 5. *Kalamazoo Gazette*, 2 September 1910, 7. *Auburn* (NY) *Citizen*, 3 September 1910, 4.
   5. *Iowa City Citizen*, 2 September 1910, 1. *Kalamazoo Gazette*, 2 September 1910, 7; 3 September 1910, 1.
   6. *Kalamazoo Gazette*, 4 September 1910, 1; 7 September 1910, 6.
   7. *Kalamazoo Gazette*, 8 September 1910, 1; 9 September 1910, 5.
   8. *Williamsburg* (IA) *Journal-Tribune*, 15 September 1910, 1.
   9. Ibid. Brockshus, "The Bird Man."
   10. *Muscatine* (IA) *Journal*, 3 September 1910, 10; 14 September 1910, 8.
   11. *Morning Democrat* (Davenport, IA), 11 October 1955, sec. 6:25. *Davenport* (IA) *Democrat and Leader*, 20 July 1924, New Home Edition, 29. *Muscatine* (IA) *Journal* 15 September 1910, 3. *New York Times*, 16 September 1910, 5.
   12. *Roanoke* (VA) *News*, 23 September 1910, 1. *Poughkeepsie Daily Eagle*, 27 September 1910, 5.

   13. *Poughkeepsie Daily Eagle*, 27 September 1910, 5.
   14. *Roanoke News*, 23 September 1910, 1.
   15. Ibid. "Rockledge Inn Once Defined Mill Mountain," *The Roanoker*, Leisure Publishing Co., Roanoke, VA, http://theroanoker.com/interests/history/rockledge-inn (7 May 2010). *The Sun* (Baltimore), 13 November 1910, 16.
   16. *Poughkeepsie Daily Eagle*, 27 September 1910, 5. *Roanoke News*, 23 September 1910, 1. *Times-Dispatch* (Richmond, VA), 23 September 1910, 6.
   17. *Oregonian* (Portland), 25 September 1910, sec. 4:5.
   18. Copy of postcard from correspondence with Whipple Manning (2004). *Poughkeepsie Daily Eagle*, 26 September 1910, 5.
   19. Department of the Navy, Naval Historical Center, "Naval Aviation Chronology 1898–1916," www.history.navy.mil/branches/avchr1.htm (14 December 2008).
   20. San Antonio Express and News, 1 April 1956, 3D. Poughkeepsie Daily Eagle, 27 September 1910, 5, 6.
   21. *Poughkeepsie Daily Eagle*, 27 September 1910, 6.
   22. Ibid.
   23. Ibid.
   24. *Poughkeepsie Daily Eagle*, 2 September 1910, 5; 28 September 1910, 5, 6.
   25. *Poughkeepsie Daily Eagle*, 28 September 1910, 5, 6.
   26. Ibid.
   27. Ibid.
   28. *Poughkeepsie Daily Eagle*, 29 September 1910, 5.
   29. *Poughkeepsie Daily Eagle*, 29 September 1910, 5, 6. *New York Times*, 29 September 1910, 1. The apparently erroneous story of DePalma's victory over Eugene Ely spread across the country nearly word for word by an unknown news service. Examples include: *Gettysburg Times*, 30 September 1910, 3. *Steven's Point* (WI) *Daily Journal*, 30 September 1910, 2.
   30. Poughkeepsie Daily Eagle, 1 October 1910, 5.
   31. *Poughkeepsie Daily Eagle*, 30 September 1910, 1, 5. *New York Tribune*, 12 October 1910, 1.
   32. *Poughkeepsie Daily Eagle*, 30 September 1910, 5
   33. Ibid.
   34. Poughkeepsie Daily Eagle, 1 October 1910, 5.
   35. Ibid.
   36. *New York Times*, 29 September 1910, 1.

## Chapter 21

1. *Poughkeepsie Daily Eagle*, 27 September 1910, 6.
2. *New York Times*, 17 August 1910, 3; 30 September 1910, 1. Curtiss, 114.
3. *New York Times*, 29 September 1910, 1. *Poughkeepsie Daily Eagle*, 27 September 1910, 6. *Albuquerque Journal*, 14 June 1910, 1.
4. *New York Times*, 2 June 1910, 1; 27 September 1910, 1. *Chicago Daily Tribune*, 25 September 1910, Metropolitan Section, H:1. *Rockford* (IL) *Morning Star*, 27 September 1910, 2. Roseberry, 289.
5. *New York Times*, 11 September 1910, 2.
6. *New York Times*, 6 July 1910, 1; 9 July 1910, 1; 1 October 1910, 1. *Washington* (D.C.) *Times*, 9 October 1910, 5. *Indianapolis Star*, 2 October 1910, 18. *Oregonian* (Portland), 10 October 1910, 5.
7. *Aeronautics* 7.5 (November 1910): 120, 160. *Springfield* (MA) *Republican*, 8 September 1910, 9. *New York Times*, 8 October 1910, 1. *The Call* (San Francisco), 10 September 1910, 1. One report in the *New York Times*, 7 October 1910, 1, says the Hudson Flyer was at Chicago for the big race, while, at the same time, the *Anaconda* (MT) *Standard*, 23 September 1910, 11, said it (or at least its motor) was with Mars in Montana.
8. *Poughkeepsie Daily Eagle*, 27 September 1910, 6.
9. *New York Times*, 11 September, 2; 14 September 1910, 4. *Anaconda* (MT) *Standard*, 23 September 1910, 11
10. *New York Times*, 4 October 1910, 1; 7 October 1910, 5.
11. *New York Times*, 2 October 1910, 1; 4 October 1910, 1; 7 October 1910, 1. *Iowa City Citizen*, 3 October 1910, 1. *Chicago Daily Tribune*, 3 October 1910, 1. *Aeronautics* 7.5 (November 1910): 160. Smithsonian Air and Space Museum, www.nasm.si.edu/research/aero/women_aviators/blanche_scott.htm (20 May 2008).
12. *Aero* 3.13 (13 January 1912): 314.
13. *New York Times*, 1 October 1910, 1; 4 October 1910, 1.
14. *Washington* (D.C.) *Herald*, 8 October 1910, 1. *New York Times*, 9 October 1910, 1. *Washington* (D.C.) *Times*, 9 October 1910, 5.
15. *Washington* (D.C.) *Herald*, 8 October 1910, 1.
16. *New York Times*, 9 October 1910, 1.
17. Ibid. Williamsburg (IA) Journal-Tribune, 6 October 1910, 2.
18. Roseberry, 291. *New York Times*, 10 October 1910, 2. *New York Daily Tribune*, 10 October 1910, 3. *Oregonian* (Portland), 10 October 1910, 1, 5. *Aircraft* 1.10 (December 1910):363.
19. *New York Times*, 10 October 1910, 1, 2.
20. *The World* (New York), 10 October 1910, 1. *Poughkeepsie Daily Eagle*, 10 October 1910, 8.
21. Ibid. *New York Times*, 10 October 1910, 2.
22. *The World* (New York), 10 October 1910, 1. *New York Times*, 10 October 1910, 1.
23. Ibid. *New York Daily Tribune*, 10 October 1910, 3. (Portland, OR) *Oregonian*, 10 October 1910, 1.
24. *New York Times*, 11 October 1910, 1. *Iowa City Citizen*, 11 October 1910, 1.
25. Ibid. *Iowa City Citizen*, 11 October 1910, 1.
26. *New York Times*, 11 October 1910, 1.
27. *New York Times*, 12 October 1910, 2.
28. Ibid.
29. *Rockford* (IL) *Republic*, 12 October 1910, 1.

## Chapter 22

1. *New Castle* (PA) *News*, 14 September 1910, 1; 15 September 1910, 3.
2. *Newark* (OH) *Advocate*, 25 March 1907, 6. *Mansfield* (OH) *News*, 20 June 1907, 6. *New Castle* (PA) *News*, 15 November 1909, 4; 13 October 1910, 12. Nancy Kertis, "Aviation Exhibit Takes Flight at the Arms Museum," *The* Jambar (newsletter of Youngstown State University) 69.53 (19 May 1989): 8. It is unclear if Gene was using the Boston Flyer or the Hudson Flyer, or some other machine. Some reports said the flyer was being sent back to Hammondsport for repairs and Gene would be using the Hudson in a month to fly from the U.S.S. *Birmingham*. After that flight, he said he hadn't flown the Hudson for over a month.
3. *New Castle* (PA) *News*, 13 October 1910, 12; 14 October 1910, 5. *Cleveland Plain Dealer*, 14 October 1910, 3. Joseph G. Butler, Jr., *History of Youngstown and the Mahoning Valley Ohio, v. 1* (Chicago: American Historical Society, 1921), 338.
4. *Evening Telegram* (Elyria, OH), 10 October 1910, 3. *Cleveland Plain Dealer*, 7 October 1910, 5; 11 October 1910, 3; 13 October 1910, 1, 2, 3; 16 October 1910, sec. 2:1.
5. *Cleveland Plain Dealer*, 9 October 1910, sec. 2:2; 12 October 1910, 4.
6. Cleveland Plain Dealer, 14 October 1910, 1, 2.
7. Cleveland Plain Dealer, 15 October 1910, 1, 2.
8. *Cleveland Plain Dealer*, 15 October 1910, 2; 17 October 1910, 2.
9. *Cleveland Plain Dealer*, 16 October 1910, sec. 2:1; 17 October 1910, 1, 2.
10. *Cleveland Plain Dealer*, 16 October 1910, sec. 2:1.
11. Ibid.
12. Ibid.
13. Cleveland Plain Dealer, 17 October 1910, 1, 2.
14. *Cleveland Plain Dealer*, 16 October 1910, sec. 2:1.

## Chapter 23

1. *New York Herald*, 23 October 1910, 1.
2. *New York Times*, 21 June 1910, 1.
3. *New York Times*, 5 August 1910, 3; 9 August 1910, 5. *Evening Telegram* (New York), 22 October 1910, 3.
4. Curtiss, 116. *Washington* (D.C.) *Times*, 17 October 1910, 7. *New York Herald*, 19 October 1910, 1.
5. *The Sun* (New York), 23 October 1910, 2. *New York Herald*, 23 October 1910, 1.
6. *Aeronautics* 7.6 (December 1910): 206. *Philadelphia Inquirer*, 14 August 1910, 6. *The Sun* (New York), 8 November 1910, 5.
7. *New York Herald*, 23 October 1910, 1. *The Sun* (New York), 23 October 1910, 2.
8. New York Times, 5 August 1910, 3. Long Beach Independent Press-Telegram, 3 May 1953, D8.
9. *The Sun* (New York), 29 October 1910, 2. *New York Tribune*, 30 October 1910, 1. *New York Times*, 28 October 1910, 2. *Washington* (D.C.) *Post*, 29 October 1910, 1.
10. *Aeronautics* 7.6 (December 1910): 200. *Washington* (D.C.) *Post*, 6 November 1910, sporting section, 4. *Globe & Commercial Advertiser* (New York), 29 October 1910, 2. *The Sun* (New York), 30 October 1910, 1–2.
11. *Aviation* 1.10 (December 1910): 354. *Philadelphia Inquirer*, 2 November 1910, 2. Curtiss, 115.

*United States Naval Institute Proceedings* 37.1 (March 1911): 163.
   12. *Globe & Commercial Advertiser* (New York), 27 October 1910, 2. *New York Times*, 8 December 1910, 4; 17 January 1912, 14. *The Sun* (New York), 23 October 1910, 1.
   13. *The State* (Columbia, SC), 4 December 1910, 5. *The Sun* (New York), 23 October 1910, 2. *The World* (New York), 22 October 1910, night edition, 1. *New York Herald*, 23 October 1910, 1. *Aeronautics* 7.6 (December 1910): 205.
   14. *Aircraft* 1.10 (December 1910): 357–358. *Aeronautics* 7.6 (December 1910): 204–206. Johnstone's Wright had a 26-foot wingspan while the Baby Wright spanned 21 feet for an 8-cylinder and 22 feet for a 4-cylinder. The standard Wright had a wingspan of 39 feet. *Aircraft* 1.10 (December 1910): 355.
   15. *Aeronautics* 7.6 (December 1910): 204–206.
   16. *New York Daily Tribune*, 28 October 1910, 5. *Washington (D.C.) Post*, 6 November 1910, sporting section, 4. *The Sun* (New York), 24 October 1910, 2.
   17. *Indianapolis Star*, 4 December 1910, sec. 2:21. *The Sun* (New York), 1 November 1910, 3. *Baltimore American*, 28 October 1910, 11; 1 November 1910, 16. *The Sun* (Baltimore), 10 November 1910, 11. *Washington (D.C.) Times*, 2 November 1910, 3.

## Chapter 24

   1. *Baltimore American*, 10 August 1905, 14. *The Sun* (Baltimore), 16 October 1910, 16; 24 October 1910, 16; 2 November 1910, 16; 3 November 1910, 12.
   2. *The Sun* (Baltimore), 2 November 1910, 1, 16.
   3. *The Sun* (Baltimore), 2 November 1910, 1, 10.
   4. *The Sun* (Baltimore), 30 October 1910, 16; 3 November 1910, 16.
   5. Ibid. *The Sun* (Baltimore), 3 November 1910, 13.
   6. Ibid.
   7. *The Sun* (Baltimore), 5 November 1910, 10
   8. *The Sun* (Baltimore), 3 November 1910, 13.
   9. Ibid.
   10. *The Sun* (Baltimore), 2 November 1910, 1, 10; 3 November 1910, 12. *Washington (D.C.) Post*, 8 November 1910, 1.
   11. *Baltimore American*, 8 November 1910, 6. *The Sun* (Baltimore), 8 November 1910, 16.
   12. *The Sun* (Baltimore), 3 November 1910, 13. *Baltimore American*, 4 November 1910, 1, 11.
   13. *Baltimore American*, 4 November 1910, 11.
   14. *Baltimore American*, 4 November 1910, 14; 5 November 1910, 1, 13. *Washington (D.C.) Post*, 5 November 1910, 4.
   15. *Baltimore American*, 5 November 1910, 13; 6 November 1910, 12.
   16. *The Sun* (Baltimore), 11 November 1910, 10.
   17. *Baltimore American*, 5 November 1910, 13.
   18. *The Sun* (Baltimore), 6 November 1910, 7.
   19. *Baltimore American*, 5 November 1910, 10.
   20. *Baltimore American*, 6 November 1910, 12; 8 November 1910, 1, 6. *The Sun* (Baltimore), 9 November 1910, 16.
   21. *The Sun* (Baltimore), 10 November 1910, 11; 11 November 1910, 10.
   22. *The Sun* (Baltimore), 11 November 1910, 10.
   23. *The Sun* (Baltimore), 10 November 1910, 11; 12 November 1910, 8.

## Chapter 25

   1. *New York Times*, 2 August 1907, 1; Sunday magazine, 16 February 1908, 7. *Cedar Rapids Evening Gazette*, 27 November 1907, 6. *The Sun* (Baltimore), 9 February 1908, 3. *Washington (D.C.) Post*, 9 February 1908, 2. *The World* (New York), 10 November 1910, 1.
   2. *Trenton (NJ) Evening Times*, 5 October 1909, 11. *Salt Lake Telegram*, 1 October 1908, 2. *The Sun* (Baltimore), 15 August 1908, 2; 31 August 1909, 4. *United States Naval Institute Proceedings* 36.4 (December 1910), 1190.
   3. *Seattle Daily Times*, 25 October 1910, 22. *Washington (D.C.) Herald*, 3 November 1910, 1. Department of the Navy, Naval Historical Center, "The History of U.S. Naval Aviation, 1–3," http://www.history.navy.mil/avh-1910/PART01.PDF (14 December 2008). Captain W. Irving Chambers, "Aviation and Aeroplanes," *United States Naval Institute Proceedings* 37.1 (March 1911): 163, 194.
   4. *Daily Eagle* (Poughkeepsie, NY), 20 February 1882, 2. Home Page of Jacob George Chambers, http://familytreemaker.genealogy.com/users/c/h/a/Melissa-D-Chambers/index.html. (11 August 2010). Kingston (NY) *Daily Freeman*, 13 February 1879, 2; 11 September 1959, 8A. Lewis Randolph Hamersly, *The Records Of Living Officers Of The U. S. Navy And Marine Corps, Sixth Edition* (New York: L. R. Hamersly, 1898), 190. Ensign W. I. Chambers, "Notes On the Nicaragua Ship Canal," *United States Naval Institute Proceedings* 11.4 (October 1885).
   5. Chambers letter to Orville Wright, 24 March 1930, The Wilbur and Orville Wright Papers, General Correspondence: Chambers, Washington Irving, 29–30, http://hdl.loc.gov/loc.mss/mwright.0305813 (August 2006).
   6. Curtiss, 116–117. *The World* (New York), 4 November 1910, 1. *New York Times*, 3 November 1910, 1.
   7. Ibid.
   8. *New York Times*, 24 November 1910, 18. (New York, NY) *The World*, 4 November 1910, 1.
   9. *New York Herald*, 5 November 1910, 1.
   10. *New York Times*, 9 September 1910, 4.
   11. *The World* (New York), 4 November 1910, 1.
   12. *The Sun* (New York), 5 November 1910, 1. *Washington (D.C.) Post*, 8 November 1910, 2.
   13. Rear Admiral George van Deurs, *Wings for the Fleet* (Annapolis, MD: United States Naval Institute, 1966), 17–18.
   14. *Washington (D.C.) Post*, 7 November 1910, 12. van Deurs, 18.
   15. Ibid., National Cyclopaedia of American Biography, v. 14, no. 1 (New York: James T. White, 1910 ), 413.
   16. *Charlotte Observer*, 12 November 1910, 1; 13 November 1910, 7. *Colorado Springs Gazette*, 12 November 1910, 2.
   17. Curtiss, 117. *New York Times*, 13 November 1910, 8. *Washington (D.C.) Post*, 13 November 1910, 8.
   18. Chambers, 174. Papers of Washington Irving Chambers, Library of Congress Manuscript MSS50799, www.loc.gov/ (April 2007). A Navy constructor, as an officer, is an engineer/architect who builds things for the service.
   19. *Baltimore American*, 12 November 1910, 8.
   20. Ibid.
   21. *The Sun* (Baltimore), 12 November 1910, 8.
   22. *The Sun* (Baltimore), 13 November 1910, 16.
   23. Chambers, 174.
   24. Ibid. *The Sun* (Baltimore),

17 August 1907, 10. "Mars Flies at Norfolk," *Washington* (D.C.) *Post*, 2 November 1910, 5. *New York Times*, 14 November 1910, 2. *Anaconda* (MT) *Standard*, 15 June 1911, 11. Norfolk Yacht and Country Club, www.norfolkyacht.com/ (18 August 2010).
  25. *Mansfield* (OH) *News*, 14 November 1910, 2. Chambers, 175.
  26. Ibid. *The Sun* (New York), 15 November 1910, 1–2.
  27. Ibid. Curtiss, 118.
  28. *The Sun* (New York), 15 November 1910, 1–2. *Democrat and Chronicle* (Rochester), 15 November 1910, 1. *Oregonian* (Portland), 15 November 1910, 3. Chambers, 176.
  29. *Baltimore American*, 16 November 1910, 9. *New York Times*, 15 November 1910, 1.
  30. *Newport* (RI) *Daily News*, 18 November 1910, 7.
  31. *Washington* (D.C.) *Herald*, 17 November 1910, 1. *Washington* (D.C.) *Times*, 23 November 1910, 3.
  32. *The Sun (New York)*, 15 November 1910, 2.

## Chapter 26

  1. *Washington* (D.C.) *Post*, 13 November 1910, 9. *Charlotte Observer*, 1 November 1910, 1. Aerofiles, "Chase-Gouverneur," www.aerofiles.com/_ca.html (20 August 2010).
  2. *Charlotte Observer*, 21 November 1910, 7.
  3. *Mansfield* (OH) *News*, 17. November 1910, 1. *Charlotte Observer*, 17 November 1910, 1; 18 November 1910, 1. *Washington* (D.C.) *Post*, 17 November 1910, 3.
  4. *Waterloo Times*, 18 November 1910, 1. *Charlotte Observer*, 19 November 1910, 4.
  5. *Charlotte Observer*, 17 November 1910, 1; 18 November 1910, 1.
  6. Birmingham Alabama Public Library, www.bham.lib.al.us/resources/government/BirminghamPopulation.aspx (21 August 2008). *Columbus* (GA) *Daily Enquirer*, 17 November 1910, 1
  7. *New Orleans Item*, 1 December 1910, 12.
  8. *Montgomery Advertiser*, 22 March 1910, 9. *Owosso* (MI) *Argus-Press*, 14 September 1954, 9. Wright & Ditson Co., *Wright & Ditson's Lawn Tennis Guide* (Boston: Wright & Ditson, 1914), 89.
  9. *Aeronautics* 8.1 (January 1911): 25.
  10. *Daily Picayune* (New Orleans), 22 November 1910, 10; 23 November 1910, 10. *Montgomery Advertiser*, 25 November 1910, 7.
  11. *New Orleans Item*, 25 November 1910, 14. *Montgomery Advertiser*, 26 November 1910, 5.
  12. *Daily Picayune* (New Orleans), 21 November 1910, 9. *Daily Herald* (Gulfport, MS), 22 November 1910, 1.
  13. *Montgomery Advertiser*, 30 November 1910, 6. *Daily Picayune* (New Orleans), 30 November 1910, 12.
  14. Roseberry, 228. Steven R. Hoffbeck, "Shooting Star," *Minnesota History* 54.8 (Winter 1995): 333. *New Orleans Item*, 25 November 1910, 14. *Daily Picayune* (New Orleans), 29 November 1910, 10; 1 December 1910, 12.
  15. *New Orleans Item*, 26 November 1910, 1; 28 November 1910, 5.
  16. *New Orleans Item*, 28 November 1910, 5; 29 November 1910, 10.
  17. *Daily Picayune* (New Orleans), 29 November 1910, 10; 1 December 1910, 12.
  18. *New Orleans Item*, 28 November 1910, 8; 2 December 1910, 14; 9 December 1910, 13.
  19. *Daily Picayune* (New Orleans), 2 December 1910, 10.
  20. *New Orleans Item*, 2 December 1910, 12. *Daily Picayune* (New Orleans), 3 December 1910, 10; 4 December 1910, 14; 5 December 1910, 8; 6 December 1910, 6. *The State* (Columbia, SC), 6 December 1910, 9.
  21. *Daily Picayune* (New Orleans), 7 December 1910, 2, 8; 11 December 1910, 14; 12 December 1910, 12.
  22. *The State* (Columbia, SC), 17 November 1910, 3; 18 November 1910, 6.
  23. *The State* (Columbia, SC), 7 December 1910, 1.
  24. *The State* (Columbia, SC), 8 December 1910, 1.
  25. *Augusta Chronicle*, 9 December 1910, A5; 11 December 1910, A8. *Macon Weekly Telegraph*, 27 July 1912, 10.
  26. *The State* (Columbia, SC), 9 December 1910, 1.
  27. *The State* (Columbia, SC), 11 December 1910, 10; 12 December 1910, 12.
  28. *Augusta Chronicle*, 16 December 1910, 2. *Columbus* (GA) *Ledger-Enquirer*, 18 December 1910, 1. *Oregonian* (Portland), 25 December 1910, sec. 4:7.
  29. *Aeronautics* 8.2 (February 1911): 60. *The State* (Columbia, SC), 21 December 1910, 5.

## Chapter 27

  1. *The Sun* (Baltimore), 3 November 1910, 12. *The Call* (San Francisco), 9 December 1910, 8; 17 December 1910, 3.
  2. *Los Angeles Herald*, 19 December 1910, 2. *The Call* (San Francisco), 14 December 1910, 7; 21 December 1910, 8.
  3. *Los Angeles Herald*, 19 December 1910, 1–2. *Seattle Daily Times*, 22 December 1910, 14. *Oakland Tribune*, 25 December 1910, 6.
  4. *Oakland Tribune*, 25 December 1910, 6.
  5. Curtiss, 118–119, 222. *New York Herald*, 24 December 1910, 1. *Muskegon* (MI) *Chronicle*, 26 December 1910, 1. *Washington* (D.C.) *Post*, 24 December 1910, 4.
  6. *Los Angeles Herald*, 9 December 1910, 1; 31 December 1910, 7. *Oregonian* (Portland), 23 December 1910, 1, 3.
  7. *Los Angeles Herald*, 11 December 1910, 1, 3.
  8. *Los Angeles Herald*, 25 December 1910, 1; 27 December 1910, 10.
  9. *Aeronautics* 8.2 (February 1911): 55.
  10. *Los Angeles Herald*, 12 December 1910, 12; 24 December 1910, 12.
  11. *Aeronautics* 8.3 (March 1911): 88. *Aerofiles*, www.aerofiles.com/_curt.html (5 February 2002).
  12. *Los Angeles Herald*, 25 December 1910, 1, 4; 26 December 1910, 12. *The Call* (San Francisco), 25 December 1910, 60. *Aeronautics* 8.2 (February 1911): 54.
  13. *Los Angeles Herald*, 28 December 1910, 1; 29 December 1910, 1; 30 December 1910, 1; 31 December 1910, 7.
  14. The Wilbur and Orville Wright Papers at the Library of Congress, Scrapbooks: December 1910-March 1914, image 29, http://memory.loc.gov/master/mss/mwright/05/05005/0029.jpg (25 April 2007). *Los Angeles Herald*, 30 April 1910, 14. *Montgomery Advertiser*, 24 May 1910, 5. *The Call* (San Francisco), 1 January 1911, 30.
  15. *The Call* (San Francisco), 14 June 1910, 1. *Los Angeles Herald*, 14 June 1910, 3. *New York Tribune*, 17 June 1910, 3. *Idaho Statesman* (Boise), 24 June 1910, 4. *New York Times*, 12 October 1910, 1. *Seattle Times*, 1 January 1911, 5.
  16. The Wilbur and Orville

Wright Papers at the Library of Congress, Scrapbooks: December 1910-March 1914, image 24. *The World* (New York), 1 January 1911, 1.

17. *Los Angeles Herald*, 10 December 1910, 1; 25 December 1910, 1, 4; 26 December 1910, 1; 27 December 1910, 1, 7. *The Call* (San Francisco), 25 December 1910, 60.

18. *Los Angeles Herald*, 27 December 1910, 1, 7.

19. *Los Angeles Herald*, 28 December 1910, 1.

20. *Seattle Daily Times*, 1 January 1911, 1, 3, 5. *New York Tribune*, 1 January 1911, 2. *The Sun* (Medford, OR), 31 January 1911, 6.

21. *Seattle Daily Times*, 1 January 1911, 3.

22. *Washington* (D.C.) *Post*, 1 January 1911, 2. *New York Tribune*, 1 January 1911, 1. *Seattle Times*, 1 January 1911, 5. *The Call* (San Francisco), 1 January 1911, 30.

23. *Oakland Tribune*, 1 January 1911, 16.

24. *Oakland Tribune*, 1 January 1911, 16.

25. *Seattle Daily Times*, 1 January 1911, 3. *San Francisco Chronicle*, 5 January 1911, 1.

26. *Oregonian* (Portland), 2 January 1911, 3.

27. *Seattle Daily Times*, 2 January 1911, 11. *Rockford* (IL) *Republic*, 3 January 1911, 2. *Oakland Tribune*, 3 January 1911, sec. 2:1.

28. *The Call* (San Francisco), 4 January 1911, 2.

29. *San Francisco Chronicle*, 5 January 1911, 1. *The Call* (San Francisco), 5 January 1911, 16.

30. *New York Times*, 1 January 1911, 1. *Oregonian* (Portland) 2 January 1911, 3. *Seattle Times*, 1 January 1911, 5. *San Francisco Chronicle*, 5 January 1911, 1.

## Chapter 28

1. *The Call* (San Francisco), 10 August 1910, 15. *Idaho Statesman* (Boise), 18 October 1910, 1.

2. *Duluth News-Tribune*, 23 December 1910, 10. *Los Angeles Herald*, 30 October 1910, 8.

3. *The Call* (San Francisco), 21 November 1910, 1; 22 November 1910, 15; 30 November 1910, 15.

4. *Los Angeles Herald*, 5 December 1910, 1; 12 December 1910, 1. *Vallejo Daily Times*, 10 December 1910, 3. *The Call* (San Francisco), 29 March 1910, 3. *Albuquerque Journal*, 16 December 1910, 1. *Annual report of the Secretary of the Navy* (Washington, D.C.: Government Printing Office, 1912), 64–72.

5. *The Call* (San Francisco), 23 August 1903, 25; 28 July 1905, 1. *Washington* (D.C.) *Times*, 10 August 1901, 5; 23 August 1903, 3. *Hawaiian Gazette* (Honolulu), 17 September 197, sec. 2:1–2. *Seattle Star*, 6 July 1907, 2.

6. *The Call* (San Francisco), 22 June 1909, 15. "Commander John Rodgers, Hawaii Aviation," http://hawaii.gov/hawaiiaviation/hawaii-aviation-pioneers/john-rodgers/commander-john-rodgers (13 October 2010).

7. *The Call* (San Francisco), 26 December 1910, 3.

8. *The Call* (San Francisco), 2 January 1911, 19; 3 January 1911, 15.

9. San Francisco Chronicle, 5 January 1911, 1.

10. Ibid. *San Jose Mercury News*, 5 January 1911, 1. *The Call* (San Francisco), 8 January 1911, 30.

11. *Oakland Tribune*, 5 January 1911, 6. *The Call* (San Francisco), 5 January 1911, 16; 6. January 1911, 6; 8 January 1911, 31–32. *Official Army Register for 1911* (Washington, D.C.: Adjutant General's Office, 1. December 1910), 382.

12. *Oakland Tribune*, 5 January 1911, 6. *The Call* (San Francisco), 5 January 1911, 16; 6 January 1911, 6.

13. Rufus F. Zogbaum, *From Sail to Saratoga* (Rome, NY: self-published, 1961), 140. "Commander John Rodgers, Hawaii Aviation," http://hawaii.gov/hawaiiavation/hawaii-aviation-pioneers/john-rodgers/commander-john-rodgers (13 October 2010). *Aeronautics* 8.3 (March 1911): 95–97. *Vallejo Daily Times*, 6 January 1911, 1.

14. *The Call* (San Francisco), 2 January 1911, 11; 3 January 1911, 3.

15. Chambers, "Aviation and Aeroplanes," *United States Naval Institute Proceedings* 37.1 (March 1911): 174, 176.

16. Chambers, "Aviation and Aeroplanes," *United States Naval Institute Proceedings* 37.1 (March 1911): 192. *The Call* (San Francisco), 10 January 1911, 3.

17. Ibid. Jack Carpenter, "Glenn H. Curtiss: Founder of the American Aviation Industry," www.glennhcurtiss.com (23 January 2003).

18. Ibid. *The Call* (San Francisco), 19 January 1911, 3. Curtiss, 120. van Deurs, 26. *Grand Forks Herald*, 24 September 1911, 2. *Neosho* (MO) *Daily News*, 8 April 1963, 3.

19. Naval History and Heritage Command, "Eugene Ely's Flight to U.S.S. *Pennsylvania*, 18 January 1911—Preparations and Spectators," www.history.navy.mil/index.html (2 November 2004). *The Call* (San Francisco), 9 January 1911, 5; 10 January 1911, 3.

20. *San Francisco Chronicle*, 10 January 1911, 5.

21. Ibid.

## Chapter 29

1. *The Call* (San Francisco), 19 December 1910, 2; 7 January 1911, 2.

2. *The Call* (San Francisco), 9 January 1911, 3; 10 January 1911, 3. California State Parks, brochure, *Mt. Tamalpais State Park*, Sacramento, 2007.

3. *The Call* (San Francisco), 8 January 1911, children's section, 1.

4. *The Call* (San Francisco), 2 January 1911, 4; 3 January 1911, 3.

5. *The Call* (San Francisco), 8 January 1911, magazine section, 3.

6. *Aeronautics* 8.3 (March 1911): 96–97. *The Call* (San Francisco), 18 January 1911, 2; 23 January 1911, 3. The Early Birds of Aviation CHIRP, November 1961, No. 67, www.rcooper.0catch.com/ewiseman.htm (21 November 2005).

7. Ibid.

8. *The Call* (San Francisco), 21 July 1910, 8; 12 September 1910, 3; 11 January 1911, 1, 3. *Evening Bulletin* (Honolulu), 10 May 1911, 10. *Herald-Republican* (Salt Lake City), 12 September 1910, 1; 4 January 1911, 10. *Evening Standard* (Ogden City, UT), 5 January 1911, 4. *Los Angeles Herald*, 31 December 1910, 7. *Salt Lake Telegram*, 8 February 10. *Aeronautics* 8.3 (March 1911): 97.

9. *Oakland Tribune*, 7 January 1911, 1–2.

10. *Oakland Tribune*, 7 January 1911, 2. *The Call* (San Francisco), 8 January 1911, 29.

11. *The Call* (San Francisco), 8 January 1911, 32.

12. *The Call* (San Francisco), 8 January 1911, 29; 9 January 1911, 3.

13. *The Call* (San Francisco), 8 January 1911, 29, 30, 32.

14. *Colorado Springs Gazette*, 2 January 1911, 1. *The Call* (San Francisco), 8 January 1911, 30, 31.

15. *The Call* (San Francisco), 6 January 1911, 6; 8 January 1911, 32.

16. Ibid.

17. *Oakland Tribune*, 9 January 1911, 3. *The Call* (San Francisco), 9 January 1911, 2, 3.
18. *The Call* (San Francisco), 9 January 1911, 2.
19. *The Call* (San Francisco), 9 January 1911, 13, 14; 10 January 1911, 1, 3.
20. San Francisco Chronicle, 10 January 1911, 5.
21. *The Call* (San Francisco), 10 January 1911, 1.

## Chapter 30

1. San Francisco Chronicle, 10 January 1911, 5.
2. San Francisco Chronicle, 11 January 1911, 3.
3. *The Call* (San Francisco), 11 January 1911, 1, 3.
4. *The Call* (San Francisco), 10 January 1911, 3. *San Francisco Chronicle*, 11 January 1911, 8.
5. *The Call* (San Francisco), 11 January 1911, 3.
6. *The Call* (San Francisco), 17 January 1911, 2.
7. Ibid. San Francisco Chronicle, 22 January 1911, 28.
8. *Daily Herald* (Gulfport, MS), 11 January 1911, 3.
9. *The Call* (San Francisco), 11 January 1911, 3.
10. *The Call* (San Francisco), 11 January 1911, 1, 3.
11. Ibid. *Oregonian* (Portland), 11 January 1911, 2. *San Francisco Chronicle*, 11 January 1911, 3.
12. *The Call* (San Francisco), 11 January 1911, 3.
13. *San Francisco Chronicle*, 11 January 1911, 8. *The Call* (San Francisco), 11 January 1911, 3. *New York Times*, 11 January 1911, 1. *Oregonian* (Portland), 11 January 1911, 2.
14. *The Call* (San Francisco), 11 January 1911, 3.
15. San Francisco Chronicle, 11 January 1911, 8.
16. *The Call* (San Francisco), 12 January 1911, 3; 15 January 1911, 33.
17. *The Call* (San Francisco), 13 January 1911, 14; 15 January 1911, 33; 16 January 1911, 2.
18. *The Call* (San Francisco), 14 January 1911, 3; 15 January 1911, 47.
19. *The Call* (San Francisco), 15 January 1911, 33; 16 January 1911, 2.
20. *The Call* (San Francisco), 16 January 1911, 3. *Herald* (New York), 16 January 1911, 2.
21. *The Call* (San Francisco), 16 January 1911, 1; 21 January 1911, children's section, 5.
22. *The Call* (San Francisco), 16. January 1911, 1, 2.
23. *The Call* (San Francisco), 17 January 1911, 1–2.
24. Ibid.
25. Ibid.
26. *The Call* (San Francisco), 11 January 1911, 3.

## Chapter 31

1. Mills interview from *The Call* (San Francisco), 9 April 1911, Sunday magazine, 8.
2. *The Call* (San Francisco), 19 January 1911, 2, 6.
3. United States Naval Institute Proceedings 37.1 (March 1911): 192–193.
4. Ibid., 195. *Oakland Tribune*, 18 January 1911, 1.
5. Rear Admiral George van Deurs, *Wings for the Fleet* (Annapolis, MD: United States Naval Institute, 1966), 20. *The Call* (San Francisco), 19 January 1911, 3; 9 April 1911, Sunday magazine, 8. *Oregonian* (Portland), 15 November 1910, 3.
6. Macon Daily Telegraph, 20 October 1911, 2. Ely's Pennsylvania helmet and his flying license have been preserved at the Hiller Aviation Museum in San Carlos, California.
7. United States Naval Institute Proceedings 37.1 (March 1911): 195.
8. Ibid. *The Call* (San Francisco), 9 September 1900, 1; 10 September 1900, 12. *Vallejo Daily Times*, 19 January 1911, 8. *U.S. Coast and Geodetic Survey: Notice to Mariners*, No. 254 (January 1900), 9. The May Flint buoy was repaired so many times the Coast Guard considered removing it; however, by 1908, the buoy played such a prominent part in society yacht races that the plan was abandoned.
9. *The Call* (San Francisco), 19 January 1911, 2.
10. United States Naval Institute Proceedings 37.1 (March 1911): 194.
11. Ibid., 193, 195. *The Call* (San Francisco), 19 January 1911, 2.
12. United States Naval Institute Proceedings 37.1 (March 1911): 195.
13. Ibid. *San Francisco Chronicle*, 19 January 1911, 1. *The Call* (San Francisco), 19 January 1911, 2.
14. San Francisco Chronicle, 19 January 1911, 1. New York Times, 19 January 1911, 1. United States Naval Institute Proceedings 37.1 (March 1911): 195.
15. United States Naval Institute Proceedings 37.1 (March 1911): 194.
16. *Vallejo Daily Times*, 19 January 1911, 1, 8. *The Call* (San Francisco), 19 January 1911, 1.
17. *The Call* (San Francisco), 19 January 1911, 2.
18. *The Call* (San Francisco), 19 January 1911, 3.
19. *San Francisco Chronicle*, 19 January 1911, 2. *Vallejo Daily Times*, 19 January 1911, 1.
20. United States Naval Institute Proceedings 37.1 (March 1911): 194.
21. *Vallejo Daily Times*, 19 January 1911, 1. *New York Times*, 19 January 1911, 1. *The Call* (San Francisco), 19 January 1911, 3. *San Francisco Examiner*, 19 January 1911, 1.
22. *The Call* (San Francisco), 9 April 1911, Sunday magazine, 8. *The Call* (San Francisco), 20 January 1911, 6.
23. *The Call* (San Francisco), 19 January 1911, 3; 9 April 1911, Sunday magazine, 8. *San Francisco Chronicle*, 19 January 1911, 1.
24. *The Call* (San Francisco), 19 January 1911, 3.
25. Curtiss, 120–124.
26. *The Call* (San Francisco), 20 January 1911, 5. *San Francisco Chronicle*, 20 January 1911, 16

## Chapter 32

1. *San Francisco Chronicle*, 22 January 1911, 8. *The Call* (San Francisco), 22 January 1911, 25. *Oakland Tribune*, 22 January 1911, 21.
2. E. E. Ennis, "Wireless Telegraphy from an Aeroplane," *Journal of Electricity, Power and Gas* 26.13 (1 April 1911): 279–280. *Crocker-Langley San Francisco Directory for the Year Commencing 1911* (San Francisco: H. S. Crocker, 1911), 579. *The Call* (San Francisco), 22 January 1911, 17.
3. *San Francisco Chronicle*, 22 January 1911, 8. *The Call* (San Francisco), 22 January 1911, 25; 23 January 1911, 2. Ennis, 279.
4. *Oakland Tribune*, 22 January 1911, 21. *San Francisco Chronicle*, 22 January 1911, 8.
5. *The Call* (San Francisco), 21 January 1911, 13; 23 January 1911, 2.
6. *The Call* (San Francisco), 25 December 1910, 31.
7. *New York Times*, 26 November 1910, 2; 29 April 1912.
8. *Oregonian* (Portland), 26 November 1910, 13.
9. *The Call* (San Francisco),

26 December 1910, 6; 27 July 1911, 1.
10. *The Call* (San Francisco), 24 December 1910, 1.
11. *San Francisco Bulletin*, 25 January 1875, 18; 9 September 1875, 2. *The Call*, 26 December 1910, 29, 30.
12. *The Call* (San Francisco), 25 December 1910, 29, 30.
13. *The Call* (San Francisco), 25 December 1910, 32.
14. *Wyoming* (NY) *Reporter*, 29 March 1911, 3.
15. *The Call* (San Francisco), 29 December 1910, 14; 1 January 1911, 32; 19 January 19 1911, 6; 23 January 1911, 1. *Oregonian* (Portland), 6 December 1910, 1. Tetrazzini's dog was a Mexican Hairless.
16. The Call (San Francisco), 21 January 1911, 24.
17. *The Call* (San Francisco), 23 January 1911, 1, 3, 2.
18. *The Call* (San Francisco), 23 January 1911, 3.
19. Ibid.
20. Ibid.
21. *The Call (San Francisco)*, 23 January 1911, 2, 3.
22. *The Call* (San Francisco), 23 January 1911, 2. *Oregonian* (Portland), 23 January 1911, 3.
23. *The Call* (San Francisco), 23 January 1911, 3.
24. *San Antonio Light*, 25 January 1911, 11.

## Chapter 33

1. Curtiss, 125.
2. Curtiss, 123, 125. Roseberry, 310–311.
3. San Diego County Quadrangle, CA, topographic map, 15 minute series, U.S. Department of the Interior, June 1904. Wallace R. Peck, "Forgotten Air Pioneers: The Army's Rockwell Field at North Island," *Journal of San Diego History* 52.3 (Summer 2006), 104. *San Diego Union-Tribune*, 7 May 1995, H2.
4. Curtiss, 124, 126–127. Peck, 104–105.
5. *San Francisco Chronicle*, 20 January 1911, 16; 24 January 1911, 7. Curtiss, 129, 221.
6. Curtiss, 130–131.
7. *The Call* (San Francisco), 27 January 1911, 4. Curtiss, 131, 132.
8 *Washington* (D.C.) *Post*, 27 January 1911, 1, 28 January 1911, 6. *The Call* (San Francisco), 28 January 1911, 13.
9. *Oakland Tribune*, 28 January 1911, 4. The U.S. Grant Hotel was built by Ulysses S. Grant, Jr. and opened October 15, 1910. Still stands (2012) at 326 Broadway, San Diego, CA.
10. *Fort Wayne Sentinel*, 28 January 1911, 3.
11. *San Diego Union*, 29 January 1911, 1. *The Call* (San Francisco), 29 January 1911, 17. *Los Angeles Times*, 29 January 1911, 19. *Aeronautics* 8.3 (March 1911): 98.
12. *Aeronautics* 8.3 (March 1911): 98.
13. Ibid. *The Call* (San Francisco), 30 January 1911, 7. *Oregonian* (Portland), 30 January 1911, 3. *Oakland Tribune*, 30 January 1911, 16.
14. *Washington* (D.C.) *Times*, 18 January 1911, 6. *The Call* (San Francisco), 18 January 1911, 2; 9 April 1911, Sunday magazine, 8.
15. The Papers of Washington Irving Chambers [part of the Wilbur and Orville Wright Papers], letter dated San Diego, California, January 30, 1911, Library of Congress Manuscript Division, Washington, D.C., http://memory.loc.gov/ammem/wrighthtml/wrighthome.html. (22 December 2006).
16. *The Call* (San Francisco), 5 February 1911, 22.
17. Papers of Washington Irving Chambers, letter dated Davenport, Iowa, February 24, 1911.
18 *Washington* (D.C.) *Times*, 28 January 1911, 1. *Times Dispatch* (Richmond), 31 January 1911, 1. *Oakland Tribune*, 5 February 1911, 1. *Salt Lake Telegram*, 17 February 1911, 12. *Goodwin's Weekly* (Salt Lake City), 18 February 1911, 8.
19. *United States Naval Institute Proceedings* 37.1 (March 1911): 201. Curtiss, 133–134.
20. *San Jose Mercury News*, 5 February 1911, 11. *The Call* (San Francisco), 6 February 1911, 7; 7 February 1911, 7.
21. Papers of Washington Irving Chambers, letter dated Washington, D.C., 9 February 1911.
22. Ibid.

## Chapter 34

1. *Medford* (OR) *Mail Tribune*, 4 June 1911, 1.
2. *Colorado Springs Gazette*, 2 January 1911, 1. The Call (San Francisco), 9 April 1911, 8. Oakland Tribune, 1 January 1911, 16. Cedar Rapids Evening Gazette, 4 January 1911, 1.
3. *The Call* (San Francisco), 20 October 1911, 2. Edward Lyell Fox, "Fatalism of The Fliers," *The Century Illustrated Monthly Magazine* 83.6 (April 1912): 846.
4. *Washington* (D.C.) *Post*, 31 August 1913, magazine section, 1. *Waterloo Evening Courier*, 21 October 1911, 1.
5. Ibid. *Weekly Sentinel* (Fort Wayne), 12 May 1913, 1.
6. *Williamsburg* (IA) *Journal-Tribune*, 28 September 1911, 6. Hill Aerospace Museum, "Flying Machines Over Zion," Chapter 2, www.hill.af.mil/library/factsheets (22 June 2006).
7. *Daily Oregon Statesman* (Salem), 6 June 1911, 1. *Cedar Rapids Evening Gazette*, 23 July 1910, 1.*Medford* (OR) *Mail Tribune*, 4 June 1911, 1. *Iowa City Daily Press*, 14 August 1911, 5. *New York Tribune*, 20 October 1911, 1. *San Antonio Light*, 25 January 1911, 11. *Fort Wayne Sentinel*, 28 January 1911, 3.
8 *New York American*, 20 October 1911, 1. *Medford* (OR) *Mail Tribune*, 4 June 1911, 6.

## Chapter 35

1. *Evening Bulletin* (Honolulu), 20 April 1911, 10.
2. Ibid. *Salt Lake Telegram*, 4 February 1911, 16; 6 February 1911, 10.
3. Ernest Victor Fohlin, *Salt Lake City, Past and Present* (Salt Lake City, 1908), 124. *Salt Lake Herald*, 21 February 1893, 8. *Goodwin's Weekly* (Salt Lake City), 4 February 1911, 4, 18.
4. *Deseret News* (Salt Lake City), 8 February 1911, 2. *Salt Lake Telegram*, 31 January 1911, 10; 2 February 1911, 1; 8 February 10.
5. *Goodwin's Weekly* (Salt Lake City), 4 February 1911, 18. *Deseret News* (Salt Lake City), 8 February 1911, 2. *Salt Lake Telegram*, 8 February 10.
6. *Deseret News* (Salt Lake City), 8 February 1911, 2.
7. *Salt Lake Telegram*, 4 February 1911, 16.
8 Hill Aerospace Museum, Flying Machines Over Zion, Chapter 2, www.hill.af.mil/library/factsheets (22 June 2006).
9. *Goodwin's Weekly* (Salt Lake City), 4 February 1911, 4. *Park* (UT) *Record*, 4 February 1911, p. 1. *Salt Lake Telegram*, 21 January 1911, 1; 9 February 1911, 10; 18 February 1911, 6.
10. *Salt Lake Telegram*, 9 February 1911, 10.
11. *Oakland Tribune*, 6 February 1911, 7. *Salt Lake Telegram*, 8 February 10.
12. *Salt Lake Telegram*, 9 February 1911, 3; 10 February 1911, 2, 7; 11 February 1911, 9.

13. *Salt Lake Telegram*, 11 February 1911, 8.
14. *Grand Valley Times* (Moab, UT), 17 February 1911, 6. *Salt Lake Telegram*, 13 February 1911, 1, 10.
15. *Salt Lake Telegram*, 13 February 1911, 10. *Logan* (UT) *Republican*, 14 February 1911, 1; 15 February 1911, 10; 17 February 1911, 12; 18 February 1911, 1.
16. *Goodwin's Weekly* (Salt Lake City), 11 February 1911, 10; 18 February 1911, 8.
17. *Salt Lake Telegram*, 13 February 1911, 10.
18 *Washington* (D.C.) *Post*, 13 February 1911, 12. *Salt Lake Telegram*, 13 February 1911, 1; 14 February 1911, 10. *Aeronautics* 8.4 (April 1911): 122. *Oakland Tribune*, 12 March 1911, 19. *Bellingham Herald*, 2 April 1911, sec. 2:14.
19. Dunlop Collection, "Oath and Enlistment Papers—Eugene Burton Ely."
20. *Salt Lake Telegram*, 15 February 1911, 8, 10; 16 February 1911, 10.
21. *Salt Lake Telegram*, 16 February 1911, 10; 17 February 1911, 12.
22. *Salt Lake Telegram*, 17 February 1911, 1.
23. *Salt Lake Telegram*, 18 February 1911, 6. *Salt Lake Tribune*, 21 February 1911, 5; 26 February 1911, 23. *Evening Bulletin* (Honolulu), 20 April 1911, 10.
24. *Salt Lake Telegram*, 18 February 1911, 6; 21 February 1911, 5. *Washington* (D.C.) *Herald*, 27 February 1911, 1.

## Chapter 36

1. *Washington* (D.C.) *Herald*, 27 February 1911, 1. *Oakland Tribune*, 12 March 1911, 19.
2. *Evening News* (San Jose), 28 February 1911, 3. Papers of Washington Irving Chambers, letter dated Washington, D.C., March 1, 1911.
3. *Evening News* (San Jose), 3 March 1911, 3. *Bakersfield Californian*, 3 March 1911, sec. 2:1.
4 *Oakland Tribune*, 10. March 1911, 4; 18 March 1911, 7. Larned would win his seventh U.S. Open title later that fall.
5. *Evening News* (San Jose), 28 February 1911, 3.
6. *The Call* (San Francisco), 4 March 1911, 1. *Evening News* (San Jose), 18 March 1911, 3.
7. *Evening News* (San Jose), 19 March 1911, 2. *Oakland Tribune*, 20 March 1911, 3. *Salt Lake Telegram*, 6 April 1911, 1.

8 Ibid.
9. *Evening News* (San Jose), 19 March 1911, 2. *New York Herald*, 31 March 1911.
10. *Covina* (CA) *Argus*, 25 March 1911, 7. *New York Times*, 16 April 1911, C8. *The Call* (San Francisco), 27 March 1911, 11. *Seattle Daily Times*, 22 March 1911, *Los Angeles Times*, 30 March 1911, I14. *Aeronautics* 8.5 (May 1911): 178.
11. *Washington* (D.C.) *Times*, 15 March 1911, 12; 16 March 1911, 3; 17 March 1911, 3. *San Antonio Light*, 30 March 1911, 1, 3.
12. *Salt Lake Telegram*, 29 March 1911, 7; 3 April 1911, 12.
13. *Salt Lake Telegram*, 1 April 1911, 1.
14. *Salt Lake Telegram*, 4 April 1911, 1; 5 April 1911, 1; 6 April 1911, 1.
15. *Salt Lake Telegram*, 5 April 1911, 1.
16. *Salt Lake Telegram*, 6 April 1911, 1.
17. Ibid.
18 Ibid. *Salt Lake Telegram*, 7 April 1911, 2. *Decatur* (IL) *Review*, 8 April 1911, 5.
19. *Salt Lake Telegram*, 7 April 1911, 2.
20. Ibid.
21. *Salt Lake Telegram*, 7 April 1911, 8; 8 April 1911, 17.
22. *New York Times*, 9 April 1911, C10. *Salt Lake Telegram*, 10 March 1911, 12. *Logan* (UT) *Republican*, 11 April 1911, 1. *Idaho Statesman* (Boise), 9 April 1911, 7. *Aeronautics* 8.3 (March 1911): 86; 8:4 (April 1911): 123.
23. *Salt Lake Telegram*, 6 April 1911, 1. *Idaho Statesman* (Boise), 9 April 1911, 7. *The Call* (San Francisco), 9 April 1911, 17. *Seattle Daily Times*, 9 April 1911, Sunday magazine, 18.
24. *Salt Lake Telegram*, 10 April 1911, 2.
25. *Salt Lake Telegram*, 11 April 1911, 12; 12 April 1911, 3; 17 April 1911, 10. *Goodwin's Weekly* (Salt Lake City), 15 April 1911, 13.
26. *San Antonio Light*, 10 April 1911, 2; 12 April 1911, 8. *New York Times*, 13 April 1911, 2.
27. *Bakersfield Californian*, 10 April 1911, 1; 17 April 1911, 1.
28 *Bakersfield Californian*, 10 April 1911, 1; 14 April 1911, 1.
29. Bakersfield Californian, 14 April 1911, 1.
30. *Bakersfield Californian*, 17 April 1911, 1, 2.
31. Ibid.
32. Bakersfield Californian, 17 April 1911, 2.

## Chapter 37

1. *Washington* (D.C.) *Times*, 21 March 1911, 1.
2. *Rockford* (IL) *Republic*, 24 March 1911, 4. *San Antonio Light*, 30 March 1911, 1, 3.
3. San Antonio Express, 20 April 1911, 7. San Antonio Light, 10 April 1911, 2. Beaumont Enterprise and Journal, 21 April 1911, 6.
4. *Salt Lake Telegram*, 17 April 1911, 10. *Idaho Statesman* (Boise), 14 April 1911, 2; 16 April 1911, 2.
5. *Aeronautics* 7.1 (July 1910): 11; 8:4 (April 1911): 130; 8:5 (May 1911): 170.
6. New York Times, 21 April 1911, 2. Beaumont Enterprise and Journal, 21 April 1911, 1.
7. *Dallas Morning News*, 23 April 1911, 8; 25 April 1911, 2. *Fort Worth Star-Telegram*, 21 April 1911, 8. *Montgomery Advertiser*, 23 April 1911, 22.
8 San Antonio Light, 28 April 1911, 1.
9. *Aeronautics* 8:6 (June 1911): 202. *Galveston Daily News*, 30 April 1911, 2.
10. *Galveston Daily News*, 30 April 1911, 2. *The Call* (San Francisco), 11 May 1911, 18.
11. *Aeronautics* 8.6 (June 1911): 213.
12. *Fort Worth Star-Telegram*, 3 May 1911, 7; 4 May 1911, 4.
13. *New York Times*, 11 May 1911, 2. *The Call* (San Francisco), 11 May 1911, 18. *Aeronautics* 8.6 (June 1911): 213.
14. Ibid. San Antonio National Cemetery (Section A, Grave 117-A), www.cem.va.gov/CEM (15 February 2010). *Kelly Air Force Base was named for 2nd Lt. George Kelly. In the San Antonio Light*, 6 April 1911, 2, James Henning is noted as "James Henning, the chief mechanician of the Curtiss factory at Hammondsport N. Y." In May 1911, he and a partner also purchased a merry-go-round for San Antonio's Exposition Park.
15. *Eureka* (CA) *Herald*, 15 May 1911, 8.
16. *Kansas City Star*, 5 May 1911, 1.
17. *Williamsburg* (IA) *Journal-Tribune*, 11 May 1911, 7. *Oregonian* (Portland), 6 May 1911, 8.
18 *San Antonio Light*, 6 May 1911, 5; 22 May 1911, 12.
19. *Kansas City Star*, 24 January 1904, 7; 10 March 1905, 5; 30 April 1911, 11. *New York Times*, 23 December 1906, SM12; 15 April 1911, 1. *Democrat and*

*Chronicle* (Rochester), 9 August 1910, 15.
   20. *Kansas City Star*, 13 May 1911, 3.
   21. *Oklahoman* (Oklahoma City), 13 May 1911, 2. *Evening Standard* (Ogden City, UT), 12 May 1911, 1. *Kansas City Star*, 13 May 1911, 3.
   22. *Kansas City Star*, 15 May 1911, 1; 16 May 1911, 4. *University Missourian* (Columbia), 21 May 1911, 1. *Railway Age* 45.8 (21 February 1908): 253.
   23. *Dallas Morning News*, 28 February 1909, 7; 10 October 1909, 44; 15 May 1911, 16; 18 May 1911, 4; 19 May 1911, 5; 21 May 1911, 12. *Dallas Morning News*, 18 May 1911, 4.
   24. Ibid.
   25. *Dallas Morning News*, 19 May 1911, 5.
   26. *Dallas Morning News*, 20 May 1911, 5, 7; 21 May 1911, 12.
   27. *Dallas Morning News*, 22 May 1911, 16.
   28. Gene left Dallas on the evening of May 21 and would make his flight in Eureka on May 27.

## Chapter 38

   1. *Eureka* (CA) *Herald*, 15 May 1911, 8.
   2. Charles Pierce Coggeshall and Thellwell Russell Coggeshall, *The Coggeshalls in America* (Boston: C. E. Goodspeed, 1930), 202–203. Leigh H. Irvine, *History of Humboldt County, California* (Los Angeles: Historic Record, 1915), 299–301. *Eureka* (CA) *Times Standard*, 23 April 1971, 5; 17 August 1975, 21.
   3. *Eureka* (CA) *Herald*, 15 May 1911, 8. *Daily Humboldt Standard* (Eureka, CA), 22 May 1911, 4.
   4. *Eureka* (CA) *Herald*, 18 May 1911, 5.
   5. *Daily Humboldt Standard* (Eureka, CA), 22 May 1911, 4.
   6. *The Call* (San Francisco), 7 January 1901, 5; 26 May 1911, 19. *Pacific Merchant Marine* 2.13 (3 July 1909): 14.
   7. *Los Angeles Herald*, 13 June 1906, 1. *Salt Lake Herald*, 13 June 1911, 1.
   8. *Daily Humboldt Standard* (Eureka, CA), 27 May 1911, 1. *Eureka* (CA) *Herald*, 27 May 1911, 1.
   9. *Eureka* (CA) *Herald*, 27 May 1911, 1, 4.
   10. *Eureka* (CA) *Herald*, 27 May 1911, 1.
   11. *Eureka* (CA) *Herald*, 27 May 1911, 1, 4.
   12. *Daily Humboldt Standard* (Eureka, CA), 27 May 1911, 8. *Eureka* (CA) *Herald*, 27 May 1911, 4.
   13. *Eureka* (CA) *Herald*, 28 May 1911, 7.
   14. *Eureka* (CA) *Herald*, 27 May 1911, 4; 28 May 1911, 1; 29 May 1911, 1.
   15. *Humboldt Daily Standard* (Eureka, CA), 29 May 1911, 1. *Eureka* (CA) *Herald*, 29 May 1911, 8.
   16. *Eureka* (CA) *Herald*, 29 May 1911, 1. *The Call* (San Francisco), 30 May 1911, 19.
   17. *Anaconda* (MT) *Standard*, 30 May 1911, 2. *Humboldt* (CA) *Times*, 28 May 1911, 1. *The Call* (San Francisco), 28 May 1911, 36; 29 May 1911, 13. *Oregonian* (Portland), 28 May 1911, 1; 29 May 1911, 4. *Medford* (OR) *Mail Tribune*, 1 June 1911, weekly edition, 5. *Nevada State Journal* (Reno), 10 June 1911, 5. Gene's manager, Norman DeVaux, would later become president of Chevrolet Motor Company of California. *Oakland Tribune*, 4 December 1918, B1.

## Chapter 39

   1. *Medford* (OR) *Mail Tribune*, 17 July 1910, 1; 1 October 1910, 1.
   2. *The Sun* (Medford, OR), 19 April 1911, 6; 21 April 1911, 1; 2 June 1911, 5. *Medford* (OR) *Mail Tribune*, 4 June 1911, 1.
   3. *Medford* (OR) *Mail Tribune*, 31 May 1911, 1; 1 June 1911, 1.
   4. *Medford* (OR) *Mail Tribune*, 2 June 1911, 6.
   5. *The Sun* (Medford, OR), 3 June 1911, 1.
   6. Ibid.
   7. Ibid.
   8. *Medford* (OR) *Mail Tribune*, 4 June 1911, 1. *The Sun* (Medford, OR), 4 June 1911, 1, 6.
   9. Ibid.
   10. *Medford* (OR) *Mail Tribune*, 4 June 1911, 5; 18 June 1911, sec. 2:11. *The Sun* (Medford, OR), 4 June 1911, 5. Elsie married Charles A. Laird, a worker with a local construction company.
   11. *Medford* (OR) *Mail Tribune*, 4 June 1911, 1. *The Sun* (Medford, OR), 4 June 1911, 6.
   12. Ibid.
   13. *The Sun* (Baltimore), 18 February 1912, 5.
   14. *Daily Oregon Statesman* (Salem), 21 May 1911, 1; 2 June 1911, 8.
   15. *Daily Oregon Statesman* (Salem), 4 June 1911, 1. *Oregonian* (Portland), 4 June 1911, sec. 2:3. *Eureka* (CA) *Herald*, 29 May 1911, 1.
   16. Ibid. *Daily Oregon Statesman* (Salem), 6 June 1911, 1. Muessig – 1910 Federal Census, Multnomah County, Oregon.
   17. *Daily Oregon Statesman* (Salem), 6 June 1911, 1. *Oregonian* (Portland), 5 June 1911, 5.
   18. *Oregonian* (Portland), 8 December 1901, sec. 4:25; 6 June 1911, 13; 27 June 1915, sec. 5:5. *Daily Oregon Statesman* (Salem), 7 June 1911, 1.
   19. *Oregonian* (Portland), 1 June 1911, 16; 5 June 1911, 16.
   20. *Oregonian* (Portland), 1 June 1911, 16; 4 June 1911, sec. 3:9.
   21. *Oregonian* (Portland), 7 June 1911, 9.
   22. *Oregonian* (Portland), 7 June 1911, 17.
   23. Ibid.
   24. Harry E. Rice, "Columbia River Kid," *Oregon Historical Quarterly* 74.4 (December 1973): 316–317. *Oregonian* (Portland), 8 June 1911, 22; 11 June 1911, sec. 4:7.
   25. *Oregonian* (Portland), 20 October 1911, 1.
   26. *Oregonian* (Portland), 20 October 1911, 4.

## Chapter 40

   1. *Anaconda* (MT) *Standard*, 16 December 1906, state sec., 15. *Springfield* (MA) *Republican*, 8 October 1883, 5. Harry C. Freeman, *A Brief History of Butte, Montana* (Chicago: Henry O. Shepard, 1900), 18.
   2. Industrial relations: Final report and testimony, submitted to Congress by the Commission on industrial relations created by the act of August 23, 1912, Volume 4, United States, Mining Conditions at Butte, Montana (Washington, D.C.: Government Printing Office, 1916), 3939, 3942. Daniel Harrington and A. J. Lanza, Miners' Consumption in the Mines of Butte, Montana, Technical Paper 260 (Washington, D.C.: Government Printing Office, 1921), 7–8, 11. *Anaconda* (MT) *Standard*, 8 March 1911, 4; 24 September 1912, 6.
   3. *Anaconda* (MT) *Standard*, 6 May 1911, 12; 10 June 1911, 6.
   4. *Anaconda* (MT) *Standard*, 10 June 1911, 7.
   5. *Anaconda* (MT) *Standard*, 10 June 1911, 7.
   6. *Anaconda* (MT) *Standard*, 15 June 1911, 11; 20 October 1911, 6. Montana Historical Society Research Center Archives, "Guide

to the Patrick A. Largey Family Papers, 1863–1965," MC 289, http://nwda-db.wsulibs.wsu.edu/print/ark:/80444/xv15060 (17 March 2011).
7. *Anaconda* (MT) *Standard*, 15 June 1911, 11. *New York Times*, 7 January 1912.
8. *Anaconda* (MT) *Standard*, 12 June 1911, 1; 13 June 1911, 1 (photo).
9. *Anaconda* (MT) *Standard*, 12 June 1911, 1, 3.
10. *Anaconda* (MT) *Standard*, 13 June 1911, 2. *Washington* (D.C.) *Herald*, 28 September 1910, 1.
11. *Anaconda* (MT) *Standard*, 13 June 1911, 2; 20 October 1911, 6. *Montana Standard* (Butte), 12 November 1972, 14.
12. *Anaconda* (MT) *Standard*, 14 June 1911, 7, 8; 15 June 1911, 6. *Evening Standard* (Ogden City, UT), 15 June 1911, 7.
13. Federal Writers' Project, *Montana: A State Guide Book* (New York: Viking, 1939), 156. *The Colliery Engineer* 29.8 (March 1909), 350. *Anaconda* (MT) *Standard*, 11 December 1910, sec. 4:3.
14. *Minneapolis Journal*, 18 February 1906, Journal Junior section, 3. *Anaconda* (MT) *Standard*, 8 December 1910, 2.
15. *Anaconda* (MT) *Standard*, 15 June 1911, 1; 17 June 1911, 2, 12; 18 June 1911, 4; 21 June 1911, 6. *Democratic Banner* (Mt. Vernon, OH), 23 June 1911, 5.
16. *Anaconda* (MT) *Standard*, 19 June 1911, 6; 22 June 1911, 5; 27 June 1910, 6.
17. *Anaconda* (MT) *Standard*, 20 June 1911, 4; 27 June 1910, 6. From the Northern Rockies Heritage Center website, *Missoulian* (Missoula, MT), 27 June 1911, advertisement; 29 June 1911, 7. www.nrhc.org/history/EugeneEly.html (22 March 2005).
18. *Missoulian* (Missoula, MT), 29 June 1911, 1, 7. From the Northern Rockies Heritage Center website, above.
19. Ibid. *Anaconda* (MT) *Standard*, 27 June 1906, 11; 15 December 1907, sec. 4:3. *The Call* (San Francisco), 25 June 1911, 26.
20. Reno Evening Gazette, 4 July 1911, 2.
21. *Des Moines News*, 21 August 1911, 5.

## Chapter 41

1. *Carson City Daily*, 23 June 1910, 1. *Nevada State Journal* (Reno), 24 May 1911, 1; 27 June 1911, 6.
2. *Nevada State Journal* (Reno), 5 July 1911, 4. *The Sun* (Baltimore), 18 April 1902, sec. 2:14.
3. *Nevada State Journal* (Reno), 27 June 1911, 6; 5 July 1911, 6.
4. *Reno Evening Gazette*, 4 July 1911, 2. *Nevada State Journal* (Reno), 3 July 1911, 1.
5. *The Call* (San Francisco), 5 July 1910, 15; 30 June 1911, 7. *Nevada State Journal* (Reno), 4 July 1911, 4, 8; 5 July 1911, 6.
6. *The Call* (San Francisco), 5 July 1911, 5. *Reno Evening Gazette*, 21 August 1965, 9. *Lethbridge Daily Herald* (Alberta, Canada), 12 July 1911, 5.
7. *Reno Evening Gazette*, 5 July 1911, 6; 11 July 1911, 4; 12 July 1911, 6.
8. *The Call* (San Francisco), 7 July 1911, 2; 16 July 1911, 61. *Reno Evening Gazette*, 7 July 1911, 10. *Oregonian* (Portland), 10 July 1911, 14. *Nevada State Journal* (Reno), 12 July 1911
9. *Lethbridge Daily Herald* (Alberta, Canada), 15 July 1911, 1, 8.
10. *Lethbridge Herald* (Alberta, Canada), 3 June 1939, 7, 34, 35; 5 August 1959, 1. *Lethbridge Daily Herald* (Alberta, Canada), 3 July 1911, 7; 8 July 1911, 14.
11. *Lethbridge Daily Herald* (Alberta, Canada), 15 July 1911, 1, 8.
12. Ibid.
13. Ibid. *Lethbridge Herald* (Alberta, Canada), 3 June 1939, 7, 34, 35.
14. *New York Times*, 15 July 1911, 1. *Cleveland Plain Dealer*, 15 July 1911, 1. *Sandusky* (OH) *Register*, 16 July 1911, 1. *Salt Lake Telegram*, 31 July 1911, 1.
15. *Seattle Times-Post Intelligencer*, 16 July 1911, 1; 21 August 1983, Pacific Magazine, 6. *Seattle Daily Times*, 26 July 1911, 6.
16. *Seattle Daily Times*, 17 July 1911, 2, 7.
17. *Seattle Daily Times*, 17 July 1911, 2. *Seattle Times-Post Intelligencer*, 17 July 1911, 1.
18. *Seattle Daily Times*, 18 July 1911, 2.
19. *Seattle Daily Times*, 20 July 1911, 1, 2, 7.
20. *Seattle Daily Times*, 20 July 1911, 1.
21. *Seattle Daily Times*, 20 July 1911, 1, 2.
22. *Seattle Daily Times*, 21 July 1911, 6, 7; 23 July 1911, 16. *Oregonian* (Portland), 21 July 1911, 15.
23. *Tacoma Times*, 24 July 1911, 1. *Wilkes-Barre Times*, 15 August 1911, 6. *Iowa City Daily Press*, 10 October 1911, 4.
24. *Baltimore American*, 27 August 1911, 12C. *Washington* (D.C.) *Herald*, 26 July 1911, 3. *Washington* (D.C.) *Times*, 26 July 1911, 6. "General Allen on Army Plans," *Philadelphia Inquirer*, 9 July 1911, 10. The College Park Aviation Museum, www.collegeparkaviationmuseum.com (April 19, 2010).
25. *Washington* (D.C.) *Herald*, 29 July 1911, 1.
26. *Philadelphia Inquirer*, 9 July 1911, 10. *Washington* (D.C.) *Herald*, 30 July 1911, 1, 2. *Washington* (D.C.) *Times*, 30 July 1911, 4. *Washington* (D.C.) *Post*, 31 July 1911, 12.
27. *Washington* (D.C.) *Post*, 1 August 1911, 2; 3 August 1911, 3; 5 August 1911, 2. *Washington* (D.C.) *Herald*, 1 August 1911, 2; 2 August 1911, 2.
28. *Aeronautics* 9.3 (September 1911): 91. *New York Times*, 22 July 1911, 2. *New York Herald*, 30 July 1911, 1.
29. *New York Times*, 6 August 1911, 1. *New York Herald*, 6 August 1911, 1.
30. Ibid. *New York Tribune*, 6 August 1911, A1.
31. *New York Times*, 5 August 1911, 5; 6 August 1911, 1. *Washington* (D.C.) *Herald*, 6 August 1911, 3. *New York Herald*, 6 August 1911, 1. *Aeronautics* 9.3 (September 1911): 91.
32. *New York Times*, 6 August 1911, 1. *New York Tribune*, 6 August 1911, A1, B14. *Aeronautics* 9.3 (September 1911): 91.
33. *Washington* (D.C.) *Herald*, 28 June 1911, 1. *Wilkes-Barre Times-Leader*, 10 July 1911, 15. *St. Johnsbury* (VT) *Caledonian Record*, 12 July 1911, 8. *Weekly Sentinel* (Fort Wayne), 12 May 1913, 1.
34. *New York Tribune*, 6 August 1911, B14.

## Chapter 42

1. *Aeronautics* 5.6 (December 1909): 215. *Aero* 2.19 (August 12, 1911): 405. James Langland, comp., *Chicago Daily News Almanac and Year-Book* (Chicago: Chicago Daily News, 1912), 362. *Aero* 2.18 (5 August 1911): 387. *Baltimore American*, 30 July 1911, 34. *New York Times*, 13 August 1911, sporting section, C7. *Indianapolis Star*, 6 August 1911, 17.
2. *Aeronautics* 9.3 (September 1911): 89–91. *Rockford* (IL) *Republic*, 11 August 1911, 6.
3. *Rockford* (IL) *Republic*, 8 August 1911, 8; 11 August 1911, 6.

4. *Chicago Daily Tribune*, 12 August 1911, 19.
5. *Iowa City Daily Press*, 14 August 1911, 5; 21 August 1911, 1. *Waterloo Times Tribune*, 23 August 1911, 4. *Williamsburg* (IA) *Journal-Tribune*, 31 August 1911, 7.
6. *Rockford* (IL) *Republic*, 11 August 1911, 1, 6, 12 August 1911, 3. *Rockford* (IL) *Morning Star*, 12 August 1911, 2. *Grand Rapids Press*, 11 August 1911, 11.
7. *Chicago Daily Tribune*, 13 August 1911, 2. *Boston Journal*, 5 September 1911, 3.
8. *Williamsburg* (IA) *Journal-Tribune*, 28 September 1911, 6.
9. *Rockford* (IL) *Morning Star*, 13 August 1911, 1. *Washington* (D.C.) *Herald*, 13 August 1911, 3. *New York Times*, 13 August 1911, C7. *Kansas City Star*, 13 August 1911, 5. *Rockford* (IL) *Republic*, 14 August 1911, 7. The *Rockford Republic* began keeping track of daily accidents.
10. *New York Times*, 13 August 1911, C7.
11. *Aeronautics* 9.3 (September 1911): 58. *Rockford* (IL) *Republic*, 29 July 1911, 3. *New York Times*, 13 August 1911, C7.
12. *The Sun* (Baltimore), 13 August 1911, 1. *Washington* (D.C.) *Herald*, 13 August 1911, 3. *Rockford* (IL) *Republic*, 14 August 1911, 7.
13. *Times Dispatch* (Richmond), 15 August 1911, 1, 7. *Rockford* (IL) *Republic*, 14 August 1911, 7; 15 August 1911, 7. *Rockford* (IL) *Register-Gazette*, 14 August 1911, 5. *New York Times*, 13 August 1911, C7.
14. Ibid.
15. *Rockford* (IL) *Republic*, 15 August 1911, 7; 16 August 1911, 5. *Elkhart* (IN) *Daily Review*, 15 August 1911, 4. *Elkhart* (IN) *Truth*, 16 August 1911, 8. *New York Times*, 11 August 1911, 2. *New York Herald*, 16 August 1911, 1, 2. The Burgess Company was the first to receive a license from the Wright brothers to manufacture their aeroplanes.
16. Goettmann Family, 1900 Federal Census, Pittsburgh, PA, Allegheny County, 14th Ward, Supervisor's Dist.: 18, Enumeration Dist.: 0174, Sheet: 1B, Line: 88. [Badger, William R.]. *Rockford* (IL) *Register-Gazette*, 16 August 1911, 10; 18 August 1911, 1. *Rockford* (IL) *Republic*, 16 August 1911, 5. *Rockford* (IL) *Morning Star*, 16 August 1911, 1. *New York Times*, 16 August 1911, 1. *Auburn* (NY) *Semi-Weekly Journal*, 18 August 1911, 7.
17. Johnstone Family, 1900 Federal Census, Chicago, IL, Cook County, 32nd Ward, Supervisor's Dist.: 1, Enumeration Dist.: 1031, Sheet: 20B, Line: 83. *Rockford* (IL) *Register Gazette*, 27 July 1911, 2; 16 August 1911, 10. *The World* (New York), 16 August 1911, 1.
18. *Rockford* (IL) *Morning Star*, 16 August 1911, 1. *New York Times*, 16 August 1911, 1.
19. Ibid. *Rockford* (IL) *Register-Gazette*, 16 August 1911, 10. *Rockford* (IL) *Republic*, 16 August 1911, 5. *Sandusky* (OH) *Star-Journal*, 16 August 1911, 1.
20. *New York Times*, 16 August 1911, 1. *Rockford* (IL) *Republic*, 16 August 1911, 5.
21. *Rockford* (IL) *Register-Gazette*, 16 August 1911, 8.
22. Ibid. *The World* (New York), 16 August 1911, 2.
23. *New York Times*, 17 August 1911, 1.
24. Ibid. *Rockford* (IL) *Republic*, 17 August 1911, 6.
25. Ibid.
26. *New York Times*, 17 August 1911, 1.
27. *Medford* (OR) *Mail Tribune*, 19 August 1911, 6. *Rockford* (IL) *Register-Gazette*, 17 August 1911, 5.
28. *Rockford* (IL) *Register-Gazette*, 17 August 1911, 5.
29. *Rockford* (IL) *Republic*, 18 August 1911, 10.
30. *Rockford* (IL) *Republic*, 17 August 1911, 6.
31. *Rockford* (IL) *Republic*, 9 August 1911, 2; 15 August 1911, 7; 18 August 1911, 10.
32. *Rockford* (IL) *Republic*, 17 August 1911, 6; 18 August 1911, 7. *Washington* (D.C.) *Herald*, 18 August 1911, 1; 21 August 1911, 7. *Cedar Rapids Evening Gazette*, 21 August 1911, 6. *Chicago Daily News Almanac and Year-Book* (Chicago: Chicago Daily News, 1912), 363.
33. *Rockford* (IL) *Republic*, 21 August 1911, 6. *New York Times*, 21 August 1911, 2.
34. *Aeronautics* 9.3 (September 1911): 89. *New York Times*, 6 August 1911, 1. *Rockford* (IL) *Republic*, 3 August 1911, 3. *Rockford* (IL) *Register-Gazette*, 21 August 1911, 5.
35. *Rockford* (IL) *Register-Gazette*, 22 August 1911, 8. *New York Times*, 22 August 1911, 2. *Philadelphia Inquirer*, 22 August 1911, 2.
36. *Des Moines News*, 21 August 1911, 5.

## Chapter 43

1. *Elkhart* (IN) *Daily Review*, 25 August 1911, 1. *Boston Journal*, 25 August 1911, 2. *New York Tribune*, 26 August 1911, 1. *New York Times*, 26 August 1911, 1.
2. John Lenger, "Conquest of the Air," *Harvard Magazine* (May-June 2003): 34–35, http://harvardmagazine.com (11 May 2011). *Times-Dispatch* (Richmond, VA), 20 August 1911, 2.
3. *Boston Journal*, 27 August 1911, 2; 30 August 1911, 2; 5 September 1911, 3.
4. *Boston Journal*, 26 August 1911, 10; 28 August 1911, 2; 29 August 1911, 2; 30 August 1911, 2.
5. *Boston Journal*, 27 August 1911, 2.
6. *Boston Journal*, 2 September 1911, 2; 3 September 1911, 2. *The Sun* (New York), 4 September 1911, 1.
7. *Boston Journal*, 29 August 1911, 1, 2.
8. *Boston Journal*, 2 September 1911, 2.
9. *New York Times*, 5 September 1911, 5. *Boston Journal*, 5 September 1911, 5. *Harvard Crimson Magazine* (20 November 1911), www.thecrimson.com (24 February 2011).
10. *Boston Journal*, 7 September 1911, 10. *Daily Register Gazette* (Rockford, IL), 1 September 1911, 16.
11. *Pawtucket* (RI) *Times*, 26 May 1898, 2. *Newport* (RI) *Daily News*, 2 September 1911, 5; 6 September 1911, 1; 20 October 1911, 4. *Boston Journal*, 6 September 1911, 12.
12. The Sun (New York), 11 September 1911, 1, 2. New York Tribune, 10 September 1911, 2; 11 September 1911, 1. New York Times, 11 September 1911, 1. Edward L Thornlike, English Composition—150 Specimens Arranged for use in Psychological and Educational Experiments (New York: Teachers College, Columbia University, 1916), 33.
13. *St. Johnsbury* (VT) *Caledonian*, 13 September 1911, 1; 21 September 1911, 1.
14. *Utica Herald-Dispatch*, 15 September 1911, 1; 16 September 1911, 2.
15. *The Sun* (New York), 17 September 1911, 4. *New York Times*, 17 September 1911, C9. *New York Herald*, 17 September 1911, 2.
16. *Evening Telegram* (New York), 17 September 1911, 2. *New York Times*, 18 September 1911, 2. *The Sun* (New York), 18 September 1911, 4. *Utica Herald-Dispatch*, 18 September 1911, 2.

## Chapter 44

1. *New York Times*, 12 September 1911, 8. *Syracuse Herald*, 14 September 1911, 5. *Evening Telegram* (New York), 24 September 1911, 2.
2. *Aeronautics* 9.4 (October 1911): 135. *Aero* 3.1 (7 October 1911): 4. *The Sun* (New York), 25 September 1911, 2; 1 October 1911, 3.
3. "Airmail Before 1918," www.centennialofflight.gov/essay/Government_Role/Pre-1918_mail/POL1.htm (11 May 2011). *Aeronautics* 9.4 (October 1911): 134. *Evening Telegram* (New York), 24 September 1911, 2. *The Sun* (New York), 25 September 1911, 2.
4. *The Sun* (New York), 23 September 1911, 4. *New York Times*, 23 September 1911, 9.
5. *Aeronautics* 9.4 (October 1911): 135. *Aero* 3.1 (7 October 1911): 1, 4. *The Sun* (New York), 2 October 1911, 12. *New York Times*, 24 September 1911, C5.
6. *The Sun* (New York), 25 September 1911, 1, 2. *New York Times*, 25 September 1911, 1. *Aero* 3.1 (7 October 1911): 2.
7. *The Sun* (New York), 25 September 1911, 1. *New York Times*, 26 September 1911, 1.
8. *The Sun* (New York), 25 September 1911, 2. *Evening Telegram* (New York), 24 September 1911, 2. *New York Times*, 17 September 1911, C9; 25 September 191 1, 11.
9. *Aero* 3.1 (7 October 1911): 1. *The Sun* (New York), 27 September 1911, 5.
10. *The Sun* (New York), 27 September 1911, 5.
11. *New York Times*, 26 September 1911, 1.
12. Ibid. *New York American*, 26 September 1911, 1.
13. *New York Times*, 26 September 1911, 1. *New York American*, 26 September 1911, 2. *New York Herald*, 26 September 1911, 1.
14. *San Antonio Light*, 26 September 1911, 8. *New York American*, 26 September 1911, 2. 9. *Lima (OH) Daily News*, 13 September 1911, 3. *Springfield (MA) Republican*, 27 September 1911, 11. *Aero* 3.1 (7 October 1911): 2. *Brooklyn Daily Eagle*, 28 September 1911, 1.
15. *Repository* (Canton, OH), 25 September 1911, 5; 26 September 1911, 8; 27 September 1911, second extra, 8.
16. *Repository* (Canton, OH), 27 September 1911, first edition, 7.
17. *Repository* (Canton, OH), 27 September 1911, second extra, 1.
18. *Repository* (Canton, OH), 27 September 1911, second extra, 1, 8.
19. Ibid. (*Repository* (Canton, OH), 27 September 1911, first edition, 7. *The Sun* (New York), 28 September 1911, 1. *Cleveland Plain Dealer*, 28 September 1911, 2. *New York Times*, 28 September 1911, 1.
20. *Repository* (Canton, OH), 27 September 1911, second extra, 8; 28 September 1911, first extra edition, 1, 7.
21. *Philadelphia Inquirer*, 30 September 1911, 4. *The Sun* (New York), 1 October 1911, 3.
22. *The Sun* (New York), 1 October 1911, 3. *Brooklyn Daily Eagle*, 1 October 1911, 7. Woodruff's reprieve lasted one week before New York Supreme Court Justice Garret Garretson denied a request that Sunday aviation exhibitions be allowed if aviators could not win prize money and no admission was charged. *Springfield (MA) Republican*, 7 October 1911, 1, 5. *The Sun* (New York), 7 October 1911, 5.
23. *The Sun* (New York), 2 October 1911, 12.
24. Ibid. *New York Tribune*, 2 October 1911, 7. *Brooklyn Daily Eagle*, 2 October 1911, 2.
25. Ibid.
26. *Aeronautics* 9.4 (October 1911): 134.
27. *The Sun* (New York), 7 October 1911, 5.

## Chapter 45

1. *Davenport (IA) Democrat and Leader*, 6 October 1911, 5. *Iowa City Daily Press*, 10 October 1911, 4.
2. Ibid. *Iowa City Daily Press*, 10 October 1911, 2.
3. *Macon Daily Telegraph*, 30 September 1911, 8; 19 October 1911, 1.
4. *Macon Daily Telegraph*, 15 October 1911, 1.
5. Brockshus, "The Bird Man."
6. *Macon Daily Telegraph*, 13 October 1911, 1; 14 October 1911, 1.
7. *Macon Daily Telegraph*, 20 October 1911, 2.
8. Ibid. *Macon Daily Telegraph*, 17 October 1911, 1; 18 October 1911, 1; 19 October 1911, 1.
9. *The World* (New York), 20 October 1911, 1.
10. *Macon Daily Telegraph*, 19 October 1911, 5.
11. *Macon Daily Telegraph*, 20 October 1911, 2.
12. *Macon Daily Telegraph*, 20 October 1911, 1, 2, 9. *The Call* (San Francisco), 20 October 1911, 2.
13. *Macon Daily Telegraph*, 20 October 1911, 1. *The World* (New York), 20 October 1911, 1.
14. *Macon Daily Telegraph*, 20 October 1911, 1, 2.
15. *Macon Daily Telegraph*, 20 October 1911, 1, 2, 9. *Iowa City Daily Press*, 24 October 1911, p. 1.
16. *Kansas City Star*, 28 April 1912, 1. *New York American*, 20 October 1911, 1.
17. *Macon Daily Telegraph*, 20 October 1911, 1, 2.
18. *Macon Daily Telegraph*, 20 October 1911, 1; 21 October 1911, 4.
19. *Macon Daily Telegraph*, 20 October 1911, 1, 2.
20. *Macon Daily Telegraph*, 20 October 1911, 2, 9.
21. *Macon Daily Telegraph*, 20 October 1911, 1; 21 October 1911, 8; 23 October 1911, 4. *The Call* (San Francisco), 20 October 1911, 2. *San Francisco Chronicle*, 20 October 1911, 1. *The Sun* (New York), 20 October 1911, 1.
22. *Macon Daily Telegraph*, 21 October 1911, 8; 23 October 1911, 12.
23. *Macon Daily Telegraph*, 20 October 1911, 1, 9. *New York American*, 20 October 1911, 1.
24. *Macon Daily Telegraph*, 20 October 1911, 1. *Williamsburg (IA) Journal-Tribune*, 23 October 1911, 1.
25. *Macon Daily Telegraph*, 20 October 1911, 1, 2.
26. *Muskegon (MI) News Chronicle*, 25 October 1911, 2. *Iowa City Daily Press*, 21 October 1911, p. 1. *The Sun* (New York), 20 October 1911, 1. *The World* (New York), 20 October 1911, 1
27. *Macon Daily Telegraph*, 20 October 1911, 1. *The Call* (San Francisco), 20 October 1911, 2. John Willard, "Eugene Ely blazes a trail in the sky," *Quad City Times* (Davenport, IA), http://qctimes.com/news/article_3ff6e13d-f9ab-5bb0-bf16-d165bcecdc28.html (14 July 2008).
28. *The Call* (San Francisco), 20 October 1911, 2, 6. *Oregonian* (Portland), 20 October 1911, 1, 4. *New York American*, 20 October 1911, 1. *Macon Daily Telegraph*, 21 October 1911, 4. *Williamsburg (IA) Journal-Tribune*, 26 October 1911, 1.
29. *Macon Daily Telegraph* 20

October 1911, 1. *New York Times,* 21 October 1911, 6.
30. *New York Herald,* 20 October 1911, 1. *Waterloo Evening Courier,* 21 October 1911, 1:2.
31. *New York Times,* 21 October 1911, 2. *Aeronautics* 9.5 (November 1911): 154. *Cleveland Plain Dealer,* 13 May 1913, 14.
32. *Macon Daily Telegraph,* 21 October 1911, 8. *Augusta Chronicle,* 9 December 1910, A5; 11 December 1910, A8. *Macon Weekly Telegraph,* 27 July 1912, 10.
33. *Macon Daily Telegraph,* 23 October 1911, 12. *Iowa City Daily Press,* 1 November 1911, 5; 8 November 1911, 1. "Eugene Ely, Birdman, Death Dip Macon Fair, Lyric Picture Today," *Macon Telegraph,* 8 November 1911, 6. An advertisement in the *Sheboygan* (WI) *Press,* 8 November 1911, 4, newspaper includes a list of all other events covered in the newsreel.
34. *Iowa City Daily Press,* 21 October 1911, 1; 23 October 1911, 4. *Waterloo Evening Courier,* 21 October 1911, 1. *Williamsburg* (IA) *Journal-Tribune,* 26 October 1911, 1.
35. Brockshus, "The Bird Man." *Williamsburg* (IA) *Journal-Tribune,* 26 October 1911, 1.
36. Ibid. *Iowa City Daily Press,* 23 October 1911, 4.
37. Ibid.
38. *Williamsburg* (IA) *Journal-Tribune,* 26 October 1911, 1.
39. *Aero* 3:9 (2 December 1911): 179.

## Chapter 46

1. *Oakland Tribune,* 20 December 1911, 1. *The Call* (San Francisco), 20 December 1911, 1, 2. Dunlop Collection.
2. *The Call* (San Francisco), 16 December 1911, 11. *Oakland Tribune,* 16 December 1911, 8. *Poughkeepsie Daily Eagle,* 24 January 1912, 5. *New York Tribune,* 25 January 1912, 1. *The Call* (San Francisco), 18 February 1912, 24. Superior Court of California, County of San Francisco, Probate Department, Probate Register of actions, 1915, vol. 38, case 18875, p. 375. *Sausalito News,* 6 November 1915, 4.
3. *The Call* (San Francisco), 14 January 1912, 19. *The Call* (San Francisco), 24 December 1911, 22.
4. *San Francisco Chronicle,* 14 January 1912, 46. *New York Times,* 7 January 1912. *The Call* (San Francisco), 14 January 1912, 19. *Aero* 3.14 (6 January 1912): 275.

5. *The Call* (San Francisco), 16 December 1911, 11. *Oakland Tribune,* 8 February 1912, 4; 11 February 1912, 35; 18 February 1912, 19. *Aeronautics* 10.3 (March 1912): 102.
6. *Oakland Tribune,* 13 February 1911, 11; 15 February 1912, 8.
7. *The Call* (San Francisco), 18 February 1912, 65, 19 February 1912, 1, 2. *San Francisco Chronicle,* 18 February 1912, 1, 24. *Oakland Tribune,* 18 February 1912, 17, 19.
8. *The Call* (San Francisco), 19 February 1912, 2. *Oakland Tribune,* 26 February 1912, 3; 12 June 1959, 12E.
9. *San Francisco Chronicle,* 18 February 1912, 24; 19 February 1912, 14. *Oakland Tribune,* 19 February 1912, sec. 2:10; 23 February 1912, Editorial Page, 6. *The Call* (San Francisco), 24 February 1912, 17.
10. *The Call* (San Francisco), 24 February 1912, 17. *Oakland Tribune,* 22 February 1912, 2; 24 February 1912, sec. 2:13.
11. *Oakland Tribune,* 23 February 1912, 1; 24 February 1912, sec. 2:13, 14. *The Call* (San Francisco), 24 February 1912, 17. *Aero* 3.23 (9 March 1912): 456.
12. Mendocino County, CA, Marriage Register, v. 11, p. 212. *Oakland Tribune,* 28 February 1911, 2:1. *San Francisco Chronicle,* 28 August 1912, 3.
13. *Oakland Tribune,* 28 August 1912, 10; 22 October 1918, 5; 25 October 1918, 3. *The Call* (San Francisco), 30 June 1912, 48. "Big Land Broker Held for Fraud," *The Call* (San Francisco), 17 January 1913, 18.
14. *Oakland Tribune,* 4 December 1918, B1.
15. Ibid. *Oakland Tribune,* 21 December 1918, 5; 30 June 1928, 24. 1920 Federal Census, San Francisco City & County, Precinct 19, Assembly District 32, Sheet: 5:B, Line: 78. (1390 Clay St.)
16. *San Francisco Examiner,* 20 November 1920, 4; 22 November 1922, 19. *San Francisco Chronicle,* 28 November 1920, society section, 9.
17. *San Francisco Examiner,* 22 November 1922, 19. Registration Location: First Judicial District County, Alaska; Roll: 1473297; Draft Board: 0. *Annual Report of the Territorial Mines Inspector (1920)* (Juneau: Alaska Daily Empire Print, 1921), 20. *Mines Handbook,* v. 15, International Edition (1922): 173. NARA, *Emergency Passport Applications, Argentina thru Venezuela, 1906–1925,* ARC Identifier 1244183 /MLR Number A1 544; Box #4392, Volume #1 [Ancestry.com].
18. *Annual Report of the Territorial Mine Inspector to the Governor of Alaska (1920)* (Juneau: Alaska Daily Empire Print, 1921), 20. *Mines Handbook,* v. 15, International Edition (1922): 173. Southeastern Alaska Mining Corporation, "Report on Jualin Mine, Berners Bay Region, Alaska" (Juneau Alaska Territorial Department of Mines, 1929), 11, 13. *San Francisco Examiner,* 22 November 1922, 19.

## Chapter 47

1. James Austin, nephew of Gene Ely, son of Madie, when asked in correspondence what he knew about the Elys.
2. *Williamsburg* (IA) *Journal-Tribune,* 2 December 1915, 3; 23 March 1916, 3.
3. *Williamsburg* (IA) *Journal-Tribune,* 18 September 1913, 8; 17 December 1914, 2; 16 September 1915, 3; 17 December 1916, 6; 23 March 1916, 3; 8 June 1916, 3.
4. *Williamsburg* (IA) *Journal-Tribune,* 12 April 1917, 8. World War I—Civilian Draft Registration Database, www.usgwarchives.org/nv/washoearc.htm (7 November 2008).
5. *Williamsburg* (IA) *Journal-Tribune,* 7 September 1939, 1. *San Francisco Sunday Examiner and Chronicle,* 12 November 1967, C13. Social Security Death Index for "H. Ely."
6. *Williamsburg* (IA) *Journal-Tribune,* 14 March 1918, 1; 7 September 1939, 1. *Davenport* (IA) *Democrat and Leader,* 26 October 1927, 11. Even though the newspaper says that Lois Gene Austin was born on Gene Ely's birthday, she was actually born the day after, October 22, 1927 (Iowa births, familysearch.com—Lois Jene [sic] Austin).
7. *Waterloo Evening Courier and Reporter,* 5 July 1918, 7. *Montgomery Advertiser,* 28 August 1918, 29. *Iowa City Citizen,* 11 May 1916, 1. *Des Moines Daily News,* 8 July 1918, 1. *Official Army Register,* "Retired List" (Washington, D.C.: Government Printing Office, 1 January 1936), 857.
8. *Biographical Directory of the United States Congress, 1774-Present,* "Hull, Harry Edward," http://bioguide.congress.gov (12 December 2009). *Iowa City Citizen,* 6 November 1918, 1. *Official*

*Army Register*, "Retired List" (Washington, D.C.: Government Printing Office, 1 January 1936), 857.

9. S. #5514, 71st Cong. (1931), S. #433, 72nd Cong. (1932), H.R. #2791, 72nd Cong. (1932), H.R. #973, 72nd Cong. (1932). *Monthly Catalog of United States Government publications* v. 38 (July 1932—June 1933): 87. *Waterloo Daily Courier*, 17 February 1933, 5.

10. Cleveland Plain Dealer, 9 August 1931, 1.

11. *Oakland Tribune*, 11 May 1932, 1; 13 May 1932, 5, 18 May 1932, 14D.

12. *Marin Journal* (San Rafael), 25 November 1926, 1. *Oakland Tribune*, 18 May 1932, 14D. *San Francisco Chronicle*, 18 May 1932, 4. Naval Historical Center photograph no. NH 77596, www.history.navy.mil (29 September 2003).

13. *San Mateo* (CA) *Times*, 12 January 1966, 51. *Independent Journal* (San Rafael), 28 March 1960, 1; 2 May 1974, 4. "Marin County Assessor History," www.calassessor.org/history/MARIN.doc (4 October 2010).

14. *Washington* (D.C.) *Times*, 22 January 1914, 16. *Washington* (D.C.) *Post*, 31 August 1913, magazine section, 1. *New York Tribune*, 15 March 1915, 1.

15. *Syracuse Herald*, 11 July 1930, second section, 17; 23 July 1930, 1. *Davenport* (IA) *Democrat and Leader*, 7 March 1941, 15. Conversations and correspondence with Whipple Manning, Whipple Hall's grandson (2004). *Evening Independent* (St. Petersburg, FL), 26 July 1944, 1. Correspondence with Debra Mieszala, a distant relative of James Mars (McBride) (2010). *Williamsburg* (IA) *Journal-Tribune*, 28 June 1945, 1.

16. *Lowell Sun*, 30 November 1954, 4; 1 February 1955, 15.

17. *Williamsburg* (IA) *Journal-Tribune*, 29 January 1953, 1; 28 January 1954, 1.

18. Rochelle Kelly, "Ely's Spirit Still Flies," *Naval Aviation* News 78.3 (March/April 1996): 30.

19. Interview with Diane Dunlop, 9 June 2013.

20. *Independent Journal* (San Rafael), 28 March 1960, 1. *Marin Journal* (San Rafael), 9 January 1919, 1.

21. *Williamsburg* (IA) *Journal-Tribune*, 25 November 1976, 2C. *Williamsburg* (IA) *Journal-Tribune*, 3 August 1961, 1.

22. Lincoln Sunday Journal and Star, 30 July 1961, 10F. Dallas Morning News, 31 July 1961, 8.

23. *Williamsburg* (IA) *Journal-Tribune*, 3 August 1961, 1; 26 October 1961, 1; 17 October 1963, 1; 12 March 1964, 1. *Cedar Rapids Gazette*, 7 August 1961, 4; 20 October 1961, 5.

24. Correspondence with Allen Haworth (January 2012).

25. *Cedar Rapids Gazette*, 24 September 2001, 6. State of Iowa-Senate Journal, 27 March 2007, p. 914, www.legis.iowa.gov/DOCS/Pubs/sjweb/PDF2/2007/03-27-2007.pdf (6 October 2010). Iowa House Resolution 31 and Iowa Senate Resolution 34 both passed March 23, 2007. Correspondence with Allen Haworth.

26. Dave Rasdal, "Eastern Iowa Life," http://easterniowalife.com/2011/01/17/still-no-stamp-for-pioneer-iowa-aviator (8 July 2010).

# Bibliography

Diane Dunlop Collection
Dunlop was married to George Hall, the son of one of Mabel Hall Ely's brothers.
Whipple Manning Collection (Manning is the grandson of Whipple Hall.)

## Newspapers

Aberdeen (SD) *Daily News*
Albuquerque *Journal*
Amsterdam (NY) *Evening Recorder*
Anaconda (MT) *Standard*
Arizona *Journal-Miner* (Prescott)
Ashland (OR) *Tidings*
Atlanta *Constitution*
Auburn (NY) *Citizen*
Auburn (NY) *Semi-Weekly Journal*
Augusta *Chronicle*
Austin (MN) *Daily Herald*
Bakersfield *Californian*
Baltimore *American*
Bayard (IA) *Advocate*
Beaumont *Enterprise and Journal*
Bellingham *Herald*
Billings *Daily Gazette*
Bisbee (AZ) *Daily Review*
Boston *Evening Transcript*
Boston *Journal*
Brooklyn *Daily Eagle*
Buffalo *Express*
The *Call* (San Francisco)
Carson City *Daily*
Cedar Rapids *Evening Gazette*
Cedar Rapids *Gazette*
Charlotte *Observer*
Chicago *Daily Tribune*
Cleveland *Plain Dealer*
Colorado Springs *Gazette*
Columbus (GA) *Daily Enquirer*
Columbus (GA) *Ledger-Enquirer*
Correctionville (IA) *News*
Coshocton (OH) *Daily Age*
Covina (CA) *Argus*
*Daily Alta California* (San Francisco)
*Daily Free Press* (Carbondale, IL)
*Daily Herald* (Gulfport, MS)
*Daily Humboldt Standard* (Eureka, CA)
*Daily Iowa Capital* (Des Moines)
*Daily Oregon Statesman* (Salem)
*Daily Picayune* (New Orleans)
*Daily Times* (Leavenworth, KS)
Dallas *Morning News*
Davenport (IA) *Daily Leader*
Davenport (IA) *Daily Republican*
Davenport (IA) *Daily Tribune*
Davenport (IA) *Democrat and Leader*
Davenport (IA) *Republican*
Davenport (IA) *Sunday Leader*
Davenport (IA) *Times*
Davenport (IA) *Weekly Leader*
Decatur (IL) *Review*
*Democrat and Chronicle* (Rochester, NY)
*Democratic Banner* (Mt. Vernon, OH)
*Des Moines News*
*Deseret News* (Salt Lake City)
*Duluth News-Tribune*
*El Paso Herald-Post*
Elgin (IN) *Echo*
Elkhart (IN) *Daily Review*
Elkhart (IN) *Truth*
Eugene (OR) *Register Guard*
Eureka (CA) *Herald*
Eureka (CA) *Times Standard*
*Evening Bulletin* (Honolulu)
*Evening Herald* (Klamath Falls, OR)
*Evening Independent* (St. Petersburg, FL)
*Evening News* (San Jose)
*Evening Observer* (Dunkirk, NY)
*Evening Post* (Frederick, MD)
*Evening Standard* (Ogden, UT)
*Evening Statesman* (Marshall, MI)
*Evening Telegram* (Elyria, OH)
*Evening Telegram* (New York)
*Evening Times* (Grand Forks)
*Evening Tribune* (San Diego)
*Fairbanks Daily News*
*Fort Wayne Sentinel*
*Fort Wayne Weekly Sentinel*
*Fort Worth Star-Telegram*
*Gainesville Sun*
*Galveston Daily News*
*Gettysburg Times*
*Globe & Commercial Advertiser* (New York)
*Goodwin's Weekly* (Salt Lake City)
*Grand Forks Herald*
*Grand Rapids Press*
*Grand Valley Times* (Moab, UT)
*Hawaiian Gazette* (Honolulu)
*Herald-Republican* (Salt Lake City)
*Homestead* (Des Moines)
*Humboldt* (CA) *Times*
*Humeston* (IA) *New Era*
*Idaho Statesman* (Boise)
*Independent Journal* (San Rafael)
*Indianapolis Star*
*Iowa City Citizen*
*Iowa City Daily Press*

*Iowa City Press-Citizen*
*Iowa State Press* (Iowa City)
*Iowa State Register* (Des Moines)
*Kalamazoo Gazette*
*Kansas City Star*
Kingston (NY) *Daily Freeman*
*Lake County Examiner* (Lakeview, OR)
Le Mars (IA) *Semi-Weekly Sentinel*
*Lethbridge Daily Herald* (Alberta, Canada)
Lima (OH) *Daily News*
*Lincoln Sunday Journal and Star*
Logan (UT) *Republican*
*Long Beach Independent Press-Telegram*
*Los Angeles Herald*
*Los Angeles Times*
*Lowell Sun*
*Macon Daily Telegraph*
*Macon Weekly Telegraph*
*Manitoba Free Press* (Winnipeg, Canada)
Mansfield (OH) *News*
*Marin Journal* (San Rafael, CA)
Mariposa (CA) *Gazette*
Markesan (WI) *Journal*
Medford (OR) *Mail Tribune*
*Minneapolis Journal*
*Missoulian* (Missoula, MT)
Moberly (MO) *Weekly Monitor*
*Montana Standard* (Butte)
*Montgomery Advertiser*
*Morning Democrat* (Davenport, IA)
Muscatine (IA) *Journal*
Muskegon (MI) *Chronicle*
Muskegon (MI) *News Chronicle*
*Nebraska State Journal* (Lincoln)
Neosho (MO) *Daily News*
*Nevada State Journal* (Reno)
New Bethlehem (PA) *Vindicator*
New Castle (PA) *News*
*New Orleans Item*
*New York American*
*New York Times*
*New York Tribune*
Newark (OH) *Advocate*
Newport (RI) *Daily News*
Oakland (OR) *Advance*
*Oakland Tribune*
Oelwein (IA) *Daily Register*
*Oklahoman* (Oklahoma City)
*Olympia Record*
*Oregonian* (Portland)
Owosso (MI) *Argus-Press*
Oxford (IA) *Leader Platform*
*Oxnard Courier*
*Paducah Evening Sun*
Park (UT) *Record*
Pawtucket (RI) *Times*

*Philadelphia Inquirer*
*Pittsburgh Press*
Portland (OR) *Spectator*
*Portland Oregon Journal*
*Post Standard* (Syracuse)
*Poughkeepsie Daily Eagle*
*Quad City Times* (Davenport, IA)
*Reno Evening Gazette*
*Repository* (Canton, OH)
*Roanoke News*
Rockford (IL) *Morning Star*
Rockford (IL) *Register-Gazette*
Rockford (IL) *Republic*
Roseburg (OR) *Evening News*
St. Albans (VT) *Daily Messenger*
St. Johnsbury (VT) *Caledonian Record*
St. Joseph (MO) *Gazette*
*Salt Lake Herald*
*Salt Lake Telegram*
*Salt Lake Tribune*
*San Antonio Express*
*San Antonio Express and News*
*San Antonio Light*
*San Diego Union*
*San Diego Union-Tribune*
*San Francisco Bulletin*
*San Francisco Chronicle*
*San Francisco Examiner*
*San Jose Mercury News*
*San Mateo Times*
Sandusky (OH) *Register*
Sandusky (OH) *Star-Journal*
Sausalito (CA) *News*
*Seattle Star*
*Seattle Times*
*Seattle Times-Post Intelligencer*
*Sioux County* (Orange City, IA) *Herald*
Springfield (MA) *Republican*
Springfield (MA) *Union & Republican*
*The State* (Columbia, SC)
Stevens Point (WI) *Daily Journal*
*The Sun* (Baltimore)
*The Sun* (Medford, OR)
*The Sun* (New York)
*Syracuse Herald*
*Tacoma Times*
*Times-Democrat* (Davenport, IA)
*Times-Democrat* (Lima, OH)
*Times Dispatch* (Richmond)
Trenton (NJ) *Times*
*Tucson Daily Citizen*
*University Missourian* (Columbia)
*Utica Herald-Dispatch*
Vallejo (CA) *Daily Times*
*Vidette-Reporter* (Iowa City)
Washington (D.C.) *Herald*
Washington (D.C.) *Post*

Washington (D.C.) *Times*
*Waterloo Daily Courier*
*Waterloo Evening Courier*
*Waterloo Evening Reporter*
*Waterloo Evening Reporter and Courier*
*Waterloo Times*
*Waterloo Times Tribune*
*Weekly Sentinel* (Fort Wayne)
*Wilkes-Barre Times*
*Wilkes-Barre Times-Leader*
Williamsburg (IA) *Journal-Tribune*
Williamsburg (IA) *Shopper*
Woodland (CA) *Daily Democrat*
*The World* (New York)
Wyoming (NY) *Reporter*

## Books

*Annual Report of the Secretary of the Navy.* Washington, D.C.: Government Printing Office, 1912.
*Annual Report of the Territorial Mine Inspector to the Governor of Alaska (1920).* Juneau: Alaska Daily Empire Print, 1921.
Baxter, Albert. *History of the City of Grand Rapids, Michigan.* New York: Munsell & Company, 1891.
*Biennial Report of the Secretary of State of the State of Oregon.* Salem: State Printer, 1911.
Blake-Alverson, Margaret. *Sixty Years of California Song.* Oakland: self published, 1913.
Bristol, Sherlock. *The Pioneer Preacher.* Chicago: Fleming H. Revell Co., 1898.
Britton, Wiley. *Memoirs of the Rebellion on the Border, 1863.* Chicago: Cushing, Thomas & Co., 1882.
Brooks, Charles Wesley. *A Century of Missions in the Empire State.* Philadelphia: American Baptist Publication Society, 1900.
Brown, Robert C., and J.E. Norris. *History of Portage County Ohio.* Chicago: Warner, Beers & Co, 1885.
Butler, Joseph G., Jr. *History of Youngstown and the Mahoning Valley Ohio, v. 1.* Chicago: American Historical Society, 1921.

Carey, Charles Henry. *History of Oregon,. v. 2*. Chicago: Pioneer Historical Publishing Co., 1922.

Castle, Henry Anson. *History of St. Paul and Vicinity, v. 3*. Chicago: Lewis Publishing Co., 1912.

Chamberlain, Newell D. *The Call of Gold: True Tales on the Gold Road to Yosemite*. Mariposa, CA: Gazette Press, 1936.

Cleland, Robert Glass. *A History of California: The American Period*. New York: Macmillan, 1922.

Cloud, Roy W. *History of San Mateo County, California*. Chicago: S. J. Clarke, 1928.

Coggeshall, Charles Pierce, and Thellwell Russell Coggeshall. *The Coggeshalls in America*. Boston: C. E. Goodspeed & Company, 1930.

Copeland, Alfred Minott. *Our County and Its People: A history of Hampden County, Massachusetts, Volume 3*. Boston: Century Memorial Publishing Co., 1902.

Cosgrove, C. N., comp. *Annual Report of the Minnesota State Agricultural Society for the Year 1910*. Minneapolis: Syndicate Printing Co., 1910.

Cram, Ralph W., ed. *History of the War Activities of Scott County Iowa, 1917–1918*. Davenport, IA: Scott County Council of National Defense, 1919.

*Crocker-Langley San Francisco directory for the year commencing 1911*. San Francisco: H. S. Crocker Co., 1911.

Curtiss, Glenn H., et al. *The Curtiss Aviation Book*. New York: Frederick A. Stokes, 1912.

Cutter, William Richard, ed. *Genealogical and Family History of northern New York*. New York: Lewis Historical Pub. Co., 1910.

*Delta of Sigma Nu Fraternity Sigma Nu*. Menasha, WI: George Banta, 1907.

Downer, E. *History of Davenport and Scott County, volume 2*. Chicago: S. J. Clarke, 1910.

Durham, David L. *California's Geographic Names*. Clovis, CA: Quill Driver Books, 1998.

Ely, Herman. *Records of the Descendants of Nathaniel Ely: The Emigrant, Who Settled First in Newtown, Now Cambridge, Mass*. Cleveland: Short and Forman, 1885.

Estabrook, Charles E., ed. *Records and Sketches of Military Organizations: Population, Legislation, Election and Other Statistics Relating to Wisconsin in the Period of the Civil War*. Madison: Democrat Printing Co. for the State of Wisconsin, 1914.

*Federal Writers' Project, Montana: A State Guide Book*. New York: Viking, 1939.

Fohlin, Ernest Victor. *Salt Lake City, Past and Present*. Salt Lake City, 1908.

Freeman, Harry C. *A Brief History of Butte, Montana*. Chicago: Henry O. Shepard Company, 1900.

Fremont, Jessie Benton. *Far-West Sketches*. Boston: D. Lothrop Company, 1890.

Fremont, Jessie Benton. *A Year of American Travel*. New York: Harper & Brothers, 1878.

French, John Homer. *Gazetteer of the State of New York*. New York: French, 1860.

Frothingham, Richard. *History of the Siege of Boston*. Boston: Little, Brown, 1873.

Gaston, Joseph. *Portland, Oregon, Its History and Builders*. Chicago: S. J. Clarke, 1911.

Greeley, Horace. *Life of John Charles Fremont*. New York: Greeley and McElrath, 1856.

Hamersly, Lewis Randolph. *The Records of Living Officers of the U.S. Navy and Marine Corps, Sixth Edition*. New York: L. R. Hamersly & Co., 1898.

Haskins, Charles Warren. *The Argonauts of California*. New York: Fords, Howard & Hulbert, 1890.

*History of Iowa County, Iowa*. Des Moines: Union Historical Company, Birdsall, Williams & Co., 1881.

Houston, George M., and H.W. Bolton, Chaplain, ed. *History of the Second Regiment Illinois Volunteer Infantry from Organization to Muster-out*. Chicago: R. R. Donnelley & Sons, 1899.

Hudson, Charles. *History of the Town of Lexington*. Boston: Wiggin & Lunt, 1868.

*Industrial Relations: Final Report and Testimony, Submitted to Congress by the Commission on Industrial Relations Created by the Act of August 23, Mining Conditions at Butte, Montana, 1912, Volume 4*. Washington, D.C.: Government Printing Office, 1916.

*Iowa County Cemetery Stones and History 1844–1975*. Marengo: Iowa County Historical Society, 1976.

Irvine, Leigh H. *History of Humboldt County, California*. Los Angeles: Historic Record Co., 1915.

Katznberger, George A., ed. *Catalogue of the Legal Fraternity of Phi Delta Phi*. Ann Arbor: Inland Press, 1898.

Kimball, Alice Windsor, ed. *The First Year at Stanford*. San Francisco: Stanley-Taylor Co., 1905.

Langland, James, comp. *Chicago Daily News Almanac and Year-Book*. Chicago: Chicago Daily News, 1912.

*Langley's San Francisco City Directory, May 1890*. San Francisco, 1890.

Lockley, Fred, ed. *History of the Columbia River Valley, v. 1*. Chicago: S. J. Clarke, 1928.

Love, William DeLoss, *Wisconsin in the War of the Rebellion*. Chicago: Church and Goodman, 1866.

*Lowell High School, San Francisco, CA. Yearbook, Red and White: Centennial Edition*. San Francisco:

Lowell High School Student Association, 1956.

Lowenstein, Major J. *Official Guide to the Louisiana Purchase Exposition at the City of St. Louis*: St. Louis. The Official Guide Company, 1904.

*Marin People, Volume 2.* "Henry Clay Hall." San Rafael: Marin County Historical Society, 1972.

*Memphis City Directory for 1901.* R. L. Polk and Company.

Moore, Albert Alfonzo. *Genealogy and recollections.* San Francisco: Blair-Murdock Co., 1915.

*National Cyclopaedia of American Biography, v. 14, no. 1.* New York: James T. White & Company, 1910.

*Official Army Register.* "Retired List." Washington, D.C.: Government Printing Office, 1 January 1936.

*Official Army Register for 1911.* Washington, D.C.: Adjutant General's Office, 1 December 1910.

*Official Army Register. January 1 1936.* "Active List." Washington, D.C.: Government Printing Office, 1936.

*Official History of the Fifth Division U.S.A. During the Period of Its Organization and of Its Operations in the European World War, 1917–1919.* Washington, D.C.: Society of the Fifth Division, 1919.

*Portrait and Biographical Album of Benton County, Iowa.* Chicago: Chapman Brothers, 1887.

*Register of Motor Vehicles and Names of Licensed Chauffeurs Registered in the Office of the Secretary of State to December 31, 1909.* Sacramento: W.W. Shannon, 1910.

*Register of the Army of the United States for 1936.* "Retired List." Washington, D.C.: Government Printing Office, 1936.

*Reports of Cases Determined in the Courts of Appeal of the State of California.* San Francisco: Bancroft-Whitney, 1914.

Ripley, Ezra. *A History of the Fight at Concord, on the 19th of April, 1775.* Concord, MA: Allen & Atwill, 1827.

Roseberry, C. R. *Glenn Curtiss: Pioneer of Flight.* Garden City, NY: Doubleday, 1972.

*Roster of Ohio Soldiers in the War of 1812, Adjutant General of Ohio.* Columbus: Press of the Edward T. Miller Co., 1916.

Southeastern Alaska Mining Corporation. "Report on Jualin Mine, Berners Bay Region, Alaska." Juneau: Alaska Territorial Department of Mines, 1929.

*Stanford Quad 1902, v. 8.* Palo Alto: Associated Students of Stanford University, 1901.

Thornlike, Edward L. *English Composition–150 Specimens Arranged for Use in Psychological and Educational Experiments.* New York: Teachers College, Columbia University, 1916.

Upton, Harriet Taylor, and Harry Gardner Cutler. *History of the Western Reserve, v. 1.* Chicago: Lewis, 1910.

Urey, Woodson, comp. *Official Report of the Proceedings of the Democratic National Convention, Held in Baltimore, Maryland.* Chicago: Peterson Linotyping Co., 1912.

Van der Linden, F. Robert. *Best of the National Air and Space Museum.* New York: HarperCollins, 2006.

van Deurs, Rear Admiral George. *Wings for the Fleet.* Annapolis: United States Naval Institute, 1966.

Weber, Erwin. *Rock Island Arsenal Golf Club: A National Historic Place.* Rock Island, IL: Rock Island Arsenal Golf Club, 1997.

Weis, Frederick Lewis. *Early Generations of the Family of Robert Harrington of Watertown, Massachusetts, 1634, and Some of His Descendants.* Worcester: privately published, 1958.

Wilbur, Ray Lyman, Edgar Eugene Robinson, and Paul Carroll Edwards. *The Memoirs of Ray Lyman Wilbur: 1875–1949.* Palo Alto: Stanford University Press, 1960.

Wise, Lu Celia. *Oklahoma's Blending of Many Cultures.* Tulsa: Metro Press, 1973.

*Wright & Ditson's Lawn Tennis Guide.* Boston: Wright & Ditson, 1914.

Zogbaum, Rufus F. *From Sail to Saratoga.* Rome, NY: self published, 1961.

## Periodicals

"Accelerating Sentiment" (serialized). *Saturday Evening Post* [1927] 200:18 (Oct. 29), 200:20 (Nov. 12), 200:22 (Nov. 26), 200:24 (Dec. 10), 200:26 (Dec 24); [1928] 200:28 (Jan. 7).

*Aero Magazine* v. 1–2 (5 August 1911–30 March 1912).

*Aeronautics Magazine* v. 1–14 (July 1907–30 June 1914).

*Aircraft* 1.10 (December 1910).

*Antique Automobile* v. 14 (September 1950).

*Century Illustrated Monthly Magazine* 83.6 (April 1912).

*Collier's* 37.9 (5 May 1906).

*Colliery Engineer* 29.8 (March 1909).

*Daughters of the American Revolution, American Monthly Magazine* 6.5 (May 1895).

Ennis, E. E. "Wireless Telegraphy from an Aeroplane." *Journal of Electricity, Power and Gas* 26.13 (1 April 1911).

Hoffbeck, Steven R. "Shooting Star," *Minnesota History* 54.8 (Winter 1995).

*Jambar* (newsletter of Youngstown State University) 69.53 (19 May 1989).

*Journal of the American Medical Association* 41.12 (1903).

*Kansas Historical Quarterly* 1.3 (May 1932).

Kelly, Rochelle. "Ely's Spirit Still Flies." *Naval Aviation News* 78.3 (March/April 1996).

*Klamath Echoes*, v. 12 (1974).

Lenger, John. "Conquest of the Air." *Harvard Magazine* (May-June 2003).

*Massachusetts Magazine* v. 2 (April 1909).

*Minnesota History* 48.2 (Summer 1982).

*Overland Monthly, and Out West Magazine* 43.4 (April 1904).
*Pacific Merchant Marine* 2.13 (3 July 1909).
Peck, Wallace R. "Forgotten Air Pioneers: The Army's Rockwell Field at North Island" *Journal of San Diego History* 52.3 (Summer 2006).
*Railway Age* 45.8 (21 February 1908).
Rice, Harry E. "Columbia River Kid." *Oregon Historical Quarterly* 74.4 (December 1973).
*Rotarian* 41.4 (October 1932).
*Technical World Magazine* 13.2 (April 1910).
*U.S. Coast and Geodetic Survey: Notice to Mariners, No. 254* (January 1900).
*United States Naval Institute Proceedings* 11.4 (October 1885); 36.4 (December 1910); 37.1 (March 1911).
*USGA Journal and Turf Management* 3.1 (April 1950).
*Weatherwise* v. 60 (January/February 2007).
*Western Field* 10.1 (February 1907); 14.5 (March 1910).

## Correspondence/Interview

Austin, James. Eugene Ely's nephew by Eugene Ely's sister, Maidie.
Brett, Jeremy. Project Archivist Special Collections and University Archives, University of Iowa Libraries.
Davenport (IA) History Museum.
Gowdy, Cathy. Marin County Genealogical Society.
Harris, Sarah N. M. Senior Associate Director, Enrollment Services Coordinator, Transcripts & Verifications, University of Iowa.
Haworth, Allen. Former Williamsburg, IA, postmaster. "The official unpaid promoter of Eugene Ely."
Insley, Debi. Gresham (OR) Historical Society.
Manning, Whipple. Whipple Hall's grandson.
Meyer, Netha M. Iowa County, IA Genealogical Society.
Mieszala, Debra. Distant relative of James Mars (McBride).
Misunas, Marla. Collections Information Manager, San Francisco Museum of Modern Art.
National Military Personnel Records Center, St. Louis, MO.
Thompson, Laurie. librarian, Ann T. Kent California Room, Civic Center Library, San Rafael, CA.
Williamsburg (IA) Public Library.

## Internet

Aerofiles, www.aerofiles.com.
"The Aeronautic Society: An Epitome of the Work of The Aeronautic Society from July, 1908 to December, 1909." Reprinted from the original, November 1958, by Bausch & Lomb Optical Co. http://earlyaviators.com/as01.htm.
Airmail Before 1918, www.centennialofflight.gov.
Altenberg, Lee. "On the Historical Contribution of the Beta Chi Chapter Of Sigma Nu." www.dynamics.org/Altenberg/SYNERGY/SynHouseHistory.html.
Ancestry.com, http://search.ancestry.com
Antique Automobiles. September 1950, http://digital.hagley.org.
Armitage, Allan M. "The American Gardener." The American Horticultural Society, www.ahs.org.
Armitage, Allan M. "A Fall Bounty of Native Asters." *The American Gardener* 85:5 (September/October 2006), The American Horticultural Society, www.ahs.org.
Big Apple History, http://pbskids.org/bigapplehistory.
Biographical Directory of the United States Congress, 1774–Present, http://bioguide.congress.gov.
Birmingham (AL) Public Library, www.bham.lib.al.us.
Brooklyn (NY) Public Library, http://sheetmusic.brooklynpubliclibrary.org.
California Assessors' Association, www.calassessor.org.
Carpenter, Jack. "Glenn H. Curtiss: Founder of the American Aviation Industry," www.glennhcurtiss.com.
Civil War Soldiers and Sailors System database, National Park Service, www.itd.nps.gov/cwss.
College Park Aviation Museum, www.collegeparkaviationmuseum.com.
Department of the Navy—Naval Historical Center, www.history.navy.mil/branches/avchr1.htm.
Dixon, Maureen. "Sleepy Hollow," PacificSun.com.
Early Birds of Aviation, http://earlybirds.org.
Early Birds of Aviation CHIRP, www.rcooper.0catch.com.
Fond du Lac County Web Ring, The History of Fond du Lac County, Wisconsin (Chicago: Western Historical Company, 1880, www.wlhn.org/fond_du_lac/towns/metomen/metomen.htm.
Gerding Theater Opening Celebration Program, Portland Center Stage, www.pcs.org/history.
Glenn Curtiss Historical Society, www.glenncurtiss.com.
Harvard Crimson Magazine, 20 November 1911, www.thecrimson.com.
Hawaii Aviation, http://hawaii.gov/hawaiiaviation/hawaii-aviation-pioneers.
Hill Aerospace Museum, "Flying Machines Over Zion," www.hill.af.mil/library/factsheets.
Historic Adobes of Los Angeles County, www.laokay.com/halac/default.htm.
Hobson, Stephen. "How Can Photographic Practice Assist Our Quest for Intimacy with an Ideal Other?" PhD diss., Griffith University Queensland College of Art, 2006, http://www4.gu.edu.au:8080/adt-root/public/adt-QGU20070824.160040.
Kansas Collection, William G. Cutler, History of the State of Kansas, "Military Record-Part 18" (Chicago: A. T. Andreas, 1883), www.kancoll.org/books/cutler.

Koontz, Giacinta Bradley. "The Flying Costume of Harriet Quimby," www.fabrics.net/joan502.asp.

Marin County Assessor History, www.calassessor.org/history/MARIN.doc.

Minnesota Department of Transportation, www.dot.state.mn.us/aero/aved/museum/aviation_firsts/minnesota.html.

Montana Historical Society Research Center Archives, "Guide to the Patrick A. Largey family papers, 1863–1965," http://nwda-db.wsulibs.wsu.edu/print/ark:/80444/xv15060.

New York Historical Society, www.nyhistory.org.

Norfolk Yacht and Country Club, www.norfolkyacht.com.

Our Campaigns, www.ourcampaigns.com.

Peerless Motor Car Club, "The Complete Peerless History," www.peerlessmotorcar.com.

Pioneer Aviation Group, "Lincoln Beachey," www.lincolnbeachey.com/lbbo.html.

Rasdal, Dave. "Eastern Iowa Life," http://easterniowalife.com.

Roanoker, Leisure Publishing Co., Roanoke, VA, http://theroanoker.com/interests/history/rocklege-inn.

St. Ann's Catholic Church, www.stannslonggrove.org/aboutus.html.

San Bruno (CA) Park School District, http://sbpsd.k12.ca.us/schoolhouse/index.html.

San Francisco Genealogy databases, www.sfgeneaology.com.

San Francisco Online Museum, www.sfmuseum.org.

Santa Rosa Recreation and Parks Department," http://ci.santa-rosa.ca.us/departments/recreationandparks/parks/lbhg.

Smithsonian Air and Space Museum, www.nasm.si.edu/research/aero/women_aviators/blanche_scott.htm.

State of Iowa Senate Journal, 27 March 2007, p. 914, www.legis.iowa.gov/DOCS

Transcript, Martha Foster Abbot Oral History Interview, 7 January 1977, by Carla Ehat & Anne Kent, Anne T. Kent California Room of the Marin County Free Library, www.co.marin.ca.us/depts/lb/main/crm/oralhistories/mfabbotft.html.

U.S. Department of Veterans Affairs, Grave Locator, www.cem.va.gov/CEM.

Vintage and Antique advertisements and products, http://mythicalplace.com.

Willard, John. "Eugene Ely Blazes a Trail in the Sky." *Quad City Times* (Davenport, IA), http://qctimes.com/news.

Williamsburg Iowa Sesquicentennial, www.williamsburg150years.com.

World War I-Civilian Draft Registration Database, www.usgwarchives.org/nv/washoearc.htm.

## Internet Manuscript

Alexander Graham Bell Family Papers, Library of Congress Manuscript Division, Washington, D.C., http://memory.loc.gov/ammem/bellhtml/bellhome.html.

Washington Irving Chambers, correspondence [part of the Wilbur and Orville Wright Papers], Library of Congress Manuscript Division, Washington, D.C., http://memory.loc.gov/ammem/wrighthtml/wrighthome.html.

Wilbur and Orville Wright Papers, Library of Congress Manuscript Division, Washington, D.C., http://memory.loc.gov/ammem/wrighthtml/wrighthome.html.

## Other Reference Sources

Brockshus, Carl. "The Bird Man, Eugene Ely." Iowa County Historical Society, Vignette No. 166, August 1994.

Brockshus, Carl. "Early History of a Part of York Twp. Known as York Center." n.d., believed to be from the Iowa County Farmer, February 1972, copy from the Williamsburg, IA, Public Library.

California State Parks, brochure Mt. Tamalpais State Park, Sacramento, CA, 2007.

## Federal Census Records.

Harrington, Daniel, and A.J. Lanza. Miners' Consumption in the Mines of Butte, Montana, Technical Paper 260, Department of Commerce, Washington, D.C., 1921.

Mendocino County, CA, Marriage Register.

Mines Handbook, v. 15, International Edition (1922).

Monthly Catalog of United States Government publications v. 38 (July 1932–June 1933).

San Diego County Quadrangle, CA, topographic map, 15-minute series, U.S. Department of the Interior, June 1904.

Social Security Death Index.

Southern Oregon Historical Society, Oral History of Seely Hall, no. 36.

Superior Court of California, County of San Francisco, Probate Department, Probate Register of actions, 1915, vol. 38, case 18875, p. 375.

Telephone Directory, San Francisco, California Pacific States Telephone and Telegraph Company, February 1903.

"A Tribute to a Young Man from Iowa County Who made Aviation History." Iowa County Historical Society, Vignette No. 122, September 1986.

# Index

Page numbers in **_bold italics_** indicate pages with illustrations.

Aerial Experiment Association (AEA) 46–47
Aero Club of America 53, 116–118, 293
Aero Club of California 53
Aero Club of Oakland, CA 52
Aero Club of San Diego 195, 197
Aeronautic Society of New York 47–48, 52, 272; *see also Golden Flyer*; Willard, Charles F.
air meets *see* aviation meet, listed by city
Air National Guard *see* Ely, Eugene Burton, California Air National Guard
air shows *see* aviation exhibitions, listed by city
USS *Akron* (ZRS-4)(dirigible) 299–300
*Albany Flyer see Hudson Flyer*
Antoinette (monoplane) 126, 150–151, 166–167, 172
Arnold, Henry (Hap) 274, 278
Atlanta, GA, aviation exhibition (December 1910) 147–148
Atwood, Harry Nelson 260, 263, 267, 274, 276–277
Austin, James (Mary Austin's husband) 299
Austin, James, Jr. (son of James and Mary Austin) 299, 324*n*1
Austin, Lois Gene (daughter of James and Mary Austin) 299
Austin, Mary (Maidie) (Eugene's sister) *see* Ely, Mary
aviation firsts: airplane flight in Canada 311*n*14; bullet fired from an airplane 90; five airplanes in air at once 90; scheduled Air Mail flight 272–273; telegraph transmission from an airplane 90–91; *see also* Norfolk, VA, aviation exhibition (November 1910), flight from USS *Birmingham*; USS *Pennsylvania* (Armored Cruiser # 4), flight to and from (January 18, 1911)

*Baby Wright* 118, 120, 151–152, 314*n*14
Badger, William 260–264
Baer, Arthur (Bugs) 35–36, 300–302
Baker City, OR, aviation exhibition (July 1911) 248
Bakersfield, CA, aviation exhibition (April 1911) 217–219
Baldwin, Thomas Scott, Capt. 150, 257, 261, 264
balloons *see City of Oakland*
Baltimore, MD, aviation exhibition (November 1910) 122–129, 133, 135
Barrington Park Aviation Meet *see* Salt Lake City, UT, air meet (February 1911)
Beachey, Lincoln 52, 75–76, 165, 202–203, 253–255, 259, 264–265, 267–268, 280, 282, 288, 294, 296, 300; front elevator removed 305*n*14
Beatty, George William 268, 270–271, 276, 279
Beck, Lt. Paul Ward 165, 167–168, 172–173, 188, 195–196, 213, 221–222, 252–253
Bell, Alexander Graham 46–47
Belmont Park, NY, aviation meet (October 1910) 85–86, 116–121, 131
Billings, MT, aviation exhibition (June 1910) 74
USS *Birmingham* (Scout Cruiser # 2) 134–135, ***137***, 160; *see also* Norfolk, VA, aviation exhibition, flight from USS *Birmingham*
Birmingham, AL, aviation exhibition (November 1910) 141, 143
Blakeslee, Henry 38, 217–218; *see also* Rosenfeld, Max
Bleriot (monoplane) 129, 150, 166, 172, 259, 268, 275
Bleriot, Louis 48–49
Boston, MA, aviation meet (August–September 1911) 267–269; *see also* Ely, Eugene Burton, accidents; Hannah, Persis Dwight
*Boston Flyer* 106, 108–111, 313*n*2
Brighton Beach, NY, aviation exhibition (September 1911) 270
Brookins, Walter Richard (Brookie) 82, 103, 118–120, 152–156, 167, 171–175, 177, 186, 188, 204, 210, 214–17, 221, 263, 277, 293; flying attire 216
Buffalo Bill *see* Cody, William Frederick
Burgess, Frederick, Bishop *see* Nassau Boulevard, NY, aviation exhibition, Sunday flights, protest of
Burkhart, John 57, 61, 63
Bush, Arthur Gladstone 15, 299
Butte, MT, aviation exhibition (June 1911) 240–243

California Air National Guard *see* Ely, Eugene Burton, California Air National Guard
Callan, Frank 136, 241–242, 283–284, 286–288, 290
Canton, OH, aviation exhibition (September 1911) 276–278

333

Cedar Point, OH *see* Cleveland–Cedar Point, OH, aviation exhibition
Chambers, Washington Irving, Capt. 99, 119, 131, 133–134, 136, 149, 158, 160–161; correspondence with Eugene Ely 198, 200; named Navy's first aviation contact 99, 131; recruits Eugene Ely for USS *Birmingham* flight 133
Chicago, IL, aviation exhibition (July 1910) 77–78
Chicago, IL, aviation exhibition (October 1910) 105
Chicago, IL, aviation meet (August 1911) 256–266; managing costs 256–257; outrage over deaths of Badger and Johnstone 262–264; *see also* Badger, William; Johnstone, St. Croix
Chicago International Aviation Meet *see* Chicago, IL, aviation meet (August 1911)
Chicago–New York Air Race (October 9–11, 1910) 86, 98, 101, 103–111
Chico, CA, aviation exhibition (July 1911) 245
*City of Oakland* 52; *see also* Mars, James Cairn
Clapp, Walker Lucas, Jr. 39–*41*
Cleveland, OH, aviation exhibition (October 1910) 113–115
Cleveland Aero Club 96
Cleveland–Cedar Point, OH, aviation exhibition (roundtrip) (August–September 1910) 95–96
Cody, William Frederick (Buffalo Bill) 8–10, 280–282, 291
Coffyn, Frank Trenholm 82, 221, 259
Coggeshall, Walter 226–228
College Park, MD, aviation exhibition (July–August 1911) 252–253
Columbia, SC, aviation exhibition (December 1910) 146–147
Conlisk, Charles 37–38
Cooke Weldon 292, 296
Coolbaugh, Robert (Bob) 304
Corbin, Austin 87–88
Covey, Howard 45, 58–62, 64
Covington, KY, aviation exhibition (November 1909) 50
Cramer, Mabel 33–34
Crane, Ned 84–85, 223; *see also* Ely, Eugene Burton, airplane vs. automobile
Cross, Mabel 292, 296–297; *see also* de Meloche, Mabel; Ely, Mabel Hall; Pierce, Mabel
Cross, Philip 292, 296–297
Curtiss, Glenn Hammond 46–50, 58, 68, 75–76, 83, 85–86, 88–90, *92*, 103–105, *107*, 111–113, 117–121, 124–126, 133, 149–152, 156, 163, 173, 197, 214–217, 252; attempt to launch airplane from ship 131–134; reaction to Eugene's USS *Pennsylvania* flight 186; refusal to defend Gordon Bennett Cup 117–118; training Navy pilots 150; *see also* Cleveland, OH, aviation exhibition; Hudson-Fulton Celebration; patent wars; tailhook, creation controversy; training military aviators; *Triad*
Curtiss, Lena Neff 89–90, 96, 125, 169–170
Curtiss Exhibition Company 10, 50, 74–75, 96, 147, 231, 290
Curtiss Manufacturing Co. 46, 48, 50
Curtiss Model D, Type 2 *see* Signal Corps Aeroplane No. 2 (Curtiss)
Curtiss Model D, Type 3 (three) 149, 151–152, 206

Dallas, TX, aviation exhibition (May 1911) 224–225
Davenport, IA, aviation exhibition (October 1911) 3–7, 280
de Lesseps, Jacques 120, 135
de Meloche, Mabel 297; *see also* Cross, Mabel; Ely, Mabel Hall; Pierce, Mabel
de Meloche, Wilford Andre 297
Demonstrating military aircraft *see* College Park, MD, aviation exhibition; San Antonio aviation exhibition
De Mott, Charles, Sheriff *see* Nassau Boulevard, NY, aviation exhibition, Sunday flights, protest of
DePalma, Ralph *see* Ely, Eugene Burton, airplane vs. automobile
DeVaux, Norman 38, 42, 45, 226–229, 231, *233*, 320*n*17
dirigibles 52, 54, 64, 299–300
Distinguished Flying Cross 299–300
Dominguez, CA, aviation exhibition (January 1910) 52–55, 58
Dominguez, CA, aviation exhibition (December 1910–January 1911) 150–156, 309*n*11
Donnelly, Walter 62, 65–67
Drexel, John Armstrong 118–119, 124–125, 135
Dutrieu, Helene 272, 274, 278

Ellyson, Lt. Theodore Gordon (Spuds) 150, 169, 195–198, 214, 217, 279

Ely & Bush *see* Ely, Nathan Dana, legal career; Bush, Arthur Gladstone
Ely, Emma Lois 3, 12–15, 19, 36, 39, 97, 287, 290–291, 298–299; divorce 19, 299
Ely, Eugene Burton (Gene): accidents 4, 7, 11, 21, 69, 74, 80, 83, 85, 96–97, 101, 110, 112, 120, 147–148, 155–156, 209, 218, 238, 243, 247–248, 252, 269, 274, 277; agrees to fly from USS *Birmingham* 133; airplane vs. automobile 84, 99–101, 141–142, 146, 223, 242; anxiety and doubts 198–199, 205, 238–239, 275, 283; automobile racing 20–21, 36–37, 41–44, 146; aviation earnings 292–293; aviation sickness 93–94; business failures 177; California Air National Guard 208, 223, 248, 252; campaigns to commemorate Eugene Ely 300–304; character and personality 5, 9, 16, 276; chauffeur 20–21, 23–26, 29, 37, 39, 296, 307*n*11; chosen for USS *Pennsylvania* flight 149; contract disputes 69, 77, 81–82; correspondence with Capt. Washington Chambers 198, 200; crashed biplane seized 290; Curtiss' tutoring of 83, 86, 104–105; death 283–284, *285*–286, 288; death in Canada, false report 81; Death Spiral (Death Dip/Spiral Dip) 3, 6, 10–11, 197, 201–202, 212, 222, 224, 235–237, 241, 280–281; description of Eugene Ely 9, 79–80, 100, 108, 123, 160, 208, 241, 276; describes flying 5–6, 9–10, 80, 96, 98, 126, 171–172, 205, 225, 282–283; Ely Glide 124, 142, 146, 193; fear of heights 176; first cross over attempt of Rocky Mountains (The Great Divide) 240, 242; first flights 67–68; flight helmet *6*, 178, 317*n*6; flying attire 108, 125, 216, 235; flying license 105, 317*n*6; friendship with Buffalo Bill 9, 281; front elevator, removal decision 11, 282, 288–289; funeral 290–291; interviews 96, 99–100, 123, 126–127, 135, 145, 176–177, 196, 201, 203, 207, 214, 228–229, 236, 241, 257–258, 277–278, 282; interviews, USS *Birmingham* flight 135–138, *137*; interviews, New York–Chicago Race 103, 106, 109–111; interviews, USS *Pennsylvania* flight 138–139,

159, 163, 178; interviews, reaction to Hoxsey's death 155; legend, college graduate 16, 306n18; legend, pal of Barney Oldfield and Eddie Rickenbacker 35; legend, San Jose, California racetrack, speed record 36, 307n7; Likely-Lakeview auto stage line 40–41; Manhattan Beach Hotel Aviation Prize 91–93, 96; marriage to Mabel 37–38; motion pictures of 182, 190, 243, 290; outrage over deaths of Badger and Johnstone 264; photographs *6*, *71*, *78*, *92*, *107*, *143*, *182–184*, *189*, *233*, *294*; pilot's license, qualified 105, 317n6; predicts airplane of future 269; recognition of 190–191, 296; relationship with father 16, 19, 81; relationship with Mabel 3, 5–7, 33, 85, 128, 143, 205, 258, 268–269; rescues earthquake victims 28; seasick 178, 228; swimming ability questioned 178; weight loss 228; *see also* Ely, Nathan Dana, correspondence with Secretary of the Navy; Georgia-Carolina Fair Association

Ely, Hubert 17, 36, 298

Ely, Julia 15, 291

Ely, Mabel Canniff von Schaezler 18–19

Ely, Mabel Hall: accident, solo flight 121; USS *Akron*, honored guest 300; anxiety and doubts 146, 171, 251; blames Lincoln Beachey for Eugene's death 52, 202, 255; correspondence 300, 302; description 100–101, 123, 125, 135, 171, 196–197, 230, 234, 242, 268, 287, 302; divorces 296–297; early life 31–34; Eugene Ely Day (February 23, 1912) 293–*294–295*–296; interviews 100, 103, 135, 169–170, 197, 203, 205–206, 230, 234, 236, 255, 258, 262; interviews, flight to the USS *Pennsylvania* 175, 205; marriage to Eugene 37–38; marriages, other 296–297, 300; passenger flight, first 89; passenger flights 268, 271, 275; photographs *143*, *182*, *189*, *233*, *295*, *301*; reaction to Eugene's death 52, 81, 287; relationship with Eugene 5, 85, 91, 100, 128–129, 143, 203, 228, 235, 237, 268, 287; *see also* Cross, Mabel; de Meloche, Mabel; Pierce, Mabel

Ely, Mary (Maidie) 3, 14–15, 36, 97, 288, 292–299

Ely, Nathan Dana 5–6, 12–19, 81, 102, 198–199, 292, 299–300; correspondence with Secretary of the Navy 198–199, 211; divorce 19, 299; legal career 14–16, 299; military service 15–16, 299; politics and congressional campaign 14–16, 299; received Eugene's Distinguished Flying Cross 299; rumors of infidelity 12, 299; *see also* Ely, Eugene Burton, relationship with father

Emeryville Aviation Meet *see* Oakland, CA, aviation meet

Eugene Ely Day *see* Ely, Mabel Hall, Eugene Ely Day

Eureka, CA, aviation exhibition (May 1911) 226–231

*Falcon* 84

Fanciulli, Jerome S. 52–53, 75, 105, 117, 220, 231

female attraction to aviators 63, 170–171, 214

First International Aviation Tournament (Rheims, Germany) *see* Rheims, Germany, aviation tournament

Foulois, Lt. Benjamin Delahauf 213, 220–222

Fremont, John C. 31

Georgia State Fair Association 283, 288

Georgia-Carolina Fair Association 146–147; *see also* Ely, Eugene Burton, crashed biplane seized

Georgian State Fair *see* Macon, GA, aviation exhibition

*Golden Flyer* 47–48, 50, 52

Gordon Bennett Cup 48, 116–119; *see also* Belmont Park, NY, aviation exhibition; Curtiss, Glenn Hammond; Grahame-White, Claude; Rheims, Germany, aviation tournament

Grahame-White, Claude 119, 267–270, 274–275, 278–279, 293; *see also* Gordon Bennett Cup

Great Falls, MT, aviation exhibition (June 1911) 243–244

Halethorpe Field *see* Baltimore, MD, aviation exhibition

Hall, Henry Clay 31–32, 287

Hall, Mabel *see* Ely, Mabel Hall

Hall, Mary Loughren 32, 287

Hall, Mercedes (Mercy) 32, 165, 227–228, 231

Hall, Whipple Spear 38, 71–73, 75–76, 78, 81, 83–85, 88, 99, *107*, 150, 166, 188, 204, 206, 210–211, 217, *233*, 300; appearance 72; buys Curtiss biplane 72; first flight as passenger 72; first solo flight 72, 310n7

Hamilton, Charles Kenney 49–51, 55, 57–58, 62–66, 77, 86, 88, 103–104, 118–120, 250, 253, 300; Curtiss sues him 86

Hammondsport, NY, aviation exhibition (July 1908) 46–47

Hanford, CA, aviation exhibition (March 1911) 213

Hannah, Persis Dwight 267–268

Harrington Family Cemetery, York Center, IA 13, 15, 290–291, 298

Harrington, Burton 13

Harrington, Emma Lois Ely *see* Ely, Emma Lois

Harrington, Orson 22–23, 25, 27–30, 79, 81, 97, 136, 233, 300; letters about the San Francisco earthquake 27–29

Harvard-Boston Aero Meet *see* Boston, MA, aviation meet

Haworth, Alan 303

Henning, James 79–80, 82, 99, 122, 135, 222, 319n14

Herzstein, Dr. Morris 25, 28–29, 39; *see also* Waldeck Hospital

Hillsgrove, RI, aviation exhibition (September 1911) 269–270

Hoff, William Henry (Bill) 218, 227–228, 241–242, 244–248, 293, 295

Hoxsey, Archibald (Arch) 102, 120, 135, 152–156, 201–202, 213, 250; falls to his death 154; funeral 156; flies President Roosevelt 152–153

*Hudson Flyer* 86, 89, 135–138, 313n2

*Hudson-Fulton* 49

Hudson-Fulton Celebration 49

hydroplane *see Triad* (Curtiss hydroplane)

*Iaqua* (Coastal Steamship) 227–229

Illinois Aero Club 256, 262–264

International Aeronautic Federation 116

International Aviation Meet, first *see* Rheims, Germany, aviation tournament

International Aviation Meet, second *see* Belmont Park, NY, aviation meet

Iowa State University (Ames, IA) *see* State University of Iowa

Jackson, MS, aviation exhibition (November 1910) 143–144

Johnstone, Ralph 121, 135, 141, 143, 156, 200, 241, 261, 304

Johnstone, St. Croix 261–264; Johnstone benefit 265, 293
*June Bug* 46–47

*Kaiserin Auguste Victoria* (ocean liner) *see* Curtiss, Glenn Hammond, attempt to launch airplane from ship
Kalamazoo, MI, aviation exhibition (September 1910) 96–97
Kalispell, MT, aviation exhibition (June 1911) 244
Kansas City, MO, aviation exhibition (May 1911) 223–224
Kelly, Lt. George Edward Maurice 174–175, 213, 221–222
Kleiser, George 57–58

Latham, Hubert 125–127, 129, 135, 150–151, 155–156, 166–167, 169, 172, 177, 234, 258
Lethbridge, Canada, aviation exhibition (July 1911) 248–249
Lewistown, MT, aviation exhibition (June 1911) 244
Likely-Lakeview auto stage line *see* Ely, Eugene, Likely-Lakeview auto stage line
Los Angeles International Air Meet *see* Dominguez, CA, aviation exhibition (1910)
Los Angeles International Aviation Exhibition, first *see* Dominguez, CA, aviation exhibition (January 1910)
Los Angeles International Aviation Exhibition, second *see* Dominguez, CA, aviation exhibition (December 1910–January 1911)
Los Angeles–Dominguez International Aviation Meet (1910) *see* Dominguez, CA, aviation exhibition (January 1910)
Loughren, Mary Hall *see* Hall, Mary Loughren
Macon, GA, aviation exhibition (October 1911) 8–11, 280–290, *281*, *285*, *289*
USS *Maine* (Armored Cruiser, ACR-1) 15, 56

Manhattan Beach Hotel Aviation Prize *see* Ely, Eugene Burton, Manhattan Beach Hotel Aviation Prize
Mare Island Naval Shipyard 159–164, *161*, 189
Mars, James Cairn (Bud) 52–53, 75–78, 83, 88–93, 95–96, *107*, 113–115, 118, 121, 127, 134–135, 151, 204, 211, 245, 248–249, 257, 262–265, 276, 283–284, 287, 292–293, 296, 300, 325n15; arranging benefit for Mabel 292–293, 296; world aviation tour 150, 204, 211, 245; *see also City of Oakland*; Curtiss, Glenn Hammond, attempt to launch airplane from ship; Ely, Eugene Burton, Manhattan Beach Hotel Aviation Prize
Mars, Marie Ethridge 52, 83, 90, 96, 245, 248, 263, 287, 292; first passenger flight 89; fears of an aviator's wife 265–266; outrage over Badger and Johnstone deaths 263, 265–266
Max Rosenfeld's Auto Livery Company *see* Rosenfeld, Max
McBride, James Cairn *see* Mars, James Cairn (Bud)
McCurdy, John A. D. (Jack) 46, 88, 90–91, 106–109, *107*, 114–115, 117–118, 121, 131–134, 140–144, 143–148, 260, 267, 276; *see also* Curtiss, Glenn Hammond, attempt to launch airplane from ship
Medford, OR, aviation exhibition (June 1910) 70, *71*, 72, *73*
Medford, OR, aviation exhibition (June 1911) 232–236
Meloche, Wilford Andre *see* de Meloche, Wilford Andre
Meyer, Secretary of the Navy 132–134, 138, 157; congratulates Eugene 138; *see also* Norfolk, VA, aviation exhibition, flight from USS *Birmingham*
military value of airplanes questioned 130–132
Mineola Field, NY *see* Aeronautic Society of New York
Minneapolis, MN, aviation exhibition (June 1910) 74–75
Missoula, MT, aviation exhibition (June 1911) 244–245
Mobile, AL, aviation exhibition (November 1910) 143
Moisant, John Bevins 119, 154–155, 261
Mudd, Frank 260, 263–264
Murray, Gordon 43–45, 308n25

Nassau Boulevard, NY, aviation exhibition (September–October 1911) 272–276, 278–279; Sunday flights, protest of 273–274, 278–279, 323n22
New Orleans, LA, aviation exhibition (December 1910) 144–146
New York Aeronautical Society *see* Aeronautic Society of New York
New York–Philadelphia Air Race, aviation exhibition (August 5, 1911) 86, 253–255

Norfolk, VA, aviation exhibition (November 1910) 129; flight from USS *Birmingham* 133–138, *137*, 143
North Island, San Diego, CA *see* training military aviators

Oakland, CA, aviation meet (February 1912) 293–296
Oldfield, Barney 20, 35, 75, 84, 99, 300
Omaha, NE, aviation exhibition (July 1910) 83
Ovington, Earl Lewis 258–260, 263, 265, 268, 272–273, 275; *see also* Nassau Boulevard, NY, aviation exhibition

Parmalee, Philip Orin *see* Parmelee, Philip Orin
Parmelee, Philip Orin 151–153, 156, 168, 170, 172–174, 177, 188, 193–194, 213–217, 220, 294–296; flying attire 216
Pasadena, CA, aviation exhibition (March 1911) 213
patent wars 46, 48, 53, 75, 117, 119–120, 264, 273
Paulhan, Louis 45, 55, 57–58, 144, 156
Peerless Automobile Company 35; *see also* Rosenfeld, Max
USS *Pennsylvania* (Armored Cruiser # 4) 4, 157–*161*, 162–163, 166, 168–169, 174, 176–187, 190, 199, 206, 209; flight to and from (January 18, 1911) 177–*180*, *181–185*, 186–187, 190; landing platform 160–162; *see also* Curtiss Model D, Type 3
*Pennsylvania* (ocean liner) *see* Curtiss, Glenn Hammond, attempt to launch airplane from ship
Petersen, Pete (Daredevil Pete) 5, 7, 20, 280, 290
Pickens, William Hickman (Bill) 35–36, 300
Pickens' Flying Circus *see* Pickens, William Hickman
Pierce, Mabel 300; *see also* Cross, Mabel; de Meloche, Mabel; Ely, Mabel Hall
Pierce, Richard 300
Pond, Charles Fremont, Capt. 158, 162–163, 177, 179, 181, *182*, 183, 190, 199
Portland Aeroplane Company 68, 310n15
Portland Automobile Club *see* Wemme, E. Henry
Portland, OR, aviation exhibition (March 1910) 62–66
Portland, OR, aviation exhibition (June 1911) 237–238

Post, Augustus 90, 104, 111, 143–145
Poughkeepsie, NY, aviation exhibition (September 1910) 99–102

Quimby, Harriet 257, 272, 278, 293

Radley, James 123, 125, 128–129, 150, 152, 155–156, 162, 166, 169, 172, 174, 177, 180; *see also* tailhook, creation controversy
Raleigh, NC, aviation exhibition (November 1910) 135, 140–141
Reno, NV, aviation exhibition (July 1911) 246–248
Rheims, Germany, aviation tournament (August 1909) 48–49; *see also* Curtiss, Glenn Hammond; Gordon Bennett Cup
*Rheims Racer* 48–49, 58, 86, 88
Rickenbacker, Edward Vernon (Eddie) 20, 35
Roanoke, VA, aviation exhibition (September 1910) 98–99
Robinson, Hugh Armstrong 162, 165, 197, 207–208, 213, 249–251, 253–254, 262, 288
Rochester, NY, aviation exhibition (August 1910) 83–85
Rock Island, IL, aviation exhibition (September 1910) 17, 97–98
Rodgers, Lt. John 158, 160, 162
Roosevelt, President Theodore 20, 99, 101–102, 152, 213
Rosenfeld, Max L. 35–38, 217; *see also* Blakeslee, Henry
Ryan, John Barry 132–134, 138

Sacramento, CA, aviation exhibition (February 1911) 199
St. Johnsbury, VT, aviation exhibition (September 1911) 270–271
St. Joseph, MO, aviation exhibition (December 1909) 51
Salem, OR, aviation exhibition (June 1911) 236–237
Salt Lake City, UT, air meet (February 1911) 204–210
Salt Lake City, UT, aviation exhibition (April 1911) 213–217
Salt Lake City International Aviation Carnival *see* Salt Lake City, UT, aviation exhibition (April 1911)
San Antonio, TX, aviation exhibition (April–May 1911) 220–222

San Diego, CA, aviation exhibition (January 1911) 196–198
San Francisco, CA, aviation meet (January 1911) 23, 34, 164, 166–190, 192–194; military maneuvers and experiments 167–168, 173–175; *see also* Curtiss Model D, Type 3; USS *Pennsylvania* (Armored Cruiser # 4), flight to and from (January 18, 1911), landing platform
San Francisco earthquake, 1906 27–30
San Francisco International Aviation Meet *see* San Francisco, CA, aviation meet
San Jose, CA, aviation exhibition (March 1911) 212
Scientific American Cup 46–47
Scott, Blanche Stuart 105, 293, **295**–296
Seattle, WA, aviation exhibition (July 1911) 249–251
Selfridge Field, CA 159–160, 165
Selfridge, Lt. Thomas 46, 130, 160
Sheepshead Bay, NY, aviation exhibition (August 1910) 88–94
Signal Corps Aeroplane No. 2 (Curtiss) 220–221
Signal Corps Aeroplane No. 1 (Wright) 220
Simon, Rene 259–260, 265
Simpson, Robert 45, 61, 67–68, 99, 166; buying Wemme biplane 67–68
single surface racer (Curtiss) 113, 117–119
Sioux City, IA, aviation exhibition (June–July 1910) 76–77
Smyth, Thomas, Father 21, 208
Sopwith, Thomas 268, 270, 273–275, 278–279
State University of Iowa (Iowa City, IA) 13–14, 306n3, 306n18
Sutherland, OR, aviation exhibition (May 1910) 68–69

Taft, President William Howard 132, 220
tailhook, creation controversy 162
Tetrazzini, Luisa 191–194, 234
Tourist Cup 42, 44
training military aviators 195–196, 212–213, 217, 220–222; *see also* San Antonio, TX, aviation exhibition (April–May 1911)
transporting 4, 70, 96, 111, 146, 220, 231, 270

*Triad* (Curtiss hydroplane) 195–196, 199, 209, 211, 213, 215–216, 251, 262
Turner, Edgar 282–284, 286–288

United States Aeronautical Reserve *see* Ryan, John Berry
University of Iowa *see* State University of Iowa

*Valkyrie* 83, 85
von Schaezler, Mabel *see* Ely, Mabel Canniff von Schaezler
von Schaezler, Otto 18–19

Waldeck Hospital 29; *see also* Herzstein, Dr. Morris
Walker, Clarence H. 165–166, 204–209; buys Eugene's original biplane 166
Walker, Lt. John C., Jr. 173, 195–196, 213, 220–222
Walsh, Charles Francis 4, 6
Ward, James (Jimmy) **107**, 144–148, 224–225, 257–258, 265
Wemme, E. Henry 5, 45, 56–62, 65–68, 99, 238–239, 287; *see also* Simpson, Robert, buying Wemme biplane
Wichita, KS, aviation exhibition (May 1911) 222–223
Willard, Charles Foster 47–48, 50, 52–53, 55, 72, 75–77, 88, 90, 104, 106, **107**, 108–109, 117, 120–125, 127–128, 135, 149, 151, 154–156, 167, 169–170, 172, 177, 199, 204–217, 221–224, 235, 237, 270, 293; flying attire 216; *see also* Aeronautic Society of New York
Winnipeg, Canada, aviation exhibition (July 1910) 78–82
Wiseman, Frederick Joseph (Fred) 43–44, 165, 272
Witmer, Charles Christian 211, 224–225, 265
Woodruff, Timothy, Lt. Governor of New York *see* Nassau Boulevard, NY, aviation exhibition, Sunday flights, protest of
Wright, Orville, and Wilbur 46–48, 53, 104, 118, 130, 133, 140, 152, 217, 273; suit against Illinois Aero Club 264; *see also* patent wars

Youngstown, OH, aviation exhibition (October 1910) 112–113

Zogbaum, Lt. Rufus F. 158, 160, 162